FAMILY BUSINESS SOURCEBOOK

FAMILY BUSINESS SOURCEBOOK

A Guide for
Families Who Own Businesses and
the Professionals Who Serve Them:

Covering Financial Planning, Growth, Management,
Psychological Issues, Succession, Women's Roles,
the Younger Generation, and Other Issues
Facing the Family-Owned Business

Edited by

Craig E. Aronoff, PhD.
Dinos Distinguished Chair of Private Enterprise
Kennesaw State College, Marietta, Georgia

and

John L. Ward, PhD.
Ralph Marotta Professor of Free Enterprise
Loyola University, Chicago, Illinois

BIP 00 2nd

Omnigraphics, Inc.

Penobscot Building • Detroit, Michigan 48226

Omnigraphics, Inc.

Eric F. Berger, *Production Manager*

* * *

Annie M. Brewer, *Vice President-Research*
Peter E. Ruffner, *Vice President-Administration*
James A. Sellgren, *Vice President-Operations & Finance*

* * *

Frederick G. Ruffner, Jr., *President and Publisher*

Family business sourcebook : a guide for families who own businesses and the professionals who serve them : covering financial planning, growth, management, psychological issues, succession, women's roles, the younger generation, and other issues facing the family owned business/edited by Craig E. Aronoff, John L. Ward.

    p. cm.

    Includes index.

    ISBN 1-55888-316-9 (lib. bdg. : alk. paper)

    1. Family-owned business enterprises—Handbooks, manuals, etc.

I. Aronoff, Craig E., 1951–.   II. Ward, John L., 1945–.

HD62.25F34 1991   90-22564

658'.045—dc20   CIP

Printed in the United States of America

Table of Contents

Table of Contents

Table of Contents

Table of Contents

Table of Contents

Table of Contents

Introduction

Family business is among the "hottest" areas of interest in business today. The media, academicians and business people increasingly recognize that family business means much more than "mom and pop." The economic and social importance of family business as well as the dynamic tension generated by the interaction of family and business processes have attracted the concentrated attention of academic researchers, those involved in family businesses, those who provide professional services to family businesses and the media.

And well it should. Over 95 percent of all businesses in the United States are family-owned. Although many family firms are small, many are major corporations including one-third of the *Fortune 500*. Family businesses produce about half the U.S. gross national product and generate half the wages paid in this country. Those are impressive statistics. They underline the importance of family businesses to our economy and to our society.

Other statistics are equally impressive if less optimistic. For example, less than twenty percent of those family businesses will survive more than twenty years. They fail or are gobbled up by other corporations. Why?

Pessimists might hold that 'family' and 'business' are inherently and implacably incompatible. Simply put, they see "family business" as the perfect oxymoron. As academicians and consultants who have studied and worked closely with family businesses, we hold a far different view. We see instead their strengths: their long-term view; the loyalty of their employees; their flexibility and adaptability; their personalized attention to customers; and their ability to maintain confidentiality.

We do not ignore the problems and conflicts that can characterize family businesses, but we believe if given the knowledge and skill to deal with the unique challenges they face, many more of these enterprises can capitalize on their strengths, cope with their conflicts and go on to succeed and endure.

But where does the family business owner seek help? How can the skilled business consultant learn to handle the business/family overlap? Where does family planning fit into business planning, and vice versa? Concentrated knowledge and skill have been difficult, if not impossible, to find in the past.

The literature of family business has been developing fairly rapidly. While the Greek tragedies and Shakespeare contain lessons relevant to the subject, with a few notable exceptions, printed material on family business topics have become increasingly produced only in the past decade. An academic journal and several newsletters and magazines focused on family business have initiated publication since 1988. Established business publications have begun to devote more space to the subject.

The quality periodical literature now existing requires its distillation and collection in one volume: *Family Business Sourcebook*. Interest in the subject has grown so dramatically partly because many founders who established their businesses after World War II now face retirement. These are entrepreneurs now vitally concerned with succession planning.

Compared to nonfamily enterprises, many young people perceive their families' firms as offering faster advancement with more significant personal and business rewards. The economic shift toward entrepreneurism over the last forty years means many more new businesses will evolve into family businesses. Given these trends, the healthy survival of family firms becomes more important than ever.

This book is valuable to those who own, work in or are affiliated with family businesses. Their recognition and understanding of the issues confronting them will be expanded, as will their capacity to deal with the challenges of family business. The book will also serve those professionals who serve family businesses: accountants, bankers, family therapists, financial planners, lawyers and management consultants. Researchers, students and academics will find that this volume eases and enlightens their efforts to understand the many subtleties of family businesses.

This volume consists of 75 articles in fifteen sections. The sections represent major interest areas within the broad family business domain including:

General Overview;

Succession;

Management and Strategic Planning;

Financial Dimensions;

Professionalizing the Family Firm;

Boards of Directors;

Family Business Growth;

Psychological Issues;

Changes and Conflict;

Family Relations;

Women in the Family Firm;

The Younger Generation;

Raising Rich Kids;

Consulting to Family Business;

and

Family Business and Society.

While the entries included here go back to 1957, all but about a dozen articles were published in the 1980s. The items selected represent more than 35 publications of considerable variety. Academic business journals from several disciplines, business magazines and newspapers, specialized publications and trade magazines are included. So are *Rural Sociology*, the *American Journal of Psychiatry*, *Partisan Review* and *The Journal of Anthropology*

Acknowledgements

Many have helped us in producing this volume. Mary Cawley organizes so much of our editorial productivity and we owe her much credit. Maureen Johnson moved massive amounts of information from pages to disks.

Others who contributed to the completion of the book include Terence Allen, Alison Allen, Betty Boswell, Shelley Browne, Peggy Fichtner, Darla Givan, and Beverly Runnels.

We owe special thanks to Dr. Pat Frishkoff and the Family Business Program at Oregon State University for the bibliographic work of her team and for so generously sharing the results of their efforts.

Many colleagues helped us to identify both their best published work and the best published work in the field. Included in this group are: Ben Benson, Irving Blackman, Rod Correll, Léon Danco, John Davis, Gibb Dyer, Wendy Handler, Barbara Hollander, Tom Hubler, Dennis Jaffe, Don Jonovic, Elaine Kepner, Ivan Lansberg, Justin Longenecker, Marion McCollom, Sharon Nelton and Ernesto Poza.

Craig E. Aronoff, Ph.D.

John L. Ward, Ph.D.

The Editors

Craig E. Aronoff, Ph.D., holds the Dinos Distinguished Chair of Private Enterprise and is professor of management at Kennesaw State College in Marietta, Georgia. The oldest son of a wholesale clothing business family, Aronoff created and directs Kennesaw State College's Family Business Forum, according to *Family Business Review,* the nation's premier model of college-based educational programs for family businesses. In 1989 he was named one of the top two post-secondary business educators in the nation by the National Federation of Independent Business Foundation.

John L. Ward, Ph.D., initiated and serves as the Ralph Marotta Professor of Free Enterprise at Loyola University of Chicago. He teaches strategic management and business leadership at Loyola's Graduate School of Business. Ward is the author of *Keeping The Family Business Healthy,* the leading book in the family business field. His research findings have been featured in many respected business and academic publications. Ward is a visiting lecturer on family business with two European business schools (IMI and IESE). In addition to speaking to more than 30 trade and professional audiences yearly, Ward has an active consulting practice focusing on family business succession, outside boards of directors and strategic planning. He currently serves on the boards of six companies.

Drs. Ward and Aronoff were co-editors of the three-volume series *The Future of Private Enterprise,* and as contributing editors for *Nation's Business,* co-author a monthly column on family business planning. They serve as frequent resources to national media on family business topics.

FAMILY BUSINESS
SOURCEBOOK

Chapter 1

General Overview

The family business has been rediscovered as the embodiment of management practices and business values required for competitiveness. But family dynamics renders firms vulnerable to rivalries and jealousies. Managing the seeming contradictions within systems that combine family and business is the key to family business survival and success.

A minor industry has now developed in helping owners of family businesses deal with the contradictions confronting them. Consultants, therapists, financial planners and researchers have become fascinated with the dilemmas of family businesses. The thoughtful prescriptions of those who have developed expertise in service of family businesses are helping to improve the odds of survival and success. Planning and communication are critical. Commitment to family values is essential as well.

Dealing with the conflicts inherent in family businesses is valuable in a societal as well as a familial sense. Real differences exist between owner-controlled and manager-controlled enterprises with the former producing greater efficiency and return on investment.

Introduction

The family business is being rediscovered as the embodiment of the management practices and business values needed to help the nation's industries regain their competitive edge. Family businesses offer many benefits including commitment to product quality, better employee relations and longer-term perspectives. They also better accommodate the next generation's talents and ambition while providing a more tolerant and supporting environment.

In the following article which originally appeared as a three-part series, the author also relates family business problems: conflicts in family businesses are dealt within the context of familial relationships and emotions, with much of the trauma centered in the succession process; in large family businesses, maintaining family control means dealing with additional stockholder and estate tax pressures.

Rediscovering Family Values

1986

By Steven Prokesch

The wallflower is becoming the belle of the ball. A decade-long debate over what is wrong with American business and how to cure it has produced a surprising model for success: the family business.

As old as America itself, the family business is being rediscovered as the embodiment of the management practices and business values needed to help the nation's industries regain their competitive edge.

The best family companies have long cared about product quality, treated employees with respect and focused on more lasting concerns than the next quarter's results. These values, business critics say, are exactly what Japan has cultivated and America has generally neglected.

"There is a tremendous amount of interest in family businesses," said James O'Toole, a management professor at the University of Southern California. "If you start looking around at well-run companies that have been around for a long time, you often find they are the work of a single individual or a family."

Family businesses, large and small, account for a majority of the jobs in the United States and for nearly half of all that America produces. Many, of course, are very small. But a great many of the nation's largest and best-known businesses are also all, or nearly all, in the family.

The family empires include Cargill, the dominant force in grain trading; S. C. Johnson & Son, popularly known as Johnson Wax; Estée Lauder, the cosmetics and fragrances company; Levi Strauss, the company that invented blue jeans, and Bechtel, the construction giant. Tabasco sauce, Mars candy bars, Stroh's beer and Schwinn bicycles are also made by family companies.

Families also hold sway over many large, publicly traded companies. The family influence at companies such as Du Pont may have withered over the decades as the family's holdings have dwindled or been diffused among the generations. Yet in many large companies families that own as little as 15 percent of the stock still remain dominant by holding prominent management positions, seats on the board and special voting privileges.

By this measure, Dow Jones & Company, the Times Mirror Company, the Washington Post Company and The New York Times Company remain family companies. The Corning Glass Works, one of the oldest enterprises in the United States, is headed by a fifth-generation member of the Houghton family, which founded the company. Descendants of the founders are still in charge at Anheuser-Busch, Marriott and McDonnell Douglas.

A growing number of universities — including Brigham Young, Pennsylvania, Southern California and Yale — are offering programs and sponsoring research on family business. Major corporations in many industries are trying to create family-like environments in their factories and offices in an attempt to get employees to work harder and smarter.

Books singing the praises of family business are starting to appear. In *The Big Time: the Harvard Business School's Most Successful Class and How It Shaped America*, one member of the famous class of '49 suggests that American industry might be much better off today if it had fewer of the sort of high-powered executives that Harvard turned out and more family-run companies "driven by a value system that's an extension of family values."

Consumers Prefer Family Companies

True or not, the public believes that products manufactured by family businesses are of higher quality than those made by companies that are not family affairs, according to a study of large and medium-size companies by John L. Ward, a professor of private enterprise at Loyola University of Chicago. Last year's sale of Richardson-Vicks Inc., which makes cosmetics and cold remedies, and this year's attempt to buy the Pulitzer Publishing Company demonstrate that the contenders in the merger-and-acquisition wars have also discovered the allures of family businesses.

In a sharp departure from the 1960's and 1970's, droves of ambitious young people are now returning to the fold of their families' businesses, both large and small.

As restructurings, mergers and acquisitions have swept American corporations, tens of thousands of white-collar jobs have been eliminated and it has become much tougher to climb the corporate ladder. And these events have coincided with a surge in demand for young managers at the family businesses created after World War II, whose founders are approaching retirement age.

"There is a perception that opportunities may not be as great in big corporations," said Peter Davis, the director of executive education at the University of Pennsylvania's Wharton School and a leading authority on family business.

At the same time, America's infatuation with the entrepreneur has turned family businesses — the vast majority of which are small or medium-sized companies — into respectable places to work. Only a decade ago, business school graduates who entered their families' businesses were often dismissed by their classmates as people who could not make it in the real world. Now their classmates are now more likely to view them with envy.

"I never realized how lucky I was until I went to business school," said Lisa M. Witomski, 30 years old, the director of marketing at her family's company, T. Frank McCall's Inc. of Chester, Pa., a distributor of janitorial supplies with sales of about $5 million. "When I described my family's business to everyone, they oohed and ahhed."

In interviews, several young men and women who had decided to go into their family businesses cited not only the security — always an allure — but also the opportunities to attain higher positions, wield more responsibility, earn more money and, of course, some day own the show.

Miss Witomski, who worked at the Pillsbury company for two years before she joined her family's business, said: "When you're working for a company like Pillsbury, the chances of reaching the top are very slim. There's security working for your family business."

Opportunities for Women

Family businesses are especially attractive to women, experts say, because of their limited success in penetrating the senior ranks of most large, publicly held corporations. In big companies, "women feel only lip service is given them regarding promotions and growth," said Dr. Matilde Salganicoff, a psychologist and family business consultant who runs a workshop at Wharton for women in family businesses.

A study of 91 women who attended the Wharton workshop found that women in family-owned businesses earn more money and hold higher management positions than do women at publicly held corporations.

Many young men and women also believe that their families' businesses are more willing than nonfamily corporations to accommodate their lifestyles and values.

"There is a resurgence of the desire for family ties," said Dr. Abraham Zaleznik, a psychoanalyst and Matsushita Professor of Leadership at the Harvard Business School, "especially given the impersonal and superficial human relationships perceived to exist in large corporations."

But Dr. Zaleznik and many other experts said that those who return to family businesses should beware. Of 59 families who operate businesses that were studied by a University of Minnesota research team, 52 reported tension or stress in their relationships because of their business involvement.

Some family businesses have been in the spotlight lately because of the well-publicized traumas that have been ripping the business — or at least their families — apart.

To put an end to bitter fighting among his three children, Barry Bingham Sr., the patriarch and chairman of the company that owned the *Louisville Courier-Journal* and the *Louisville Times*, put the family-owned newspaper and broadcasting on the auction block. Dissident family shareholders of Pulitzer Publishing tried to force the management members of the family to sell the company. And in the wine country of California, members of the Sebastiani family have feuded publicly over operation of their winery.

Family businesses have to deal with the generational disputes, sibling rivalries and the jealousies and tensions that divide so many families in addition to normal business problems. And in a family business, the death of the patriarch may not just be a personal trauma, but may set off a power struggle for control of the business.

A Respect for Tradition

The current fascination with family businesses, however, runs deeper than the public's love of a good family spat. It is also an appreciation of their values.

At Levi Strauss, S. C. Johnson, Marriott, L. L. Bean and other widely admired family companies, concern with quality, employees and the communities in which they have roots are not fads to be adopted today and abandoned tomorrow. They are family values handed down from one generation to the next and preserving them is often deemed as important as anything else.

Leon L. Bean, who founded the 74-year-old mail-order house that bears his name, died in 1967. But his grandson, Leon A. Gorman, the company's president, keeps alive the founder's tenet that the customer is always right. Even temporary employees go through a training program that includes a film on "L. L." and his philosophy. And to this day, dissatisfied Bean customers have the same privilege as those who bought L. L.'s original Maine hunting shoes: They may return merchandise with no questions asked.

Levi Strauss & Company is widely known for philanthropy and enlightened treatment of its employees. For Robert D. Haas, the president and chief executive, and his cousin Peter Haas Jr., a company executive and director, these are not beliefs learned at business school, but the values with which these two great-great-grand-nephews of the founder, Levi Strauss, were raised.

Both were expected, when growing up, to donate a portion of their allowances to charities. And when Robert's father, Walter Haas, Jr., was running the company, the kinds of business-related matters he discussed at home were the company's moves to integrate its plants in a still-segregated South or the ashtray that a worker had brought him from the Kentucky Derby. "What I drew from that was there aren't big and little people, just people, in an organization, and everybody counts," Robert said.

Certainly not all family businesses are well run. The Marriott Corporation may rank as one of the best-managed hotel and food-services companies around, but J. Willard Marriott Jr., its chairman and the son of its founders, said it took him 20 years to ease out unproductive relatives and family friends.

The late August Sebastiani may have built Sebastiani Vineyards into the nation's 11th-largest winery. But to hear his sons tell it, he was a tyrant who mistreated employees, family and non-family alike. He did not especially care about the welfare of the community in which he did business, they said, and he grossly underinvested in plant, equipment and staff, a practice that has come back to haunt the winery.

Some of the most venerable family-controlled or -run businesses—including Levi Strauss, S. C. Johnson, Corning Glass Works and the Weyerhaeuser Company, the timber and wood products giant—have had their share of troubles in recent years. To varying degrees, all four allowed bureaucracies to take root, tolerated mediocre or sloppy performance and were slow to adapt to changes in their industries. As a result, some of these companies had to restructure extensively and a couple had to resort to layoffs.

An examination by *Fortune* magazine of 10 large family-run companies whose stock is publicly traded found that their return to shareholders in the past decade in many instances lagged behind the average return in their respective industries. The mediocre earnings and stock performance of Richardson-Vicks, which had been run by the Richardson family for 80 years before it was sold last year to the Procter & Gamble Company, undoubtedly helped make it a takeover target.

On the other hand, several family companies were among those that had returned the most to their shareholders in the past decade. Shareholders of Hasbro Inc., the toy maker, fared the best of any *Fortune 500* company. Two other family companies—Herman Miller Inc., the office-furniture company based in Zeeland, Mich., and Tyson Foods of Springdale, Ark.—ranked fourth and fifth, respectively.

Some management experts insist that the larger, publicly traded family companies tend to outperform their competitors over the long haul. "If I'd want to make a quick killing, I'd probably not invest in them," Professor O'Toole of the University of Southern California said of family companies. "But if I wanted to have a secure investment that I could pass on to my children or grandchildren, I probably would."

Chief executives of nonfamily corporations, of course, often argue that they would like to take a long-term view toward their business. They want to take more risks in developing new products, they say, and they would show more commitment to their employees and communities if they could. Wall Street, with its pressure to keep up earnings, is the villain, they say.

Most family businesses, though, also have to contend with pressure to increase short-term earnings. Many have stock that is publicly traded. Even privately held family companies often have passive investors to worry about: relatives and foundations who may have no interest in management, but plenty of interest in their dividends.

Yet many of these companies believe they answer to a higher authority—to family traditions and the communities in which they live and conduct business.

That was a key reason why after 14 years as a public company, the descendants of Levi Strauss took the company private last year in a leveraged buyout. The family feared that Levi—and its long history of placing social concerns above profits—would fall victim to the acquisition wars sweeping corporate America, Robert D. Haas said.

The story is similar at other family companies. In selling their Louisville newspapers, one condition that the Binghams established was that the buyer express a willingness to continue to contribute five percent of the

9

newspapers' pretax profits to local charities and maintain their pay, benefits and employment levels. When the Gannett Company agreed last month to buy out the Binghams, it offered the most assurances of any prospective buyer, the family said.

Take Care of Employees'

Although Marriott has grown in the past 59 years from a single root-beer stand to a hotel and food-service giant with sales of $4.24 billion, its guiding philosophy has not changed: "Take care of employees and customers," Mr. Marriott said. "My father knew if he had happy employees, he would have happy customers and then that would result in a good bottom line."

The philosophy appears to be working. The driver of an airport-shuttle van in the Washington area said the simple reason why he feels lucky to be a Marriott employee is that "they take care of their people." Customers apparently feel the same: Corporate travel managers and travel agents surveyed last year by *Business Travel News* ranked Marriott hotels as "the best over all in the United States."

Other family companies view their responsibility to employees with equal importance. The century-old Johnson Wax—one of the nation's largest family-owned and -run companies, with sales of $2 billion—was one of the first companies in the country to give its employees paid vacations, pensions, profit-sharing and group life insurance. And it still has a no-layoff policy.

Herman Miller has a program that encourages workers (or "participative owners" as it calls them) to suggest ways to lower costs and raise productivity by giving them a portion of the savings. All of its 3,000 full-time employees in the United States who have been with the

company a year or more are shareholders.

While many other apparel companies have moved production overseas, where labor costs are much lower, the Phillips-Van Heusen Corporation maintains half of its production in the United States. "These people have worked for this company for generations," Lawrence S. Phillips, the company's president and the great-grandson of the Polish immigrant who started the company by selling woolen shirts to Pennsylvania coal miners, said with emotion.

Passions run equally high when the family business executives talk about the products and services their companies provide. Why do they seem to care more about their products than other companies? And why do consumers perceive their products to be of higher-quality than those that non-family companies turn out? "It's your name on the product," said Professor Ward of Loyola. "It's your pride. It's your integrity. It's your love. That's why."

The pride was evident as Mr. Phillips explained why his company refuses to sell its apparel lines to discounters. "We didn't spend all this time and money to build a brand just to make a quick buck by selling opportunistically and materialistically," he said.

Such family concerns as Herman Miller and Estée Lauder will often spend years developing new products or markets and will stick with them long after most other companies would have given up on them. Estee Lauder, for instance, swallowed losses for 10 years in Japan, until it became "a very, very successful" market for the company, said Leonard A. Lauder, the president and chief executive of the cosmetics company named for his mother.

Often, the most venerable family businesses are led by men who know their companies inside and out because they grew up with them. Max O. De Pree, the chairman and chief executive of Herman Miller, swept floors at the company "as a kid," he said, and later was a master upholsterer. So was his older brother, Hugh, who succeeded his father, D. J. De Pree, as chief executive in the early 1960's and then stepped down himself at the end of 1979.

Leonard Lauder's career began at age 10, when he collected sales receipts from beauty salons that sold his mother's cosmetics. In high school, he helped with bills and taking orders.

Mr. Marriott's first "real job," at age 14, was clipping invoices together in the finance department, he recalled. But his first big contribution came during the gas-rationing days of World War II, when his father asked him to help him figure out how to lure bus riders into the company's drive-in restaurants. He was then nine years old.

When the Relatives Fall Out

His wife, Vicki, stands stone-faced and silent, but Sam Sebastiani cannot hide his anguish as he chews a Tums in his home in the hills of California's wine country and mourns the loss of his job and his family. After he spent six years struggling to save his family's winery following his father's death, he said bitterly, his mother, brother and sister have rewarded his efforts by throwing him out.

Ernest D. Key Jr., the owner of the Atlanta Belting Company, is a man with a shattered dream: to pass on his small manufacturing company to his children, even as his father had passed it on to him. After disputes with two sons-in-law and a daughter, they quit the business. Now, he talks about selling it to employees.

"I thought the family that worked together, stayed together," he said. "I have proved that when a family works together, it is destroyed."

Family businesses. They can be the stuff that American dreams are made of. But as Sam Sebastiani, Ernest Key, and plenty of others can attest to, they can turn into nightmares as well.

Only 30 percent of family businesses survive their founders and make it into the second generation, according to most authorities on the subject. The rest are sold or go bankrupt. And the statistics grow grimmer with the passage of time. Only half of these companies that live through the transition to the second generation will survive as a family business into the third or fourth generations.

Moreover, just because they survive does not mean they thrive. John L. Ward, professor of private enterprise at Loyola University of Chicago, studied what happened to 200 family businesses during a 60-year period. He found that while 26 survived as privately owned family businesses, only six continued to grow and prosper.

Businesses run by families face many of the same challenges that confront non-family companies: handling leadership succession; keeping shareholders happy without milking the business dry; attracting and developing capable managers; forging a management consensus on the company's direction, and treating all employees, including women, fairly in terms of promotion and pay.

But in family businesses these issues can quickly assume highly emotional dimensions because they involve two distinctly different but equally demanding organizations: the family and the business.

"Often we tend to think of family businesses as some kind of unified structure in which what's good for the family is good for the business and vice versa," said Paul C. Rosenblatt, professor of family social science and psychology at the University of Minnesota and co-author of *The Family in Business*. "But the goal of the business is profitability, survival and cornering a share of the market, and the goal of the family is to keep people sane and getting along O.K. The actions you might take to make sure that everyone gets along, such as keeping relatives in the business who aren't doing the job, might undermine the profitability of the business," he said.

When Decisions Must Be Made

If anything, being in business together makes it tougher — not easier — for relatives to get along, Professor Rosenblatt and other experts said. Doling out raises or selecting a successor may be a difficult decision for any chief executive.

It is doubly difficult when the boss has to choose a son over a daughter — or reject both in favor of a more deserving outsider. All chief executives complain about how hard it is to keep investors happy. It is much more complicated when those shareholders are siblings, uncles or cousins.

When power, money and prestige are mixed in with the personal tensions common to most families, all too often the family business turns into a battleground that pits fathers against children, brothers against sisters and cousins against cousins.

"One of the biggest problems, if not the biggest problem, in family business is family members getting along with each other," said J. Willard Marriott Jr., chairman, chief executive and son of the founder of the Marriott Corporation, the multibillionaire hotel and food-service company of which the Marriott family owns 21 percent.

The well-publicized fight for control of the Louisville-based media empire owned by the Bingham family may have looked like an instance of women struggling to claim their rightful place in a business world that still largely discriminates against them. But in this case the man denying them their place, on the board happened to be their brother. To try to restore family peace, their father decided to sell the business.

Relatives Judged by Relatives

Mr. Key of Atlanta Belting said that his family blowup illustrated how difficult it could be for one family member to sit in judgment on the performance of another. When he criticized the work of his two sons-in-law, his daughters sided with their husbands, and Mr. Key's wife sided with the children, he said.

After his father, August Sebastiani, died in 1980, Sam Sebastiani became head of Sebastiani Vineyards. But he did not succeed his father in becoming the company's major stockholder. And perhaps even more important, he did not succeed him in becoming the head of the family. From accounts provided by both Sam and his younger brother Don, Sam's difficulties in getting along with his brother and sister quickly turned the business into a battleground.

But his fatal mistake may have been the way he handled his relationship with his mother, Sylvia. He acted more like a chief executive than the attentive son she had wanted following her husband's death. Sam began to communicate with her by memos, sent by intermediaries to keep her posted on the business. And he made his wife the winery's first lady, a role his mother had held.

All this not only hurt his mother's feelings. It also lost him the support of the company's controlling shareholder, his mother. And that cost him his job. "I should have seen the signal," he now says.

The Trauma of Succession

To varying degrees, the trauma that the Sebastiani family business suffered is well known to thousands of other family businesses: the trauma of succession. Because so many of the G.I.'s who came back from World War II to start up a business are nearing retirement age, an unprecedented number of family businesses are in the process of being passed from one generation to the next.

But to hear psychologists, consultants, academic experts and those in family businesses tell it, the vast majority of these companies will handle the transfer miserably. And as the statistics indicate, most of these businesses will leave the family fold.

Peter Davis, director of executive education at the University of Pennsylvania's Wharton School and a leading authority on family business, said succession was "the most difficult transition" that family companies face. Dr. Norman L. Paul, a Boston psychiatrist, called it "the main problem" for family businesses and one "that is sloppily handled in general."

The same business owners who say that their dream is to pass on the fruits of their labor to their children somehow cannot bring themselves to groom a successor and minimize estate taxes – both vital steps for insuring that the business stays in the family and thrives.

Why? Because many business founders view the task of giving up the enterprise as tantamount to planning for their own funerals.

"They look upon retirement as somewhere between euthanasia and castration," said Léon A. Danco, president of the Cleveland-based Center for Family Business, a consulting firm. Ivan L. Lansberg, an organizational behavior specialist at Yale University, said that many equate stepping down from the family business with surrendering their power, compromising their standing in the community and losing their identity.

Another Battle in Oedipal War

Some psychiatrists and psychologists see the struggle for control of the family business that often occurs between fathers and sons in particular as but another battle in their unresolved Oedipal war. Only now, the company is the mother figure both are fighting to possess.

John A. Davis, an organizational behavior specialist at the University of Southern California, said the best time to begin dealing with succession is when a father is in his 50's and his children are in their late 20's or early 30's. "Match them in this period, and you've got a teacher and a student," he said.

But match a father in his 40's who is undergoing midlife crisis and a son in his early 20's who is trying to assert his independence and the results can be disastrous. Another bad mix: When a father is in his 60's or older and is suddenly confronted with the frightening fact that his life is nearing an end, and his son is in his late 30's and is obsessed with making his own mark.

In many successful situations, Professor Davis said, "The son wants to take control of his own life and the father happens to be in the way." He added, "The father wants to maintain control over his own life and live out his dreams. What we have here is a battle between the two men's developmental needs."

This may explain why Dan Bishop, the 34-year-old vice president of operations of a Los Angeles-based rubber products company founded by his great-uncle, is full of anxieties. Succession plans at the company are in limbo. Meanwhile, Mr. Bishop favors an aggressive diversification program to reduce the company's dependence on its traditional product line of tire-repair materials. But his 60-year-old father, and boss, favors a slower approach.

"Change is harder for him," the younger Mr. Bishop said. "He did his risk-taking 50 years ago. I'm starting my risk-taking now." He added that "out of my frustration" he founded with his wife, Carol, a therapist, the National Family Business Association, one of many support groups for people in family businesses that have sprung up in recent years.

The Concern for Security

The problem is common. As business leaders enter their 60's, they often become risk-averse. Financial security suddenly becomes of paramount importance. Handing over the business to a son or daughter eager to prove him or herself will jeopardize that security, they fear.

The story of John Paul Getty, the billionaire who was frightened to let go of his money, is legendary. But it seems that every consultant who works with family businesses has a comparable tale to tell.

The impact of not reinvesting in the business and not permitting the up-and-coming generation to spread its wings can be devastating, Professor Ward of Loyola said. He found that those few family companies that have managed to prosper and grow over the decades also were the ones that had given each new generation the room to prove itself by taking the business in a new direction.

As his official biography puts it, J. Willard Marriott Sr., the co-founder of Marriott, "shunned credit like the spotted fever." Nonetheless, he decided to let his oldest son, Bill, take on the debt needed to finance a big push into the hotel business — and transform a business with sales of less than $100 million into a corporation whose sales hit $4.24 billion last year.

While still in his 20's, Samuel C. Johnson, the current chief executive of S.C. Johnson & Son Inc. and great-grandson of the company's founder was allowed by his father to orchestrate the company's entry into the insecticide business. Today, insecticides are one of its most profitable businesses, with sales of more than $200 million.

Now he wants his children to carry on the tradition. So far, Mr. Johnson has coaxed two of his four children to join the company: His eldest son, S. Curtis Johnson 3rd, who is 31, is involved in a new venture capital business that he convinced his father to create. And a daughter, Helen, 29, is marketing new hair products. "I'm looking to the fifth generation to bring new perspectives and new inputs into the company," Mr. Johnson said.

Only too often, though, fathers cannot or will not face the fact that the son or daughter who is a manager in the business is capable of handling responsibility. Until his death in 1980, August Sebastiani ran what had become the nation's 11th-largest winery as a virtual one-man show.

"You had to be 55 before you could gain business credence with my father," Sam Sebastiani said. "If you did something 99 percent perfect, he concentrated on the one percent that was wrong."

Keeping Control Gets Harder

Last year's sale of Richardson-Vicks Inc. to the Procter & Gamble Company for $1.22 billion sent shock waves through other family businesses. If Richardson-Vicks was vulnerable, their leaders reasoned, what family company was not?

The]Richardson family had managed the 80-year-old maker of cold remedies and personal-care products for four generations and had been united in its desire to keep the company independent. It controlled directly and indirectly a third of the company's stock. In times gone by, that would have been more than enough to quash the fancies of any would-be acquirer. But now even family-controlled businesses are vulnerable if their performance falls short in the eyes of the market.

As the fall of Richardson-Vicks amply demonstrated, times have radically changed. In a period when the values and traditions of family businesses are being held up as a model for American industry, it has never been tougher for families to hang on to their companies and to manage them the way they want. Judging from what the leaders of the biggest private and public family companies say, there is no safe haven for a family business of any size from the takeover wars and intensifying competition sweeping corporate America.

S. C. Johnson & Son Inc. may be one of the largest privately held family companies, with sales of $2 billion. Even so, its chairman, Samuel C. Johnson, worries about his century-old consumer-products company being overpowered in the marketplace by what he called "agglomerating competitors" such as Procter & Gamble, which can rely on the stock market to finance its mega-mergers.

On the other hand, J. Willard Marriott Jr. the chairman of the publicly traded Marriott Corporation, envies the likes of S. C. Johnson. Although his family controls 21 percent of the company, Mr. Marriott complains about the compromises he must make to raise his company's stock price. He would like to own more of his hotels, rather than just manage them. And he would spend more on advertising, if only he dared. "If we were a private company, we would do a lot of things differently," he said.

As the family leaders of companies, ranging from the giant Marriott to the relatively small McIlhenny company, the maker of Tabasco sauce, readily acknowledge, this is an age that honors merit. In an era when the takeover sharks will start circling at the first sign of weakness and shareholders — even those who are relatives — may be more than willing to sell for the right price, lineage and tradition are no longer deemed an adequate substitute for raw talent and outstanding performance. A high stock price and a healthy dividend seem to be all that matter these days.

"One of the reasons we're around is we are profitable and pay a good dividend," said Edward M. Simmons, the president and a member of the fourth generation of the founding family to manage McIlhenny, based in Avery

Island, La., which is owned by 90 descendants of the company's founder or their spouses.

Estate Taxes are Burdensome

Even before the merger and acquisition boom, family tensions and the weakening of family bonds over time made it exceedingly difficult for most business families to maintain their ownership and management grip on their companies. If family squabbles did not cause the sale or breakup of a family business, estate taxes often would.

To settle with the tax man, the]Wrigley family had to sell the Chicago Cubs baseball team. The Coors family had to sell shares in its beer company to the public. And confronted with the double whammy of five years of losses and a steep estate tax bill, the Sebastiani family of Sebastiani Vineyards has had to consider selling its winery.

Of course, the family influence at Du Pont, Procter & Gamble and thousands of other one-time family businesses has withered as their founders' descendants became too numerous or simply lost interest in the company over the years. As the business passed to the third, fourth or fifth generation, the priority of family members not active in management often becomes maximizing income rather than holding on to the business. That is why the Rockefeller family recently decided to cash out of Rockefeller Center by, in essence, selling a large portion of the famed Manhattan complex to a real estate investment trust. And it is a major reason why such newspaper publishing companies as the Tribune company of Chicago have gone public.

Another reason so many family companies are selling these days is because of the lofty premiums that acquirers are now frequently willing to pay. "Family members are saying: 'Our business may never be worth this much again. Maybe we ought to sell while we're at the top of the market,'" said John L. Ward, professor of private enterprise at Loyola University of Chicago and an authority on family businesses.

At the Mercy of the Market

Even if a family wants to keep its businesses, the trusts and foundations that often hold their shares for them may have no choice but to sell if the bid is high. In a legal case arising from the LTV Corporation's attempt to buy the Grumman Corporation in 1981, a judge ruled that pension fund trustees who helped Grumman thwart LTV were personally liable for not acting in the best interest of their beneficiaries. Although an appeals court dismissed the case (because a rise in Grumman's stock price had eliminated the fund's paper loss and rendered the issue moot), the lower court ruling was still seen as setting a precedent.

"That scared the dickens out of a lot of family businesses," said Martin A. Siegel, a managing director and co-head of the mergers and acquisitions department at Drexel Burnham Lambert Inc. "Now unless 51 percent of the company is in the hands of one person who is young, in good health, has money outside of his investments in the company and doesn't live in a community property state, it's vulnerable."

If Richardson-Vicks failed to take precautions before it was too late, plenty of other companies are fighting back.

Mr. Johnson of S. C. Johnson plans eventually to transfer his majority ownership to one of his four children to protect the private company from family squabbles that have sparked the sale of other family businesses.

The descendants of the founder of Levi Strauss & Company, the blue jean and apparel maker, took their company private in a $2 billion leveraged buyout last summer. The move pre-empted any possible takeover attempt and also allowed the company to buy out 60 percent of its family shareholders. As a result, the worry of family shares passing into possibly unfriendly hands "is going to be a problem for another generation to contend with," said Robert D. Haas, the president and chief executive and a great-great-great-nephew of the company's founder.

Marriott purposely keeps its debt level high and requires that any acquirer has to obtain the backing of two-thirds of its shareholders. The Phillips-Van Heusen Corporation, which has been considering going private, just this week adopted a "stockholder rights" plan aimed at making it prohibitively expensive for an unfriendly suitor to buy the company.

Dow Jones & Company, the publisher of *The Wall Street Journal*, recently adopted a bylaw mandating its directors to take into account non-economic issues in considering any takeover bid. In a more dramatic move that has stirred controversy, Dow Jones is in the process of issuing a special class of stock to shareholders aimed at insuring that voting control of the company remains with the Bancroft family, which owns 54.7 percent of the company.

Companies Alter Voting Structures

Many other companies, non-family as well as family-run, are doing the same. "At least 50 companies on the three major stock exchanges have substantially altered their voting structures over the past two years and a number of others have proposed similar changes," said John Pound, a senior financial economist at the Securities and Exchange Commission.

Many family businesses have long had various classes of stock with different voting rights to insure that even if family ownership fell below the 50 percent mark, it would still control the company. But several of these businesses, including the New York Times Company, created their separate classes of stock before they went public.

What is controversial about what Dow Jones and other companies have done or are doing is that they are changing the rules in the middle of the game," said Mr. Pound, who is involved in an S.E.C. study of whether such changes hurt shareholders.

For its part, Dow Jones "feels very strongly that the journalistic independence that we operate under as a result of the Bancroft ownership is something very critical to the company's continued success," said Lawrence A. Armour, Dow Jones' director of corporate relations. Under increasing pressure from competing exchanges, the New York Stock Exchange, which had frowned on such recapitalizations, is reconsidering its regulations.

Even as family businesses are embracing these protective measures, though, many are taking steps to improve the quality of their management. At a time when thousands of young men and women are rediscovering their families' businesses as great places to work, many would-be successors are expected to "prove themselves" first in the outside world.

Giving Children Some Choices

Fathers who had been forced by their fathers to go into the business are now going to extremes to make sure that their children are not torn by the same doubts that they endured.

Lawrence S. Phillips, the president and chief executive of Phillips-Van Heusen, lamented that he had "no choice" about going into his family's apparel company. And he recalled his "embarrassment" at being made a vice president at age 29 because "I didn't deserve to be vice president nearly as much as executives who were not related to my father," Seymour J. Phillips, now the company's chairman. Now, he said, he will consider allowing his son, David, 26 years old, to join the business only after he has worked for five to 10 years someplace else.

William and Gary Lauder, the two sons of the president of Estée Lauder Inc., decided to get some career training outside the family. William, 26, is an associate merchandiser for Macy's, while Gary, 24, is a venture capital analyst for a small investment bank.

In another sign of the times, many family business leaders of bigger companies assert that no child of theirs should assume that he or she has an automatic claim to the throne. Mr. Marriott noted that his two sons and a son-in-law are beginning in low management positions and "there have been no promises" one will ever get to the top job.

Attracting and retaining outside management talent is also critically important for family businesses, and it is often a difficult task.

Some executives shun family companies for fear of getting caught in a family fight. Don Sebastiani, the chairman and chief executive of Sebastiani Vineyards, said he thought such fears were one reason why several executives he had approached about becoming president of the winery would not consider the job.

Non-family managers are frequently reluctant to devote themselves to a company in which they will never be able to obtain an ownership stake or have a shot at the top job. "A lot of professional managers say, 'This is a good place to get started in but I wouldn't want to stay here for a career,'" said W. Gibb Dyer Jr., an organizational behavior specialist at Brigham Young University who has studied professional managers in family businesses.

Some family companies have been able to keep high-powered executives by paying them a premium. One such company is Mars, the family-owned candy giant, according to Peter Davis, the director of executive education at the University of Pennsylvania's Wharton School and a leading authority on family business. At Mars, he said, "managers know they will never own part of the company, but they are paid above the industry norms and in some cases, significantly above industry norms."

At least one family company has decided that not even money is enough of an incentive. When Max O. De Pree, the 61-year-old chief executive of Herman Miller Inc., retires, management control of the successful furniture maker will pass from the family, which has run the company since 1919.

What is unusual about this transfer is that it stems from neither a lack of heirs nor family interest. Rather, the De Prees decided that only by barring the third generation from the business could they attract the management talent that Herman Miller needed to grow.

Protecting the Family Jewel
Actions by four family-owned companies to safeguard family control.

Levi Strauss & Company
> The Haas family, descendants of the company's founder, took the business private in a $2 billion leveraged buyout in 1985.

Phillips-Van Heusen
> The board adopted a stockholder rights plan this week to make an unfriendly acquisition bid prohibitively expensive. The company has also been considering a leveraged buyout.

S. C. Johnson & Son
> Samuel C. Johnson plans to transfer his majority ownership to one of his four children to protect this private company from family squabbles that have sparked sales of other family businesses.

Dow Jones & Company
> The company announced plans in 1984 to issue a second class of stock with special voting rights that will maintain control by the Bancroft family, which now owns 54.7 percent of the company. A shareholder suit delayed the move but the case was settled in the company's favor on May 29.

Note:
On April 16, [1986] Dow Jones changed its bylaws to discourage unfriendly suitors. It staggered the terms of its board; required any prospective buyers to make the same dollar offer to all stockholders, and allowed the board to consider non-economic issues in a takeover offer.

Introduction

Is family management contrary to American principles of freedom and equality? Is there real value in a tradition of family management? Does family influence contradict all precepts of professional management? Is it foolish to attempt to perpetrate family influence in any firm? Robert L. Donnelley poses these questions and then takes a dispassionate look at family business to identify some of its advantages and disadvantages.

The Family Business
1964

...has both strengths and weaknesses. The important thing is to understand them.

By Robert G. Donnelley

- Is family management contrary to the fundamental American creed advocating free competition, equality of opportunity, and the best man for the job?

- Is the value of a tradition of family management largely illusory — a product of self-interested rationalization by the families involved?

- Does family influence contradict all precepts of professional management?

- Do the complexities and demands of today's business environment make it foolish to attempt to perpetuate family influence in any firm?

Doubts like these about the effectiveness — if not the morality — of family management of businesses are typical of prevailing attitudes among businessmen, consultants, and educators. In some enterprises, the family interest is a source of serious weakness. But whether the very presence of family members in an organization is per se an indication of mismanagement is definitely open to question. In fact, if one takes an objective look at the success of some family enterprises, he may wonder whether the effectiveness of the typical reward-punishment system underlying nonfamily businesses has not been greatly overrated.

In this article, I will attempt to take just such a dispassionate look at family business and to identify some of its advantages and disadvantages, hoping that these will serve as guideposts for

What Is A Family Business?

In this article a company is considered a family business when it has been closely identified with at least two generations of a family and when this link has had a mutual influence on company policy and on the interests and the objectives of the family. Such a relationship is indicated when one or more of the following conditions exists:

Family relationship is a factor, among others, in determining management succession.

Wives or sons of present or former chief executives are on the board of directors.

The important institutional values of the firm are identified with a family, either in formal company publications or in the informal traditions of the organization.

The actions of a family member reflect on or are thought to reflect on the reputation of the enterprise, regardless of his formal connection to management.

The relatives involved feel obligated to hold the company stock for more than purely financial reasons, especially when losses are involved.

The position of the family member in the firm influences his standing in the family.

A family member must come to terms with his relationship to the enterprise in determining his own career.

members of the business and financial community who wish to understand such enterprises more fully. I hope that this article will be of particular interest to those who are currently employed by, or are considering being employed by, or who now manage family firms.

In view of the fact that what are strengths in one company may be weaknesses in another, the most that any outsider can contribute to people within a particular firm is to provide insights that will help them understand their situations so they can then work out their own courses of action.

My observations are based on a study of 15 successful family companies, supported by personal interviews with family managers and other interested businessmen and educators.

Weaknesses to Avoid

Let us look first at the negative side of the picture, in terms of actual case examples, and then go on to examine the impressive instances where, in contrast, strengths have developed. Among the

weaknesses of family management, the following seem most prevalent:

1. Conflicts occurring between the interests of the family and those of the enterprise as a whole.

2. A lack of discipline being exerted over profits and performance in all parts of the organization.

3. A failure to rise quickly to meet new marketing challenges.

4. Situations where nepotism rules unchecked by objective standards of meritorious managerial performance.

Conflicts of Interest

In a family company, the family almost always has the proprietary and/or management power to pursue its own objectives and aspirations, even when they are at variance with the best interests of the enterprise. By contrast, the competing interests and values of members of a "public" corporation check or condition those of the individual (and his family); and the corporate leadership tends to develop, perpetuate, and emphasize the institutional values of the firm over those of the individual through formal systems of measurement and incentive.

Of course, this situation in the public corporation does not always result in a balance. Sometimes, the organization will dominate the individual and his family. The popular concept of the organization man with his organization wife and children is an example of this danger. Such domination will sometimes directly affect the public interest, as was exemplified in the price-fixing case involving General Electric, Westinghouse, and some other producers of electrical equipment. While the public corporation may have problems, its corporate machine at least enforces in its members a sense of responsibility to the heads of the organization.

In a family enterprise, this organizational enforcement is not native to the system, at least as it applies to family members. The balance between family interests and company interests is usually a psychological one, stemming from the family's own personal sense of responsibility toward the firm. The fact that most successful family enterprises have developed elaborate institutional restraints on family prerogatives, backed in most cases by rigid family traditions, does not obviate this fact, for in each of these cases, the restraints had to be initially effected by the family members themselves. E. I. du Pont de Nemours & Company, Inc., almost universally considered the epitome of a well-administered, successful organization, is an example:

"Despite the fact that members of the du Pont family represent a substantial ownership interest in the company and are present in its management and policy making, family relationship, quite obviously, has not been the sole reason for promotion. This restraint on family prerogative, however, stems from Pierre du Pont's deliberate rejection, in 1910, of the "long-entrenched, inherited attitude that the firm was managed for the family and the family was to manage the firm . . . . . Pierre did appoint family members . . . to senior posts . . . but only after they had proven themselves managerially competent." [1]

In less successful organizations, however, the immunity from institutional restraint allows important company needs to be thwarted by family considerations. Such a situation may lead to one or more of the widely catalogued problems of family firms, including capital shortages, misguided financial secrecy, ingrown company policies, a lack of profit discipline, ineffective utilization of nonrelated management talent, nepotism, and, most seriously, family conflicts.

These abuses, moreover, are not unnatural, especially in a family that has failed to develop consciously a sense of company responsibility. Unlike the company value system, which ideally determines a person's authority, responsibility, status, and financial benefits on the basis of his demonstrated competence in accomplishing the goals of the firm, family norms usually stress the obligation of providing for the needs of the family. In the resulting confusion of values, company requirements may lose out to family obligations. Such a situation is demonstrated by the case of the Cole Hardware Company* (the names of this and subsequent companies designated by an asterisk, and the individuals involved, are disguised, but they represent actual cases):

Reasoning from his obligation to the other family members, Peter Cole, the president and sales manager, felt required to give his brothers and brother-in-law positions in the firm, despite their incompetence. "The thing to do would be to let them out," he stated, "but I can't do that with my own brothers. Furthermore, if my brother-in-law isn't employed here in some sort of a job, I'll just have to find another way of supporting him."[2]

Cole's expressed obligation to his relatives is in direct contrast to an employer's normal responsibility which requires him to reward only performance and to penalize the lack of it. In the case of the Cole company, the president ignored the company need—a competent management group—to solve a family problem. This confusion of family interests with those of the firm is also the source of other problems in family firms.

In those situations where the company is considered the family exchequer, an excessive secrecy over financial matters may result, stifling the development of adequate business controls and sound planning techniques and allowing ineffective methods and policies to remain long undiscovered. Here is an example:

> In one large eastern family manufacturing firm, the family managers excluded—even from the treasurer—any knowledge of the company's financial position, because the family's financial interests were so interrelated with those of the business. In such a situation, the company treasurer was not able to perform even the most basic

functions normally accorded the job.

Poor Profit Discipline

Another problem found in family firms (but also common to close corporations in general) is lack of profit discipline. Like a close corporation, a family company may tend to concentrate on product quality, excessive plant and equipment improvement, civic affairs, sales "empire building," and personnel relations beyond the contribution of these factors to the long-term profits of the company. This emphasis may lead to poor cost-control systems and other lax accounting procedures, or to management's unwillingness to take the necessary corrective action when company accounting procedures indicate that its "pet projects" are out of line.

Although the impact of this problem is hard to estimate statistically, the top officers of two major Chicago banks cited "good accounting systems" and the "willingness to take quick corrective action when costs are out of line" as the major differences between successful and unsuccessful family enterprises. And it is interesting to note that a recent comparison of a group of small companies (of which 80 percent are closely held) with their publicly owned counterparts revealed that those belonging to the closely held group generally had lower profit margins—one-half that of their publicly owned competitors. Since family firms are generally more conservative than public firms in their financial reporting, and since family firms, for competitive and tax reasons, may bury profits in many ways, these figures must be suspect.

Nevertheless, there is something to consider here for managers of family-owned companies who may question the sharpness of their profit discipline.

How Prevalent Is Family Ownership?

An estimated 20 percent of **Fortune's** list of 500 largest manufacturing companies show evidence of significant family management and/or proprietary interest.

In many industries — including chemicals, drugs, textiles, grain brokerage, meat packing, investment banking, glass making, liquor distributing, printing, publishing, advertising, and retailing — family-identified firms play a significant, if not dominant, role. These enterprises include such successful organizations as Du Pont, Seagrams, Cargill, Corning Glass, Upjohn, Firestone Tire and Rubber, Winn-Dixie Stores, Joseph Magnin, Cabot, Inc., and Lykes Bros. Steamship.

A 1955 **Fortune** survey of 175 of the largest U.S. corporations revealed that no less than 55 percent of the companies had close relatives or in-laws holding management jobs in the same firm.

A 1952 study based on a survey of 8,000 executives made by Professors W. Lloyd Warner and James C. Abegglen (**Big Business Leaders in America**, New York, Harper & Bros., 1955) revealed that two out of every five men whose fathers were top-ranking executives, and three out of every five men whose fathers were owners of large businesses, had positions in their fathers' companies. Significantly, these researchers found that the proportion of sons and major owners in the same firms as their fathers reflected an increase over that found in a survey conducted 24 years before. Professors Warner and Abegglen also noted a decline in the number of sons holding the top position of president or chief executive in the same firms as their fathers but found this "more than offset by the increase in sons among vice-presidents and below" compared with a generation ago.

Immobile Marketing

Too much involvement with family interest may prevent a company from capitalizing on new market developments or on major growth opportunities. This attitude is illustrated in the case of the Howard Wine Company :

> To meet a developing national market for its products, the company needed additional equity financing. Even though the firm's projected growth would have more than covered its equity dilution, the Howard family opposed the move, according to the financial consultant, solely because they felt "it wouldn't be right, having outsiders meddling in our affairs."

When a family identifies too closely with a particular product or function, another problem may arise: the company may be particularly vulnerable to the effects of changes in the market. Such a situation was true of the Hollowell Glove Company :

> Through the years, the father had trained his son to equate quality with a specific glove style. Despite a change in taste which made this particular style unacceptable, the son was unable to lead the firm in adapting to the new market condition. In this particular case, the son hopefully believed that customers would return to the old style and thought that any change in the product "would only cheapen the company's reputation for quality that my father took such pains to develop."

This problem does not exist in all family firms. Nevertheless, while some of the executives and business educators interviewed commended successful family companies in general for their "firm policy of defining their product and staying within the definition," many noted a wide-spread marketing weakness in family firms. As the president of a major Chicago bank put it:

"With respect to the less successful enterprises, it is our observation that their production is usually fairly efficient. Their problems are most apt to center around marketing and the development of new and improved products. Thus, these companies tend to lag behind their competition and lose market position. Recovery of a deteriorated competitive position is a slow and difficult process which usually cannot be achieved by the management that permitted the deterioration to occur."

Excessive Nepotism

A less subtle problem of family companies is nepotism, which according to one dictionary definition is "the advancement of relatives on the basis of family rather than merit." So much has been written on this subject alone that there is danger of its being overly stressed in any discussion of family enterprises. As noted in *Fortune*, "The overriding fact is . . . that competition and the demands of the marketplace soon take care of any company that relies on incompetent relatives in management."[3] Despite this fact, every family-identified firm must be concerned with possible favoritism built into its personnel policies, since popular opinion almost automatically suspects such an abuse in nearly all family businesses.

In firms where it is practiced, nepotism develops from the family's imposition of its own values and membership criteria on the business, regardless of the question of competence. When this occurs, the opportunities that can be offered to nonfamily management talent are restricted. This, of course, places the company at a disadvantage with respect to its competitors who can draw on wider markets for their personnel.

At the same time, nepotism weakens the firm's present managers, forcing them both to carry the dead weight of the incompetents and to assume the burden of the job left undone. Even more seriously, nepotism may lead to a management system that stresses family politics rather than accuracy. When this occurs, the essential task-orientation of the firm is destroyed considerably, jeopardizing the company's long-term prospects for survival.

The type of thinking that creates nepotism is also conducive to internecine feuds—the most serious problem in family enterprises. Arguments and serious differences of opinion are not unique to family firms. Nevertheless, the normal mechanism of inheritance can create strongly competing minority interests and disagreements which, when they do occur in a family firm, seem to involve the emotions of all the parties to an exceptionally high degree.

Tradition and company identification, as well as proprietary interest, cause each family member to view himself as a spokesman for the business, with a right to decide corporate policy equal to that of the other family members. Thus is created the paradox of one such company where the authority stemming from the position in the company is circumvented—so much so that the policies instituted by the president are challenged by the executive vice president.

When, in addition to nepotism, other abuses are present, the potential danger of family conflict is enhanced. In companies where out-and-out nepotism exists, the system of measurement and rewards based on family relationship rather than competence diminishes the institution's ability to cope with internal stresses and strains. Each decision becomes a subjective and highly charged "family problem," instead of a settlement based on the external objective standard of contribution to company goals. In the Everett Hardware Manufacturing Company :

> The senior executives, Paul and Peter Everett, agreed to treat their respective sons alike, despite the demonstrated greater competence of one of them. When the fathers died, however, the firm's operations became paralyzed, as neither branch of the family allowed the other any control. Since the company was treated as a family inheritance rather than a family responsibility, the fathers provided no system of weighing the claims of the cousins. Such a system, however, became important when family harmony was lost.

Strengths to Seek

Even though these problems exist in some family firms, one should not overlook the significant advantages that may be realized by the organization that can successfully capitalize on the assets such a relationship supplies. After all, family self-interest is similar to any other human factor that competes with or otherwise interferes with corporate objectives. Parkinson's Law, for example describes a common bureaucratic situation in which a manager will satisfy his own need for prestige by adding superfluous employees. The situation in which workers restrict output despite a company's formal system of incentives and measurement is an example of powerful human forces at work on a lower level.

When, however, such self-interest is controlled in a family firm and the family equates its long-term best interest with that of the company, a rare harmony is achieved between the normally competing values within the individual and the organization. Reinforced and perpetuated by family pride, identification, and tradition, this unity of purpose has been a fundamental, though intangible, factor in the success of many family firms. It is also the basis of all the other advantages accruing to such an enterprise. Among these are the following:

1. The availability of otherwise unobtainable financial and management resources because of family sacrifices.

2. Important community and business relationships stemming from a respected name.

3. A dedicated and loyal internal organization.

4. An interested, unified management-stockholder group.

5. A sensitivity to social responsibility.

6. Continuity and integrity in management policies and corporate focus.

Personal Sacrifice

It is paradoxical that family interest, a source of financial weakness in some firms, is in other circumstances a major element of financial strength. Many family companies have been built on the tradition of minimal dividends and personal sacrifice, and family pride and loyalty have been responsible for continued operation through periods of hardship when considerations of profit and loss might well have dictated closing down. According to a noted business historian, it was just these factors that caused the early owning families behind Weyerhaeuser to sustain 40 years of losses so that the company could grow into an industrial giant.

The extent of this loyalty is evident in a wife's reminiscences of the early struggles behind another major industrial leader:

> "Our good times were always five years ahead. Whenever I wanted some new furniture, my husband said, 'Not now. We need a new machine.'"

In other cases, family pride and identification cause company obligations to be honored beyond the family's legal responsibility. The bankruptcy debts against many firms are repaid for these reasons. In one major company, the owning family even paid out of its own pocket the firm's obligations to its employees during a period of substantial financial losses.

Sometimes, a well-established family not only contributes financial support but also draws upon management skills in its other organizations to help the firm in solving a serious problem. In several of the cases studied, particularly those dealing with closely held firms, this type of emergency pooling of resources is found to be quite prevalent. Take the case of the Roger Distributing Company* :

> Throughout the war years, this company had rapidly expanded by providing accounting and distributing services to industry. Most of its business, however, was tied up in one major account. In the postwar changeover to a new system of record keeping, the company developed serious production and administrative difficulties in servicing this key account. Unsolved, these problems would not only have caused the company to lose a substantial amount of business, but would also have reflected on the firm's reputation in the industry. The necessary engineering help was found, however, in another company run by the Roger family. The owning family itself came to the rescue by making the necessary arrangements; it did not leave the solution up to the two competing management groups within the organization.

Much criticism is leveled against family executives who inherit plush administrative positions with little or no effort on their parts. Little credit, however, is given to the family manager who takes over an organization that is "too messy" or "too hopeless" to attract the so-called competent outsider. Witness the case of the Horwitz Machine Company,* a small midwestern manufacturer of heating products:

> In this company, the nonrelated president attempted to ruin the firm so that he could own it outright. This action was instigated despite the favorable stock option plan provided the president on his acceptance of a position in management and without regard to the other employees or to the community within which the company was located. After a considerable personal investment, the family stockholders were able to squeeze out the president. When no one could be attracted to

manage the company, an experienced family member undertook the job as part of his "family responsibility."

Valuable Reputation

In concluding its article on the Rothschilds, *Time* noted, ". . . to face the future, they [the Rothschilds] have one advantage from the past, the Rothschild legend — in itself a very bankable asset."[4]

Not only may a family's reputation have a beneficial influence on community relations, but it may have a direct and obvious impact on the company's operations. In many cases of struggling manufacturing companies, the owning family's reputation is an important factor in receiving loans from local banks. In spite of the uncertainty of these ventures, the banks believe that their risks are lessened in view of their past experience with the family.

Family ties may also be important in establishing the trust necessary to conduct business — especially in situations where the stakes are high and the companies involved are not protected by a unique competency, a special expertise, or by legal sanctions against a breach of faith. The fast-moving, risky field of investment banking seems to be an example of such a situation. Several New York investment houses are connected by family ties which may be important in the establishment of joint ventures where the returns may be substantial and the competitive relationships highly informal.

In some cases, the benefit derived from a family relationship may be more subtle. In those areas of business where informal relationships are crucial to the conduct of the enterprise, the firm's identification with a family may have a direct bearing on its marketing activities. A closely held brokerage house, for example, may retain or attract customers because of its identification with a prominent family or families. Such a relationship may play a role in instances where all other factors are comparable or the results of the services provided are intangible.

Employee Loyalty

The value of a family relationship is not limited to the family's role in the firm's business and its public relations. Such involvement may also play a large role in the internal organization of the enterprise. To the small firm, family management can avoid disastrous executive turnover and ensure that the company's particular competitive skills will remain unique to it.

In recent years, business has become increasingly aware of the problem of the high turnover at the executive level. One New York consultant firm estimates that 75,000 to 100,000 of the nation's executives in middle and upper management change their jobs yearly. The size of this turnover led one writer to comment:

> "Although it cannot be shown in dollars and cents on a profit-and-loss statement, turnover at the executive level is . . . one of the most costly hidden items borne by the modern corporation."[5]

What is expensive to the large firm may be disastrous to the small one, where such turnover disrupts the management organization and threatens the firm's competitive livelihood. A nonrelated executive is held to a small firm only by his self-interest. If he finds an opportunity that suits him better, he will go elsewhere. If he joins a company in another area, he represents a considerable loss in terms of the time and expense spent in training him--resources that are severely limited in the small enterprise. More likely, he will join a competitive firm or go into business for himself and thus represent a major threat to his former company.

Unlike a large organization, the small firm does not have the security of size or of an extensive research and development program. Normally, its competitive strategy is based on the ability to perform certain services better than or faster than other, often larger, firms. Usually, a small company's resources are special techniques or product improvements which are not patentable. When one of its executives goes to work for a competitor, the small company may find its own techniques or product innovations used against itself and its position in the industry seriously jeopardized.

In contrast to the nonrelated executive, a relative is effectively blocked from the temptation of greener pastures. Once he decides to work in the family firm, the convergence of expectation, training, and family pressure ties him to the enterprise. If a relative does seek a job with another firm in the industry, his family connections, moreover, cause the firm's competitors to treat the relative with suspicion--another factor restricting his outside business opportunities.

Within the organization in general, a succession of competent family managers can develop a strong feeling for the company. Despite the current tendency of many observers to sneer at paternalism, several family companies apparently believe that relatives are particularly helpful in the area of employee relations, judging from the number of cases where relatives are used in this capacity. Such a finding seems to be supported by a *Fortune* article dealing with the pros and cons of hiring relatives. In noting that some companies consider the presence of family members an advantage when dealing with employees, the article quotes Charles Heinz, then vice president of industrial relations at H. J. Heinz Company, as saying, "I think the fact that I'm in the Heinz family helps make for a better climate in labor negotiations." [6]

In some family companies, the loyalty of employees and nonrelated managers to the family and the company is found to be particularly significant. Unlike the loyalty felt toward non-related managers, it is not lost when the recipient retires but tends to be carried over to his son and through him to the company. Sometimes, this loyalty is so great that the other company employees will actively attempt to perpetuate family control. In the case of a small metal-treatment company, for example, the employees [became actively concerned] about training the owner-manager's son because they did not want "outsiders" owning and managing the organization.

Management-Stockholder Unity

When a family closely identifies its own best interests with those of the firm, the company may realize a significant benefit from the resulting community of interest between stockholder and management groups. Such mutuality has been cited as the major defense of employee stock-ownership plans.

Not only is such a dual perspective nearly always automatically present in family managers, but because of the hold of family tradition, it normally extends beyond the sometimes limited self-interest of cashing in on a special stock option plan. Family members are usually extremely reluctant to sell their ownership in the family firm. This attitude seems to cause many such managers to place greater stress on the company's best interests in the long-term.

Because of their ownership influence, moreover, family managers may be less sensitive to criticism based on short-term performance, and may be freer to focus on the long-term aspects of the company moves. Many family executives, moveover, commented at length on moves that their firms made when considerations of short-term performance might well have dictated a more conservative policy. Several executives attribute their company's early emphasis on research and development to the ability to stress long-term goals.[7]

In some cases such as the following two examples, the assurance of a loyal stockholder interest apparently enables a firm to make key moves that critically affect its long-term strength.

- In the Hopwell Fabricated Material Company, according to the family president, such loyalty was a major factor in the firm's decision to embark upon a national merchandising campaign that caused the firm to dominate its field. "At its inception, the project called for annual expenditures equaling one-third of the company's annual sales," he said. "Without substantial stockholder support, the directors and the firm would have been much more conservative."

- In the Wray New England Printing Company, the president believed that family ownership was essential to his company's ability to "go for broke" in its fight to win the right to adopt technological improvements without prior union approval. This right was accepted only after a major strike which proved so costly in the short term that the owner-manager was convinced that the company would have failed without the stockholder support guaranteed by the family ownership interest. "We knew the family believed as we did, and were willing to take the risk," recounted a nonrelated manager about the situation. "With substantial outside stockholder interest, we might have viewed our responsibilities somewhat differently when faced with such severe losses."

The presence of a *responsible* family ownership interest may also play an increasingly important role in another respect. In companies where the family tie is primarily a proprietary one, the knowledge that there is an interested stockholder with enough stock to make his voice heard may make those charged with the management of the firm think extra long about their stockholder responsibilities. This role may be a significant one in view of the increasing immunity of management from stockholder control where ownership is widely scattered. A substantial outside ownership interest ensures some review of management policies. When such an interest is tied to the firm by family identification, the protection afforded may be even greater, since the stockholder is less likely to sell out when difficulties arise.

Besides these possibly unique advantages, several company managers believe that family-owned companies benefit, as do other forms of close corporations, from a greater flexibility than their more public competitors. Although such an advantage seems more attributable to the type of centralized organization that family ownership encourages than to family ownership per se, several family managers cited specific examples where their ability to move quickly on major policy decisions has resulted in important long-term gains. Because of this flexibility, a meat packing firm, for example, was able to make a major purchase of processing plant on six hours' notice, entering the processing part of the business at a very opportune moment.

This flexibility, however, may not always be an advantage, especially in cases where it interferes with good management principles. "A situation in which the family dominates the firm," noted one textile executive, "may encourage a 'yes man' management team and a captive board of directors, resulting in an improper review of company moves." Agreeing with this opinion, the executive of a family paper company observed, "Our family influence may enable management to move quickly, but every time we have, the results have been disastrous."

Similar to other forms of close corporations, family-owned companies may also have an additional advantage of secrecy. Although secrecy about company operations may interfere with management functions if carried to excess, several company executives cited the ability to restrict operational information as an important competitive advantage. A former family company, for example, based its decision to remain closely held partly on "the lessened ability of outside interests, particularly competition, to appraise the effect of company actions" which such ownership provided.

In some family businesses, as the following example shows, the ability to restrict information is considered crucial:

In ten years the Lambrecht Machinery Company grew from one-fourth the size of its major competitor to two-thirds its size. "if our competitor had realized how rapidly we were expanding,"

the president said, "he would have prevented us. He knew we were establishing new plants but, without financial statements, he did not know how successful our ideas really were."

Social Sensitivity

Family pride and identification with the company may cause management to be more sensitive to its social responsibility and thereby contribute to the firm's long-term strength. The rigid profit consideration inherent in nearly all business organizations is a powerful one. Unchecked, it may lead to actions not always in the public's best interest.

When an individual employee is asked to participate in such actions, he may find himself in the untenable position of obeying his best judgment *only* at the sacrifice of his job and his family's security. But because of "the name on the door," a family management (many of the family executives interviewed believe) is less able to justify acts contrary to the community's best interests either to itself or to the public. Attitudes like the following are not uncommon:

"How could I explain a price-fixing scandal to my son?" asked a paper manufacturer. "Such a situation would do considerable damage to the family's reputation, as well as that of the company."

As in the case of the other advantages cited, the importance of having a family name associated with a company is hard to substantiate statistically. While most executives interviewed agree in general that this is a potential advantage, almost all point out that whether or not it is realized depends on the family linked with the firm. "I have dealt with many a family," noted the treasurer of a large textile concern, "who had the ethics of

31

thieves. And the conduct of their business reflected it."

Several executives were also quick to point out that this advantage may be diminishing in importance. "Twenty-five years ago," added the president of a large industrial material manufacturing company, "I would have agreed completely that social sensitivity was a strength of the family company, but today nearly every company has recognized the importance of a good reputation in the community."

Despite these qualifications the evidence appears to indicate that the family companies, because of the family involvement, tend generally to weigh the social aspects of decisions more heavily that do comparable public firms.

Continuity and Purpose

There is an overriding advantage that a succession of competent family managers can provide to a business enterprise — continuity and a deeply felt sense of corporate purpose. These two elements seem to be increasingly important in a society where change and the break-up of traditional institutions are normal.

Every company tends to have a number of corporate "myths" or traditions which entrench particular objectives and capabilities. When a family management tradition exists, these important myths are considerably strengthened by the family's involvement in them, since each guiding principle becomes part of a continuum stemming back to the firm's founding, with the family manager providing the unifying factor between the company's past and its present.

While a family manager's most important contribution in this area may be an intangible one, a family association may have a major value in enabling a firm to absorb large-scale operational changes without disrupting important organizational values or the essential unity of the firm. For example:

- The chief executive of a large manufacturing concern believes that the presence of a family management tradition has helped his organization preserve its historical stress on quality despite an increasing mechanization in its production processes. The founder of the firm built the reputation of the company on its quality workmanship, and, according to the executive, the succession of family managers has tended to perpetuate this dedication to quality within the organization.

- The effect of family identification on a company's ability to absorb major changes was also noted by a nonrelated treasurer of a weaving firm. Since the war, his company has grown rapidly through acquisition. Despite this rapid growth, the treasurer believes that the sense of unity provided by the managing family, which traces its connection with the organization over three generations, has prevented a severe case of organizational indigestion. "Despite our growth and despite our absorption of many different firms," he added, "the diverse management elements have remained united through the mutual respect for the family members who head the company."

A family association, however, may be valuable for more than its influence on a firm's internal organization. Sometimes, this association may be directly related to a firm's unique competitive competency.

One steel company president noted that family management may be important in perpetuating the value of "personal service." When a firm is founded on the value of personal service (which often is linked to the activities of the original proprietor), its possibilities for expansion are limited. Yet the use of other family members may allow the firm to expand beyond one man's capabilities while still retaining the company's unique competitive ability. Such thinking underlies a well-known New England restaurant's stress on family management in its advertising.

In several other cases, family management seems to have been an element in a firm's public image. The Findlay Art Gallery, for example, prides itself in representing the experience of "three generations in art"; the Oscar Mayer Company, with sales of $279 million in 1963, communicates its emphasis on quality by referring to its family management in its motto: "A tradition of quality from our family to yours." A similar use of tradition is developed in a series of ads run by the H. J. Heinz Company. In these ads, Chairman Henry Heinz personally pledges the company to the maintenance of his grandfather's guiding principle of using only the finest quality ingredients. The tradition of family management and Chairman Heinz's ability to appeal to this tradition tend to reinforce the company's reputation for quality in the eyes of the public.

The family manager may also have several advantages in executive development over his nonrelated counterpart. Among these may be dedication, experience, unusual access to management, and immunity from organizational pressures.

The point was repeatedly made by those interviewed that many sons and other family members will tend to work harder, to be more enthusiastic, and to be more loyal to the company than their nonrelated counterparts. Also, having grown up in the company environment, they may have an extensive knowledge of the company before they begin working. Once in the firm, they may benefit from a greater willingness on the part of senior management to spend time with them. Finally, family members may be able to develop themselves without jeopardizing their relations with others. A family supervisor noted: "Because I am in the family, I can set my own pace without others feeling that I am playing up to my boss." For these reasons, a family member, provided he is interested, may have an unusual opportunity in a family company to develop his management potential to the utmost.

Caveats to Consider

So far we have seen that the family participation is not always a source of weakness. What is weakness in one firm seems to develop, under competent management, into a major strength in another. But the experience of organizations where family participation is a source of strength indicates that this is true only when:

1. The family understands that its personal objectives can be realized only by the long-term success of the enterprise.

2. Family managers are willing to establish policies and formal restraints to ensure that family participation is limited to the extent of its contribution to the firm's long-term strengths.

The histories of many of the most prominent firms indicate that their present positions are in large part attributable to the recognition of the importance of these two factors. Such recognition, however, is often precipitated by a family or company crisis. In several cases, these conditions were met only after a family member had to be fired. In others, they were the result of the company's growth, which forced the family to come to terms with the needs of the enterprise. Paradoxically, by giving up some elements of control, the family apparently strengthened its own position of leadership and, at the same time, improved the firm's chances for profitable operation.

Checks on Favoritism

To ensure a positive balance between family and company interests the managements of most successful family firms seem to delineate clearly between traditional family prerogative and that belonging to management. While recognizing that the family association may give a relative some claims to employment and/or management preferences, many of these firms have ensured, through the establishment of formal checks as well as informal traditions, that these claims will not dominate. Here is a case in point:

> The Thompson Manufacturing Company* is a large material-processing firm. Its family executives believe that some family participation in management is important, because it adds to the firm's internal unity. This intangible strength is supported, moreover, by every practical consideration. Through their stock ownership, the family branches control the company, and the Thompsons believe that some family participation in management makes it more likely that this stock will be voted in the company's best interests. For these reasons, blood ties are a consideration in employment

and in subsequent management selections.

Nevertheless, this consideration has not been allowed to dominate, for the family executives believe that the right to manage has to be earned by family members in the same manner as by nonrelated employees. "A relative's name may get him in the door," noted the president, "but the rest is up to him." To ensure that such a condition is carried out, the company has a strict policy that, where sons are involved, all evaluation and supervision are under the control of others. The father is not even allowed to ask how well his sons are doing.

In line with this personnel policy, the company exerts further control over family self-interest. A majority of the directors are not related to the Thompson family, although management encourages all family branches, including those not in management, to represent their stock on the board. When there is a company problem that involves family interest, such as management succession and compensation, these outside directors play an important role in ensuring that the needs of the enterprise are met despite sometimes conflicting family interests.

While allowing some family privileges, the owner-managers of the Thompson Manufacturing Company recognize the need to accept some limitations on family prerogatives in order to obtain a stronger management organization. Because of this willingness to take such action, the firm has risen to a position of dominance within an industry where family mismanagement is the rule.

Barriers to Employment

In the Thompson company, there are no special restrictions on family employment other than the general condition that the relatives measure up to the company's employment standards. Among companies studied, this situation tends to be the exception. Many of the family companies which recognize the importance of limiting family prerogatives tend to be more restrictive in their initial employment policies. A few family firms have even adopted a policy of employing no relatives at all.

The value of such a rigid policy, however, is uncertain. In general, the tendency to make exceptions to rules against hiring relatives seems to be most marked where the family retains stock control, such rules become self-defeating as the family becomes less willing to place company interests above family interests. In the more typical situation, families try to limit, but not eliminate, family employment.

In some companies employment restrictions are based on blood ties and/or age. Many families tacitly exclude in-laws, despite the fact that within several firms, including those where such restrictions are currently practiced, the experience with in-laws had in the past been favorable. In many of the companies studied, the firm is currently managed by the eldest son of the former chief executive. Such situations suggest that primogeniture exists in some companies. Since most of these sons are named after their fathers, the situation may be attributable to greater family expectation and pressure on such individuals to enter the firm.

In other companies, family members who wish to enter the family firm are required to measure up to standards more rigid than those applied to nonrelated management talent. A long-established family firm, located in New England, stipulates that a relative may work for the company only after he has been "invited in" by the present managers. Several companies require that family members be successful elsewhere before entering the firm.

One of the companies having such a condition is the Pillsbury Company, whose chairman, Philip W. Pillsbury, commented: "I have had a policy of not having sons work for the company unless they have established themselves somewhere else for a period of years." In advocating such a policy, a family executive in a bank noted that this requirement provides the family member with an important business perspective and helps develop the individual's self-confidence.

The Thompson company is typical of a second approach to the problem of limiting family prerogatives. The managers hope that the family management tradition will be maintained, but they neither arbitrarily restrict nor force family participation in the company. The family management is especially careful not to pressure family members to join the business. The family helps its members who have outside interests to get started in other careers, and, because the stock of the company is publicly traded, no relative who embarks on another career is faced with the difficult problem of having his and his immediate family's financial well-being under another's control.

Since the employment of relatives is not restricted in the Thompson company, the family managers give special attention to the problems of developing and objectively evaluating the administrative skills of the members entering the firm. Although some family companies establish special development programs for family members, the Thompsons are treated in a fashion similar to other management trainees. They participate in management development meetings and are required to work up through the normal levels of management.

Spurs to Performance

Establishment of impartial measures of the performance of family members is not unique to the larger firms such as the Thompson company. One family distributorship, for example, places its family employees on sales contracts, thereby making their compensation and success in the organization strictly dependent on their selling ability.

A similar approach can be noted in the case of a sporting goods manufacturing concern. In this firm, the son has been given complete responsibility over the development of a new product line. This project provides the son with valuable management experience, and at the same time it tests his competency in all phases of the operation. In another family firm, the trust officers managing the family trust have been specifically charged with evaluating the boss's son. If he proves not capable, they are required to sell the firm.

Executive Evaluation

While their methods vary, many of the more successful firms seem to realize that the best interests of both the firm and the family require objectivity in the executive development of family members. This objectivity is particularly important to the company because the family employees tend to personify the organization's chief vices and virtues to

the public, to the company's customers, and to the entire staff of the firm.

From the viewpoint of the family member being evaluated, such objectivity may prevent the relatives from unwittingly discriminating against him. Henry Ford for example, allowed his son, Edsel, little management influence out of the misguided belief that he lacked the "toughness" necessary to run the company. History has indicated that the Ford Motor Company had outgrown the father's brand of "toughness" and that, at the time, the son's approach was what the company needed.

Thus, this type of objective appraisal may allow the family relative to be himself, rather than a junior edition of the senior family members, a situation which benefits both the company and the individual. Finally, when the family member is required to earn his position, his own doubts about his abilities are lessened, the challenge of a career with the firm is increased, and his problem of winning the acceptance and confidence of the organization is minimized.

Coexistent with the policy of limiting family prerogatives, wiser companies, such as Thompson, place strong emphasis on attracting and developing nonrelated management talent. In the Thompson company policy was developed initially when growth pressures had convinced the family of the impossibility of filling all the management needs from within the family. Currently, nonrelated executives outnumber the Thompson family in top management and are widely represented in the executive committee. Nonrelated executives participate in a liberal stock option plan and, as the chairman noted, many of the nonrelated executives have made their fortune in the company. In the past, nonfamily managers have even been president of the company. Such willingness ensures that the company is well managed, regardless of the stage of executive development of family members. It also partly explains the company's reputation in its industry as a "good place to work."

The owning family's willingness to open top company positions to nonrelated management talent seems to be a common attribute of most of the longer-lived family companies. Three of the five past presidents of a five-generation, $300-million manufacturing firm, for example, were not related to the owning family. A similar situation exists in a family bank studied, as well as in many of the longer-lived firms researched. When such opportunities are made available to all employees, regardless of family ties, the family company seems to have little problem in attracting the necessary executive talent.

Conclusion

Popular opinion has it that when family and business are interrelated, a less efficient business enterprise generally results. But a close examination of the subject suggests that this belief may be unfounded. It ignores the fact that effective administrative practice is founded on an understanding of all human relationships as they affect an organization and not on a denial of them. Where such understanding is present, the family firm has generally evolved organizational procedures and traditions, bordering on law, that have capitalized on those aspects of the interrelationship which are of direct value to the long-term interests of the firm and family.

The success of many family companies indicates that ignorance of the relationships involved *and not family participation per se* is a key factor in the success or failure of such firms. Understanding the contribution a family may make to the firm's long-term strengths, analyzing the weaknesses involved, and implementing organizational restraints to control such problems, all are aspects of the manager's problem in a family firm.

Notes

1. Alfred D. Chandler, Jr., *Strategy and Structure* (Cambridge, Massachusetts, Massachusetts Institute of Technology Press, 1962), p. 64.

2. C. Roland Christensen, *Management Succession in Small and Growing Enterprises* (Boston, Division of Research, Harvard Business School, 1953), p. 175.

3. Perrin Stryker, "Would You Hire Your Son?" March 1957, p. 228

4. December 20, 1963, p. 74.

5. Judith Dolgins, "A Good Man is Hard to Keep," *Dun's Review and Modern Industry*, May 1963, as quoted by *The Executive*, August 1963, p. 21.

6. Perrin Stryker, op. cit., p. 228.

7. See Arnold C. Cooper, "R & D is More Efficient in Small Companies," *Harvard Busines Review.* May-June 1964, p. 75.

Introduction

"It is a daily miracle that there are any owner-managed businesses left in the world with so few making plans for their own continuity," says Léon Danco. This article discusses the problems confronting family businesses and reports Danco's blunt advice on the subject. Danco, perhaps the nation's senior family business authority, is also profiled.

The SOB's
1980

By Randall Poe

The fathers have eaten a sour grape, and the children's teeth are set on edge

Jeremiah 31:29

If family business is not the backbone of the American economy, it is certainly the prime rib. The more than 10 million family-owned businesses employ half of this country's private work force. A new President's Report shows that small businesses (those with under $100 million in sales or 500 or fewer employees) currently generate 43 percent of our gross national product. During a recent six-year period (1969-76), businesses with 20 or fewer employees created 67 percent of this nation's new jobs.

But the founders and operators of family businesses are up against the wall.

They are being squeezed by union pressures, government regulations, taxes, and inflation. But the biggest problem they face — and one of the least publicized — is that of succession: keeping their business in the family.

Despite all the easy talk these days about the efficiency of modern management, many business entrepreneurs are watching their firms either sold out from under them or self-destruct because they have not planned for their own succession. Only 30 percent of all family businesses survive into the second generation. "There is no doubt about it," says George Abbott of the National Family Business Council, "the succession problem is the most important issue facing family business."

Recent talks with business owners, their offspring, and informed outsiders suggest three central reasons for the succession quandary. Business owners (1) are too busy keeping their businesses alive to plan their own exit; (2) don't have any real confidence in their offspring, even though many expect their sons to replace them; and (3) do not see family perpetuity as a major concern.

"Family business is peculiar," notes Abbott, "because it is private and carries the total personality of the entrepreneur. The real problem with succession is that so few kids are like their parents. They are just as good, even better educated, but they are different. The father is beginning to slow down a little just as the son reaches 25 or 30 and is raring to go. If the father resents change and keeps stifling the son's drive and creativity (and it happens all the time), the son gets angry or gives up. He may even stop talking to his father altogether. Then you've got problems."

Léon Danco—president of University Service Institute and founding director of the Center for Family Business (see end)—who is widely considered to be the country's leading authority on family businesses, observes: "It is a daily miracle that there are any owner-managed businesses left in the world with so few making plans for their own continuity. The toughest thing for the business owner to realize is that time is running out on him. Most owners don't plan because they don't think they are going to retire or die. The hairy chested mesomorph who has built a successful business comes to believe he is divine. He cannot face the myth he has created, which is of his own immortality. Because he has not taken time to prepare a successor, he takes his business right into the grave with him."

Many family firms are operated not as mere businesses but as royal preserves. When a 107-year-old southern food-supply firm names a new son president, he dons a cape embroidered with the family coat of arms and accepts a three-foot torch from the outgoing chief. Explains Danco: "Since family businesses are like monarchies, the oldest brother becomes president and succeeding brothers or husbands of daughters assume roles based on order of birth. Comparative ability is a second consideration. The oldest son may be a perpetual drunk and the youngest a mathematical wizard, but this doesn't change their positions in the company. Similar inequities occur when the bright sister of two stupid, lazy brothers marries a competent, hardworking man. The chances of his becoming president over the two brothers are roughly 1,000 to 1."

Rarely are sons similar to their fathers: most are worse, and a few are better...

Homer

The failure to plan creates anxiety and hostility in many business families. It has been called the SOB (sons of bosses) Syndrome. Many SOBs have grown tired and angry waiting for their fathers, the founders of the family business, to step down or lay the groundwork for an orderly transition of power.

Troubled by his own succession problems a decade ago, and discovering that his own anxieties were shared by others, a young Massachusetts executive named Gerald Slavin founded a group comprising solely bosses' sons. And, yes, he called it the SOBs. The idea proved to be such a popular one that it soon spread across the country.

"The big problem with business fathers is that they want perfect carbon copies of themselves rather than imperfect originals," Slavin notes. "There is a widespread feeling that since they've done things one way for 30 years or so, it damn well ought to be right. But there are a lot of ways to skin the cat."

While the SOBs have been charged with being too brash and confrontational, they are also credited with bringing some deep problems out of the business closet and raising the consciousness of both founding fathers and their offspring. Danco, no fan of SOB militancy, although he has consulted for the organization, says: "Too many of them were interested only in confrontation. Many were bright and decent, but too many were just bright and cruel. They have real problems, but their way of handling them was to get rid of their old men and put them out to pasture."

I recently spent an evening with the senior vice president of a California electronics firm, which is owned by his father. The company has 210 employees and had sales of $426 million last year. The son, who is 33, makes $92,000 a year, but he is bitter.

"There is no trust or faith in me," he says. "The 'Bear' [his nickname for his father] treats me like I was still a kid. I make a half-million-dollars' worth of decisions every month, most of them the right ones, and am still second-guessed. He doesn't do that with the other executives. I'll be president, I'm sure of it because I'm qualified, but I may die or go nuts before it happens. He has promised to retire and semi-retire for the last 10 years. I've laid it on the line. One more year of this and I walk. It's a bad scene."

The father, who is chairman and president, started the business with $45,000, which he borrowed from *his* father in 1951. He is now 66. The business, he told me, demands his presence. "I've built this thing up by myself. It's my life. I know exactly what would happen if I left. It would survive, but it wouldn't

grow properly. Stephen [not the son's real name] will follow me as president. He knows that. He's good and he's learning, but he's not ready."

While the situation may seem extreme, it is loudly echoed across the country. It is an age-old conflict — the impatience of youth colliding with the implacability of age. Some family business dramas seem like classical tragedies — a mix of Sophocles' *Oedipus Rex* and Turgenev's *Fathers and Sons*.

Perversely, family discord is frequently caused by those very same, much-admired personality traits that have forged the successful business. As management authority Harry Levinson puts it: "The most successful executives are often men who have built their own companies. Ironically, their very success frequently brings to them and members of their families personal problems of an intensity rarely encountered by professional managers. And these problems make family businesses possibly the most difficult to operate."

Danco's advice to both fathers and their offspring is blunt, simple, and old-fashioned. To business fathers, he says: *Understand that the hairs on your chest are numbered and that your primary goal is not to generate more money and sales than anybody else but to perpetuate your business.*

To offspring, he advises: *Understand your father's drive, recognize his accomplishments, and help him keep his dream alive.*

And he continues: "The business owner has been the giver of life in America. When he closes his doors and sells out to people who don't care about the business, it is a disaster. I deal with business owners by the thousands, and they are the most wonderful and decent people on earth. Many are the unaccepted, the unwashed, the unlettered. Nobody with a Ph.D. starts a family business. They are rejects from the Establishment; immigrants who were accepted; salesmen, managers, and technicians who weren't appreciated; iconoclasts who say, 'The hell with it, I'll do it myself.' And they do. And yet they sow the seeds of their own destruction with their secrecy, with their unwillingness to accept competent advice, and in the mistaken belief that they will live forever."

Still, signs of change are in the air, evidenced, for example, by the growing lineup of consultants, gurus and advisers to family businesses. Danco's seminars, for owners and their wives and their offspring, provide a full range of services, including financial and estate planning and succession strategies. Other comprehensive programs are run by the National Family Business Council, in conjunction with Danco's Family Business Center and the business schools at Harvard and Wharton, by Connecticut-based Educational Systems and Design, by SOB-founder Slavin, and by several dozen consulting firms.

The most positive thing happening right now is that business owners are realizing they have a problem," explains Emmett Wallace of Educational Systems and Design. "They have been so busy running from crisis to crisis that they just haven't done a good job of planning. So many successful businesses were started just after World War II, and the founder are now reaching retirement age. Many are worried about their businesses; most are counting on sons or sons-in-law to take it over. That's their dream, but they've done little to make that dream come true. In some cases, as we tell them, the best thing to do may be not to keep the business in the family

at all but to sell it. But the owner has got to do something he's been reluctant to do: face the problem and resolve it."

A few dirty battles never hurt any family.

John Wayne

While many family businesses are living harmoniously, there is enough evidence of deep-seated hostility to suggest that many others still have a long way to go. For example: A New York son removed his father by gunpoint from his office. . .a father had his son kidnapped and held hostage until he agreed to leave the firm. . . a wife, siding with her son in a succession struggle, hired a professional hit man to terminate her husband (the husband was injured, but continues to run his company).

Few family feuds go public. But it happens. The 21-year-old head of an $8 million clothing firm in New York recently filed suit in Manhattan Supreme Court asking that his 54-year-old father be prohibited "from entering upon the premises" of the family business. The son alleges that his father's reputation, resulting from two bankruptcies, is damaging the business.

The father says his son told him, "'You're so bad, nobody wants you. . . You're so bad, Dad.' I said to him, 'For 21 years I wasn't too bad for you.' I got him bar mitzvahed, I got him a minibike, a $10,000 Jaguar, his own apartment when he was 18."

"I think I've seen it all," says Danco. "Siblings beating on siblings, even killing each other, wives siding with one side or the other, sexual favors withdrawn, physical takeovers of the old man's office when he leaves town. One of the cruelest things I've seen involved a bright young man who told his father that if he was not made president the old man would never see his grandchildren again. The father refused the ultimatum, but it has torn the family apart. After a big family knockout, the son moved away. It has left the father an emotional wreck, destroyed him."

While each family problem is different, many have a similar ring. Egos and ambition are working overtime, and father-son rivalry shines through.

A friend recently introduced me to a 32-year-old man who is an executive in his father's small, successful chemical firm. They had sales of $5.5 million last year and employ 61 people. The son had worked more than two years for a major chemical company and one year for an export-import firm before joining his father's firm. According to the son, the father has done an excellent job of estate planning. The father also continuously reassures him that he is being groomed to succeed him. But..."I'm worried that I will not be in a position to replace him because he keeps me totally in the dark about this company. I run the second most profitable division, but don't even set or control my own budget. He says he doesn't want to worry me with details and wants me to concentrate fully on marketing. I have an MBA and got outside experience at his request so I would contribute something, but he makes all the important decisions. He asks no advice from me. I feel it's not my role to go to him. He expects me to be a younger version of him, but I see things differently. I know I could take us into some new markets we should be in, but he won't change. We do things the way we always have. Our board of directors consists of my father, me, my mother, who is treasurer, and my brother-in-law, who is operations vice president. We meet three times a year, but we don't make any real decisions. We drink coffee and listen to

my father tell us how tough business is. I know it's tough, but it's not so bad as he makes it out. I need to make decisions and be on the inside of all this company's business. All I'm told is that I'm progressing fine. I'm constantly reminded that worse times are coming, how credit is tight, and how I should save more. Then he reminds me that other people would love to have the estate he's leaving my sister and me. Well, I don't want a damn estate. I want a chance to prove myself."

His lament is not new. As Alfred C. Fuller, the original Fuller Brush man used to say: "Father never let us forget that every apple had a cash value and every fork of manure held a potential for part of next year's living."

Grievances are common in all employee-employer relationships, but the problems of family succession can inflict real pain. The mixture of business and family almost ensures discord. As one observer explains it: "With the family business, the cuts are always deeper and the blood redder." There are nearly as many explanations and proposed solutions as situations.

The plain fact is, many family business conflicts are caused, basically, by a lack of communication. As consultant Frank Butrick explains it: "There is a surplus of thoughtless, vain, overbearing, misleading and dishonest talk, and never enough earnestness and honesty. It's usually the son who throws up the barrier and it is the father who must eventually tear it down. It is not easy for a father to take hat in hand and begin to build a friendship with his own son. A father's sense of rightness, supported by an ordinary amount of adult pride, makes him feel that his son should come to him. Unfortunately, this seldom happens, and when it does, it all too often is an attack rather than a groping for understanding."

To stimulate family business continuity, Danco prescribes large injections of humility. He also calls for owners to begin sharing decision-making with their successors. At his seminars he tells them to try an experiment: "The next time you face a business decision, the next time there is a problem, call in your successor and ask him to help you work on the solution. Don't tell him how you plan to solve it and then ask him what he thinks. That's just mousetrapping him. Share with him the same information you have about the problem and then take time for a good old-fashioned buzz session on the subject. Doing this is going to be damn hard for awhile because it hasn't been your style to ask anyone for help. But practice the experiment anyway. Each time you try to work out solutions together, the process will become easier. You may be surprised to discover just how smart your son or daughter is. They, in turn, will be amazed at the care and precision required of a manager in making decisions. Half the time they thought you just flipped half-dollars or decided with a dart board."

He is also a strong believer in outside boards of directors—nonfamily members—for family businesses, and has helped hundreds of firms establish them. "Most family-owned businesses do not have real boards of directors. They have a group of melon splitters and co-conspirators—mother's and dad's old cronies, sons, a few management employees who rubber-stamp the decisions the boss makes, or relatives employed in the company. The business owner-manager doesn't want and cannot use a rubber-stamp board. The business owner has to balance off the self-interests of family and employees with outsiders—businessmen who are engaged in enterprises different from his own, who both appreciate and understand the risks he shoulders, whose judgement he respects and who respect him."

It is not only what we have inherited from our fathers that exists again in us, but all sorts of old dead ideas and all kinds of old dead beliefs and things of that kind. They are not actually alive in us; but there they are dormant, all the same, and we can never be rid of them.

Henrik Ibsen

It's clear that those who found and run successful businesses aren't everyday people. Studies reveal that they are significantly more achievement-oriented than the general population; one study suggests that people who found family businesses possess "more drive and more need to control their environments" than even professional executives. "The small businessman is unique, a counterrevolutionist," said William H. Whyte, Jr., author of *The Organization Man*.

And some founding fathers may be wrestling with father demons of their own. Harry Levinson observes: "The entrepreneur characteristically has unresolved conflicts with his father, research evidence indicates. He is therefore uncomfortable with being supervised and starts his own business both to outdo his father and to escape the authority and rivalry of more powerful figures."

It has been widely suggested that the long-range salvation of family business is professional management. Some authorities have recommended that trusts be set up for family members, removing them from direct business operations, while providing funds for them to develop new business ventures. One staunch advocate of professional management has been Levinson: "In general, the wisest course for any business, family or nonfamily, is to move to professional management as quickly as possible. . .I know of no family business capable of sustaining regeneration over the long term solely through the medium of its own family members."

Others, however, stress that many family businesses do not want and cannot afford professional management. "There is no damn way in the world," says one analyst, "that a $3 million family business with 35 employees can get real professional management."

The call for more professionalism in family business frequently carries two suggestive maxims: (1) personal lives and business don't mix, and (2) nepotism generates inefficiency. But these theses, too, have been challenged. A *Harvard Business Review* analysis in 1976 observed:

> Historically, the main problem with this rational argument is that most companies lean more heavily on family and personal psychology than they do on such business logic. The evidence is overwhelming. There are more than one million corporations in the United States. Of these about 980,000 are family dominated, including many of the largest. Yet most of us have the opposite impression. . .The human tradition of passing on heritage, possessions, and name from one generation to the next leads both parents and children to seek continuity in the family business. In this light, the question of whether a business should stay in the family seem

less important, we suspect, than learning more about how these businesses and their family owners make the transition from one generation to the next.

An earlier *Harvard Business Review* analysis noted: "The success of many family companies indicates that ignorance of the relationships involved *and not family participation per se* is a key factor in the success or failure of such firms." As one observer told me: "I wish we wouldn't keep treating family businesses as if they were baby seals. Some of them are screwed up, but they are not an endangered species. Family business will be with us forever."

In the murky maze of family business, one fact does seem clear: the longest running family firms seem to be those that open top management slots to people who don't live on the family tree.

If the very old will remember, the very young will listen.

Chief Dan George

Despite all the confusion and contradiction, there are encouraging signs that both business owners and their families are beginning to take hard, practical steps to perpetuate their businesses. As noted earlier, family-business workshops and seminars across the country are drawing growing numbers of participants. More and more firms are upgrading their professional staffs and the quality of their advisers. Many are setting up outside boards to improve their auditing and review procedures. A surprisingly large number of family firms are now gliding smoothly into their second generation.

The biggest breakthrough, many analysts say, is simply getting more

owners and their families to take time off from their business grinds to plan

Family Business Sourcebook

their successions. Some families are holding periodic meetings to evaluate management progress and to set specific goals for family members; something many have been reluctant to do in the past. A family engineering firm in New York, for instance, brings in two outside consultants every quarter to measure the progress of four family executives.

The National Family Business Council has established a "swap" program in which sons and daughters are loaned to outside firms to broaden their skills. The program's aim: to prevent the unbred thinking that has maimed many family businesses. "It's working very well," says Abbott, "especially when both fathers and sons are involved." The Associated General Contractors of America has a similar project, swapping sons and daughters among noncompetitive companies for periods ranging up to five years.

Virtually all small family-business experts say that sons and daughters should get outside experience before joining the family firm. As the owner of a small manufacturing firm told me: "I wouldn't hire my son until he worked for someone else for three years. I've seen 'em come in after school and they have nothing to contribute. They just become little yes-men very fast."

And Danco's appraisal: "I'm only a little more optimistic now than I used to be. Most business owners are still going to have to learn the hard way, but an awareness is growing. If the owner can just convince himself that his business will live but he won't, he'll be on the right road. As they grow older, they must stop priding themselves on being the oldest and hardest working employee in the firm and become teachers. Their chief pupil must be their successor, and that person must be

treated as a successor — not as a pet or some assistant to the president. In a time of technological change, so-called experience isn't what owners think it is. It's not 40 years of experience, as they tell me. It's more like 20 years of experience, repeated twice. Or even 10 years experience repeated four times. The owner has so much to teach, but if he doesn't start sharing that knowledge, the company will close its doors when he dies. Then the family will begin hiring gladiators called lawyers and bankers, and they will decide what to do with the business on the way home from the funeral — about four cars back from the flowers."

Advisers are telling owners to cool the "you're-not-ready" and "you're-not-tough-enough" lectures to their sons. They note Henry Ford's refusal to turn over critical management decisions to his son, Edsel, because he lacked "toughness." It is now widely cited as a classic father-son blunder, with many observers concluding that a change in management style was exactly what the company needed at that time. And the files are full of similar episodes.

But business history also ripples with success stories involving sons who were given opportunities and took their firms beyond their fathers' wildest dreams. To name only a few: Howard B. Johnson, Edgar M. Bronfman of Seagram Co., August A. Busch, Jr. of Anheuser-Busch, and Willard Rockwell, Jr. of Rockwell International.

Howard Johnson pinpoints his father as the reason for his own success. "Dad gave me every chance to be whatever I wanted," he notes. "But I am one of the few fortunate young men who felt strongly at the age of 12 what I wanted to do with my life. I wanted to run the company. Still, it isn't every father who

45

8# Family Business Sourcebook

their successions. Some families are holding periodic meetings to evaluate management progress and to set specific goals for family members; something many have been reluctant to do in the past. A family engineering firm in New York, for instance, brings in two outside consultants every quarter to measure the progress of four family executives.

The National Family Business Council has established a "swap" program in which sons and daughters are loaned to outside firms to broaden their skills. The program's aim: to prevent the unbred thinking that has maimed many family businesses. "It's working very well," says Abbott, "especially when both fathers and sons are involved." The Associated General Contractors of America has a similar project, swapping sons and daughters among noncompetitive companies for periods ranging up to five years.

Virtually all small family-business experts say that sons and daughters should get outside experience before joining the family firm. As the owner of a small manufacturing firm told me: "I wouldn't hire my son until he worked for someone else for three years. I've seen 'em come in after school and they have nothing to contribute. They just become little yes-men very fast."

And Danco's appraisal: "I'm only a little more optimistic now than I used to be. Most business owners are still going to have to learn the hard way, but an awareness is growing. If the owner can just convince himself that his business will live but he won't, he'll be on the right road. As they grow older, they must stop priding themselves on being the oldest and hardest working employee in the firm and become teachers. Their chief pupil must be their successor, and that person must be

treated as a successor — not as a pet or some assistant to the president. In a time of technological change, so-called experience isn't what owners think it is. It's not 40 years of experience, as they tell me. It's more like 20 years of experience, repeated twice. Or even 10 years experience repeated four times. The owner has so much to teach, but if he doesn't start sharing that knowledge, the company will close its doors when he dies. Then the family will begin hiring gladiators called lawyers and bankers, and they will decide what to do with the business on the way home from the funeral — about four cars back from the flowers."

Advisers are telling owners to cool the "you're-not-ready" and "you're-not-tough-enough" lectures to their sons. They note Henry Ford's refusal to turn over critical management decisions to his son, Edsel, because he lacked "toughness." It is now widely cited as a classic father-son blunder, with many observers concluding that a change in management style was exactly what the company needed at that time. And the files are full of similar episodes.

But business history also ripples with success stories involving sons who were given opportunities and took their firms beyond their fathers' wildest dreams. To name only a few: Howard B. Johnson, Edgar M. Bronfman of Seagram Co., August A. Busch, Jr. of Anheuser-Busch, and Willard Rockwell, Jr. of Rockwell International.

Howard Johnson pinpoints his father as the reason for his own success. "Dad gave me every chance to be whatever I wanted," he notes. "But I am one of the few fortunate young men who felt strongly at the age of 12 what I wanted to do with my life. I wanted to run the company. Still, it isn't every father who

GOSHEN COLLEGE LIBRARY
GOSHEN, INDIANA

would name his son president at the ripe old age of 26."

One observer says that what seems to be happening lately is that more business owners "are making 'readiness' a question rather than a sermon." But many informed insiders suggest the real key to success depends on early action. Danco observes: "An owner must have his succession plans in order by the time he's in his late fifties or the game is over. There is not time to catch up. Business owners must realize that their time is finite. A working lifetime is really less than 500 months. Too many fathers, I'm afraid, think their kids are never going to be ready. I was given a command of a Navy ship when I was 21. If that ship had been my father's, no way that would have happened. It's amazing, but I had an 89-year-old businessman, still running his company, come to me to shape up his son. 'Talk to him,' he told me. The 'kid' was 57. Damn it, somehow we've got to rename retirement. We've got to think of it as renaissance, not rejection."

The Declarations of Danco

Leon Danco—part evangelist, part business mentor—is the man many family business owners turn to for succession help. His Cleveland-based University Services Institute and Center for Family Business have become a training ground for both owners and their heirs. His persistent message is something not all of them want to hear: family business is in trouble and the chief enemy is not the government but themselves. "He is our shrink," says George Abbott of the National Family Business Council. "Nobody knows more about the problems of family business."

Danco got his Ph.D. in economics from Case Western Reserve University and an MBA at Harvard Business School. He is an adjunct professor of business administration at John Carroll University. He started his family business program in the basement of the university library in 1963. Few took him seriously at first. "Business owners thought I was a nut," he told me, "talking about the need to perpetuate family businesses. Hell, I wasn't even invited to lunch." But Danco has quickly become one of the highest paid business advisers in the country, the Billy Graham of the family business.

"I sure didn't invent family business, but I will never stop telling those who will listen that the perpetuation of family business is one of the most important callings on earth."

A fast-thinking man of 5 foot, 6 inches, he is perpetually in motion. His business costume is a blue blazer, gray slacks, and a strategic Timex watch. ("Who argues with a man who wears a Timex?") To slow him down, his wife, Katharine, once give him a five-minute recording of nonstop applause for his birthday accompanied by this note: "Why don't you just stay home for a while and talk to the children and me?"

He honed his speaking style from watching his father, an executive with McKesson-Robbins. "He had flowing white hair and loved the girls. He was a tremendous speaker, with a true gift for persuasion and a great sense of humor. I used to watch him double people up at sales meetings. I learned so much from him. In fact, I look very much like him."

Danco's wife and daughter, Suzanne, work closely with him at his seminars. His wife writes regularly for his information-packed monthly newsletter.

"The Family in Business." His son, Ty, recently competed in the two-man luge competition at the Winter Olympics, finishing first among all Americans and eleventh overall. He has little interest, however, in following his father in the family business.

Danco is on the road speaking or consulting three weeks a month. His consulting fees alone net him over $250,000 a year. His book, *Beyond Survival*, a kind of New Testament for family business owners, brings him steady and sizable royalties. He is the keynote speaker at hundreds of trade groups: addressing pest controllers, accountants, attorneys, salvage owners, and Italian restaurateurs. He has been on the same bill with jugglers, strippers, and auctioneers, and with Bob Newhart, Flip Wilson, Richard Nixon, Gerald Ford, and the late Bishop Sheen, to name a few.

His all-time favorite audience: Jewish scrap dealers. "They all have diamond cufflinks, alligator shoes and $350 silk suits, and open-necked shirts," he tells you, "and they are the most confident group of people I've ever gotten to know. I enjoy their earthiness, their joy for living, their realness. If I were not a Catholic, I would be a Jew. I dislike addressing the bland and uncertain. I like secure people."

Attending Danco's seminars, as I did recently, is like being invited into the inner sanctum of a brilliant guru. His seminars feature experts on taxes, estates, accounting, and financial planning, but the star is Danco himself. His subject range is stupendous. He moves nimbly from medieval history to the latest OSHA regulations, from inventory control to Benjamin Spock and John Kenneth Galbraith, from movies and opera to cash flow. He asks owners and their sons and daughters to draw their firm's organization charts, which he then flashes on a screen. They are usually a constellation of boxes straight out of *Roots*, filled with the names of fathers, sons, daughters, cousins, nephews, even grandfathers.

"What these charts show is that there is no organization," he point out. "It's neanderthal art masquerading as organization. This is cave drawing, and if it wasn't serious, it would be a joke. What most family-business organization charts show is destruction in the making. It shows owner-managers are depending on second-class advisers, a nonfunctioning board of directors, and an accounting system that wouldn't look good in a call house."

The average life expectancy of any business is now 24 years, he emphasizes, which doesn't include the vast majority of firms that expire within the first 10 years. Danco's overriding sermon is that family business organizations must become more professional if these numbers are going to change.

He strongly pushes family firms to get competent outside advisers. Most owners, he says, are surrounded by what he calls Rasputins. Danco: "They are the bankers, insurance people, and accountants who have been with the owner since the beginning when he couldn't afford competent advice. But the Rasputins comprise by far the majority of advisers to family business. They are destructive because their main role is to show the owner how to screw the IRS. I'm no Pollyanna on taxes, they are a very real problem, but, damnit, taxes come second. Growth and the family business come first. Business owners in the beginning are the most marginal clients on earth, so they get the most marginal advisers. The business owner can't pay much in the beginning, so these are the people he gets stuck with. A lot of owners tell me they can't get rid of these people because they've been there so long. I tell them that paid advisers don't deserve loyalty because they have obsolescence built into their fees.

Danco continues: "Business just can't make it today without great advisers - bankers, lawyers, accountants, and insurance experts. Family business badly needs 35-year-old, button-downed CPAs who work for first-class firms. The owner should stop fooling himself that his accountant is stupid because he only earns a pittance of the money the owner does and doesn't understand the business. Advisers aren't there to take the owner's risks and rewards. They are there to provide fiscal discipline."

Recently, on a consulting assignment, an owner told Danco that his attorney said he didn't need outside advisers. "I told him that he needed a new attorney," Danco relates. "Then I told him one of us must go because I do not want to be seen in his kind of company. I'm always willing to leave. I have only terminal arrangements. You've got to be like the terrorist – willing to die."

Some of Danco's wide-ranging thoughts on family businesses:

On semiretirement: "The most common thing I hear from owners is that they are planning or are already semiretired. They tell me they leave work a little early now and take a few months off to play golf in Florida. What they're really saying is that their glasses are slipping down on their noses a little more and they don't hear so well and can't eat all the food and drink all the booze they used to and that the only thing left is to come into the office and bang on the table, intimidate the help, alienate the customers, and in general screw up the business part time. This is called semi-retirement. I'm not going to tell you what their sons call it."

On nepotism: "There is nothing wrong with nepotism. It's the only way to go in family business. People talk about nepotism as if it were incest. Well, it isn't. But it all depends on selecting the right 'nepots.' They can be sons or daughters or sons-in-law or cousins. And you can have corporate 'sons' – managers you have raised in the business who become your heirs. But the basic urge to leave a growing business behind you must be there."

On the four final options for family business: "The president-owner has four final choices for his business. He can liquidate, close the doors, turn the assets to cash, and call the movers. That's corporate euthanasia. Or he can work out a means for stock participation and acquisition among his management and maybe induce his adopted successors to continue on the job and build the future. Or he can try to sell out or merge with a larger economic entity, cop out on his responsibilities and blame it on estate liquidity or tax minimization or something. Or, fourth, he can try to keep the family jewels in the family vault. For my money, this is the best solution of all. The jewels were created for the family in the first place."

On business sons: "Business owners' sons are usually oversold and underdeveloped. Few people understand or sympathize with kids born with silver spoons. But sons interested in the family business need to be tested before they assume control of the firm. The problem is that so many don't get the chance and become embittered and emasculated. They end up being noneconomic beings – playboy, dilettantes, or just bums."

Introduction

What makes successful family businesses successful? Veteran consultant Ben Benson suggests the following: value systems that balance the interests of the business and the family; a true sense of partnership in which family members make personal sacrifices for the benefit of all; established ground rules about entry to the business, compensation and stock ownership; preventive maintenance through regular family discussions of issues confronting the business including long-term objectives, management succession, estate planning, performance evaluation; and use of an independent board of directors.

Preventive Maintenance for the Family Business
1988

By Benjamin Benson

Over the years Bob Smith has built a highly successful travel agency, and his aspirations to build a lasting family business appeared to be fulfilled when his son, Adam, and daughter, Molly, joined in the business. But it was not to be so easy.

Bob loves both his children dearly, but is convinced that Adam is only there because it is a haven from the real world where he would have to compete on merit. Molly, on the other hand, helped in the office during high school, has earned the respect of employees and customers, and is making a solid contribution to the business.

So, should Bob allow each of his children equal pay, status and authority in the business? Should his estate plan provide that they inherit equal shares of stock? If he treats them equally he may be tolling the death knell for the business. If he doesn't it may cause turmoil in the family.

There are over 14 million businesses in the United States. Over 98 percent of these are privately-owned, with the vast majority consisting of family-owned businesses. These businesses produce a major portion of the gross national product, provide most of our job growth and directly influence the lives of most Americans.

The mortality statistics of FOB's are grim reminders that building an enduring FOB is a monumental task. It's estimated that less than 30 percent ever reach the second generation, with fewer than 13 percent going to the third generation. A major reason is the conflicting needs of the business and the family.

Yet some families find a way to walk the tightrope and achieve both business success and family harmony. Their business provides them, and future generations, with opportunity for work fulfillment, financial security and status in the community. Their family lives are also enhanced by the sharing of both sacrifices and benefits in a common endeavor.

These families are not immune from conflicts, but they have found a non-destructive way to resolve them. In one highly successful family business, two brothers shared adjoining offices. "We've never had a door between us," one brother said. "From the beginning we've known that if you win a fight, it means you're no longer partners." The other brother said, "Both of us are strong-willed individuals. We've been disagreeing successfully for 30 years."

"All happy families are like one another," said Tolstoy. "Each unhappy family is unhappy in its own way." So what do successful FOB's have in common?

The value systems of successful families tend to place an appropriate balance on both the best interests of the business and the well being of the family. They also tend to treat the business as a true family partnership, with family members willing to make personal sacrifices for the benefit of the family and the business.

This relationship may be defined in a family creed which articulates the family's relationship to the business. For example, the creed would state that

conditions under which a family member could enter the business, be compensated and own stock. Although the creed may vary widely with each family's attitudes, it is appropriate for all family businesses, large and small, to establish these ground rules [turmoil flourishes in ambiguity].

In a survey conducted by our firm, we inquired about the owners' attitudes toward important issues such as management succession, compensation, stock ownership, rivalry among relatives and competition for authority. Predictably, a majority of the respondents indicated that these issues were not considered to be a serious problem.

Our experience indicates, however, that the problems are there and building—*they just don't know it.* These owners may be compared to a man standing at the edge of an incoming tide. The water may be ankle or knee deep and present no danger—when it gets to chin level it is generally too late. (If you don't believe this, take another look at the mortality statistics.)

Preventive Maintenance

Much like having a medical examination, which is intended to detect disease before it becomes untreatable, practically any family business can benefit from preventive maintenance.

Most owners/managers are so immersed in the everyday pressures of fighting fires that they rarely take the time for a long term view and take it too much for granted that the family understands what's going on. Meetings to discuss the family's relationship with the business are rare. Problems such as sibling rivalry, real or perceived inequities about compensation and stock ownership are avoided. There is no easy answer, it is reasoned, and maybe

50

the problems will go away by themselves. (They won't.) This can be the first step of a healthy transition from communication by emergency to a unified family dialogue.

The best place for such a meeting is at a family retreat, away from the shop and the telephone. (This may be a good time to use that cabin in the woods.)

Participants should include all family members, both active in the business and passive. It's probably a good idea to invite in-laws as well, so that they can learn what's going on directly, rather than second hand.

The purpose of the retreat is to provide a forum for introspection, problem-solving and policy-making. For some participants this will be their first opportunity to talk about their concerns in a non-confrontational atmosphere.

Has the family agreed on its long-term objectives; whether to keep the business in the family, sell it, or be acquired? Do the seeds of serious conflict exist? What are the most important challenges facing the business and family? All of these issues should be allowed to surface so that they may be faced. A family which is emotionally healthy should be able to deal with these sensitive issues openly. Families which are already experiencing severe conflict should seek help of another kind.

Impartial Outsider Provides Guidance

The chances of a successful retreat are greatly enhanced by the engagement of a facilitator to run the meeting. This brings the guidance of a professional, who is experienced in helping family-owned business, to share his experience, help identify issues, and

keep the atmosphere non-confrontational.

The right agenda is important to the success of the meeting. The agenda must be tailored to each company's unique needs. The facilitator usually accomplishes this by interviewing the firm's principals and developing questionnaires to be completed by the participants in advance. A preliminary agenda is based on the responses with additional issues added at the meeting, if necessary.

In addition to their own unique concerns, every family should consider the following issues:

Management succession —

Has the present owner/manager faced the reality that nobody lives forever, and that successful transition to the next generation may depend on his ability to identify, train and install a successor during his lifetime?

Estate planning—

Has the controlling stockholder not only provided for the estate tax impact, but for an intelligent transfer of power to future generations? Does it consider the possibility of stock falling into hostile hands and the differing perspectives of children who are active in the business as compared to those who are passive?

A family creed —

Has the family established a written creed defining the ground rules for family participation in the business, including entry into the business, standards of expected performance and compensation and stock-ownership policy?

Strategic business planning—

Does the company have a written strategic business plan which defines short and long-term objectives, establishes strategies to achieve those objectives and assigns responsibilities for action to be taken?

The reward system —

Does the company's reward system (money, status and perquisites) encourage or discourage high levels of performance?

Performance evaluation —

Does management establish mutually agreed-upon job objectives with family members and key employees? Do they get their periodic constructive feedback as to their performance?

Communication within the family—

Does the family meet periodically to discuss business-related family issues in an unhurried atmosphere away from the business? Does the environment exist for a free flow of ideas, and do family members have a forum in which to express concerns?

Preparing adult children to enter the business—

Are children encouraged to obtain the appropriate educational background and outside experience before entering the business?

The use of an independent board of directors —

Does the company have the benefit of an independent board of directors or advisory board?

It should be noted that the retreat is not the end of the preventive-maintenance process, but the beginning. Where consensus is obtained by the participants, policy should be set, courses of action established and responsibility for implementation assigned.

Where agreement cannot be reached, further discussion should be planned, possibly with the continued assistance of the facilitator.

One important outgrowth of the meeting should be the establishment of periodic family meetings in the future, so that the dialogue may continue.

After this program, families such as Bob Smith's should be in a considerably better position to face the future together as a unified family, rather than as a group of individuals who happen to be related.

Introduction

Two studies presented in this article indicate both performance and policy differences between large owner-controlled and manager-controlled firms in the same industry. Firms controlled by their owners have both much higher rates of return on investment and lower dividend payouts. The owner-controlled firms appear more efficient, yet are gradually being eliminated. This becomes a problem of both private and public concern. Managers and directors can hardly ignore this challenge to their internal operations: what goals are they attempting to achieve? And government officials should investigate a neglected area of significance for public policy: should the relative social responsiveness of the two types of firms be considered in enacting taxation and antitrust laws?

Ownership and Management: The Effect of Separation on Performance

1969

By R. Joseph Monsen

Reprinted by permission of **Business Horizons**. August, 1969, pp. 46-52, Vol. 12, No. 4. Copyright ©1969 by **Business Horizons**; All rights reserved.

The separation of ownership from control in the large corporation has been recognized for many years. What has not been understood, however, is the effect of such separation on the performance of the firm. Evidence now indicates that large owner-controlled companies outperform manager-controlled ones in terms of return on investment by a significant degree.

A few economists in the past, including the author, have suggested that the separation of ownership from control of the corporation creates a quite different motivation between owners and managers. Such difference in motivation may be ascribed to goal conflict of owners and managers that exists in our modern economic system because of the asymmetry between risks and rewards. This asymmetry appears to take the form of greater incentives and rewards for owners than managers in terms of risk-taking. Since recent research has suggested that motivation has far greater consequences upon economic efficiency than economists or others have commonly supposed, differences in goals and motivations between owner-managers and nonowner managers may indeed explain the differential performance between the owner- and manager-controlled companies.

If owners and managers are motivated differently do these differences affect corporate policy? In other words, we may ask whether owner- and manager-controlled companies are basically different in terms of goals, outlook, and policies, or are differentiated only because owner-controlled firms try harder to produce a higher rate of return on their investment? The research cited offers inconclusive proof on this point. However, some recent evidence suggests that there are very basic policy differences between owner-controlled and manager-controlled companies beyond mere return. The author has assembled data which show that dividend policies are very different between the two types of companies. It now appears that manager-controlled firms tend to have higher earnings/payout ratios than firms controlled by their owners. While the industry in which the firm is located has a significant effect upon its dividend pay-out, the type of control appears to be even more significant in explaining the difference in dividend policy.

Such differences appear quite understandable if we look at the goals and incentives of both owners and managers. Due to the tax differential between capital gains and dividend income, a preference for a smaller dividend pay-out and greater earnings retention is a reasonable policy for a company controlled by a wealthy owner-manager. Further, there are noneconomic reasons (desire to rule a financial empire or continuance of family name or tradition) that can supply other explanations as to why an owner-managed firm would prefer to finance itself through high retained earnings rather than risk loss of control by participating extensively in outside capital markets.

Thus it appears that overt policy decisions, such as dividend pay-out, are influenced significantly by what type manager controls the company. Differences between these two types of firms in both performance and policy suggest that fundamentally there are quite separate goals and motivations at work for owners and managers. Such differences in outlook result in distinctly different behavior patterns between the two types of firms.

If we admit such differences do in fact exist, what are the implications? A number of questions come to mind.

Is motivation really the crux of the issue? Is motivation sufficiently crucial for efficiency that it affects the firm as strongly as our data suggest?

Are professional managers themselves merely less proficient than the owner-managers in large firms? Are business schools training professional but inefficient managers? Could this account for the difference in performance and behavior we observed?

Would different compensation schemes for management alter their behavior and goals? If so, what kind of a system could be devised that might be successful?

Most critically for the economy, are current tax policies eliminating the most efficient firms, forcing them to merge with and become manager controlled? Is profit becoming less important to the largest corporations?

If owner-controlled firms are more efficient in terms of return on investment, are manager-controlled firms more responsive to the demands of workers, consumers, and government? Which is better?

These questions will be explored briefly after we have examined in more detail several of the studies mentioned above.

Summary of Results

In an attempt to shed some light on the behavior of owner-controlled and manager-controlled large firms, 72 corporations were studied from *Fortune's* list of the 500 largest industrial firms by sales in this country for a twelve-year period (1952-63). Six firms (three owner-controlled and three manager-controlled) from twelve different industries were compared. A firm was considered owner-controlled if 10 percent or more of the corporation stock was owned by one party. An analysis of the data revealed that the owner-controlled group of firms outperformed the manager-controlled firms by a considerable margin. The net income to net worth ratio was 75 percent higher for owner-controlled corporations over the twelve-year period. This indicates that these firms provide a much better return on the original investment, and suggests a better-managed capital structure and more efficient allocation of resources.

The effect of the type of industry on the net income to net worth ratio was statistically significant but only one-third the strength of the control-type effect; the size of the firm was not a significant factor. No other effect, including the control plus industry interaction, was statistically significant, indicating that *the owner- or manager-control factor affects all industries tested.*

In an attempt to look at policy differences, particularly dividend policy, 69 owner- and manager-controlled firms were studied from among the 200 largest nonfinancial corporations in this country. Again, owner control was defined as a minimum of 10 percent stock ownership in the corporation by one party, and firms of roughly the same size and same industry were compared. Utilizing an analysis of variance statistical technique, as in the first study, the results were once again quite clear. The type of industrial classification to which a firm belonged did influence the firm's dividend pay-out ration. However, the ownership type of the company had an even stronger effect, statistically, upon the dividend policy than the type of industry to which the firm belonged. Further, no evidence was found that industry interaction with ownership type produces special effects upon dividend payout ratios. Thus, the evidence supports the existence of distinct dividend pay-out policies between owner-controlled and manager-controlled firms of approximately similar size in the same industry.

These two studies support the idea that the type of control strongly affects both the performance and the policy decisions of a company. In this sense, the traditional economic approach addressing firms from this aspect as simply one aggregate of behavior is seriously oversimplified.

Why, in the first study, should the owner-controlled firms outperform the manager-controlled firms? And why, in the second study, should the two types have very different and distinct dividend policies? The answer that seems most convincing is that two quite different motivational incentive systems are at work, emanating from the pursuit of different goals. It would seem that our business system is not generally structured to provide the same set of motivations or goals for both owners and managers. As a result, the behavior of our largest firms differs widely depending upon what group controls them.

Some Practical Implications

Motivation

In the past, economists have tended to ignore the effect of motivation upon economic activity. Only recently have some studies been made which yield evidence that motivation is considerably more important in influencing efficiency in the economy as a whole than economists traditionally have believed. Thus, the effect of the modern separation of ownership from management may have a motivational impact upon the performance of the firm—perhaps of greater consequence than allocative efficiency, which has been the main concern of past economic efficiency studies.

If motivation does have a significant effect upon the performance of the firm, what factors influence motivation? Does the separation of ownership and control in most large corporations have an effect upon motivation of management? Does such motivational difference, if it exists, between owners and managers affect the behavior of the firm? The data of the studies we have cited here certainly do suggest that owner- and manager-controlled firms behave differently. The differences in goals and motivations that we have posited seem the most plausible explanation. However, while the differences in behavior of the two types of firms can be observed empirically, our motivational explanation, sound as it may seem, is not definitely established. We can in final analysis only suggest explanations that seem consistent with the data.

While traditional economic theory recognizes only one motive for firm management—to maximize profit—economic theorists have recently suggested that the large firm attempts to maximize sales, growth, or the management's own lifetime income. In fact, different types of firms may pursue one or a combination of these and other goals, and in the real world the owner-controlled firm appears more likely to fit the picture of the world painted by traditional economic theory. Distinguishing between types of firms is important because the behavior of each firm with respect to profits depends upon certain elements of its internal structure.

The professional manager, unlike the owner-manager, is probably more responsive to pressures from the various constituent groups of the firm such as workers, consumers, suppliers, stockholders, and the government. The professional manager is apt to respond to conflicting demands from these groups by balancing one off against the other or by utilizing compromise as an issue-settling device. The owner-manager, who views each dollar given to workers, suppliers, consumers, or the government as coming from his own pocket, is less likely to compromise. Further, the position of the owner-manager is a good deal more secure regarding his tenure in office than that of the professional manager. For, although professional management is generally autonomous in the large corporation, an executive may be sidetracked or replaced if he makes a bad blunder. The owner-manager, because of his stock ownership, seldom faces this problem. The risk and reward system for owners and managers is therefore quite different.

Because of these basic differences in the security and financial reward of their respective positions, the strategy to maximize the income of an owner-manager may be considerably different from that of a nonowner manager. Given the same goal, to maximize their wealth, the strategy, policies, and performance of the firm would probably be quite different depending on whether the company was owner- or manager-controlled.

Further study may reveal that there are also differences in behavior between various subtypes of owner- and manager-controlled firms. Mutually owned corporations are a specific category needing further research, for they appear to form a quite distinct category of their own. All told, if motivation is a major factor influencing firm behavior, we could hypothesize that wherever the motivations of corporate leadership patterns have a distinct character, firm behavior should reflect that fact. Finally, if motivations and behavior are different between groups of firms, should this cause any change in current tax or antitrust policies to either encourage or discourage certain forms of economic behavior?

Professional Managers Less Proficient?

Two questions are associated with the idea that owner-managers seem to be outperforming professional (nonowner) managers. First, is there any reason to feel that the ability level differs between the two groups? One is hard put to see why one group should be any more able than the other. If anything, one might suspect that the professional manager who has worked his way up in the company without benefit of family or financial interest might actually be more capable. However, we have already noted that the professional manager's goals, motivations, incentives, and range of alternatives for company policy might be quite different from that of owner-managers. Since

there is no reason to believe otherwise, the latter factors, rather than intrinsic ability, would seem most likely to explain the behavior differences found in our data.

The other question that comes to mind is whether the business schools are training professional but inefficient managers. Again there is no particular reason to suspect that business schools only train nonowner-type managers. Yet the suspicion does remain that the modern business school has created its own ideology and technique of business management that may, in effect, be stifling creativity and entrepreneurship. Are the business schools merely turning out business bureaucrats? Is this the type of individual who is rising to positions of leadership in the major corporations? Frankly, the business schools have not examined their products or their program with this possibility in mind. Most of the major schools in this country seem largely concerned with justifying their present approach or system. Their own ideology has thus far gotten in the way of their looking objectively at their impact and effect upon the business system — except to enthuse over it for fund-raising purposes.

It could well be that business schools are basically turning out business bureaucrats who know how to rise in the corporate bureaucracy but lack the motivation of owner managers. Therefore, nonowner managers may make decisions that prevent the company from performing as profitably as the owner-controlled firm. Why should they make such decisions? A number of possibilities can be suggested, many of which could be significant. Does the professional nonowner manager prefer to minimize risk? lead a quiet life? make the firm overly conservative by using compromise techniques in decision making? grow and merge for the sake of growth or his own vanity (and possibly higher salary in a larger company) rather than for potential return on investment? All of these possibilities cast the manager in a negative light. Yet the results themselves, in terms of lower return on investment, cast aspersions upon either the management-controlled firm's efficiency and competence or its goals.

Compensation Schemes

If we assume that the difference in performance between owner- and manager-controlled firms is due basically to different strategies to achieve their individual goals, then we must ask whether incentives can be developed that would tend to bring together the goals of both owners and managers in manager-controlled firms. Is it possible to devise incentives that would induce managers to maximize the rate of return on owner's investment when they themselves are not major owners? It would be most interesting to investigate whether the various compensation schemes of large companies are directly correlated with the performance of the firm as to rate of return. However, there now appears to be little major difference between the compensation schemes for officers of the country's largest corporations, at least not enough to expect substantial differences in incentives. Could marginal differences in incentives and clear-cut goals of the corporation (particularly constraints upon decisions) have a significant effect?

The problem may involve not only the goals of the corporation, but also the range of decision alternatives managers feel they possess. Altering incentives may do no good if the bureaucratic system of the corporation itself effectively prohibits managers from making

the same kind of decisions that owner-controlled firms can make. If less risk, flexibility, and internal decision-making coherence is possible within the manager-controlled firms, altering incentive systems may have no appreciable effect upon present performance.

Let us assume, however, that manager-controlled firms would perform as owner-controlled firms if the compensation system is altered so that the manager income is largely related to the company's return on investment. Is there any chance that this might merely cause an overly great concern for short-run profits and that the firm might suffer in the long run? This is a possibility, of course. The twelve-year span of our original study on the rate of return on investment is hardly what might be called a long-run period. Yet, at the same time, this is not a short-run period as far as management tenure is concerned. Plenty of "birds would have come home to roost" during our period of observation if an overly great concern on short-run return was typical. Certainly some reflection of the damage to these firms might be evident within the space of twelve years.

A serious problem not previously considered is that owner-controlled firms may not pay sufficient attention to the interests of their public consumers, workers, suppliers, and the community. It may be that, on the average, manager-controlled firms may not pay sufficient attention to the interests of their public — consumers, workers, suppliers, and the community. It may be that, on the average, manager-controlled firms are more responsive to the demands of the public and their communities. If this is the case, we then face the problem of having to decide between firms internally efficient or firms externally responsive to their constituency and environment. At present there is no way of empirically proving that the large managerially-controlled firm is consciously or even inadvertently accepting smaller rates of return on the owner's capital in order to satisfy demands from other groups upon the firm. Or, put another way, we have no evidence to determine whether the manager- or the owner-controlled firm is the most responsive to social demands of the public and its community environment.

It is possible, however, that just such a choice between (1) efficiency and social responsibility or (2) between the redistribution of return on owner's investment and the public may be the crux of this issue. No investigations have yet been made that can answer this perplexing and disturbing questions.

Tax Policies

Our data reveal that the owner-controlled firms, which appear most efficient in operations in terms of return on investment (the usual definition of efficiency for firms), are gradually being eliminated from among the largest corporations. Tax policies make it very difficult to pass on working control of these large corporations. Further, the huge size of these firms, due to mergers and internal growth, make the money required for working control increasingly exorbitant. These factors, when coupled with division among heirs, tend to gradually eliminate the large owner-controlled firms from among the largest 200 or 500 corporations in this country. Further, the ranks of new owner-controlled firms among these top corporations are not replenished as easily as before due to the above reasons, particularly because smaller firms have to merge for competitive reasons, for owner's diversification of holdings, and for estate tax payment.

All told, the trend toward the elimination of owner-controlled firms seems inexorable, yet these firms may be the most efficient ones in our economy. By allowing them to disappear we may be reducing our over-all level of efficiency and economic growth. Since the trend is so pronounced and well-known, it may seem strange that there has been no research by government or private sources to determine whether policies which permit and promote this trend are sound for society as a whole.

Perhaps (just as antitrust laws prohibit mergers and practices that reduce competition within an industry) we should also prohibit the elimination of owner-controlled firms by manager-controlled ones. Competition is not the only major value. If, however, further research could provide additional evidence that manager-controlled firms were more socially responsible, such evidence might tend to offset our findings of greater efficiency on the part of owner-controlled firms.

The entire area of government policy needs greater study to determine what the actual (rather than intended) effects of legislation and policy are upon the society and economy as a whole. At present our national policy is too haphazard and untested to be able to say with confidence that our values and goals are being furthered by present public policy. Further research in this area is badly needed, and should be sponsored by the government as well as by private sources.

Managers More Responsive to Society?

This, of course, becomes the crux of the issue of public policy changes. If it could be shown that manager-controlled firms are more responsive to the needs and demands of their public environment, then the gradual elimination of owner-controlled firms might be considered socially appropriate. Our society at this stage of development would probably opt for firms that would be more concerned about local community and social problems, the safety of their products, and the pollution of the streams and air they use. Such criteria might well rank with or above greater efficiency and return on the owner's investment in a society such as ours.

However, the firm that shows itself more efficient in its use of resources and shows a higher rate of return in the competitive market should benefit society materially by being able to produce more goods at less cost. Yet, in an affluent society where the problem is indifference rather than lack of resources, we might indeed be further ahead in terms of society's total welfare to exchange some efficiency for more social responsiveness.

The question we cannot answer at this moment, however, is whether the manager- or owner-controlled firm is the more socially responsive — if, indeed, there is any difference at all between them. If the owner-controlled firm proved to be socially more responsible — along with its superior efficiency record — our public policy would need to be drastically revised.

Property ownership in our society now appears to be of considerable significance in determining how resources are used. This is as true for the use and development of urban land in our major cities as it is for the use of corporate resource. Yet whether society should be encouraging certain types of ownership use and discouraging other types has not been clearly thought out in our public policies. Studies that are available have yet to be translated into relevance for tax policy, for example.

The implications of the studies mentioned here suggest that managers, owners, general investors, and the makers of public policy need to look carefully into the performance and policies of corporations where ownership control may provide different goals and motivations for different groups of firms. We have argued here that current public policies do not take these factors into account in the developing of tax or antitrust legislation and policy.

Conclusions

The studies discussed here offer empirical evidence that the separation of ownership from control has indeed produced different and distinct types of economic behavior. Both performance and policy differences are observable. Large owner-controlled firms in the same industry have much higher rates of return on investment and lower dividend pay-outs than manager-controlled firms. The first finding may or may not be the result of conscious policy; nonetheless, the performance differential is certainly there. The finding on dividend pay-out is the conscious result of policy decisions.

Our observation that the owner-controlled firm is more efficient but is gradually being eliminated was suggested by both Berle and Means in their original study nearly forty years ago and confirmed by Larner's recent one. Since this is a problem of both private and public concern, it should be investigated to see if the public policy which encourages it should be changed.

At the very least, managers, directors, investors, and government officials should give immediate attention to the reasons why owner-controlled firms have higher rates of return than comparable manager-controlled firms.

There may be considerable opportunities for increasing the rate of return in manager-controlled companies. Managers and directors can hardly ignore this challenge to their internal operations, and government officials should not let this opportunity pass to investigate a neglected area of significance for public policy. Could a case be made that manager-controlled firms should be constrained from acquiring owner-controlled ones? What would be the total effect upon our economy and society? The relative social responsiveness of the two types of firms could settle argument as to whether large owner-controlled firms should be gradually eliminated from our economy as present public policy encourages.

The main justification for the present public policy is either (1) that redistribution of economic power is encouraged by permitting managers to replace owner in controlling our largest firms, or (2) that manager-controlled firms have a higher social worth to society in some way, perhaps in greater social responsiveness to environmental problems. As we have said, the latter has yet to be established. Thus, this whole area of public policy needs investigation. It may well be that drastic changes in our taxation and antitrust laws need to be made. It is time, as well, that directors and management looked into their own motivation to determine what goals they are attempting to achieve and in what order of

preference. The data here certainly cast suspicion on the assumption that manager-controlled firms are placing return on investment as their prime goal. If they are, they are inexplicably less efficient in pursuing this goal than the owner-controlled firms. It would seem more likely at this stage of investigation to posit motivational and goal differences between owner- and manager-controlled firms as the critical factors in influencing their performance and policies.

We can only hope that the studies cited here will create greater concern and further research. Both pubic and corporate policy may be badly in need of overhauling – how and where is the next question.

1. H. Leibenstein, "Allocative Efficiency vs. X-Efficiency," *American Economic Review*, LVI (June, 1966).

2. R. J. Monsen, J. S. Chiu, and R. J. Pulliam, "Dividend Policy and Corporate Control: Some Implications for the Theory of the Firm" unpublished.

3. R. J. Monsen, J. S. Chiu, and D. E. Cooley, "The Effect of Separation of Ownership and Control on the Performance of the Large Firms," *Quarterly Journal of Economics*, LXXXII (August, 1968). The findings of D. R. Kamerschen in the June, 1968 issue of the *American Economic Review* appear inconclusive on this subject due to the design and methodology of the study.

Introduction

The family company has several unique inherent attributes. Each attribute is a source of benefits and disadvantages for owners, family members employed by the business and non-family employees. The authors label "bivalent" attributes which contain both benefits and disadvantages and maintain that family business success or failure depends on how well these features are managed.

Bivalent Attributes of the Family Firm
1982

By John A. Davis and Renato Tagiuri

Most firms in the U.S. are family businesses — organizations where two or more extended family members influence the direction of the business through the exercise of kinship ties, management roles, or ownership rights. While most family companies are small, some are relatively large and several are giants in their respective industries. Taken together they contribute about 40 percent of the gross national product and over half of our national employment (Beckhard and Dyer, 1983). It is vital, given the prevalence and importance of family-controlled organizations in our society, that we understand the characteristic behavior of the family members who influence these firms.

Most writings on these organizations appear in the business and trade press, and generally focus either on a particular family or on a specific issue, such as the son's entry into the company or the rivalry between relatives who work together.[1] As it stands today, the family business has not been extensively researched or described. Some systematic study has been done, however, on the social structure and the particular strengths and weaknesses of family companies,[2] on the psychology of the owner-manager,[3] on nepotism,[4] and on management succession in these firms.[5]

This paper builds upon insights found in the above writings, and it also incorporates observations from our on-going study of family firms. In this discussion we deal only with those family-controlled companies where two or more individuals are simultaneously members of the owning family, owners and managers. More specifically, this includes any company that is (a) ownership controlled by one family,[6] (b) includes at least two family members in

Figure 1. Overlap of Family and Ownership and Management Groups

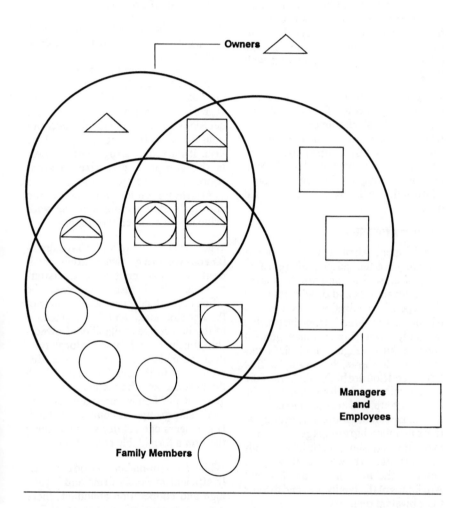

its management, and (c) also has non-family employees.[7] The graphic representation of this set of relationship is displayed in Figure 1.

Our purpose in this paper is to show that the family company has several unique inherent attributes, and that each of these attributes is a source of benefits and disadvantages for owning families, non-family employees and family employees. As a result of their latent negative and positive potential, we call these inherent features Bivalent Attributes. When one considers that only 30 percent of family firms survive to the second generation (Poe, 1980), and that their average life span is only 24 years

(Danco, 1977), the concept of Bivalent Attributes is a reminder that the success or failure of any family firm will depend upon how well these inherent features are managed. Their successful management will also affect the well-being of the family and the family's relationship with employees and with the greater community.

We propose a theory here which will conceptually account for many important behavioral characteristics of the family company, and which will incorporate and build upon previous descriptive and conceptual work done on family businesses. Hence, our major contribution in this work is a conceptual one.

Bivalent Attributes

The Bivalent Attributes of the family company are the unique, inherent features of these firms and are the source of the advantages and disadvantages of this type of organization. Bivalent Attributes derive directly from the overlap of family, ownership and management memberships. Figure 1 displays this overlap. It shows, for example, that Father and Son are both members of the same family, are both members of the owning group, and are both members of the management group. The overlap of these membership groups generates the many distinguishing features of family companies. In what follows, we describe the most important Bivalent Attributes of the family firm and discuss their bivalent qualities.

Simultaneous Roles

Because of their overlapping memberships, family members working in the family firm can have three simultaneous roles: as relatives, as owners and as managers. As family members they are concerned primarily with the welfare and the unity of the family; as owners they are interested in return on investment and in the viability of the firm; as managers, they work toward the firm's operational effectiveness.

Relatives' simultaneous obligations to the family, company, and shareholders, and to each other as relatives, managers, and owners, can serve to bond them loyally to each other and to the business. The loyalty can involve standing behind one another's decisions, making personal contributions for each other, the family, and the firm. It can reduce struggling for power in the company, give rise to great cooperation and trust, and create a sympathetic understanding of one another's shortcomings, along with pride in one another's strengths.

When one or more relatives have simultaneous roles (e.g., owner-father-president) this can centralize decision-making, which, in turn, can increase the efficiency, effectiveness and privacy of the decision-making process. Because of the immediate availability of ownership, business and family information, decision-makers can quickly and discretely act in the best interest of both the business and the family. When the goals of the family, management, and ownership groups are compatible, family managers can act decisively, making the firm a formidable competitor.

While decision-making can be especially efficient in family firms and loyalty high and cooperation abundant, there can also be negative outcomes that flow from simultaneous roles.

In general, norms about behavior in business and norms about behavior within families are opposed. Families traditionally seek internal unity and try to repress or deny rivalry among members whereas businesses often strive for a healthy level of internal competition.

64

In this framework of double-norms, either competitiveness within the firm, or family unity may be sacrificed to protect the company or the family. Even in the best of cases we find the owner-manager-relative periodically suffering the anxiety that results from what we call "norm confusion."

Because of simultaneous roles, family considerations can easily intrude on business decisions, and vise versa. Family ownership, and business issues can get mixed up; business discussions may be transformed into highly charged arguments about family issues, while family decisions may be made on the basis of company needs. Consequently, companies can suffer from a lack of marketplace objectivity and poor profit discipline, and families from a feeling that relatives are sacrificed for the good of the firm.

Because of the overlap in social systems, relatives can retreat into whatever roles give them the greatest power in conflict situations. A founder-father-president can retreat into his role as father, and treat his son-subordinate like a child, for example, to maintain his position or power. The movement in and out of roles can obscure the reasons underlying disagreement and prolong and inhibit the resolution of conflicts. Nonrelatives doing business together are less able to retreat into non-business roles and more likely to handle business decisions objectively.

Complicating the situation further is the possibility that family members, regardless of their positions in the family or business, may each consider themselves as spokespersons for the business. When this is compounded by rivalry that is carried from the family setting into the business, it can lead to conflicting orders being given to the company, family members trying to undermine

each other's authority in the company, and a general lack of clarity about responsibilities.

Shared Identity

Relatives who work together share a sense of identity. While this Bivalent Attribute may seem obvious, it is nevertheless a meaningful and important influence on relatives' behavior both on and off the job. Since work and family domains are intertwined in family firms — a result of the overlap — each action of every employee-relative carries both business and family meaning.

The family name, for example, is an identity for family members and has a meaning to people inside and outside the family. Family ties define a bond and rules of behavior for relatives. Outsiders come to associate certain traits with the family and expect to see that behavior. If one or more family members are loud, unruly, bossy, the whole family may be suspected of having a potential for the same behavior. The same could also be true for good, constructive behavior. One relative's behavior can influence the reputation of others in the family and the reputation of the business as well.

Both on the job and off the family polices the behavior of its members to insure that they are acting in an acceptable manner toward friends of the family, customers, suppliers, and employees. This concern with image and the consequent policing may do much to increase awareness among family members and also to define family standards and a mission around which relatives can rally and find a reason for mutual loyalty.

On the other hand, the policing may be stifling to some family members. Even very creative expression may be

65

discouraged if it does not fit the family mold. Family members may feel that they are being watched in and out of the company and resent their lack of freedom. At the same time, family members who try to maintain the family image may be angered by relatives who do not.

The pressure to act in ways that enhance the reputation of the business can offset the influence of the family in the management of the company and restore some objectivity to decision-making. On the other hand, it can add to the pressure to conform to roles more tightly prescribed than ordinary executive roles and foster resentment toward family and business authority.

A Lifelong Common History

The behavior of blood relatives working together is influenced, in part, by the fact that they lived with one another all the life of one of them. Out of this time comes considerable common experience, even though each family member has his or her own recollections of that experience.

From their time together, relatives learn a great deal about each other's strengths and weaknesses. They can use this knowledge, when working together, for constructive or destructive purposes. They can try to draw out one another's strengths and work to complement one another's weaknesses or they can point out their relative's weaknesses to undermine his or her standing in the firm.

The relationship's history includes a mixture of happy and disappointing experiences and these do much to shape the pair's expectations concerning working together. A strong foundation for the relationship (where the two have learned both how to support and how to be in conflict with one another) can

mean that the two will endure considerable adversity and remain loyal to one another. Early disappointments, on the other hand, can reduce trust between the relatives and complicate work interactions. One family member, for example, might avoid certain work situations with a relative for fear of being let down again.

Because the relationship between two blood relatives begins in the family, when one or both are infants, the two practice for many years certain ways of behaving around each other. Many of the impressions that the two have of one another are unconscious, well-established, and difficult to change. When the two begin to work together it is easy for them to lock into their old mutual, reciprocal ways. Each acts as a cue to the other to resume their well-practiced respective roles. If the history of the relationship is positive and constructive, the ease and speed with which the mutual patterns come into operation is an advantage, an economy. But if the relationship has been difficult, the rapid locking is a disadvantage out of which it seems very difficult to escape.

Emotional Involvement and Ambivalence

As a result of the combination of benefits and constraints that relatives present to one another throughout the history of their relationship, family members hold concurrent and powerful positive and negative feelings for each other. That is, they feel ambivalently toward each other.

Given the potential for greater love and greater hate among family members, it is not surprising that emotions between relatives often surface more easily than between non-related individuals. Because of the emotional content of their bond, relatives working together may find it difficult to interpret one another's actions and words objectively. Instead, communications are often interpreted in terms of their meaning in a family context and they can elicit the same response they did at an earlier time in life.

Not all emotion between relatives is expressed openly. On the contrary, there are generally strict psychological prohibitions against open conflict among family members. Once emotion (love or hate) rises from the unconscious to consciousness, the family member must decide whether to express or suppress the feeling.

On the positive side, the expression of love can generate unusual motivation, cement loyalties and increase trust among relatives. The prohibition against public conflict can be a norm among family members that can eliminate embarrassing conflict situations. This, in turn, can put family members at ease in public situations which can aid work relationships.

Powerful feelings of hate and resentment and the accompanying sense of guilt can greatly complicate work relationships. The denial of negative feelings can result in the suppression of discussions about quite natural differences of opinion, and lead to covert expressions of hostility such as undermining each other's confidence, withholding emotional support, avoiding one another (particularly around sensitive family issues), and issuing conflicting orders to the organization. The expression of a relative's negative feelings toward a family member can damage the work and family relationship and greatly disrupt the company.

The Private Language of Relatives

An interesting feature of the work interactions among family members is the relatives' private language. Over the many years of shared experiences relatives evolve special words, phrases, expressions, body movements that have agreed upon meanings. Private languages, "family languages," allow family members to communicate more efficiently than is generally possible among nonrelatives, even among close friends. This can permit relatives to exchange more information with greater privacy and arrive at decisions more rapidly than can two nonrelatives.

On the other hand, aspects of this private language can trigger sensitive, painful reactions that can distort communication. A private language can keep non-family people uninformed and can also be a weapon in an on-going family struggle. It is an interesting paradox that in even the most embattled family company, there is often strong adherence to even the most painful family language.

Mutual Awareness and Privacy

Family members have an especially keen awareness of each other's circumstances: what pressures they are under, what makes them happy or angry, how they are feeling physically, and so on. This awareness is created through three channels. First, there is the explicit communication among family members. This can be greater for relatives than for nonrelatives since relatives may see each other more often in many types of business and social settings. Second, family members have a private language which aids this awareness of each other. Third, family members share relatives who may pass on information from one relative to another.

Increased awareness can improve communication between relatives and help to temper business decisions with an understanding of their implications for family members. It can give relatives insights on how to support one another.

On the other hand, increased awareness can lead some family members to feel trapped or overwatched. Since family members who work together have relatively little time apart and since they have a heightened awareness of each other, they may feel as if they are "living in a fishbowl." The "fishbowl" is often hidden from the world's view, but these relatives may feel very exposed to one another. The combination of heightened awareness and emotional intensity may add up to a feeling that personal privacy is not available in a family company system. Moreover, because of this feature, family members often *are* vulnerable to the attacks of relatives.

Meaning of the Family Company

Depending on the generation of the company and the length of the family's association with it, the organization takes on particular meanings for members of the owning family. The firm (especially a first generation company) is typically regarded as a part of the family and relatives can often have strong feelings about it. To a founder-father it often represents a wife, mistress, or child. For a son (especially if he grew up with the firm) the company is the father's creation or mistress and the son becomes its guardian, sibling, or suitor. Later generations can also feel strong personalized attachments to the organization but this seems to occur more infrequently.

It has been our observation that in a family system where there is adequate security and abundant nurturance, the family company will not be perceived as a threatening rival or interloper. However, in a family where there is a prevailing struggle for security and a perceived lack of emotional resources, the family firm may be perceived as a displacing family member who takes away status and resources from real family members.

The meaning of the company for a family member and the corresponding attachment to it are important influences on work relationships between relatives. Father and son can become fierce rivals for the possession of this nurturant symbol. A founder can fight to maintain control over the company and seem to love the firm more than he loves his son. When strong attachments exist, discussions about organizational control can become subjective and highly-shared emotional confrontations.

Conversely, if relatives are strongly attached to the organization, they can be united in their goals for it and in their willingness to contribute to it. Ultimately this symbolism can define a sense of mission for the organization that non-family companies rarely match.

Conclusions

For managers in family companies, or for those who interact with such companies, it is crucial to recognize, as this conceptual note has pointed out, that the *same* organizational features of these firms account for both their strengths and their weaknesses. Thus it is necessary to recognize the potential for positive and negative consequences in each of these features which we have called Bivalent Attributes . See Table 1 for a summary of these characteristics. It is not possible for management to eliminate the presence of the Bivalent Attributes — they derive directly from the defining overlap of membership groups. The challenge in these organizations is to manage the

Table 1. Bivalent Attributes of the Family Firm

Disadvantages (–)	Attribute	(+) Advantages
Norm confusion and anxiety. Family, business and ownership issues can get mixed up. Lack of business objectivity.	Simultaneous Roles	Heightened family and company loyalty. Quick, and effective decision-making.
A stifling sense of being overwatched. Resentment toward family and business.	Shared Identity	Heightened family and company loyalty. A strong sense of mission. More objective business decisions.
Family members can point out weaknesses and undermine relatives. Early disappointments can reduce trust in work interactions.	Lifelong Common History	Relatives can draw out relatives' strengths and complement their weaknesses. A strong foundation can encourage a family to weather adversity.
Lack of objectivity in communication. Resentment and guilt can complicate work interactions. Covert hostility can appear.	Emotional involvement and ambivalence	Expression of positive feeling creates loyalty and promotes trust.
Can trigger sensitive reactions that can distort communication and encourage conditions for conflict.	Private Language	Allows for more efficient communication with greater privacy.
Can lead relatives to feel overwatched and trapped.	Mutual Awareness and Privacy	Improved communication and business decisions that support the business, owners, and family.
Fierce rivalries can develop between relatives.	Meaning of the Family Company	Company symbolism can define a strong sense of mission for employees.

inherent Bivalent Attributes to maximize their positive and minimize their negative consequences.

The concept of Bivalent Attributes, we argue, is a useful tool for the study of all organizational forms. Each organization will have unique, inherent features that will lead to either advantages or disadvantages. Because the family firm is composed of social systems whose goals, norms and other features can be in such stark contrast, perhaps its Bivalent Attributes are more apparent than for other kinds of organizations. We encourage organizational researchers to derive more Bivalent Attributes for family companies and to test the usefulness of this concept on other organizations.

Footnotes

1. cf. Altman (1971), *Business Week* (1966, 1967), Butrick (1977, 1978a,b,c,d), Danco (1967, 1975, 1976, 1978), Folger (1969), Groseclose (1975), James (1975), Loving (1975), Martin (1975), Minard (1976), Poe (1980), Shaw (1959), Sheehan (1966), Steele (1979), Time (1976), Tysick (1967).

2. Barry (1975), Becker and Tillman (1978), Calder (1961), Davis P. and Stern, D. (1980), Davis, P. (1983), Donnelley (1964), Edison (1976), Folger (1969), Kepner (1983), Lansberg (1983), Levinson, H. (1971, 1983), Levinson, R.E. (1975), Miller and Rice (1973), Tilles and Contas (1965).

3. Brockhaus (1979), Brockhaus and Nord (1980), Collins, Moore and Unwalla (1964), Danco (1977), Day (1980), Deeks (1976), Greenfield, Strickon and Aubey (1979), Kets de Vries (1977), Mancuso (1973), Naumes (1978), Schein (1983), Sexton (1980), Smith (1967), Zaleznik and Kets de Vries (1975).

4. Benshahel (1975), Cambreleng (1969), Ewing (1965), Florsheim (1970), Gaffey (1966), Levinson, R. E. (1976).

5. Barnes and Hershon (1976), Beckhard and Dyer (1983), Christensen (1953), Davis, J. (1982), Davis, S. (1968), Hershon (1975).

6. For most smaller companies, ownership control means 51 percent ownership, but for larger companies, it is possible to own less than a majority of the shares and elect a board of directors that will support the controlling family's goals.

7. While the firms discussed here are a subset of all companies which are ownership controlled by one family, most writing on this subject deals with this type of situation.

Bibliography

Altman, H. Coming in with dad. *Nations Business*, June 1971.

Barnes, L and Hershon, S. Transferring power in the family business. *Harvard Business Review*, July-August 1976, 105-114.

Barry, B. The development of organization structure in the family firm. *Journal of General Management*, Autumn 1975, 42-60.

Becker, M. and Tillman, F. A. *The family owned business*. Chicago: Commerce Clearing House, 1978.

Beckhard, R. and Dyer, W. G., Jr. Managing continuity in the family-owned business. *Organizational Dynamics*, Summer 1983, 5-12.

Benshahel, J. Playing fair in a family firm. *International Management*, February 1975, 30(2), 37-39.

Brockhaus, R. H. Psychological and environmental factors which distinguish the successful from the unsuccessful entrepreneur: A longitudinal study. Proceedings of the Academy of Management, 1980.

Brockhaus, R. H. and Nord, W. R. An exploration of factors affecting the entrepreneurial decision: Personal characteristics versus environmental conditions. Proceedings of the Academy of Management, 1979.

Business Week. When your real job is 'son'. October 15, 1966, 98.

Business Week. Keeping their success in the family. December 9, 1967, 96-98.

Butrick, F. M. Passing the reins gracefully. *Convenience Store Merchandiser,* September 1977.

When father and son collide. *The Packer,* December 30, 1978a.

Father and son in business. *Best's Review,* February 1978b.

Communication and planning and prerequisites for son's entry. *The Packer,* September 2, 1978c.

Your wife's role in the family business. *Screen Printing Magazine,* June 1978d.

Calder, G. H. The peculiar problems of a family business. *Business Horizons,* Fall 1961, 93-102.

Cambreleng, R. W. The case of the nettlesome nepot. *Harvard Business Review,* March-April 1969, 14-17, 22-25, 28, 32, 34, 170-171.

Christensen, C. *Management succession in small and growing enterprises.* Doctoral dissertation, Graduate School of Business Administration, Harvard University, 1953.

Collins, O. F., Moore, D. G., and Unwalla, D. B. *The enterprising man.* East Lansing: Michigan State University Press, 1964.

Danco, L. Why family owned firms fail. *International Management,* November 1967, 22, 57-58.

The sterile hybrid. *Retail Control,* August 1975.

Family owned business — an endangered species. *Inland Printer American Lithograph,* February 1976.

Beyond survival: A business owners guide for success. Cleveland: The University Press, Inc., 1977.

Portrait of a business owner. *Restaurant Business,* June 1978.

Davis, J. *The influence of life state on father-son work relationships in family companies.* Doctoral dissertation, Graduate School of Business Administration, Harvard University, 1982. Ann Arbor: University Microfilm No. 8219510.

Davis, M. Entrepreneurial succession. *Administrative Science Quarterly,* December 1968, 402-416.

Davis, P. Realizing the potential of the family business. *Organizational Dynamics,* Summer 1983, 47-56.

Davis, P. and Stern, D. Adaptation, survival and growth of the family business: An integrated systems perspective. *Human Relations,* 1980, 34(4), 207-224.

Day, P. J. Charismatic leadership in the small organization. *Human organization,* Spring 1980, 50-58.

Deeks, J. *The small firm owner-manager: Entrepreneurial behavior and management practice.* New York: Praeger, 1976.

Donnelley, R. The family business. *Harvard Business Review,* July-August 1964, 83-105.

Edison, B. As the family business grows, or why didn't grandfather tell us? In J. D. Glover and G. A. Simon (Eds.), *Chief executive's handbook.* Homewood: Dow Jones Irwin, 1976, 273-290.

Ewing, D. Is nepotism so bad? *Harvard Business Review,* January-February 1965, 23-32.

Florsheim, H. Nepotism and the family run company. *Business Management*, June 1970.

Folger, J. H. The case for the family owned business. *New England Business*, April 1969.

Gaffey, E. *Neponistic and non-neponistic firms and performances.* Doctoral dissertation, University of Arkansas, 1966.

Greenfield, S. M., Strickon, A., and Aubey, R. T. Entrepreneurs in cultural context. Albuquerque: University of New Mexico Press, 1979.

Groseclose, E. You have problems? Consider the plight of the nation's SOB's. *The Wall Street Journal*, March 20, 1979, 1.

Hershon, S. *The problem of management succession in family businesses.* Doctoral dissertation, Graduate School of Business Administration, Harvard University, 1975.

James, R. D. Bill and Mel Lane follow their father's policies at Sunset Magazine. *The Wall Street Journal*, January 17, 1975, 1.

Kets de Vries, M. The entrepreneurial personality: A person at a crossroad. *Journal of Management Studies*, 1977, 14, 34-57.

Kepner, E. The family and the firm: A coevolutionary perspective. *Organizational Dynamics*, Summer 1983, 57-70.

Lansberg, I. S. Managing human resources in family firms: The problem of institutional overlap. *Organizational Dynamics*, Summer 1983, 39-46.

Lessner, M. and Knapp, R. R. Self actualization and entrepreneurial orientation among small business owners: A validation study of the POI. *Education-al and Psychological Measurement*, 1974, 45, 455-460.

Levinson, H. Conflicts that plague the family owned business. *Harvard Business Review*, March-April 1971, 90-98.

Consulting with family businesses: What to look for, what to look out for. *Organizational Dynamics*, Summer 1983, 71-80.

Levinson, R. E. What to do about relatives on your payroll. *Nation's Business*, October 1976, 64 (10), 55-60.

Making your family business more profitable. *Michigan Business Review*, May 1975, 27(3), 24-29.

Loving, R., Jr. Outsider in the throne room at Kaiser. *Fortune*, March 1975, 127.

Mancuso, J. Fun and guts: *The entrepreneur's philosophy*. Reading: Addison-Wesley, 1973.

Martin, R. Reeces of Reece Corp. put in some time on the bottom rung. *The Wall Street Journal*, January 24, 1975,1.

Miller, E. and Rice, A. The family business in contemporary society (Ch. 9), Constraints on growth and change in the family business (Ch. 10). *Systems of Organization*, New York: Harper & Row, 1973, 103-126.

Minard, I. In privacy they thrive. *Forbes*, November 1, 1976, 38-40, 45.

Naumes, W. *The entrepreneurial manager in the small business: Text, readings, and cases*, Reading: Addison-Wesley, 1978.

Poe, R. The SOB's. *Across the Board*, May 1980, 23-33.

Schein, E. H. The role of the founder in creating organizational culture. *Organizational Dynamics*, Summer 1983, 13-28.

Sexton, D. L. Characteristics and role demands of successful entrepreneurs. Paper presented at Academy of Management Conference, 1980.

Shaw, R. What about family owned corporations that have 'gone public'. *The Magazine of Wall Street*, January 17, 1959, 411.

Sheehan, R. There's plenty of privacy left in private enterprise. *Fortune*, July 15, 1966, 223.

Smith, N. *The entrepreneur and his firm.* East Lansing: Michigan State University Press, 1967.

Steele, N. Brothers war for control. *New York Post*, January 29, 1979.

Tilles, S. and Contas, A. F. Planning in the family firm. Unpublished paper by the Management Consulting Group, Boston Safe Deposit and Trust Co., 1965, 1-31.

Time. Bitter grapes. September 13, 1976, 49-50.

Tysick, J. Following father in the family firm. *The Director*, May 1967.

Zaleznik, A. and Kets de Vries, M. Myth and reality of entrepreneurship. *Power and the Corporate Mind*, Boston: Houghton-Mifflin, 1975.

Chapter 2

Succession

It has been said that the three most important issues confronting the family business are succession, succession...and succession. To remain a family business, each generation must be succeeded by the next, the ultimate management challenge.

Even among large, public businesses the effort to achieve family management succession remains amazingly strong in our society. This tendency is somewhat surprising in light of the myths that exist about family business succession and of what can be described as the succession conspiracy—forces aligned to resist succession planning.

To achieve familial succession, the generation in power must let go and the inheriting generation must desire involvement. Fortunately, guidelines and advice are available about navigating the succession process so that fewer family businesses will confront the reality of being the last generation.

Introduction

Perpetuating the family business is the ultimate management challenge. To succeed, a business owner must simultaneously deal with business, family, succession and estate challenges. This article suggests approaches to help make it happen.

Perpetuating the Family Business
1984

By John L. Ward

For many small business owners, passing the business on to children is a warming motivation. At some point it helps to make worthwhile the ups-and-downs, the hassles and the long hours away from home when the children were young. For other small business owners having younger relatives work in the business is the best opportunity available for the relatives. For these business owners family succession almost becomes an inevitable consequence even if not originally sought.

Perpetuating the family business into future generations, to me, is the ultimate — most difficult — management challenge. Not only do you have to see to it that the business stays healthy long term, but unlike publicly held businesses you have to face the possible dilution of resources from estate/inheritance taxation. Further, you have to effectively train and install your successor from a very select group of family alternatives. Finally, successors very often come with siblings which require effective preparation for co-management or "partnership"-type ownership and management. Any one of these management challenges is a subject for life study. Yet the family business owner must face them all almost simultaneously.

This article is to focus on *the family* — what can be done to make *family succession* more possible and more successful? The following is a checklist from studies of successful family businesses.

The Role of the Owner-Manager

- Am I committed to the family succession? Is it a dream I deeply feel?

- Do I have personal financial security for me and my spouse after retiring from the business?

- Do I have a clearly chosen successor and an announced retirement date?

- Do I have a new challenge or group of interests that will keep me satisfied so I never look back or go back to the business?

- Am I willing to take the chances of delegating many decisions and authority?

- Am I still willing to take new business risks?

- Am I willing to share full financial information with top managers, family members and advisors?

Family Participation in the Business

- Are there known rules for "who" from the family can join the business with what qualifications?

- Do we place family members in meaningful and definitely needed jobs?

- Are our most business-competent children in the most responsible positions?

- Do we pay family only what their job is worth in the open market?

- Do we have a way to formally and objectively review and reward family member performance?

- Are we willing to keep business ownership only (mostly) in the hands of the family members who manage the business?

Successor(s) Development

- Does our successor have worthwhile business experience other than in our business to gain fresh ideas and to learn the "grass isn't greener?"

- Is our successor being taught and mentored by someone other than their parent?

- Does our successor have independent, personal opportunity to make a visible difference in our business now?

- Is our successor continuing to be educated more than just on-the-job?

- Are we purposefully and tirelessly teaching our successor our business history, philosophy and strategy more than anything else?

- Does our successor have outside-of-the-business chances to be a leader and gain respect?

- Does our successor have a clear, sensible rationale for why he/she wants to work in the family business — one that sustains him/her when things get tough?

- Does our successor have opportunity to be with other family business successors with whom to share interests and concerns?

The Role of the Family

- Does the family perceive the business owner(s) as enthused, stimulated and challenged by the business as they grow up?

- Does the family value all vocations equally — in or out of business?

- Do family members believe that participation in the family business is purely voluntary but quite welcome?

- Does the family actively teach in-laws about the business — especially if they *do not* work for the business?

- Does the family and the business afford fun times for the entire family to be together?

- Does the family teach savings, sacrifice and investment in the young?

- Does the family have a clear philosophy of how it plans to take care of its needy?

For the most part these questions are common sense but need reminder and vigilance. Other of these questions are tougher to face, to solve and to talk about openly with family. To bring regular attention, credibility and caring help to these issues, family businesses are much more frequently turning to a board of *outside* directors or board of advisors for assistance. Your problems and troubles are really not that unique nor secret; others who own and manage family businesses can share their experience and their empathy through a board-type excuse to hold regular, quarterly meetings to plan for our family-in-business future.

There is no greater challenge nor more proud and meaningful ambition.

Introduction

In tracing the succession of leadership during the history of 105 major industrial corporations, Thomas R. Navin gains insights into both executive evolution and family succession. He finds that the manner in which these corporations choose their top leadership tends to pass through five distinct stages: Initiator, founder, heir, technician and professional. The duration of each stage is influenced by the company's growth rate (the more immediate its success, the more likely the founder will be entrenched) and perpetuation of family involvement (the longer the family produces managerial heirs, the longer succeeding stages will be delayed).

Navin also found that a one-third factor appears to operate in famiy involvement. In each generation, the probability of famiy succession is abut one in three.

Passing on the Mantle: Management Succession in Industry
1971

By Thomas R. Navin

Considering the key role that management plays in the success of business ventures, it is curious that so little attention has been given to the process of management succession. The Library of Congress catalogue does not even list the term as a subject heading. It may be that each instance is regarded as unique and that no generalization is possible. Perhaps the selection of a new chief executive officer is typically so surrounded by secrecy that research on the subject has not been thought practical. Or maybe the whole process is commonly regarded as Elijah-like and there is nothing further to say about it; the chief executive officer just picks his successor and passes on the mantle.

The classic works on the origins of America's business elite were principally concerned with the social and educational backgrounds of business leaders and gave little attention to the selection of successive chief executives.[1] The writers based their conclusions on an extensive compilation of quantifiable data (much of it now eighteen and twenty years old); they did not delve into the process by which the leadership of an enterprise evolves from the initial inception of the venture down to its present status as leading industrial.

This article is a by-product of research into the origins of some of America's most successful industries. It is based on hypotheses concerning the basic ways in which leadership has evolved as the organizations have grown larger and older.

Method and Hypotheses

Since the study on origins involved a selected group of today's top-performance companies, it seemed advisable to take the hypotheses derived from that study and compare them with the behavior of a list of companies that contained some random factor and some companies that had once been large. Therefore, the supporting data listed all companies beginning with the letter *A* in the following categories: the top 500 industrials in 1917; the top 500 industrials in 1955 (the first year of the now-famous *Fortune* list); and the top 1,000 industrials as published in *Fortune*'s most recent listing in June, 1970.[2] This selection, obviously not a sample in the usual statistical sense, has the advantage of including companies that have been on the top list for over fifty years and others that have risen to prominence only within recent years.

The resulting list contains a total of 130 firms, distributed as follows:

10 in the top 100 industrials in 1970

50 in the 101 – 500 industrials in 1970

39 in the 501 – 1,000 industrials in 1970

5 no longer large enough to make the 1970 list of 1,000

12 failures (7 during the Great Depression)

20 sold to other industrials

2 no longer classified as industrials by *Fortune*.

The total list proved difficult to work with for several reasons. To achieve perspective over a long span of years it was important to work with a group of companies that had spent a major part of a rather long existence as Big Industrials. The list of 138 contained a number of companies that did not serve this need. It included sixteen conglomerates that had grown large only in the last five or six years and, although most had started as industrials a number of years ago, they had all remained relatively small until their recent explosive growth through merger.

In addition, two companies made *Fortune*'s list only because of large sales volume; in terms of assets and number of employees, they did not belong on the list. Two were spin-offs from large companies, later reabsorbed by their parents. One was a cooperative and therefore had an owner-manager relationship different from that of other firms. And, finally, twelve had failed some time ago under circumstances which made information about their management succession difficult to obtain and generally not pertinent. The unsuitable examples were eliminated; the remaining companies totalled 105.

The next task was to trace the 105 companies from their origins to the present, taking care to focus on the chief executive officer of each. This also proved difficult, and, as a consequence, the data may contain a number of unintentional errors. Until recently, companies did not distinguish clearly between the chief executive officer and the chief operating officer. Sometimes executive power resided with the president and sometimes (increasingly so) with the board chairman. When a particularly influential officer moved from the presidency to the chairmanship, it is presumed, in the absence of information to the contrary, that he continued to be the chief executive officer.

The following seven hypotheses are intended to apply principally to companies that have enjoyed enough success to be rated among the nation's largest industrials. They also apply principally to conditions existing since 1880, largely because few Big Industrials existed before that time.

First, the manner in which Big Industrials choose their top leadership tends to pass through five distinct stages. The sequence appears inherent in the nature of big business and can occur in any epoch including, presumably, the present and immediate future when some Big Industrials are just beginning their rise to success. The five steps are:

Initiator stage

Founder stage

Heir (family or surrogate) stage

Technician stage

Professional stage

Second, the duration of each stage may be subject to increasing compression, that is, strongly influenced by the date of founding of the enterprise; more recently founded companies pass through each stage more rapidly. The duration is probably also influenced by two other variables; rate of growth of the company in its climb to success (the more immediate its success, the more likely the Founder will become entrenched) and perpetuation of family involvement (the longer the family continues to produce managerial heirs, the longer the succeeding stages will be delayed).

Third, something like a one-third factor (similar in concept to the half-life phenomenon in physics) appears to operate in family involvement. For every three Founders, one will pass along the business to his son; for every three sons, one will pass the business to a grandson; for every three grandsons, one will pass the business to a great-grandson. (In the control group there are 58 founders, 19 of whom were succeeded by a second generation, 7 by a third, and 4 by a fourth.) This process is independent of ownership, and may continue even after family holdings have dwindled to less than 1 percent of the outstanding stock.

Fourth, the combined Founder-Heir stages reached their zenith during the 1920's when over half the leading industrials passed through those phases. The two phases have been occurring less frequently among Big Industrials since the 1920's, but it is important to note that approximately 20 percent of today's Big Business is still in the Founder-Heir phase of development. This figure may stabilize at around 10 percent because of the constant renewal from below of recent Big Industrials still in their Founder stage.

Fifth, the Technician stage of management succession is most frequently encountered today. This stage began to be important at the turn of the century but was not brought to the attention of the academic world until 1932 and of the general public until 1941.[3] The phase passed its peak during the 1960's when over 70 percent of the Big Industrials could be said to be passing through it. Though this stage seems to be declining in importance, it will probably not be superseded by the next phase until the 1990's.

Sixth, although much has been written about the Professional Manager in the last decade and a half, he is no more prominent today in the top leadership of Big Business than was the Technical Manager in 1900. Nevertheless, the Professionals can already be conceptualized, and some can be found in the echelons of business just below the top.

Seventh, the fact that Big Industrials are operated today by cooperative oligarchies is gaining wide recognition. But the hypothesis that oligarchic rule in Big Business has existed much longer than is generally recognized is supportable at present only by inference and needs further study to establish its validity.

The Five Stages

The Initiator

To appreciate the Initiator's role in establishing the line of management succession, it is helpful to review briefly the conditions that prevailed before Big Industrials came into being. In the period immediately before the Industrial Revolution, new businesses were the undertaking of individuals. These men performed a variety of roles; in addition to being initiators, they were organizers, administrators, production heads, sales managers, and so on.

In a word, these men were entrepreneurs, and it would be helpful if we limited that overused word only to such situations. As Gough as written, "...the archetypal entrepreneur is not only the man of initiative, but the man who 'runs his own show'."[4] If the successful entrepreneur was not succeeded by his own son (a 33 percent probability?), the business was dissolved or sold.

During the Industrial Revolution, business undertakings became more complex. The partnership form of The partnership form of organization became more common. Partnerships not only served as a convenient means of gathering enough capital to float the enterprise and spread the risk, but also served to assemble the needed skills. Typically, the partners were evenly matched in capital and, in a complementary sense, in expertise as well. Which partner eventually became dominant was often a direct consequence of which produced the heirs to carry on the business. All of the pre-1880 firms on the list (23) began as partnerships, and all but four survived into the twentieth century in the hands of descendants of one of the partners. Like the proprietorship, the partnership produced an heir or was dissolved.

By 1880 when Big Industrials began their rapid increase, the partnership form began to yield to the corporation as the favored way to launch a venture. The incorporators, in contrast to the partners, brought to the enterprise different degrees of skills, different kinds of experience, and different amounts of capital. The leader was not always obvious at the outset, but one of the incorporators was almost always the Initiator, the man with an original idea or the initiative to get the others to enter upon a common venture. This man often lacked the disciplined administrative quality required to build a successful organization and frequently did not last long in the role of chief executive.

The founding of the Beech-Nut Packing Company, now Squibb Beech-Nut, illustrates the diacritical role played by the Initiator. The original Beech-Nut product, a cured ham, was developed by a man named Ephraim Lipe. But it was a son, Raymond, who perceived the market potential of the product and who, with a brother Walter (later the operating head), induced several of their associates to put money into the venture. Among the associates was

Bartlett Arkell, the 21-year-old son of a successful manufacturer of paper bags. The company was still in its formative stage when the depression of 1893-97 nearly wiped it out. Only an infusion of funds from the senior Arkell staved off bankruptcy. In 1899 young Arkell became chief executive officer, a post he retained until his retirement forty-seven years later. Arkell is generally regarded as the Founder of the company; the Initiator was clearly young Lipe.

The Initiator, of course, can be the Founder; it has happened. But a word to the wise is in order. Anyone investigating the early history of a successful company should beware of the blinding glory of the company Founder as related in retrospect (often by the founder himself). With diligence one often finds a predecessor.

How the transition from Initiator to Founder occurs is seldom clear. Usually it takes place during a crisis as in the Beech-Nut experience of 1893-97. Since a beginning venture is likely to experience crisis after crisis, the opportunities for transition arise frequently.

Generally, Initiators only remain in office from a few months to a few years. Occasionally, one survives for several years as a modest success until his fellow investors realize that he is missing important opportunities. But instances of this type are rare; no examples appear among the 105 companies on the list. However, the experience of Gerber products illustrates the possibility. The original company was called Fremont Canning Company (Fremont, Mich.) and was organized in 1901. One of the initial but nonactive investors was Frank Gerber, owner (with his father) of a tannery in Fremont. In 1904 Gerber began to devote some time to the management of the Fremont Canning Company, and after 1906 spent full time

on the job. He did not become president, however, until 1917 and did not enter the baby food business until 1928. The company name was changed to Gerber Products in 1941.

Gerber retained the key position in the company for forty-six years, until his death in 1952 at the age of 79, after which he was succeeded by his son. But he did not supersede the initiator of the business until sixteen years after the founding.

Initiators can be categorized into five groups:

Those who launch a venture of no great economic significance and for no better reason than to fulfill a desire to make a living by doing his "own thing." (Of the Initiators in the table, 22 percent fall in this category.) That such a venture ultimately achieves great success is sometimes due to fortuitous circumstances that do not evolve until a later date.

Those who find a way to improve on existing technology by "building a better mousetrap" often at a lower cost (21 percent).

Inventors holding patents on products which give a protected opportunity to gain a foothold before competition sets in (21 percent).

Those so familiar with the workings of the economic system that they see profit opportunities before they are generally recognized. These are often men of means, maturity, and established success (34 percent).

Those who devise a new "system" of doing business, a difficult performance to pull off since the matter of timing is so crucial (2 percent).

The Founder

Nearly every Big Industrial has a Founder and/or a Founder Myth. American Book and American Bank Note are two clear-cut exceptions on the list if one excludes the 14 companies that are legally discontinuous but organizationally uninterrupted continuations of former ventures (4 foreign branches, 5 spin-offs, and 5 mergers). The Founder is the person under whom the enterprise takes its viable form. As explained previously, the Founder is not necessarily the Initiator. Evidence shows that 30 of the companies in the group had Founders who succeeded Initiators; an intuitive assessment suggests a much larger figure, perhaps 50.

The Founder, like the Initiator, is often a member of the original group. Typically, the organization group quickly sees the need for a spokesman. If the group envisages early and great success, the spokesman may be their strongest member. If, however, prospects are for a long hard pull the more experienced man may be too busy to take on the leadership task and it may be left to a lesser member of the group, possibly the Initiator himself. Since a company destined to succeed often enjoys a spurt of prosperity early in its existence, this early success can reflect credit on the man in charge, whoever he may be.

If he has the ability to cope with the rising demands of a growing organization, he is on his way to becoming the acknowledged Founder. If, in addition, the original organizers fall to quarreling, as they often do in the early years of travail, the founder may be given a chance to "make a market" for dissident stockholders, thereby becoming not only the Founder but also the dominant stockholder.

Viewed in retrospect, these events usually seem to have a certain inevitability about them, a forward movement that ignores the many turnings of the ways not taken. The strong-arm elements of the sell-out by dissidents are, for instance seldom set down for historical view unless a lawsuit results, as in the case of the Addressograph Company. The faults or weaknesses of the Founder may be overshadowed by the great success of his company, for which he is given principal credit. The existence of a predecessor, the Initiator, may be completely forgotten. And so there frequently develops a Founders' Myth; sometimes its validity cannot be established. The existence of such myths has been commented on by various authors, but the common tendency for these myths to arise has not been properly recognized.

The ages of Founders at the time the companies on the list were formed indicate that the average age for founding a company is 35 and that any substantial deviation can be accounted for only by special circumstances. At the this end of the age range, one can find few Founders who took leadership at over 50. Only one, Jose de Navarro of Atlas Portland, was over 53. De Navarro was a wealthy man of earlier achievement and was both Initiator and Founder, belonging to the category of men able to see an economic opportunity and seize it before it is generally recognized by others.[5]

At the lower end of the age scale — those in their early twenties — are three general categories of Founders. Some, junior members of a consortium, rise to fame with the spurting success of their enterprise; some, the sons of businessmen who back them in a youthful venture, eventually become on-the-spot spokesmen for the venture and take full credit for its founding; others are bona fide Initiator-Founders who, through sheer drive and ability, take a venture from unpromising beginnings to great success.

The Founder of a successful company inevitably enjoys enormous prestige, which provides a bulwark against adversity. It is almost unthinkable that a Founder be fired. The list included only 6 founders who, if not fired, at least were allowed to resign their positions as chief executive officer (at American Chicle, Acme Cleveland, American Sumatra, Aeronca, Ampex, and American Viscose). In 5 of the 6 cases, the companies had become public enterprises and had fallen on bad times; an especially vulnerable period was created by the depression of 1921. As a result, the Founders were eased out as chief executive officers by critical boards of directors. In the sixth instance, a British founder was replaced when the company was taken over by American interests as a result of lend-lease arrangements early in World War II.

Company Founders are not only usually exempt from being fired, they are also exempt from retirement. Most of them die in office. Consequently, a commonplace of the founding era in a company's history is the long duration of leadership by the chief executive officer. The average tenure of Founders in the list, not including those still active, is 32.4 years. In addition to the prestige-building factors already referred to, the lengthy tenure of leadership is likely to generate an unassailable eminence.

The creation of a Founder myth does not require that company be outstandingly successful at the outset; so long as it has a success that is demonstrable, the tradition will germinate. Occasionally, the company will remain modestly successful for years and then suddenly experience a period of rapid growth long after the Founder has dies; in that case, the Founder will usually still receive the honor for the company's success, not the chief executive officer at the time of the rapid growth.

For instance, Avon Products did not surpass $2.0 million in sales volume during the first fifty years of its existence. Then, in 1954, after both the Founder, David H. McConnell, and his son had passed from the scene, it began a period of rapid growth, doubling its size every three or four years. Nevertheless, for those who know the company, it is the McConnells who hold the position of reverence, not their successors.

The above observations are not intended to deny that a Strong Man may come to the rescue of a faltering company and lift it up to great success. When this phenomenon occurs within the early years of a venture's existence, it should be classified as part of the Founder phenomenon. But there are instances when Strong Men come to the fore after what would normally be regarded as the end of the founding period. Maxwell Motor Car Company, one of the first and largest automobile manufacturers, went through two financial crises before bringing in Walter P. Chrysler from General Motors, who turned it into the Chrysler Corporation of today.

The time span of the Founder's leadership generally exceeds by a wide margin the span of any of his successors. Occasionally, at a later date, a Strong Man will come along and dominate the venture for an extended period, but this usually grows out of some type of financial crisis or abrupt change in ownership. As explained later, it takes some such discontinuity to bring in a person young enough to have a prolonged impact on the venture.

The Founder's Heirs

It has often been observed that highly successful men become so egocentric that they behave as though they were immortal in that they make no provision for their succession. The evidence is that this circumstance rarely occurs, but that when it does the consequences attract considerable attention. The only conspicuous example on the list is the American Sugar Refining Company, which groped for leadership for five years after the death of H. O. Havemeyer.

Usually the Founder has an heir (family or otherwise) who is so strongly entrenched that no combination of opposing forces is able to unseat him. Because of the long tenure of the Founder it is natural that he should develop a chief assistant; in fact, the more successful the company, the more easily the Founder can delegate all operating responsibilities. It is not necessary for the Founder to declare his assistant or son to be heir apparent; if the Founder's death is sudden, no one else may be available who has anything like the chief assistant's knowledge of the company's operation. A dramatic example occurred in the history of Crown Cork & Seal when the Great Man's personal secretary, who also happened to be the executor of his estate, succeeded him in the presidency with nearly disastrous results.

Not much need be added to the familiar story of the Founder who is succeeded by his son or son-in-law except to remark that the Family Heir tradition remains amazingly strong in our society. It has, in fact, survived transitions to public ownership. Nearly all the companies on the list are publicly owned, and yet 14 are still headed by chief executive officers who are Family Heirs. Furthermore, we are beginning to see surprising instances of reversion to family leadership; companies sometimes pass on to later forms of management succession only to return to family management when a new heir comes to the fore. Armco and International Harvester are recent examples.

The type of heir almost completely ignored by historical literature is what might be called the Surrogate Heir, a phenomenon almost as common as the Family Heir but one generally treated in company histories as though it were unique and therefore of no historical import. One of the reasons why the Surrogate Heir had been overlooked is that his existence is often overshadowed by the Founder. In some instances, where the Founder and his Surrogate Heir retire simultaneously, the key function performed by the heir is never recognized.

What is so intriguing about the Heir phenomenon is the probability that it has done much to perpetuate the founding philosophy of the company, commonly expressed as "the way we do things around here."[6] There is strong tendency for heirs to continue slavishly the policies of the Founder. Earlier it was noted that the Founder Heir preponderance in American Big Industrials extended into the 1930's; therefore, it may be presumed that a large number of those now in charge spent their formative executive years in the Founder – Heir environment. Small wonder, then, that Big Industrials tend to have individual "personalities" which are passed along to the new and younger executives when, during their indoctrination period, they are coached in "the way we do things around here."

The Technicians

A business that has been in existence for forty or fifty years, grown big and neared the end of its normal Founder-Heir experience, generally becomes institutionalized. Within its large central headquarters a kind of bureaucracy has developed; a constellation of Technicians has evolved into a managerial team; complex relationships, sometimes of long standing, have ripened among the top executives; and certain functional areas have achieved greater influence than others. In a company like Avon Products, the sales function dominated; in Allied Chemical, the controllership; and in American Bakeries, personnel management. Observant junior executives soon learn that the best path for advancement lies within the department with dominant prestige.

As a result of this natural evolution, the choice of a successor to the Heir (or the last of the Heirs) is likely to be determined from within. The more successful the company, the more likely the board will accept the choice of the oligarchy. Frequently, it appears that the president is the person making the choice (and, of course, sometimes he is) but often his choice is strongly influenced by the apparent preference of the executive group. In less happy circumstances, he may have to choose between leaders of opposing factions within the hierarchy. Only rarely does he run the risk of imposing his personal choice upon the organization in full knowledge that the choice is unwelcome.

Usually, the chosen person has been head of the department of greatest prestige. Because of the time involved in his rise to the top, he is usually not a young man. Because it is easier for the oligarchy to agree on an experienced older man than on an untried younger one, the Technician is usually well along in years. Since such a man may never have had top administrative experience he sometimes proves a disappointment and is soon replaced. Thus an abrupt break occurs in the pattern of leadership span between the last of the Heirs and the first of the Technicians. Where long spans previously were common, short spans (typically less than seven years) now predominate.

Foreseeing this trend, Newcomer felt that continuity in Big Business was going to be increasingly difficult to maintain.[7] But she was overlooking the role of the oligarchy, and, in fact, the reverse has taken place. As the oligarchy became entrenched and proceeded to promote one after another of its senior members to leadership, the ability of any one person to deflect the movement of the organizational mass was minimized. Instead, the inertia of the organization tended to delay change. One can surmise that change, when it came, was probably long overdue.

Incidents are the only evidence to substantiate the point, but one is led to hypothesize that the inertia of the oligarchy has been reinforced by the nature of the Technician's background. Though he may have had a broadening college education, his range of experience is likely to have been narrow. Surprising as it may seem, the typical Technician is, administratively speaking, a "virgin," the term used by the Japanese for a person who, without previous experience, enters a company and rises to the top. (The Japanese prefer it that way. If not a virgin, he is at least chaste, having worked for only one or two other companies before settling down in the company of his final choice.)

Even today, 25 of the chief executive officers on the list belong to one or the other of these restricting categories (and this does not include the 14 family heirs and 7 founders, most of whom are also one-company men). The most astonishing example in the Aluminum Company of America, which is reputed to have one of the most inbred executive corps in American industry. In its eighty-two years of existence, and with a single minor exception, no chief executive officer of Alcoa has ever worked for anyone else.

One might conclude from these facts that American business has been poorly managed by its Technicians. The opposite is true. The Technicians rose to leadership during a period when intense specialization was needed for competitive survival. A well-trained Technician with extensive experience in his company could not be improved upon as a chief executive officer so long as conditions remained fairly stable, or so long as business remained profitable, enough (as it did during the last decade) to be protected even when it was slow to adjust to changing conditions. (Singer, for example, required nearly a decade for rejuvenation.)

In the minds of many board members, the Technician is not, and perhaps never has been, the *beau ideal* of a chief executive officer. In many instances, boards of directors faced with an indication (usually declining profits) that the ruling oligarchy is not to be trusted will name their own choice of a successor. In these instances, the board almost always opts for a generalist. Addressograph–Multigraph brought in the president of a similar but smaller firm, General Fireproofing Company. Or the board, when looking outside for a president, may select a corporation lawyer, presumably because he has many of the attributes of the generalist. This view is frequently ill-founded, for the corporation lawyer, when contrasted with the Professional Manager, is conceptually a Technician who has specialized in a particular type of generalist activities.

A second type of generalist brought in from the outside by board action is the Business Aristocrat. This person has inherited substantial blocks of stock in several corporations and has developed a high level of sophistication about business matters, although mostly at second hand. Since he may be widely known in social circles frequented by board members (indeed, he may be one of the board members of the troubled company), it is not unnatural for a board to turn to such a man for leadership. Although this phenomenon was common in nineteenth century New England and is still common in many parts of Europe today, it has rarely occurred among the Big Industrials of twentieth century America. There are only 4 examples on the list.

The Professional Manager

The ideal Professional Manager is easy to conceptualize, but it is difficult to point to one in the flesh. *First,* a Professional is a businessman who has had specific education for his administrative role, preferably to the extent of an advanced degree. He has spent about twenty years acquiring broad experience, working in various functional areas, in various companies, and in various industries, or he may have taught for a while or served as a management consultant.

Second, about the time he is 45 he should have settled on the company of his choice and spent the next decade or so thoroughly familiarizing himself with its workings. The Professional should spend a number of years getting to know the organization that he may some day head because only thereby can he gain the expertise that will give his judgements the requisite weight with other members of the oligarchy. And only thereby will he be able to build the other members of the oligarchy. And only thereby will he be able to build the kind of interpersonal relationships that will give him insight into the pervasiveness of "the way we do things around here."

Third, on the ideal path to leadership the Professional should head a division or a profit center or subsidiary — some post in which he can experience at firsthand the full range of responsibilities that fall to a man in a top executive position. A number of today's Professionals have acquired this experience while chief executive officers of a company that was later acquired by a larger corporation.

Fourth, the professional executive should have had some experience with government relations.

The background of few executives include all five criteria. Not a single company on the list is headed by a man with the full set; the 16 men on the list referred to as Professionals are simply individuals who meet some of the criteria. The most common shortcoming is specific education.[8] But a change is coming, though slowly. Of the 16 Professionals on the list, 10 arrived at the top only in the last five years; 5 arrived there during the preceding five years, and only 1 before that. The single early arrival, at Atlantic Refining, is worth commenting on for Atlantic was not only the earliest company on the list to move in the direction of professionalized leadership but is now the closest to achieving that goal.

In 1952 Atlantic elevated to its presidency an individual who was, surprisingly, not an oil man. He was Henderson Supplee, Jr., and his experience was acquired in a milk company. After a postgraduate year at Wharton School of Finance, Supplee joined the family firm of Supplee-Wills-Jones Milk Company, and for the next twenty years was involved in its management, half that time as president. In 1947, he was brought into the Atlantic organization to understudy Robert H. Colley, a Technician who had come up through the finance area. On Colley's retirement in 1952, Supplee was named chief executive officer.

Supplee had many attributes of a Professional, though none in marked degree. He had had some graduate education in business, some experience outside the oil industry, some experience as a chief executive (but not in a big business setting), some chance to familiarize himself with the operations of the company before taking over, and some experience with the federal government (though principally because of his aristocratic connections). He was indeed a mixture of the Professional and the Business Aristocrat.

Four years after becoming president, Supplee brought into his management group, again in the finance area, Thornton F. Bradshaw, an archetypal Professional Manager. Eight years after joining Atlantic, he was made chief operating officer. The role of chief executive officer at Atlantic is filled by Robert O. Anderson, whose age is the same as Bradshaw's and whose background is completely complementary since he is an oil-man enterpriser and Atlantic's largest single stockholder. (His company, Wilshire Oil, had been acquired by Atlantic on a stock deal.) It may well be, therefore, that Bradshaw will never make it to the position of chief executive officer.

The arrival of Professionals in the top ranks of Big Industrials probably has been delayed by the prosperity of the 1960's. Had the diversification difficulties of the 1950's been followed by severe economic strain, it is probable that many of our leading companies would have made major changes in their top leadership, bringing in men of more sophistication, broader experience, and greater ability to cope with the problems of diversification. But the strain on profits in the 1960's was not general. Indeed, thanks to a high price-earnings ratio, many companies were able to solve their diversification needs by acquisition rather than internal creativity.

As a result, management was not put to the severe test of having to cope with a diversity of problems in a declining economy. The oligarchs remain in control, and the Professional Managers remain in the lower levels of management. If business conditions remain prosperous through the seventies, there may be no great rush toward professional management.

It should be pointed out, if it is not by now apparent, that the dynamics of American business have created a current scene of great diversity. The 105 companies included in the sampling represent all stages of development, and consequently reveal a variety of conditions surrounding the decisions that are going to be made in the near future about who will succeed the current chief executive officer. The breakdown of the 105 sample companies includes

43 in the Technician Stage

16 in the Professional State

14 in the family Heir Stage

7 in the Founder Stage

5 in the Surrogate Heir Stage

20 merged into other Big Industrials

Clearly, the decision in each case is going to be influenced by the stage of the company's development. What remains an untested part of the hypothesis earlier posed is the fixedness of the progressions from one stage to the next. To date, few companies have skipped a stage. But as the duration of each stage compresses and as the availability of Professional Managers extends, it may well be that some companies especially those established since 1945, will go directly from the Founder to the Professional Stage. We shall have to be alert to the possibility and wait and see.

1. Frank Taussig and Carl Joslyn, *American Business Leader* (New York: The Macmillan Company, 1932); Mabel Newcomer, *The Big Business Executive: the Factors That Made Him — 1900–1950* (New York: Columbia University Press, 1955); W. Lloyd Warner and James C. Abegglen, *Big Business Leaders in America* (New York: Harper & Row, Publishers, 1955).

2. For description of first category, see T. R. Navin, "The 500 Largest American Industrials in 1917," *Business History Review*, XLIV (Autumn, 1970). Detailed information concerning the supporting data is available from the author.

3. A. A. Berle and Gardiner C. Means, *The Modern Corporation and Private Property* (Chicago: Commerce Clearing House, Inc., 1932): James Burnham, *The Managerial Revolution* (New York: The John Day Company, Inc.), 1941.

4. J. W. Gough, *The Ruse of the Entrepreneur* (New York: Schocken Books Inc., 1970), p.17.

5. Another company on the list provides an even better example, although it relates to an Initiator. Robert C. Pruyn, son of the second American ambassador to Japan, became interested in welding because of his investments in the iron and steel industry. Learning of French advances in the use of oxyacetylene, he formed the Air Reduction Company with the financial backing of Percy A. Rockefeller, nephew of John D. Rockefeller, and the technical assistance of Herman Van Fleet. After some early misadventures, he arranged to have the presidency taken over by a protege, who came to play the Founder role in the company.

6. See the chapter by this title in Marvin Bower, *The Will to Manage* (New York: McGraw-Hill Book Company, 1966).

7. In data collected in 1950, Newcomer found that the average span of the chief executive officer was less than ten years (*The Big Business Executive: the Factors that Made Him*). One might conclude that the turnover rate is accelerating, but the coming of the professional manager may arrest or reverse this trend.

8. Paul E. Holden, Carlton A. Pederson, and Gayton E. Germane, *Top Management* (New York: McGraw-Hill Book Company, 1968), p.238. They estimate that only 4 percent of all top executives had M.B.A. degrees in 1967. However, Austin J. Gerber and George L. Marrah, in their article "How Our Key Executives Have Been Educated," *Business Horizons* (February, 1969), pp.51–55, found in their sample that the number of vice-presidents with M.B.A. degrees had risen from 3 percent in 1945 to 20 percent in 1967.

Introduction

Don't leave your children's careers to fate. Show the opportunities offered by the family business, share your enthusiasm, get them involved. Rather than presenting the family business as the fallback position, make other careers the secondary choices. A family business owner debunks myths with his own experience.

Myths About Succession
1986

By Marshall Paisner

Reprinted with permission of **Inc.**, October 1986, Vol. 8, #10, pp. 146-147. Copyright ©1986 by Goldhirsh Group, Inc.,38 Commercial Wharf, Boston MA 02110; all rights reserved.

Until 10 years ago, I had the same attitudes as most business owners about passing my company on to the next generation. I figured my two sons would find professions more interesting than running my chain of car washes, and I'd eventually sell the business and retire.

And, as my sons entered college in the mid-1970s, our lives seemed to be headed that way. Bob, my oldest son, was intent on becoming a dentist. Dan, two years younger, seemed inclined toward a career in sales. But while they were in college, both the family and the business got lucky. Bob took a pre-dental biology course and realized that perhaps he didn't really want to be a dentist after all. I asked him whether he might want to join the business. Within a couple of years, he decided to come aboard full-time. At that point, Dan confessed to me that he had always assumed he'd be joining the company as well.

Today, Bob and Dan run ScrubaDub's operations, while I am its chief executive officer. Thanks to their involvement, the business has grown and prospered, going from three car washes to six, with two more on the drawing board. Sales have more than tripled. My wife and I are very proud of our sons. Bob is vice-president of operations, and has substantially improved our quality and speed over the past few years by incorporating the latest technology from various industries. Dan is vice-president of sales and marketing, and has raised our unit sales to one of the highest in our industry. Our image, employee spirit and direction have never been better.

The whole experience has made me realize that I was wrong to adopt a hands-off attitude toward my sons' involvement in the business. I should have been more aggressive from the very beginning, rather than leaving the outcome entirely to fate. I have also become convinced that many myths exist about succession in a family business. These myths encourage parents to play a passive role, on the theory that, by following their own inclinations, kids will turn out happier and better adjusted. But such an approach overlooks the important opportunity that business owners can offer their children. It's not just an opportunity to earn lots of money. It's an opportunity to accomplish important milestones, to preserve and expand the business as a symbol of family pride and accomplishment.

Granted, my experience is limited and my sons are still young. Some unanswered questions remain. How well will they get along without us around? What effect will their own families have upon their work habits and obligations to the company? Will they be prepared for the inevitable setbacks that await them? Will they keep the business in the family, or eventually sell it and move to the Sunbelt?

Myth #1: Don't talk business at the dinner table.

As our children were growing up, my wife, Elaine, and I had a running battle on the subject of talking business over dinner. I liked to discuss the business simply because I was enthusiastic about it. My wife, who has been actively involved in ScrubaDub, felt that we should leave the business behind when we sat down for meals. Nevertheless, we sometimes discussed company matters anyway, and, in retrospect, those conversations were significant. When I talked about satisfying customers and exploiting emerging opportunities, the children got a sense of the business as a challenge and commitment.

I suppose that people preach the dinner rule because too often the talk about the company concerns crises, difficult

customers and other bad news. Innocent and liberal minds can be poisoned early on a diet of unhappy stories. They wind up turned off not only to the business, but to their parents as well. But if the conversation centers on enjoyable subjects – such as employee relations, successful marketing, and expansion plans – children will grow up with good feelings about the business. Besides, talking positively about the family business makes great dinner conversation.

Myth #2: Let the kids choose their own careers – there's always the family business.

Our business schools have helped foster a cultural bias against family businesses by suggesting that the real action is in large corporations. Professors seldom recommend that their students consider the family business their first choice of a career. Of course, parents usually reinforce this attitude by encouraging their children to build careers outside the business, and to view the family company as a fall-back alternative in case they fail.

I believe strongly in the eagles-ducks theory: when you send the children out to test their wings, the eagles soar off and continue soaring, while the ducks return, hoping to learn to become eagles. Sometimes they screw up the family business in the process. To keep the eagles at home, I believe in encouraging children to consider the family business as a primary, rather than a last-ditch, career choice. If it doesn't work out, they can then move on to something else. With this approach, surprisingly, children almost always wind up liking the family business, and they offer it new vitality and vision as well.

This isn't to say you shouldn't send the children off for some outside experience, but do it with a purpose in mind. You might, for instance, arrange for them to work in companies where they can learn how to improve the family business. While my son Bob was still in college, I had him spend a summer working for a top-quality car-wash chain in Germany. After he returned, he traveled around the country visiting what I considered to be the 10 best car washes in America, spending a day or two at each. He came back from the two trips extremely enthusiastic and full of ideas for improving ScrubaDub's operations—how, for example, we might solve our chronic problem of getting employees to wear their uniforms regularly. He also had a new appreciation of the importance of keeping our grounds neat and attractive. At his suggestion, we installed underground sprinkler systems at all locations, to maximize the benefits we get from planting flowers and grass.

Another approach is to have the children work in an allied industry. My other son, Dan, went to work for a car-wash equipment manufacturer before joining ScrubaDub. There he learned about the wholesale side of the business, which we are involved in, and came back with ideas for improving our car-cleaning performance through the use of better equipment.

Myth #3: Start your children at the bottom, so that they can earn the respect of employees.

The question here is timing. Certainly it helps to know a business from the ground up, but kids can start at the bottom only if the time is right. More often than not, the right time is during high school and college. When they get out of school armed with newly acquired business or technical skills, they are ready to take on real responsibility. At that point, it can cause problems to start them at the bottom, True, they are better able to cope with real responsibility if they have already spent time working at the bottom. My son Bob made the transition fairly smoothly because low-level employees knew and respected him from his earlier days at the car wash.

For Dan, though, the situation was trickier, since he had put little time into the car wash during his teens. When he came into the business after college, one of his first projects was to examine our merchandising sales approach. Rather than let him sink or swim, I got involved, pushing him to experiment. He put together some direct-mail, discount-priced specials that increased sales substantially. Inspired by that experience, Dan wrote our organization's first sales-training manual. I estimate that profits rose by about $100,000 that year thanks to the consistent and effective sales tactics our employees began using as a result. As for Dan, he was well on his way to respectability in the organization.

There's a lesson in that. Once the kids take on responsibility, early success is essential, because respect comes from results.

Myth #4: Give equal pay to all your children who work in the business.

Most employees are paid according to their responsibilities and the quality of their work. The owner's children, however, usually receive equal compensation, regardless of performance and effort, simply because they are siblings. My feeling is that salary should be based on performance. My sons feel that salary should also reflect effort. No one, they argue, should be unhappy with a partner who works hard, but just lacks the smarts.

So far, they've been able to work things out according to this philosophy. Bob started in the business two years before Dan, who then came in at a lower salary. After three years, the two of them decided that equal in responsibility, contribution to the business, and effort, and should get equal pay. They've stayed on the same pay level ever since. They know, however, that they can't remain equal forever. We constantly discuss and debate who will succeed me as CEO. Right now, Dan believes that Bob probably will.

My sons also feel strongly, as do I, that family considerations are paramount in deciding how to manage responsibilities. For several years, Bob went to night school for his M.B.A., which he completed in 1985. Dan often had to cover some of Bob's responsibilities during exam periods. Recently, Dan went through a personal crisis that distracted him from his job for a few months. Bob went out of his way to fill in for Dan, as well as to provide support in dealing with the problem. It's now resolved, and the two are probably closer for having handled these situations as they did.

Myth #5: Divide the stock equally among all your children, whether they work in the business or not.

The conventional wisdom holds that the owner's children should receive equal shares of the family business, whether they're in the business or not. This practice invariably leads to the dilution of ownership and, I believe, causes more family businesses to be sold than any other factor. I don't think that the practice makes sense. Why give the company's stock to individuals who have no ability to increase its value?

I'm not suggesting that you divide your estate unevenly. Leave other assets to children not in the business. If the company's assets make up the bulk of the estate, then allow the children in the business a one-way option to buy back any outstanding stock from their siblings over a period of time.

That's the approach I've taken. The bulk of my assets are in ScrubaDub, and I have one daughter, who is not in the business. My will states that, if nonbusiness assets do not constitute one-third of my estate, she'll get part of the business, with the proviso that Bob and Dan can buy her out at the market price; she can't sell to outsiders unless her brothers decide not to exercise their option.

In any event, it is very important to talk with your children about these issues. Tell them about your plans for turning the business over to them, and explain the sequence of events.

Myth #6: Make sure you're ready to turn complete control over to your children, because that's the hardest part.

We have all heard the stories about Dad refusing to give up the reins and not trusting his children to exercise responsibility and authority. In some cases, I suppose, that's a real problem, because some individuals do have an emotional need to keep total control, but control itself is not necessarily an all-or-nothing proposition. I've found some real benefits in passing operating responsibilities to my sons. For one thing, I have more time to travel and sail. For another, I can use the time I spend at work concentrating on long-range issues.

For example, I've spent the last couple of years computerizing our main office. Now, nearly everyone in our company uses computers, from the payroll person to the sales manager. I also carried out one of Bob's ideas, which involved funding two car washes through a limited partnership. My current project is to computerize each of our six car-wash locations. The computers will relieve us of many of the control problems inherent in a cash business and will make ScrubaDub one of the most technologically advanced companies in its industry.

In making the transition from operations to planning, an owner has to work out an agreement and a timetable with the children. My agreement with my sons has moved me out of operations over a five-year period ending later this year. We have stuck with the plan, and it's worked out well. They're operating the company, and I'm getting things done for the business that wouldn't otherwise get done.

Introduction

The lack of succession planning has been identified as one of the most important reasons why many first-generation family firms do not survive their founders. This article explores some of the factors that interfere with succession planning and suggests ways in which these barriers can be constructively managed.

The Succession Conspiracy
1988

By Ivan Lansberg

Reprinted from **Family Business Review**. "The Succession Conspiracy," Ivan Lansberg, Summer 1988/Vol. 1/No. 2. San Francisco: Jossey-Bass, Inc. Used with permission of the publisher.

Max Weber, the great German sociologist, was among the first to identify the importance of having the founder of an organization turn over power to a successor who could solidify the administrative structures required for the continued development of the enterprise. Weber (1946) referred to this process as the institutionalization of charisma and saw it as one of the greatest challenges of leadership.

In family firms, the problem of succession and continuity acquires an even greater significance. Consider the following findings: Available estimates (Dun & Bradstreet, 1973) indicate that approximately 70 percent of all family firms are either sold or liquidated after the death or retirement of their founders (Beckhard and Dyer, 1983). The failure of these businesses to continue as family firms beyond the tenure

of their founders has serious social and economic consequences.

The firms that are sold to large bureaucratic firms are subject to the self-interest and standardized bureaucratic policies of the purchasing organizations. Research suggests that many of the positive characteristics associated with family ownership and management, such as concern for quality, long-term investment perspective, and strong community relations, are easily lost as a result of acquisition by larger firms (Astrachan, this volume).

The liquidation of a family firm constitutes a loss not only to the proprietary family, which often has most of its assets tied up in the firm, but also to the employees and surrounding community, whose economic well-being depends on the survival of the business.

Demographic patterns suggest that the number of business owners confronting the realities of succession and retirement is rapidly increasing throughout the economy (Sonnenfeld, 1986). Today, there are more than 24 million Americans over 65 years of age. More important, this group constitutes the fastest-growing sector of the United States population (U.S. Bureau of the Census, 1977). In the coming decade, a large number of postwar business start-ups that weathered the economic and organizational challenges of their entrepreneurial years will face the exit of their founders.

The research that is available (Christensen, 1953; McGivern, 1974; Trow, 1961, Hershon, 1975; Barnes and Hershon, 1977, Tashakori, 1977; Ward, 1987; Dyer, 1986; Rosenblatt, de Mik, Anderson, and Johnson, 1985) shows that one of the most significant factors determining the continuity of the family firm from one generation to the next is whether the succession process is planned. Succession planning means making the preparations necessary to ensure the harmony of the family and the continuity of the enterprise through the next generation. These preparations must be thought of in terms of the future needs of both the business and the family.

First-generation family businesses are heavily dependent on the founders not only for their leadership and drive but also for their connections and technical know-how. Failure to plan for succession needlessly deprives the business of these crucial managerial assets (Christensen, 1953, Danco, 1982; Hershon, 1975; Tashakori, 1977; Beckhard and Dyer, 1983; Whetten, 1980). Moreover, if succession planning is avoided, the founder's unexpected death can force a major upheaval in the pattern of authority and ownership distribution. In this situation, conflict among the founder's heirs often becomes so intense that they are unable to make the strategic decisions needed to ensure the future of the firm. Failure to plan for succession also threatens the family's financial well-being by leaving many thorny estate issues unanswered; a distressed sale of the firm is often the result.

Yet, in spite of all the rational reasons for planning the founder's succession, experience and research suggest that leadership succession is seldom planned in family businesses (Christensen, 1953; Trow, 1961; Hershon, 1975; Tashakori, 1977; Lansberg, 1985; Rosenblatt, de Mik, Anderson, and Johnson, 1985).

While much has been said about the high incidence and detrimental effects of the failure to plan succession, little attention has been given to the issue of why planning is so often avoided. This paper provides an analysis of the critical forces that interfere with succession planning in first-generation family firms. I describe the condition of the system as it approaches the succession transition and provide some preliminary explanations for why the planning process is so vehemently avoided in first-generation family firms. The basic argument is that each of the constituencies that make up the family firm experiences poignantly ambivalent feelings about the inevitable succession transition. This ambivalence prevents key decision makers from engaging constructively in planning for the exit of the founder. One underlying premise of this article is that gaining awareness of the reasons for resistance among the various constituencies is an important first step toward mobilizing the planning process. While my focus is predominantly on diagnosis, the last section considers intervention strategies that can help to mobilize the system in the direction of succession planning.

The ideas presented here arise from three sources: my own personal experience as the son of an entrepreneur who chose to plan his succession, my consultation with family businesses facing the succession transition, and my research on family firms that successfully completed the transition to the next generation and on firms that were either sold or liquidated.

Ambivalence Toward Succession Planning

The succession transition imposes a wide variety of significant changes on the family firm: Family relationships need to be realigned, traditional patterns of influence are redistributed, and long-standing management and ownership structures must give way to new structures. To further complicate matters, the timing of the succession transition tends to coincide with life cycle changes in the family as well as changes in the firm's markets and products (Davis and Stern, 1980; Ward, 1987). These changes are anxiety provoking and create a need to resolve some of the uncertainties surrounding the future of the family enterprise. At the same time, resolving these uncertainties makes it necessary to address many emotionally loaded issues that most people would prefer to avoid or deny.

People in family business adopt different ways of coping with their ambivalence toward succession planning. One common response is to compromise opposing feelings by enacting a number of self-defeating behaviors. For example, consider the case of a founder who chooses his oldest daughter to be his successor but undermines her authority by refusing to give her the coaching and training that she needs in order to perform competently

in the top position (Rogolsky, 1988). Nominating his daughter as the successor addresses the founder's desire to "do something" about the continuity problem. Passively sabotaging the daughter's professional development placates the founder's need to remain in control of the firm. The two sets of behaviors prevent any real movement toward the design of a feasible succession plan.

Another way in which people attempt to cope with their ambivalent feelings toward succession is by projecting the side of ambivalence that they feel least comfortable with onto others (Smith and Berg, 1987). In succession planning, such splitting tends to occur across generational lines, with the older generation becoming the primary defender of the status quo and the younger generation becoming the sole advocate of change. In these situations, each group enacts an opposing side of the ambivalence; together, they prevent the system as a whole from making any progress in planning for the future. Consider the case of a founder who is repeatedly badgered by his oldest son about the absence of a succession plan. With every attack, the founder becomes increasingly defensive and moves to reassert his control over the family firm by procrastinating further. As the conflict escalates, the son becomes increasingly unaware of some of his own misgivings about the future (for instance, any doubts that he might have about his ability to perform competently in the top position or his fear of his father's death). Likewise, the founder loses sight of his reservations about preserving the status quo (for example, his secret yearning to retire from day-to-day operational management). The result of the struggle is that the two cancel each other out. Unless each of the critical actors comes to terms with the side of the ambivalence that is being denied, it will be difficult to reach the level of cooperation needed in order for planning to take place. Let us examine the issues that the succession transition raises for each of the constituencies that make up the family firm.

Stakeholders and Their Perspectives

In order to understand the impact of succession on a family firm, it is necessary to differentiate the perspectives of the various stakeholders that make up the system. Figure One constitutes a pictorial representation of a family firm. It depicts four basic constituencies: the family, the owners, the managers, and people external to the firm. (Similar frameworks have been developed by Davis and Tagiuri, 1986 and by Davis, 1983.)

Each constituency tends to have different goals and expectations (Lansberg, 1983). For example, family members often view the firm both as an important part of the family's identity and heritage and as a source of financial security that will enable them to satisfy their life-style expectations. This view of the firm is rooted in their membership in the family and in a symbolic representation of the firm as a "mother" whose function is to provide nurturance and a sense of connectedness among family members. In contrast, those in management see their careers as tied to the firm and tend to regard the business as a vehicle for professional development and economic achievement. From their perspective, the firm's primary goal is not to look after the needs of family members but to generate profits and ensure them continued career growth. Accordingly, those involved in management expect that the firm's resources will be allocated to those who contribute directedly to its growth. Finally, owners view the business predominantly as an investment from which they want to receive a fair return. Their expectations stem

Figure 1. The Family Firm System

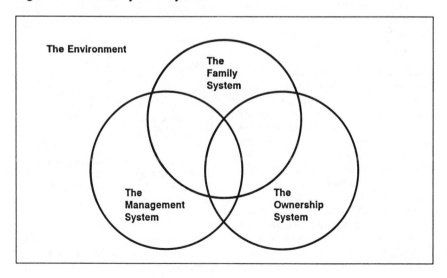

from an ownership right that is often difficult to exercise in the context of a family business. It is also important to note that individuals can belong to more than one group at the same time. It is, therefore, possible for the same person to hold conflicting views about the ultimate goals of the firm (Lansberg, 1983).

While I assume that each constituency will be ambivalent toward succession planning, my primary focus will be on the negative side of the ambivalence, because the available evidence indicates that the forces against planning tend to dominate in the majority of cases.

The Founder. Throughout the development of the family business, the founder tends to be the only person who is a dominant player in all three constituencies. (Throughout this article, I will be referring to founders as male, since the vast majority of entrepreneurs facing succession within the next decade are males, and our data is predominantly from male-run firms.) This position of centrality gives the founder a pervasive influence over the family firm system, making his own strongly felt ambivalence toward succession planning particularly problematic.

While founders are often aware of many good reasons for developing a succession plan, they also experience strong psychological deterrents to managing their exit. One difficult deterrent to succession planning is the founder's reluctance to face his own mortality. For a founder to plan succession, he must come to grips with death. This is not an easy task for anyone (Becker, 1973), least of all for an entrepreneur who typically has guided his life in the firm belief that he controls his own destiny (Gasse, 1983; Brockhaus, 1982). Succession planning forces founders to

go through a kind of premature death ritual. As one founder I interviewed commented, "Planning my succession was like being actively involved in all of the arrangements for my own wake."

In her work on death and dying, Elizabeth Kübler-Ross (1969) proposes that the process of coming to terms with impending death follows a predictable sequence of stages: denial, rage, depression, negotiation, and finally acceptance. Succession planning requires that founders go through this difficult cycle at a time when they are still feeling strong and vital – when those around them continually remind them that they are the indispensable hub of the family firm. Under these conditions, it is very difficult for founders to move beyond the denial stage. Consider, for instance, Armand Hammer, the ninety-year-old entrepreneur who is legendary for his unwillingness to plan his exit from Occidental Petroleum, the firm he has run for the past thirty-one years. Asked by a *New York Times* reporter to comment on why he had not chosen a successor, he said, "'And if I pass' – and here he paused, caught himself, and amended his statement – 'When I pass, the board of directors will pick my successor. They are a good group.'" (Williams, 1984, pp. 1-3).

Frequently, founders develop a complex set of rationalizations and compromises that prevent them from engaging in succession planning. The most destructive maneuver is used by the founder who repeatedly goes through the motions of choosing successors only to undermine their authority and fire them after a given period on some capricious pretext.

Founders also resist succession planning because it entails letting go of their power to influence the day-to-day running of the business. In many cases, founders became entrepreneurs precisely because of a strongly felt need to acquire and exercise power over others. Surrendering power over the firm is thus experienced as the first step toward losing control over life itself. Founders' strong needs for power and centrality are evident in the way they structure their businesses (Hershon, 1975; Tashakori, 1980). Researchers have documented the tendency of founders to make themselves indispensable to their businesses by resisting the delegation of authority and insisting that they be involved in decisions that would be better handled at lower levels in the organization (Tashakori, 1980; Hershon, 1975; Dyer, 1986). This self-reinforcing tendency for centrality leads many founders to develop an exaggerated image of the disastrous consequences that their retirement would bring. This image is frequently shared by others in the family firm, and it often becomes an integral part of the family firm's culture (Dyer, 1986; Schein, 1985). The gloomy outlook, in turn, creates a powerful rationale for avoiding succession planning and reinforces the founder's need to remain involved in day-to-day decisions. While it might be true that the founder is indispensable at any given point in the life of the family firm, the fact remains that the founder has the power to break the dependency cycle, since he is largely, though not entirely, responsible for perpetuating it.

The fear of losing control of the business is often compounded by the thought that retiring from the firm will lead to a demotion from one's central role within the family. As a successor in one company put it, "My father refused to let go because he feared that after retirement he would no longer be Papa—no longer the patriarch that all his children would look up to and

depend on. He wanted to die ruling the family and the firm, and, unfortunately for all of us, he did."

It is interesting to note, in this regard, that even those founders who do plan their succession out of management of the business often retain ownership control of the firm until their death. They do so in spite of the considerable estate tax advantages of passing control of stock ownership to heirs while the founder is still alive.

In addition to the loss of power, founders also resist succession planning out of fear of losing an important part of their identity. For an entrepreneur, his organization defines his place in the community and in the world at large. Moreover, the firm forms an integral part of his sense of self (Levinson, 1971; McGivern, 1978). The business is often his most significant creation. And, unlike his children and, possibly, his wife, it is a loved one he can keep. Thus, founders suffering from the empty nest syndrome at home can become even more attached to their businesses (Rogolsky, 1988). At a time in life when the founder is struggling to come to terms with the meaning of his life's work, when there is too little time to redo some of his life choices, the thought of separating from the organization is disturbing and painful. Even founders who have gathered the courage to forge ahead with a succession plan often find themselves disoriented after their plan is made public. In one family company that I studied, the founder worried that he would be ignored and cast aside by the financial community and by his business associates after he announced his succession plan. Whether or not he was invited to business gatherings and conventions became a major preoccupation, as did the title that he would put on his business cards. He also worried a great deal about whether he could keep his office in the company's building, even though he was still the sole owner of the firm.

Finally, as Levinson (1971) and others have indicated, founders struggling with succession often experience powerful feelings of rivalry and jealousy toward potential successors. Some psychoanalytic researchers have suggested that for a male entrepreneur the firm may constitute an unconscious representation of his mother. For example, Levinson (quoted by Goleman, 1986, p. 30), says, "The son symbolically defeats the father by starting his own business. He simultaneously builds and marries his organization; it represents the mother he could never win away from his father."

Succession triggers in the founder the same rivalry he experienced toward his father in the early stages of his life. This time, however, the struggle is reenacted with the successor, a younger rival who waits to take over the founder's place with his beloved organization. Simultaneously, the founder may be experiencing similar displacement in his daughters' affections through their choice of younger male partners (Rogolsky, 1988). These feelings become evident in a persistent distrust of the successor's competence and ability. In one company that I studied, the founder's mistrust and rivalry with his successor reached a point where the founder spent most of his time minutely documenting every decision the successor made in order to build a convincing case for not retiring. The fact that the company was actually making a sizable profit under the successor's leadership was not sufficient evidence of managerial competence. Instead, the founder argued that until the successor learned to take care of the details (like turning the lights off at night and using

good grammar on internal memos) he would not be fit to assume the management of the firm. After a painful struggle for control, the successor left the company, and the founder has since repeated the cycle with two other successor candidates.

Most analysts of the succession problem limit their attention to the founder. While the founder is unquestionably the critical actor in succession planning, it is important to realize that the founder is not alone in resisting the planning process. The founder's own family frequently exerts strong pressures to avoid the emotion-laden issues of succession.

The Family. In order to understand the family's reaction to succession planning and the reasons why its members might want to avoid the planning process, it is important to consider the stage in the life cycle at which a family is likely to be at the time of succession. The need to start thinking about succession planning does not typically arise until the founder and his spouse enter the last stage in the life cycle (around age sixty). Family theorists (McGoldrick and Carter, 1982) have described some of the issues confronting married couples at this juncture in their lives. By this time, the last of the children has left home, and the couple is struggling to adjust to the vacuum produced by the empty nest. Unresolved marital difficulties that for years had lain dormant, masked by the continuous pressures of child rearing and business startup, reemerge during this period. The death or illness of the couple's parents, who are by now well into old age, exerts additional pressures. The thought of growing increasingly dependent on others is especially difficult for couples who place a strong value on managing for themselves.

Retirement and the changes of status that come with it further exacerbate these difficulties. Couples at this stage resort to emotional strategies, such as denying the need to deal with succession, refusing to relinquish power, and reasserting their authority and centrality in both the family and the business hierarchies. For the offspring, this is also a time of stress and adjustment, as they are themselves adapting to the multiple demands of the adult world, including marriage and (for many) divorce, careers, and parenthood. In addition, the children are eager to establish their own financial independence and autonomy at this stage of their lives. These conditions make it unlikely that the offspring will be patient and supportive of the parents' attempts to assert their power over family members. On the contrary, the offspring may resort to displacing their own difficulties with succession onto the founder, who is viewed as the only obstacle to their own advancement within the firm. Often, those among the younger generation who most eagerly want to bring about the exit of the founder experience a good deal of unconscious guilt that leads them to sabotage their own chances of being effective successors.

Many of the developmental challenges of this stage interfere with the family's ability and willingness to engage in an open discussion of succession issues. For the founder's spouse, the succession transition creates a complex set of challenges and uncertainties. On the one hand, spouses may worry a great deal about the economic and emotional future of the family and continuously work to mediate conflicts that emerge between the founder and the next generation or among the siblings themselves. For this reason, spouses are often supportive of succession planning

and in many cases serve as a powerful influence in mobilizing the founder to confront his difficulties in facing the transition. On the other hand, the founder's spouse faces a number of issues that can deter her from addressing the succession issue. For the spouse, too, the firm constitutes an important center of activity and a major component of her identity (Rosenblatt, de Mik, Anderson, and Johnson, 1985). Like the founder, she may be confronted with letting go of many important roles she has played in and around the business over the years. These roles vary significantly from firm to firm and include anything from running a part of the business or managing the company finances to helping employees with their family problems and organizing social activities for clients (Rosenblatt, de Mik, Anderson, and Johnson, 1985). At times, spouses can discourage succession planning because they fear that a substantive discussion of the future of the family business will disrupt the family's harmony. In one family business that I studied, the founder's spouse played the role of emotional guardian of the family, constantly shielding the family from the emotionally upsetting issues of succession. By actively discouraging any of the children from engaging in discussions about the future of the family business, the spouse enabled the founder to continue procrastinating on development of a succession plan. Sometimes, the founder's spouse resists bringing in an outside consultant because this would violate the privacy of the family and expose the family's dirty laundry to public view.

Many other family factors can interfere with the open discussion of succession. For example, as the result of such factors as gender and birth order, the parents can differ significantly in their preference for the children. These differences have a powerful effect on each parent's assessment of which child should be the founder's successor, and they heighten the chances that the choice will be experienced as preferential treatment. While the emotional response to the choice of successor is often mediated by such factors as the family's ethnic background and traditions (in particular with regard to primogeniture) as well as by the configuration of family coalitions and the developmental stages of the key participants, the decision tends to be emotionally loaded for the majority of business families.

In addition, most Western cultures have norms regulating family behavior that discourage parents and offspring from openly discussing the future of the family beyond the lifetime of the parents. This is particularly true of economic and financial matters, such as estate planning, an open discussion of which is typically viewed as a breach of etiquette or as denoting self-interest and a lack of mutual trust. These norms are functional in ensuring that relationships within the family are guided by personal caring, not by such motives as economic opportunism. However, when businesses are operated by families, the same norms can serve to discourage the necessary discussions of succession planning.

Other investigators have noted that many families have difficulty talking about inheritance and the economic future of the family. For example, Rosenblatt and his associates (Rosenblatt, de Mik, Anderson, and Johnson, 1985, p. 192) argue that the anxieties about succession and inheritance may also result from the fact that the stakes (financial and otherwise) are high for the founder's heirs: "What people will inherit or fail to inherit is not only something of financial value but also an occupation, a status, and a place in the community." Families fear that an open discussion of these issues might only serve to fuel invidious comparisons among the heirs that could destroy the fabric of the family.

Finally, the younger generation sometimes avoids succession planning because it arouses strong fears of parental death, separation, and abandonment. In one case, an entrepreneur's adult son told me that "deep down inside" he did not even want to think about what life would be like in the absence of his parents. He feared that addressing succession would be so upsetting that it might actually bring about the death of his father, who, incidentally, was in very good health. Given the anxiety that the succession transition generates, it is not unusual for family members to harbor very negative expectations of what would happen if succession issues were to be openly discussed in the family. While it is unquestionably true that families differ in their ability to cope with the stress brought about by succession planning, such fatalistic expectations often prevent even the healthiest of families from confronting the need to plan.

The Managers. The difficulties with succession are not limited to the founder and the family. The firm's managers are also confronted with difficult emotional issues that lead them to resist planning. This section discusses the senior nonfamily cadre of managers who constitute the upper echelons of the firm. This group is often composed of older managers who have worked with the founder from the start of the firm.

Many senior managers are reluctant to shift from a personal relationship with the founder to a more formal relationship with a successor. In most cases, these managers have developed unique ties with the founder that extend well beyond the parameters of a contractual work arrangement. Over the years, the founder may have personally managed each senior manager's training, evaluation, and compensation and tendered personal favors to the managers and their families. For example, in several of the firms that I studied, the founder had helped secure loans to the senior managers for the purchase of their homes. For many senior managers, personal ties with the owner constitute the single most important advantage of having worked for a family firm over the years. The founder's succession may also confront the older managers with the reality of their own aging and retirement. In conflictual situations in which the founder and the younger generation are struggling for control, the older managers not infrequently side with the founder in favor of the status quo. The families of senior managers may also have personal ties to the founder and his family, so that the shifting hierarchy in the founder's family may stimulate changes in the families of senior managers. In many cases, several members of a single family are employed by the firm, so that a change in leadership can threaten the employment of these families as well. In some of the larger family firms, the senior managerial ranks include younger professional managers with shorter tenure in the firm who aspire to formalize the structure of the firm (Dyer, 1986). These managers are often eager to purge the firm of relatives both of the owners and of the other managers) who in their view are not contributing to the growth and development of the firm.

Regardless of his or her competence and skills, a successor is seldom able to replace the entrepreneur in the eyes of the older managers. With the change of leadership, it is not only inevitable but also appropriate and necessary for many of the functions that the founder performed to become institutionalized (Greiner, 1972). Senior managers often expect that formal controls, such as budgets, management information systems, and personnel systems, will restrict their autonomy and influence. These expectations lead them to resist both the planning and the implementation of the succession transition. It is not unusual, therefore, to find the senior managers colluding with the founder and members of the family in avoiding serious discussions about succession.

The Owners. Besides the family and the senior managers, the owners also encounter difficulties addressing succession planning. In most first-generation businesses, the founder has given or sold some ownership interest to older managers, relatives, or both, either to give them an incentive to further their involvement with the business or to limit estate taxes. In these cases, the founder typically retains ownership control of the business. In larger firms, the founder has often secured the financial backing of outside investors who are given some share of the ownership in return for their investment. Typically, these outside investors are old friends of the founder and themselves owner-managers of other family firms in the community. Still other family firms are dealerships or franchises in which larger firms have a direct ownership involvement. Like other stakeholders in the family firm, the owners, in whatever capacity they serve, also experience difficulties actively engaging in or mobilizing the succession planning process.

For owners who work in the firm, whether they are family members or not, the difficulties typically stem from the way in which they acquire their share of ownership. Often, the founder has passed along some share of his ownership to these individuals as a paternalistic gesture of goodwill or in recognition of some special contribution that these people either have made or are expected to make. However, this gift or sale carries with it an implicit expectation of loyalty and allegiance to the founder that makes it very difficult for internal minority owners to raise questions about succession planning without appearing to be disloyal.

Outside minority owners who are old friends of the founder are often themselves involved in resisting succession planning with their own firms and as a result tend to avoid discussions of succession planning altogether. As one founder whom I interviewed put it, "The moment I announced I had finally decided to do something about succession, my partners and business colleagues jumped on me and told me that I was crazy. They inquired whether I had received bad news from my doctor. It took me a while to figure out that what I was doing confronted them with their own succession anxieties."

Not all founders have the wisdom to separate their own anxiety about succession from that of others. The problem of succession is a generational issue that confronts all members of the same cohort at about the same time. The reluctance of the founder's partners and peers to face up to succession often reinforces the founder's own resistance to planning his departure from the firm.

Family firms that belong to the dealer network of a larger firm are seldom constructively encouraged to plan for the succession of the founder. At best, large firms deal with the succession issues of their dealer principals by

specifying in their contract that a "suitable successor" (*suitable* is usually left undefined) must be found in order for the franchise agreement to be renewed beyond the tenure of the dealer principal. It is evident in many cases that the head office does not have much understanding of how the complex interaction of family and business affects the dealers' ability to cope with succession. In the parent organization, management succession is typically handled through a formal process that has been institutionalized for a considerable period of time. Often, the parent organization expects that dealers will approach succession with the same degree of bureaucratic rationality that is presumed to be used to handle management succession at headquarters. While the threat that the dealership agreement will be terminated does raise awareness of the need to do something about succession, the bureaucratic rationality imposed from headquarters actually serves to inhibit consideration of the way in which the personal dynamics of the founder and the founder's family might be interfering with succession planning. In addition, the imposition of vague contractual limitations in the absence of supportive processes and structures serves only to increase the tensions that are characteristic of dealer-headquarters relations. Headquarters frequently becomes a target onto which the founder and others in the family firm can displace much of the anxiety and anger that they experience as a result of the succession situation.

The Environment. Resistance to the succession planning process is not limited to the individuals who are directly involved with the family firm system. Environmental forces also create barriers to succession planning. These forces consist of the clients and suppliers who have grown dependent on the founder as their primary business contact in the firm.

These people know that the founder is the person to whom they must speak when they want action. Although it is clearly in the client's long-term interest that the firm plan for its healthy continuation, clients and suppliers worry about losing their connection to the top and frequently side with the founder in avoiding the effort to plan succession. In one company that I studied, the founder had retired and moved a thousand miles away and was still getting and responding to daily calls from clients three years after his departure from the firm. In service businesses, in which the founder's personal network is one of the firm's most critical assets, the founder's connections can become a powerful reason for perpetuating centrality. In many cases, the founder's network results from a lifetime of shared experiences with members of his cohort who do not easily develop links with the successor and others of his or her generation.

It is worth noting here that our cultural values do not generally support leaders who plan their succession. In fact, until fairly recently, management scholars have not paid much attention to the generic problem of leadership succession. As Sonnenfeld (1986, p. 321) has indicated, "How a leader leaves office is as important to his or her constituents as how the office is acquired. Nonetheless, our attention is not balanced between these events. We hear regularly of the violent warfare surrounding prominent cases of corporate executive succession struggles, yet that is where the discussion begins and ends. The collective wisdom on leadership departures does not appear in the best-selling management guides, research reports, or classroom texts."

The stereotypes that we carry are of legendary leaders who have "died in the saddle" or "gone down with the ship," not of leaders who have thoughtfully planned their exit. Perhaps our own collective ambivalence toward authority interferes with our ability to come to terms with the fact that leaders do not just fade away—they die. In this context, succession planning is viewed more as a sign of weakness or as a deficiency of character than as an essential component of responsible leadership. Since founders view themselves as centrally responsible for the well-being of their families and their firms, they do not take such cultural messages lightly.

Mobilizing the Succession Planning Process

The preceding analysis presents a preliminary answer to the question, Why do so many first-generation family firms avoid planning the exit of their founders? The question is important because the lack of a succession plan is a critical factor in the failure of many family firms. I have painted a picture of a gridlocked system, in which critical stakeholders experience a great deal of ambivalence toward the planning process and consequently tend to procrastinate, compromise, or get stuck in nonproductive conflicts with one another. Although only some of the obstacles that I have identified may be operating in a given situation, it is critical for decision makers and consultants to be attentive to the ways in which these forces can interfere with stakeholders' willingness to participate in constructive planning for the founder's exit. An important first step in the effort to develop strategies for mobilizing the development of a succession plan is to diagnose the resistance from the perspective of each critical constituency.

This section suggests a number of interventions that can help to loosen the resistance toward succession planning. These ideas are aimed at those who may be able to help bring about change, including consultants, lawyers, accountants, directors, and other key decision makers directly involved with the firm. As the available data on the rarity of succession planning suggest, systemwide resistance to succession is a powerful force. Mobilizing the development of a succession plan requires a great deal of patience, skill, and persistence. It is important for those who attempt to bring about the design and implementation of a succession plan to have the credibility and legitimacy needed to work with all the critical constituencies. In recognition of the complexity of the problem, the ideas presented here should be viewed not as a recipe for "fixing" the succession situation but as suggestions that must be tailored to the specific conditions of any given case. They are based on the assumption that the family is a healthy one in which any conflicts and difficulties that do exist result not from serious pathology but from normal life cycle stressors (Walsh, 1982).

I shall first present some ideas that can help to mobilize the founder to undertake succession planning. Subsequently, I explore system-level interventions. Most of these suggestions are based on the idea that, in order to mobilize the system, we need to find ways of strengthening forces that favor succession planning while simultaneously weakening or redirecting the forces that work against it.

Working with the Founder. Given the centrality and influence of the founder, his willingness is a necessary, though not a sufficient, condition for effective succession planning to take place. At the very least, getting the founder to accept the need to plan should be an important priority during the early phase of any planned intervention effort. Let us examine what can be done to strengthen the founder's willingness to address succession, paying particular attention to his emotional and cognitive needs.

It is important to address the founder's emotional needs and insecurities about succession first, since these typically constitute a major obstacle to the development of a plan. The principal aim here is to create conditions that may help the founder to work through his most critical resistances to the planning process.

One option is to help the founder develop a support network of founders who have themselves done succession planning and as a result understand what the process entails. Conversations with these peers may help the founder to gain some perspective on his own resistances to succession. More important, comparing experiences with others increases the likelihood that the founder will understand his reluctance to let go as a common response of any founder faced with the succession transition — as a hurdle generic to the situation that can and should be overcome. Peers and elders who have successfully planned their succession and thereby ensured the continuity of the family business are most likely to transmit to the founder a sense of pride and accomplishment about having faced up to the challenges posed by succession.

Interestingly, many of the founders whom we interviewed who had planned their succession had recently had a close encounter with death, such as a heart attack, a near fatal accident, or the death of a close friend or relative. The interviews suggest that contact with death, either directly or vicariously, helped to mobilize these founders to face their own mortality and plan their succession. Being attentive to the occurrence of such events may help interveners to identify times when the founder is more receptive to the idea of planning his own succession. Once a founder has had time to grieve and work through the loss of a close friend or relative, he may be less guarded and more willing to come to terms with the consequences that his death could have on his own family and business. Here, too, a support network can help a founder to work through his fears by offering help from peers who have faced similar circumstances. For instance, founders who have planned their exit often envision the institutionalization of the firm as a realistic way of perpetuating their values and beliefs—a more tangible form of immortality. This perspective may help the founder to reframe the succession process as something that he would be doing for himself as well as for others. In addition, founders can also gain much from others who can serve as role models and describe the process they went through to plan their exit as well as their feelings about their new roles.

It is important for the family to understand how difficult and painful it is for the founder to let go. The entrepreneur is the symbol of strength and self-sufficiency in the family. This image may make it difficult for the family to perceive and empathize with the founder's difficulties around these issues. Helping family members to understand what succession means emotionally for the founder will help them to develop ways of supporting him through this painful transition. This process can take the form of helping the family to reframe

"erratic" or "irrational" behavior as a natural reaction to the process of letting go. For example, a successor-to-be who is attentive to the founder's emotional difficulties with succession is more likely to react constructively to attempts by the founder to interfere with the transfer of power. By being firm and supportive rather than adversarial, the successor-to-be may help the founder to take the necessary steps.

Sharpening the founder's awareness of the need for planning is also important. Frequently, it is helpful to sensitize the founder to the degree to which the family business is dependent on him. The critical diagnostic questions at this stage are, What would happen today if the founder died unexpectedly? What is likely to happen in the family? What is likely to happen in the company? What would happen from the point of view of the ownership and estate taxes? How would the outside world (for example, banks, critical suppliers, clients) react? Typically, these questions help to create a sense of urgency about the need for planning.

It may also be helpful to strengthen the founder's sense of responsibility as a father and CEO by validating the fact that succession planning is the leader's highest duty. For example, it may be useful to expose the founder to case studies of family firms in which the founder assured the continuity of the family and the enterprise through a carefully planned and orchestrated succession.

The raising of awareness must be coupled with concrete ideas about what to do about the problem. The basic tasks involved in succession planning include

• Formulating and sharing a viable vision of the future in which the founder is no longer in charge of the family firm.

- Selecting and training the founder's successor as well as the future top management team

- Designing a process through which power will be transferred from the current generation of management to the next

- Developing an estate plan that specifies how family assets and ownership of the enterprise will be allocated among the founder's heirs

- Designing and staffing the structures appropriate for managing the change, including a family council, a management task force, and a board of directors

- Educating the family to understand the rights and responsibilities that come with the various roles that they may assume in the future.

While it is beyond the scope of this paper to explore the preceding list in depth, it is important to stress that, unless the founder understands the specific tasks involved in succession planning, his resistance to the process is likely to be heightened.

It is also beneficial to help the founder to develop a clear vision of his future roles both inside and outside the family business. Founders who develop strong interests in activities other than management of the family firm have an easier time planning their succession. For some founders, this means pursuing new careers outside the firm. For example, a founder who longed to be actively involved in teaching became a highly successful management professor at a local college. Another retired to pursue a career in music. He is now the conductor of the town's symphony orchestra. Still another founded a consulting firm and spends his time advising other founders on the subject of family businesses and succession.

It is also important for founders to design the interim or transitional role that they will occupy after they turn over management of the firm to their successor. Clarifying this role helps to reduce uncertainty about the future and appeases the founder's fear that he will be totally disconnected from the firm on retirement. This transition role may vary significantly from one case to another. In some of the firms that we studied, the founders were out of operational management but continued to serve as chairmen emeriti in an advisory capacity on new projects or on overall policy matters. Others served as elder statesmen who worked to promote the firm in new and established markets. Still others managed to design an internal role well insulated from day-to-day management. One founder whom we interviewed is a highly successful engineer who invented an important manufacturing process. Basic research is his first love. He turned over the running of the firm to his son (also an engineer) and, at age seventy, returned to the bench. Now eighty-three years old, he has developed a number of new patents since his return to research. Needless to say, there is a very real risk during the transitional period that a departing founder may infringe on his successor's territory and autonomy. It is important for the boundaries around the founder's involvement to be drawn very clearly and both the founder and the successor to monitor this aspect of the transition carefully. Clarifying future roles (both external and internal) facilitates succession planning by reducing uncertainties about the future. In addition, if the founder is drawn out of day-to-day management by his own excitement over new activities, the pain of surrendering power is mitigated by the attractiveness of the new challenges ahead.

Working with the Family. In order to help a family to overcome its resistance to succession planning, it is helpful to structure a process that brings together different subgroups of the family to discuss succession. The timing of these meetings is important.

During the early phases, it is important for the founder and his spouse to reach a mutual understanding about the necessity of planning. First, the couple should articulate what they would like to gain from the planning process. Together, the founder and his spouse constitute the leadership of the family business system. It is critical, therefore, that they develop a shared vision of the future. This vision should include a statement of their aspirations for themselves and the rest of the family as well as a list of the specific activities that they would like to share in the future. The primary aim is to help the couple to support each other throughout this process and to help them realize that they can be instrumental in achieving a good life in the future. This is important, because unless they feel empowered to design and implement a succession plan, it is unlikely that they will be able to exercise their leadership effectively and help others in the family and the firm come to terms with the challenges posed by succession. Sometimes, couples find it beneficial to seek marital counseling and advice on personal financial planning before they address succession planning. In these cases, helping the couple to make such a decision can be an important first step in mobilizing succession planning.

Once the founder and his spouse have had a chance to clarify their expectations and issues, it may be useful to create a family council. This group can be composed of all family members who are key to the future of the business, including the founder, his spouse, and children as well as other relatives who have a significant stake in the family business. The council comes together with the purpose of discussing issues that arise as a result of the family's involvement with the business (Ward, 1987). These issues include, Should the family perpetuate the business, and if so why? How will family members in and out of the business benefit from perpetuating the firm? What are the family's shared values? How should these values be represented in the firm? How can the family give support to relatives who choose not to work in the business? Structurally, a family council should operate only as an advisory body to the company's board of directors. That is, the family council's function is to articulate the views of the family so that those in the board can make decisions and design policies that protect the overall values, needs, and wishes of the family owners.

For the family, the council provides a setting in which differences can be aired and worked through without interfering in day-to-day management of the business and without contaminating the family's non-work-related relationships. In the council, family members can articulate their expectations of one another and explore the specific roles that they expect or wish to play in the future. A family firm that I work with has made very effective use of such a family council. The council is made up of the founder, his wife, their children, and the children's spouses. In one of the early meetings of the council, each person wrote a description of himself or herself and the family business in five years. I encouraged them to think about this future scenario from the perspective of ownership, manage-ment, and family. Individuals then met with their spouses to share their in-dividual expectations for the future. Each couple presented the conclusions from its discussions to the others. This was the first time that the family had come together to discuss their profes-sional and family expectations. Moreover, the meeting served to clarify the views that family members had of one another. As one of the second-generation participants commented, "This was very helpful, since it allowed me, for the first time, to appreciate the professional aspirations and the capabilities of my siblings."

The family council can also serve to bring together subgroups within the family that do not usually communicate. In one business, the founder and his son were the only family members directly involved in management; the other three siblings had long been kept in the dark about the true financial status of the firm. As a result, these family mem-bers had unrealistic expectations about the economic health of the business and about the financial benefits that it could provide. The family council made it possible for the founder and his son to educate the rest of the family about the financial constraints on the firm. This in turn helped those in the family who had not been involved with the firm to bring their expectations for the future into line with reality.

The family council is also a forum in which family members can come to terms with the end of an era in the family's history—that of the creation of the business under the leadership of the founder. Having an opportunity to discuss, enjoy, and mourn the pains and joys of this period in the life of the family helps to pave the way for succession planning. As numerous authors on

human change have argued, the ability to achieve closure on a given period of life enhances successful transitions to the next phase (Bridges, 1980; Tichy and Devanna, 1986; Smith and Berg, 1987). Finally, a family council gives the next generation of leaders in the family an opportunity to become reacquainted with one another as adults. All too often, siblings unconsciously per-petuate early patterns of behavior. In family council meetings, siblings have an opportunity to rediscover one another by working on a common prob-lem. The creation of the council may by itself be one of the most significant ways of mobilizing the system to engage con-structively in succession planning.

Working with the Managers. Senior managers also need an appropriate forum in which to discuss succession issues openly and frankly. One option is to create a special task force whose mission is to develop a five-year management continuity plan. Ideally, such a plan addresses the problem of continuity not just in terms of finding a replacement for the founder but also in terms of training individuals to fill criti-cal senior management positions in the future. In other words, such a group has primary responsibility for designing and staffing the management structures needed to institutionalize the firm. Thinking about continuity from a sys-temic perspective requires an assess-ment of the future needs of the family business. What kind of organization do we want to have in the future? What skills should top leaders have in order to manage this organization effectively? Do we have the people in place who can perform effectively in that future or-ganization? If so, what kinds of training do they need in order to manage the future system competently? If we do not have the people internally, how will we go about recruiting appropriate candidates? These are some of the critical questions that need to be addressed.

In order to reduce resistance to addressing the critical issues, it may be helpful to structure some special incentives into the design of this task force. For example, the succession task force can be treated as a prestigious group in which only the founder's most trusted managers are invited to participate. In may also be useful to give members of this task force some financial incentives for their service.

It may also be beneficial to create some incentives for older managers to address their own retirement issues. These incentives can include an early retirement plan or career and outplacement counseling. In addition, it may be desirable to create incentives for managers to train and develop their replacements as an integral part of their regular job responsibilities.

Working with the Owners. The most effective way of mobilizing the owners to develop a succession plan is to activate the board of directors. Typically, family businesses underutilize their boards. Founders often assign board responsibilities only to inside employees. Often, these individuals are too dependent on the founder to be able to serve effectively as advisers.

A well-designed board of directors can provide a much-needed source of expertise and perspective during succession planning. More important, the board can serve a continuous monitoring function by overseeing that the transfer of management responsibilities from one generation to the next goes according to plan. When structuring a board, it is important to keep in mind that its primary function is to safeguard the interests of the owners by ensuring

that the enterprise is effectively managed in keeping with its mission. It is important, therefore, for decision makers to be attentive to both the design and the composition of the board.

From the design point of view, it is desirable for the responsibilities of the board to be clearly articulated and for the board to have the power and authority necessary to fulfill its duties effectively. It is generally recommended (Ward, 1987; Danco, 1982) that such a board be predominantly staffed with outside directors who can provide an external and relatively unbiased perspective and that the size of the board be kept to a reasonable number (seven, plus or minus two). While this is sound advice, it is not always possible to structure an entirely external board. For one thing, many family firms cannot afford the cost of a totally external board. These businesses may have to work very hard at encouraging independence in the board by carefully selecting, training, and endorsing thoughtful insiders.

Ultimately, whether the board works effectively depends on the willingness of the founder to design it well and to abide by its recommendations. Some founders do use their boards effectively. For example, one founder in our study explicitly charged his board with the task of alerting him to any unconscious attempts on his part to undermine the design and implementation of a succession plan. In this case, the founder was aware of his own needs to resist the succession process and recognized the value of developing a process for monitoring his own behavior in the context of succession.

Finally, it may be helpful to bring together representatives of the family council, the succession task force, and the board of directors to work on specific problems. If these exchanges are appropriately orchestrated, they can be an extremely useful way of educating people in the various groups about each other's needs and perspectives. For example, family members in the council who have never worked in the firm may learn about the professionalism and technical knowledge required to manage the business effectively. Managers have an opportunity to know the family as a whole and to get information about how the family is likely to treat management when the founder is no longer involved with the firm. It may also be useful to bring together the family council and the

board from time to time. For example, the board may benefit by hearing directly from family members about their values, goals, and expectations as these pertain to the mission of the family enterprise.

Summary

In this paper, I have analyzed the forces that interfere with succession planning in first-generation firms. My purpose has been to provide a set of hypotheses that can help us to understand the often cited failure of first-generation family firms to plan the exit of their founders. The central theme has been that the founder, the family, the owners, the senior managers, and other

Figure Two. Strategies for Mobilizing Succession Planning

Strategies for Mobilizing the Founder

Help the founder to develop a supportive network of peers who can empathize and share leanings.

Be attentive to timing, paying particular attention to how the founder is coping with his fears of death.

Heighten the sensitivity of the family to the needs of the founder.

Provide the founder with specific data about the steps involved in the development of a succession plan, and, if possible, get him to develop a timetable.

Help the founder to design a role for the future that will motivate him to let go of his present involvement in operational management.

Strategies for Mobilizing the Family

Help the founder and his spouse to develop a shared vision of the future.

Help the founder and his spouse to seek marital counseling if needed.

Develop a family council that facilitates meetings of the family in which members discuss their values and expectations for the business and for one another.

Strategies for Mobilizing the Managers

Create a succession task force and build in incentives that reward serious involvement in the development of a succession plan.

Encourage planning for succession for senior managers as well as for the founder.

Strategies for Mobilizing the Owners

Create a board of directors that is appropriately staffed and that provides an independent perspective that can safeguard the interests of the owners.

Family Business Sourcebook

stakeholders typically experience poignantly ambivalent feelings toward succession planning. I have argued that these feelings cause the constituents in family firms to procrastinate in developing a plan. If they wait until the founder's death, it is often too late to rescue the firm, and the family undergoes tremendous stress.

The resistance to succession planning is difficult to change. Nonetheless, I have provided some suggestions for mobilizing the planning process. Figure Two summarizes these recommendations. I argue for a systemic approach to succession planning and for multiple interventions aimed at addressing the resistance of the founder and his spouse, the family, the senior managers, and the owners. Contrary to common practice, I maintain that is essential to develop structures, such as a family council, a board of directors, and a succession task force, that can involve those whose cooperation is critical for the development and implementation of a continuity plan. In the final analysis, it is very unlikely that a first-generation family firm can mobilize itself for succession planning unless the founder is willing. In a very real sense, the founder retains his power to perpetuate or destroy his life creation right up to the very end.

References

Barnes, L. and Hershon, S. "Transferring Power in the Family Business." *Harvard Business Review*, July-August 1976, pp. 105-114.

Becker, E. *The Denial of Death*. New York: Free Press, 1973.

Beckhard, R. and Dyer, W. G., Jr. "Managing Continuity in the Family-Owned Business." *Organizational Dynamics*, Summer 1983, pp. 5-12.

Bridges, W. *Transitions: Making Sense of Life's Changes*. Reading, Mass.: Addison-Wesley, 1980.

Brockhaus, R. H. Sr. "The Psychology of the Entrepreneur." In C. A. Kent, D. L. Sexton, and K. H. Vesper (eds.), *Encyclopedia of Entrepreneurship*. Englewood Cliffs, N.J.: Prentice-Hall, 1982.

Christensen, C. R. *Management Succession in Small and Growing Enterprises*. Boston: Graduate School of Business Administration, Harvard University, 1953.

Danco, L. A. *Beyond Survival: A Business Owner's Guide for Success*. Cleveland, Ohio: University Press, 1982.

Davis, J., and Tagiuri, R. "Bivalent Attributes of the Family Firm." Unpublished manuscript, University of Southern California, 1986.

Davis, P. "Realizing the Potential of the Family Business." *Organizational Dynamics*, Summer, 1983, pp. 47-56.

Davis, P. Presentation at the annual meeting of the Academy of Management, Boston, 1984.

Davis, P. and Stern, D. "Adaptation, Survival and Growth of the Family Business: An Integrative Business Perspective." *Human Relations*, 1980, 30 (4), 207-224.

Dun & Bradstreet. *The Business Failure Record: 1972*. New York: Dun & Bradstreet, 1973.

Dyer, W. G., Jr. *Cultural Change in Family firms: Anticipating and Managing Business and Family Transitions*. San Francisco: Jossey-Bass, 1986.

Gasse, Y. "Elaborations on the Psychology of the Entrepreneur." In C. A. Kent, D. L. Sexton, and K. H. Vesper (eds.), *Enclycopedia of Entrepreneurship*. Englewood Cliffs, N.J.: Prentice-Hall, 1982.

Goleman, D. "The Psyche of the Entrepreneur." *New York Times*, February 2, 1986, p. 30.

Greiner, L. E. "Evolution and Revolution as Organizations Grow." *Harvard Business Review*, July-August 1972, pp. 37-46.

Hershon, S. A. "The Problem of Management Succession in Family Businesses." Unpublished doctoral dissertation, Harvard School of Business Administration, 1975.

Kübler-Ross, E. *On Death and Dying*. New York: Macmillan, 1969.

Lansberg, I. "Managing Human Resources in Family Firms." *Organizational Dynamics*, Summer 1983, pp. 39-46.

Lansberg, I. "Family Firms That Survived Their Founders." Paper presented at the Annual Meeting of the Academy of Management, San Diego, Calif., 1985.

Levinson, H. "Conflicts That Plague Family Businesses." *Harvard Business Review*, March-April 1971, pp. 90-98.

McGivern, C. "The Dynamics of Management Succession." *Management Decision*, 1978, 16, 32-46.

McGoldrick, M., and Carter, E. A. "The Family Life Cycle." In F. Walsh (ed.), *Normal Family Processes*. New York: Guilford Press, 1982.

Rogolsky, S. "Daughter Successors: Last Resorts or Lost Resources?" Unpublished manuscript, Yale School of Organization and Management, 1988.

Rosenblatt, P. C., de Mik, L., Anderson, R. M., and Johnson, P. A. *The Family in Business: Understanding and Dealing with the Challenges Entrepreneurial Families Face*. San Francisco: Jossey-Bass, 1985.

Schein, E. H. *Organizational Culture and Leadership: A Dynamic View*. San Francisco: Jossey-Bass, 1985.

Smith, K. K., and Berg, D. N. *Paradoxes of Group Life*. San Francisco: Jossey-Bass, 1987.

Sonnenfeld, J. "Heroes in Collision: Chief Executive Retirement and the Parade of Future Leaders." *Human Resources Management*, 1986, 25 (2), 305-333.

Tashakori, M. *Management Succession*. New York: Praeger, 1980.

Tichy, N., and Devanna, M. A. *The Transformational Leader*. New York: Wiley, 1986.

Trow, D. B. "Executive Succession in Small Companies." *Administrative Science Quarterly*, 1961, 6, 228-239.

U. S. Bureau of the Census. "Estimates and Projections of the Population: 1977-2050." *Current Population Reports*, July 1977, p. 25.

Walsh, F. "Conceptualizations of Normal Family Functioning." In F. Walsh (ed.), *Normal Family Processes*. New York: Guilford Press, 1982.

Ward, J. *Keeping the Family Business Healthy: How to Plan for Continuing Growth, Profitability, and Family*

Leadership. San Francisco: Jossey-Bass, 1987.

Weber, M. *The Theory of Social Economic Organization*. (T. Parsons, trans.) New York: Oxford University Press, 1946.

Whetten, D. A. "Sources, Responses, and Effects of Organizational Decline."

In J. R. Kimberly and R. H. Miles (eds.), *The Organizational Life Cycle: Issues in the Creation, Transformation, and Decline of Organizations*. San Francisco: Jossey-Bass, 1980.

Williams, W. "The Uneasy Peace at Occidental." *New York Times*, September 9, 1984, pp. 1-3 (business section).

Introduction

The style of departure of a retiring leader has implications for the quality and depth of the internal pool of leaders. Older leaders who will not step aside become out of phase with their own generation and in conflict with the next. Retirement from corporate leadership is part of the leader's responsibility for the continuing well-being of the firm by providing future opportunities for others.

When the Old Gods Won't Let Go
1986

By Jeffrey Sonnenfeld

Reprinted by permission of Across the Board, December 1986. Copyright ©1986, Conference Board Inc.; all rights reserved.

Like a parade of marching bands passing the judges, our business executives can be viewed as a procession of passing generations. For a brief period, perhaps a decade or two, each generation enjoys displaying its finest effort before the reviewing stand. When the show is over, the band performs its rehearsed routines with less fervor as it marches on down the road. Organizations that survive and flourish across generations have succeeded in passing on the band major's baton from leader to leader of succeeding generations. By setting the pace of the procession, the leader orchestrates the speed of his or her replacement in the spotlight.

The spotlight moves to the new incumbents and their likely successors. Unlike other creatures, human beings are aware of tomorrow and want to be prepared for it. The rising leader represents tomorrow for us today. Leaders bring us, among other managerial qualities, a prophetic vision. We struggle to shape the development of leaders in an effort to shape our future.

The leader, then, much like a folk hero, offers to guide us with a new map of the future. The departing leader exits with his or her maps tucked away in a pocket, because successful or not, these maps represent only plans for the past. Society cares most about the history of the climb of leaders and their reign when it can provide lessons for future rulers. What lessons can there be in the exit of the outgoing leader?

The style of departure of a retiring leader has implications for the quality and depth of the internal pool of leaders, the continuity of accumulated executive wisdom, and the degree of human turbulence experienced by insiders and outsiders. Winston Churchill warned in a speech to the House of

120

Commons: "If we open a quarrel between the past and the present, we shall find that we have lost the future."

Daniel Levinson, a psychologist at Yale University and author of *The Seasons of a Man's Life*, has argued that leaders over age 65 create career plateaus down the line through their mere existence, and thus retard the development of future leaders. Levinson thought that late-aged executives should leave office. If the leader does not leave, Levinson wrote, "he is 'out of phase' with his own generation and he is in conflict with the generation of middle adulthood who need to assume greater responsibilities...even when a man has a high level of energy and skill he is ill-advised to retain power into late adulthood. He tends to be an isolated leader in poor touch with his followers and overly idealized or hated by them. The continuity of the generations is disrupted."

The leaders responsible for grooming future leaders can therefore spiritually sabotage their own executive-development programs. If the company's mission no longer includes the fulfillment of a manager's dreams, why then work to fulfill the collective dreams of the company? A boss filled with despair over his or her own lethargic career may be a destructive mentor. The grand fanfare designed to excite and cultivate new leaders can aggravate the resentment of lost opportunity. New high-potential managers appear as threatening rivals. Training for longer-term payouts is discouraged with an emphasis on the present. Bosses thus warn subordinates to meet today's performance and leave the career dreaming for some other time. Initiative is dismissed as foolish naivete. Ambition comes to be seen as opportunism.

This jealousy by the old is read by the intended proteges as selfishness and stodginess. Vast reservoirs of accumulated wisdom remain untapped as the young seek to bypass those who obstruct the free flow of the career stream. Instead of being perceived as valuable reservoirs of learning, older superiors can be seen as dangerous rapids to circumnavigate. This intergenerational hostility only intensifies as the manager realizes that he or she is perceived as merely a hindrance to the careers of others. The response is to intensify the campaign to prove one's centrality and insure survival — thus perpetuating the cycle.

The tensions across generations are based upon the premise that we can take the full continuum of work ages and divide it into homogeneous clusters. Just as mass society has been segmented into 20-year epochs, so can the members of specific institutions be. Researchers across disparate fields reach uncommon agreement in acknowledging the profound differences of interest at early, mid-, and late career. Some believe that the differences are based on our interactions with the changing opportunities and challenges.

The more internal distinctions across generations have to do with different stages of evolving life structures. This concept of the life structure is the overall design of a person's life at a given time. Personal priorities change as we redefine our existence relative to our job, family, friendships, and health, and to the wider society. The changes we experience do not have a mere transitory impact. Rather, their force is cumulative. We gain greater personal insight, we recognize hidden limits, and we appreciate previously obscured strengths. Confidence over different life sectors shifts, and personal priorities are rearranged accordingly.

How a leader leaves office is as important to his or her constituents as how the office is acquired. Nonetheless, our attention is not balanced between these events. We hear regularly of the violent warfare surrounding prominent executive-succession struggles, yet that is where the discussion begins and ends. The collective wisdom on leadership departures does not appear in best-selling management guides, research reports, or classroom texts. Our classic literature on leadership has been far more concerned with the ascent and contribution of leaders than with their descent. The making of presidents, the rise up the corporate hierarchy, the effectiveness of top corporate leaders, the ethics of the top executives, the genius of entrepreneurs, and the courage of turnaround experts reflect the range of such frequent published discussions. The discussions of leadership have inspired the debate and programs needed to spark revitalization of our institutions. These discussions, however, reveal the common concern with the future that is shared by society at large.

Thus, when we consider corporate leadership succession, we see a special aspect of retirement that is not always present for other public figures. This is the leader's responsibility for the continuing well-being of his firm. Perhaps, then, we must appreciate retirement from such offices as more critical than from other occupations. The CEO's challenge is not merely to remain a lively individual contributor. Rather, the challenge is to provide future opportunities for others who are blocked by the leader's mere existence. Personal questions concerning another's age, tenure, and health are not invasions of privacy when the discussion concerns those with substantial control over the destiny of many others. Such discussions of leaders' health and departures

have been heightened in public due to the historical records set regarding the ages of national leaders - for example, Ronald Reagan, who is roughly a decade older than most of his predecessors were.

Armand Hammer's frequent "execution" of probable successors at Occidental Petroleum is legendary, according to *Business Week*. *Fortune* commented on Harry Gray's "firing squad" approach to management turnover during his reign as chief executive of United Technologies. His dismissal of Robert Carlson, the company's president, was followed by Carlson's unsupported charges of electronic surveillance. At Chock Full O'Nuts, the bedridden octogenarian chief executive had entrusted the daily management of the company to his personal physician, much to the dismay of a large group of shareholders.

The succession story at Puritan Fashions is far more tragic than those above. When Carl Rose, the 62-year-old chief executive, contemplated his retirement from the firm he had run for 36 years, he found that he had no internal reservoir of senior talent to groom for the top job. Since taking over after his father's death in 1947, Rosen had shown a marked inability to retain his senior executives. He hired an outside successor, Warren Hirsch, from his leading competitor. Rosen signed a contract to pay Hirsch more than $1 million, and announced to the public that the future was in Hirsch's hands. After some sudden reported skirmishes with the company's designer, Calvin Klein, who was also a major shareholder, during the first two months on the job, Hirsch was dismissed with his full $1 million for eight weeks' work.

Two years after Hirsch's dismissal, Carl Rosen learned that he had cancer. His son Andrew was hastily groomed to take over; more experienced potential heirs had left in frustration with Rosen's "one-man-show" style. Just before his death, Carl Rosen acknowledged that his son was an unproven, inexperienced successor. "I never knew him until about four years ago," he said. "I was never there when any of the children were born. I was always working.

"I really devoted my life to this company, and they paid me very well. But as you get older, and you put on the scale what you gained and what you lost, you wonder if it all was worth it. This industry is tough."

Within a year, this sad story was rounded out by the removal of young Andrew Rosen by dissident shareholders — again led by Calvin Klein. The thought of succession to Carl Rosen was like suggesting death. When death was actually imminent, it was too late to find a successor.

In essence, the chief executive's name becomes figuratively hyphenated with the name of the firm. His or her personal career dreams have become the common property of the firm, the guiding organizational vision. When a new leader and a new dream are selected, the departing leader is left with a deflated sense of purpose, since his purpose was fulfilled through the mission of the group. When an orchestra conductor retires, it is unlike the retirement of any of the other performers. All the others can leave with their instruments and continue to play solo or in ensembles. But the conductor leaves only with memories, as his instrument, the orchestra, remains behind. In 1960, Eugene Ormandy, music director of the Philadelphia Orchestra, said, "The Philadelphia Orchestra sound is me,"

and music critics resoundingly agreed. He served as music director from 1948 until his reluctant retirement at age 80 in 1980. On this occasion he complained, "One retires when one is dead or ill." His diminished eyesight, reduced hearing, and heart complications left him no other option.

Our best modern executive-development programs strive to locate and groom promising young stars drifting somewhere in the seas of management within large corporations. Succession planning, the development of subordinates, and fast-track programs are the common activities used to identify and cultivate new leaders. The hidden message of many of these programs is that executive development stops at mid-career. You are out of the tournament once you begin to stagnate in a position. Pre-retirement counseling, ample pensions, and retiree clubs are growing to ease the exit from leadership roles. A switch into a new field late in an executive's career is not commonly seen as a shrewd investment within most companies. Such changes generally require the older person to leave the firm to locate new opportunities.

Many firms facing a career-system problem, such as logjam in the promotion stream or a retrenchment crisis, have turned to early-retirement incentive programs as the most humane and least disruptive option. Career stagnation and massive layoffs have been minimized through such voluntary severance programs. Such firms as Exxon, IBM, Polaroid, Du Pont, Uniroyal, Crown Zellerbach, Firestone, Metropolitan Life, Sears, B. F. Goodrich, A&P, Eastman Kodak, Travelers Insurance, American Can, Pan Am, American Airlines, and United Airlines have successfully thinned their ranks through fair and attractive early-retirement programs.

Despite the lucrative lure of the programs, firms have been astounded by the stampede of enthusiastic workers. Following a 45 percent drop in profits in the first nine months of 1981, Polaroid designed an especially tempting exit program. It encouraged the exit of 934 employees, 7.2 percent of the domestic work force, well in excess of the 6 percent target. On average, the departing workers were 53.4 years old with 18.4 years of experience. All parties - participants and nonparticipants - reported that the program made them feel more positive about the future of the company. Several key employees left, including the top marketing executive and an heir to the presidency. Nonetheless, the firm was pleased. Polaroid renewed the program four years later.

Similarly, lagging sales growth and an unfavorable report on employee productivity relative to competitors led Du Pont to prune "deadwood" in 1985. In the spring, the company chairman, Edward Jefferson, announced a program that encouraged 12,000 early retirements, or a shocking 8 percent of the work force. This was twice the projection of 6,000 departures, with the company losing some of those employees it had hoped to keep. Gaps in some places required the hiring of less experienced workers. Senior managers, about 800 people, were excluded from the program. The company estimated that the program would save $230 million after taxes the next year.

Late-career exit quandaries are resolved through various degrees of continuity in one's job. Some people maintain their careers full throttle until the engines of life just give out. Others withdraw gradually and pursue other careers. Still others scale back their involvement in the same career and allow more time for leisure. Finally, there are those who completely disengage and become uninterested in occupational life. One's health, personality, family needs, and opportunities dictate the likely amount of energy for one's career late in life.

Thus, at the extremes, we see that some top executives cling to a position late in their careers as if hanging on for dear life, while other eagerly leave, happy to break free of the role imposed upon them from without. A distinguishing feature between these two clusters of older people is that some people are content with the impact they have had on others, while some still seek greater impact.

To some extent, this satisfaction may be determined by the distance one has traveled in one's life. The resources with which we have been provided relative to whose we have developed and utilized help to calibrate our yardstick of success. In the popular film *Cocoon,* aliens called Antarians offer resident of a Florida retirement community an escape to a land of not only eternal life, but eternal *productive* life. Most eagerly accept this escape from their decaying purposeless existence. A character named Bernie, however, firmly declines the Antarian gift despite the pleading of his friends. As he has said earlier in the film, each of us is dealt our hand of cards, and it's not fair to want to reshuffle the deck. Bernie's memory of his late wife's drifting awareness but constant loving appreciation serves as a reminder of a life filled with little regret. He is grateful and content. He does not want to relive his life.

Similarly, some leaders want to relive and rework their careers if they feel that they did not achieve the truly great heights that were in their grasp. Chief executives, as folk heroes, are driven by more than the desire to use what they have been given. As many of the rest of us do, they seek to be net contributors rather than net consumers in life.

Our failure to appreciate retirement as a special hardship for leaders causes us to inadvertently aggravate resentment across generations.

Introduction

From the inheritor's perspective, succession looks quite different from that of the current owner. This research asks potential successors for their views on the family firm. Most saw their firms as authoritarian in management style. Over forty percent had no intention of joining the firm. Most felt free to make their own decision.

Succession in the Family Firm: The Inheritor's View

1986

By Sue Birley

Reprinted by permission of **Journal of Small Business Management**, July 1986, Vol. 24, No. 3, pp. 36-43. Copyright © 1986 by **Journal of Small Business Management**; All rights reserved.

In recent years, the small firm has enjoyed much public prominence; it has been seen as a hope for the future, the source of new jobs, new wealth, new products and services. Indeed, a healthy small firm sector is seen by many as a prerequisite for economic growth.[1]

Despite this, the small firm is essentially short-lived — many cease to exist within the first two years, and only a few survive beyond five years.[2] Moreover, although more than 98 percent of corporations in the U.S. are family owned, it is estimated that only 30 percent continue into the second generation, and only 15 percent into the third.[3]

While this decline is due in part to the inherent viability of the firm, another cause is found in the desires and attitudes of each generation. Does the owner wish to pass the firm to his children? If so, when? Are the children interested in the firm? Do they wish to pledge their futures to it? At what point in his or her career does a child wish to join the firm? The answers given to questions such as these can be crucial to the long-run survival of the family firm.

Much has been written about the issue of succession in the family firm, and about the heartaches and feuds which often follow. Most writers, however, have taken the perspective of the incumbent — the current owner. In this paper the issue will be examined from the viewpoint of the children who inherit the business.

Related Literature

In reviewing the literature on succession in family firms, two main streams emerge. The first concentrates on the issues associated with the choice of a successor, and the second with the period of transition after the retirement or death of the founder.[4]

Choosing a Successor

Succession in the family business refers to the replacement of the owner/manager of the firm—the CEO or president. However, despite the CEO's obvious pre-eminence, almost all general literature on leadership and succession deals with a lower level in the firm, often the supervisory level.[5] Moreover, there is very little which looks at the particular problems of the family firm. Nevertheless, a number of small business studies point to the fact that one of the major issues faced by the firm is the question of choosing a successor,[6] a problem magnified by the presence of potential successors within the owner's family.[7] Many writers conclude that this issue is so difficult for owners to deal with that they abdicate responsibility, leaving the decision to the last moment without planning for succession or training the successor.[8]

A number of reasons for this reaction are suggested. Beckhard and Dyer explain that managing change in a family-owned company is often complicated by such factors as resistance to change by the leader.[9] Lopata concludes that such decisions are complicated by the degree to which social life, leisure life, and business life are intertwined.[10] Whiteside adds a further dimension: the perceived competence of the family successor.[11] As a result of the owner's apparent unwillingness to make a decision, a number of authors prescribe the need for outside intervention during both the planning process and the eventual transition period.[12]

General agreement emerges on at least one point—that the primary successor is usually the eldest son,[13] and that both generations of the family view him as holding this responsibility. Bindley, a

second-generation owner, was expressing this attitude when he wrote:

In 1965 my father asked if I would like to come back and try the family business. I thought, being the eldest son, I guess I owed it to them, or to him, to try it.[14]

Historically, daughters have apparently escaped this particular form of family responsibility. Indeed, in 1982, *Business Week* reported that only 500 women were operating family businesses, although this number was forecast to "soar by 1990."[15]

The Transition Process

Golden argues that as the family and the firm are so inextricably interwoven, the transition period is often fraught with emotion and problems.[16] Further, in his graphic article, "The SOBs," Poe remarks, "Many wait impatiently—the impatience grows as they become middle-aged—for the founding father to let go."[17] As a result, rivalry and resentment grow,[18] sometimes to the point of public debate.[19] Indeed, Barnes and Hershon, in their study of transition in 32 companies, conclude that "the healthiest transitions are those old-versus-young struggles in which both the family managers and the business change patterns,"[20] a point reinforced by Crist in her study of a North Carolina firm.[21] Moreover, Barnes and Hershon emphasize the importance of all members of the family and the extended family (the employees) in this process.

Limitations of Previous Research

Much of the literature on succession in the family firm is taken from the perspective of the owner. The viewpoint of the successor, the pressures he or she feels, and the choices he or she makes are reported second-hand. Indeed, many articles imply that the children have no choice but to return, and are raised to that end. For example, Longenecker and Schoen outline a seven-stage succession model in which three of the stages take place during childhood, and thus prior to entry into the family firm.[22] Despite such a lengthy indoctrination period, many firms do not survive beyond the first generation,[23] although it is not known how often this is due to the inheritor's reluctance to continue the firm and how often to poor management.

In his study of 53 companies which went out of business, Ambrose[24] found that the perceived limited interest on the part of the children of the family firm was a factor in the owner's decision to cease operations, a point reinforced by Nelton.[25] This may not be the only reason, however. When appointed CEO of Puritan Fashions on the death of his father, 27-year-old Andrew Rosen is quoted as saying:

I was always afraid of my father. I was never really that close to him, but I was always around him . . . If I try to do things like my father, I won't succeed.[26]

Thus many different motivations and emotions can be expected to influence potential successors when making decisions about taking over the management of a family business.

Method

The purpose of this study was to explore the emotions and motivations of children from family firms during their last year of formal university education, when they are making choices about future jobs and careers. This choice is made in a context which presents returning to the family firm as only one of many options; and peer pressure may lead many to prefer the option of a new

job, which may be perceived as both more lucrative and exciting than the family firm.

Drawing upon the issues discussed above, the research survey was designed to answer the following questions:

1. What proportion of respondents had decided to return to the family firm?

2. Did they have any idea of the timing of their return?

3. To what extent did they feel pressure to return from their parents?

4. How interested were they in the firm, its products, markets, and strategies?

5. To what extent do the answers to the above questions depend upon factors such as size of the firm, pressure from parents, or the educational attainment of the child?

To test these questions, a multiple-choice questionnaire was designed and issued to 221 students in four senior B.B.A. classes (mean age 21) and two second-year M.B.A. classes (mean age 25) of the University of Notre Dame (see table 1). Although Notre Dame draws from a national population, the sample may not be representative of all prospective inheritors of family businesses, nor of those in the total student population. This sample of students at a private university have higher than average academic backgrounds and presumably can afford the substantial cost of their college education. Many of these students, therefore, probably come from families which own very successful family firms — firms in which options for the inheritors are likely to be greatest. For these reasons, the study is clearly exploratory.

The first part of the questionnaire concerned the student's aspirations to own a firm of their own and the second their attitudes toward risk. The third part addressed students from family-owned firms. Care was taken to preserve the anonymity of this group. Interestingly, the percentage of students from family firms within each class group was remarkably similar—27 percent for the B.B.A.s and 30 percent for the M.B.A.s Results are based on preliminary analyses of responses given by 61 potential inheritors using a significance level of 5 percent or less.

Table 1
Total Number of Students Surveyed

	Family Firm	Not Family Firm	Total
M.B.A.	19	45	64
B.B.A.	42	115	157
Total	61	160	221

Results

The Firms

Of the 61 companies, all but one was owned by the respondents' parents, rather than grandparents or other relatives. Consequently, "owners" are referred to as "parents" throughout. Although firms varied widely by sales levels and industry, all employed fewer than 500 people (see table 2).

Respondents were asked to rate their families' firms on a scale of 1 to 7 for three factors—the extent to which both systems and structure were appropriate to the needs of the firm, and the extent to which they saw the style of management to be autocratic (1) or democratic (7). The mean scores for systems and structures were 3.1 and 3.7, respectively, with standard deviations of 1.8 and 1.7 (no significant difference between the means). Thus, the size and type of

firm were unrelated to perceptions about the appropriateness and effectiveness of firm systems and structures. Fully 70 percent of students, however, scored their families' firms 1 or 2 on management style, indicating highly authoritarian styles of management.

Future Intentions

The inheritors were asked their intentions with regard to the family firm: did they *wish* to return; did they think they *would* return; and did they think it was *expected* of them by their parents or family? The results are shown in table 3.

Approximately 20 percent of the respondents wanted to return to their family firms within five years; another 38 percent believed they would return at some unspecified time; and the remaining 42 percent had absolutely no intention of returning. A very similar pattern of response held for the question about whether students *thought* they would return. The older M.B.A. students appeared to be more inclined to return to the family firm than undergraduates (p .05), a result which suggests that these particular M.B.A. students may be pursuing their degrees in anticipation of operating the family firm.

Over 50 percent of the respondents claimed that the decision as to whether to join the firm was completely up to them—their parents expected them to join the business only if they wanted to. Another 20 percent said that their parents did not expect them to join the firm at all. To explore this question further, respondents were asked to describe the amount of pressure which they felt from their parents. Five seven-point scales were constructed to describe various aspects of the pressure to join the firm. These aspects are listed

Table 2
Characteristics of the Family Firm

	M.B.A.	B.B.A.	Total
Number of Employees:			
Range	4–450	1–80	1–450
Mean	80	27	44
Median	33	17	20
Sales:			
Range	$50,000–$40M	$60,000–$20M	$50,000–$40M
Mean	$5.94M	$3.06M	$4.12M

Table 3
Intentions of the Inheritors

	Do you want to return? (percent)	Do your parents expect you to return? (percent)	Do you think you will return? (percent)
On graduation	10	13	12
Within five years	10	7	10
Sometime in the future	38	8	36
Only if you want to	NA*	52	NA
Never	42	20	42

in table 4, which also shows the mean scores for fathers and mothers.

In order to avoid bias in the scale results, students were told to consider a score of 4 as a neutral position between the two extremes. The mean scores of the respondents were all significantly different from 4 (p .05). They described the pressure which they felt from their parents as inclined to be soft, absent, unintended, or implicit, all of which reinforces the previously stated view that the decision was left up to them. Moreover, they saw their parents' attitudes as distinctly positive rather then negative (scale 5).

These results contradict the traditional view that parents wish their children to return and make their views about this known, and that they are insistent and perceived by their children as difficult. No significant differences were found between the mean scores for father and mother, supporting the conclusion that, overall, inheritors did not perceive any disagreements between their parents. Mothers, however, were seen as somewhat "softer" (scale 1) than fathers (p .10).

Sibling Position

Despite the fact that 20 percent of the respondents were eldest children, their perceptions of parental influence did not differ significantly from those of younger siblings, suggesting that parent's attitudes tend to focus on the needs and interests of the child rather

Table 4
Parental Pressure

Scale	Score 1	Score 7	Father	Mother
1	Hard.................... Soft		4.6	5.2
2	Present................ Absent		4.5	4.8
3	Intended........... Unintended		4.9	4.6
4	Overt................. Implicit		4.7	4.3
5	Positive.............. Negative		2.7	3.1

than their sibling position. This applied equally to sons and daughters, although there were differences in siblings' intentions. All the females indicated that they would either never return or that it would be "sometime in the future." However, perhaps the most surprising result of all was that not one of the inheritors who intended to return on graduation, or in the near future, was an eldest child.

Interest in the Firm

The decision to return to the family firm is influenced by a sense of responsibility to the family and by the degree of interest in the firm. It has been suggested that inheritors are more likely to be interested in systems and strategy than in particular products and markets.[27] This should come as no surprise, for with the different backgrounds of parents and children, there is no reason to believe that specific product interest should span generations. the respondents were therefore asked to indicate their personal level of interest, on a seven-point scale, in the firm's products, markets, personnel, systems, and strategy. A score of 1 indicated "no interest," a score of 4 "neutral" and a

score of 7 "fascinated." The mean scores are shown in table 5.

The results fall into three areas:

1. Personnel — the score is not significantly greater than the mean, indicating overall indifference to this aspect of the firm.

2. Products, markets, and systems — these scores are significantly greater than the mean score, indicating fairly strong interest in these aspects of the firm, whether or not inheritors intended to return.

3. Strategy — as expected, the interest in this aspect of the firm was significantly greater than in other aspects listed. Moreover, it was not confined to those intending to return, nor to those in the M.B.A. group, nor to those representing larger firms in the sample.

Are You Needed?

To assess the sense of responsibility toward the firm, students were asked whether they were needed to assist with managing the business. Responses were not related to firm size or perceptions about the adequacy of firm systems and structure. The reasons given by those who felt they were needed (48 percent) *all* reflected a personal responsibility to the family, and thus to the firm. Reasons cited ranged from the need to compensate for parents' lack of education (a possibly arrogant view not confined to the younger B.B.A.s), through "they don't know what they are doing," to a belief that family firms should continue, and finally to a sense of family duty.

Table 5
Inheritor's Interest in the Firm

Aspect of Firm	Mean Interest Score
Products	4.7*
Markets	4.8*
Personnel	4.2
Systems	4.4*
Strategy	5.8**

*p < .05.

**p < .005.

Conclusion

Perhaps the most surprising result of this study is that this group of inheritors appears to explode the myth that responsibility for the family firm lies solely with the eldest child. Clearly, all siblings felt a strong need to make a decision, and the decisions which they made did not reflect their sibling position. Nor was it an indication of their level of interest in the firm; those who intended to return were as interested (or disinterested) in the products, markets, systems, and personnel as those who did not. As might be expected of business students, however, their chief interest was in the firm as an entity—its goals, its direction, its strategy.

These results suggest that the parental view reported by Ambrose,[28] i.e., that children are not interested in the business; is not altogether so; they may be interested even though they have future interests elsewhere. Indeed, a number of inheritors indicated that, while they did not intend to return to the family firm full-time in the near future, they did intend to participate in decisions, if only at an advisory level.

The prospective inheritors in this sample believed that their parents take an even-handed and open approach to their career choice. Most of the respondents felt little pressure was being exerted to induce them to join the family firm. Moreover, there was no evidence to suggest that fathers applied more pressure than mothers, or vice versa. This is contrary to previous views that parents expect children to join the business and that they pressure them to do so.

Although it is dangerous to generalize from a sample drawn from one institution, Notre Dame is a private university which attracts students from families nationwide and from a variety of ethnic groups. Consequently, there is no reason to believe that the parents of these students are more understanding than any other group of parents who choose to send their children to college. Clearly, therefore, these results suggest that a sense of responsibility to the family is as much self-imposed as imposed by parents.

The results of this exploratory study differ from those reported elsewhere. They do, however, identify a large group of students who face career choices very different from those faced by other students. These issues are too often totally ignored in curriculum design at all levels in the educational system. Further research should be conducted to:

- ascertain whether these results can be replicated elsewhere, e.g., in other universities and colleges; for younger inheritors not yet faced with an initial career choice; for inheritors who have initially chosen employment elsewhere; for those from different ethnic backgrounds.

- study the attitudes of matched groups of parents and children to investigate the extent to which communication between the generations contributes to a smooth transition from one generation to another.

- ascertain the relationship between the type and level of education chosen, the size of the firm, and the level of interest expressed by the inheritors.

- ascertain whether firm size and management are related to the perceptions of both parents and children regarding the need for inheritors to return to the family firm.

1. U.S. Small Business Adminstration, *A Report of the President* (Washington D.C., Small Business Administration, 1984).

2. D. Birch, "The Job Generation Process," in *MIT Program on Neighborhood and Regional Change* (Cambridge, Mass.: MIT, 1979).

S. J. Birley, "New Firms and Job Generation," *Entrepreneurship Research* (Babson Park, Mass.: Babson College 1984).

3. B. Benson, "The Enigma of the Family-Owned Business,"*Perspective*, vol. 10, no. 1 (1984).

4. See, for example: D. M. Ambrose, "Transfer of the Family-Owned Business," *Journal of Small Business Management*(January, 1983).

5. D. Norburn, "Gogos, Yoyos and Dodos: Company Directors and Industry Performance," *Strategic Management Journal.* (Winter 1985).

6. J. Dewhurst and P. Burns, "Starting and Succeeding in Business," *Rydges* (February 1984).

7. L. B. Barnes and S. A. Herson, "Transferring Power in the Family Business," *Harvard Business Review* (July/August 1976).

8. R. Poe, "The SOBs,"*Across the Board* (May 1980).

9. R. Beckhard and W. G. Dyer, "Managing Change in the Family Firm — Issues and Strategies," *Sloan Management Review* (Spring 1983).

10. H. Z. Lopata, "Work, Play, Family and Dreams," *Loyola Business Forum* no. 1 (1978). See also C. McGivern, "The Dynamics of Management Succession," *Management Decision*, Vol. 16, no. 1 (1978).

11. M. Whiteside, "Building Successful, Enterprising Families: 1," *Loyola Business Forum* (Summer 1983).

12. See, for example, J. F. Bulloch, "Problems of Succession in Small Business," *Human Resource Management* (Summer 1978), pp. 2-6; R. B. Peiser and L. M. Wooten, "Life-cycle Changes in Small Family Businesses," *Business Horizons* (May/June 1983), pp. 58-65; J. W. Peters and E. A. Mabry, "The Personnel Officer as Internal Consultant," *Personnel Administrator* (April 1981); and P. B. Dimsdale, "Management Succession — Facing the Future," *Journal of Small Business Management* (October 1974).

13. H. Levinson, "Conflicts that Plague the Family Business." *Harvard Business Review* (March/April 1971).

14. W. Bindley, "Entrepreneurship and the Family," *Loyola Business Forum* (Summer 1983).

15. *Business Week*, "When a Daughter Takes Over the Family Business," (March 29, 1982).

16. S. Golden, "Building Successful, Enterprising Families: 2," *Loyola Business Forum* (Summer 1983).

17. *Ibid.*

18. *Ibid.*

19. *Wall Street Journal*, "All in the Family: How Third Generation Came to Take Control at Puritan Fashions," (September 6, 1983).

20. Barnes and Herson, "Transferring Power in the Family Business."

21. I. Crist, "Family Forms Business, Enters Business in More Ways Than One," *Business Forms Reporter*, vol. 19, no. 2 (February 1981).

22. J. G. Longenecker and J. E. Schoen, "Management Succession in the Family Business," *Journal of Small Business Management* (July 1978).

23. *Ibid.*

24. *Ibid.*

25. S. Nelton, "Shaky About Joining the Family Firm?" *Nation's Business*, vol. 71, no. 11 (November 1983).

26. *Wall Street Journal*, "Drama in Texas: Keck Family Feud, Not Economics, Largely Paved Way for Mobil's Plan to Buy Superior" (March 13, 1984).

27. S. J. Birley, "Corporate Strategy and the Small Firm." *Journal of General Management* (Winter 1982/83).

28. *Ibid.*

Introduction

Should a family business stay in the family? The question is really academic, since families appear to be in business to stay. But, when the management moves from one generation to the next, the transition is often far from orderly. In addition, as the company develops, there is a need for a management style that goes beyond survival thinking and entrepreneurs tend not to be reorganizers. In fact, while a sometimes bitter power struggle is peaking, the fortunes of the company may be sliding downhill. In other cases, power struggles are part of a healthy transition. According to these authors, family and company transitions will be more productive when they are simultaneous. The eternal problem involves the older generation's making use of the flexibility and new ideas of the succeeding generation. Third party involvement may help to prevent irreparable family rifts and company stagnation. Dialogues between all the parties — family managers, relatives, employees, and outsiders — can also help.

Transferring Power in the Family Business
1976

By Louis B. Barnes and Simon A. Hershon

One of the most agonizing experiences that any business faces is the moving from one generation of top management to the next. The problem is often most acute in family businesses, where the original entrepreneur hangs on as he watches others try to help manage or take over his business, while at the same time, his heirs feel overshadowed and frustrated. Paralleling the stages of family power are the stages of company growth or of stagnation, and the smoothness with which one kind of transition is made often has a direct effect on the success of the other.

Sons or subordinates of first generation entrepreneurs tell of patient and impatient waiting in the wings for their time to take over the running of the company. When the time comes, it usually comes because the "old man" has died or is too ill to actively take part in management, even though still holding tightly to the reins of the family business. Often this means years of tension and conflict as older and younger generations pretend to coexist in top management.

As one second generation manager put it, speaking of these problems: "Fortunately, my father died one year after I joined the firm." Concerning another company, a prospective buyer said: "The old man is running the company downhill so fast that we'll pick it up for nothing before the kids can build it back up."

The transition problem affects both family and non-family members. Brokers and bankers, professional managers, employees, competitors, outside directors, wives, friends, and potential stock investors all have more than passing interest as a company moves from one generation to the next. Some of these transitions seem orderly. Most, however, do not. Management becomes racked with strife and indecision. Sons, heirs, key employees, and directors resign in protest. Families are torn with conflict. The president–father is deposed. Buyers who want to merge with or acquire the business change their minds. And often the company dies or becomes stagnant.

The frequency of such accounts and the pain reflected in describing the transfer of power from one generation to the next led us to begin a more formal research inquiry into what happens as a family business, or more accurately, a family *and* its business grow and develop over generation. Specifically, what happens in the family and company between those periods when one generation or another is clearly in control but both are "around"? In addition, how do some managements go through or hurdle the family transition without impeding company growth? And can or must family and company transitions be kept separate?

The research project on these questions began in June 1974 and is still continuing. It has included interviews with over 200 men and women and multiple interviews in over 35 companies, not all of which went beyond the first crucial transition test. This article contains some of the initial findings and conclusions.

Professional or family management?

Some observers and commentators on family business believe that the sooner the family management is replaced by professional management in growing companies, the better. The problems just described can lead to disruption or destruction of either the family or the business, sometimes both, in the long run. Furthermore, the argument goes, an objective, professional management will focus on what is good for the business and its growth without getting lost in the emotions and confusions of family politics.

This rational argument for professional management in growing companies has man strong advocates. It has been suggested that the family members should form a trust, taking all the relatives out of business operations, thus enabling them to act in concert as a family.[1]

Like any argument for objectivity, the plea for professionalism has logic on its side. It makes good business sense, and in a way, good family sense as well. It guides a business away from mixing personal lives with business practices, and it helps to avoid the evils of nepotism and weak family successors who appear so often to cause transition crises.

Historically, the main problem with this rational argument is that most companies lean more heavily on family and personal psychology than they do on such business logic. The evidence is overwhelming. There are more than one millon businesses in the United States. Of these, about 980,000 are family dominated, including many of the largest. Yet most of us have the opposite impression. We tend to believe, after a generation or so, family businesses fade into widely held public companies managed out outside managers with professional backgrounds. The myth comes partly from a landmark study of big business by Adolph Perle and Gardner Means, who maintained that ownership of major U.S. companies was becoming widely diffused and that operating control was passing into the hands of professional managers who owned only a small fraction of their corporation's stock. This widely publicized "fact" was further used by John Kenneth Galbraith to build a concept which he called the "technostructure" of industry, based in large part on the alleged separation of corporate ownership from management control.[2]

There is evidence to the contrary, though. A study reported in *Fortune* by Robert Sheehan examined the 500 largest corporations on this question. Sheehan reported that family ownership and control in the largest companies was still significant and that in about 150 companies controlling ownership rested in the hands of an individual or of the members of a single family. Significantly, these owners were not just the remnant of the nineteenth century dynasties that once ruled American business. Many of them were relatively fresh faces.[3]

The myth is even more severely challenged in a study of 450 large companies done by Philip Burch and published in 1972. By his calculations, over 42% of the largest *publicly* held corporations are controlled by one person or a family, and another 17% are places in the "possible family control" category. Then there is one other major category of large "privately" owned companies — companies with fewer than 500 stockholders, which are not required to disclose their financial figures. Some well-known corporate names are included in this category: Cargill,

Bechtel Corporation, Hearst Corporation, Hallmark Cards, and Hughes Aircraft, among others. Burch notes that contrary to what one might expect, the rather pervasive family control exercised is, for the most part, very direct and enduring. It is exercised through significant stock ownership and outside representation on the board of directors, and also, in many cases, through a considerable amount of actual family management.[4]

When one thinks more closely about families in big as well as small businesses, some well-known succession examples also come to mind, suggesting that family transition and corporate growth occur together even through there may be strain in the process. For example:

- H. J. Heinz was founded by Henry J. Heinz to bottle and sell horseradish, and today H. J. Heinz II, a grandson, heads the billion dollar concern.

- Triangle Publications owns the *Morning Telegraphy*, *TV Guide*, and *Seventeen*. It was founded by Moses Annenberg. He was succeeded by his son, Walter, and a daughter, Enid, is now editor-in-chief of *Seventeen*.

- The Bechtel Corporation was begun by Warren A. Bechtel, for building railroads. His son, Steve Sr., directed the firm into construction of pipelines and nuclear power plans. Today, Steve Jr. heads the $2 billion company, which is now further diversified.

- Kaiser Industries, built by Henry J. Kaiser, includes Kaiser Steel, Kaiser Aluminum and Chemical, Kaiser Cement and Gypsum, Kaiser Broadcasting, Kaiser Engineering, and Kaiser Resources. The present industrial giant is headed by Henry's son, Edgar, now over 65 years old. An obvious successor is Edgar Jr., president of Kaiser Resources Ltd.

Should a family business stay in the family? The question now seems almost academic. It is apparent that families *do* stay in their businesses, and the businesses stay in the family. Thus there is something more deeply rooted in transfers of power than impersonal business interests. The human tradition of passing on heritage, possessions, and name from one generation to the next leads both parents and children to seek continuity in the family business. In this light, the question whether a business should stay in the family seems less important, we suspect, than learning more about how these businesses and their family owners make the transition from one generation to the next.

Inside and outside perspectives

What are the implications when the transition from one generation to the next includes both business and family change, and what are the consequences also if business and family, though separate, remain tied together in plans, arguments, and emotions? In considering these questions, it might be helpful to examine two perspectives in addition to age difference. One is the family, the other is the business, point of view. Both of these can be viewed from either the inside or the outside.

Exhibit I shows these four different vantage points from which to observe family and business members. One viewpoint is that of the "family managers" (inside the family and inside the business) as seen by both old and young generations. When they forget or ignore the other three perspectives, they can easily get boxed into their own concerns. This kind of compulsion includes hanging onto the power for the older generation and getting hold of it

for the younger. To both generations, it implies the selection, inclusion, and perpetuation of family managers.

A second perspective comes from "the employees," again older and younger, who work inside the business but who are outside the family. Understandably, they face different pressures and concerns from those of the family managers, even though many are treated as part of the larger corporate family. The older employees want rewards for loyalty, sharing of equity, and security, and they want to please the boss. Younger employees generally want professionalism, opportunities for growth, equity, and reasons for staying. Both age groups worry about bridging the family transition.

A third perspectives comes from "the relatives," those family members who are not in the active management of the business. The older relatives worry about income, family conflicts, dividend policies, and a place in the business for their own children. The younger, often disillusioned brothers and cousins feel varying degrees of pressure to join the business. Both generations may be interested, interfering, involved, and sometimes helpful, as we shall see later on.

Finally, the fourth perspective comes from "the outsiders." These are persons who are competitors, R & D interests, creditors, customers, government regulators, vendors, consultants, and others who are connected to the business and its practices from the outside. They have various private interests in the company which range from constructive to destructive in intention and effect.

A curious irony is that the more "outside" the family the perspective is, as shown in *Exhibit I*, the more legitimate it seems as a "real" management problem. Yet the concerns in the left column boxes are typically just as important as, and more time consuming than, the outside–the–family problems on the right. These inside–the–family problems tends to be ignored in management books, consultant's reports, and business school courses. Ignoring these realities can be disastrous for both the family and the company.

Our studies show that the transfer of power from first to second generation rarely takes place while the founder is alive and on the scene. What occurs instead during this time is a transition period of great difficulty for both older and younger generations. For the founder, giving up the company is like signing his own death warrant. For the son or successor, the strain may be comparable. As one of these said:

"I drew up the acquisition papers to buy my father out, because for a long time he has been saying he did not care about the business anymore. However, when it was all taken care of, and we presented him with the papers, he started to renege. Everything was done the way he would like it. Yet he would not sign. He finally told me he did not think he could do it. He felt it awfully hard to actually lose the company. He said he felt he still had something to give."

And another commented:

"I can't change things as fast as I would like to. It is absolutely clear to me that things need to be changed. However, it is not easy. First of all there is the function of age and experience as well as being the boss's son. Every other

officer in the company is in his fifties. What I am talking about now are deep sources of dissatisfaction. I would like more ownership. Now I have only 7%, my father has 80% and my family another 13%. In my position, I just cannot move the company fast enough. We argue a lot, but nothing seems to change. I have set a goal for myself. If I cannot run the company within two years, I am leaving. I'll do something else."

The company transition

While family managers feel the multiple strains as the generations overlap during the periods of transition, another related process is occurring as the company grows and develops. Various authors have tried to describe this process.[5] But, where one describes a smooth procedural development, another sees a series of difficult crises. For some, a series of growth stages is important. For others, it is the merging of functions with processes that count. Most writers do not tie business growth or decline to family transitions. However, the following points stand out for us in relation to company transitions.

1. Organizational growth tends to be nonlinear. Organizations grow in discrete stages, with varying growth rates in each stage.

2. Periods of profound organizational development often occur *between* periods of growth. These slower periods often are viewed with alarm, but they force managers to examine what the company has grown toward or into. These periods of development are the transition periods which appear less dramatic (i.e., there is less growth) but may be most crucial to a company's preparations for its own future.[6] The apparent floundering can provoke

Exhibit I.
Pressures and interests in a family business

	Inside the family	Outside the family
Inside the business	**The family managers** Hanging onto or getting hold of company control Selection of family members as managers Continuity of family investment and involvement Building a dynasty	**The employees** Rewards for loyalty Sharing of equity, growth, and successes Professionalism Bridging family transitions Stake in the company
Outside the business	**The relatives** Income and inheritance Family conflicts and alliances Degree of involvement in the business	**The outsiders** Competition Market, product, supply and technology influences Tax laws Regulatory agencies Trends in management

useful learning once management begins to adopt and encourage new practices and procedures.

3. A typical management response to transitional strains is a total or partial reorganization of the company. This sometimes helps shake up old habits but rarely resolves a transition crisis. What is needed is time for the social and political system of the company to realign themselves into new norms and relationships.

Exhibit II shows how a later growth stage differs from and builds on the

Exhibit II.

Characteristics of company growth

Organizational characteristic	Patterns of the first stage	Patterns of the second stage	Patterns of the third stage
Core problem	Survival	Management of growth	Managerial control and allocation of resources
Central function	Fusion of diverse talents and purposes into a unified company	Fusion of general authority into specialized functions	Fusion of independent units iinto an inter-dependent union of companies
Control systems	Personal (inside); survival in marketplace (outside)	Cost centers and policy ormulation (inside); growth potential outside)	Profit centers and shared abstract performance criteria(inside); apital expan-sion potential (outside)
Reward and motivation	Ownership, membership in the family	Salary, opportunities and problems of growth	Salary, p erform-ance bonus, stock options peer prestige
Management style	Individualistic direct management	Integrating specialists collaborative management	Integrating generalists collective management
Organization:			
Structure	Informal	Functional specialists	Division organizations
CEO's primary task	Direct supervision of employees	Managing specialized managers	Managing generalist managers
Levels of manage-ment	Two	At least three	At least four

earlier ones. The first stage is charac-teristic of an entrepreneurial company with direct management. The second is typified by a rapidly growing product line and market situation with second level management set up in specialized functions. The third stage has divisional operations with a diverse line of products and markets. Whereas the management style of the first stage is highly personal and direct, the second tends to become the more collaborative style of a boss and specialized peers. The third stage typically involves a looser, impersonal, collective style, with the chief executive managing generalists as well as functional specialists. Under the patterns of the first stage, the core problem for a small company is survival. The patterns of the roughly defined second stage show a size and scope requiring such specialized functions as finance, production, marketing, and engineering.

As the company's size continues to increase, it is likely to evolve toward third-stage patterns of growth. At this point, different product lines become separate companies or divisions, while, in multinational firms, the separation may also be on an area basis (e.g., Europe, North America, Latin America, Middle East, Far East) as well.

In between the box–like stages of growth shown in *Exhibit II* appear the transition phases which help to prepare an organization for its next stage. To cross the broken lines separating one growth stage from another in *Exhibit II* requires time, new interaction patterns, and an awkward period of overlap. In effect, the broken vertical lines of *Exhibit II* represent widened time zones of varying and irregular width.

As we have seen, family transitions and company transitions can occur separately and at different times. However, we found that they usually occur together. As a company moves from the problem of survival to one of managing rapid growth, it must develop new control, motivation, and reward systems. It also requires a management style that can integrate specialists and their functions. This development cannot occur without a top management that wants to take the extra step beyond survival thinking. That is where an eager younger generation comes in. He, she, or they are more likely to want to go beyond traditional practices. This pent-up energy seemed to be a major factor in getting beyond company transitions in 27 out of 32 businesses we studied where the company had gone beyond the first growth stage.

Another kind of transition occurs between the second and third growth stages. Company and division units in stage three had general managers in both the head office and the decentralized units who had learned to work with both other general managers and functional specialists. This meant that they had to have or develop a sense of the complex interdependence that characterizes most major companies today.

These dual transitions seemed best catalyzed when the old management forces somehow helped to pave the way for the new. The following is a good example:[7]

- When Max Krisch came to America in 1851, he brought an expertise in baking and an old family recipe for bread. Soon after settling, he established a small bakery. The business grew, and Max got help from his three sons as soon as they were old enough to operate the ovens after school and on weekends. When Martin, the oldest, graduated from college in 1890, he joined the business and soon started suggesting changes which he was convinced were good for the company's growth. His father refused, and the two men would often end up in disagreement. Sometimes the arguments were long and bitter.

Eventually, Max's wife abandoned her role of neutrality and intervened on Martin's behalf. She begged Max to give Martin a chance to implement his ideas. Reluctantly, Max agreed and let Martin take the first step.

Martin's idea was to sell bread to milk peddlers who would offer it for sale to their milk customers. It was a new concept at the time, and it worked. The demand for Krisch's Bread increased sharply.

At this time, too, the second brother, Peter, was ready to join the company. Martin realized that the company's production capability would soon be unable to keep up with the increasing sales. He hoped that Peter could take over, modernize, and expand production, but again Max reacted strongly. He argued that the baking of Krisch's Bread could not be done in volume without ruining the quality. Martin and Peter eventually promised their father that if the new methods harmed the bread's quality they would discontinue them. Over time, Max again agreed to go along with the change, and Peter worked closely with his father to increase production while still maintaining quality. Again, too, the mother was behind the scenes trying to keep peace in the family.

When the third brother, Kurt, joined the firm, Martin gave him the responsibility for bookkeeping and financial affairs. Fortunately, Kurt had a good head for figures and did the job well.

As Max became less active in the business, Martin was in charge, with Peter heading production, while Kurt handled the financial end of the business. The business flourished. Occasionally, the three sons felt hampered by Max's continuing strong opinions on some aspects of the business. At these times, the boys' mother would often referee the disagreements. Partly because she was a sensitive person and a good listener, she was usually able to help the father and sons arrive at some mutually satisfactory solution to their problems.

Our studies show that when the familial and organizational transitions occurred

together, as in the Krisch case, they typically took place in an atmosphere of strain and uncertainty. Quite often, a mother was a behind-the-scenes influence. More often, though, the transitions were not managed well either inside the family or inside the business. In the Krisch case, Martin guided the company into its second growth stage. But it was his mother's sensitive management of the family relationships that eased that process and eventually permitted the brothers to achieve an outstanding growth record for the firm. Although Max's time-tested ways and methods fell by the wayside as his sons took over, he became a useful adviser once both he and his sons accepted Martin as head of the business though not head of the family. The transfer of power inside the business took place when Max moved into a new working relationship with his sons and a new family relationship with his wife. With Martin managing the business transition and his mother helping to hold the family together, Krisch's Bakeries made both transitions.

The second transition period for Krisch Bakeries is also instructive. After an impressive growth record over a 30–year period, Martin Krisch and his brothers set the wheels in motion for the transition to the third generation. Martin's son, Max Krisch II, was the most obvious successor.

By 1925, the company had established an executive committee of both family and nonfamily managers who made decisions by consensus. The brothers believed that such an arrangement helped keep the family together and provided valuable inputs from nonfamily members on the executive committee.

In preparation for the transition, Martin, who was then 55, hired an outsider who suggested that a new role of coordinator be set up for the committee which he took on initially and then passed on to Max II, who had just been brought onto the committee as a member. Soon after, Martin was advised by the outsider that he should get off the committee and out of the company as much as possible.

Thus Martin began spending more and more of his time away from the company in civic, volunteer, outside boards, and other business activities. At times, he was frustrated and unhappy over not being in the mainstream of the business, but he gained some satisfaction in watching Max II develop into a manager who set new wheels in motion for the company's expansion and diversification into new areas of business. New product lines were developed, the company was broken into divisions and a chain of other businesses was started. All seemed to be going well until the company was hit by an anti-trust suit which restricted and delayed some of its ambitious plans.

Though the Krisch Bakeries' plans for wider ownership, diversification, and expansion were stalled for a number of years, it seemed to again make the dual transition on both the family and the business levels.

The single transition

Even though most of the companies we studied changed top management and growth stages together, other companies showed one transitional change at a time. A stagnant company can get that way when the older generation gives way to the younger without any company transition. The Quinn Company was one of these.

- In the Quinn family business harmony had been difficult to achieve. The founder, Josiah Quinn, established his industrial supply company

in 1911. He began the business with a partner, and it grew steadily. As business improved, the partner took a less active role, and Quinn soon began to resent the partner's equal salary and taking of the profits.

When his wife suddenly died, Quinn impulsively sold the business to his partner and took his five children West. After several years there, he returned home and began a new business, remarried, and had two children by his second wife.

Eventually, Quinn's oldest children joined the firm. They worked well together, and the company prospered. When his second set of children also joined the company, however, jealousy and resentment increased. Conflict began to disrupt operations daily. The problems flowed over into family life, where his wife took the side of "her" children against "his." Finally, Quinn decided to set up a separate company for his wife's children. He founded it under another name, brought customers from the other company, and enjoyed helping it get started.

When World War II broke out, Quinn's most capable son in the first company was drafted. He was sent out West, married, and eventually set up his own company in San Francisco. This left the first company without a really capable successor, though the departed son's brothers and brothers–in–law worked to keep the company going. Again, dissension increased. While the company continued to operate after Quinn died, its performance levels never rose over the next 30 years.

The Quinn Company's transition from first to second generation was influenced by a major split within the family, by the loss of its key young successor, and the divisive role taken by

Quinn's second wife. The family conflicts seemed to keep Quinn and his heirs from dealing with company transition problems, since all their energies were spent on inside-the-family problems. The result was a family transition without a simultaneous company transition. Such single transitions were even harder for those inside the family and the company than when the two transitions occurred together. Today the Quinn Company is heading painfully into another transition, its second generation having apparently suffered much, but having learned little from the first one. The older family managers find it hard to let go as the 66-year-old president steps aside uneasily, only to be replaced by a 68-year-old in-law whose sons wait impatiently and sometimes irresponsibly for their turn. Meanwhile, the company suffers.

Another type of single transition occurs when a company moves from one growth stage to the next within one management generation. Such growth occurs rarely, it seems, in the first generation, partly because entrepreneurs tend not to be reorganizers, and growth requires reorganization along with a shift in management styles. We found these company transitions without a family transition to occur more often during the second generation. Whereas first generation entrepreneurs had trouble shifting to high growth strategies and more collaborative styles, the sons were more flexible, possibly because the shift from a second to a third stage growth pattern involves letting go of less personal ties or possibly because they had more help in making the shift. Here is an example of such a transition:

• When Well Thomas died, his hardware supply business passed on to his two sons, Paul and Bing. Paul handled production, and Bing worked in sales. The two brothers built the family firm into a major hardware supply house. Paul became chief executive officer, and he and Bing eventually diversified the business into retail hardware stores, medium equipment companies, an electrical manufacturing company, and several unrelated businesses. Along the way, they brought in six third-generation members of their own and their sister's families, but these young family members never quite made the grade. Paul, with Bing's approval, fired five of the six and handed the presidency of the corporation over to a man who had been president of one of the acquired companies.

His justification for discharging his sons, nephews, and sons-in-law was the good of the family business, and therefore in the long run the interests of all family members. Nevertheless, he had created a split in the family that never healed. Meanwhile, the new company president admitted that Paul had become like a father to him, and it was apparent that the father-son parallel was very strong for both of them. There was still one nephew in the company, and although he had an important position, it was clear that he had no inside track on succession plans.

Thomas Enterprises moved faster than most companies do in its growth cycle, possibly because Paul Thomas was willing to sacrifice family harmony for what seemed to be business efficiency. Ironically, though, the fired family members each went on to successful careers in outside jobs, most of them pleased in retrospect to get out from under Paul's reign. Whether any one of them could have taken over the sprawling company is hard to judge at this stage. What is clear is that Paul found another "son" who became heir apparent. In an artificial way, the "succession" transition actually came along only slightly behind company transition.

The three patterns shown in the Krisch, Quinn, and Thomas cases suggest some overall advantages of family and business transitions occurring at the same time. The Quinn and Thomas cases also show what happens when family managers, relatives, employees, and outsiders cannot form a power coalition to protect either the family or the business transition, whichever is jeopardized by family conflicts. In the Quinn case, the family managers withdrew in the face of destructive family pressures typified by Quinn's second wife. She not only divided the family but had a strong hand in dividing the company into two separate enterprises, each also competing with the other. In effect, the microcosm of family conflict became replicated in the macrocosm of the two companies. With capable second generation managers, the original Quinn business never got beyond the first growth stage.

In the Thomas case, the opposite occurred. The relatives retreated "for the good of the family business," as Paul Thomas put it. They helped to destroy the family by abdicating in favor of the dominant older family managers, Paul and Bing Thomas. In the process, some competent family managers were lost. However, the point is not whether Paul and Bing were right or wrong, it is only that they made sure that they were never really tested or questioned by the intimidated relatives. Neither employees nor outsiders found a way to help either.

Under the distorted dominance of either family managers or relatives, not only crippled transitions but regression can set in. Consider one more case:

- In the Brindle Company, a father had handed the business over to a son-in-law, did not like the results, and reclaimed the company, even though the son-in-law had done an impressive job of managing the company in terms of growth and expansion. Several years later, with the son-in-law out of the business, but still with a small ownership stake, Mr. Brindle sold the company at a fraction of the price that the same buyer had offered while the son-in-law was running the business. The business' growth had stalled and declined. The company had gone from second generation back to first generation, and the family was shattered to the extent that the two youngest grandchildren born to the son-in-law and his wife had never been permitted to meet their grandparents.

Managing the two transitions

If, as in the Brindle case, a single dominant power force tends to cause lopsided transitions or regression, how can a constructive pattern be built for creating and managing both transitions? The answer seems to lie in a power balancing setup that prevents polarized conflict. Only in the Krisch case, of those described earlier, was this power balancing done effectively. Yet it also happened in at least some of the other companies we studied. It may help to look at some of the assumptions and mechanisms that were used to encourage and manage the two transitions.

The company will live, but I won't

The key assumption for growth was an almost explicit decision by senior managers that "the company will live, but I won't." This assumption, so often avoided by older family managers, is almost built into the forced retirement programs of established companies. But an entrepreneur or even his sons, as they get older, must somehow consciously face and make the decision that, even though they will die, the company will live. Often, that decision occurs not because they are pushed into it, or out of the company by the younger family managers, but because of the intervention of relatives, noncompeting employees, or trusted outsiders, who may find a way of helping to pull the old family manager into a new set of activities.

At some point, a critical network of family managers, employees, relatives, and outsiders must begin to focus upon the duality of both family and business transitions. Such talks should, in our opinion, begin at least 7 to 8 years before the president is supposed to retire. Even though the specific plans may change, the important assumptions behind those plans will not.

Mediation vs. confrontation

Time after time we saw cases in which an entrepreneur's wife played an important role in bridging the growing gap between father and sons, as happened in the Krisch case. It also happened that an entrepreneur's widow would step in as a peacemaker for the younger generation. But when it came to helping both transitions occur, the wife was more important than the widow. As in the Krisch case, she would help or persuade her husband to look toward the (children's) future instead of his own past. In effect, she provided a relative's outside-the-business perspective. Such outside perspectives turned out to be crucial in transition management, because they helped to heal and avoid the wounds of family conflict.

In some management circles over recent years, a cult of confrontation has been built. Confrontation is regarded

as calling a spade a spade, not in anger, but as a way to move beyond conflict toward problem solving. The approach is reasonable and works in many business situations.

As we pointed out earlier, though, families and their businesses are not necessarily reasonable. The primary emotions tend to be close to the surface, so that conflicts erupt almost without reason. Attempts at confrontation by one party often fail, because they are seen as open or continuing attacks by the other.

When such nerve ends are raw, partly because of family jealousies and partly because of historical sensitivities, a third party or outside perspective can provide mediation and help to soften hardened positions. Relatives, outside directors, friends, and key employees all take this role in family companies. But they do something else that is equally important. They can help to begin a practice of open dialogue that cuts not only across age levels, but across the different perspectives of family managers, relatives, employees, and outsiders. The dialogues can aid in manpower planning and in managing the transitions. The question is how to develop such dialogues so as to include all the relevant perspectives.

Mechanisms for dialogue

None of the dialogue mechanisms we observed or heard of is a cure-all. But each brought different important combinations of people together. One company management had periodic family meetings for family managers and relatives. Another combined family managers and employees into project teams and task forces. Outside boards of directors, executive committees, and nonfamily stock ownership(to be sold back to the company at the owner's death or departure) brought together family managers, employees, and outsider consultants on major policy problems in a number of companies. One family company had in-company management development programs, but invited outside participants and also gave periodic progress reports to the financial and civic community for comment and review. At one extreme, family managers and key employees did set up a series of confrontation sessions, but only after detailed planning. The ground rules were carefully worked out and over the years both family and company transitions made good progress. At the other extreme, companies would hold various lunches or social events where the open dialogue opportunities were limited but sometimes possible in an informal setting.

Future role building

Unwillingness to face the future stalls both family and business transitions, since in one sense the future can only mean death for an older family manager. But in a more limited sense it implies new but separate lives for the manager and his company. If some of the above assumptions and mechanisms begin to take hold, they will lead to the building of new roles. The older managers learn how to advise and teach rather than to control and dominate. The younger managers learn how to use their new power potential as bosses. Family managers take steps to learn new roles outside the business as directors, office holders, and advisers. Employees learn new functional management skills as well as new general management skills. Relatives learn how to take third party roles to provide an outside perspective.

Beginning near the end

We have been describing one of the most difficult and deep-rooted problems faced by human organizations. Family owned and managed concerns include some of the largest as well as most of the smallest companies in the United States and possibly the world. It seems pointless to talk about separating families from their businesses, at least in our society. Families are in business to stay.

However, as one management generation comes near its end, the life of the business is also jeopardized. Meanwhile, critics, scholars, and managers like to pretend that the "real" business problems lie outside of the family's involvement. This may be true in some cases, but it can also lead to and perpetuate four sets of tunnel vision. Family managers, relatives, employees, and outsiders adopt separate perspectives and separate paths.

Our studies, however, suggest that the healthiest transitions are those old-versus-young struggles in which both the family managers and the business change patterns. For this to happen, "the old man*" must face the decision of helping the company live even though he must die. If he can do this, the management of transitions can begin. In effect, a successful family transition can mean a new beginning for the company.

Writers like to think that their work and words will have a lasting impact upon the reader. However, the history of the topic we are discussing provides little cause for such optimism. In fact, a truly lasting solution may come only from experience such as that described by an entrepreneur who said:

"I left my own father's company and swore I'd never subject my own children to what I had to face. Now my son is getting good experience in another company in our industry before coming in to take over this one. Within five years of the day he walks in that door, I walk out. And everyone knows it — even me."

1 Harry Levinson, "Conflicts That Plague the Family Business," *HBR,* March-April 1971, p. 90.

2 Adolph A. Berle and Gardner C. Means, *The Modern Corporation and Private Property* (New York: Harcourt Brace & World, 1968) and John Kenneth Galbraith, *The New Industrial State* (Boston: Houghton Mifflin, 1971.)

3 Robert Sheehan, "Proprietors in the World of Big Business, " *Fortune,* June 1967, p. 178.

4 Philip H. Burch, Jr., *The Managerial Revolution Reassessed* (Lexington, MA: D. C. Heath, 1973.)

5 George Strauss, "Adolescence in Organization Growth: Problems, Pains, Possibilities," *Organizational Dynamics,* Spring 1974, p. 3; Robert B. Buchele, *Business Policy in Growing Firms,* (San Francisco: Chandler Publishing Co., 1965); Theodore Cohn and Roy A Lindberg, *Survival and Growth: Management Strategies for the Small Firm* (New York: AMACOM, 1974); Lawrence L. Steinmetz, "Critical Stages of Small Business Growth," *Business Horizons,* February 1969, p. 29; Bruce L. Scott, "Stages of Corporate Development — Part I," Harvard Business School Note 9-171-291, BP 798.

6 Larry E. Greiner, "Evolution and Revolution as Organizations Grow," *HBR* July-August 1973, P. 17.

7 This and all following cases are based on real circumstances, but fictitious names and industries are used.

Introduction

From childhood, successors in family businesses are prepared in many subtle and direct ways for future leadership. This article presents a model of management succession in the family business that seems to account for the complexity of the process. The perspective adopted is one of long-term socialization.

The parent-offspring succession process is described in terms of seven stages: 1) pre-business, 2) introductory, 3) introductory/functional, 4) functional, 5) advanced functional, 6) early succession and 7) mature succession. The first three stages occur prior to the successor's full-time entry into the firm. The last two occur after the successor has assumed the leadership role. Each stage is described.

Management Succession in the Family Business
1978

By Justin G. Longenecker
and John E. Schoen

Reprinted by permission of **Journal of Small Business Management**, Vol. 16, No. 3, July 1978. Copyright ©1978 **Journal of Small Business Management**; all rights reserved.

We recently visited the young president of a family-owned business. His father had founded the company in the late 1930s and retired several years ago due to a serious illness. At one point during our conversation, the president opened a desk drawer and produced a yellowed photograph.

As we looked at the picture, he said: "I guess I really have been preparing for the presidency since I was a little boy. See in the picture—that is Dad and me on a motorscraper at the factory in Illinois—it was just after World War II, and I must have been 6 or 7 years old.

In fact, with the exception of the two years I spent in the military, I have worked either on a part-time or full-time basis in the business since 1952. And believe me, some of the jobs Dad gave me were not much fun! On the other hand, I suppose those jobs made a better man out of me."

The comments of this young president and those of many other successors indicate an awareness of preparation for leadership that begins long before the successor enters the business, and that continues beyond the point of succession.

A Model of Management Succession

Throughout childhood, adolescence, and adult years, successors are prepared in many ways, formally and informally, to accept the mantle of leadership at some time in the future. Some influences are subtle; others are more direct. Conditioning for future leadership includes specific training assignments prior to taking over the business, but it also includes much more. The process is apparently far more complex than would be indicated by a picture of transition based on a succession agreement between parent and child, followed by a brief orientation for the successor.

This article suggests a model of management succession that recognizes the complexities of the succession process.

The basic proposition may be stated as follows:

Parent-child succession in the leadership of a family-controlled business involves a long-term, diachronic process of socialization, that is, family successors are gradually prepared for leadership through a life-time of learning experiences.

The model provides an intuitively appealing explanation of successor preparation. Although some preliminary field studies have been conducted, no empirical data are presented here to support the model. It is desirable, of course, that the accuracy and practical implications of the model be explored by further research.

Limitations in Studies of Succession

Major studies of leadership succession have concentrated on the process by which the new leader, once selected, stabilizes himself in power.[1] These studies have been primarily concerned with short-run organizational

effectiveness after the transfer of the leadership position.[2]

While analyses focusing on post-succession periods are useful, they also have several limitations. For example, the background and preparation of the successor for leadership have been ignored in most succession studies. In fact, the studies recognize neither the relationship between the development of the successor and his subsequent level of performance in the leadership position, nor the possibility of a developmental relationship between the incumbent and the successor.

Gouldner[3] and Guest,[4] however, have stated that managerial succession involves a number of stages and that analyses of succession should utilize the concept of stages. In a similar discussion, Grusky[5] noted the need to study succession as a developmental process rather than as an equilibrium process. According to these theorists, everything in succession does not occur at one time; some key variables are activated at different points in time. According to Gouldner, the limited time span and focus of inquiry found in the bulk of the succession research has contributed to an overly simplified view of managerial succession as an event rather than to its understanding as a long-term step-by-step process.

When a son or daughter succeeds a parent, it is clear that an extended relationship exists between the incumbent and the successor. To the extent that the relationship is directed toward the development of the child for the presidency of the organization, family succession can be described as a process of socialization. Indeed, the specialized learning of the successor and the relationship to the incumbent appears to occur both inside and outside of the organization and to extend over many years from the successor's childhood into his adulthood.

The central proposition of this article represents, therefore, an attempt to: (1) lengthen the time perspective of managerial succession, (2) emphasize the socialization or developmental aspects of succession; and (3) note the possibility of distinct periods of learning and activity for the successor. Although the term "father-son succession" is frequently used for the sake of simplicity, the description may apply equally well to father-daughter, mother-daughter, or mother-son succession.

Theoretical Foundations of the Succession Model

Although it has unique features, the proposed succession model has its antecedents in early succession theory. The long-term nature of managerial succession was emphasized by Davis when he observed that the transfer of leadership in business organizations may take a decade or more to complete.[6] Trow[7] and Christensen[8] also indicated that succession may involve an extended period of time and suggested the importance of the temporal dimension to the study of succession.

Stages in the succession process were mentioned by Trow,[9] Carlson,[10] and Levenson,[11] Christensen[12] and Davis[13] likewise described periods of selection and development for the successor prior to the transfer of the leadership position.

Socialization has been defined by Cogswell as the process by which individuals prepare for participation in a system or society.[14] Several contributors to succession theory including Grusky,[15] Levinson,[16] and Hodgson, Levinson, and Zaleznik[17] have used the concept of socialization in their discussions of successors and their development.

The course of socialization, referring in this case to the development of the successor, is seen as a complex chain of events which ideally expose the individual to experiences that help him to perform successfully in the leadership position. The process of socialization typically requires the successor to fill several successive preparatory positions or roles. The successive steps necessitate the continued mastery of knowledge and skills as well as changes in the personal and social identity of the successor. In such a process of socialization, the incumbent (father) is typically cast as the chief socializing agent (developer) and the successor (son) as a novice (learner).

Among the writers who describe the development of an individual as process of socialization, many offer insights to the dynamics of the incumbent-successor relationship. Branett and Tagiuri,[19] Crites,[20] and Edler,[21] imply the usefulness of the father-son or familial relationship in promoting the successor's interest and knowledge of the family business during his childhood and adolescent years, often culminating in a career choice to enter the organization. Similarly, the importance of the father-son relationship to the development of the successor after he formally joins the organization has been suggested by the writing of Becker and Strauss,[22] Brim,[23] Cogswell,[24] and Wheeler[25] in adult socialization.

In family business literature, there are also discussions of socialization and the long-term nature of father-son succession. Writers such as Levinson,[26] Calder,[27] Donnelley,[28] and Lazarus[29] described managers who began to indoctrinate and train their sons at an early age to replace them as the head of the family business. In such situations, childhood, adolescent, and adult socialization apparently occurred in the process of father-son succession. Thus, a systematic analysis emphasized a series of developmental steps or stages in family succession seems appropriate.

A Diachronic Framework for the Analysis of Father-Son Succession

Since the study of succession as a process differs from earlier succession studies, a new framework for analysis relating to stages in the process of father-son succession is required. Such a framework of analysis, organized on the basis of the "activities-learning experiences" of the successor, is presented in Figure 1.

The proposed framework represents a model of father-son succession and consists of seven stages including: (1) pre-business, (2) introductory, (3) introductory-functional, (4) functional, (5) advanced functional, (6) early succession, and (7) mature succession, as shown in Figure 1.

The stages are related to two important events in the family succession process: (1) the entry of the successor into the organization as a full-time employee and (2) the transfer of the leadership position to the successor. As shown in Figure 1, the "pre-business," "introductory," and "introductory-functional" stages are considered to occur prior to the successor's entry into the firm. In a similar manner, the "functional" and

Figure 1. Framework of Analysis — Stages of Father-Son Succession

Pre-business	Introductory	Introductory-Functional	Functional	Advanced-Functional	Early Succession	Mature Succession
		Entry of Successor $\|\|$		Transfer of Presidency $\|\|$		
Successor may be aware of some facets of the organization or industry. Orientation of successor by family members, however, is unplanned or passive.	Successor may be exposed by family members to jargon, organizational members, and environmental parties prior to part-time employment in firm.	Successor works as part-time employee in organization. Gradually, the work becomes more difficult and complex. Includes education and work as full-time employee in other organizations.	Successor enters organization as full-time employee. Includes first and all subsequent non-managerial jobs.	Successor assumes managerial position. Includes all supervisory positions prior to becoming the president.	Successor assumes presidency. Includes time successor needs to become leader of organization or more than "de jure" head of organization.	Successor becomes "de facto" leader of organization.

"advanced functional" stages relate to the development of the successor between becoming a full-time member of the organization and assuming the presidency. The last two stages of the typology, "early succession" and "mature succession," relate to activity and learning of the successor after the transfer of the presidency.

The first and last stages of the framework, "pre-business" and "mature succession," are included primarily to serve as boundaries for the actual process of a successor's development. In other words, the development of the successor for the presidency has a beginning and an end in each company although the exact points may be indeterminable and may occur with some variation among the organizations.

In one sense, the "pre-business" stage, therefore, simply establishes the boundary for subsequent stages in which substantial development occurs. On the other hand, the socialization of the successor may have started through a type of unplanned, passive orientation and conditioning that results from visits to the company and from play around equipment related to the business.

Like the "pre-business" stage, the "introductory" stage includes developmental experiences of the successor that occur before he is old enough to work in the family business. The "introductory" stage differs from the "pre-business" stage, however, in that the incumbent and other family members actively and intentionally introduce the successor to various facets and persons associated with the organization.

The "introductory-functional" stage begins when the successor first engages in part-time work in the family business and continues until he joins the organization as a full-time employee.

During this state, the successor completes his formal education and perhaps works as a full-time employee of other organizations or serves in the military service.

The successor enters the "functional" stage upon joining the family business on a full-time basis. This period includes the successor's initial assignment and all non-managerial positions held by the successor.

The "advanced functional" stage commences as the successor is promoted or brought into a managerial position by the incumbent and continues until the son succeeds his father in the leadership position. The successor may hold several managerial positions in the company before occupying the presidency.

When a son replaces his father as president of the family business, succession in the leadership position has, of course, taken place in the organization. On the other hand, a major conclusion of succession studies has been that the leadership role of an organization does not transfer as easily or absolutely between the incumbent and successor as does the leadership title. In a similar manner, Bailey[30] and Learned[31] have suggested that the development of a successor is seldom completed at the point he becomes president. Thus, the "early succession" stage denotes the period after the successor assumes the presidency, but before the time he masters the complexities of the position and gains the control associated with the leadership role.

The final or "mature succession" stage, then, serves as a boundary for the actual process of succession. That is, the major portion of a successor's development or socialization is considered to be completed when two conditions are

154

met: (1) the successor has assumed the leadership role in the organization as well as the leadership position and (2) the successor is relatively autonomous in that role, particularly in terms of his relationship to his predecessor father. Since the determination of a "mature" successor is difficult to make and will vary in timing from individual to individual, the "mature succession" stage is defined as beginning two years after the transfer of the presidency.

Summary

Management succession in the family-owned business involves a lengthy, almost life-long period of development. This article has proposed a model to identify seven stages of this succession process. These stages are, in turn, grouped according to two key events — the entry of the successor into the business and the successor's assumption of the leadership position. Thus, the model conceptualizes management succession in the family-owned business as a long-term, diachronic process of socialization.

1. Bernard Levenson, "Bureaucratic Succession," in Amital Etzioni, ed., *Complex Organizations* (New York: Holt, Rhinehard and Winston, Inc., 1966), pp. 362-63.

2. Oscar Grusky, "Administrative Succession in Formal Organizations," *Social Forces*, Vol. 39 (December 1960), pp. 105-06.

3. Alvin W. Gouldner, "Comment," *American Journal of Sociology*, Vol. 68 (July 1962), pp. 55-56.

4. Robert H. Guest, "Rejoinder," *American Journal of Sociology*, Vol. 68 (July 1962), p. 56.

5. Grusky, p. 106.

6. Stanley M. Davis, "Entrepreneurial Succession," *Administrative Science Quarterly*, Vol. 13 (December 1968), p. 403.

7. Donald B. Trow, "Executive Succession in Small Companies," *Administrative Science Quarterly*, Vol. 6 (September 1961), p. 232.

8. C. Roland Christensen, *Management Succession in Small and Growing Enterprises* (Boston: Division of Research, Graduate School of Business Administration, Harvard University, 1953), pp. 3-4, 11-14, 17-30.

9. Trow, 1961.

10. Richard O. Carlson, "Succession and Performance among School Superintendants," *Administrative Science Quarterly*, Vol. 6 (September 1961), pp. 212-13.

11. Levenson, 1966, pp. 363-67.

12. Christensen, 1953.

13. Davis, 1968, pp. 403-404, 407.

14. Betty E. Cogswell, "Some Structural Properties Influencing Socialization," *Administrative Science Quarterly*, Vol. 13 December 1968), pp. 418 and 421.

15. Grusky,, 1960, pp. 106-110 and his "Managerial Succession and Organizational Effectiveness," *American Journal of Sociology*, Vol. 69 (July 1963), pp. 25-31.

16. Harry Levinson, "A Psychologist Looks at Executive Development," *Harvard Business Review*, Vol. 40, No. 5 (September-October 1963), pp. 69-71.

17. Richard C. Hodgson, Daniel J. Levinson, and Abraham Zaleznik, *The Executive Role Constellation* (Boston: Division of Research, Graduate School

of Business Administration, Harvard University, 1965), pp. 37-48.

18. Cogswell, 1968, pp. 419-21.

19. Rosalind C. Branett and Renato Tagiuri, "What Young People Think About Managers," *Harvard Business Review,* Vol. 51, No. 3 (May-June 1973), pp. 106-18.

20. John O. Crites, "Parental Identification in Relation to Vocation Interest Development," *Journal of Educational Psychology,* Vol. 53 (1962), pp. 262-70.

21. Glen H. Edler, Jr., "Parental Power and Legitimation and its Effect on the Adolescent," *Sociometry,* Vol. 26 (1963), pp. 50-65.

22. Howard S. Becker and Anselm L. Strauss, "Careers, Personality, and Adult Socialization," *American Journal of Sociology,* Vol. 62 (November, 1956), pp. 253-263, and Becker, "Personal Change in Adult Life," *Sociometry,* Vol. 27, No. 1 (March 1964), pp. 40-53.

23. Orville G. Brim, Jr. "Aduilt Socialization," in John A. Clauseu (ed), *Socialization and Society* (Boston: Little, Brown and Company, 1968), pp. 183-225, and his "Socialization through the Life Cycle," in Orville G. Brim, Jr. and Stanton Wheeler, *Socialization after Childhood: Two Essays* (New York: John Wiley and Sons, Inc., 1966), pp. 3-49.

24. Cogswell, op. cit., pp. 417-37.

25. Stanton Wheeler, "The Structure of Formally Organized Socialization Settings," in Orville G. Brim, Jr. and Stanton Wheeler, *Socialization after Childhood: Two Essays* (New York: John Wiley and Sons, Inc., 1966), pp. 53-116.

26. Harry Levinson, "Conflicts That Plague Family Businesses," *Harvard Business Review,* Vol. 49 (March-April 1971), pp. 91-93 and 96-97.

27. Grant H. Calder, "The Peculiar Problems of a Family Business," *Busines Horizons,* Vol. 4 (June 1961), pp. 96-97.

28. Robert G. Donnelly, "The Family Business," *Harvard Business Review,* Vol. 42 (July-August 1964), pp. 102-105.

29. Charles Y. Lazarus, "From Family Management to Professional Management," *Indiana Business Paper No. 8,* n.d., pp. 3-5.

30. Joseph C. Bailey, "Clues for Success in the President's Job," *Harvard Business Review,* Vol. 45, No. 3 (May-June 1967), pp. 97-104.

31. Edmund P. Learned, "Problems of a New Executive," *Harvard Business Review,* Vol. 44, No. 4 (July-August 1966), pp. 22-24.

Introduction

Smooth succession in family business is a contradiction in terms. Nonetheless, much can be done to improve the odds that a family business will survive to the next generation. Education, training and planning are keys. Parents should create some separation between themselves and their business, begin to institutionalize the firm, let people know where they stand, create great development plans for potential successors including outside experience, develop personal interests and assure financial security. Children should express their interest in the family business, take responsibility for their development, get a mentor and gain experience outside the firm.

Making Sure Your Business Outlasts You
1986

By Sharon Nelton

Television viewers know her as the mother of Kate Jackson in "Scarecrow and Mrs. King," and many remember her as Fred MacMurray's wife on the long-running series, "My Three Sons." In real life, Beverly Garland *is* a wife and a mother.

She is also an entrepreneur, and she shares a goal common to America's estimated 13 million family business owners: keeping the business in the family.

Most entrepreneurs dream of turning control of a business over to a daughter or son who will run it with the same love and attention. But sometimes children either do not want, or are unable, to run the business. Then, to keep ownership in the family, alternatives — such as hiring professional managers — must be found.

Desire to pass a family enterprise on to the next generation may be strong, even passionate. But even in the most harmonious of families, making the transition is not easy.

"The concept of 'smooth succession' is an oxymoron [contradiction in terms]," observes Peter Davis. Director of executive education at the University of Pennsylvania's Wharton School, Davis says that succession in a family business "is probably the most complex management challenge anybody faces." Not only is it a highly charged emotional issue, but it often requires changes in the structure and culture of an

157

organization as well as changes in the people involved.

One thing that might make the process easier for Garland and her partner, husband Fillmore Crank, is that they began early to take steps to attract their children to their business and prepare them to take over.

Despite more than 200 film and TV roles, Garland found out long ago that being an actress does not always mean steady work, and she wanted a hedge against down times in her career. She and Crank, a general contractor, decided to go into the hotel business, building the 262-room "Beverly Garland's Howard Johnson's Resort Lodge" in North Hollywood, Calif., in 1973.

Crank was a widower with a teen-age son, Fillmore, Jr., and daughter, Cathleen, when he and Garland married. They have a daughter and son — Carrington, now 21, and James, 17.

Fillmore, Jr., returned from Vietnam when the hotel was nearing completion, and Garland and Crank put him to work as manager. Garland says there have been times when, short on help, she has done the hotel laundry herself, and Crank has cleaned the rooms and made beds. "We're the kind of people that if something has to be done, you just pitch in and do it," she says.

The family business expanded to a second hotel in Sacramento. Young Fillmore oversaw its construction and has been manager of the 207-room facility for five years. Cathleen, who had been housekeeper of the Howard Johnson's, took over as manager of that hotel until she left to have a baby.

Garland's and Crank's hotels now do $9.4 million worth of business a year and keep 300 people employed. Crank is 64,

and Garland is in her mid 50s. And, as Cleveland family business consultant Léon Danco would bluntly remind them, they aren't going to live forever: "Although we might like to believe we are divine, we cannot live out the ultimate myth, our own immortality."

As family businesses go, the situation that Garland and Crank find themselves in is a common one. Like other business owners, they must plan a transition of ownership, management and wealth — or it will be done for them by courts and heirs after they die.

One issue they are considering is fairness. Fillmore, Jr., 37, is the only member of the second generation deeply involved in the business and the one most clearly prepared to take over. To provide him with an incentive besides salary, Garland and Crank have begun, in the last year, to transfer interest in the company to him under a tax provision that permits each to give him $10,000 a year tax-free.

With continued planning — and luck — Garland and Crank may be able to avoid the heartbreaking rifts so many families go through when a new generation takes over. Danco recalls a daughter-in-law who, on learning that her husband was not to be his father's successor, told her father-in-law that he would never see his grandchildren again.

For more than 20 years, Danco's Center for Family Business in Cleveland has been running seminars to help families deal with the many highly charged issues centered in their businesses.

A seminar on managing succession in November drew more than 100 participants from 33 companies. Some were founders and spouses who had attended a Danco meeting before and now had grown children in tow. Others came in droves as families, bringing as many as 9 or 10 members. Still others reported being unable to persuade a reluctant parent to come.

The meeting room was filled with concerns, some stated openly, others admitted quietly over dinner. Sons expressed fears that their fathers would never retire. Daughters and wives spoke of men who would not let them share in running the business. One young woman said she had been disowned because of business differences with her parents. A son-in-law, the obvious successor in one business, said he did not wish to inherit family problems with the business. "I don't want to be the savior of my wife's family," he said.

Although the seminar did not directly help families solve the burning emotional issues, it did help them get some of the issues out in the open. And it covered such topics as getting the company organized for succession and ownership transfer techniques.

Successful transition is not just a concern of the families themselves. Obviously, employees have a stake in seeing the business continue and prosper. But so do large corporations and entire industries. Franchise stores and distributorships are frequently family owned, and corporations that depend on them are concerned about the stability of the families involved.

Almost all the 800 Allied Van Lines agencies across the country, each doing anywhere from $100,000 to $25 million in business annually, are family owned, according to Allied training specialist Mary England. (Allied is not a franchisor – all stock in the corporation is owned by the agencies.)

"Right now a large percentage of our agencies are going through succession," England says. "If a smooth transition doesn't take place in ownership, and the next generation hasn't been prepared for the business, at the worst, that agency would go bankrupt and Allied would possibly no longer be represented in that market. At the other extreme, maybe the agency would no longer grow, which once again hurts everyone involved."

Allied already offers accounting help for families going through succession, and England is developing a broader program aimed at helping agencies make a successful transition.

Succession in a family business is a two-part equation, according to the Wharton School's Peter Davis. One part consists of the founder or owner letting go and turning the company over to a successor. The other consists of the potential successors developing themselves to take over.

Davis says planning a succession takes at least five years. The process should begin by the time the entrepreneur is in his or her mid 50s, with the children possibly in their mid 20s. Here are some guidelines for both parents and children, as suggested by consultants, educators and members of family businesses themselves:

Parents

- Look at how you can alter your relationship to the company so that you are not so central to it and it is not so dependent on you. Stew Leonard, Jr., notes that his father used to come into his Norwalk, Conn. supermarket, Stew Leonard's, every day. Now he is delegating more and coming into the business less often.

"We are in here, putting out the daily and weekly fires, while he is getting more strategic, starting to think down the road five years rather than worrying that the windows are not clean in front of his building," says young Leonard.

- Develop an organization chart and put it on paper for all to see. This is part of delegating and structuring the organization so that you can learn to let go. "The business has to be more than you," says Davis. You must "institutionalize" it so that there is something to hand over when the time comes. Your organization chart should include key nonfamily members as well as family members.

- Plan for more than one successor. It is too risky to depend on just one potential heir to the throne—he or she might be run over by a truck or suffer a debilitating illness.

- Let everyone know where they stand. It should not come as a bitter surprise to someone who is ultimately not chosen. Career alternatives need to be discussed with those who are not going to be successors. Malcolm (Mac) Donley, 30, of Donley's, a Cleveland construction firm, says that while it is his goal to succeed his father as head of the company, he knows he is not the only contender. "There are other good people here. I have to be just as good and maybe better than they are to get that position."

- Have a clear personal development program for your potential successors. Teach them all you know, and support their efforts to develop themselves.

- Encourage your successor to get worthwhile experience outside your business. And don't fret if your offspring wants to leave the company for a while. Experience outside the family enterprise will bring back fresh perspective and head off any

concerns that the heir might wonder later "what it's like out there."

Dorothy Roberts, who succeeded her first husband as president of Echo Design Group, Inc., a New York fashion accessories company, says that her son Steven felt obligated to come into the firm when his father died. "I don't think he intended to come into the business," says Roberts. He worked for two years, but, she says, "I knew he really still had that wanderlust and wanted to get out and travel and explore other areas." She suggested that he take a sabbatical, which he used to work on an M.B.A. in France.

"I did it because I felt that I owed it to him, but I also did it because I think when a son or daughter of an owner works in a business, they have to love that business and want to be there." Steven, 29, is back in the company as vice president of sales, and his sister, Lynn, 32, is in charge of advertising and publicity.

- Don't neglect your daughters. In a study on family businesses, Paul C. Rosenblatt and a team of University of Minnesota researchers found that most entrepreneurs preferred passing a business on to nonrelatives instead of a daughter. But when they don't give daughters a chance, entrepreneurs lose 50 percent of potential offspring successors. Rosenblatt says in a book called *The Family in Business* (Jossey-Bass). "If one would like to pass a business on to a blood relative, and one wants to maximize one's chances of finding somebody willing and competent, it seems self-defeating, even if one has sons, to fail to consider daughters."

- Develop personal interests so that you have something to retire *to*. Going to Florida to sail and play golf is not enough, warns Davis. Entrepreneurs who do that "get bored, and they come back and get into mischief."

Consider, instead, spinning off part of your existing business and starting a new business.

Or, suggests Davis, use the opportunity to "re-energize" your creative talents. He describes the founder of a machinery company whose 33-year-old son said, "Either I take over now, or I leave." The father did not want to lose the son—he was too valuable. So the father handed over control to the son and started a consulting firm in design engineering, the creative work he had done in the beginning. And the company he had turned over to his son became his sole contractor.

- Make sure you and your spouse have enough income once you retire.

- Keep your plans up to date. Reading, Pa. management consultants Patricia and Edward Langiotti say they are working with a particularly tricky situation. A family in a retail business is facing a third generation transfer where, because of succession agreements made by the partners, the business could fall into sole ownership of uninvolved family members. A cousin has made a career out of running the business and does not know, because the family has kept it secret, that he may end up out in the cold.

The Langiottis have the task of helping the partners see that the agreement they drew up long ago, providing that the living partner would buy out the deceased partner's share, is not only unfair but out of date. It does not take into account the way the offspring in the

third generation have developed and what their interests are.

Children

- If you are interested in having a role in the family business, make it known. Discuss your goals with your parents so they, with appropriate educational and development steps, can support you in achieving them. If a parent wants you in the business but is reluctant to delegate real responsibility so that you can get the necessary experience, the Langiottis suggest you get tough and insist on an employment agreement.

It could set forth the fact that you are making the company your career choice with the goal of eventually owning and managing it. The agreement should then set up a series of accomplishments that can yield more and more of a management decision-making role as you show, through your performance, that you can handle this level of responsibility. It should also include a plan for distribution of stock to you or some kind of profit sharing that ensures that you reap the benefit of your work.

- Take responsibility for your development. Davis says you must first go through an apprentice phase, where you learn something about the business. Then you need to specialize, getting a specific skill under your belt. It could be accounting, finance or sales, for example, and it will give you something to fall back on "if the old man sells the business." Finally, you must become a generalist, learning to manage.

"Those stages need to be planned, they need to have goals at each step along the way, and they need to be evaluated," says Davis. You also should be under the supervision of someone other than your parents.

• Get a mentor. Again, says Davis, this should not be the parent—he or she has too many roles to play with you. You need somebody who can give you support throughout the development process, says Davis, "preferably a respected, experienced outside person who can counsel you and give you the advice you need on your longer term career development skills."

• Get experience outside the firm. This not only helps you gain self-confidence, knowledge and new ideas, but it often enhances your credibility with employees in the family business, who know you "made it" somewhere else.

A few last words to parents:

Give your children room to make mistakes, but find the right balance between coming down too hard on them just because they are your children and overlooking their errors. Be as fair with them as you would with a nonfamily employee.

"Entrepreneurs somehow expect their children to have the management skills that the parents took 20 years to develop, and the willingness to sacrifice financial rewards for many years, and the willingness to work the 12-hour days that they did when they were starting up," says Sharp Lannom, president of DeLong Sportswear in Grinnell, Iowa.

"None of those things do they expect from somebody from the outside."

Lannom, 47, went into the family business 25 years ago when his father died and his mother and three younger brothers needed his help. He had intended to pursue a different career, partly because, like many children of

business owners, he found it hard to work with his father.

Parents should take their children into the family business only if they really enjoy it, counsels Ralph E. Stinson, chairman of Bettcher Manufacturing Corporation, a Cleveland metal stamping firm.

"To come into the business because someone else wants you to be there would be something like a prison sentence," he says.

Stinson's son, David, is Bettcher's vice president of manufacturing and a likely successor.

Agree on clearly defined responsibility, suggests Pat Langiotti, "so that you don't have the younger person thinking he has authority that Dad is yanking out all the time. That's something we see over and over."

Tom Kilpatrick, 27, expects to succeed his 65-year-old father as head of the Kilpatrick Investment Company in Oklahoma City. Tom has delayed marriage to devote himself to the business and learn as much as he can over the next few years. "Out of respect for that," he says, "I would like to have my father consider me not as a kid climbing the ropes but more as a partner and teammate."

Ultimately, experts caution, you must be honest with yourself about a child's ability. If he hasn't got what it takes, he can still own the company, but management should be turned over to a nonfamily professional.

"How do you get a family business to last 200 years?" asks Philadelphia consultant James E. Barrett. "You never put it in the hands of an incompetent kid just because you love him!"

Introduction

A 70-year legacy ended when Lou Mazel sold the family business. Aging leadership, lack of a successor, needed new investment and new employees led to the decision to sell. But adjusting to the change in his life is another matter.

The Last Generation
1985

By Hank Gilman

Lou Mazel is standing in the blouse department in Gayne's, a discount store he sold just 15 hours ago.

Clearly, he is not pleased. "My wife wants me to jump up and down," says the 72-year-old Mr. Mazel. "But letting go of something like this is like losing a member of the family."

The decision to sell the family business to a Massachusetts discount chain was a long, painful process; after all, the store had been part of the Mazel family for 73 years. But because Mr. Mazel had failed to groom a successor, there was no one to replace him. "I didn't delegate enough authority in the early years," he concedes. "My thinking was that whatever you do yourself, you do better."

Mr. Mazel's predicament is shared by many family business executives facing retirement. "Most of them feel like they're going to go on and on, and they feel that finding a successor is something they can resolve quickly," explains Norman Rachlin, a Miami accountant. That approach, he contends, "usually results in a sale." In fact, only about 30% of the country's family businesses are passed onto second generation family members, and only 15% make it to the third generation, says Nancy Drozdow, project manager for the Family Business Program at the Wharton School of Business.

It was a particularly hard decision for Mr. Mazel. He and his brother, who died in 1971, had built up the family business that their father had begun by selling housewares door-to-door from a horse-drawn buggy. By last year, the store was producing more than $10 million a year in sales and had never been more profitable.

But it became apparent to Mr. Mazel that it was time to sell. The store needed both a major facelift and an infusion of young and aggressive employees. "We had an excellent nucleus," Mr. Mazel says of his store's aging staff. "But the nucleus was beginning to show cracks."

An unlikely vehicle for a family fortune, Gayne's made plenty of money for the Mazels. The cavernous store recalls the musty discount outlets of the early 1960s, replete with pipe rack displays, bargain-blaring signs and harsh neon lighting.

But the store is legend in these parts. Mr. Mazel says shoppers drive from as far as Montreal, about 100 miles away, to buy its eclectic mix of discount merchandise: refrigerators, dog food, even Vermont's biggest camera department.

The store's roots go back to 1914 when Mr. Mazel's father, Morris, moved his horse-and-buggy business into "Amazin Mazel's," a small general store in downtown Burlington. During the Depression, Lou Mazel and his brother, Sidney, worked in New York City to help keep the family afloat. In 1936 they returned to Burlington and joined the family business.

In 1959, the Mazels opened Gayne's, named after a heavily advertised dog food brand (a recognizable name, Mr. Mazel figured). Their father was semi-retired and the brothers were convinced that discounting was the wave of the future. And just to reassure their customers that little would change, the brothers announced that the elder Mazel would "call in three times a day" to make sure the store was being run in the Mazel tradition.

The store more than tripled in size over the next 10 years as the Mazels' discounting formula took hold. But in 1969, Lou Mazel was faced with his first succession quandery. Sidney was ill and there were no family members or employees to replace him. "My brother hadn't been well for several years." Lou

Mazel recalls. "He wasn't strong enough (to continue) at the time and he was thinking of selling. But I was very strong and there was no question that I wasn't going to sell." Mr. Mazel became a one-man show. He worked 80-hour weeks while operating the store, buying merchandise and writing weekly ads.

Meanwhile, there was not much time for Mr. Mazel to consider his own successor. He figured he would not have to worry; indeed, one of his four daughters was studying marketing in college.

But by 1980, Mr. Mazel was thinking about selling Gayne's. The store's lease was expiring, and he was, after all, 67 years old. To make matters worse, Mr. Mazel still had not groomed a successor, and his daughter was not ready to join the family business. "A couple of occasions he asked if I had any interest in the business," recalls Nancy Mazel-Tiffany, then a buyer for Filene's department store in Boston. "But I was getting good training and I was single and I wasn't ready to come back to Burlington."

Another possible successor was Joe Sussman, the Gayne's store manager and a Mazel family employee for 35 years. But, "It was too much for Joe," says Mr. Mazel. "He was getting tired too."

Mr. Mazel decided to continue working full time and bought the Gayne's building, but he finally realized that he had not adequately prepared for retirement. "A business as large as this one needs two or three backups," Mr. Mazel says. "I realized that three, four years ago. But it was going so well without bringing in someone else and upsetting the applecart."

Mrs. Mazel-Tiffany, now married, finally returned to Burlington in 1983 to work at Gayne's. At the same time, Mr. Mazel decided to work part time, hoping that his daughter soon would be ready to run the business. But time was running out. The store needed a $500,000 renovation. And Mr. Mazel's lower-level managers, some of whom had worked for the family for 35 years, could not keep up the long hours and energy to compete with other retailers.

"Joe (Sussman) and I both knew we were going just great, but you just couldn't sit on your hands," Mr. Mazel says. "We had to move up. The store needed a whole new appearance. We needed a whole new influx of people." Adds Mrs. Mazel-Tiffany: "We were at a crossing point, and I think that swayed him. He realized he would have to come back into the business if he wanted to train me. It was just bad timing."

Mr. Mazel had to make a decision: sell Gayne's, liquidate the business, return full time, or hire someone to run the store.

About a year ago, Mr. Mazel contacted an old friend, Paul Kwasnick, president and chief executive officer of Mars Stores Inc., a small, but growing discount chain based in Brockton, Mass. "I think Lou wrestled with the problem of selling the family jewels for quite awhile," says Mr. Kwasnick. "It was becoming a personal burden to him." Last January, Mr. Mazel agreed to sell Gayne's to Mars for a price that was not disclosed. Mars retained the Gayne's name. Mr. Mazel kept the real estate and an office on the store's top floor.

Letting go was the hard part. The night before the closing. Mr. Mazel locked himself in the store after taking the final inventory. The day after the sale, Mr. Mazel was back at Gayne's as if he had never left. He talked with employees and even lent $35 to Margaret Ross, who had been the store's first customer back in 1959. Mrs. Ross wanted by buy a portable stereo for her grandson, but a salesclerk was refusing to set it aside until the end of the week, when Mrs. Ross would get her paycheck. This was not the Gayne's that Mrs. Ross had come to know. "Not a good start," Mr. Mazel confided to her. "It's only been a few hours."

Corrine, Mr. Mazel's wife, is trying to soften the blow. She scheduled a month's vacation in Mexico and the Caribbean. "He's been reacting with very mixed feelings," she says. "But we had reached a point where it was necessary to change the major focus of our lives from what's going to happen to the business to other things. I think we're happy to get on with other things."

Mr. Mazel does not seem as sure. Sitting in his car outside a local shopping mall, he talks about his new life: the civic organizations, more time for tennis and real estate ventures. But, he is reminded, he will not be a retailer. Mr. Mazel looks straight ahead and slowly shakes his head from side to side. He is not smiling.

"No good," says Mr. Mazel.

Chapter 3

Management and Strategic Planning

The managerial issues confronting family firms differ somewhat from those facing non-family businesses. Personal and family goals, emotions, and impact on relationships are much stronger considerations in family business management and strategic planning.

Many family businesses fail to engage in meaningful strategic planning. Articles contained in this section seek to demystify the process, showing how to engage in strategic planning and how to adapt the strategic planning process to family and business goals.

Finally, the chapter includes a management checklist for family businesses which incorporates planning considerations.

Introduction

Management problems in a family-owned business are somewhat different from the same problems in a non-family business. When close relatives work together, emotions often interfere with business decisions. In some family companies, control of daily operations is a problem. In others, a high turnover rate among non-family members presents difficulties. In still other companies, growth creates challenges because some of the relatives are unwilling to plow profits back into the business. This article discusses such problems from the viewpoint of the family member who is the company's manager. It offers suggestions that should help family business leaders manage effectively and profitably.

Problems In Managing a Family-Owned Business
1987

By Robert E. Levinson

Originally printed as U.S. Small Business Administration Management Aid #2.004, Office of Business Development, 1987.

When you put up your own money and operate your own business, you prize your independence. "It's my business," you tell yourself in good times and in bad times.

However, "it's our business," in a family company. Conflicts sometimes abound because relatives look upon the business from different viewpoints.

Those relatives who are silent partners, stockholders, and directors see only dollar signs when judging capital expenditures, growth, and other major matters. Relatives who are engaged in daily operations judge major matters from the viewpoint of the production, sales and personnel necessary to make the company successful. Obviously, these two viewpoints may conflict in many instances.

This natural conflict can be aggravated by family members who have no talent for money or business. Sometimes they are the weak offspring of the founders of the company—sons and daughters who lack business acumen—and sometimes they are in-laws who must be taken care of regardless of their ability or the company's needs.

Basically, the management problems that face the manager of a family-owned business are the same as those which confront the owner-manager of any small company. But the job of the "family manager" is complicated because of the relatives who must be reconciled to the facts of the market place, the factory, and the counting house.

The Sparks Fly

Different opinions do not always produce discord, but sometimes they cause "sparks to fly"—especially in a family-owned company. Emotion is an added dimension as brothers and sisters, uncles and aunts, nephews and nieces, and fathers and children work together in such a small business.

For the individual who must head such a company, the important thing is to recognize this dimension of emotions and to make objective decisions that are difficult to come by in such situations.

Many times when members of a family are active in the business, it is hard to make objective decisions about the skills and abilities of each other. For example, one says about another relative, "He was lazy when we were kids, and he's still lazy." Or a disgruntled wife says about an aunt, "What does she know about the business? She's only here because of her father's money."

If such emotional outbursts affected only the family, the manager might "knock a few heads together" and move along. But often it is not that easy. The quarrels and ill feelings of relatives have a way of spreading out to include nonfamily employees.

Then the manager's problem is to keep the bickering from interfering with work. You cannot afford to let the company become divided into warring camps. You have to convince nonfamily employees that their interests are best served by a profitable organization

rather than by allegiance to particular members of the family.

Another aspect of the emotional atmosphere is that often nonfamily employees tend to base their decisions on the family's tensions. They know how their bosses react and are influenced by this knowledge.

Is The Manager Really In Control?

The president of a small company is not always necessarily the person in charge. In many family-owned businesses, the elder statesman of the family becomes president or chairman of the board of directors. But day-to-day management is in the hands of other members of the family.

In some cases, even the best hands are tied as the family member tries to manage the business. For example, the ceiling on the amount of money that can be spent without permission from the rest of the family may be too low for the situation confronting the company. Having clear operating expenditures may mean missing opportunities for increased profits, such as taking advantage of a good price on raw materials or sales inventory.

In other cases, a manager may be in a bind because of emotional involvement. For example, you may feel that you have to clear routine matters with top family members because "Uncle Bill never lets you forget your mistakes." Personalities and emotional reactions create bottlenecks that work against an efficient operation.

Efficiency may be reduced also by relatives who indulge in excessive family talk during working hours. The manager should set the example and insist that relatives refrain from family chit-chat on the job.

In some family-owned companies, the day-to-day manager may be a bottleneck. You may be a bottleneck because you do not have the ability to delegate work and authority. You may be the manager because of age or the amount of capital you have in the business without regard to your qualifications. In other instances, you may hold up progress because you do not listen to others in the company.

One solution is for other members of the family to persuade such a manager to let someone else run the day-to-day show, perhaps a hired manager.

If a member of the family has to be in charge of operations, he or she should be capable of using efficient management techniques and be thick-skinned enough to live with family bickering and tough enough to make his or her decisions stick.

One way to obtain objective control in a family-owned business is to hire an outsider to manage the day-to-day operations when the company can afford it. Any manager may become as biased as any other family member. With a hired manager, the family members will have their hands full in setting policies and in planning for growth. An efficient hired manager will see to it that all employees—family and nonfamily alike—know to whom to report at all times.

Such definite lines of authority are even more important when a member of the family manages operations with other relatives filling various jobs. The responsibilities of family members should be spelled out. "Family employees" should discipline themselves to work within the bounds of these lines of authority. Even then, it is wise to have a nonfamily employee high in the organization so that he or she can be

involved in operations and help smooth out any emotional decisions which family members may make.

The manager's authority to suspend or discharge flagrant violators of company rules should also be spelled out. Management control is weakened if special allowances are made for "family employees."

An important question connected with authority is: Who takes over when something happens to the family member who heads the business? A position may be "up for grabs" if the family hasn't provided for an orderly succession. This need is especially critical when the top family member is approaching retirement age or is in poor health.

Your Brother-In-Law Needs a Job?

One of the most common problems in a family business is the hiring of relatives who do not have talent. But what are you to do when your sister or another close relative says, "Bob needs a job badly"? The emotional aspect of such family relationships is hard to fight. But try to go into it with your eyes open. It will be hard to fire Bob if he turns out to cost you more money than his presence is worth.

The main thing is to recognize the talent or lack of it. Suppose your brother-in-law, for example, has little or no ability as far as your company is concerned. Perhaps you can put him in a job where, in spite of his weaknesses, he can make a contribution and not disturb other employees.

The major concern is not necessarily the relative but how he or she affects other employees. In some cases, a relative can demoralize the organization by his or her dealing with other employees. For example, he or she may loaf on the job, avoid unpleasant tasks, take special privileges, and make snide remarks about you and other relatives.

If you are stuck with such a relative, try putting him or her in a job where he or she will have minimum contact with other employees, out of the mainstream of decision making. For instance brother-in-law Bob might be placed in a sales office in another city some distance from the company's headquarters where he will be under the supervision of a top producer. Another alternative is to change his attitudes by formal or informal education.

The key is to see that the nontalented relative does not affect the relationship that you, the manager, have with other members of your staff. Other employees will respect you for keeping relatives in line.

Strange things sometimes happen. There is always the chance that the non-talented relative may be under your direction and turn into an asset for your company.

Is Nonfamily Turnover High?

Some family-owned companies are plagued with a high turnover among their nonfamily top people. Sometimes relatives are responsible. They resent outside talent and, at best, make things unpleasant for nonfamily executives.

In other cases, top-notch managers and workers leave because promotions are closed to them. They see your relatives being pushed into executive offices.

The exit interview is a useful device for getting at the root of this type of turnover. A key employee who has decided to leave may be eager to tell you the true story—or at least enough of the facts to help you develop a course of action.

When a manager has the facts, he or she may have to confront the trouble-causing relative with an unpleasant story. What comes out of the confrontation is anyone's guess. Rare is the owner-manager who can fire a troublesome and close relative and make it stick. One way to remove such a thorn from the side of key executives is to help the relative start a business in a non-competing line—provided he or she has the management ability that is necessary for success. Another way is to "exile" him or her to a branch office or find a job with another company.

Spending to Save Money?

Many times, as the owner-manager you feel that you must make an expenditure to improve efficiency, yet other family members oppose the expenditure. They view it as an expense rather than an investment. They feel that funds spent for items, such as more efficient equipment, encroach on their year-end dividends.

One way to help these relatives see that "you have to spend money to make money" is to base your arguments for the expenditures on facts and figures that nonfamily employees have gathered. Suggest to the opposing family members that the matter be settled on a cold dollar basis: for example, "by spending money for this machine, we can increase our profits and get our money back in four years."

If the opposing relatives refuse to accept your projection, try calling in outside business advisers. Relatives will sometimes believe advisers, such as your banker, accountant or attorney, when they won't accept your judgment. But keep in mind that outside advisers who are personally close to other family members, should not be included among your counselors.

Paid consultants can also be useful in proving the worth of an expenditure. Such help is particularly valuable on specialized projects that require more research than you or your regular advisers have time to do.

Status Quo Blocks Growth

When some of the relatives in a family-owned business grow older, they develop an attitude of status quo. They don't want things to change and are afraid of risk. With this attitude, they can, and often do, block growth in their family's business.

The solution to such a problem is to urge or suggest that the status quo members slowly disappear from the scene of operation. One way to do this is to dilute their influence in management decisions. For example, the status quo relatives might be given the opportunity to convert their stock in the corporation to preferred stock. Or they might sell some of their stock to the younger relatives.

It might also be possible for the status quo relatives to think in terms of gradual retirement. Their salaries can be reduced over several years, and they can relinquish some of their interests. With the proper legal advice, it might be possible for a small corporation to recapitalize. A new partnership agreement might be drawn up when the company is a partnership.

Such actions can take into account all of the growth of the business to that particular point and can enable the retreating members to recover their equity. Meanwhile, the manager and active relatives can renew their efforts toward expanding the business.

How Is The Pie Divided?

Paying family members and dividing profits among them can also be a difficult affair. Many persons feel that they are underpaid, but what about relatives who comment as follows:

"Uncle Jack sits around and gets more than I do."

"Aunt Sue goes to Europe on the returns of money her husband put into the business before he died ten years ago."

"Your brother goofs off and rakes in more than you do."

How do you resolve such complaints? You don't entirely. But if the business is a small corporation, certain equalizing factors can be accomplished by stock dividends. By recapitalizing the company, some stockholders can take preferred stock with dividends.

Salaries are best handled by being competitive with those paid in the area. Find out what local salary ranges are for various management jobs and use these ranges as a guide for paying both family and non-family personnel. When you tie pay to the type of work that the individual does, you can show disgruntled relatives the value that the industry puts on their jobs.

Fringe benefits can also be useful in dividing profits equitably among family members. Benefits, such as deferred profit sharing plans, pension plans, insurance programs, and stock purchase programs, offer excellent ways to placate disgruntled members of the family and at the same time help them to build their personal assets.

How the pie is divided is vital to growth in a small business. Profits are the seedbed for expansion, and lenders are influenced by what is done with profits.

173

What banker wants to lend to a company a substantial amount when its earned surplus is drained off by relatives?

Where Do You Go For Money?

Another major problem in managing a family business is that of obtaining money for growth. Generally speaking if the company is profitable, you can get funds from your bank.

But when the growth is substantial, a company often outgrows its local bank. When you see the prospect of expansion looming ahead, the managing relative should begin to plan for it. You will need to consider techniques for financing, such as the following. Planned financing may be a combination of these items:

Taking out a mortgage on the company's building.

Asking suppliers to extend credit on purchases.

Factoring the company's receivables and inventory financing.

Borrowing on a note basis from friends.

Borrowing the cash surrender value of relatives' life insurance policies.

Contacting an insurance company for a long-term loan.

Contacting the Small Business Administration for a business loan. In some areas, the manager can get financing from a Small Business Investment Company.

If the business is a small corporation, the following techniques also offer possible sources of money:

Selling a portion of the stock to the company's employees for cash.

Selling some of the stock to another company for cash. In a merger, you can use the credit of the larger company.

Contacting a regional investment banker who may privately find a lender, using some of the company's stock as collateral.

Contacting a national investment banker who would underwrite some of the company's stock. This would be "going public."

Effective budgetary controls are important in seeking growth funds. Such controls help the managing relative to determine the company's needs. Lenders also regard them as evidence of good management.

Exchange Information

Fortunately, in most communities, the manager of a family-owned business is not alone. Other individuals operate small companies for their families and may provide a source of information and help.

The managing relative should seek out and cultivate counterparts. You can exchange ideas with them and learn how they solved problems in which their relatives were involved.

In a small corporation, the thinking can be stimulated by having outsiders on the board of directors--directors who are not relatives and who are from other types of businesses.

State and national trade associations are also good sources of information and help. Through them, the managing relative can get facts from non-competitors.

174

Introduction

All businesses have strategies, but some take the trouble to plan theirs. While strategic planning sounds intimidating to smaller businesses, it is simply the process of setting clear, long-term goals and developing objectives to achieve them. This article shows how to organize the planning process through phases of analysis, definition, development, control and reevaluation.

Strategic Business Planning for the Small- to Medium-Sized Company
1987

By Steven M. Lurie

In the present economic environment, strategic business planning could be the key difference between companies which will lose ground in the coming years and those that will position themselves for future success.

Strategic business planning is sometimes incorrectly perceived as an esoteric activity undertaken by only the largest companies with highly trained staffs. In fact, the strategic planning process works particularly well in smaller, growth-oriented organizations, because the entrepreneur is able to provide strong, direct input and support for the plan and because of the ease of communication.

What is Strategic Business Planning?

All businesses have strategies, which are simply the methods used to make and sell products or perform services. Often, however, the strategies are determined only by a company's reaction to events beyond its control, rather than through planning.

Strategic business planning is a company's "game plan" for the future. It is an organized effort to set clear, long-term goals and to develop methods or strategies, for achieving them. The goals of most businesses are usually clear—maximize profits and return on investment. But, just as a football team without a game plan is unlikely to win, a company without clearly defined

175

strategies probably won't meet its objectives. Strategic business planning is more than an attempt to forecast the future; it is an attempt to influence it. Through strategic planning, management can think ahead, taking advantage of opportunities rather than reacting to problems. The planning process helps provide lead time for management action.

Organizing the Planning Process. Companies of all sizes can benefit from organizing the strategic planning process. The larger the company, the more formalized the process becomes.

For a smaller company, strategic planning may be nothing more than an organized long-range thought process, which may not even be communicated to others in the organization. Where the management team consists of the entrepreneur, a sales executive and a production executive, those individuals might informally meet to set goals and to plan strategies.

A larger company would usually benefit from a more structured planning process. And, when input from middle-management is needed or when strategies are complex, smaller companies would also benefit from an organized effort. A planning committee is often useful, and might include representatives from administration, marketing, production, research and finance. It would have primary responsibility for developing overall goals and strategies. Sub-committees from each discipline could help take advantage of middle managers' ideas.

Regardless of the extent of organization, the planning process is the same. While the process is continuous, it can be divided into these distinct stages:

- Analyze the business.

- Define the entrepreneur's goals.

- Define the business's goals.

- Develop strategies.

- Develop and implement plans.

- Monitor performance.

- Reevaluate goals and strategies.

Analyze the Business. For management to be able to decide where the company should go and how to get there, it must first know where it is; such an analysis is the foundation for strategies designed to take advantage of opportunities and solve problems.

The planning team needs to have a frank discussion about the company's business and past performance, searching for answers to question such as:

- What are the company's marketing strengths and weaknesses? Where is its sales and distribution network strong? Where is it weak? Does the company have a good track record for developing new customers? Are customers loyal? What is the company's reputation for quality products? Are the prices competitive?

- What is the company's plant capacity and utilization, cost position relative to its competitors, labor force availability, technological competitive position and ability to produce new products or modify existing ones?

- What are the company's production strengths and weaknesses? Does the company produce high quality products? Are there quality control problems? Is the labor force stable and experienced? Is employee turnover too high? Is the company a low or high cost producer? Are facilities and equipment "state of the art"? Are they old and inefficient? Is the company able to meet promised delivery dates? Does it have a reputation for failing to meet such dates?

- What are the company's financial strengths and weaknesses? Does it have access to significant new sources of funds, either through debt or equity financing? Are sources of funds exhausted or prohibitively expensive? Is trade credit dependable? Is the company faced with restrictive credit limits from suppliers?

The result of this planning effort should be an analysis of the company's business, its market and its resources. It also should enable management to catalog the business's strengths and weaknesses, and put it in a better position to develop goals for future profits and plans for achieving them.

Define the Entrepreneur's Goals. Once management focuses on what the company is, it can decide what it should be. In the smaller business, however, before the company's goals are defined, another step is often necessary — defining the entrepreneur's goals for the business.

The entrepreneur with a small business is likely to have personal, possibly unstated, goals for the business. Some entrepreneurs are primarily interested in maximizing their after-tax income in the short-term. Others may be willing to make sacrifices now to produce a greater long-term return. Many entrepreneurs are also concerned with "successorship," which could have different meanings to different entrepreneurs. It could mean:

- Selling the business either to outsiders or key employees.

- Maintaining or building the business for his family to run.

- Providing for continuity of management by non-family members for the benefit of his family.

The entrepreneur should know what he wants from the business before broader goals are established, because strategies will differ depending on those goals.

Define the Business's Goals. Having defined the entrepreneur's personal goals for the business, the business goals can be developed. The goals should be well defined and clearly understood by the management team. Otherwise, company goals may be viewed differently by individual employees who may work at cross-purposes with each other. In smaller businesses, the entrepreneur will usually first set the company's broad goals, such as:

- Significantly improve profits and return on investment.

- Achieve significant volume growth.

- Maintain present market position in spite of increased competition.

The broad, stated goals should be consistent with the entrepreneur's personal goals for the business. For example, to improve the stability of his business, the entrepreneur might state the company's goals as maximizing profits and achieving growth. He might also want to improve the company's management team, which can make the business more attractive to potential buyers.

After the entrepreneur has decided on broad business goals consistent with his personal goals, more specific ones would be developed. These goals should be:

- Designed to take advantage of the company's strengths while neutralizing weaknesses. For example, a business with a reputation for producing high quality products would ordinarily not decide to compete with discounters. On the other hand, a discounter with a reputation for low quality might establish a goal to overcome its reputation, but would probably decide not to compete with high quality, high priced competitors.

- Realistic and achievable within a reasonable time. However, they should also be challenging and require significant effort to achieve; in that way, the entire company will be geared to their accomplishment. Impossible goals will lead to frustration, but if they are too easy to achieve, the program will not be meaningful, and the company will be an underachiever.

- Specific enough to permit an objective appraisal of results. For example, a company desiring to increase profitability might state its goals as, "to achieve pre-tax income of 10 percent of sales" rather than "to increase profitability."

Developing Strategies. Developing the company's strategies to achieve its goals is the exciting part of the strategic business planning process. Here, "brainstorming sessions" are useful. During these sessions, team members are encouraged to be creative and freely express their ideas. The objective is to elicit as many ideas from the group as possible, as individuals will have different perceptions. From these sessions, innovative ideas are often developed about what the company can

do over the next few years. Even if the company does not develop radical new ideas, it should at least provide a few new ideas about actions the company could take to improve its market position, productive capabilities, management or financial strength.

Develop and Implement Plans. A three-year plan with specific action programs should be developed based on the company's goals and strategies. Based on that plan, the company should determine what it intends to do during each of those years and develop short-term budgets. Budgets are not meant to change or form the company's strategy as much as to provide a measure of accomplishment toward reaching the company's longer-term goals in an organized manner.

Monitoring Performance. Monitoring results of the strategic business plan is a continuous activity. Budgets are useful for comparing financial results against the plan. In addition, non-financial information is often needed by management to monitor the planning process. For example, information about equipment utilization, quality control, and employee turnover could relate to management's goals and strategies. Systems may be needed to report such data in a timely manner.

Reevaluate Goals and Strategies. Change is inevitable, so modifications in the plan are almost always necessary for the company to achieve its broader goals. Management should not hesitate to reconsider its strategies. Management could also discover that its goals are unrealistic. If so, they should be restated. Strategic business planning is a management tool and should not be allowed to supersede needed changes.

Introduction

Strategic planning is particularly important in family businesses because it is the secret to keeping the business in the family long term. Family firm strategic planning involves the needs and interests of both the family and the business. As members of the next generation assume leadership, strategic planning is a key to regenerating the business while implementing their program. As generations change, so do priorities. So must strategy, most often by building on the strategic foundation set by the previous generations.

To engage in strategic planning, write down three or four key words representing business goals. Then take a long-term view, understand the company's environment, get the management team involved, and focus on the company's strengths in relation to its environment. Examples given of families and family business using strategic planning include: a snack food maker, a funeral home chain, a supermarket, a cabinet maker and an automotive dealership.

Strategies for Family Firms

1986

By Sharon Nelton

When Michael W. Rice succeeded his father as president of Utz Quality Foods, Inc., it was a nice little potato chip and pretzel company with 325 employees and an annual growth rate of five to 10 percent. From its location in Hanover, Pa., it served three markets: Baltimore, Washington and south-central Pennsylvania.

Now, nearly eight years later, Utz is a *bigger* nice little company with 550 employees and an annual growth rate of more than 20 percent.

Why has this family business, founded by Rice's grandparents in 1921, grown and prospered so?

Because Rice, 43, did some strategic planning.

First, he decided he wanted more rapid growth. "My grandfather and father were content with a slow rate of growth," he says. "They liked to control things very closely and felt that if they grew faster, they'd lose the control. I felt that if you developed your managers properly, you could achieve growth but still maintain the quality and basic strength that got you where you were."

He expanded the company's geographic reach to encompass Virginia. He added new products, including corn chips and other corn snacks, because he could see that corn-based snacks were gaining popularity in the mid-Atlantic region. He stepped up marketing and, to make Utz more manageable, he bought out a sister's interest in the company, leaving himself and his mother, Arlene Utz Hollinger, as sole owners.

One thing he did not change was quality. Utz snack foods are more costly to produce, but Rice believes he has a better product than most of his competitors.

Rice has proved to himself what a number of other business owners are coming to learn — that strategic planning in family businesses pays off. Most of the planning concepts involved apply to non-family enterprises, too.

Strategic planning should not be confused with day-to-day operational planning, advises William P. Anthony, professor of management at Florida State University.

In his recently published *Practical Strategic Planning* (Quorum Books, Westport, Conn.), he says it includes five key elements:

• Long-term focus, usually three to five years but sometimes as long as 20.

• An understanding of the outside environment in which the business operates.

• Involvement of top management.

• Commitment of large amounts of organizational resources.

• A setting of direction for the organization by focusing on its identity and its place in a changing environment.

Anthony says a good strategic plan can help a company answer such questions as: Are we growing enough? Are some of our products and services obsolete? Should we add new ones? What type of personnel should we hire?

Charles Gueli, Jr., 40, chairman of the Gueli Organization, a diversified family-owned business in New York, says he found that when members of his family simply talked about their hopes and dreams for the company, it often made them better prepared to take advantage of opportunities that arose. Since making that discovery a few years ago, Gueli has instituted more formal planning procedures and is working to improve them.

Matthew J. and Richard J. Lamb, brothers who own Blake-Lamb Funeral Homes, Inc., in Oak Park, Ill., have turned to strategic planning to help them remain competitive in a fast-changing industry. They are also using it to help ensure that their business stays in the family.

Marvin "Mickey" Weiss has used strategic planning to weather the bad times that have beset the steel industry in northern Indiana, where WiseWay Super Food Centers, his independent supermarket chain, is located. Over a 2 1/2 year period, he phased out the four least profitable of his eight stores, losing only a third of his volume in the process. Now the company is ready to expand again.

Other families do strategic planning because their business has reached a stage when plans must be made if the business — and consequently the family — is not to suffer. Herb H. and Kenneth Seilkop of Economy Pattern & Castings Company, a Cincinnati firm that serves the foundry industry, say they finally decided they had to grow.

"We're too big to operate as a little company and too little to operate as a big company," Ken says of the $4.5 million-sales firm. He and his brother have brought in an outside board of directors to help them clarify and achieve their strategic objectives.

Harvey J. Beaudin did no strategic planning for Miles Fox Office Products Company, in suburban Detroit, throughout the 1970s. Even during Detroit's darkest days, the office supply industry was booming — and it still is. Miles Fox (named after the founder) grew fast enough to absorb three of the four Beaudin children and has now outpaced even their ability to manage it without becoming more professional. It had 16 employees and revenues of $660,000 in 1968, the year Beaudin bought it; now there are over 70 employees and annual revenues of $12 million. The Beaudin family is using strategic planning to create a more professionally run organization.

"A strategic plan is a business' formula for success," says John L. Ward, professor of free enterprise at Loyola University of Chicago and author of *Keeping the Family Business Healthy*, to be published by Jossey-Bass, of San Francisco, next fall.

Michael J. Kami, of Corporate Planning Inc., a Lighthouse Point, Fla., consulting firm, suggests that the phrase "strategic planning" be abolished because it smacks of reports that are put together and then ignored. He prefers to call it strategic management with strategic thinking."

He explains: "'Management' is doing something, and 'thinking' means don't be stupid."

Though strategic planning in publicly held corporations is concerned only with the needs and interests of the business, John Ward points out that there is a second dimension to such planning in family businesses: the needs and interests of the family.

With time, for example, Mike Rice may find that planning does more than help the Utz company improve its performance. It may also help him, his mother and his wife, Jane — Utz's public relations director — transfer leadership of the company to the fourth generation.

Fewer than 15 percent of family businesses stay family-run that long, according to Ward. "The average life expectancy of the once very successful family business is 55 years," he says. After that, they either close or change hands.

"Perpetuating the family business is the most difficult, most challenging management task that anybody can undertake," contends Loyola University's Ward. He has conducted research on 200 family businesses, and, he says, "The secret to keeping the business in the family is to take the long view — to think and plan strategically."

Ward is interested in helping family businesses avoid living out the "shirtsleeves to shirtsleeves in three generations" syndrome in which the first generation builds the business, the second maintains it, and the third loses interest in it. Sometimes, the second generation milks the business, consuming all its wealth so that nothing is left for the third generation.

Family businesses that have been most successful over the years, Ward says, are those that have found ways to regenerate themselves with new strategies each time they reach a plateau.

In a family business, "you're dealing with two different issues," says Matt Lamb, board chairman of Blake-Lamb Funeral Homes. "A family is forgiving; a business is bottom-line oriented. How do you really meld those two together and still have a successful business and a loving family?"

Business people like the Lambs, who include the future of the family itself in their strategic planning, find it not only results in a better business but also makes it easier for family members to clarify their roles in and out of the business, helping them to face directly such touchy issues as who will own and run it.

Matt and Dick Lamb bought their 106-year-old funeral home company from their father, who had acquired it from the founding Blake family in 1928. The $7-million-a-year firm includes 11 metropolitan Chicago funeral homes.

The brothers began to formalize strategic planning about five years ago.

"We had gotten very aggressive in acquisitions, but we really felt the need to have an overall picture of where we were going and where the industry was going," says Dick, 45, the president. A decade ago, the Lambs began to see their industry moving from one of family-owned companies to one made up of large conglomerates.

In the past couple of years, competition from the conglomerates has become more and more aggressive, and the environment, says Matt, 54, has become "hostile to a family-type, small operation. One of the main decisions that we had to make was whether we wanted to sell out or to persevere in this kind of environment."

They decided to persevere.

But they wanted help, and two years ago they created an advisory board of three Chicagoans in unrelated fields: Schwinn Bicycle Company President Edward R. Schwinn, Jr., because of his experience in running a family company that had undergone many changes in recent years; Ronald L. Taylor,

president of the Keller Graduate School of Management, who could bring an academic overview to the operation; and Mark A. Levy, a restauranteur and real estate developer, for his knowledge in acquisitions, service, quality control and personnel development. Levy is in business with his brother, a fact that was important to the Lambs, who wanted to know more about how other brothers with different interests get along in a rapidly growing company.

"The most important thing the advisory board does for us," says Dick, "is to make us focus on the really important things for our future rather than strictly on putting out fires today.

"We found we could no longer just be in the business of providing caskets, limousines, funeral facilities and funeral services. We found that in the light of the changing environment, changing competition and new ideas, we were really in the business of providing services to families at the time of a death."

Their board has helped them build on the strength of outreach services that they were already offering, such as programs to help people cope with the death of a loved one. They have also moved into joint ventures with cemeteries and a flower company. And they are developing a computer software business-management package and insurance programs that they expect to market to new customers—other funeral homes.

lake-Lamb is growing 25 percent a year, but the Lambs are keeping in sharp focus the vision of their company as one that can respond to new ideas and still treat grieving clients as individuals.

Simultaneously, the Lambs have been paying attention to developing the company's future management. Three of Matt's four children have chosen to join the company, and one of them, Rosemarie Lamb, 29, has already been singled out as the successor in leadership. As chief operating officer, she is running the company on a day-to-day basis, and Matt and Dick are beginning to involve her in developing the programs for growth as well.

Within the past few years, Matt's family has periodically held structured meetings in which both family issues and business issues are discussed. They get such items on the table as why one family member is paid more than another and why the oldest daughter was chosen chief operating officer.

"Everyone has to leave their egos and prejudices outside the room," says Matt. "Then you just get into it. There is never anything unsaid between us."

Dick's five children are younger, the oldest being 20, and it remains to be seen whether any will join the family business. The family does not have formal meetings yet, but there are discussions around the dining table. Dick says, "The issues at this point are, 'Should I go into the business?' "What happens if I don't go into the business — will you still love me?'"

Still open is the question of future ownership of the company — an issue the Lamb brothers say is hard to get into while the company is growing so fast. With nine children between them, however, the growth and increasing complexity of the company may make ownership decisions easier. Because the company has more facets to it and more subsidiaries, Dick says, ownership can be "shared in ways that were not possible for us in the past."

Another set of brothers who are conscious of the need to account for the

family in their strategic planning are the Seilkops of Economy Patterns & Castings in Cincinnati. But their problems are quite different. It is uncertain whether anyone from the next generation will take over Economy.

Herb is 57, and neither of his two children, now in their 30s, expect to join the family business. Ken is 48; his older daughter, a college sophomore, has expressed interest in joining the company in an accounting position someday, while the younger, a high school senior, has indicated no interest.

Because of the uncertainty, the Seilkops have taken several steps to assure the continuity of the business. For the time being, their plan calls for the company to remain in the family but to be run by professional management if Ken and Herb are not available to run it. They have brought in an outside board of directors empowered to see that the company has good management. And they have identified their vice president, C.B. Green, as their successor, if the board approves.

In families where succession is uncertain or family members are especially young, reliance on trusted lieutenants like Green can be vital. At 27, Donald Weiss is the youngest of four Weiss children and the only one involved in WiseWay food stores. He is the clear-cut successor. But his father, Mickey Weiss, is 63, leaving a larger-than-usual generation gap and, although Mickey plans to be around awhile, there is some question about whether there will be enough time for him to train the younger generation.

"When there's a case where there's a big gap in ages, like my own," says Don, "non-family business members are very important — both for filling the gap between generations and also bringing in some professional management expertise." Mickey recruited managers from other chains who, Don says, have contributed their experience and given the company stability. Mickey and Don also rely heavily on their long-time vice president, Patrick O'Malley, who handles day-to-day operations. Don, who has a Columbia University M.B.A., has been able to learn much about the supermarket business under the tutelage of these valued managers.

Ask family business owners if they can recall a time when lack of strategic planning hurt the business, and most will say yes.

Mickey Weiss thinks he missed an opportunity by not getting into discount supermarkets earlier. He and his son will try to recoup by making their next store, now in the planning stages, a discount operation.

Ken and Herb Seilkop at Economy Pattern & Castings believe they missed out on good acquisitions they could have made if they had started strategic planning earlier.

Inability to come up with a new strategy, in fact, caused Wolferman's, a grocery chain based in Kansas City, Mo., to close its doors. It began as a downtown grocery store in 1888, when Kansas City streets were filled with horses, wagons and cowboys, and became the premier grocery chain in the area, offering high quality products, charge accounts and home delivery.

"It was a high-overhead business — that was one of our problems," says Fred Wolferman, whose grandfather and great-grandfather founded the company. After World War II, supermarkets came on strong, getting better at merchandising. The need for stores like Wolferman's dwindled. The stores were liquidated in 1972, four years after

Fred Wolferman, now 41, went to work for the company.

"It would have taken a radical reorganization of the business to adapt it to the changing market," he says.

But he did keep a piece of the company: the famous, extra-thick English muffins that the family had been producing since the early 1900s. He went into the industrial real estate business, but he also went into partnership with the head of the old company's bakery to continue producing muffins for wholesale.

When his partner retired in 1976, Fred Wolferman quit the real estate business and went into muffins full-time. His wife, Kristie, is not actively involved in the business, but she came up with the strategic idea that put the company back on the map again. Do mail order, she urged.

Fred placed the first mail order ad in *Bon Appetit* in 1977, "and darned if it didn't sell a lot of muffins," he says. The ad launched Wolferman's into a venture that increases 30 percent to 40 percent a year, helping to boost the revitalized company's annual sales from $600,000 in 1981 to over $4 million last year. Now getting back into retailing, Fred recently opened two stores, each combining a restaurant with a specialty food shop.

Loyola's John Ward observes that among the family businesses that survive over the long term, you see a change in strategy with each new generation. The new leadership does not necessarily abandon the old strategy but often adds to it.

The Gueli Organization was launched as a woodworking company in Brooklyn 40 years ago by Charles Gueli, Sr., a master craftsman who learned his trade in Italy. When Charlie, Jr., joined the company in 1964, it was basically the same woodworking business his father had started, doing $800,000 a year in sales with the help of 50 Old World craftsmen. "They could build cabinetry better than anyone and always had a backlog of work," Charlie recalls.

Inadvertently, the company began to do other kinds of construction-related work, such as painting or drywall, simply because it was asked to do so by contractors who did not want those jobs themselves.

Only when Charlie was well-versed in the business did the Guelis actually start to seek clients for the new areas of work they were getting into.

Since Charlie, who has been chairman since 1976, joined the business, it has grown to seven companies involved in such fields as construction, architectural management and maintenance, all extensions of the original woodworking operation. Charlie's brother, Robert, joined the firm in the mid-1970s, to be followed by Robert's wife, Connie, who is in sales, and a cousin, Charles A. Gueli, who opened a Washington office and helped the company get started in the real estate development field, its big new growth area.

Charlie, Jr., feels the company has found its real estate niche in smaller commercial projects in suburban locations. In just three years, its holdings have grown to $35 million. The Gueli Organization itself is doing $30 million in annual sales and has grown to 140 employees.

Another successor who brought a new strategy to a company is Thelma Hausman Dunlevy, 55, who became president of Hausman Motor Company, a Louisville, Ky, Jeep dealership, after her father died in 1982.

Charles Hausman had been in business for 60 years and, says Dunlevy, "he had earned the community's respect for his integrity." That was an image she did not want to change, but she did begin to advertise much more aggressively and make the company more visible by sponsoring community events and participating in trade and community organizations.

Sales of new Jeeps jumped from 35 to 70 the year she took over. Now the dealership sells 100 annually, even though, because of the demographics of the area, the manufacturer's projections indicate sales should be only 32.

The Hausmans might have lost the opportunity to keep the business under family management if Dunlevy and her sister, Joan H. Campbell, who is office manager, had not pushed their way into the business. Dunlevy says their father was a "warm and loving patriarch." Their mother, Loretta W. Hausman, now 83, has been involved in the business in the office since the 1940s. Dunlevy says she and her sister, with their mother's help, convinced their father "that we could serve as a bridge to carry the business on into the fourth generation."

Even as small children, says Dunlevy, the sisters planned how they would run the company when they were grown up. It was a long time before Dunlevy's ambitions were realized, "because women weren't supposed to get into sales." She became a teacher first and did not join the family firm until 1977. Only six months before Dunlevy's father died could her mother persuade him to incorporate. Dunlevy and her sister got stock for the first time, and also for the first time, she says, "the tax lawyer, accountant and banker became acquainted with the daughters."

Now that it is her turn, Dunlevy is not leaving succession to chance. Seven of the 13 Hausman employees are family members, including three of Dunlevy's six children. Two of them, sons, are being groomed to take over. Meanwhile, Dunlevy says, "Mother, my sister and I have worked hard to show one and all that women can pick up the torch and carry it."

Members of the younger generation speak with special appreciation of parents who face up to the succession issue and start planning it early.

Richard M. "Rick" Beaudin, 31, president of suburban Detroit's Miles Fox, says "one of the things you've really got to give credit to my father for" is that he drew up a buy-and-sell agreement with his children as soon as Rick graduated from high school. "He wants to make sure the company stays with the family," says Rick.

By helping his son get a bank loan, Mickey Weiss has made it possible for Don to buy one of the WiseWay stores.

To begin the strategic planning process, Mike Kami advises, family business owners should collect their thoughts at 2 o'clock in the morning, when it is quiet and put down three or four words that are most important for the business or for themselves.

He says: "Maybe it's 'security' or maybe it's 'power.' Maybe it's 'lots of money' or 'give my son or daughter a career.' What is the absolutely most important?"

Suppose you choose "lots of money." Then, says Kami, "maybe the plan should be to make the company profitable short-term and sell it to a conglomerate. If you say you want power, then you may want to run a good company and use the money to run for political office."

Once you have made the big decisions, he says, "then, derivatively, you make the little decisions." But your decisions cannot be contradictory, he warns. For example, you must choose either "quality" or "cheap," because each calls for a completely different strategy.

Family businesses tend to change leadership only every 25 or 30 years, notes John Ward. He says this can be a problem in a world where non-family firms change leadership more often and where, studies indicate, the average business life cycle (the move from start-up to maturity to early decline), which once tended to last 30 or 40 years, has dropped to less than 20.

It is not feasible for a family business to change leadership every 10 or 15 years, Ward says. But today's rapid pace does mean that a family business can no longer wait from one generation to another to change its strategy. "We need to see family business leaders who are able to bring to fruition two or three new strategies to their business every generation," says Ward.

For some family business leaders, this may be difficult, if not impossible.

For others, it is the perfect situation. Ward finds that some people are not satisfied by building one business to a point where they are wealthy and socially accepted. They like to keep on charging, because they love the challenges of managing and of change — even more than they love the products and services they have created.

Perhaps that is what keeps Mickey Weiss going. Since he started WiseWay in the early 1940s, he has outlasted the national supermarket chains that came and went in his Indiana area. He has outlasted many of his independent grocery competitors. Now, with the help of his son, Don, he is preparing to outwit and outlast his discount competitors.

Mickey would never have been content to stop at age 45 and live comfortably on what he had built, says Don. "He is not a person who is happy with the status quo."

Whether new strategies are introduced by one high-energy business owner, by the younger generation or by top-notch non-family managers, they must be frequent enough and timely enough to meet the challenge of competition and change, experts say. At the same time, the leaders of enterprise must be deft enough to meet family needs.

Sums up Loyola University's Ward: "The future of any family business depends on two key factors. There must be an atmosphere that encourages personal growth and harmonious succession. And there must be effective management with both short- and long-range views."

Neither factor, he cautions, comes about by accident. They require planning, commitment and investment of money and time *now* to reap the benefit in the future.

Introduction

Most family-owned businesses struggle to survive beyond a single generation. Strategic planning—for both business and family—can help to strengthen the family enterprise and extend its lifespan. The author offers a six-step process toward implementing strategic planning: family commitment; business health assessment; identification of business alternatives; family and personal goal consideration; selection of business strategy; and assessment of family interests and capabilities.

The Special Role of Strategic Planning for Family Businesses

1988

By John L. Ward

Reprinted from **Family Business Review**, Summer 1988 No. 2 Vol. 1. San Francisco: Jossey-Bass, Inc. Used with permission of the publisher.

Strategic planning for family-owned businesses differs from planning for other types of companies largely because the family firm must incorporate family issues into its thinking.

Family concerns and preferences can influence the choice of business strategy and often make the family reluctant to embrace more formal goal-oriented discussions and decisions. Further, family considerations can limit the strategic aggressiveness of the family firm.

While our research revealed several reasons for this hesitation among family businesses, it also pointed to the critical need for strategic planning and the special benefits to those who undertake it.

That research consisted of three studies of strategy in family firms. Ward (1987) has detailed information on this research. In the first study, 200 privately owned firms that were at least five years old and that employed at least twenty people in 1924 were selected at random from the *Illinois Manufacturers Directory*. (The year 1924 was selected because 1919 was the earliest date of meaningful data.) Interviews at the surviving firms in 1984 documented the family ownership and leadership succession patterns and the evolution of the companies' strategies.

The second study compared the strategies and results of firms that were closely held or family-controlled with the strategies and results of public firms not controlled by families. For this study, we subdivided the PIMS data base (Strategic Planning Institute, Cambridge, Massachusetts) into 300 business units of privately controlled firms and 1,500 units of publicly held firms not controlled by families and studied their strategic profiles to determine the extent to which private companies selected different strategies, competed in different environments, and obtained different results. We explored hypotheses on the long-term orientation of private and family-controlled companies, the emphasis on quality, and so on.

In the third study, we recruited twenty family firms to apply the strategic planning framework to their own businesses. Each business assessed its industry, market, and environmental threats and opportunities. Each firm also assessed its strengths and weaknesses. As a result of these assessments, the businesses selected strategic alternatives that were most appropriate to their situations. Then, they described their current strategies. In nearly every case, their current strategies were less aggressive than their self-determined strategic potential. Last, each family identified the factors that it believed to have contributed to the conservativeness of its choices. The explanations included questions bearing on estate tax and personal financial liquidity and uncertainty over the eventual success of future family leaders.

With this paper, I hope to stimulate research exploring the special role of strategic planning in the family firm; to provide professionals who serve family businesses with some insights on how families in business approach strategic planning; and, most important, to outline a strategic planning framework for the family business. I want to encourage a formal approach to strategic planning. Many contend that strategic planning is merely one quick vehicle to "strategic thinking" — conscious regular

attention to key issues affecting the future of the business. They argue that formal planning is not necessary if "strategic thinking" is present, especially for smaller firms. I prescribe a formal process for three reasons: First, not all family businesses are small. Second, for most family businesses, strategic planning is the necessary groundwork for active "strategic thinking." Third, formal planning meetings and review help to promote the healthy, open, shared decision-making so often needed in the family enterprise. Brandt (1981) and Steiner (1969) are two good references on formal strategic planning.

This paper begins with an argument urging strategic planning in family businesses. Then, I define this process for families and identify the particular questions they must address. Next, I illustrate how family issues often influence the choice of business strategy, and I outline a strategic planning framework integrating family and business. I then suggest several unique competitive characteristics of family companies that can influence the choice of business strategy. I conclude by noting the reasons that I believe explain the reluctance of family business owners to plan and the additional benefits of planning specific to family businesses.

The Need for Strategic Planning

A family that perpetuates its company from generation to generation is rare. The study of 200 family-owned Illinois manufacturing firms found that only 13 percent lasted through the third generation. Of these, just a small minority—3 percent (N=3)—actually prospered, as evidenced by an increase of 10 percent or more in their employee base over the sixty years between 1924 and 1984. The results of this study are summarized in Figure 1.

Figure 1. Life Expectancy of 200 Successful Privately Owned Manufacturing Firms, 1924-1984

No longer surviving	80%
Same name still surviving as independent companies	20%
Of the 20% still independent:	
Sold to outsiders	5%
Went public and no longer controlled by the founding family	2%
Still owned by the same family as in 1924	13%
Of the 13% still owned by the same family:	
Grew significantly	3%
Did not grow	3%
Declined	7%
Of the 80% that did not survive:	
Ceased when 0 to 29 years old	33%
Ceased when 30 to 59 years old	36%
Ceased when 60 to 89 years old	16%
Ceased when 90 years old and over	15%

There are several possible explanations for the high failure rate. First, many family businesses are small and lack the staff and financial strength of larger companies. Second, the family itself can become a stumbling block as the rigors of business sharpen such problems as sibling rivalry and generational succession. Relatedly, the funding of family estate planning, retirement, divorce, and other personal projects often tempts business owners to harvest the company's profit rather than to reinvest it in additional business growth. Third and most important, many owners of family businesses lack a conceptual framework for assessing their company and planning for its future. They often do not take advantage of modern analytical tools that can help them to conquer the challenges of family business continuity. The most critical of these tools is planning—to guide both the company and the family.

My research noted one important pattern among the family firms that had not only survived but prospered: these firms had renewed or regenerated their business strategies several times over the sixty years studied. They added new strategies to their past ways of doing business as market and competitive pressures required response. For example, one food service distributor began in the early 1900s with its founder selling fresh fish to restaurants from a seaport's docks. With the advent of refrigeration technology, the company began using coolers to store and truck fresh and frozen fish and frozen vegetables. Next, the company enlarged its geographic range and added warehouse space for dry goods in order to compete more effectively. Now, the firm is exploring national markets and even export opportunities. Another successful firm began as a stationery supplier to businesses. Then, the firm added furniture to its line, which also moved the business into interior design services. Now, the company is opening multiple outlets for retail stationery, gifts and cards, and it is considering the acquisition of a discount office furniture retail store. The key point from these examples is that prospering firms plan actively and add new strategies to their businesses as their environments change. The successful firms in our research pursued change continually.

The research noted another important pattern that was related to the family: Often, the new business strategies came about as a result of changing family influences. In some cases, the new directions were an expression of a successor's interests. In other cases, the plans provided sibling partners with opportunities to "do their own thing" or to obtain some "healthy distance" from each other.

I believe that the best way both of addressing the changing environment and of coping with shifting family circumstances and needs is through a strategic planning process that incorporates both.

What is Planning?

The term *strategic planning* typically refers to the process of developing a business strategy for profitable growth. It is designed to create insights into the company and the environment in which the company operates. It provides a systematic way of asking key business questions.

Such an inquiry challenges past business practices and opens the way for choosing new alternatives. The result should be a well-prepared strategic plan—usually a written document—that spells out specific steps to improve customer satisfaction, increase profit, and revitalize and prepare the company for the next generation. The plan also states the chosen mission of the business, identifies the direction of future growth, and describes programs that can help to achieve that growth. It thus indicates ways in which the business can compete more effectively.

This approach to strategic planning does not assume that business growth occurs automatically. Instead, it assumes that growth occurs only if specific steps are taken to encourage it. The purpose of the planning process is to determine these steps by asking three questions: in what markets do we want to compete? how can we compete effectively in those markets? and how aggressively do we want to reinvest our corporate and family resources?

The approach advocated here is similar to the sort of strategic planning practiced by most companies. However, the family business must consider the other dimension: the preparation not only of a business strategic plan but of a family strategic plan. The family plan spells out long-term personal and professional goals for family members. It also establishes a process whereby family goals and issues can be explored at regular intervals.

Family strategic planning addresses four questions: *First,* why is the family committed to perpetuating the business? For example, why not sell the company? What benefits does the family see in keeping the business? *Second*, how does the family see itself and the company in years ahead? Does the family envision that many family members will be active in the firm, or will they be passive owners? Does the family see the business creating spin-off ventures for family members? *Third*, how will the family build or maintain strong relationships, resolve conflicts and work for harmony? How will the family and the business resolve questions of family compensation? *Fourth*, what are the specific steps required to accomplish the family's personal and professional goals each year? Is this the year to discuss and establish rules, such as expecting outside work experience? Will the family begin regular "family fun" activities, such as group vacations?

Answers to these questions are important, because in a family enterprise they shape business strategy in ways that other companies do not need to consider. Should family members in the company work together in one business and location or apart in separate businesses and locations? How much money does the family need from the company? Are older family members confident that their sons and daughters can run the company well? In its strategy, the company's plan must reflect these considerations.

This weaving together of business and family plans represents a special challenge for the family business, because it means that the business and the family plans are highly interdependent. The business plan requires the family to determine the extent of its commitment to the company. That commitment depends on the prospects for the business that the planning process reveals. As a result, the family cannot separate strategic business planning from family strategic planning. It must undertake

both in a connected and simultaneous way.

Realizing the Company's Full Potential

Some owners resist the idea of combining family with business. They believe that business decisions are best and most cleanly made when the decision makers ignore the personal interests of the family. But, those who subscribe to this school of thought should consider the following: In 1982, we studied twenty family concerns representing a variety of industries and locales that were willing to share their planning process with us. The owners were asked to assess their companies through a comprehensive, strategic planning process. Much to their surprise, the majority of the business owners discovered that they were performing below their strategic potential. That is, they were pursuing strategies less ambitious than their own business assessments would justify.

For example, a company supplying food vending machines and products to businesses was the leader in its market. It was very profitable, and it faced no particular competitive or technological threats. Yet, for several years the firm had been plodding along doing nothing different except refining operational procedures, such as developing sales commission systems and computer programs that provided more detailed information on delivery and repairs. Although the opportunities for growth —in new cities, in cafeteria food service, in new product lines, and other areas— were bountiful, the company did not have a vision. The stagnation came from wanting to limit the possibility of dispute among the three brother owners, to wait until the plans and capabilities of the next generation were clear, and to avoid a business spending commitment while their own personal financial plans were unaddressed.

Owners offered two explanations for the disparity between their strategic potential and their actual—less ambitious—strategic choices. First, they were unsure of the way in which family members might influence their businesses. For example, they did not know whether all members would want to work together under a single roof or whether they would prefer to work apart in autonomous business divisions. They did not know whether those in the business would have to provide financially for those outside the business. They did not know whether they as parents might wish to set cash aside for the new ventures of entrepreneurially-minded offspring.

Second, owners were unsure of their own commitment to the company's future. They were unsure because they had not explored or settled such key issues as the amount of money available for new projects or the amount of managerial talent that potential successors possessed. As a result of these uncertainties—all related to their families—the owners selected more cautious, conservative business strategies. They did this despite self-avowed confidence in the underlying strengths of their companies.

This study demonstrates that family issues strongly influence the choice of business strategy in a family business. Family issues shape business judgement whether the fact that they do is formally recognized or not.

How Planning Begins

When a family business faces almost any setback, a specialist in strategic planning may well be called in. The problem can be characterized in such terms as these: "We're not as innovative as we should be." "We're losing profitability." "We're wasting a lot of energy debating where we should be going." The first efforts of the planner, as he or she begins to intervene, are usually to profile the current situation, using financial analysis or competitive analysis or customer analysis, and to interview the senior managers on what they see as the key strategic issues facing the firm.

The first entry into the business can offer insights on its health and aggressiveness. The interviews often uncover all sorts of family business issues, such as uncertainty about succession, rivalries among family members, and discrepancies between position and performance.

In any case, the planner or consultant looks for opportunities to generate enthusiasm about the planning process. The hesitancy to undertake strategic planning often results from fear that it is an unfamiliar process and that it may reveal confidential data, expose weak management communication practices, and surface past errors and current family issues. The planner is asked to propose a process that gets strategic planning going.

Step One: The Commitment of Family

In a family business, the ideal starting point for the planning process is the family itself. The first step is for the family to establish its level of commitment to the future of the business and to planning as a way of securing that future. Is the family willing to sacrifice short-term material gains in order to invest money in the company? Will family members spend the time it takes to build a business? Can they work together? Do offspring have the necessary qualities of leadership? Are parents willing to let go of the company when the time comes?

Figure 2. The Interdependence of Family and Business Planning

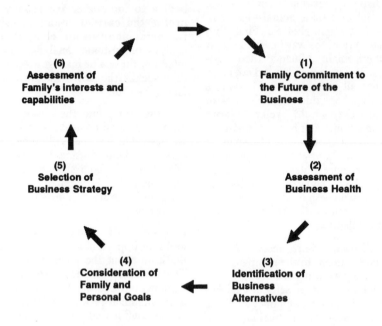

If family members reach a consensus on these issues, they can write a preliminary statement of commitment. Such a statement might say, "We are fundamentally interested in the long-term future of this business. We want this business to last forever. And, we will do what it takes to accomplish that!" Whatever the resolve and rationale, the family's statement of commitment is a necessary first step. As Figure 2 shows, the rest of the planning process flows from this commitment.

Step Two: Assessing the Firm's Business Health

Next to the family's commitment, the foundation for planning lies in a financial and market analysis of the business. Such an analysis is common in firms that practice strategic planning. It shows whether the company is gaining or losing market share, using cash efficiently or inefficiently, and increasing or decreasing its productivity. Such analysis has an additional significance for the family business. Among other uses, it reveals whether the family is reinvesting sufficiently in the business to help ensure a vital future or whether it is financing personal needs at the expense of the company.

Natural forces within the family business probably encourage disinvestment from the business over time. So-called excess cash from the business is often used to reward the family for years of sacrifice with an improved standard of living. Or, it is used to meet such perceived needs as retirement and inheritances or to retire debt or reward loyal employees.

Most successful families are unaware of the damage done by these financial "harvesting" practices. They assume that all is well if profit is strong and sales are rising. They think they can afford high levels of personal spending. Yet, successful businesses must have a certain amount of reinvestment if they are to continue to grow. In fact, the longer family members want the business to live and the more prosperity they want to enjoy in the years ahead, the higher their rate of current reinvestment must be. Families that spend the company's profit elsewhere set in motion forces that silently weaken the firm, often in ways that will not show up on the bottom line for years. At that point, it may be too late to reinvest and turn the company around.

Financial analyses uncover potential soft spots. They illustrate just how much money is going into such areas as family bonuses and how much is being plowed back into the enterprise. The most important of these analyses figures the rate of reinvestment in the business.

Approaches to the calculation of rate of reinvestment range from figuring debt-to-equity ratios to judging the number of strategic experiments under way. One of the most useful approaches compares the return to the owner with the return to the business. This approach figures family salaries, bonuses, and perquisites as a percentage of the total sum available for future business opportunities. That sum is typically measured by net income before taxes.

To figure the percentage, owners divide family salaries plus perquisites by that sum. Family salary and perquisites should usually be no more than 33 percent to 50 percent of operating income for midsize companies with more than twenty employees. If the figure is significantly higher, the family is milking the business for short-term; gain. It is withdrawing more funds than public companies typically pay out in dividends to their shareholders.

To be sure, milking or harvesting the business may be desirable for some families. Perhaps a family has concluded that the future of the company is dim or even hopeless for reasons beyond its control. If that is the case and the family still wants to find a long-term, prosperous role for itself in business, the family should harvest profit and seek other ventures in which its members can invest. But, if the family has concluded that its firm is a satisfactory investment, the harvesting of profit clearly compromises the future vitality of the family business.

Step Three: Identification of Business Alternatives

The next step is to identify possible business alternatives; enter new geographical areas, increase the quality of service, hire strong managers to generate sales or improve productivity, and so on. At this stage, family businesses can consider some of their possible uniquenesses or advantages.

Truly clever strategies capitalize on market insights and the relative competitive strengths that the individual business enjoys. Good family businesses will share some strengths by the very fact that they are family businesses. The following insights were supported by the study that compared the strategies and performance of nearly

300 family companies with the strategies and performance of 1,500 public companies.

Many family firms enjoy the benefits of a long-term orientation. They rarely have outside shareholders to whom they must justify quarterly performance in sales and earnings; no stock market will judge them harshly if they increase expenses for worthwhile strategies. They can afford to focus their vision on the future. They also tend to have a flexible organization, with fewer bureaucratic layers that can stall a needed market response. The company's motivation for quality, born of having the family's own name on the door or in the board room, often produces quick service and top-notch products. The company is adaptable to smaller markets. It is often willing to invest in people. And, if the family provides a unified culture at the top of the organization, it becomes easier to establish business direction and to get everyone pulling together in that direction. Clear direction increases a company's chances of success.

The strengths just listed have clear implications for the strategic direction of any family business. The strategies that are suitable to these particular strengths include exploiting smaller markets, market niches, ethnic or regional markets, declining or more mature markets that yield profit through personal effort, and emerging markets. Smaller companies can also emphasize craftsmanship or customized services or products.

These strategic directions suggest that the smaller family business does best by seeking out the "hidden customer" - the buyer whom others have somehow overlooked or ignored. Of course, big and small companies alike desire that customer. But, the family business has some specific advantages that can help it to win even when it competes with companies that have larger staffs, more financial clout, or both. Its very smallness gives it the ability to respond quickly. The personal involvement of the owner tends to seal the loyalty of employees and customers alike. And, if it is physically close to its market, there is the potential for such extra services as emergency delivery and personal tracking of customers' tastes.

These possibilities also suggest some relative weaknesses of the smaller family business, such as limited access to large amounts of capital, naivete of management, or inattention to cost-cutting measures. In the business strategic planning process, I encourage attention to the relative strengths and weaknesses of family ownership. Explicit recognition of these characteristics should improve the choice of strategy.

Reluctance of Family Business Owners to Plan

The planning process outlined in this paper often seems threatening to business owners. Many think of planning as a straitjacket that will constrain their instinctive survival skills and limit business flexibility. The nature of the planning process also requires these independently minded business owners to share decisions – and private financial statements – with others in the company. These statements represent power and information that many owners would rather keep to themselves.

Others object to planning because they think the future is too uncertain to make the effort worthwhile. Rapidly changing markets, an unpredictable economy, and the unclear career interests of offspring are just a few of the unsettled issues that they foresee.

Family Business Sourcebook

Perhaps the greatest threat is the association of planning with change. This association seems to create nearly unresolvable dilemmas, because change requires compromises. For example, satisfying the demands of customers for a new product may require the business to divert money from successful projects that have a guaranteed return to experimental activities whose return is unknown. Executing the changes suggested by planning also often requires business owners to tailor their products to specific customers in specific markets. Such tailoring destroys the "Be All Things to All Customers" principle that guides so many businesses in their early years, a principle that is especially attractive to the business owner who sees a variety of customers and products as a way of diversifying risk from any one category of product or customer.

Executives in non-family businesses are often exposed to more businesses over time, and they may have more experience with sophisticated planning systems. More important, they are less likely to see the stability of the business as critical to the preservation of their own family wealth and well-being. In any case, my experience suggests that the mature business owner who owes his or her personal wealth and life-style to a strategy that he or she has built or designed is reluctant to change the successful formula.

Benefits of Planning

As we have seen, formal planning helps to prevent family businesses from "undershooting" their strategic potential by articulating assumptions and perceptions. Planning encourages commitment from family members as a part of the process. It provides techniques that help managers to assess the company's rate of reinvestment and assure that the business is retaining sufficient cash for a solid future.

The very nature of planning requires a variety of people to be involved. Those who report directly to the chief executive will contribute to the business plan. Members of the immediate, and often, the extended family will be involved in the family strategic plan. As a result, the planning process increases business knowledge throughout the company and the family and provides outstanding training for offspring, who are the successors and future leaders of the company.

Planning provides one other key benefit. Because it requires the participants to answer tough questions about competition and reinvestment, the planning process helps all managers and family members to develop a common understanding—that is, the same assumptions—about the world in which the company operates. Consequently, at the very least, business planning should encompass everyone who reports to the business owner and every family member with a key management role in the present or future.

Such a common undertaking is critical, because conflict in family businesses is often caused by differences in basic assumptions of values, especially among family members involved in guiding the business's direction. For example, consider the father and son who are arguing about whether to install up-to-date manufacturing equipment. The argument may be less about the value of technology than it is about the relative value of change and consistency. The young often argue for change; the old, for the status quo. Typically, they will not attempt a straightforward resolution of such underlying differences. Instead, they may begin to argue about

197

personalities or management styles. Such discussions can easily cause emotional pain. The original objective — to decide whether or not to install new equipment — is forgotten.

The Special Role of Personal Values and Family Communications

Even within families, values are bound to vary. They shape the choice of goals, modify the ability to tolerate risk, and influence ideas about teaching and learning. They show up in family decisions that in turn mold business strategies and the approach to strategic planning. How much money does the family need for security? The answer to this question affects the level of investment in a business strategy. To what degree should family differences be openly discussed and tolerated? The answer to this question affects the ability to debate business facts and perceptions. How close should family relationships be? The answer to this question affects decisions on geographic expansion.

All these questions are critical examples of how family factors influence the choice of strategy in a family business. Answering these questions can lead to conflict. Understanding that there is no absolute right or wrong in many of these issues is one step toward compromise. Strategic planning is a valuable tool that helps to build such qualities as the ability to work toward consensus, team management, and shared decision-making. It identifies the fundamental business and family assumptions in a constructive way.

Strategic planning strengthens the ability to share decisions and value orientations. Both are critical requirements for success in perpetuating the family business. So, in addition to providing a framework for evaluation and choice of a business direction and family goals, strategic planning is a process that prompts healthy communication on critical family business issues.

Conclusion

To keep a family business moving forward requires a spirit of reinvestment; a confident eagerness to commit funds for the sake of future family benefits. Motivating the family requires a compelling vision — a commitment to a family dream — that everyone shares. When such a commitment has been made, the family can aggressively invest family funds in a business strategy.

There are many challenges to sustaining a family's emotional investment in an enterprise from generation to generation. Deliberate strategic planning is one key to success. It helps to create motivation that can sustain the family and business through inevitable differences in individual perspectives. Good planning releases energy that the family can use to fulfill the dream of many family businesses: creating and sustaining a healthy family enterprise for the next generation.

The insights gained from the three studies outlined at the start of this paper and from personal experience suggest how strategic planning in the family business differs from planning in non-family business. It is clear that business and family strategic planning promote continuity in family businesses.

References

Brandt, S. C. *Strategic Planning in Emerging Companies*. Reading, Mass.: Addison-Wesley, 1981.

Steiner, G. S. *Top Management Planning.* Ontario: Collier-Macmillan Canada, 1969.

Ward, J. L. *Keeping the Family Business Health: How to Plan for Continuing Growth, Profitability, and Family Leadership.* San Francisco: Jossey-Bass, 1987.

Introduction

No small business is easy to manage, and this is especially true in a small family business. It is subject to all the problems that beset small companies, plus those that can, and often do, arise when relatives try to work together.

The family member who is charged with managing the company has to work at initiating and maintaining sound management practices. By describing what is to be done and under what circumstances such practices help prevent some of the confusion and conflicts that may be perpetuated by self-centered family members. Such relatives sometimes regard the company as existing primarily to satisfy their desires.

The questions in this checklist are designed to help chief executive officers to review the management practices of their small family companies. The comments that follow each question are intended to stimulate thought rather than to include the many and various aspects suggested by the question.

Management Checklist for a
Family Business
1976

By Benjamin M. Becker
and Fred Tillman

Originally published as a U. S. Small Business Administration "Management Aid," 1976.

Is executive time used on high priority tasks?

Yes ☐   No ☐

The time of the owner-manager is one of the most valuable assets of a small business. It should not be dribbled away in routine tasks that can be done as well, if not better, by other employees. Never lose sight of the fact that you, as owner-manager, have to make the judgments that will determine the success of your business. You may want to run a check on how your time is used. You can do so by keeping a log for the next several weeks. On a calendar memorandum pad jot down what you do in half hour or hour blocks. Then review your notes against the questions: Was my time spent on management tasks such as reviewing last week's sales figures and noting areas for improvement? Or did I let it dribble away on routine tasks such as opening the mail and sorting bills of lading? You may want to ask your key personnel to run the same sort of check on their time.

Do you set goals and objectives?
Yes ☐   No ☐

Goals and objectives help a small company to keep headed toward profits. Goals and objectives should be specific and realistic. In addition they should be measurable, time phased, and written. In getting a list of your goals and objectives start by writing them out for your present successful operations. Objectives that are written out in straight-forward language provide a basis for actions by your key personnel. For example, state that you will sell a certain number of units this year rather than saying you will increase sales.

Do you have written policies?
Yes ☐   No ☐

Flag this question and return to it later. Working through this checklist should suggest changes that may be needed if you have written policies. By the same token, your review of your business will provide input for writing out policies if there are none in writing.

Is planning done to achieve these goals and objectives?
Yes ☐   No ☐

In a sense, planning is forecasting. An objective, for example, for next year might be to increase your net profit after taxes. To plan for it you need to forecast sales volume, production of finished goods inventory, raw materials requirements, and all the other elements connected with producing products and selling them. Moreover, while planning your forecasts, you will want to make provision for watching costs, including selling expenses. If there are key employees who can provide input into the planning, ask

them to become involved in that process.

Do you test or check the reality of your goals and plans with others?
Yes ☐   No ☐

Outside advisers may spot "bugs" that you and your people did not catch in the press of working through the details of goal setting and planning.

Are operations reviewed on a regular basis with the objective of reducing costs?
Yes ☐   No ☐

Costs must be kept in line for a profitable operations. Review operations periodically such as weekly or monthly, to insure that overtime is not excessive, for example. And what about quality product acceptance by customers? Costs may be excessive because of obsolete methods of machinery that has seen its best days. And what about plant layout or materials flow? Can changes be made that will save time and materials? Determine the frequency of your reviews for the various types of operations and place a tickler on your calendar to remind you of these review dates.

Are products reviewed regularly with the objective of improving them?
Yes ☐   No ☐

Products as your customers benefit from them are the key to repeat sales. A regular review of your products helps to keep them up to the expectation of your customers. Feedback from customers can be useful here. To reduce costs sometimes a product can be modified without sacrificing use and quality. If product obsolescence is a hazard, what plans are being made to substitute new products as existing ones become obsolete?

Do you ask outside advisors for their opinions and suggestions on products and operation procedures?
Yes ☐   No ☐

Outside persons, such as friends in non-competing lines of business and management personnel from local colleges and universities can help you see the facts about your products and operating procedures. They can provide a fresh viewpoint – the viewpoint of persons who are not involved in the products and operations as are you and your key personnel. The suggestions and counsel from a local management consultant may provide benefits far in excess of his or her cost. In this area some small companies set up a board of directors to satisfy the law concerning small corporations. But that is the end of it. Members of the board are not used for their knowledge and skill in business. They can make valuable contributions and the owner-manager should use all possible opportunities for getting such concerned opinions about the various phases of the company.

Are marketing and distribution policies and procedures reviewed periodically?
Yes ☐   No ☐

The best made product in the world can run into trouble if marketing and distribution policies and procedures are not right for it. Periodical checks can help you to be aware of changes that may be taking place in the channels through which you distribute. One approach is to check your competition; does it seem to be changing channels and policies? Can you still meet the requirements of your customers by

using your traditional channels of distribution?

Are there periodic reviews of profit and loss statements and other financial reports?
Yes ☐   No ☐

In these reviews you can compare your operating ratios to those for your industry. It is also helpful to review your cash flow projections to see what, if any, changes are needed in your financial planning.

Do you have an organization chart?
Yes ☐   No ☐

You may need only a simple organization chart to show accountability and to establish a chain of command. In a family business, accountability and chain of command should be spelled out so that the one who is the chief executive of the company has the "mandate" he or she needs for managing.

Do you use job descriptions for your key personnel?
Yes ☐   No ☐

When you and your key personnel write descriptions for their jobs, you and they have a clear understanding of what is to be done and by whom. Such an understanding is essential in any small business but especially critical when relatives are involved. Spelling out duties may not prevent conflicts with you and an in-law, but such detail can help you resolve misunderstandings, if and when they occur. In addition, when, and if a key person leaves, the job description is a helpful tool in recruiting and training a replacement.

Do you periodically compare performance of key personnel with their job descriptions?

Yes □   No □

Periodical comparison of performance helps your key personnel to be efficient. It also helps to pinpoint weak spots for you and them to work on for improvement.

Do you provide opportunities for key personnel to grow?

Yes □   No □

Your aim should be to help key personnel stay alert to new and more efficient ways to do things. Conferences, seminars, and workshops which trade associations and agencies, such as the Small Business Administration, sponsor can help key personnel to grow in their management skills and outlook. Rotating job assignments is a way to make key personnel aware of the problems that their counterparts face. Include in your budget an amount that can be spent during the year for personnel training and education.

Do you face the issue when key personnel stop growing?

Yes □   No □

Some owner-managers try to avoid the unpleasant task of facing the fact that a key person has stopped growing. It may be the result of not matching personnel and the job. Or in some family businesses, the cousin or brother-in-law never was interested in personal growth or any aspects of management. If there is little or nothing you can do about such a mismatch, face it and don't waste time trying to do the impossible. On the other hand outside problems may be crowding in on the key person. Once you know why he or she stopped growing, you can determine what needs to be done. In some cases, additional training is the answer. In other cases, the motivation that results from broadened job responsibilities resolves the problem.

Are there policies and plans for motivating employees?

Yes □   No □

Working through others is by no means an easy task. First of all, people are not puppets that can be moved by strings. Life may be a stage, as the poet said, but most people in small business are reluctant to submit to directors. Look for ways — good communications, respect for their viewpoint, incentive pay, and so on — to encourage people to *want* to do what you *need* them to do as employees in your company.

Do you have adequate employee benefit plan?

Yes □   No □

This includes life and health insurance, major medical, and pension. Benefit plans often are necessary to meet competition for skilled employees. Substantial plans can help to hold non-family key individuals in a family-owned business.

Do you have key personnel insurance on yourself and is your family protected against your untimely passing?

Yes □   No □

If these precautions are not taken, your death could result in the rapid dissolution of the business.

Is there lack of communication among key personnel?

Yes ☐   No ☐

The routine passing of information among you and your key personnel may be all that you want it to be. But what about disagreement? Do key personnel refrain from expressing disagreement with you? Good communications should provide a forum for exchanging ideas and for airing differences of opinion. Possible an early morning meeting once a week with you and your key personnel would provide a forum for exchanging ideas.

Does your recordkeeping system present a realistic picture of your business? Is this the same type of recordkeeping system that other companies in your industry commonly use?

Yes ☐   No ☐

Appropriate records should give the owner-manager answers to questions such as: Is there sufficient cash to operate the business? To pay back the bank? To pay taxes? Is too much capital tied up in inventory? Are accounts receivable being collected promptly? Bankers and other lenders need a realistic picture. Corporate records, if your company is a corporation, should be up-to-date including corporate minutes and record books. In checking out your recordkeeping, keep in mind that a poor system can result in excessive and meaningless information.

Do you seek legal and financial advice on major transactions?

Yes ☐   No ☐

The fine print in contracts causes trouble for some small business owners. They did not realize until it was too late what they had agreed to do. Legal and financial advice at the appropriate time can help the owner-manager to comprehend the full scope of his company's contractual obligations and allow time to make decisions based on facts rather than assumptions. Whenever possible use your standardized contract in making contractual obligations.

Do you document informal agreements with customers, suppliers and others?

Yes ☐   No ☐

"He's as good as his word," is a fine attitude to have about customers, suppliers, and others with whom you work on a daily basis. But think a moment; in being as "good as your word," how often do you forget? Memory slips. A note to yourself, or to a supplier to confirm a telephone conversation for example, helps both of you to recall what you agreed, or did not agree upon, and prevents misunderstanding and hard feeling. Keep dated copies of all correspondence you send out. At some later period these copies could be invaluable.

Do you plan your major financial decisions with the help of your accountant, lawyer, and other tax advisers?

Yes ☐   No ☐

An owner-manager cannot ignore the impact of Federal and State income taxes, as well as other taxes, on his business. He should plan his major financial decisions with the help of his accountant, lawyer, and other tax advisers.

Do your plans include self-development projects for yourself?

Yes ☐   No ☐

Sometimes an owner-manager sets up training for everyone in his company except himself. Because conditions change so rapidly he should set aside some time for activities that will help him to keep abreast of his industry and the economic world in which his company operates. Your trade association should be a source about meetings, conferences, and seminars which you can use in such a program for yourself.

Are there plans for succession in the event of the untimely death of the family member who manages the company?

Yes ☐   No ☐

The successor may not be the same person who substitutes when the chief executive officer is sick or on vacation.

Whether the successor is a family member or a nonfamily employee, the business should make the transition smoother when the family agrees upon a successor ahead of time. Such agreement is necessary if the business is to bear the expense of grooming the successor.

Chapter 4

Financial Dimensions

While the human and relational dimensions of family businesses get tremendous attention, they are businesses after all. As businesses, their financial dimensions are of extreme importance. Financial performance of family firms, financial planning in them, and the financial perspectives of significant entities outside the business—like the bank or the IRS—are the themes of some articles contained in this *Sourcebook* chapter.

Other articles look at financial options available to owners of family businesses such as employee ownership or going public. Ideally, however, family business owners want to maintain ownership in the family. Under such circumstances, the desire is to transfer the business from one generation to the next in a manner most positive and least injurious to the family and the business. This goal requires estate planning that is both sensitive and smart.

Introduction

When the family keeps a close eye on the business, the business performs better. Forbes research shows that common sense axiom holds for large, publicly traded companies as well as mom-and-pops. Considering 50 randomly selected companies with significant family ownership, the study shows that family businesses outperform their industry groups by a rate of nearly two-to-one.

All in the Family
1983

By Paul Bornstein

Did you ever notice that the most successful restaurants usually seem to be those where the owner is always around? Sure, it's one thing to watch the chef and the headwaiter, and another to run a company with sales of hundreds of millions. But we wondered if it pays to invest in large corporations where a family owns a big chunk of stock and is actively involved in management.

To answer that question, we set up a simple test. First, we searched corporate records to find 50 firms in which one family or individual owned or controlled at least 30 percent of the common stock. Then we looked at the stock performance of these companies over the past 10 1/2 years. We then compared this individual company performance with the performance of the relevant industry group as represented by the Media General Industrial Stock Indices.

The results are encouraging for all-in-the-family investors. From our random sample we found that it can indeed pay to buy firms where the owners are on hand and calling the shots. In fact, we discovered that, of the 50 companies on our list, 31 did better than their industry groups, while only 19 didn't do as well.

In terms of absolute gains, the results are particularly impressive at Bruno's, a food store chain; Flightsafety International, a firm offering high-technology training services; Manor Care, which runs nursing homes; and Wang Labs, manufacturer of computers and word processors. Since the end of 1972, the stock of each of these firms has gained more than 2,000 percent.

The amount of control, however, doesn't seem to be closely correlated with price movement. The Coors family has 100 percent voting control but

Where the owners watch the store

Here is a list of 50 companies, all owned 30% or more by members of one family. Over the past 10 1/2 years, 31 have outperformed their industry groups, and the results for many have been quite good. The other 19 haven't done as well. But there is always a chance for new blood.

Company/Industry	Name of family	% control or stock ownership	Recent price	—Stock Performance— company since 12/29/72	industry Index since 12/29/72	Relative movement company vs industry
Adams Drug/retail drug stores	Salmanson	69.9%	21 1/2	-9.5%	78.1%	0.51
HF Ahmanson/savings and loan	Ahmanson	70.1[1]	34	11.5	69.6	0.66
Air Express Int'l/freight handling and shipping	Mailman	37.7	13	205.9	73.7	1.76
Bandag/rubber and plastic	Carver	46.2[2]	54 7/8	56.8	26.8	1.24
Bruno's/retail food stores	Bruno	42.0[2]	20 1/8	2376.9	190.0	8.54
Carter-Wallace/drugs	Hoyt	51.4	24 1/8	-9.0	34.5	0.68
Adolph Coors/distillers and brewers	Coors	100.0[2]	25 1/8	-18.5	93.8	0.42
Cox Communications/broadcasting	Cox	40.8	47 1/4	426.8	240.2	1.55
Dollar General/retail – discount	Turner	44.2	33 1/2	570.0	78.1	3.76
Far West Financial/savings and loan	Belzberg	67.3	27 5/8	96.7	69.6	1.16
First Charter Fin'l/savings and loan	Taper	34.7	33 1/4	23.7	69.6	0.73
First City Properties/real estate investments	Belzberg	69.0	9 1/4	-62.5	-20.6	0.47
Flightsafety Int'l/personal services	Ueltschi	38.8	32 7/8	2112.3	86.2	11.88
Hechinger/retail	Hechinger/ England	65.3	27 1/4	967.8	218.3	3.35
Hillenbrand Inds/health	Hillenbrand	63.0	46 1/4	180.3	90.8	1.47
Illinois Tool Works/machinery – light equip	Smith	42.4	54	61.8	89.4	0.85
Lance/food, pkgd goods	Van Every	43.8	28 1/2	78.1	38.9	1.28
Lawson Products/retail	Port	32.9	35 3/4	133.2	218.3	0.73
Longs Drug Stores/retail drug stores	Long	33.7	46 3/4	19.1	78.1	0.67
Lukens Steel/metals – iron and steel	Huston	34.0	14 1/4	-4.6	114.4	0.44
Manor Care/health services	Bainum	43.9	22 1/2	3016.3	90.8	16.33
Mary Kay Cosmetics/cosmetics	Kay	34.6	31 3/4	669.7	-47.2	14.58
Meredith/publishing	Meredith	44.0[4]	38 3/4	481.3	261.4	1.61
MITE/machinery – light	Blinken	35.7[2]	35 1/2	735.3	89.4	4.41
Molex/electronics	Krehbiel	50.4	70 1/2	693.1	216.1	2.51
NCH Corp/chemicals	Levy	47.5	19	-56.3	52.1	0.29

Where the owners watch the store (continued)

Company/Industry	Name of family	% control or stock ownership	Recent price	Stock Performance— company since 12/29/72	Industry Index since 12/29/72	Relative movement company vs Industry
AC Nielsen/business services	Nielsen	55.7	35 3/4	108.8	94.2	1.08
Nordstrom/retail apparel	Nordstrom	52.0	42 1/4	805.4	298.8	2.27
Northwestern Steel& Wire/ iron/steel	Dillon	63.1[2]	24	-30.4	114.4	0.32
Omark Inds/machinery--light equip.	Gray	30.0	26 3/8	358.7	89.4	2.42
Playboy Enterprises/publishing	Hefner	67.1	11 5/8	-36.7	261.4	0.18
Petrie Stores/retail – apparel	Petrie	63.2	36 7/8	41.8	298.8	2.27
Premier Indl/automotive	Mandel	62.3	34 1/4	608.6	-5.1	7.47
Presley Cos/building, building materials	Presley	34.9	20	221.5	62.9	1.97
Roadway Services/freight handling, shipping	Roush	36.4[1]	64 1/2	387.9	73.7	2/81
AH Robins/drugs	Robins	36.3	25 1/2	-32.4	34.5	0.50
GD Searle/drugs	Searle	32.0[1]	48 1/8	40.9	34.5	1.05
Shapell Inds/building, building materials	Shapell	44.6	47 3/8	129.7	62.9	1.41
Standard Register/business services	Sherman	76.0[2]	32 1/2	473.5	94.2	2.95
Times Mirror/publishing	Chandler	31.2[1]	76	196.6	261.4	0.82
Tyson Foods/food – meat and dairy	Tyson	61.4	11 3/4	735.6	77.6	4.70
United Inns/hotels, motels	Cockroft	35.2	32	4.1	86.3	0.56
Vermont American/machinery/machinery – light equip	Thomas	44.9	20 1/2	531.0	89.4	3.33
Wang Labs/business data processing	Wang	40.2[2]	39 1/8	2714.8	66.8	16.88
Wean United/machinery – heavy	Wean	50.0[1]	7 3/4	82.4	51.3	1.21
Weis Markets/retail food stores	Weis	73.0	40	583.5	190.0	2.36
Winn-Dixie Stores/retail food stores	Davis	53.4[1]	56	78.8	190.0	0.62
Jack Winter/textiles – apparel	Winter	59.0	11 1/8	156.7	211.6	0.82
Wometco Enterprises/broadcasting	Wolfson	36.0	36 1/4	482.8	240.2	1.71

[1] Including related trusts. [2] Voting control. [3] Less than ten years. [4] Including related Bohen family. [5] Including market value of Lanier Business Products.

Source: Media General; Standard & Poor's.

Coors shares went flat during the period covered by our analysis. Since this brewer went public in 1975, the stock has declined 18.5 percent, vs. a 93.8 percent gain for Media General's brewing and distilling industry. On the other hand, Omark Industries, with the smallest amount of owner control in the table below, performed much better than Media General's light equipment industry group, 358.7 percent vs. 89.4 percent.

The last column in the table relates stock performance to industry performance. It indicates how a dollar invested in the individual company would compare with a dollar invested in a cross section of companies in its industry.

Look, for example, at Mary Kay Cosmetics, controlled by Mary Kay and her son. A dollar invested in Mary Kay over the 10 1/2 year period outperformed a dollar investment in the Media General cosmetic industry group by almost a 14.6-to-1 margin. Mary Kay's stock appreciated 669.7 percent, while the cosmetic industry declined 47.2 percent.

Of course, not all family-owned outfits were able to outshine their peers. Hugh Hefner's Playboy Enterprises didn't do well for investors. While publishing stocks gained 261.4 percent, Playboy lost 36.7 percent. NCH Corp., run by the Levy family, lost 56.3 percent, while the index for the chemical group was up 52.1 percent. And Northwestern Steel & Wire, 63.1 percent owned by the Dillon family, was also a poor performer.

There is another potential negative for investors in family-controlled businesses. Takeovers are difficult, if not impossible, without at least some cooperation from the family shareholders. That isn't to say that these companies are invulnerable to merger activity. Tax or estate considerations, family squabbles or an offer that is simply too good to refuse can sometimes put a family-owned firm on the block.

The Taper family, for example, which has a one-third interest in First Charter Financial, a savings and loan association, has agreed to merge with Financial Corp. of America. But Air Express International apparently won't be going to the altar with Consolidated Freightways because of a union veto—even though J.L. Mailman, who holds 37.7 percent of the firm's stock, apparently favored the sale.

The Belzberg family controls two of the companies in our table but, so far, the Belzbergs have been better at banking than at real estate. Far West Financial, a savings and loan, has gone up 96.7 percent since 1972, but First City Properties declined 62.5 percent in that same period.

Family ownership, of course, is no guarantee that a company will outperform others in its industry. But when the principals have a major part of their personal fortunes at stake, their best interests and those of company shareholders are often one and the same. Over the period we examined, family-owned companies outperformed their industry groups by a ratio of nearly two-to-one. Those are the kind of odds we like.

Introduction

Planning for long-term business success and achieving it means that the owners of private companies must devote a year or more to determining their objectives for the firm, for themselves (whether active or inactive in the business), and for key managers and employees. Only in this way can the business be kept independent and passed to capable owners and managers. Five areas are discussed that owners must carefully evaluate, develop plans for, and coordinate if the business is to be financially rewarding to them and their families or partners. The five areas are: capital, control, bringing in the next generation of leaders, reaping rewards, and estate planning.

A Question for Business Owners: "Are You Prepared for Success?"
1982

By Peter Moffitt

Reprinted by permission of SAM Advanced Management Journal, Autumn 1982. Copyright ©SAM Advanced Management Journal 1982; all rights reserved.

In spite of the present difficult economic climate, many owners and CEOs of private companies who are now deeply involved in the problems of business survival are also preparing for long-term business success.

An independent businessman, who had built a successful $25 million company in which he had hoped his two sons would be actively involved, stated the problem this way: "At 68, I am too old to manage this company by myself. I built it for the children, and none of them wants to work here. It's too small to go public, and I don't want to sell because I have nothing else to do. I can't afford to pay gift taxes so I can't give it away, and I don't dare die owning 100 percent of the company. Tell me what I should do now."

The reader will undoubtedly recognize elements that concern owners of all closely held businesses today. Some owners plan for business success and achieve it, and at the same time they arrange their personal finances so that they may pass the business on to their children and others without unnecessary taxation or interference from outside shareholders. However, many do not devote sufficient time to study all facets of the problems (both business and personal) that arise from being very successful in their private companies.

A son of deceased owner recently merged his $30 million manufacturing business with a larger company at $6.50 per share although the stock had been valued at $10.00 per share in his parents' estates ten years earlier and the company had later gone public at $15.00 per share. What went wrong?

First, the father had correctly estimated that his estate would require $3 million to pay estate taxes, and he had $3 million set aside in certificates of deposit to cover the expense of a stock redemption. However, since the father left half his estate tax-free to the mother, he had neglected to anticipate that when the mother died, there would also be a $3 million liability for estate taxes.

While the son was totally competent to manage the company, he was not prepared to have the three elderly executors of his parents' two estates (which controlled 96 percent of the company) call a special shareholders' meeting to elect themselves to the board. The three executors then directed the son to manage the business, not to maximize profits, but to raise the $3 million required to settle taxes in the mother's estate. The result was the son became so frustrated that he had a serious heart attack, was forced to retire from active management, and the business floundered for five years because there were no competent younger managers trained to run the company. Thus, because of inadequate planning by the father, the family's inheritance was reduced 60 percent, managers were quickly terminated by the new owners, and the son is still disabled. This is certainly not the happy result that the father contemplated when he built the company.

May I suggest that the problems of business ownership today are difficult but not impossible to solve if the owners are willing to devote sufficient time to determine their objectives for the firm, for themselves (whether active or inactive in the business), and for key

managers and employees. Most owners complain about our enterprise system and taxation but do not devote sufficient time to defining objectives and to planning how the business can be kept independent and passed to capable interested owners and managers. Since complex issues are involved, this planning can take a year or more, and it should be reviewed every few years, which is a difficult commitment for a busy owner and president.

In my experience first as the son of an owner, later as a commercial and investment banker, and for the past 18 years as a consultant to private companies, almost every private business has five areas of concern that must be carefully evaluated, planned for, and responded to if the business is to be successful and financially rewarding to the owner an his family or partners.

1. The question of capital

In the current period of historically high interest rates, many businesses are learning to their dismay that they pay more in interest on borrowed money than they earn as profit before taxes for the owners. Inflation increases the need for capital, growth requires more capital, and the typical owner lacks the expertise to measure and manage the capital employed in his business.

Stated simply, invested capital employed in the business is defined as the owner's net worth plus all borrowed money (including leased capital), and total return is defined as the after-tax cost of interest paid plus net profits after taxes. To survive and grow in today's economy, the total rate of return on total invested capital should be about 1.67 times the prime rate. Thus when the prime rate was 6 percent, a successful firm required a total return of 10 percent. Now, however, with the prime rate averaging 15 percent and not expected to go much below 12 percent, a business must earn 20 to 25 percent in order to finance its operations. Ask yourself how your return on invested capital (ROIC) measures up against a 25 percent requirement.

ROIC can be divided into two parts: net profit as a percent of sales and turnover of total capital. The first part involves decisions that affect the P&L statement, sales quantities, prices, cost control, and cost avoidance. The second part requires careful management of the balance sheet, maximizing the turnover of not only cash but also receivables, inventory, fixed assets, and current liabilities.

In many businesses today, management is trying to carry too great a variety of styles or colors that result in large and slow-moving inventories without achieving increased profits to compensate for lower inventory turnover. The financial group also allows customers to delay paying bills for 60 to 90 days, which results in slow turnover of receivables, again decreasing available capital. Managements must increase the turnover of fixed assets and equipment to increase their turnover of capital and to improve ROIC to more satisfactory levels. If this doesn't occur, sale of excess investment in equipment may be necessary to finance growth.

But for owners, there is also a personal side to the capital question.

In planning their personal affairs, most business owners anticipate a redemption of stock from their estates to help pay their estate taxes and administrative expenses (as provided in Section 303 of the Internal Revenue code). This kind of plan transfers the estate tax upon the owner's death from the heirs to a reduction in capital for the business (which is probably undercapitalized).

Life insurance can help to provide the necessary funds, but as the business grows and the estate value increases, additional insurance often becomes an uneconomic use of company capital. Thus an owner of a rapidly growing business should ask his advisers how he can slow down the growth of his estate without slowing down the growth of the business. It can be done without too much difficulty, and it is always much easier than it is to reduce the value of the estate once the growth has reached $20 million or $50 million. Reducing the value of the estate at that point would reduce the size of the stock redemption later to pay estate taxes.

2. How to maintain control

Many times in older private companies, inactive shareholders (descendants of the founder) own as much or more stock than those managing the business. These two groups are bound to have different objectives, particularly as the company grows and adds more shareholders in each generation. The needs of the shareholders will change with advanced age. But there are two useful strategies for dealing with divergent interests of shareholders of private concerns.

The first option is to recognize that some shareholders should be given the opportunity to sell their stock back to the company for cash and/or notes. These notes can bear interest (tax deductible) and be repaid over five to 15 years. The tax laws can be a problem in these lifetime redemptions since the business and selling shareholders may unwittingly fail to strictly follow the tax laws, and the proceeds are later considered by the IRS as a dividend to the sellers taxable at maximum income tax rates rather than as capital gains. However, by carefully following the procedures in the tax laws and regulations (and with expert tax and legal advice), it is almost always possible to work out a redemption on a capital-gains basis. In any event, it is a good policy to review the shareholder list regularly and buy out inactive shareholders to avoid problems later.

The second course to maintain control is to divide the common shares into voting and nonvoting classes, both of which have equal economic values and identical dividends, but only a small number of which carry authority to vote at shareholders' meetings. (Corporation laws vary, and some states do not permit this. However, you can always organize a new corporation in a state that does allow nonvoting stock and register the new corporation in your home state.) Also, make sure all shares are covered by a stockholders' agreement that requires that shares must first be offered to the company and then to the other shareholders before they can be sold to an outsider.

Often it is desirable to place the entire small block of voting shares in a permanent trust or holding company so that the voting control is unified. It is also beneficial to have the key family managers as trustees of the voting block and to elect several experienced businessmen as directors who can use their influence to help the owners make strategic plans, to represent the interests of *all* shareholders, both active and inactive, and to prevent abuses of power. In the event of an untimely death, these directors can make the best decisions on the appointment of a successor.

3. Bringing in younger managers and family members

Although most parents like to feel that all younger family members have the education and qualifications to manage

the enterprise, in real life it is often necessary to look outside the family to provide the skills needed to run the company successfully. Therefore, it is desirable for both family and managers to have a clear agreement on the initial qualifications for employment, the definition of acceptable performance, and the need to let ineffective managers depart gracefully while they are still young enough to begin a new career. There is nothing worse than a 50-year-old incompetent relative on the payroll whose lack of ability should have been recognized and dealt with 20 years earlier.

If top management has a clear understanding of the goals for the business and for its financial success in terms of ROIC, incentive programs can be developed so that key employees can earn bonuses payable in either cash or nonvoting common shares. A profitable business should also begin to fund a profit-sharing or pension plan to permit older employees to retire so that younger managers can look forward to moving into positions of responsibility and building their own capital.

However, the biggest change usually required in making the private company an attractive place to work for family and nonfamily managers alike is in the way that the owner manages as the CEO. When he founded the business, the entrepreneur made all the decisions and all employees reported directly to him. However, if the company is to grow and be successful, the owner must recognize that his way of managing when the company was small will stifle managers' development, and the most capable candidates will probably leave within a few years. The owner needs to take the time to learn the requisites of being an effective CEO at different company size levels. Primarily, he shall need to spend more time on organizational development, planning, and controlling and leave more of the actual decision making to subordinates who are closer to the activities affected by the decision.

4. Getting your eggs out of the basket

As discussed earlier, it is usually desirable to find a way for inactive shareholders to get cash for their shares. Similarly, every business owner should plan how he can achieve some independent capital outside the company during his lifetime. This lessens his dependence upon the business and makes him more willing to let go of control, frees up top jobs for younger qualified individuals, and makes the estate planning problems of the owner easier to coordinate with the business's objectives.

A word of caution is advisable since stock redemption transactions are fraught with tax traps. However, with sufficient advance planning, it is usually possible to withdraw a substantial amount of capital from the company for the retiring president. Our advice is to start this kind of planning at age 50 so as to be financially independent at 65 or 70 at the latest.

For example, a man who built a fine distribution firm wished at age 60 to withdraw about $2 million from the business and turn its control over to his two sons who at 36 and 40 had been running the company for the last five years. Many attorneys whom he consulted told him that if he took $2 million from the company, he would face the risk of having that amount taxed as a dividend and not as a capital gain.

However, a close evaluation of all the facts showed that the father met the four tests required by the Internal Revenue Service for what is called "a total termination of interest" under Section 302. The tests are: (1) He had no transactions in the company's shares for the prior ten years. (The sons were given their shares when they reached age 21.) (2) He agreed to resign as an officer and director and not be on the payroll in any capacity, such as a consultant. As such, he could collect his pension or profit-sharing benefits. (3) He agreed to take unsecured notes from the company in partial payment for his stock because IRS regulations prohibit secured notes in this kind of transaction. (4) He filed a statement with the IRS that he would not reacquire a stock interest in the company for a minimum of ten years after the redemption. By meeting these tests, he qualified for capital gains treatment, even though the remaining shares in the company were owned by his two sons. Importantly, he had an independent valuation of his shares so that there was no question of his having made a gift of capital to his sons by undervaluing the shares he redeemed.

5. Solving the estate problems

If the owner has done a good job on the first four items, he will have built a profitable business, staffed it with excellent family and outside managers, and gotten some of his capital out of the business. He also will have had discussions with his attorney and other advisers and realized that although he built a sizable business, figuring out how to pass it on to future generations is a much more complex and time-consuming process.

First, let us recognize that estate planning for the owner should encompass his remaining active years with the company, his retirement, and his possible disability, as well as how to protect his surviving spouse and children. Therefore, he should strive for maximum flexibility to meet changing conditions, and the plan should be tailored to meet his unique personal situation and objectives. This means he has to provide much of the leadership in developing the plan because only he knows his real goals.

It is necessary to remember that the estate tax levied on transfers of capital at the time of death serves to remove capital not only from the family but also from the business. This is because most estate plans of business owners contemplate a redemption of stock from their estate in an amount sufficient to pay all the taxes and expenses of settling the estate. This is the redemption permitted under Section 303 of the Internal Revenue code.

Even though estate taxes are being reduced over the next four years to a maximum of 50 percent, the owner of a large business faces the challenge of reducing the capital that will have to come from the owner's estate and also from the business. However, one noted expert has called the estate tax "a voluntary tax." In other words, the owner may arrange his estate and business affairs in such a way that he does not have to pay any more estate tax than he really wants to.

At some point in time, most business owners become agreeable to a "freeze" on the capital values in their estate so long as they can maintain a voice in the control of the business.

The message should be clear to the business owner: If he wishes to minimize capital drain that will occur in his estate (and in the company from a Section 303 redemption), then he should arrange his affairs during his lifetime so that his estate will not increase at all or not increase as fast as the growth of the total business.

For example, the owner may exchange *all* of his common stock for preferred stock of equal capital value based on an independent valuation. The preferred stock may have voting rights but since it will not increase in value as the company grows, he can then fix precisely the potential estate tax against the value. When dividends are paid, he will receive them first and also have a salary continuation contract. Taken together, these sources will supply his income for a retirement period.

In his eventual estate, there sill be no valuation problem since the preferred stock cannot be worth more than par value or its call price. The executors can determine the amount of the Section 303 redemption, and in consultation with the company treasurer, they can decide whether it is better to pay all the taxes when due or to elect the 15-year installment option in the tax law. The remaining preferred shares will provide income to his widow and also be used to fund her estate taxes through another redemption. Generally, it is better to pass the preferred shares to those children who are not active in the business so that they will receive income on their inheritance, and later these shares can be redeemed if desired.

Meanwhile, exciting things are happening for the remaining voting and non-voting common shareholders: They are receiving the benefit of all the future growth in the business after payment of dividends to the preferred stockholders. This offers a real incentive for the younger family members and managers.

An additional option for the owner is that instead of making charitable donations in cash, he can give the shares of his company to local charitable causes. These stock gifts benefit him by reducing his eventual estate. By giving him a current charitable deduction on his tax return, his net income is increased. Gifts of this kind must be made only to publicly supported charities (not to private foundations) and are limited to 30 percent of income. When the charity needs cash, it can make arrangements with the company treasurer, but in the meantime it receives dividends on the shares.

Introduction

Intangible assets, going-concern values, minority discounts, comparable public corporations, fair returns on assets, unusual or non-recurrent items, adjusted profit and loss statements, company size, and restricted share marketability are some of the factors that come into play when a family business is valued by the IRS for estate tax purposes. The IRS usually values high while owners value low. Courts, where such matters are resolved, come out in the middle.

The article also provides some ways of reducing taxes due when an estate contains a substantial family business. While a few points in this article have been outdated by changes in tax law, it remains a useful overview.

Valuation: IRS-Style
1985

By Jonathan Plutchok

A true valuation of a corporation's stock will include the value of all of its intangible assets. Goodwill — the loyalty of customers, favorable public reputation and recognition of the business' name — is an important intangible. Others are patents, trademarks and franchises, all of which can be important asset enhancements.

The value of a company's goodwill and similar factors is accounted for when the company is valued under an earnings-oriented method. The firm's historical earnings on which predictions are based must necessarily include those earnings attributable to the intangible assets: if it doesn't generate income it is probably not an asset.

Intangible values become significant, therefore, only when other valuation methods that do not rely on earnings are employed. This will most often be the case when a real estate or investment holding company is being assessed. With these, asset values take precedence over earnings, so intangible assets must be accounted for separately.

Goodwill is generally estimated by examining external factors such as the number of years the business has operated at its location, presence of a recognized trade name, customer loyalty, etc. If these prove inconclusive the IRS has set forth a special method of valuing goodwill and other intangibles (Rev. Rul. 68-609, 1968-1 CB48).

Rev. Rul. 68-609 suggests that the IRS calculates the company's historical average tangible asset values over a representative recent period — say, five years or so. Then the assessor will compute what appears to be a fair return on that asset value over the same period (usually, somewhere around 8 to 10%). The excess of the company's earnings over the fair return is attributed to intangibles.

For instance, let's assume that Churning Title Corporation is a real estate holding company that is well established in its community. Over the past five years its tangible asset holdings — primarily real estate — have had an average worth of $5 million per year. A fair return on $5 million, says the IRS in valuing Churning, would be 8% or $400,000. Yet Churning earned an average of $500,000 (excluding, of course, unusual and nonrecurrent items) over the same period. The IRS would conclude that the additional $100,000 was attributable to Churning's goodwill or other intangibles.

The goodwill that some businesses enjoy may not be transferable or may not survive the death of the company's owner; this is often the case when the firm depends heavily on the services and reputation of a particular individual, such as a doctor or lawyer. Goodwill will be a negligible issue in these cases.

"Going-concern value" is another intangible that sometimes is lumped together with goodwill. Going-concern value reflects the worth to a buyer of having the company's assets already assembled and functioning at the time of purchase. There is intrinsic value, obviously, in not having to assemble the

assets, establish a new company to operate them, train employees, and so forth. The amount that might be attributed to going-concern value is generally unique to a specific business and can vary widely from case to case.

A controlling block of stock in a closely-held corporation is worth more than a minority interest: The majority owner can actually run the company, while a minority owner generally must go along or sell out — and the latter can be just about impossible to do. The logical inference may seem abundantly obvious, but it is not in the eyes of the IRS.

The IRS usually does not allow majority premiums or minority discounts for shares in family-owned corporations. The IRS assumes that a spirit of cooperation and a congruence of interests characterizes family relationships, and these do not jibe with the fractiousness implied by the minority discount. Only when there is evidence of hostility among shareholding family members will the IRS consider the possibility of discounting noncontrolling shares. The IRS' hard-nosed position has won precious few adherents in court, however, especially in estate tax cases. Most courts will allow some discount — from as little as 10% to as much as 50% — to minority interests.

In theory, when a husband and wife own a business equally and jointly a discount should apply to the interest of each. One spouse's undivided interest in the company generally is not marketable and usually constitutes a noncontrolling or minority interest.

If there have been any recent sales of the client company's stock they can guide the appraiser or IRS agent in setting the company's value. However, the sales must have been arm's length transactions between unrelated parties for their prices to have any validity; such a situation is rare among closely-held corporations.

The last but definitely not least item on our IRS valuation checklist under Rev. Rul. 59-60 is comparable public corporations. If an appraiser can find a company that is very similar to the one being valued but with publicly traded stock, its price would be an excellent guide in figuring the subject corporation's worth.

The two businesses must, however, be truly comparable. The "benchmark" company should be in the same line of business as the one being valued, in the same size range and with a similar capital structure and vital financial ratios—especially those concerning earnings. Finally, the benchmark company's stock must be freely and fairly traded on an open market. The IRS prefers listed stocks, but those traded over the counter will do if no exchange-listed corporations can be found.

Of course, even if an ideal benchmark firm is located a closely-held corporation frequently will be afforded some discount from apparent market value due to its smaller size and restricted share marketability. Some other adjustments may be necessary depending on the particulars of the situations of the benchmark and valued companies.

The IRS agent gets to have his say when he applies the principles of Rev. Rul. 59-60 to determine the value of a client's firm. How his estimate fares, however, when the client disagrees strongly enough to challenge it in court is another question.

A Small Business Administration study has shown that, within the flexible parameters of Rev. Rul. 59-60, the IRS has tended to choose whichever valuation approach would produce the highest value and thereby the greatest revenues for the Treasury. (The same study accused taxpayers of assigning unrealistically low values—surprise, surprise.)

Much as the courts might applaud the revenue agents' patriotic zeal, they seldom endorse the high valuations that result. Courts appear to favor compromise valuations, which are generally closer to the realistic figures anyway. In Tax Court, for example, the IRS has valued business interests 2.06 times higher than the executors in estate tax cases while the court only inflated the executors' figure by an average of 1.45.

There are many techniques that help prevent the value of a client's business from blowing his estate taxes out of proportion. Here's a quick survey of some of the most popular and effective tax-cutting methods:

Recapitalization. The client can "freeze" the value of stock in his estate as well as pass the baton to the next generation by rearranging the company's capital structure. He keeps preferred stock with a steady income, while his intended successors get new common stock that will reflect all the company's future growth.

Put a lid on earnings. Use of various accounting and inventory methods can keep the company's earnings low, which will help bring the valuation down.

Go public. Owners can encourage arm's length sales and purchases of their firm's stock. Creating a market this way can help in setting a value.

Buy-sell agreement. A valid, binding buy-sell agreement covering the corporation's stock, which incorporates a reasonable formula for valuation, will usually be recognized by the IRS as fixing the company's estate tax value.

The buy-sell must control lifetime stock dispositions as well as testamentary ones, and must be an arm's length, bona fide transaction.

Special-use valuation. If the technical requirements are satisfied, real estate in a closely-held family business can be valued by the executor of the owner's estate according to its present use in the business, rather than at its highest and best use.

Alternate valuation date. The executor may elect to value an estate's assets as of six months after the date of death instead of on the date of death itself. The value of a closely-held business is often significantly lower on the alternate valuation date, since the owner's death can depress the worth of the company.

More often than not, the client, his company or his estate will seek to reduce the tax value of the business. A lower tax value will facilitate a more generous lifetime gifting program and will cut the exposure to estate taxes faced by the estate of the owner. Financial planners should not jump to the conclusion, however, that a lower valuation is desirable in all cases—the opposite may often be true.

The overall tax burden on the family unit that owns a closely-held business may be smaller if a high valuation is chosen. That's especially likely if the business or its assets in the near future; low value may find the owners caught on the thorns of income taxes.

The tax basis of an estate's assets is "stepped up" to their fair market value on the date of the deceased owner's death (or the alternate valuation date, if that's elected). A higher estate-tax valuation means a higher basis. A higher basis means a lower income tax when the property is sold or otherwise disposed of. It also leads to higher depreciation deductions for business equipment.

For some estates and beneficiaries, the income-tax savings of a high estate valuation will more than outweigh increased exposure to estate taxes. And with the rising unified estate-and gift-tax credit and the unlimited marital deduction, fewer estates will be exposed to estate tax liability at all.

An estate valuation on the high side can bring other benefits besides income-tax savings. Raising the value of a business interest may help it qualify the estate for installment payment of estate taxes (if any are due) under Section 6166, or for a special stock redemption to pay estate taxes under Section 303. To be eligible for either tax break the business interest must exceed 35% of the estate's total value.

While many clients' interests are best served by a low valuation of their business interests for calculating estate tax, planners should remain aware that at times a high valuation can actually be beneficial. The crucial starting point, however, is a clear understanding of the basic principles of valuation for tax purposes.

Introduction

Family-owned and owner-managed businesses represent a substantial portion of every local business community and can be a major source of commercial loan business. However, they can be fraught with problems directly related to the type of business ownership. This article points out the substantial contribution that the loan officer can make to these businesses. It discusses not only the lending relationship but also management prototype, psychological insulation, succession planning, and business structure and conflicts that characterize these smaller businesses.

Owner-Managed and Family Businesses: Special Considerations for the Loan Officer
1983

By Sam H. Lane, Ph.D.

Reprinted by permission of **The Journal of Commercial Bank Lending.** August 1983, Vol. 65, No. 12, pp. 51-58. Copyright ©1983 by Robert Morris Associates; All rights reserved.

Commercial loan officers must be able to work with a wide variety of business organizations. Family-owned businesses and owner-managed businesses present special challenges and merit particular consideration. In many important ways, these businesses are very different from professionally managed organizations in which the person managing the company does not own it.

The commercial loan officer may encounter a new loan application from a potential customer representing an owner-managed company. Or the lender may need to handle a situation in which the company already has a loan and is in trouble. Last, an increased understanding of the special characteristics and needs of these types of businesses will aid loan personnel working with owner-managers who are good customers.

These three situations take on special meaning because it is estimated that 70% of owner-managed businesses never reach the second generation. Some are sold, but many more simply fail.

Why Most Never Reach the Second Generation

An entrepreneur who is an owner-manager is vulnerable to a special set of management pitfalls that can lead to problems later in the life of a business. These pitfalls usually are realized only "after the fact" when the damage has been done. In some cases, an aging founder realized too late he has not properly planned for the continuance of his company after he retires. He *is* the company, and there is no business organization or structure. In other cases, the founder dies suddenly, leaving a widow and children to try to figure out what to do with a business no one knows much about.

Bringing a second generation into a business has its own set of problems. Ideally, there will be one heir who has been groomed and is ready to step into the top management position. More typically, there are several children who must work out an equitable sharing of responsibilities, positions, and salaries"all of whom need to be matched with a desire to work and appropriate business skills and aptitudes.

The Owner-Manager Prototype

Typically, an owner-manager is a hard-driving, tenacious entrepreneur who has struggled long and hard for success. At some point, he or she has done every job in the company and has endured the pressures and uncertainties of starting and nurturing a business. This past history clouds objectivity; there is no power greater than the entrepreneur's. There is no mechanism for ensuring management transition if it becomes necessary. Thus, he will dominate"for better or for worse"the workings of the company for a long time.

The owner-manager may have family or close friends as employees. In that case, it is inevitable that business and personal issues will get confused. Key management persons may be hired or retained on criteria other than performance. A premium is placed on loyalty.

Psychological Insulation

Independent perspective and advice from others, such as expert senior vice presidents or a board of directors, are typically not available in an owner-managed environment. The owner-manager is responsible for the whole enterprise. He or she must evaluate every situation and make a decision. Like many leadership positions, it is "lonely at the top." Self-reliance becomes a habit. Questioning the owner-manager's decisions is not encouraged because it resembles competing, being negative, or impeding the effort"a threat to the success of the enterprise.

The result is owner-managers become psychologically insulated; their perspectives narrow and they become totally self-informed. They are the forest and the trees. Because they have limited experience from working in only one setting, they are aware of few alternatives and options.

Because of inclination and personality, the owner-manager is less likely to set up and use formal, numerical information systems. He or she relies more on informal input which can be distorted, incomplete, and not available when needed.

Reduced Planning, Problem Solving, and Decision Making

These factors all diminish the owner-manager's capacity in three management areas critical to a successful business:

Planning.

Problem solving.

Decision making.

Each area suffers because of lack of systematic, continuous, and timely information systems. Objective criteria against which progress can be measured do not exist. A full range of ideas are not explored because they are not available.

Rational solutions to problems may be rejected because of personal relationships; pet ideas of favored few may get preferential treatment. People who should be key to the process are not, and peripheral people may be influential. A good solution or plan may not even be advanced because it is not "popular" with the founder.

Another related result is reduced capacity in all three areas at the middle and lower levels of management. Past experience for these people has been to advance ideas or suggestions only to have the owner-manager ignore them and do what he or she wants to anyway. These people quickly experience futility, and skill development ceases. Important questions and issues will always be kicked upstairs for the owner-manager to make a decision.

The end result is that the owner-manager deals with symptoms rather than causes. The lack of a good data information base, limited personal perspective, and lack of independent input prevent accurate analysis and decision making.

Family-Owner Business Prototype

Most family-owned businesses have similar predictable problems. The emotional strains of mixing family with business can be monumental. When Dad is still in charge, it may be difficult, if not impossible, for him to give up his business. He feels that no one can do as good a job as he can, and he thinks he will live forever. The most difficult task he has is to "let go" psychologically. This strong and pervasive theme ranges from resisting any kind of succession planning to not being able or willing to delegate day-to-day managerial responsibilities.

The Hard Task of "Letting Go"

Letting go of the business requires the founder to confront and realize that if the grand dream is going to survive, it is going to have to do so without him at some point. The vast gulf of uncertainty about the future coupled with a strongly felt and habitual "grow and build" theme make this a difficult insight to grasp. The founder and the business are psychologically inseparable. It is an extension of himself and provides personal gratification; it is also an affirmation of personal power. Giving up his business is like giving up a part of himself.

Some founders never face reality, and heirs are left to sort things out among themselves as best they can, aided by an expensive array of lawyers, accountants, and trust officers. Not having a carefully developed succession plan supported by carefully coached and tested support personnel is similar to not having a will. The likelihood of a rational distribution of assets is minimal. The process is left to whim or family political maneuvering and reasoning based on emotion and personal relationships rather than rational thought and good business judgment.

There is no question that founders who do plan for their own succession face a complex and sometimes painful task. Old issues have to be confronted and resolved; questions requiring difficult answers have to the raised; decisions have to be made that have been put off for years. Family business consultants working with these situations really have three clients: the founder, the family, and the business. Each set of interests is inextricably interwoven, and the final solution has to work for all three.

Family Business Sourcebook

Informal Structure and Conflict

If Dad is gone and the family is left to run the business, certain other factors come into play. Families tend to have outdated views of each other. Even though children grow up, early mistakes are remembered and not easily set aside.

Unusual managerial structures develop to settle squabbles or inheritance "rights." In an attempt to placate individuals involved, responsibilities are shared, some people are paid to stay out of the way, or the family members become so friendly that they overcompensate and hard business decisions don't get made. No one wants to criticize brother, uncle, or cousin.

Thus, the informal structure, not a formal organization chart, is far more powerful in an owner-managed company than in a professionally managed company. Familial relationships, with all their complexity, determine the outcome of many decisions.

Perhaps it is not surprising that conflict is one of the biggest threats to a successful family-owned business. Many times, the conflict is resolved by altering the ownership of the business. Sometimes this is a successful strategy. More often, the conflict is avoided and all parties are appeased based on a labyrinth of personal and business understanding and decisions. The bookkeeper can not be fired because she is Aunt Jane, even though the monthly statements are always late.

The key is for the family to develop skills to resolve issues and problems that have implications for the business as well as for family relationships. These issues that cut both ways are the ones that give family-owned businesses the most difficulty. However, hard business decisions must be made in a way that does not materially deteriorate the cohesiveness of the family.

Succession Planning

Another major issue facing family-owned businesses is succession planning. Consultants working with family businesses usually find one of three patterns of succession:

1. Strong father, disinterested children.

2. Conservative father, ambitious children.

3. Branches of the families.

Each pattern presents a different set of problems and issues.

In the first case, the father is, always has been, and always will be, a forceful, hard-driving entrepreneurial type of person. He is personally dynamic and charismatic, in general, a hard act to follow. Usually, his children do not have much interest in the business because they have no desire to compete with their father. This is a tough situation because someone other than one of the children usually has to assume control of the business when the founder steps aside.

In the second pattern, the founder has retired on the job and wants to enjoy the fruits of his labor. The children are ambitious and are willing to take risks to expand the business. The founder doesn't want to take risks that will threaten his good life. The status quo makes good sense to him. The children, however, feel suppressed and may even leave the company for a perceived better opportunity. This is a more optimistic pattern because the change in attitude required is not as great as in the first situation. Conservative founders can come to see that ambitious children do need opportunities.

The third pattern is where two or more brothers (partners) have founded a business and succession follows family lines. Even though the founders successfully divided the labor, responsibility, and power, it is almost impossible for the next generation to achieve the same balance of relationships. The easiest solution is when one family can buy the other out. A second possibility is for the business to be split into two separate companies.

Evaluating "Organizational Health"

Several critical dimensions can be useful criteria for the commercial loan officer working with owner-managed and family-owned businesses to evaluate their "organizational health." Organizational health refers to the degree to which the business is well managed, its prospects for continued growth and viability, and how stable it is currently. Unfortunately, these criteria cannot be quantified and put into an equation. the loan officer must judge how much to weight each factor and which is the most important in any given situation.

These criteria can be framed as a set of five questions that can be asked about any owner-managed or family-owned business.

1. *Is the current leadership capable?* In most cases where the founder is in good health and functioning, little question exists as to capability. He or she made the company what it is. However, the answer is quite different if the founder is senile or incapacitated but may "live forever." Another problem occurs when the leader of the business is a family member who has little business experience but wants to run the company. In this case, the company evolves into being managed by a diverse array of business advisers, and direction is diffused or inertia sets in.

2. *Does a succession plan exist?* In the case of an aging founder, the question is what will happen to the company after he or she moves on. In some cases, founders have totally resisted even thinking about it and have no plans at all. Thus, it is likely the company will fall into quick disarray and confusion in the founder's absence. Alternatively, the founder may have done rather elaborate estate planning without really thinking through the implications for the management of the company. For example, a widower can leave controlling interest in a company to children who are not interested in, or capable of, running it. The question quickly moves beyond the mere existence of a succession plan to one of whether the succession plan provides for continuity of capable management.

3. *Is independent input available and used?* At a minimum level, there should be some evidence that the owner-manager listens to and acts on information given by senior people in the organization. If the founder does not respect their judgment or if secrecy characterizes the organization, then it is unlikely much independent advice is received. The next level is that the owner-manager is surrounded with and listens to competent business advisers. This usually boils down to an acknowledged willingness to call on outside expertise as the need arises. The best situation is the existence of an active, functioning outside board of directors that meets regularly to review progress and chart future direction.

4. *Is there a business organization in place?* This criteria has three parts. One is the existence of necessary and appropriate controls and reporting procedures. The second is an active planning and progress monitoring process to ensure decisions are made rationally and systematically. The third

aspect is the existence of competent managers at the middle levels of the company who are rewarded fairly. Too often competent managers quickly see that their futures are limited and seek their fortunes elsewhere. Or a manager sees large discrepancies in compensation between his or her level and family members at the same management level and is not motivated as a result.

5. *What is the pattern of family and business relationships?* If the family has a long history of acrimonious conflict, it is a bad sign. It will be difficult to make hard business decisions that negatively affect family members. In addition, a good prediction is that personal issues will spill over into business decisions and planning. Another aspect is the overlay of the ownership of the business onto the pattern of familial relationships. It would be difficult for two brothers who never got along to own and manage a company they inherited from their father. By the same token, it will be difficult to manage a company if substantial ownership is spread among several family members not actively associated with the business. The last aspect of this criterion is the amount of functional overlap among family members in the business. The best case is where family members have equal but mutually exclusive responsibilities. The worst case is family members with substantially overlapping responsibilities.

Working With The Business

Commercial loan officers may use the above questions to guide their decisions about making a loan in the case where they are only concerned with lending and are not interested in helping the business resolve problems. The criteria serve as a rough indication of whether the loan will be repaid. Alternatively, if the loan officer is motivated to assist the people in their business, the questions are a good beginning to determine what needs to be done. However, solutions are not pat and do not come easily.

In the case of a founder who is getting older and refuses to plan ahead, it falls to whomever has the "king's ear" to persuade him to begin long-range plans for the company. This may be one of the children, yourself, a close friend, or a business adviser. It is critical that the source be trusted and credible so the message will be heard and understood. No force on earth can *make* the founder hear it; it has to come from within. If a founder does not perceive a problem exists, then there is no market for a solution.

Another strategy is to nip problems in the bud by doing things differently earlier in the life of the company. However, young entrepreneur-founders tend to give this low priority because they are struggling for survival and see little need for this kind of help.

One hope for owner-managed and family businesses in the early and middle growth stages is that today's entrepreneurs are better educated and are more likely to accept professional counsel. Increased awareness among loan officers, accountants, and lawyers also make them more alert to trouble signals.

Conclusion

Family-owned and owner-managed businesses represent a substantial segment of every local business community. They can be a major source of loan business. However, working with these businesses can be particularly challenging for loan officers. At times, it is difficult to assess accurately the various dynamics and influences on the business such as family relationships or the temperament of the founder. Sometimes, it may seem the situation is so confused and in conflict that there is no hope.

But loan officers need to develop the skills and abilities necessary to size up and work with these types of businesses. Not only do they need to evaluate these smaller businesses in terms of loan risk but they also may be called on to give advice regarding difficulties such businesses commonly encounter. Their overall level of effectiveness in this area is directly dependent on their adeptness at dealing with the unique situations and people they will encounter.

Introduction

While the use of Employee Stock Ownership Plans (ESOPs) in public companies is widely publicized, over half of all ESOPs are established by private firms—often to purchase shares of a retiring owner.

Benefits an ESOP brings to a company include substantially reduced after-tax borrowing costs and creating a market for a closely-held company's stock. In addition to financial benefits, properly structured ownership leads to increased sales growth, employment growth and decreased turnover.

An ESOP can have special benefits to family firms. A retiring owner can receive up to 1.8 times as much after-tax cash by selling to the ESOP rather than selling only to the company's management group. By selling a portion of stock to the ESOP each year, the owner can provide a time frame for transition. By structuring the ESOP so that employees have to agree to a sale of stock from the ESOP to a potential acquiror, the chances of the company remaining independent is dramatically increased.

Family Businesses and Employee Ownership
1988

By John Weiser, Frances Brody,
and Michael Quarrey

Reprinted from **Family Business Review**, Vol. 1, No. 1., 1988. San Francisco: Jossey-Bass, 1988. Used with permission of the publisher.

Employee stock ownership plans (ESOPs) make headlines when they are used to bail out plants threatened with closure or to prevent hostile takeovers. However, these uses of ESOPs are in fact fairly rare. The predominant use for ESOPs—accounting for approximately half of all ESOPs—is to purchase the shares of the retiring owner of a closely held corporation (Chelimsky and others, 1986, p. 20).

Why is this? What makes employee ownership attractive to so many family business owners? We find that it is a mix of financial and organizational benefits. The financial benefits of employee ownership are dramatic and widely touted. Although the organizational benefits are less publicized, they are equally important, and they make employee ownership a particularly good fit with the culture of many family firms.

Financial Benefits

The financial benefits fall into two categories. The first major benefit is a reduction in the cost of borrowing money. If a company borrows money through an ESOP, the company can deduct both interest and principal from taxable income when repaying the loan, subject to certain limitations. This fact substantially reduces the company's after-tax cost of borrowing. In addition, any bank or lending institution that lends funds to an ESOP can exclude 50 percent of the interest income received from the ESOP from taxable income. As a result, some institutions have made loans to ESOPs at rates as low as 80 percent of prime. The combination of a lower tax payment and a lower interest rate can lead to a net after-tax reduction in loan costs of 30 to 40 percent per year. The reduction in the cost of borrowing may make it attractive for a company to use an ESOP to borrow for expansion or for the purchase of stock.

The second major benefit is the creation of a market for stock in a closely held firm. The company stock in an ESOP is appraised every year, and a market value is assigned to the stock. The ESOP can buy company stock during the year from any individual at the market price. In addition, if the ESOP holds 30 percent or more of the company stock after the sale transaction, the seller can roll over the proceeds of the sale into another qualified investment and avoid tax on any gain on the sale. The tax avoidance becomes permanent if the qualified investment stock is held throughout the seller's lifetime. This makes an ESOP a particularly attractive purchaser for the stock of a retiring owner, who would otherwise face significant capital gains tax on the sale.

Organizational Benefits

Even though the financial benefits are substantial, it is the organizational benefits that most strongly distinguish employee ownership from other methods of raising funds and purchasing stock. It has been shown that

properly structured employee ownership leads to increased sales growth, increased employment growth, and increased productivity. No other method of raising funds and purchasing stock has been shown to have such positive organizational effects.

Research conducted by the National Center for Employee Ownership (NCEO) has uncovered two key factors that together create higher sales growth and productivity: the creation of an "ownership attitude" among the employees and the involvement of the employees in shop-floor decision making (Rosen, Klein, and Young, 1986, Quarrey, 1986).

For the company, the shift from an employee attitude to an ownership attitude can be a key benefit of employee ownership. The dichotomy between employees and owners can be broken down. Employees become more interested in seeing the company succeed financially and become proud to own stock in the company. Turnover decreases. For example, turnover last year of New York Health Care Associates, a 100 percent employee-owned company, was only 38 percent of the industry average.

The ownership attitude does not arise simply from the fact that employees own stock. The stock must have value, and it must comprise a significant proportion of the employees' total compensation. Ownership of stock leads to an ownership attitude only when the ownership of stock has a meaningful financial impact. To put it in monetary terms, if you make $15,000 per year as an employee and $150 per year as an owner, you probably do not feel much like an owner. Moreover, you probably will not develop much of an ownership attitude until your ownership starts earning you $1,000 or more per year (Rosen, Klein, and Young, 1986).

In addition, in order to foster the development of an ownership attitude among employees, management must be committed to employee ownership as an end in itself. Research conducted by NCEO has shown that employees are more motivated, more satisfied, and more apt to develop a strong ownership attitude in companies where ownership sharing is part of the management philosophy than they are in companies where ESOPs are installed purely for tax or financial reasons (Rosen, Klein, and Young, 1986). The more dedicated the company is to the idea of ownership, the more likely the employees are to act and feel like owners.

The second factor necessary to gain the full positive organizational effect from employee ownership is the involvement of employees in shop-floor decision making. Such involvement can include quality control, work methods, purchasing, labor-management relations, or budget and goal setting. In its research, NCEO found that companies that had a high level of employee participation in shop-floor decision making reaped substantial benefits when they instituted employee ownership, while companies that had a low level of employee participation did not after they instituted employee ownership (Quarrey, 1986).

Employee ownership can lead to a higher level of commitment and enthusiasm, but commitment and enthusiasm translates into greater productivity only when the employees have ways of participating in efforts to improve how the company does business. When an ownership attitude comes together with the opportunity and the responsibility for improving the

operations of the company, productivity, commitment, and sales increase. At the O & O supermarkets in Philadelphia, employee ownership has been brought together with employee involvement in all phases of store operations. The result: labor costs per sales dollar are lower, and sales per employee hour are significantly higher than they are at comparable stores in the Philadelphia area.

In addition to increasing sales growth and productivity, employee ownership can be used to heighten the sense of family in a family firm. If the employees own a portion of the stock of a family firm through an ESOP, there is an increased identity of interest between family members and employees. Each employee has in effect become one of the family. This effect is enhanced by the fact that the ESOP covers all long-term employees. Everyone who stays with the firm long enough will eventually become an owner and one of the family.

Employee Ownership and Family Firm Values

Employee ownership can be an important method for increasing commitment to the mission as well as to the unique values of the family firm. David (1983) notes that family firms are more likely to have the following strengths than non-family firms: a concern for the long run that measures results over decades rather than years or quarters, a commitment to quality, an emphasis on maintaining the value of the company's name, and a high level of concern and caring for the needs of the employees as individuals.

Employee ownership can help family firms to capitalize on these strengths. As will be described in detail later in this article, employees who own stock through an ESOP cannot receive the cash value of their stock until they retire or leave the company. This leads them to take a long-run perspective on company growth and profitability. What matters to most employees in an ESOP is the value of the company's stock many years into the future, not next quarter.

Employee ownership, particularly in conjunction with participatory decision making, can lead to an increased emphasis on quality and the value of the corporate name. Employees involved with production are often very aware of the quality of the product and the timeliness of shipping, because they see these aspects of the business every day. As owners, production workers become more concerned with these issues and devote personal efforts to improving them.

Companies that involve employees in the business as owners are able to use shared ownership to underscore the importance of each individual employee. Ownership is important, and shared ownership givers evidence of the importance that the company places on each employee. In these and other ways, employee ownership can enhance unique elements of family firm culture.

Pitfalls of Employee Ownership

While employee ownership can confer substantial advantages on family-owned firms, there are some serious pitfalls that must be avoided. ESOPs can be expensive and complex, far out of proportion to the benefits that they confer for smaller businesses. First, the installation of an ESOP generally costs no less than $7,000, and it usually costs considerably more. Ongoing administration of the ESOP is also expensive, costing anywhere from $5,000 to $25,000 per year for smaller businesses. In addition, ESOPs are subject to areas of pension and tax regulation that are both complex and frequently modified. A general rule of thumb is that a business must have a payroll that exceeds $500,000 per year and pretax profits that exceed $100,000 per year before an ESOP becomes cost effective.

Second, although employee ownership is sometimes perceived as an answer to the problems of failing businesses, it is not a magic wand that can turn a losing business into an instant winner. The well-publicized failures of Rath Packing Company (an employee-owned meat-packing company) and Hyatt-Clark Industries (an employee-owned manufacturer of bearings for rear-wheel-drive vehicles) offer clear evidence of this fact. In both situations, employee ownership extended the life of the company for several years, but it was not enough to overcome the problems of declining markets and severe labor-management strife.

Several family business owners whom we have advised have expressed concerns over involving employees as owners in troubled businesses. The decision to sell a financially troubled firm to their employees was influenced in part by the importance to the employees of being able to extend their jobs for a few more years. The family business owners were also influenced by the level of financial risk that the employees were prepared to bear in order to become owners.

The benefits of employee ownership may not compensate for a shift in the value of real estate that makes liquidating a company more attractive than selling it as an operating concern. This is particularly true in such areas as New York City, where dramatically rising land values have led to the liquidation of many family-owned businesses.

The final pitfall is that the installation of an ESOP can dilute the earnings per share of the company, which can depress stock value. This development is particularly likely in situations where the company is issuing new stock to be placed into the ESOP. Although the long-term impact may be favorable, the short-term effects can be severe enough to cause current owners to pressure the company not to adopt an ESOP. The effects of potential dilution must be planned for, and offsetting benefits must be made clear to owners.

Employee Ownership and Retirement

The organizational and financial benefits make employee ownership of interest to family firms in many situations. However, in our experience, employee ownership is particularly attractive to family firms when there are no heirs who are interested in continuing in the business. In such situations, the family business owner is often faced with either selling the business to outsiders or liquidating it. Employee ownership offers a third option. Employee ownership can allow the retiring owner to leave a legacy — a healthy, independent firm that continues the business and the traditions of the family. The ESOP binds the employees together into a unit like the family. It also allows the retiring owner to leave behind an intact firm without sacrificing his or her ability to cash in on a lifetime of investment in the business.

Selling a family firm to outside investors can be an attractive option. However, as Astrachan (1985) points out, there can be negative consequences for the firm and the community that are not immediately obvious. These consequences can be particularly severe when a family business is sold to a large firm that is not family owned and managed. Astrachan (1985) argues

that the culture of family firms often differs in important ways from the culture of non-family firms.

These cultural differences can lead to severe management problems as the bureaucratic culture of a large, non-family-owned firms is imposed on the more personally oriented culture of a smaller family-owned firm. In addition, family firms often play important roles in their communities, roles that bureaucratically organized firms outside the community in which the family firm operates are less able and less willing to play. In this case, the sale of the family-owned firm can have a negative impact on the community as well. A sale to the employees allows the company both to maintain its own culture and to continue to play an important role in the life of the community.

But, will the business be able to survive after the owner retires? Family business owners are usually key players in the management of the firm, and their departure is often a significant blow to the business. Many owners are worried that their companies will perform poorly if they retire and sell to the employees. Research indicates that, with proper preparation, employee-owned companies can perform well after the owner retires.

Cohen and Quarrey (1986) studied the performance of companies in which the owners sold their stock to an ESOP and retired from active management. The study measured the performance of the ESOP companies relative to other companies of similar size in the same industry. Because most of the companies examined were closely held, the study used sales growth and employment growth rather than growth in profits to measure company performance. Cohen and Quarrey (1986) found that annual percentage growth in sales for the ESOP companies was 1.3 times as great as the annual percentage growth in sales for similar companies, and annual percentage growth in employment was 1.7 times as great as the annual percentage growth in employment for similar companies.

An ESOP allows great flexibility in structuring a purchase of a retiring owner's stock, because there is no requirement that the ESOP purchase all or any particular percentage of the retiring owner's stock. In addition, managers and employees can purchase stock individually at the same time that the ESOP purchases stock on behalf of all employees. Finally, an ESOP can provide an incentive for reductions in employee compensation or for direct employee equity investments in the corporation. When it is clear that a cut in pay or a cash investment will be used to repay a loan that is buying stock for their own accounts, employees often are much more willing to accept a pay cut or to invest than they would be in other situations. However, in our experience, employee investment is most likely to happen when the employees have a compensation package that more than covers their basic needs.

The contrasting effects of different levels of compensation on willingness to invest can be seen by comparing two companies, whose names will be withheld to protect the confidentiality of financial information. Company A had a wage-and-benefit package averaging approximately $18.10 per hour when the company was formed. The employee owners invested $4,000 apiece in the company and agreed to a wage-and-benefit reduction of $3.84 per hour. Company B's employees receive a wage-and-benefit package ranging from $5.60 to $14.75 per hour. The employees made no initial investment, and they have accepted a much

smaller wage deferral, of 65 cents per hours, which is being used to fund the purchase of stock through the ESOP. The willingness and ability of the employees to make sacrifices in order to become owners can be a key element in making possible an ESOP purchase of stock. It is worth noting that Company A employees, who made a much greater investment, anticipated a much higher potential return in future profit growth.

The financial benefits of an ESOP can dramatically enhance the company's ability to purchase a retiring owner's stock. For example, compare a sale of stock to the members of the management group without an ESOP; with a sale of stock to the management group and the employees through an ESOP. Assume that in both instances most of the funds for the purchase will be borrowed from a bank and secured by the assets of the business. In such a case, sale to the ESOP allows the company to generate significantly more cash for the seller than sale to the management group. The cost of borrowing funds is substantially reduced, so the company can afford to borrow more and hence pay more to the seller. In addition, the seller has to pay capital gains tax on a sale of stock to the management but can defer the tax on a sale of stock to the ESOP if the sale is properly structured. The net effect is that the retiring owner can receive more than 1.8 times as much cash from the company after taxes by selling to the ESOP than by selling only to the management group.

The ESOP can be used to place a time frame on the transition in ownership. For example, the retiring owner can agree to sell a certain portion of his or her stock to the ESOP every year and even to make the stock sale contingent on the achievement of certain performance goals by the company. This agreement can allow the retiring owner to continue to exercise control over the company even while turning over the reins to the next generation.

A retiring owner also may be interested in assuring that the company will continue to be an independent concern and not be acquired in a hostile takeover after his or her retirement. An ESOP can help the retiring owner to achieve that goal. The ESOP can be structured in such a way that the employees have to agree to a sale of stock from the ESOP to an acquiring company. Such a condition dramatically reduces the likelihood that the company can be acquired in a hostile takeover.

Case Study: M. W. Carr Company

All these themes can be seen in the case of the M. W. Carr Company, a manufacturer of high-quality picture frames that has captured approximately 20 percent of the market (Quarry, Blasi, and Rosen, 1986). M. W. Carr was founded by Martin Wales Carr in 1896, and the company had been owned and managed by family members for three generations when Louis Carr became president in 1946. At that time, the company faced severe problems associated with rising costs for materials and labor. Louis decided to address these problems by taking steps to get the shop-floor workers involved in building a more productive and profitable company. To achieve this end, Louis changed to a pay system that provided incentives for better performance and instituted a series of monthly dinners in which he met with employees representing the various shop-floor areas.

The innovations, together with the postwar recovery, led to a much higher level of profitability. In 1954, Louis decided to continue to increase the involvement of the shop-floor work force

in the company by adding a profit-sharing plan. He also instituted a no-layoff policy to create further sense of security and belonging among the work force.

In the early 1970s, Louis became interested in employee ownership. He felt that having a portion of the profit sharing paid out in stock, which would rise in value if the company did well and fall in value if the company did poorly, would further increase the employee's commitment. He decided that an ESOP might be a useful tool, and he spent several years studying the idea, getting the management team on board, and working with them to develop the details of the plan. The ESOP was installed in 1977, replacing a portion of the profit-sharing plan.

During the several years after the plan was installed, Louis started to think about retirement. His children were not interested in taking over the management of the company. He had been approached by several outside investors who were interested in acquiring the company. Louis did not want to sell his company to an outsider; he wanted it to remain independent. He was concerned that a new management team from outside the company would not treat his employees properly. He also felt that the employees who had helped to build the company should benefit from the company's future success. So, in 1981, he sold the rest of his stock to the ESOP, and the employees became the owners of M. W. Carr. In 1983, the last year for which numbers are available, the profit-sharing plan and the ESOP together were worth approximately $5.5 million. Top management owned 22 percent of the stock, foremen owned 21 percent of the stock, shop-floor workers owned 51 percent of the stock, and the remainder was unallocated stock held in the ESOP.

Employee Ownership Details

How does employee ownership work in the day-to-day operations of a company, such as M. W. Carr? The stock that the employees own through the ESOP is held in a trust called the *employee stock ownership trust* (ESOT). The ESOT can acquire the stock in either of two ways. The first way is for the ESOT to purchase the stock from stockholders with cash that it receives from the company or that it borrows from a lending institution with a loan guaranteed by the company. The company receives a tax deduction, up to certain limits, for the cash that it contributes to the ESOT and that the ESOT uses to purchase stock or to repay a loan used to purchase stock. The second way for an ESOT to acquire stock is for the company to contribute stock to the ESOT directly. The company receives a tax deduction for the market value of the stock at the time of the contribution, up to certain limits.

If the company is privately held, the stock in the trust is appraised every year by an outside valuation expert, who sets a market price for the stock. Each employee participating in the ESOP has an individual account in the ESOP and receives a statement each year of the value of the stock in his or her account. The stock that the ESOT acquires is allocated to individual accounts each year according to an allocation formula, which is set when the ESOP is put in place. The allocation formula may distribute stock in proportion to compensation, years of service, or certain other approved measures.

The stock remains in the ESOT until the employee retires or leaves the company. Employees may not withdraw stock from their accounts prior to that time, nor may they use the stock as collateral for a loan. Individuals "vest" — that is,

acquire rights to the stock in their accounts — according to a predetermined schedule. If individuals leave the company before they have fully vested, they forfeit a portion of the stock in their individual accounts. Vesting schedules can be set in a variety of formats at the time when the ESOP is installed, but they cannot be easily changed once the ESOP is in place.

When employees leave the firm, the company may distribute to them either cash or stock. If the company is privately held, it must give the employees the right to sell the stock back to the company itself or the ESOT at the appraised value. Although the company is not legally obligated to do so, it may write into the original ESOP documents a requirement for the employees to sell the stock back to the company or the ESOT at that point. The obligation of the company to repurchase the stock of retiring and departing employees is referred to as the *repurchase liability*, and it can pose a significant cash drain on the company if employees retire in large groups at one time. Financial instruments similar to insurance stop-loss policies are available to protect against unusually large repurchase liabilities in any one year.

It is important to realize that employee ownership does not mean that the employees necessarily have a say in the operations of the company. The laws governing employee ownership require the appointment of a trustee for the ESOT, who votes the shares in the ESOT. The trustee can be appointed by management, the employees, or both. The trustee's responsibilities are determined by ESOP and pension law. In general, the trustee is free to vote the stock in any way that he or she determines to be in the best interests of the employees covered by the ESOP. On a

238

few very important issues, voting rights must be "passed through" to the employees. That is, in these areas, the employees must be allowed to direct the trustee's vote. The specific issues requiring direct employee votes vary from state to state, but they generally include such major corporate decisions as the decision to dissolve the corporation, to merge with another corporation, or to sell substantially all the assets of the business.

Although ESOP law does not require the employees to have a voice in how the company is run, research shows that companies that include employees in decision making receive more benefit from employee ownership than companies that exclude employees from the decision-making process. There are many different ways in which employees can be included in decision making. Our experience indicates that the key to including employees in decision making is to specify from the outset exactly which decisions are open to employee-owner input and which are reserved to management, the ESOT trustee, and the board of directors.

Deciding to Pursue Employee Ownership

Although employee ownership has some very attractive features for family businesses, the decision to incorporate employee ownership into a family business is not one that can be made lightly. Employee ownership is most successful when the management of a company is committed to involving employees in the company and to sharing ownership as an important method for creating involvement. The decision to pursue employee ownership should be made only after a careful review of the goals and needs of both the family and the business.

The first step in deciding about employee ownership is to gather information about the alternatives that can be used to achieve the goals and meet the needs of the family and the business. In the case of a retiring owner, these alternatives might include sale to outside buyers, liquidation of the business, and sale to the employees. A preliminary assessment of the costs, risks, and benefits of each of the alternatives must be made in order to determine which of the options should be pursued further. If, for example, it turns out that a competitor who is very interested in purchasing the business is willing to pay far more than the employees could ever manage to pay, it may not be attractive to pursue employee ownership.

There are national and state centers for the support of employee ownership that can assist owners in developing a preliminary assessment for the firm. These organizations also maintain lists of government programs and consultants who specialize in employee ownership.

As part of the initial assessment, the attitudes of management, employees, and union (if there is one) toward employee ownership will need to be ascertained. The management will be a key factor in any ownership structure. If managers are opposed or indifferent to employee ownership, it can be very difficult to complete a sale to the employees, and employee ownership is not likely to have the kind of positive effect on productivity and commitment that has been seen in businesses where management supports employee ownership. Management needs to be positively in support of employee ownership in order for the greatest benefits to be achieved. In many successful employee ownership efforts, as at M. W. Carr, the owner has worked with the management team for a period of several years to build enthusiasm for and commitment to the concept of employee ownership before attempting to develop a structure for employee ownership.

If employee ownership appears to be worth pursuing after the initial assessment period, the next steps are to conduct a feasibility study for employee ownership and to choose the appropriate structure for employee ownership in the business. The feasibility study is an in-depth analysis of possible structures for employee ownership that determines the costs and benefits for the owners, the company, and the employees under each of the different structures. The variables that differ from structure to structure include what percent of stock is sold to the ESOP, when the stock is sold, whether the ESOP borrows money to purchase the stock, and how the stock will be allocated to the individual accounts.

In the feasibility study, the cash flows associated with stock contributions, stock purchases, and debt service are calculated. The tax effects of the various transactions are analyzed, and the impact on the financial statements of the company is computed. Finally, the value of stock over time in the ESOP, the potential benefits to employees, and the repurchase requirements for the company are estimated. All these calculations allow the owners to evaluate the different possible structures that can be used for employee ownership and to choose the one that best meets their goals.

Feasibility studies can be conducted by company management, or a consulting firm can be hired to perform the analysis. At the end of the feasibility study, the owners should have a clear

sense of what they will gain by pursuing employee ownership, what employee ownership will cost, what major hurdles will need to be overcome, and what the appropriate structure for employee ownership in their company would be. At this point, the owners can decide whether and how to institute employee ownership. If a decision is made in favor of employee ownership, a plan for handling the transition should be devised.

There are several important tasks that need to be accomplished for the transition in ownership to achieve the owner's goals. The most important of these tasks is communication. The employees, the management team, and the company's customers and suppliers all need to understand what the changes will mean to them. Particularly in the situation where a key owner is retiring, the shift in ownership can unsettle long-standing relationships and cause tremendous anxiety about future roles. A well-considered communication program will address the concerns of all affected parties and give them a clear understanding of the role that they are expected to play in the new ownership structure.

A second key task is negotiating the details of the ownership transfer. Exactly how much will be paid, when, and by whom must be negotiated to the satisfaction of all the parties involved. If there is a loan, a financing application must be made, and all the loan documents must be reviewed. The ESOP papers must be prepared, and a summary of the ESOP must be submitted to the Internal Revenue Service and to the Department of Labor for review. If a key owner is retiring, there may be a consulting contract between the owner and the company that specifies the compensation, rights, and responsibilities of the owner after the sale.

Once the details have been settled, the ESOP can be installed, and the transition in ownership can be finalized. As already noted, one attractive feature of the ESOP is that it can place an explicit time frame on the transition process. Particularly where a key owner is retiring, the new owners will need to learn what ownership means and what their rights and responsibilities really are. Members of the management team will need to be coached and guided in their new, expanded roles, a process that can continue over a period of time that ranges from a year to five years or more, depending on the company.

The relationship between a retiring owner and the company is similar to the relationship between a parent and an adolescent. The parent is letting go of control, and the adolescent is assuming his or her adult role. However, the adolescent still is quite inexperienced and in need of guidance. The relationship can become stormy as the adolescent explores new ways of doing things and new ways of relating to the world. Eventually, the adolescent develops a fully adult style that is his or her own but that also incorporates much of what the parent taught. Likewise, the management and employees must develop their own strategy for the business, and they may explore ways of relating to customers and markets that are quite different from the way in which the former owner operated. With proper guidance, the company will settle into a new strategy that recognizes its unique strengths and weaknesses while preserving the best elements of the culture created by the retiring owner.

Employee ownership has much to offer the family firm. Because many of the benefits of ESOPs are uniquely suited to the needs and financial situation of a retiring owner of a closely held firm, it is not surprising that many of the ESOPs created to date were created by business owners at retirement. The reduced cost of borrowing, the creation of an incentive for employee investment, and the rollover of capital gains tax are all powerful incentives for using ESOPs as a way of selling stock at retirement. And, most important, the ability of employee ownership to help a retiring owner create a legacy—a healthy, independent firm that carries on his or her name and traditions—can make a sale to an ESOP a particularly satisfying way of retiring.

References

Astrachan, J. H. *Family Firms and Community Culture: An Optimal Fit.* Yale School of Organization and Management Working Paper, New Haven, Conn.: Yale School of Organization and Management, Yale University, 1985.

Chelimsky, E., and others "Employee Stock Ownership Plans: Benefits and Costs of ESOP Tax Incentives." General Accounting Office, GAO/PEND-87-8. Washington, D.C.: U.S. General Accounting Office, 1986.

Cohen, A., and Quarry, M. "Performance of Employee-Owned Small Companies: A Preliminary Study," *Journal of Small Business Management*, 1986, 24(2), 58-63.

Quarrey, M. *Employee Ownership and Corporate Performance.* National Center for Employee Ownership Research Paper. Oakland, Calif.: National Center for Employee Ownership, 1986.

Quarrey, M., Blasi, J., and Rosen, C. *Taking Stock: Employee Ownership at Work.* Cambridge, Mass.: Ballinger, 1986.

Rosen, C., Klein, K., and Young, K. *Employee Ownership in America: The Equity Solution.* Lexington, Mass.: Lexington Books, 1986.

Introduction

This article explains the process of going public and discusses the advantages and disadvantages of doing so.

The Pros and Cons of Going Public
1985

By Pauline Krips Newman

Reprinted by permission of **SAM Advanced Management Journal**, Winter 1985. Copyright ©1985 SAM Advanced Management Journal; all rights reserved.

"Going public" creates an aura of success for the men and women who are instrumental in bringing a company to such a milestone. There are, however, several important considerations that need to be evaluated before the decision to go public is made. This article will examine those considerations.

An initial public offering (known as an "IPO") is normally underwritten on a best efforts or firm commitment basis. The characteristics and names of these two types of underwritings match. In a best efforts underwriting, the underwriter acts as the company's agent, using its best efforts to place as much of the stock as it can. In a firm commitment underwriting, once the regulatory requirements are met and certain conditions satisfied, the underwriter will actually buy all of the stock being offered (subject to withdrawal in the face of market conditions) and then resell the stock as a principal. From the company's perspective, a firm commitment underwriting is preferable and, in most instances, is the form of underwriting the company should anticipate. Although the selection of an underwriter is beyond the scope of this article, it is important to note that the company should select an underwriter able to provide marketplace support for the stock after the offering.

A company's first public offering is usually of common stock and accomplished by registering the stock under the Securities Act of 1933 and the securities laws of the various states in which the stock will be offered and sold. The process of registration is costly, both in terms of the actual dollars and top executive time that must be invested. It would not be unusual for a small public offering (in the $3 million range) to cost the company $200,000 or more. Without an adequate management team available to tend to corporate business during this period, the business may suffer. Top management will be involved in the long and arduous process of preparing the registration

243

statement, cleaning up the corporation's legal and accounting matters and negotiating the terms of the underwriting arrangements. Top executives will also be required to participate in what are commonly referred to as "dog and pony shows" or "road shows." These are meetings with groups of potential underwriters (the selling syndicate) in key states where the securities are to be sold. These top executives will be making presentations and answering questions about the company. In a typical IPO, the dog and pony or road show will take as long as a full week and will occur shortly before the anticipated effective date.

The time and cost considerations are, in this author's opinion, the most critical ones for a company in the pre-public offering stage. Although there are also post-public offering considerations (discussed below), they are less impelling than the key management time and dollar costs a company incurs in preparing to go public. These initial considerations loom even larger when weighed against the risk that if market conditions or the company's business change adversely, the offering could fail to occur. In such instance, the company will find itself saddled with a large debt and loss of substantial amounts of its top executives' time that can never be regained.

As with any important decision, however, the company must balance the costs and risks in going public against the ultimate benefits.

Advantages of Going Public

Most obviously, the public offering of a company's securities will result in a significant infusion of capital. In fact, depending on the stage of the company's development, the capital infusion resulting from a public offering may be larger, less expensive and

involve less dilution than might be the case in a private placement.

After the public offering is consummated, the company will have an improved balance sheet, which can be expected to increase the company's borrowing power and enhance its ability to reduce its borrowing costs.

Once the stock is trading freely (whether on an exchange or in the over-the-counter market), it will have a liquidity and a market valuation unavailable to a privately-held company. The insiders who built the company and now own a large number of its shares will have a measurably increased net worth. Subject to applicable securities laws (discussed below), these insiders will be able to sell shares in the newly created public marketplace. In some cases, insiders may have sold shares in the offering itself. Whether or not there is a secondary offering of stock by corporate insiders will depend on the nature of the offering, the underwriter, market conditions and the strength of the company.

A company with publicly traded stock has a prestige and glamour that a privately held company lacks. This should, over time, produce greater publicity for that company which, in turn, will benefit its product or business.

It is likely that the investment banker that takes a company public will require representation on the board of directors for a period of time. As discussed below, this may be viewed as an erosion in the control of the board by the insiders. On the other hand, the expertise and business acumen of that investment banker's representative will generally be advantageous to the newly public company.

Finally, the quantifiable value and ease of trading of the stock of a public company provides the company with an increased ability to attract and retain employees through stock incentive programs and to expand through acquisitions by use of its stock.

Disadvantages of Being Public

As stated above, the primary obstacle to going public is the large investment of both top management time and costs that must be incurred before the public offering can be launched, even though there is a risk that the offering could ultimately abort. If a company can absorb these time and dollar costs, the advantages of going public are clear. On the other hand, once a company goes public, its operating environment will be very different from that of its privately-held days.

Reporting, Information and Other Compliance Requirements

A public company must comply with complex and costly reporting requirements which, if not accurately fulfilled, will subject the company and certain insiders to liabilities under the securities laws. These reports range from the initial filing with the Securities and Exchange Commission (SEC), to reports on the public offering proceeds and expenses, to continuous annual quarterly and significant event reports. These annual reports (10-K's) will require audited financial statements; the quarterly reports (10-Q's) will require unaudited financial statements.

Registration of the company's publicly-held securities under the Securities Exchange Act of 1934 ("1934 Act") may be required by the underwriters and will be statutorily required when the company achieves a certain level of shareholders and dollar amounts of assets. After such registration, the Company will be subject to the proxy rules of the 1934

Act, which include additional filing requirements and the delivery of an annual report to stockholders.

The stock of most first time public companies will be traded over the counter and will be listed in the National Association of Securities Dealers Automated Quotation System (NASDAQ). This will subject the company to the filing requirements of the National Association of Securities Dealers, Inc. (NASD), which include reports on such events as a change of corporate name, an increase or decrease of 5% or more in outstanding common stock or declaration of a cash dividend or a stock split.

The company will be required to release important information on a timely basis (although during the 90-day period immediately following the IPO, there are limits on the type of information that can be released without amending the prospectus delivered in the public offering). Assuming the stock is listed with NASDAQ, the NASD guidelines for timely public disclosure of information must be followed.

The underwriting agreement signed in conjunction with the public offering most likely will require that the company deliver certain of its reports to the underwriters and make generally available to the company's shareholders an earnings statement for a 12-month period beginning after the effective date of the registration statement.

The company will be subject to the Foreign Corrupt Practices Act ("FCPA") which will affect the way the company makes and keeps its books, records and accounts and which will require the company to devise and maintain a system of internal accounting controls complying with the requirements of the FCPA.

Loss of Control and Flexibility

As stated above, the investment banker that takes the company public may require at least one representative on the company's board of directors. The company is also well advised to include other outside (non-management) directors on its board. These outside directors (as well as the investment banker's representative) can contribute a great deal to the company. Their presence, however, will erode the pre-public control and flexibility of the board.

Once public, the company will have a larger shareholder base than before, comprised mainly of "strangers." Gone are the "good old days" of shareholder action by quick phone calls or written consents. When the company is required to comply with the proxy rules of the 1934 Act, the calling and holding of a shareholders' meeting will be complicated even further.

The myriad of securities law disclosure requirements hold the actions of insiders up to public scrutiny. For example, the salaries and other perquisites of top executives and transactions among the company and corporate insiders become public information.

Increased Costs

The reporting and other compliance requirements of a public company will obviously result in a substantial increase in legal, accounting and printing costs, as well as in the time commitment of top corporate personnel. In addition, the public company will use a transfer agent and registrar, making stock transfers significantly costlier than before the public offering. Stock transfers under Rule 144 (discussed below) require even more paperwork and result in even more expense.

Key executives will discover that a surprising amount of their time is required for shareholder relations, public relations generally, and meetings with security analysts. The company may ultimately decide to retain a public relations firm or hire additional personnel to handle some or all of these matters.

Restrictions on Insiders

For the company first going public, the stock that was issued before the public offering will generally constitute so called "restricted securities." Generally speaking, restricted securities can be "dribbled out" in the public marketplace (under Rule 144) by those who have owned them for a period of at least two continuous years. Holders of Rule 144 stock who are not "affiliates" of the company will be effectively free from the restrictions of Rule 144 after they have owned the stock for three or more continuous years. "Affiliates" (who, in broad terms, are the officers, directors and shareholders who own 10 percent or more of the company) will be subject to the restrictions of Rule 144 no matter how long their holding period.

The underwriting agreement may have required a "lockup" of the shares of stock of key insiders. This means that these insiders will not be able to make any sales of their stock for an agreed upon period of time, which normally would not exceed 120 days after the date of the offering.

The anti-fraud provisions of the securities laws apply to anyone who has so called "inside information" (information not disclosed to the public). Anyone possessing such information is precluded from purchasing or selling the company's securities until the public has had adequate access to such information. Recently enacted legislation (the Insider Trading Sanctions Act of 1984) enables the SEC to seek treble damages against someone trading on undisclosed material inside information. In addition, criminal fines now can be imposed up to $100,000 per violation.

After the company has registered its securities under the 1934 Act, its officers, directors and 10 percent or more shareholders must file reports with the SEC disclosing their beneficial ownership of the company's securities and any change in this beneficial ownership. These same officers, directors and shareholders will also become subject to the so called "short swing profit" provisions of Section 16(b) of the 1934 Act and are required to disgorge any "profit" resulting from sales and purchases or purchases and sales of the company's securities made within 6 months of each other. Since the "profit" determination is made by matching sales and purchase transactions on the basis of lowest purchase price and highest sales price, a "profit" may be statutorily determined even though the insider suffered a loss. Caution is urged for directors, officers of 10 percent or more shareholders who hold options on the company's securities since option exercise is deemed to be a purchase for these purposes.

Persons who own or acquire 5 percent or more of the company's stock will be required to file a schedule of their holdings (and of changes therein) with the SEC. Purchases of the company's securities in the public marketplace by the company or its officers, directors or 10 percent or more shareholders will be regulated and officer, directors and 10 percent or more shareholders will be prohibited from "selling short" any of the company's securities.

Liabilities

The company, its officers and directors are increasingly exposed to liability— under the Securities Act of 1933 with respect to materially inaccurate disclosures (or omissions) in the registration statement used in the public offering and under the 1934 Act with respect to materially inaccurate disclosures (or omissions) made in reports filed under that Act, as well as with respect to regulated transactions (relating to the company's stock, inside information, FCPA and the like).

In conclusion, going public has many rewards, but it is a costly and time consuming procedure for which a company must be prepared, both before and after the offering.

Introduction

For those involved, the transfer of control or ownership of a closely held business is their single most important lifetime transaction. Fraught with complexity, the transfer requires a clear understanding of personal, family and business objectives as well as tax law. This article is a guided tour that helps you gain the information with which to reach your goals.

How To Transfer Your Corporation to the Next Generation
1988

By Irving L. Blackman, C.P.A., J.D.

Adapted and reprinted by permission of the author from Blackman, Kallick & Bartelstein's **Special Report 11.** Copyright ©1988, Irving L. Blackman.

Sooner or later the control of every closely held family business must be transferred. Sometimes the control is transferred to members of the next generation within the family. At other times, transfers are made to new management people who are a "next generation of nonfamily management."

In practice, we get specific problems with real people, real businesses, and real objectives. Then we must use the tax law, together with known techniques, to solve the problems and meet the objectives.

Almost without exception, the transfer of control or ownership of a closely held business is the single most important lifetime transaction for the people involved. It transcends not only life and

death planning, but it does so for a group of people, rather than a single person. The dollars involved usually represent numbers that are big, will get bigger and ultimately must be split up among family members. More often than not, some of the family members are active in the business while other family members are not active in the business.

Sizing Up the Problem

Let's size up the tax problem. Suppose today's book value of your business is $500,000. Suppose your growth—both real and inflationary combined—is projected at 10 percent a year; the book value of your business will double every seven years. Assume the book value and real value (the price a buyer would pay) are the same. Have you ever made a chart showing what the transfer cost might be? It would look something like the following table.

Family Business Sourcebook

Time Frame	Value of Business	Transfer Tax	Next Bracket
Today	$500,000	$155,800	37%
In 7 Yrs	$1,000,000	$345,800	41%
In 14 Yrs	$2,000,000	$780,000	49%
In 21 Yrs	$4,000,000	$1,775,800	50%*

*55 percent is the highest rate until 1993, when 50 percent will be the highest rate.

The following table assumes you are single and have $600,000 in other assets. Why $600,000? Because the first $600,000 of an estate is tax free. Now, let's add up everything you own on the date of death and see what the actual estate tax might look like. Again, assume you are single (if you had a wife, she went to heaven before you). Your tax chart would look like this:

Size of Estate	Actual Tax
$600,000	None
$1,000,000	$153,000
$3,000,000	$1,083,000
$5,000,000	$2,083,000
$10,000,000	$4,583,000

More assets or liabilities, marital status and other factors have an impact. But the above charts give you an idea of the size of your tax problem today and also what it might be tomorrow. Unquestionably, the government tax machine is most efficient when family wealth is transferred *en masse*.

However, the government-transfer-tax machine can be beaten.

A variety of tax-saving transfer of ownership techniques (strategies) have been used by so-called "sophisticated business people" for generations. Their use has been limited to those fortunate few who have been able to find professionals capable of translating family objectives and applicable tax law into a workable plan. That's it—*a workable plan*—and the sooner the plan is put ito effect, the greater the tax savings.

Simply put, the easiest way to beat the government transfer tax machine is by *lifetime planning*. (Remember, you ain't dead yet.)

As practiced in my office, transfer of ownership is an organized approach to:

1. Restate the business owner's questions and problems into a series of short- and long-range objectives.

2. Identify and discuss the techniques that meet those objectives.

3. Develop and implement a lifetime plan.

4. Dovetail the estate plan with the lifetime plan.

5. Maximize the after-tax wealth of the family unit.

Questions

Lifetime planning brings a flood of questions.

Do I sell to the kids?...Give them the business?...Who keeps control—while I'm alive? And after I die?...How much will the IRS get when the kids take over?

And when I die?...How will the IRS value my business?

The answers tend to change every time a different person asks the questions. The answers sometimes change even if asked by the same person, because circumstances have changed—your son decides to go into the business or not to, business gets substantially better or worse, or a child gets married or divorced.

Other questions are asked to identify the objectives of the client. Here's a typical set of questions:

• Who will operate the business after you retire? Is there a competent family member or employee within the corporate group at the present time? Should an outsider be considered?

• How will you maintain the income flow you and your family require after you retire? Will it be through dividends or payments from an established pension or profit-sharing plan? Should such a plan or plans be set up now? Can you provide the income flow by renting real estate or other property to the corporation?

• Are you interested in selling the business? If so, is the business salable to some outside third party, and if so, at what price?

• Is the business likely to grow in value in the future to the extent that it creates a prohibitive estate tax liability?

• If the business continues to grow, will it have the cash available to pay the resulting estate tax?

• Do you want to control the management of the business for as long as you live? Or do you want to pass control to someone else while you are still alive?

• Do you think the best interests of the family will be served by passing control to nonfamily management only after your death?

• Consider family members who are not active in the business. Might any of them become active? Do they get equal or unequal shares? Do they share in future growth? How will their interests be turned into cash?

• Can current income tax or gift tax on the transfer be avoided? If not, how much will it be?

• Is there room for flexibility in your plan if your objectives change?

There are many other questions that might be asked. All the skill and experience of the practitioner must be used to make sure that all pertinent questions are asked.

Using the Questions to Set and Accomplish Objectives

All of your objectives must be listed before the next step in developing an overall plan is attempted. Often the founder's wife (or husband) must be consulted to make sure all objectives have been considered and listed. Objectives have a way of dividing themselves into two types—first, the personal objectives, and second, the tax objectives. Many clients are more interested in the personal objectives and feel that taxes play second fiddle; their eyes are on the family and the family's welfare. Other clients are just the reverse; they have their eyes on the tax bill, and cutting taxes is the only way to turn them on. Both types of objectives can be served if the plan is properly conceived and implemented.

A typical set of objectives might look like this:

1. Joe Founder's (Joe's) objectives:

    a. Continue to work until age 60 (Joe is now 57).

    b. Then slow down, but remain active in a consulting capacity.

    c. Keep day-to-day control of company until my oldest son, Joe Jr. (who is now 30) can assume total responsibility and control.

    d. Have a steady flow of income for retirement without necessity of any compensation from the company after age 65.

2. Corporation's objectives:

    a. Build a strong management team headed by Joe Jr.

    b. Make sure the company can survive if Joe cannot be active for any reason.

    c. Make sure that none of the corporation's assets would be needed to pay taxes when Joe dies.

3. Family's objectives:

    a. Joe's wife can continue to live in the manner in which she is accustomed if Joe should die first.

    b. Joe's other two children (Tom, aged 32, and Mary, aged 27) would each receive a fair share of Joe's estate. (Neither Tom nor Mary is likely to become involved in the business. Tom is a successful doctor. Mary married a millionaire who doesn't like you, your wife, or your business.)

    c. Make sure that all nineteen grandchildren have an educational fund set up for them.

    d. None of the family's real estate or business assets should be sold to pay death taxes.

With our list of specific objectives, we are ready to develop a transfer plan and select the transfer tools to accomplish those objectives.

The Transfer Plan

In most cases, planning the transfer of a closely held corporation simply means accomplishing the founder's objectives while minimizing the tax cost. The client attempts to freeze his estate at its current level and divert future growth (to the extent possible under the law) to the natural objects of his bounty (usually his children and grandchildren). As this report develops, you will see that it is far easier to divert future growth than it is to disgorge wealth that has already been accumulated. A good transfer plan is part of an overall lifetime plan that attempts to get the asset-freezing process into place as soon as possible. Also, it dovetails with the estate plan. Obviously, if you can cut off (transfer) wealth before it accumulates, serious tax problems can be avoided.

The Transfer Tools

A number of tools have been developed to accomplish the transfer of ownership and asset freeze objectives. They include:

1. Sale of stock,

2. Stock bonus to employees of the corporation,

3. Gifts,

4. Redemptions,

5. Redemptions with appreciated property owned by the corporation,

6. Preferred stock dividends,

7. Recapitalization (no longer viable),

8. Personal holding company, and

9. Combinations of the above methods.

In addition to these methods, others can be used to meet transfer objectives. While not covered in this article, the most important are:

1. Buy and sell agreements,

2. Private family annuities,

3. Employee stock option trusts, or "ESOPs," as they are commonly called,

4. Other qualified deferred compensation plans (profit-sharing or pension plans),

5. Nonqualified deferred compensation plans,

6. Family partnerships,

7. Multiple corporations,

8. Life insurance as required to protect the family, pay estate taxes, fund buy and sell agreements, and so on, and

9. GRIT (Grantor retained interest trust).

Setting up a transfer of ownership plan that covers all the bases is a complex procedure that requires the help of an expert. This article cannot give you all the answers. It will get you started and show you how to avoid the tax collector's heavy hand.

Sale of Stock

The sale of stock from one family member to another should only be used when one of the other methods discussed in this chapter will not work. Tax consequences make this method prohibitive for two reasons: (1) The selling family member must pay tax on the profit, and (2) the buying family member must use after-tax dollars to make the payments, which are not deductible.

The stock of a closely held corporation is usually sold in either an outright sale (usually to outsiders) or a buy-sell agreement between stockholders. In an outright sale, terms are agreed on at a specific point in time at or near the time of sale. With the buy-sell terms have been set forth, usually at some point in the past, to be triggered by a certain event.

Buy-sell agreements between a founder and members of his immediate family (spouse and children) usually are not necessary, because typical objectives can usually be accomplished better by another method. In addition, most buy-sell agreements set up stringent rules that are not flexible enough to meet changing family objectives. Buy-sell agreements make sense between brothers, uncle and nephew, unrelated fellow stockholders or in other relationships, but not between parents and children.

If the stock has not been transferred to the son during the father's life, there should be some prearranged assurance that the value of the father's stock is on hand in terms of the money to make the purchase after his death. Normally the only way to accomplish this with the required certainty is by having life insurance. However, the age of the founder might make it prohibitively expensive for either the corporation or the son to own and pay for life insurance. Further, the father might be uninsurable.

Whether the corporation purchases stock, via a redemption, or the son purchases the stock, neither will get a deduction for the purchase price.

Other problems come with the setting of the purchase price.

Since the price of stock (or the formula for determining the price) must be fixed in advance, the founder is on the horns of a dilemma. A high price will increase both his estate and the financial burden on the family business and the son. If the price is set too low, it will jeopardize the funds needed to support the founder's wife and could become unfair to children not in the business. Often, such children must look to the stock value as the sole mechanism for receiving their "fair" share of the estate. A price lower than fair market value can run afoul of Section 2036(c).

Finally, IRS attribution rules are designed to turn distributions from a corporation to certain related parties into dividends, taxed as ordinary income (instead of tax-free distributions or capital gains). If your family corporation bought $200,000 of stock from your estate or your wife, the entire $200,000 could be taxed as a dividend.

An outright sale of stock can be made either for cash or on an installment basis.

The easiest way to understand the impact of a sale is by running through the cash flow results of a cash sale. Refer to Exhibit I. Let's run through the exhibit together.

Assumptions

Joe Founder's corporation is worth $500,000. Joe wants to sell his son John 1 percent of the stock. John does not have any funds with which to make the purchase. All parties—the corporation, Joe and John—are in a 30 percent income tax bracket. Joe's estate will be in a 50 percent estate tax bracket.

Look under column headed "Corporation." To get John the money to buy the stock, the corporation pays him a $10,000 bonus. Assume there is no

Exhibit I. Cash Flow—Outright Sale

Details	Corporation	John	Joe
1. During Life			
a. Portion of salary	($10,000)	$10,000	– –
Tax – Saved	$3,000		
– Paid	– –	($3,000)	– –
Net after tax	($7,000)	$7,000	– –
b. Purchase of stock	– –	($7,000)	$7,000
Tax–assume cost of $1,000, profit of $6,000 x 30%	– –	– –	($1,800)
Net after-tax	($7,000)	$None	$5,200
2. Estate tax at death of Joe	– –	– –	($2,600)
Net after income and estate taxes	($7,000)	$None	$2,600

reasonable compensation problem. Notice that the $10,000 is shown opposite "Portion of Salary" as outgoing from the corporation. Since the corporation deducted the $10,000 on its income tax return, the "Net after income and estate taxes" is a net out-of-pocket $7,000 to the corporation.

Next, look at the column under "John." John received a $10,000 salary/bonus, paid $3,000 in taxes and had a "Net after-tax" balance of $7,000. He immediately wrote a check to his father for $7,000 to purchase 1 percent of the stock. Joe's tax cost for this stock was $1,000, resulting in a $6,000 profit. At a 30 percent tax rate, Joe's tax is $1,800, leaving Joe with $5,200 in cash. Upon Joe's death, that $5,200 will be included in his estate, resulting in a $2,600 estate tax cost. Joe's "Net after income and estate taxes" is therefore $2,600. When all the smoke clears, the net result of the entire transaction—from the $10,000 bonus to John to the final amount left in Joe's estate—is a $4,400 *cash outflow*, or $7,000 out of the corporation, less $2,600 left in Joe's estate.

Every time you think about selling the stock of a closely held corporation to a family member, it is imperative that you work the proposed figures through a tentative cash flow. In almost every case, you will wind up with a negative cash flow. Then, make a projection of what the cost of the loss of the use of money might be. Remember, Joe paid an $1,800 tax on the $6,000 profit.

Just how much could the family unit have earned with the $1,800 if Joe lived for 20 more years after the sale to John? The loss of the use of money may ultimately be a greater cost than the immediate tax cost.

An installment sale usually gives better results than an outright sale, but the tax

pill will still be bitter. Here are some of the advantages and disadvantages of using an installment sale.

Advantages include: The future growth of the stock unquestionably has been transferred to the son. The principal and interest on the installment sale will provide a flow of income to the father. Assuming the stock was sold at fair market value, there is no current gift tax or use of the unicredit. The son gets a stepped-up basis for the stock. There is great flexibility in the amount of present and future payments. Payments can be adjusted via the interest rate, the amount of each principal payment, by adding a prepayment privilege, or by providing for a balloon payment down the road.

Disadvantages include: If the father retains an interest in the corporation, the sale will not be effective for estate tax purposes under Section 2036(c). The portion of the gain realized each year will be subject to an immediate tax. Although this gain can be deferred by making the initial principal payments small and putting a balloon at the tail end, sooner or later the tax on the gain must be paid.

If the father dies before receiving full payment of the installment obligations, the obligation is not only included in his estate for estate tax purposes, but the remaining collections will be subject to income tax as collected. This is called "income in respect of a decedent," causing, in effect, a double tax on the same note receivable. The taxes paid on the lifetime installment sale are actually a waste. They could have been avoided if the stock had been held until death.

The interest the son pays to his father could be classified as investment interest, which can only be deducted against investment income. If the son has no investment income, the interest is, in effect, non-deductible. Electing S-corporation status will make the interest deductible.

Once the sale is completed, certain other questions must be asked and dealt with immediately. "What happens if the son cannot make the payments?" Certainly, he can renegotiate the contract with his father. This might become a necessity if the value of the stock goes down significantly.

But what if the son dies and one of the objectives was to provide a cash flow to the father? Unquestionably, life insurance is an essential consideration for solving this problem. Because the son is a generation or so younger than his father, term insurance for the son will provide an inexpensive and certain solution for satisfying this particular family objective.

In most cases, the employee will be the son or daughter of the founder or some other close family member active in the corporation. Suppose we give a bonus to Joe Founder's son, John, who is an employee of the corporation. The bonus is in shares of stock of the corporation. Assume there is no unreasonable compensation problem when the value of the bonus stock is added to John's other compensation.

It is not commonly known that when a corporation issues shares of its stock to an employee the employee must pay income tax on the fair market value of the stock he receives. The corporation can deduct the fair market value of the stock that it gives to the employee as compensation. This gives Joe, John and the corporation a tremendous tax advantage.

Which is best? A sale of stock from Joe Founder to John or use of the stock bonus method? Obviously, Joe's objectives would have an impact on the answer. A comparison between a sale of stock from Joe to John as opposed to a stock bonus shows which method best

Exhibit II. Cash Flow—Partial Stock Bonus

Details	Corporation	John	Joe
1.During Life			
a. Cash salary	($5,000)	$5,000	– –
b.$5,000 of stock as salary	– –	– –	– –
Tax (on $10,000 salary)			
Saved	$3,000	– –	– –
Paid	– –	($3,000)	– –
Net after tax	($2,000)	$2,000	$ None

meets Joe's objectives. Remember Exhibit I where Joe sold $7,000 worth of stock to John, who had received a cash salary of $10,000; paid a tax of $3,000, resulting in a $7,000 after-tax amount to John; and finally, transmitted $7,000 to Joe.

Now take a look at Exhibit II. John receives $5,000 in cash and $5,000 in stock as a salary/bonus, a total of $10,000. Look under the column headed "Corporation." Remember, all parties are in 30 percent tax brackets.

The corporation is out-of-pocket $5,000 because of the cash salary and is in-pocket $3.000 because of the $10,000 it deducted as compensation. The "Net after-tax" cash flow is $2,000. Now look under John's column. He received the $5,000 in cash plus $5,000 in stock for a total of $10,000 in compensation and must pay $3,000 income tax for a "Net after tax" of $2,000. What about Joe? He is not even involved in the transaction. He did not make a gift. He had nothing to do with it, other than sitting on the Board of Directors and voting for the transaction.

As a matter of fact, Joe has reduced the value of his interest in the corporation. Assume Joe owned 100 percent of the corporation before the stock bonus, represented by 100 shares of stock. After the stock bonus of one share to John (since this share is worth $5,000, the total value of the corporation is approximately $500,000), the corporation has 101 shares issued and outstanding. Joe still owns the same 100 shares, but only 99.01 percent of all the stock. In effect he has transferred almost 1 percent of the corporation's value — all without a real transfer and, best of all, with zero tax cost.

Gifts

The primary advantage of an annual gift program, with either the operating or nonoperating children, is its very simplicity. In certain cases, a gift program can be used to accomplish all the family objectives. In most cases, however, because of the high value of the stock involved gifts alone cannot do the entire job.

These items should be considered when contemplating a gift program of stock. You can make a $10,000 gift to each person each year without any gift tax consequences. If your wife consents to the gift, the amount is doubled to $20,000. Property that is likely to appreciate over time (like stock in a closely held corporation) is the perfect gift to be made to members of a younger generation. Future appreciation is removed from the estate of the donor without any tax cost.

While the founder would like to transfer the ownership of the stock so that it will be removed from his estate, he might not want to transfer control to his children. Perhaps the children are minors. Perhaps adult children are active in the business, but their managerial capabilities aren't fully established and Dad wants to hang in there. Worst case, perhaps there are adult children but they are not active in the business and who cannot handle ownership responsibilities.

These problems can usually be solved by putting the stock into a trust, issuing nonvoting stock, or keeping enough stock to stay in control. Using those methods can be very technical. Your professional advisor must be involved.

Simple lifetime gifts can seldom be looked to as the sole tool needed to fulfill family objectives. When the amount of gifts becomes high enough, tax consequences result. Gifts usually are used in combination with other methods to transfer the stock of a closely held corporation.

The combinations of methods for transferring corporate stock are limited only by the imagination. One example should make the point.

Let's go back to Exhibit II and change the facts just a bit. Assume John was given two shares of stock as a bonus (no cash) with a value of $10,000. Now the corporation would be in-pocket $3,000, and John would pay $3,000 in income tax. Joe makes a $3,000 cash gift to John so he can pay his income tax liability. Joe's $3,000 gift does not have any tax consequences.

If we assume the corporation has a fair market value of $500,000, then Joe has managed to move approximately 2 percent of the future growth of the corporation to his son without any current out-of-pocket cost to the family. Why? The corporation is $3,000 in-pocket (because of the $10,000 salary deduction), while Joe and John together are out-of-pocket $3,000 (because the gift to John was used to pay John's current tax liability—30 percent of the $10,000 value of the bonus stock). Net effect: The family, including the corporation, comes out even.

There is an additional estate tax saving. Joe's estate will be reduced by about $13,000 ($10,000 for the approximate current value of the stock plus $3,000 in cash). In a 50 percent estate tax bracket, the family will save another $6,500. Of course, future appreciation of the stock owned by John after the stock bonus also will escape inclusion in Joe's estate.

An employee stock bonus plan, continued over a period of years and combined with cash gifts from the founder,

can be very effective in moving substantial portions of stock to one or more members of the family who are employed by the corporation.

Redemptions

A redemption occurs when a corporation uses its property to acquire its own stock from one or more stockholders. The vital question really is, "What will the tax treatment be to the redeeming stockholder—a dividend or capital gain?" Every cent of a dividend, to the extent of retained earnings, is subject to tax. A capital gain, on the other hand, is tax free for the full amount of the tax bases (usually cost) of the stock.

The Internal Revenue Code provides a clear answer. If the redemption qualifies as a sale or exchange, the excess of the proceeds over the taxpayer's basis is a capital gain. If the redemption does not qualify, the entire amount of the proceeds is a dividend. Of course, the amount of the dividend is limited to the earnings and profits of the corporation at the time of the redemption. The Code provides four redemption methods of attaining capital gain treatment: complete redemption; substantially disproportionate redemption; redemptions not essentially equivalent to a dividend; and certain redemptions involving railroad stock or bankruptcy situations.

For example:

Joe Founder owns 70 percent of the stock; the other 30 percent is owned by an unrelated business associate. The corporation, J. F. Inc., is worth $1,000,000. J. F. Inc. redeems 10 percent of Joe's stock for $100,000. Joe is stuck with a $100,000 dividend. Since it is not a "complete redemption," and it flunks the complex requirements for a "substantially disproportionate redemption." If, however, J. F. Inc.

257

redeems all of Joe's stock for $700,000, Joe's profit is a capital gain.

The redemption price may be paid in a lump sum or in installments. In practice, the rule is complex and can trap you into a dividend. Seek professional guidance.

Quite often, a family-controlled corporation owns property that has appreciated substantially over the years. Although the corporation may be rich in terms of appreciated property (in the form of vacant land, improved real estate or something else), there may be no cash with which to redeem a retiring or selling founder.

Have the redeeming stockholder (using a complete redemption) exchange his stock for the appreciated property. The corporation treats the transaction just like a sale to a stranger; the stockholder walks off with both a capital gain and the appreciated property. Where real estate is involved, the stockholder can lease the property back to the corporation.

Recapitalizations

The term "reorganization" as used in the Internal Revenue Code is very different from the general meaning of the term; the use is different than a corporate financial arrangement or "rearrangement" of a corporation that is in financial trouble. Although there are six types of reorganizations, our concern here centers around what is commonly referred to as a "recapitalization."

Before Congress placed Section 2036(c) into the IRS Code, recapitalization was a straightforward process.

The corporation issued as its only class of voting stock, voting preferred stock that will be owned and retained by the founder. This stock has a small value.

The second class of stock to be issued by the corporation is non-voting preferred stock. This stock is structured in so that it constitutes almost all of the value of the corporation's assets at the time of the recapitalization. The third class of stock under the plan is nonvoting common stock. It constitutes the entire residuary value of the corporation but has little or no present value. This stock automatically becomes the beneficiary of the future growth of the company. Its ownership goes to those persons (the kids) in the family who will enjoy the future growth. The result was a tax joy. The value of the founder's preferred stock was frozen, yet he was still in control. The future growth went to the kids who owned the common stock.

I could cry. Congress killed recapitalizations as an effective way of freezing the estate of an owner of a closely held corporation. The new law, via Section 2036(c), is broad and sweeping and stops the use of recapitalizations, as described above. If you hold a 10 percent or more interest in the voting power or income stream of a business, you can be affected. If you transfer the potential appreciation in that interest (typically common stock) and retain a significant interest in the income (typically the preferred stock), the value of the transferred interest will be included in your gross estate at death.

The new law is a complex maze. Not only is it technical, but it probably will be years before final regulations will be issued by the IRS. The law is so broad that it has an impact not only on recapitalizations, but in many other areas of transfer including gifts, sales and redemptions.

There is no easy way to explain Section 2036(c). Here is exactly the way the section appears in the Internal Revenue Code:

"[Sec. 2036(c)]

(c) Inclusion Relation to Valuation Freezes. —

(1) In General. - For purposes of subsection (a), if —

(A) any person holds a substantial interest in an enterprise, and

(B) such person in effect transfers after December 17, 1987, property having a disproportionately large share of the potential appreciation in such person's interest in the enterprise while retaining an interest in the income of, or rights in, the enterprise, then the retention of the retained interest shall be considered to be a retention of the enjoyment of the transferred property."

Now, it is only fair to tell you that the above quotation is only the beginning of the section. It rambles on for almost four full pages. The rest of the section gives you a series of definitions, special rules and exceptions.

The intent and the effect are simple. Any attempted freeze (usually to younger family members) is treated like a transfer with a retained life interest. As a result, upon the death of the transferor (usually, the business owner), the transferred interest will be included in the estate of the transferor at its value on death. In addition, that value is includable if the retained interest is disposed of during the three-year period prior to the date of the decedent's death. Also, it may be includable even if the retained interest is sold for its fair market value during the three-year period.

The new section has seven important operating rules:

1. *An individual and his spouse* are treated as one person.

2. The term *family,* for these purposes, means, with respect to any individual, the individual's spouse, any lineal descendant of the individual or the spouse, any parent or grandparent of the individual and any spouse of any of the foregoing. Relationship by adoption is treated as one by blood.

3. *A transfer encompasses,* but is not limited to, all transactions whereby property is passed to or conferred upon another, regardless of the means or device employed in its accomplishment. Sales for full and adequate consideration, other than to family members, are exempt from the new rules. Appropriate adjustments in the value of the estate will be made for sales which are not exempt. When an interest is sold for less than full and adequate consideration, the amount included in the estate will be reduced by the consideration received by the decedent. Sales to family members are deemed to be for less than full and adequate consideration. The Technical & Miscellaneous Revenue Act of 1988 (TAMRA) carves out an exception for family sales if the transferor receives "qualified debt." Basically, this is fixed interest debt due within 15 years of the issue date. The debt cannot be subordinated or converted to stock and cannot have voting rights.

4. *A person holds a substantial interest* in an enterprise if he or she owns, directly or indirectly, 10 percent or more of the voting power or income stream or both in the enterprise. For these purposes, an individual is treated as owning any interest in an enterprise owned, directly or indirectly, by any

member of his or her family. According to the Conference Committee Report, interests held indirectly by a person include interests held by an entity in which the person has an interest.

5. Although the term *enterprise* is not defined by the new law, the Committee Reports say that an enterprise includes a business or other property which may produce income or gain. This makes it clear that partnerships, as well as corporations, are included.

6. *A disproportionately large share of potential appreciation* is any share of appreciation in the enterprises greater than the share of appreciation borne by the property retained by the transferor. Rights in the enterprise are voting rights, conversion rights, liquidation rights, warrants, options and other rights of value.

Example

Success Co. is owned 100 percent by Joe Founder. Success has only common stock. Joe gifts 51 percent of the stock to his son, John. John has more potential appreciation than Joe in the stock of Success. Result: Joe's estate will include the value of John's stock.

What to Do

As long as Joe Founder wants to keep on working in the business, he should not transfer more than 50 percent of the stock to his children.

The Conference Committee Report explains that if a share of appreciation borne by the transferred property is disproportionately large, but only with respect to part of the transferred property, only that part of the transferred property is includable in the estate.

Example

Joe owns a substantial interest in an enterprise. His holdings consist of 100 shares of common stock and 100 shares of preferred stock. He transfers 80 shares of the common stock and 20 shares of the preferred stock. Only 60 shares of the transferred common stock are included in Joe's gross estate. The transfer of the 20 shares of preferred stock, in effect, cancels the transfer of the 20 shares of common.

If the taxpayer retains preferred stock with the income stream or voting rights, Section 2036(c) will sweep the attempted freeze back into the taxpayer's estate.

When Founder Wants to Retire

Once the founder really wants to retire — quit working in the business entirely — here are two ways to still accomplish a freeze of the future growth.

The family sale (possibly using an installment sale) may become one of the most popular estate-freeze techniques. The disadvantage of this technique is the loss of the tax-free step-up in basis on death. Of course, the buying family member gets a step-up to the purchase price. Incurring income tax at the 28 percent rate may be much better than a 55 percent estate tax cost in some cases. The sale should be for cash, or an installment sale could be used to defer the income tax cost. On an installment sale, since the debt is from the shareholder and not the enterprise, it need not be qualified debt.

The sale should be made at fair market value.

A sale of part of the stock for qualified debt to a family member in tandem with a complete redemption in cash (or qualified debt) is an excellent way to bail cash out of the corporation and transfer the remaining value and all future growth to the children or grandchildren. Sales for full and adequate consideration are not gifts and therefore are not subject to the generation-skipping transfer tax. Again, make the sale/redemption at fair market value.

New Capitalization-Like Opportunity...Use of S Corporation and Gifts

S Corporations have many uses. But whoever would have thought this form of corporation could pull off an effective estate plan (corporate freeze) ploy? Well, it can. Here's how.

An S corporation can have nonvoting as well as voting common stock. (Two classes of stock – preferred and common – are prohibited.) A two-step procedure allows you to shift current value and future growth to the next generation while still maintaining absolute control of the corporation.

Exchange a portion of your voting common stock for nonvoting common stock. After the exchange, immediately begin an annual gift-giving program of the nonvoting stock to the younger generation. At the rate of $10,000 ($20,000 if married) per year per done, this method can be an effective estate tax-saver. Be careful not to transfer more than 50 percent of the stock.

A Final Word

To cover every aspect of how to transfer control of a closely held corporation would take several large volumes. Even then, the volumes would not contain every nuance, exception, rule and tax problem.

Furthermore, every transfer of ownership plan is always a little different than any other plan. Why? The reason becomes obvious when you stop to think that each plan involved *real* people, with *real* family problems and *real* tax problems.

Remember, any type of transfer that is attempted by the owner of a closely held business requires a valuation of the entire business. Sooner or later, the owner of a closely held corporation and his family must face the valuation problem. It is easier to face the problem while the owner is alive and healthy. It is also easier to face the problem before the corporation has appreciated substantially in value. Delay favors the IRS.

Also remember, tax planning saves dollars. Do it. *Now.*

Introduction

For a business family, forms of estate planning include business continuity, personal financial security, equitable treatment of the next generation and tax savings. This article suggests means and processes by which a business family can successfully engage in estate planning. Succession hazards are pointed out so they may be avoided.

Estate Planning for the Family-Owned Business: It Is Not Really "Mission Impossible"

1988

By Glenn R. Ayres

Estate planning, or perhaps more accurately for the family-owned business, ownership planning, is all too often shrouded in legal and tax mysteries and conducted exclusively in the confines of the professional's office. There is an almost tangible aura of confidentiality surrounding these efforts and a stifling seriousness associated with dealing with such emotionally-loaded topics as "money," "death," and "family."

Even if it does get "finished," the task may be seen as thoroughly distasteful and as a result the planning is often incomplete or frequently languishes for years without adequate review or update.

It does not have to be this way. However, the process of change has to be initiated by the business owner. Most lawyers, accountants, financial planners and trust officers have been taught to operate as experts, not as process consultants. The client presents a problem and they have one, two, or a dozen immediate solutions waiting on the shelf or in the word processor. The priority is to get the job done, bill the file and go on to safer, other work.

Financial experts struggle daily to keep abreast of an ever-evolving tax system; their markets are extremely competitive; and it is their perception that they get paid for results, not talk. Spending much time in the murky and emotional waters of death, money and family simply doesn't make good economic sense when they hear the client say over and over again, "keep it simple and get this done as quickly as possible."

The first order of business, then, is for you, the family business owner, to change the ground rules. The client is always in control of the relationship and if that control is exercised, most professional advisors will welcome an open and direct approach rather than one which is critical and guarded.

Begin with a review of your priorities before the first visit and then clearly establish those priorities with your consultant. Certainly tax planning is important, but viewed from a family business perspective, the following list might be a lot more productive:

1st Priority: Continuity of the Business

2nd Priority: Your Personal Financial Security

3rd Priority: Equitable Treatment of the Next Generation

4th Priority: Tax Savings

Continuity of the Business

Continuity of the business, seen both as a family and a business issue, deserves top billing. Viewed in this way, questions of management and ownership can be separated and the topic of succession planning broadened to deal with all aspects of what is good for the company. It is fair game in this contest to talk about selling the business, involving non-family employees, or even utilizing outside management resources. In short, by placing continuity of the business at the top of your priority list you have put this area back into the contest of business planning. This is an area you know well and one in which you have participated, if not directed, for years. Solid answers in this area will direct and focus the rest of the estate planning process.

Your Personal Financial Security

It is amazing how often this priority is left off the list entirely. Yet the best tax advice is utterly useless if it runs counter to your own needs and *desires*. The vast

majority of estate plans, no matter how sophisticated, do not save a penny of taxes for the current generation so it is vitally important that you assess your own needs early on in the process.

Consider this abbreviated list:

• What does your life style demand in the way of financial support?

• How large a reserve do you need to feel safe, comfortable and independent?

• When the business no longer occupies you on a full time basis, what will it cost to pursue the activities and interests you have?

• What is your personal risk tolerance? Can you step back and let someone else make the big business decisions, even if you are not at risk financially?

• Do you have responsibilities or financial commitments to others outside the business?

Equitable Treatment of the Next Generation

Note this does not say *equal* treatment. Your children are not fungible and you have never treated them "equally." Parents strive to treat their children as unique individuals, each with their own business, family and personal goals. Why all of a sudden must everything be divided down to the last penny and piece of silver?

Perhaps this problem of absolute equality stops more good planning from going forward than any other single factor. Most surprising to many parents is the realization, usually brought to time by their own children, that the children neither want nor expect absolute equality. "Of course Bill and Sue should ultimately get the business," voices a brother, "they've been working there all their lives and a good measure of our family's success has to be attributed to their involvement and commitment."

Even without the next generation's recognition of fairness as opposed to equality, the concept needs to be accepted if the first and second priorities are to be achieved in most planning situations. Almost invariably the business represents the most significant element in your balance sheet, and unless a sale, merger, or public offering is a part of the plan, it simply will not be possible to effectuate absolute equality in your estate plan and still serve the best interests of the business. And this is not to say that there are not a number of ways a healthy business can financially serve non-action family members. But the goal must not be equality at all costs.

Assuming the business is sufficiently sound to permit some financial participation by non-active family members, it is important not to saddle involved family members with the uncontrolled "arm chair quarterbacking" of a non-involved parent or sibling. Such second guessing can, with good planning, be turned into active and knowledgeable board participation, but passive policy making is touchy business at best. If attempted, it should be carefully structured, involve outside directors, and include some clear lines of responsibility in addition to a system of evaluation for both board members and management.

All of this protecting of the active family members is not just for the benefit of management. On the flip side, a gift of a minority interest that does not carry enough weight to influence management is not a great bonanza to non-active shareholders. Family or closely held company stock normally pays no dividends; there is no market for the stock; and it often represents an

appreciating asset on a non-active child's balance sheet that will someday cause an estate tax problem with no off-setting financial gain.

If the financial benefits from the company are to be used to assist non-active family, consider structuring those benefits around passive assets, like land or equipment, or use the business to bolster your own non-business resources so that your future gifts will not impact on the management structure. Listed below are some ideas the financially healthy company might employ:

1. Net-Net Lease: Assuming the real estate used by the company is owned outside the corporation, giving this property, subject to lease, to a spouse or non-active children creates a passive income stream for the owner while assuring the company that it will have predictable costs it can rely upon. The "net-net" feature in such a lease merely places the burden for maintenance, insurance and taxes on the company rather than the non-active owners. (Equipment leasing is yet another variation on this theme.)

2. Recapitalization: While recent legislation has limited some of the tax benefits of capital reorganization, it is still a viable way to separate passive income (dividends) from corporate control (voting rights). This technique permits the splitting up of the corporate stock into blocks that typically carry with them corporate control (voting common stock) and blocks that have no vote, but rather carry an annual dividend stream (preferred stock). Used judiciously, this is one way for the current generation to replace some of their salaried income with dividend income while allowing day to day control to pass to the now active generation. Such dividend paying preferred stock can also be given to the next generation

of non-participating family members, while at the same time allowing those active in the business a free hand in running its affairs. (In the partnership context, the use of a family partnership can serve much the same purpose.) As with all major planning devices, care must be taken to insure that the operational as well as the tax ramifications are well understood prior to implementation.

3. Insurance: This type of asset can be used by the business to retire the senior generation's stock or the policies can be owned directly or in trust by non-active children as a substitute for corporate assets.

4. Corporate Benefit Packages: Concepts like deferred compensation, profit sharing, pension plans and even bonus plans, can play an important role in building non-business assets for the use of a surviving spouse or non-active children pursuing other career options.

Used most creatively this type of asset serves as a substitute for a stock buy-out between generations by using business dollars generated by son's management efforts to build a fund for mom and dad. Done in this manner, the stock can now be gifted to the active son rather than sold; dad and mom have replaced an illiquid asset with a highly liquid one, and a pool of divisible funds has been created for use in planning for the children not involved in the business.

5. Consulting Agreements: These contracts permit the senior generation or other children involved in related enterprises, to tap into corporate compensation in a programmed and complimentary manner that takes into account their individual skills while at the same time not being an intrusion on management.

Tax Savings:

Taxes should be one of the tests of whether the plan is, or is not, workable. However, they must not be the focus of the planning. In many respects, estate taxes are equivalent to the cost of the project. Like any cost factor, if the price is too high, another alternative will be chosen. The only real distinction here is that "not buying" should not be considered an option.

This part of the analysis should be left to the expertise of your lawyer or accountant. First decide what is in the family's best interest, and then look at the tax cost of the project. If the cost is too high, a framework will then exist for you and your advisor to discuss alternative techniques. the objective is to lower the cost without doing serious damage to how you want your affairs and the affairs of your business ordered.

Through this process you will gradually work down from an ideal plan that is too expensive to a compromise plan. It will be an affordable plan that still carries out your essential wishes. Keep in mind that the most tax effective plan is really not very cost effective if it results in a ruined business, an impoverished spouse, or conflict between the brothers and sisters.

Having settled on your new list of priorities, one other new ground rule needs discussing: *Confidentiality.* There is probably nothing as private in our legal traditions as the preparation of a will. This is neither incorrect nor inappropriate in many situations, but for the family business owner the maintenance of strict confidentiality that excludes the family makes the job a whole lot tougher. Consider:

• The impact the business is having and has had on your entire family.

265

- Whether it is to go to all the children or none of them.

- Whether your spouse will succeed you or sell out.

The disposition of a family-owned business affects everyone in the family. Your daughter may fear working for her mother who has not been involved in the business, or your son may be looking for other options if he doesn't get some signal from you soon. The family-owned business is truly more than a business; it has been part of your lives together and even the most passive of children need to be heard on this issue. Equally important, you need to know their thinking if business continuity and family harmony are to be achieved through your decisions.

Business owners say, "But, I can't discuss this topic at home, it would be World War III!" But if you do not exercise the leadership to solicit views and facilitate some collective understanding of these issues as only a parent can do, it will just as surely be World War III after you are gone.

No one is suggesting that estate planning discussions are easy, particularly if the family does not manage their differences well already, but any old probate hand will tell you that fights which erupt during the probate more often than not will leave permanent scars. Opening these discussions to your entire family may, in the final analysis, be the most important legacy of all.

If you choose to involve your family in the estate planning process, help is available. Your lawyer, accountant, financial planner or trust officer will be pleased to participate in a planning process that has clear priorities and an openness initiated by you.

Such an advisor may be able to solicit more candid responses from your family than even you can and he or she can set the tone for the process by making it clear that this is *your* planning. The participation of your children is to be encouraged and welcomed, but the ultimate decisions must remain your own. As a third party, the advisor can also often facilitate discussions that would not be productive or even possible for a family member. And, of course, the advisor has the technical skill to help you translate your business and family decisions into an effective estate plan and explain the operation of that plan to your family and management team.

Such a process can take any number of forms, but here is one suggested format:

1. Hold an initial meeting with your advisor where your priorities are laid out, your tentative business decisions communicated, and your family concerns expressed.

2. Schedule interviews between your advisor and the next generation (and perhaps selected non-family employees) to solicit their views, goals and concerns.

3. Hold a family planning meeting chaired by you and facilitated by your advisor where the concerns and objectives of the family are reviewed in a non-personal way and where the advisor presents the outline of an estate plan designed to address these issues.

4. Have the advisor prepare the documents necessary to memorialize this plan. Schedule a review and approval meeting for the two of you.

5. Convene a family signature conference where the instruments are executed with your family present. Have the advisor explain their operation and

impact on the business and individual family members.

Yes, it costs more up-front to do it this way, and yes, it may at first be more than a little intimidating to all concerned. But carried through to completion in an open and respectful manner this kind of planning will produce an estate plan that addresses your priorities and has the support of the entire family, whether they are involved in the family-owned business or not.

Certainly Uncle Sam will change the rules on us again, children will change their minds, and you may even decide to move to Phoenix. But updating your estate planning will never be as difficult or as mysterious as it once appeared and it certainly won't be viewed as "Mission Impossible."

Family-Owned Business Succession Hazards

Owners of family-owned businesses, like everyone else, find it difficult to openly confront the emotionally sensitive topics of death and money. Estate and succession planning can only be done if both subjects are discussed in detail. Avoidance easily sets in.

Avoidance is also fostered by complexity. Family business owners are surrounded by complexity. Protection of self and spouse, distribution to offspring, and tax considerations are essential concerns, but only if the business continues to exist. The priorities of continuity, protection, distribution and taxes are often in conflict with each other. Avoidance can be a line of least resistance when trying to sort out the confusion.

Avoidance results in failure to take action, secrecy, poor communication and incompleteness. The result can be a harsh and undesired emotional and economic legacy for future generations. the cost of avoidance is high.

Use the following list of "Succession Hazards" to check out your avoidance of estate planning.

1. "Doing nothing at all." An unprepared family in the midst of grief has to deal with the task of taking over business operations and sorting out the legal hassles.

2. "Behind closed doors." Secret discussions with legal advisors mean surprises for the survivors at a time when emotions are already spent and surprises are not easily managed.

3. "Equality at all costs." Confusing expressions of love and affection with the distribution of assets may burden the business and leave wounded feelings.

4. "It's no one's business." Neglecting to take into account the impact of decisions on the lives of the next generation and overlooking the possibility of communicating about needs and wishes can leave loved ones feeling discounted and unimportant.

5. "Our family has always done it this way." Tradition may mean issues of competence, interest and suitability are overlooked, hurting the business and thereby neglecting talent and interest within the family.

6. "No one else can do it right." Difficulty in valuing differences and in recognizing the contributions of others can rob the business of potential growth and creativity and can prevent appreciation and validation from being felt among family members.

Chapter 5

Professionalizing the Family Firm

Business growth or successful generational transition ultimately requires an evolution from an entrepreneurial to a professionally managed organization. This evolution occurs not only in terms of managerial practices, but also in terms of the firm's cultural values.

Professionalization of the family firm helps to overcome the emotional and psychological contradictions inherent in family business systems.

Introduction

Business growth or successful generational transition ultimately requires an evolution from an entrepreneurial to a professionally managed organizational system. This article offers guidelines for small-to-medium-sized companies seeking to make the transition. A successful transition should be planned and executed carefully and gradually in four stages: analysis and evaluation of existing business strategy; formalization of decision-making and information systems of the firm; selection and training of key individuals and development of middle management; and constant monitoring of change to insure a smooth transition.

The Transition to Professional Management: Mission Impossible?
1984

By Charles W. Hofer and Ram Charan

Reprinted by permission of **Entrepreneurship: Theory and Practice,** formerly the **American Journal of Small Business,** Vol. IX, No. 1, Summer 1984. Copyright © 1984 Baylor University.

Introduction

Since the pioneering work of Schumpeter [23], the study of entrepreneurship and enterprise development has attracted considerable interest in both academic and professional circles. This interest has been further stimulated by later research that showed the significant impact entrepreneurial activity has had on technological growth [14]. Until recently, this interest was channeled into two related, but separate lines of inquiry. The first focused on various characteristics of the entrepreneur. Here the hope was to find those traits or other factors that differentiated successful entrepreneurs from other individuals, for if this could

be done, our limited national and organizational resources could be more effectively directed to those persons most likely to succeed. The second line of inquiry involved an examination of the evolution of new enterprises over time. Here the purpose was to discern those characteristics that distinguished successful from non-successful enterprises at each "stage" of their development.

The importance of such work is further accentuated by the ever unfolding sequence of current events that increasingly dramatize the limitations on our natural and organizational resources and the consequent need to use them wisely. Such constraints make it critical that we increase our understanding of the enterprise development process so that we can reduce the extremely high failure rate of new ventures and thus reduce the amount of resources we need to allocate to risk-taking activities. At the same time, we also need to further improve our knowledge of the downstream aspects of enterprise development because recent research has indicated that, after the starting difficulties have been overcome, the most likely causes of business failure are the problems encountered in the transition from a one-person, entrepreneurial style of management to a functionally organized, professional management team. Accomplishing such transitions is a difficult task, however, especially because of the psychological makeup and personality traits of most founding entrepreneurs [3][6][8]. It is, in fact, so difficult that Barnes and Hershon [2] have concluded that the best way to make such transitions in organizational evolution is to pursue them when the entrepreneur retires or dies and a new generation of management takes over the direction of the organization. While this may be so, the need to improve our use of organizational resources demands that we develop models for successfully making such transitions without resorting to such a drastic expedient. It is the purpose of this paper to present one such model.

Enterprise Development and Evolution

There are, of course, already numerous models of organizational development and growth. Starbuck, for example, identified models of organizational growth that he felt could be grouped into four broad categories, i.e., "cell division models; metamorphosis models; will-o'-the-wisp models; and decision making process models." [26].

In the policy area, most of the organizational development and growth models proposed to date would combine characteristics of Starbuck's cell division and metamorphosis categories. Because of this overlap, we have found it more useful for our own research to reclassify such models into one of the following four categories: (1) life cycle models, (2) stages models, (3) evolutionary models, and (4) transition models.

The life cycle models, including those of Steinmetz [28] and Kroeger [17], represent organizational development and growth as following a pattern directly analogous to biological life cycles. While intuitively appealing, such models have a number of weaknesses. First, organizations do not display the time consistency of development found in biological models. Thus, few of these models stipulate when one phase of the life cycle ends and another begins, even though such specification is necessary for improving management practice. Second, the development portrayed by such models is invariant in sequence, yet most studies of organizational development indicate no such invariant sequence in real life. And, third, not all organizations die as postulated by such models or at least not in time periods relevant to the entrepreneur. The stages models, including those of Filley [12], Scott [24], Buchele [3], Lippett and Schmidt [19], Salter [22], Thain [26], Collins and Moore [10], and Straus [29], attempt to get around these difficulties by postulating a series of "stages" through which organizations evolve over time. Unlike the life cycle models, however, the movement of an organization from one stage to another in these models is dependent on a number of factors other than time. Thus, it is not necessary that an organization ever move out of Stage I, and, even if it does, there is no prescribed time at which this must occur. Equally important, organizations need not go through every stage, and there are several possible sequences in which they may move from stage to stage. These models also permit several alternatives to death for the alternate development of the firm. The two most critical weaknesses of stages models are that, with one or two exceptions, they do not indicate the details of the process or the problems involved in making the transition between stages, and that they do not agree on a common set of stages. Thus, Straus has only two stages, while Buchele has seven. Moreover, their stages do not simply collapse into one another. Instead, Collins and Moore, Filley, and Buchele present several stages that precede Stage I of the Scott, Salter, and Thain models, while the latter contain at least one or two stages that follow the last stages of the Collins and Moore and Buchele models. Nonetheless, the stages models are a great improvement over the life cycle models, even though more research is needed so show that the patterns of organizational structure and systems they recommend for each stage do indeed produce better organizational performance than other patterns of structure and systems for that stage of development.

The evolutionary models of organizational development and growth proposed to date are both stronger and weaker than the stages models. Their major weakness is that while they contain most of the "stages" of development described by the stages models above, they propose an invariant linking of the different stages in the same way the life cycle models linked the different phases of the life cycle. In fact, Greiner [15] goes so far as to propose that "each phase is both an effect of the previous phase and a cause of the next phase." And, as we noted above, this proposition does not square with actual field observations even though there are some organizations for which it may be

true. The strength of these models is that they explicitly recognize the existence of, the importance of, and the difficulty of the transitions between stages. Unfortunately, however, they do not go on and develop any detailed models of how these transitions may be accomplished. This limitation is especially critical since the management problems encountered in making such transitions are more severe than those involved in selecting the optional structure and systems once the transition is accomplished. Similarly, more scarce resources are consumed by the firms that fail while trying to make these transitions or that retard their growth because they fear they will be unable to make the transition than are lost by firms which continue to operate with an inefficient structure once the transition is completed.

One problem in developing transition models is that it may be necessary to construct a different model for each different transition that is possible between different stages. Christensen [6], for example, has developed a model that focuses on the problems of management succession in entrepreneurially managed firms. Among the different transitions that are possible, probably the most difficult to achieve and also perhaps the most important for organizational development is that of moving from a one-person entrepreneurially managed firm to one run by a functionally organized, "professional" management team. Little research has been done on this topic, and most of what has been done has focused on the non-behavioral aspects of the transition. One exception is Barnes and Hershon's work [2] on the management succession-organizational development linkages in closely held firms. In general, they conclude that it is much easier to move from one stage of organizational development to another at the same time that a transition is made in the top management of the organization than at any other time. They also note that such transitions are more easily achieved from the second generation onward as each succeeding generation has some appreciation for the problems of such transitions since they went through such an experience themselves. Except for timing and perspective, however, Barnes and Hershon offer no further prescriptions for how such transitions might be accomplished. Nonetheless, their observation that the psychological makeup and personality traits of the entrepreneur pose equal, if not greater, barriers to the transition to professional management than do limitations on organizational resources and environmental opportunities is a major contribution to the development of improved models of this process.

The Entrepreneurial Process of Decision Making

Before beginning a discussion of our propositions on how to most effectively implement the transition to professional management, it is necessary to examine the key characteristics of entrepreneurially managed firms that will need to be modified in the transition process. The most important of these are: (1) a highly centralized decision making system, (2) an over-dependence on one or two key individuals for its survival and growth, (3) an inadequate repertoire of managerial skills and training, and (4) a paternalistic atmosphere.

It is impossible, of course, to centralize all decision making in any firm. Typically, though, most decisions about the acquisition and allocation of capital

resources, the selection and compensation of key personnel, pricing, purchase of raw materials, development of new products, loans and credit arrangements, labor negotiations, and diversification are made by one or two individuals including the entrepreneur him/herself in the Stage I firm.

At the same time, these individuals usually also get heavily involved in many of the day-to-day operating activities of the firm. This characteristic of the entrepreneurial firm permits it to respond quickly to environmental opportunities and threats. However, it also inhibits the development of subordinates' decision making skills – a situation that oft-times makes the organization too dependent on the top few individuals. Another possible danger arising from this tendency of the top individuals to get heavily involved in day-to-day activities is that such activities will begin to cut into the time the entrepreneur and his/her top executives should be spending on strategic decision making.

The failure to develop subordinates, coupled with the entrepreneur's personal limitations, and the fact that the entrepreneur usually feels he/she cannot afford to hire high-salaried functional personnel generally produces a number of major gaps in the range of skills possessed by the entrepreneurial firm. For example, since its inception fifteen years ago, Lawn King Products, Inc., a $40 million mideastern organization that manufactures and markets garden tractors, has been highly dependent on its owner/president's personal abilities for its high brand image and extensive distributor dealer network. Additionally, it is the owner himself who does all the selling. However, in recent times the owner has been feeling the limitations of his lack of knowledge and training with regard to broader marketing concepts, internal control through accounting and competitive strategies against larger companies, and this has begun to show up in the company's performance.

The final key characteristic of entrepreneurial firms is their highly paternalistic climate. Because they are small and have a relatively stable group of "core" employees, these firms develop a high sense of family among their members. In addition, the entrepreneur, through his/her attitudes and actions, encourages every employee to seek his/her advice whenever problems of a personal nature arise. Though the loyal paternalism that results from such behavior does account for part of the success of the entrepreneur in developing his/her company and personnel, it can also have long-term counter-productive effects.

Before proceeding to describe our model, it should be noted that the four characteristics discussed above are often important and in many cases essential to the success of the small, entrepreneurially managed firm at least up to a point. Beyond that point, however, they can become barriers to the firm in its efforts to capitalize on further market opportunities. For example, Breitman & Company, a manufacturer and marketer of women's belts and handbags, expanded its sales and profits over 3300 per cent during its first 10 years of operations because of the genius of its president as a designer and the selling talents of its vice president. During this time neither man changed his style of management and the company continued to use the same systems and procedures it had developed at start up. Over the next four years, however, its profits remained constant even though sales more than doubled because of the increasing inefficiency of these systems, and less than two years

later the firm went bankrupt when its costs had risen even more and its sales had dropped sharply because of customer dissatisfaction with its ever increasing delivery times.

Moreover, when these characteristics start turning into barriers, they begin to tax the physical and mental capabilities of the entrepreneur. It is, therefore, at this juncture that he/she must realize that the mode of managing his/her business requires a change from entrepreneurial to professional management.

A Model for the Transition to Professional Management

A professionally managed Stage II firm is one which has a functional organization structure based on its current needs, permits delegation of appropriate day-to-day decision-making authority to its subordinate managers, utilizes formal information analysis and the intra-firm consultative process to make administrative decisions, reflects in its routine operations stable corporate and business strategies that recognize both the long and short-term needs and goals of the organization, is free from excessive dependence on any particular individual or individuals for their skills and talents, and displays a certain degree of interchangeability among its components.

Given the characteristics of the typical entrepreneurially managed Stage I firm described above, it is not likely that successful transitions to professional management will occur very often unless they are planned carefully and implemented gradually.

The transition itself will usually involve five or more of the following seven steps [See exhibit 1 for a conceptual overview of the process].

1: *The entrepreneur him/herself must want to make the change and must want it strongly enough to make major modifications in his/her own task behavior.*

2: *The day-to-day decision making procedures of the organization must be changed.* Specifically, participation in the decision making process should be expanded, and the consultative process should be introduced. Greater emphasis should also be placed on the use of formal decision techniques.

3: *The two or three key operating tasks which are primarily responsible for the organization's success must be institutionalized.* This may involve the selection of some new people to supplement or replace those 'indispensable' individuals who have performed these tasks in the past.

4: *Middle level management must be developed.* In general this means that specialists will need to learn to become functional managers while functional managers are learning to become general managers.

5: *The firm's strategy should be evaluated and modified if necessary to achieve growth.*

6: *The firm's organizational structure and its management systems and procedures should be modified slowly over time to fit the company's new strategy and senior managers.*

7: *The firm must develop a professional board of directors.*

In general, the transition process is slow since it involves organizational and personal learning and because it is necessary to preserve old strengths while developing new ones. It must also be handled carefully because of all the psychological contracts that will have been built up over time. Moreover, the relative importance of these steps varies as is indicated by the following set of propositions about the transition process:

P1: If the entrepreneur does not want to change, the probability of successful transition is almost nil.

P2: If the entrepreneur is unwilling to change his/her day-to-day behavior, the probability of a successful transition is very low.

Some support for these propositions is provided by the experiences of Breitman & Company which was unable to make a successful transition in spite of successfully completing steps 4-5 of the transition process because its top managers were unwilling and unable to make such changes in their behavior. At the same time, several other steps of the transition process are also critical to successful transitions as is indicated in the following propositions:

P3: If the day-to-day decision making procedures are not changed and the top two or three key operating tasks are not institutionalized, the probability of a successful transition is almost nil.

P4: If sufficient numbers of middle managers are not developed, the probability of a successful transition is very low.

P5: If the firm's strategy is not consistent with moderately large and rapid growth, the probability of a successful transition is almost nil.

Some support for propositions P4 and P5 comes from the experiences of the Blakeston & Wilson Company which went bankrupt because of strategy problems and a lack of effective middle level managers even though its top management was so enthused about growth prospects that it easily met propositions P1 and P3 as well as P7 below.

P6: If a firm's top management is desirous of growth and willing to change its behavior and if the firm changes its day-to-day decision making procedures, institutionalizes key tasks and adopts a strategy consistent with moderately rapid growth, then the probability that it will successfully complete the transition process is quite high.

P7: Firms that try to complete the transition process too quickly or that take excessive time to complete it are less likely to be successful than firms that proceed at an intermediate rate.

Propositions P6 and P7 are supported by the experience of the Wilton Oil Equipment Company which met the conditions stipulated in propositions P1, P2, P3, and P4 but which did so only after a prolonged period of time so that

TABLE 1. PROPOSITIONS ON THE TRANSITION PROCESS

COMPANIES		P_1	P_2	P_3	P_4	P_5	P_6	P_7
Dansk Designs		V_w	V_w	V_w	V_w	V_w	V_s	N_s
Breitman		V_s	V_s	V_s	Vs	X	V_w	V_s
Wilton Oil		V_w	V_w	V_w	V_w	X	X	V_s
Vappi		V_w	V_w	V_w	V_w	V_w	V_s	X
Solartron Electronic Group		X	X	V_w	N_w	V_w	N_s	V_s
Vermont Tubbs		N_w	N_w	V_s	V_s	X	V_w	V_s
Blakeston & Wilson		V_s	V_s	V_s	V_s	V_s	V_w	V_s
Duralast		N_w	V_s	V_s	V_s	V_s	V_w	V_s
Hedblom		V_w	V_w	V_w	V_w	V_w	V_s	N_s
Superb Biscuits		V_w	V_w	V_w	V_w	X	X	V_s
Saltwater Farms		V_w	V_w	V_w	X	V_w	X	V_s
Total	V_s	2	3	4	4	2	3	8
	V_w	6	6	7	5	5	4	0
	N_w	2	1	0	0	0	0	0
	N_s	0	0	0	0	0	1	2

Key:

V_s indicates the situation provides strong direct evidence that the proposition is valid.

V_w indicates that the situation provides weak, indiret evidence that the proposition is valid.

N_w indicates that the situation provides strong, direct evidence that the proposition is not valid.

N_s indicates that the situation provides weak, indirect evidence that the proposition is not valid.

X indicates that the situation neither supports nor refutes the proposition.

it did not enjoy the measure of success it might have had.

Testing the Model

Quite clearly it is not acceptable to use single item anecdotal observations such as those above to test either individual propositions or the conceptual scheme from which they were derived. On the other hand, we were reluctant to establish the type of large scale research program that would be needed to comprehensively test each of our propositions until we were more confident of the general validity of our model. Consequently, we decided to test our ideas on a small scale basis first to see whether they appeared to have sufficient validity to warrant a more complete testing program.

As our sample, we chose ten different case studies on the transition process that are currently available from Harvard Case Services. We then asked a three person group to evaluate the degree to which each of the case studies supported or contradicted our propositions. (See Table 1)

Since not all cases provided direct evidence with respect to the validity of the different propositions, the sample size for most of the propositions was insufficient to permit strong statements about the statistical validity of the proposition even though, in all cases, the evidence that was available did support the propositions. On the other hand, taken as a group, our data provided rather strong support for our overall conceptual model, i.e., 26 out of 29 directly relevant observations are supportive of the propositions developed from our model while 33 of the 36 tangential observations also support our propositions.

One could question, of course, whether one should cluster the data relating to different propositions together as we have done. Clearly such a procedure would be inappropriate if all propositions were not related to each other in any way. However, since they were all developed from the same conceptual scheme, such a grouping gives a rough test of the statistical validity of the conceptual scheme as a gestalt even though the sample size for each individual proposition precludes making any final judgments about the statistical validity of our propositions on an individual basis.

Summary and Conclusions

Overall, this preliminary study suggests that our conceptual model of the transition process involved in moving from a one person, entrepreneurial style of management to that of a functionally organized team of professionals is a useful tool for predicting whether such transitions will be successful. It also indicates that it may be possible to assist the entrepreneur who would like to make such a change to do it successfully, i.e., that it is not necessary to wait for a new generation of management to take over before making such changes as Barnes and Hershon suggest. On the other hand, it would be inappropriate to put excessive faith in our model at this time since our sample size was not large enough to produce statistically significant results for any individual proposition.

Perhaps equally as important as the initial testing of our model, however, was the idea of testing the validity of our conceptual scheme in the aggregate. It would be incorrect to suggest that such a procedure should ever be considered as a substitute for the large scale testing of a model and its associated hypotheses—it is not! However, in those circumstances in which a series of propositions are all derived from one model or conceptual scheme, this procedure provides a way to get some rough assessment of the overall validity of the model or conceptual scheme before incurring the high cost associated with gathering a large-scale sample.

The Next Steps

Since this study has indicated that our conceptual framework may have merit, the next steps are to sharpen up the individual propositions and to develop the larger scale sample needed to test

EXHIBIT I. A Schematic Prepresentation of the Transition Process Showing the Relative Time Dimensions Involved in the Change

Recognition and awareness of need to change													
	Entrepreneur wants to change												
		Entrepreneur tries to change his own day-to-day behavior											
		Analyses of existing decision making procedures											
			Stabilization and formalization of decision making procedures										
						Broadening of participation in decision making & use of consultative procedures							
			Identification of key tasks	Institutionalization of key tasks									
				Development of middle level management									
				Assess adequacy of existing strategy		Implement new strategy							
						Evaluate org. structure		Check with others	Implement new structure				
									Hire and fire new personnel				
										Develop Board			
			Constant monitoring of change process through observation of key indicators										

| 0 | 3 | 6 | 9 | 12 | 15 | 18 | 21 | 24 | 27 | 30 | 33 | 36 | 39 | 42 |

Time (Months)

each proposition individually. When gathering this sample, we will need to take care that we get observations on a variety of different types of organizations since our present sample consisted mostly of manufacturing firms. In addition, we shall also need to get data on those situations not in the public record in which the transition was not successful since such firms are likely to be smaller than those we have studied and may indeed have different needs and requirements during the transition process.

References

1. Ansoff, H. I. and R. G. Brandenberg. "A Language for Organizational Design: Parts I and II." *Management Science*, 17(12): 705-31.

2. Barnes, L. B. and S. A. Hershon. "Transferring Power in the Family Business." *Harvard Business Review*, 54(4): 105-114 (July/August, 1976).

3. Buchele, R. B. *Business Policy in Growing Firms*. Scranton, Pennsylvania: Chandler Publishing Company, 1967.

4. Cannon, J. T. *Business Strategy and Policy*. New York: Harcourt, Brace and World, 1968.

5. Chandler, A. D., Jr. *Strategy and Strategy and Structure*, Cambridge: MIT Press, 1962.

6. Christensen, C. R. *Management Succession in Small and Growing Firms*, Boston; Harvard University, 1953.

7. Clarke, P. *Small Business*. Sydney: West Publishing Company, 1973.

8. Clifford, D. K. "Growth Pains of the Threshold Company." *Harvard Business Review*, 51(5): 143-154 (September/October, 1973).

9. Cohn, T. and R. A. Lindberg. *Survival and Growth: Management Strategies for the Small Firm*. New York: AMACOM, 1974.

10. Collins, O. and D. C. Moore. *The Organization Makers*, New York: Appleton-Century-Crofts, 1970.

11. Dun and Bradstreet. *The Business Failure Record Through 1972*, (New York: Dun and Bradstreet, 1973), p. 9.

12. Filley, A. C. *A Theory of Small Business and Divisional Growth*. Unpublished doctoral dissertation. Ohio State University, 1962.

13. Glueck, W. F. "An Evaluation of Stages of Corporate Development in Business Policy," Paper presented to the Midwest Academy of Management, Kent, Ohio, April 26, 1974.

14. Gough, J. W. *The Rise of the Entrepreneur*. New York: Schocken Books, 1970.

15. Greiner, L. E. "Evolution and Revolution as Organizations Grow," *Harvard Business Review*, 50(4): 37-46 (July/August, 1972).

16. Kotler, P. "A Theory of Market Evolution." Unpublished working paper July 23, 1976.

17. Kroeger, C. V. "Managerial Development in the Small Firm." *Business Horizons*, 17(1): 41-47 (Fall, 1974).

18. Levinson, H. "Conflicts that Plague a Family Business." *Harvard Business Review*, 49(2) (March/April, 1976).

19. Lippett, G. L. and W. H. Schmidt. "Crises in a Developing Organization." *Harvard Business Review*, 45(6): 102-112 (November/December, 1967).

20. McGuire, J. *Factors Affecting the Growth of Manufacturing Firms*. Seattle: Bureau of Business Research, University of Washington, 1963.

21. Mueller, D. C. "A Life Cycle Theory of the Firm." *Journal of Industrial Economics* 20(3): 199-214 (July, 1972).

22. Salter, M. S. "Stages of Corporate Development." *Journal of Business Policy*, 1(1): 23-27 (Autumn, 1970).

23. Schumpeter, J. A. *The Theory of Economic Development.* New York, Oxford Press, 1961.

24. Scott, B. R. "Stages of Corporate Development – Parts I and II." Boston: Harvard Case Services, #9-371-294 and 5.

25. Starbuck, W. "Growth and Development." In March, J. (ed) *Hand-book of Organizations.* Chicago: Rand McNally, 1965.

26. Thain, D. H. "Stage of Corporate Development." *Business Quarterly,* Winter 1969, pp. 33-45.

27. Steinmetz, L. L. "Critical Stages of Small Business Growth." *Business Horizons,* February 1969, pp. 29-36.

28. Straus, G. "Adolescence in Organizational Growth: Problems, Pains, Possibilities." *Organizational Dynamics,* 2(4): 1-12 (Spring 1974).

Introduction

A study of forty family firms shows that the family business's culture helps to determine success in the firm's survival into the second generation. Researcher W. Gibb Dyer of Brigham Young University found four common family business cultures: paternalistic, laissez-faire, participative, and professional.

In the first generation 80 percent of family businesses were found to be paternalistic and 10 percent each were laissez-faire and participative. Only one firm had a "professional" culture. In succeeding generations, two-thirds experienced cultural change, the majority becoming professional cultures. Since paternalistic cultures do not prepare the next generation well for leadership responsibilities, successful leadership transfer generally appears to require evolution from paternalistic culture to one of the other three available patterns

Culture and Continuity
in Family Firms
1988

By W. Gibb Dyer, Jr.

Reprinted from **Family Business Review**, Vol. I, No. 1, Spring 1988. San Francisco: Jossey-Bass, 1988. Used with permission of the publisher. All rights reserved.

In today's turbulent times, family firms lead a tenuous existence. Few are able to survive beyond the first generation. The reasons for the demise of these firms include poor economic conditions, lack of capital and resources, and incompetent management. However, my study of more than forty family firms indicates that the culture of the family business plays an important role in determining whether the firm continues successfully beyond the first generation.

In this paper, I will describe the kinds of cultures found in the business side of the family firm (as opposed to the culture of the family or the board of

directors), outline the advantages and problems associated with each cultural pattern, and discuss how one might go about changing the culture if that is deemed to be necessary.

Culture and Continuity

To gain an understanding of why some family firms succeed and others fail, my research team and I systematically examined the histories of more than forty family firms. Some firms were rather well known, such as du Pont and Levi Strauss, while others were much smaller mom-and-pop businesses. We gathered data from a variety of sources, such as corporate histories, annual reports, memoirs of former leaders, interviews, and minutes of board of directors meetings. As we gathered data from these sources, we began to create "maps" of the cultures of the firms in our panel. Dyer (1986) describes the method. By studying these firms historically, we sought to discover the kinds of cultures found in these firms and to determine the kinds of cultural patterns that tended to be associated with family firms that had been successful over time.

What is Culture?

The culture of any group can be viewed on four levels: artifacts, perspectives, values, and assumptions (Schein, 1985; Dyer, 1986). Artifacts are the more tangible aspects of culture. They are physical — the dress, physical layout, company logo, and other emblems used by a group; verbal — the language, jargon, stories, and myths shared by the group; and behavioral — the common rituals, ceremonies, and behavioral patterns. Artifacts are the most visible manifestations of culture, but to fully understand a culture, one must decipher the shared meanings behind them.

Artifacts can be thought of as the symbolic representations of the next level of culture, socially shared perspectives. A perspective is "a coordinated set of ideas and actions a person uses in dealing with some problematic situation" (Becker, Geer, Hughes, and Strauss, 1961). Perspectives are the norms and rules of conduct that the group deems acceptable for handling such problems as developing a new product, giving a performance appraisal, hiring and training new employees, or gaining a promotion.

While perspectives are situation-specific rules, values are broader principles, such as Serve the Customer, Be Honest, or Do Not Question Superiors.

Values are both formal and informal, and they can often be found in the "philosophy" espoused by the group. Since groups do not always act in accordance with espoused values, distinguishing between the ideal and real values is critical in doing a cultural analysis.

At the foundation of the culture are the group's basic assumptions. The other three levels of culture are based on this most fundamental level. Assumptions are the premises on which a group bases its world views and on which the artifacts, perspectives, and values are based. In family firms, certain kinds of assumptions are often found regarding the nature of relationships, human nature, the nature of truth, the environment, time, the nature of human activity, and whether preferential treatment should be given to certain individuals. Figure 1 describes these categories of assumptions and the kinds of orientations associated with each category. In each of the firms that we studied, we mapped the firm's artifacts, perspectives, and values and then made inferences regarding the underlying pattern of assumptions.

Cultural Patterns in the Family Business

The cumulative set of assumptions that a group holds is called the *cultural* pattern of the group. Indeed, the core of any culture is this pattern of interlocking assumptions that creates a unique belief system. Because basic assumptions are the key to understanding culture, my research team used them to broadly define the kinds of family business cultures that they found. We observed four common business cultures: the paternalistic culture, the laissez-faire culture, the participative culture,

283

Figure 1. Categories of Cultural Assumptions

1. **The Nature of Relationships.** Are relationships between members of the organization assumed to be primarily lineal (that is hierarchical), collateral (that is, group oriented), or individualistic in nature?

2. **Human Nature.** Are humans considered to be basically good, basically evil, or neither good nor evil?

3. **The Nature of Truth.** Is truth (that is, correct decisions) discovered from authority figures, or is it determined by a process of personal investigation and testing?

4. **The Environment.** Is there a basic belief that humans can master the environment, that they must be subjugated by the environment, or that they should attempt to harmonize with the environment?

5. **Universalism/Particularism.** Should all members of the organization be evaluated by the same standards, or should certain individuals be given preferential treatment?

6. **The Nature of Human Activity.** Are humans basically active (**doing** orientation)? Are humans passive and unable to alter existing circumstance (**being** orientation)? Or, is a person's primary goal the development of self as an integrated whole (**being-in-becoming** orientation)?

7. **Time.** Are members of the organization primarily oriented to the past, the present, or the future?

---

and the professional culture. Figure 2 presents the basic assumptions underpinning these cultures.

The orientations outlined in each category indicate how leaders of family firms use very different assumptions in operating their businesses. For example, the paternalistic pattern is founded on assumptions that emphasize personal and charismatic characteristics of the founder and family, while the professional pattern emphasizes impersonal rules as the means of getting work done. In the next four sections, I will describe each pattern in detail and identify its strengths and weaknesses.

The Paternalistic Culture

The paternalistic pattern was the most common culture in the family firms that we studied. In this pattern, relationships are arranged hierarchically. The

leaders, who are family members, retain all power and authority and make all the key decisions. The family distrusts outsiders and closely supervises the employees. Moreover, family members are afforded preferential treatment. Employees are assumed to have a "doing" orientation; that is, they are supposed to carry out the family's orders without question. The stance toward the environment tends to be proactive in developing new markets or products. However, the family may also create a particular market niche and prefer to stay within it. The paternalistic firm also seems to have one of two orientations around the time dimension. Some paternalistic firms tend to be oriented to the past. Carrying on the founder's and family's legacy is the primary aim of the owning family. Thus, time-worn traditions are at the center of the culture. Other paternalistic firms tend to be very present oriented. Although

Figure 2. Cultural Patterns of the Family Business

	Paternalistic	Laissez-Faire	Participative	Professional
Nature of relationships	Lineal (hierarchical)	Lineal	Collateral (group orientation)	Individualistic
Nature of human nature	People are basically untrustworthy	People are good and trustworthy	People are good and trustworthy	People are neither good nor evil
Nature of truth	Truth resides in the founder family	Truth resides in the founder/ family although outsiders are given autonomy	Truth is found in group decision making/ participation	Truth is found in profess- ional rules of conduct
Orientation toward the environment	Proactive stance	Harmonizing/ proactive stance	Harmonizing/ proactive stance	Reactive/ proactive stance
Universalism/ particularism	Particularistic	Particularistic	Universalistic	Universalistic
Nature of human activity	Doing orientation	Doing orientation	Being-in- becoming orientation	Doing orientation
Time	Present or past orientation	Present or past orientation	Present or future orientation	Present orientation

they maintain some traditions, they focus on current problems and needs and quickly change to meet new threats.

One company that illustrates the pater-nalistic pattern was National Cash Register under the direction of John Patterson. Patterson and his family controlled the firm for almost a half century. Patterson charted his own course after he bought the company for $6,500 in 1884. He did not follow the advice of local business leaders and rarely listened to his subordinates. He believed that salesmanship was the key to success and developed the most sophisticated training school for salesmen at the time. His salesmen wore white shirts and dark suits — a forerunner of the IBM image. In fact, Thomas Watson received his initial training at NCR Patterson often acted in what many would consider to be an arbitrary and capricious manner: He would give an employee a raise one week and fire him the next. He had his top managers arrive for work early in the morning for horseback riding and calisthenics. He viewed himself as a pioneer and a conqueror—he rode a white horse because Napoleon did. He claimed to be an expert in topics ranging from health to religion. He also created one of the first "welfare" industrial organizations in the United States, building parks, theaters, and other amenities to bring the employee's entire family into the NCR fold. As one observer at the time described Patterson, "he was so intent on helping that often he insisted on minutely regulating the lives of those with whom he came in contact. He was perfectly willing to override the objections of the individual if he believed that the individual's objections were against the best interests of both the individual and of society. He thought there was only one best way of doing anything and that everyone ought to be taught that best way and then be forced to follow it" (Crowther, 1923, p.9). John Patterson built an amazing empire with this cultural pattern until his death in 1922.

The paternalistic pattern tends to work well when the leader of the family business has the necessary expertise and the information needed to manage all aspects of the business. In this kind of culture, there is little uncertainty regarding who makes the decisions. Thus, decisions can be made quickly, and resources can be mobilized to meet competitive threats. Since the leaders in a paternalistic culture are often highly charismatic figures, there tends to be high commitment on the part of the followers to carry out the leader's vision. This commitment has a positive effect when a business is small and struggling for survival.

However, a number of potential problems are associated with the paternalistic culture. First, the business often relies too much on the leader for direction. Hence, the firm is in jeopardy if the leader dies or is incapacitated. Second, training and development for the next generation are often neglected. Third, the leader may not be able to manage ambiguity or complexity as the business grows or as the environment becomes turbulent. Fourth, since the leader makes all the key decisions, many members of the family business may have feelings of incompetence or powerlessness. Given these potential problems, the paternalistic culture generally is best able to succeed when the business is small and the environment is fairly stable. As the firm grows, the leader's family matures, and as the environment becomes more volatile, the family business culture often must evolve into a new cultural pattern.

The Laissez-Faire Culture

We have called another cultural pattern that we have studied the *laissez-faire* culture. This pattern is similar to the paternalistic pattern in many ways. Relationships are hierarchical, family members are afforded preferential treatment, and the employees are expected to achieve the family's goals. Moreover, the orientations of these two cultures toward the environment and time are similar. Where they differ is in their assumptions about human nature and the nature of truth. In the laissez-faire culture, employees are seen as being trustworthy, and they are given responsibility to make decisions. While the ultimate truths regarding the firm's mission and goals rest in the hands of the family, employees are given a great deal of authority and discretion to determine the means of achieving those goals. As a result, the laissez-faire firm is quite unlike the paternalistic firm, where the family determines both the ends and the means.

Levi Strauss and Company has historically followed this laissez-faire tradition (Cray, 1978). The founder's daily routine emphasized the responsibility that he delegated to his subordinates. Levi Strauss would typically leave for his morning walk to work at nine o'clock and arrive around ten—long after the store was opened. Trusted employees opened the store. He would check the sales figures for the previous day and spend the rest of the day chatting with his salesmen, who called him by his first name. He left the store in the late afternoon to visit a local tavern and have a drink with some friends. Employees stayed until closing time, and the trusted bookkeeper locked up the store.

The Strauss family and their descendants have also been known for their willingness to take care of their employees during times of trouble. For example, the family paid the doctor bills of one employee who became ill with diphtheria. They also gave him $1,000 to pay his debts. This employee eventually became the plant manager. Thus, from Levi Strauss down to the current leadership of the Haas family, the family has attempted to provide a secure place of work for employees, and it has provided overall direction and guidelines, but it has allowed employees great latitude in making decisions and influencing company affairs.

The laissez-faire culture is more amenable to business growth and individual creativity than the paternalistic pattern is, since the family delegates a great deal of responsibility to employees. Such a pattern is appropriate if the family is not able or willing to oversee all the day-to-day activities of the business, and the business requires employees to use their initative and change quickly in order to meet new conditions.

The major danger of the laissez-faire culture is that employees may not act consistently with the family's basic values and assumptions. Such was the case of Levi Strauss. Although the company was able to grow very rapidly by giving autonomy to plant managers, it began to have serious problems with product quality in the 1970s when some plants produced garments that did not meet the company's standards. Without appropriate review, employees working in a laissez-faire culture can lose sight of the company's goals, and the business can run out of control.

The Participative Culture

The third pattern that we studied is the participative culture. This cultural pattern is relatively rare in a family firm. We found only four organizations in our panel that had developed such a pattern at some point during their history. The participative pattern is based on assumptions that vary dramatically from the first two patterns that I have described. Relationships tend to be more egalitarian and more group oriented. The status and power of the family tend to be de-emphasized. Employees are deemed to be trustworthy, and the family attempts to give employees the opportunity to magnify their talents. "Doing" is not enough. Employees must accomplish their work in such a way that other people will be involved and personal growth and development will result. Participative cultures tend to be proactive in managing their environments. They attempt to get at the truth and to make proper decisions by eliciting employee input. No one is assumed to have all the answers. The participative culture is present-focused but also oriented toward the future. Nepotism and other forms of favoritism are formally disdained.

One of these unique participative cultures is found at W. L. Gore and Associates. Founded by Bill Gore, a scientist from du Pont who developed a variety of applications of Teflon, the company has created a culture that seems to have a number of advantages: high commitment and morale, the ability to respond quickly to changes in the environment, and the ability to innovate.

To create this kind of culture, all 4,000 people who work for the company are called *associates* rather than *employees*. Terms like *boss, manager,* and *supervisor* are replaced by words like *leader* or *sponsor*. This practice is intended to de-emphasize the use of titles and status symbols and to create a feeling of community. There are no job descriptions to speak of, nor are there organization charts. The associates become part-owners of the company after one year of service. Bob Gore, Bill's son and the current president, constantly reinforces the belief that status, rules, and hierarchy inhibit communication and group decision making (Pacanawsky, 1985). Hence, the Gore family is committed to an egalitarian climate, and it has attempted to foster a sense of freedom and responsibility in employees that is seldom found in a family firm.

In a participative culture, employees are generally able to be creative to develop their talents and abilities. Through participation in decision making, they become more able to understand and internalize the values of the company, and they are more committed to the decisions that are made. Such a pattern seems to succeed in environments that are complex and changing and that require employee input from many levels in order to make the right decisions.

The major weakness of the participative culture is also found in its decision-making processes. It often takes a great deal of time to come to a participative decisions. Important decisions can be delayed or undermined by the process of gathering input from employees. Hence, the challenge of those working in a participative culture is to differentiate between the decisions that need to be made rapidly with minimal discussion and the decisions that must receive more time and employee participation.

The Professional Culture

The term *professional culture* is not intended to mean that this type of organization is more professional than the others but that this cultural pattern is generally found in firms where the owning family decides to turn the management of the business over to nonfamily, professional managers. The professionals often bring with them a set of assumptions that are quite different from those in the other three patterns. Relationships are individualistic, meaning that employees focus on individual achievement and career advancement. Competition is keen in this kind of culture. Professional managers often take a rather impersonal, neutral stance toward employees, who are evaluated on their ability to contribute to the profits of the business. The owning of family's involvement in the business that characterizes the other cultures often disappears with the advent of professional management. The professionals rely on their years of professional training to make rational decisions. The result typically involves the creation of various programs to improve efficiency and cut costs. Employees are encouraged to do their jobs quickly and efficiently; personal development of employees is a secondary concern. Since professional managers are frequently brought into a family firm in order to turn it around, they may find themselves in a reactive mode — forced to put out fires — or they may take a proactive stance in cutting costs by instituting "modern" management techniques, restructuring the company, or laying off employees.

One company that developed this professional pattern was International Harvester. Founded by Cyrus McCormick at the turn of the century, International Harvester was run in the paternalistic tradition of the family. When the company fell on hard times in the 1970s, the president Brooks McCormick (a descendant of Cyrus), hired Archie McCardell, chief operating officer at Xerox, to turn the company around. McCardell replaced the previous management with his own team (see Harvard Business School Case no. 9-381-053) and encouraged the new managers to compete with one another in carrying out his cost-cutting programs. Bonuses and other incentives were given to those individuals who succeeded. *Efficiency* and *cost control* were the watchwords of the McCardell regime. Unfortunately for McCardell, the impersonal nature of the cost-cutting programs created a great deal of ill will among union members and precipitated a bitter strike. Eventually, the union ended the strike, but it was able to force the board of directors to fire McCardell. Thus, the assumptions of the professional culture proved to be short-lived at International Harvester.

The advantage of the professional culture is found in the new ideas and management techniques that the professional managers can often bring to the firm. The outsiders can often improve the firm's accounting, marketing, or other operating systems and make the business run more efficiently. Furthermore, they have fewer ties to the past, and thus they are able to see new possibilities that can move the firm in new directions.

The major weakness of the professional culture is that it tends to alienate the employees who were used to working for the family under a different set of assumptions. Absenteeism, turnover, unhealthy competition among individuals and among departments, low morale, and low commitment are often the negative side effects of the change to professional management.

Ensuring Continuity in the Family Firm

The preceding descriptions of family business cultures illustrate the variety of culture in family firms. While not every family firm may fit exactly the patterns of assumptions listed in Figure 2, we were able to categorize the family firms in our panel according to the four patterns.

The paternalistic pattern was the pattern most commonly found among the family firms that we studied. This procedure was particularly true of first-generation firms: Approximately 80 percent of the firms in our panel had a paternalistic culture in the first generation. The firms with participative and laissez-faire cultures each accounted for 10 percent, and only one firm was deemed to have a professional culture in the first generation. In succeeding generations, more than two-thirds of the paternalistic firms experienced culture change, the majority becoming professional cultures. It would seem that in order for the family firm to transfer leadership to the next generation successfully, the paternalistic culture must evolve into one of the other three patterns. Paternalistic cultures do not prepare the next generation well for leadership responsibilities and give them little chance to develop their leadership skills. The experience of the firms in our panel suggests that family firm cultures do indeed change as new leadership takes over.

As we have mentioned, all cultural patterns—not just the paternalistic pattern—bring their own set of problems and challenges for management, and they may need to change in order to meet new conditions in the external environment, in the business, or in the owning family. For example, family firms that face an increasingly turbulent environment often need to foster assumptions of the participative culture in order to respond quickly to changes, develop new ideas, and improve decision making. Companies experiencing the negative effects of nepotism may need to move to professional management. Family firms experiencing rapid growth generally must delegate authority and responsibility to nonfamily employees, thus becoming more laissez-faire in nature.

At some point in time, most leaders of family firms are faced with the question: How do I change the culture of my business to make it more effective? The answer to this question can be threatening, because leaders of family firms often must change their own assumptions and behaviors. The experience of most family firms is that such assumptions change only when there is a major crisis in the firm. However, if the leaders wait for a crisis to occur before they begin to change, the outcome is generally not favorable either for the family or for the business. That is why many family firms fail. Despite this rather pessimistic assessment, there are some actions that leaders of family firms can take to initiate culture change. These activities can include analyzing the culture and planning for change, changing the assumptions of the leaders, or developing new leadership through the use of hybrids and

outsiders. The planned change approach represents a method for changing the culture incrementally, while the other two approaches represent more drastic remedies where change is more abrupt.

Analyzing the Culture and Planning for Change. One method for changing culture is, first, to create a "map" of the organization's artifacts, perspectives, values, and assumptions; second, to determine the consequences of this cultural pattern; and, third, to plan for change (Schein, 1985; Wilkins, 1983; Dyer, 1986).

To conduct such an analysis and change effort typically involves the creation of an action-research team involving members of the organization as well as outside consultants. The insiders help the outside consultants to understand the subtle nuances associated with the culture, while the outsiders—often by asking "dumb" questions about surprises they encounter—attempt to make the more tacit dimensions of the culture overt.

This inside/outside team interviews individuals and observes behavior at various levels and locations throughout the organization. Usually both an insider and an outsider conduct the interviews in order to foster joint inquiry. The team lists what appear to its members to be the significant artifacts of the culture, then attempts to discover the routines and rules of the culture that make up the perspectives shared by members of the organization. Often such questions as who succeeds and who fails here? What are sins in this organization? and How are decisions made here? are used to gather data (Dyer, 1986). Career histories are also useful, inasmuch as interviewees often discuss the kinds of problems they encountered as they attempted to adapt to the culture. The team also attempts to uncover organizational subcultures — groups holding different beliefs — by asking interviewees which individuals or groups hold opposing views. Often, the problems in family firms are the result of subcultures in conflict, such as the first generation versus the second generation or family members versus nonfamily employees.

When the more overt artifacts, rules, and norms are discovered, the research team must begin to build hypotheses about the company's values and tacit assumptions. As mentioned earlier, these more tacit beliefs must be inferred, since members of the organization may be unable to articulate them clearly. This is particularly true of members of the owning family. What we can hope that the action-research team will arrive at is a map of the culture that lists the key artifacts, perspectives, values, and assumptions. Once this has been done, the team can identify the kind of cultural pattern — paternalistic, laissez-faire, participative, professional, or some other — that prevails.

Once the culture map has been created, the action-research team can begin to focus on the question, what are the consequences of this kind of culture for the company now, and what will they be in the future? The team should attempt to articulate how the culture helps or hinders the organization's strategy and its effectiveness, as well as how it affects employee motivation, productivity, and development. Through this analysis, the team can begin to pinpoint where the problems are and whether there is a need for change.

If change is needed, the team then can develop specific actions that reflect a different set of assumptions. For example, succession planning and estate planning can be used to push a family firm to become more future oriented. New guidelines for decision making and delegation can move the firm to become more participative in nature. Reward systems can be altered to discourage nepotism. Conflict management mechanisms, such as asset management boards, can be set up to manage family disagreements (Beckhard and Dyer, 1983).

If this approach to change is used, it needs support from the family and top management if it is to succeed, because the changes may reflect new assumptions, and they may be strongly resisted. Change in the way power is distributed often accompanies culture change. Some are likely to gain and others to lose in the process. I have found it useful in generating support for any proposed changes to include key members of the family and nonfamily employees in the action-research team. Although such an approach can seem quite attractive, I have found through working with a number of family and nonfamily businesses that attempts to change via this method are easy to resist, undermine, and misunderstand. Thus, we must look at other change strategies as well.

Changing the Leader's Assumptions. One of the greatest problems facing leaders of a family firm is their lack of awareness of the impact of their assumptions and behavior on those around them and of the kinds of cultural patterns that their behavior promotes. Since the leaders of family firms have often created the culture, the culture can change if the assumptions of the leaders change. By becoming aware of their own assumptions and the impact of their assumptions on those around them, leaders can begin to take the often painful steps needed to change them.

To gain such self-awareness, family leaders can do a number of things. For instance, they can sit on the boards of directors of other family firms. By observing the problems of others, they can gain insight into their own. They can also find competent board members and advisers for their own company who can help them to grapple with difficult problems and give them honest feedback on their performance.

Leaders can use data gathered via interviews, questionnaires, and group meetings to obtain feedback about themselves. Outside consultants can also help leaders to understand how their behavior affects their business and their family. In one family firm that we studied, I gave the president of the company a detailed description of the culture. One of the main problems seemed to be the difference in management style and philosophy between the president, who favored a participative culture and his chief operating officer, who was attempting to foster the assumptions of a professional culture. Of this study, the president said: "I got it [the study] at the office one day and took it home to read. While I usually sleep soundly, I woke up at one o'clock in the morning and began to read, finishing it at dawn. It was gripping to read, like a novel. While there were few surprises about how I ran things, the differences [the professional manager] had made did surprise me. I hadn't appreciated how different our styles really were." Using this new information, the president eventually fired the chief operating officer and took steps to correct some serious problems.

In some cases, workshops, seminars, or sensitivity training sessions offered by specialist organizations can also prove helpful. A number of organizations have been created to provide the heads of family firms with information and programs to help assess their problems.

Therapy and counseling are other alternatives for those who seek insight, experience anxiety or depression, or find serious schisms in their families. In one family firm, the son of the founder was constantly plagued by the ghost of his father and by employees who reminded him that his father "wouldn't have done it that way." To deal with this pressure, the son enlisted the help of a competent therapist. The therapist finally convinced the son that the business was his —not his father's. Armed with this insight, the son has been able to change the culture and expand the business. His anxiety and fears have also been alleviated. Therapy is often the only way in which individuals and families can gain insight and help with serious emotional or psychological problems.

Change Through Hybrids and Outsiders. If the family leader is unwilling or unable to change his or her own assumptions, there are alternative ways of changing the firm's basic values and assumptions. One option that Edgar Schein (1985) has discussed is to promote individuals who share most of the basic values and assumptions of the leaders but vary on one or two dimensions. These individuals are enough like the leader to gain acceptance but different enough to introduce change. For example, a new manager could share all the assumptions of the leader of a paternalistic firm with the exception of the assumption about human nature. The new manager could believe that people can be trusted and given responsibility. If such hybrids are promoted and encouraged, the culture can eventually change to become a laissez-faire or participative culture.

If the culture needs to be changed more quickly, replacing the top management with outsiders who have different assumptions is another option. This method of introducing change is often used during crisis periods where a quick turnaround is needed. We have seen a number of cases where professional managers quickly changed the culture when they were brought in to solve a crisis. The disadvantage of this approach is the fact that many of the traditions, routines, and skills that had helped the firm in the past can be lost. Also, long-term employees who are passed over for promotion may become disgruntled and demoralized when outsiders are placed in leadership positions.

Conclusion

It is difficult to change the culture of any business, and to attempt any of the activities that have just been described requires leadership that is committed to change. Since the leaders largely create and shape the cultural patterns of the business, they must understand the effect of those cultures and take steps to ensure that they foster cultural patterns that will allow the business and family to grow and thrive. Family business cultures can either contribute to success or be a major stumbling block. To understand and manage the opportunities inherent in family business cultures is not easy, and it is not often done in family firms, but it is essential for leaders who wish to ensure the continuity of their businesses and the well-being of their families.

References

Becker, H.S., Geer, B., Hughes, E. C., and Strauss, A. L. *Boys in White*. New Brunswick, N.J.: Transaction Books, 1961.

Beckhard, R., and Dyer, W. G., Jr. "Managing Continuity in the Family-Owned Business." *Organizational Dynamics*, 1983, 12 (1), 5-12.

Cray, E. *Levi's*. Boston: Houghton Mifflin, 1978.

Crowther, S. *John H. Patterson: Pioneer in Industrial Welfare*. New York: Doubleday, 1923.

Dyer, W. G., Jr. *Cultural Change in Family Firms: Anticipating and Managing Business and Family Transitions*. San Francisco: Jossey-Bass, 1986.

Pacanavsky, M. Personal communication, June 29, 1985.

Schein, E. H. *Organizational Culture and Leadership: A Dynamic View*. San Francisco: Jossey-Bass, 1985.

Wilkins, A. L. "The Culture Audit: A Tool for Understanding Organizations." *Organizational Dynamics*, 1983, 2 (2), 24-38.

Introduction

Despite their diversity, all family firms exist on the boundaries of two qualitatively different social institutions: the family and the business. Each has its own distinct, often contradictory, rules of conduct. These structural contradictions affect the founder's ability to effectively manage the firm, particularly as it matures and grows. The founder experiences psychological stress as a result of conflicting social norms. Specific conflict areas confronting family business owners include: selection of employees, compensation, equity, performance appraisal, and training and development.

The author recommends that founders gain understanding of the contradictions confronting them, make others in the system more aware, and then to affect the separation of management and ownership.

Managing Human Resources in Family Firms: The Problem of Institutional Overlap

1983

By Ivan S. Lansberg

Reprinted from **Organizational Dynamics**, Summer 1983, pp. 39-46. Copyright ©1983 American Management Association, Periodicals Division; reprinted by permission of the publisher, AMA, 1983.

Since the early beginnings of capitalism, the family has constituted a primary vehicle of economic production. In spite of the many significant technological changes that have taken place since those early times, recent surveys show that the family remains a critical force behind many modern work organizations. In the United States alone, for example, over 90 percent of all

corporations (including 35 percent of the *Fortune 500*) are either owned or controlled by a family.

Yet despite the prevalence of family businesses, our understanding of this type of organization remains rather limited, particularly with regard to its fundamental structure. In response to this state of affairs, this article examines some basic sociological properties of family firms, focusing on how structural contradictions that are built into their fiber affect the founder's ability to effectively manage relatives who work in the business. The article also provides some practical guidelines for entrepreneurs who head family firms.

Institutional Overlap: A Fundamental Problem

Family firms come in many shapes and forms, ranging from the local "Ma and Pa" store to the huge multinational. In addition, family firms vary widely in their missions and strategies and in the markets in which they operate. Despite this diversity, however, one undeniable fact holds true for all family firms: These organizations exist on the boundaries of two qualitatively different social institutions – the family and the business. Each institution defines social relations in terms of a unique set of values, norms, and principles; each has its own distinct rules of conduct.

These institutional differences between family and business stem primarily from the fact that each exists in society for fundamentally different reasons. The family's primary social function, on the one hand, is to assure the care and nurturance of its members. Thus social relations in the family are structured to satisfy family members' various developmental needs.

The fundamental *raison d'etre* of the business, on the other hand, is the generation of goods and services through organized task behavior. As a result, social relations in the firm are, on the whole, guided by norms and principles that facilitate the productive process.

In their formative years family firms often benefit from the overlap between family and business principles. During this stage, the firm's social dynamics are still highly organic, with all employees reporting directly to the founder/entrepreneur. The informal nature of familial relations is frequently carried over into the firm, serving to foster commitment and a sense of identification with the founder's dream. In addition, during these early days the family often provides the firm with a steady supply of trustworthy manpower.

As the business matures, however, and more complex organizational forms emerge, institutional overlap between family and firm begins to generate conflicts in the organization. Typically, these conflicts manifest themselves in the form of normative contradictions whereby what is expected from individuals in terms of family principles often violates what is expected from them according to business principles.

The Founder

In most family firms, the person who experiences these institutional contradictions most strongly is the founder (usually the founder/father), who sits at the head of both the family and the task systems. Typically the founder finds him- or herself operating under conditions of high normative ambiguity in which incongruent values, norms, and principles erode the ability to manage effectively.

Take, for instance, the following case:

> Harry Peterson is the founding father of a highly successful service business. Now 65 years old, Harry is beginning to consider the prospect of retirement. In so doing, he confronts the difficult task of picking his successor. Harry knows the importance of technical expertise in determining the success of a chief executive officer (CEO) in his business. Harry's son has worked in the business for the past five years. While being bright and hard working, his son lacks the technical knowledge to assume the responsibilities that

295

such a position would require. From a business point of view, Harry feels he should choose one of his senior managers to succeed him. This person is highly competent as a professional and is well acquainted with all the technical aspects of the business. From a parental perspective, however, Harry feels that he should give the job to his son. After all, the son deserves an opportunity to follow in Harry's footsteps and develop into a full-fledged professional. What should Harry do?

Although these problems are structural in nature – that is, they result from conflicting social norms existing independently of the founder – he or she often experiences personal psychological difficulties as a result of the conflicting pressures. Founders frequently experience a great deal of stress from "internalizing" the contradictions that are built into their jobs as heads of the family firm.

Moreover, the psychological stress induced by this conflictive situation reduces the entrepreneur's ability to manage effectively and sets the stage for the firm's eventual downfall, which typically occurs about the time when the founder leaves the business. It is interesting to note that the average family firm exists for approximately 24 years, a period that happens to coincide with the average tenure of most founders.

Human Resources Problems

Contradictions between the norms and principles that operate in the family and those that operate in the business frequently interfere with the effective management of human resources in family firms. Let's examine some characteristic ramifications of this institutional overlap.

Problems of Selection

Typically, relatives feel entitled to "claim their share" of the family business; they flock to the firm demanding jobs and opportunities regardless of their competence. The rationale rests on the family principle that unconditional help should always be granted to relatives who are in need. From a business standpoint, however, the founder knows that the firm cannot be allowed to become a welfare agency. The hiring of too many incompetent individuals (whether they are "family" or not) would certainly threaten the effectiveness and possibly even the survival of the business.

Founders often find themselves in the difficult situation of having to choose between either hiring (or firing) an incompetent relative or breaking up their relationship with some part of the family.

Problems of Compensation and Equity

In the area of compensation, remuneration of relatives who work in the firm also creates difficult problems for the founder. The conflict here again is structural in nature and exists "independent of the founder's will." Let us examine some research findings that shed light on the dynamics underlying the giving and getting of rewards in the family and in the business.

Sociologists tell us that the norms and principles that regulate the process of giving and getting (that is, the exchange of goods and services) in the family are qualitatively different from the norms and principles that regulate the same process in the firm. The exchange of resources in the family is guided by implicit affective principles that focus each person's attention on the needs and long-term well-being of the other, rather than on the specific value of the goods and services being exchanged.

By contrast, the process of giving and getting that operates in the firm is regulated by economic principles that oblige individuals to be explicit about both the market value of the goods and services exchanged and the time frame within which the exchange will take place. Hence the notion of "a fair day's work for a fair day's pay."

Given the problems inherent in mixing the principles of exchange in family and business, it comes as no surprise that many founders have difficulty discussing terms of compensation with their relatives. This is particularly the case with their children who work in the firm. As a result, compensation for relatives is often based on ambiguous principles deriving from a hybrid of family and business criteria and they generate all sorts of dysfunctional processes in the firm.

For instance, contrary to commonly held beliefs about nepotism, studies have shown that founders tend to underreward their relatives who work in the firm. While this practice is relatively harmless during the formative stages of the firm, it creates considerale problems in the mature family business. Underrewarding relatives, regardless of their competence, may lead to a situation in which incompetent family employees are retained while competent family employees are driven to seek employment elsewhere.

Founders repeatedly justify such undercompensation by arguing that family members "have an obligation to help out" in the business. Moreover, founders frequently feel that rewarding relatives in terms of market rates would be perceived as favoritism by nonfamily employees. Clearly, both of these rationales reflect some confusion about principles of exchange that should operate in the context of the firm.

In compensation, the problems created by the institutional overlap of family and business are not limited to incongruent principles of exchange. Perhaps one of the most difficult problems faced by the founder in this area stems from the fact that family and firm are regulated by different norms of fairness.

In the context of the family, two dominant norms of fairness operate. In vertical family relationships – that is, the relationship between parents and their children – the dominant norm of fairness is the concept of need. Parents have a moral obligation to allocate their resources so that the children's needs are met. In horizontal family relationships, such as the relationships among siblings, equality is the dominant fairness norm. Thus it is assumed that in allocations among siblings, each individual is entitled to an equal share of resources and opportunities.

However, the norm of fairness that operates in the firm is based on the concept of merit. Ideally, the level of rewards an employee receives is determined by his or her competence in accomplishing organizational goals. Given the fundamental task orientation of the business, it is more functional in this context to allocate resources so that those who are most productive receive proportionally larger shares of the resources available in the system.

The mixed nature of family business makes it difficult for founders to resolve allocation problems in a way consistent with both the norms of fairness that operate in the firm and the norms of fairness that operate in the family.

The clash between the principles of fairness that operate in the family and in the firm lies at the heart of the problem of nepotism. Seen from the overlapping systems perspective, nepotism occurs when the ground rules that define fairness in the task system are violated — that is, when family are given rewards and privileges in the firm to which they are not entitled on the basis of merit and competence.

Problems in Appraisal

The institutional overlap between family and firm also interferes with the appraisal process. Frequently, founders experience many difficulties when trying to evaluate the performance of a close relative who works in the firm — particularly when it comes to objective evaluation of their own children.

First of all, the very concept of appraisal (that is, objective assessment of an individual's contribution and worth) in the context of a family system seems a preposterous idea. In a family system individuals are, by definition, seen as ends in themselves. The standing of an individual in a family is determined more by who the individual "is" than by what the individual "does." Applying a set of objectively derived criteria to evaluate a family member's performance goes against the very principles that regulate and define social behavior in the family.

In the firm, on the other hand, the process of appraisal seems fully congruent with the requirements of a system whose primary function is economic productivity. In this context, looking at individuals more as means than ends enables us to identify those who contribute most to the achievement of organizational goals.

It is not surprising therefore, that a founder faced with having to assess the managerial competence of his or her own offspring experiences a great deal of stress because it is not possible simultaneously to do justice to the norms and prescriptions that operate in the family and in the business systems. Moreover, the founder's difficulties in making such appraisals are frequently compounded by informational problems. These problems emerge when nonfamily employees cover up a relative's incompetence — either to curry favor or to avoid "crossing" the founder.

Problems in Training and Development

The clash between family and business principles also impacts the founder's ability to manage effectively the training and development of family members. In this instance, founders frequently find it difficult to separate individual needs from organizational needs. From a family point of view, the relative's training should focus on "whatever is best for him or her." From a business point of view, training should emphasize learning experiences that will increase the individual's ability to attain organizational goals. Very often, however, individual relatives' needs do not coincide with the firm's needs. Moreover, founders are frequently willing to invest organizational resources in ventures that, while being risky or even outright incompatible with the organization's core mission, are intended to provide their offspring with an opportunity to grow and develop.

Coping Mechanisms

Caught in the midst of these conflicting institutional prescriptions, founders often have trouble adopting clear and explicit management criteria. This is particularly true in these areas of human resources management in which family and business principles come directly into conflict. To cope with the stressful double bind in which they find themselves, many founders adopt one of two strategies.

One is to adopt decisions that compromise between conflicting family and business principles. These compromises, however, often lead to decisions that are suboptimal from a management point of view. For example, one founder who was unable to choose between his son and a professional manager as his successor decided to split the office of chief executive into two distinct offices, giving one to his son and one to the professional manager. In this case the founder's "solution" led to a power struggle between the two that threatened the firm's long-term survival.

Another coping strategy for dealing with the institutional contradictions that confront them is to indiscriminately oscillate between family and business principles. Founders often arbitrarily behave strictly in accordance with business principles in some instances and strictly in accordance with family principles in others, without laying down a set of criteria or guidelines that specify when family or business principles are appropriate. This constant oscillation between business and family principles often leads to discontent both among employees and among relatives, all of whom perceive the founder as being inconsistent and unpredictable in his or her managerial approach.

Solutions To These Problems

It is evident from the foregoing analysis that the institutional contradictions facing the founder are built into the very nature of these organizations, so the problems entailed can never be fully resolved as long as the firm remains a family business. From our perspective, the best that founders can hope for is to develop procedures for managing more constructively the contradictions inherent in their role as founders.

As an important first step toward the development of constructive coping strategies, founders need to gain the awareness that a fundamental part of the stress they experience is environmentally induced. Research evidence on what is typically referred to as "role conflict" suggests that understanding the problem's structural roots would significantly reduce their stress and enhance their ability to manage these institutional contradictions more effectively.

Similarly, founders need to make significant others (both in the family and in the firm) aware of the contradictions that are built into the family firm's structure. Shifting the problem's source from the founder to the system would stimulate the formulation of procedures for separating family and business issues and would set the stage for collaborative problem solving among all the parties concerned.

The key to developing effective procedures for managing these contradictions is the separation of management and ownership. Basically, this entails examining the relatives who work in the firm from two distinct perspectives: an "ownership" perspective and a "management" perspective. From an ownership perspective, relatives would be subject to all the norms and principles that regulate family relations; from a management perspective, relatives would be affected by the firm's principles. Let us briefly examine how this separation would work in terms of the various human resources problems discussed earlier.

First of all, the separation of ownership and management issues in terms of personnel selection would call for accepting into the firm only those relatives who, on business grounds, were thought to possess the skills needed to perform effectively on the job. Hence from a management perspective relatives would be treated just as others are treated when they apply for a position. From an ownership point of view, on the other hand, relatives interested in working in the firm would be given the opportunity to acquire the necessary skills to meet the firm's standards. These opportunities could take many forms, including sponsored apprenticeships in other firms, formal educational training, and so forth. The funds to cover the necessary training expenses would come from the family's assets rather than from the business. In this way relatives could be taken care of in a manner consistent with family principles without necessarily compromising the firm's sound management standards.

Second, in terms of the compensation process, a similar distinction between management and ownership needs to be made if we want to develop more constructive ways of managing the institutional overlap. In this case the separation of management and ownership would entail rewarding relatives working in the firm strictly on the basis of business principles. Any additional rewards, advantages, or opportunities for relatives would be allocated under the ownership umbrella quite independently from the relatives' standing in the firm. For instance, under these conditions a founder wishing to provide a son or daughter with an expensive life style would make the necessary income available to him or her by way of stock dividends, not by inflating the offspring's salary beyond his or her professional worth in the market. Such an arrangement would ensure honoring the offspring's privileges as an owner while maintaining an effective merit-based reward system.

With regard to the appraisal process, the separation of ownership and management implies that relatives working in the firm would be subject to evaluation on professional grounds, like everyone else working for the firm. To deal with the potential conflicts between family and business principles, the appraisal of family members would include the opinions of subordinates, peers, and superiors rather than just the potentially biased opinion of founder or family.

Finally, the separation of management and ownership has important implications for managing the training and development of family members who work in the firm. From a management perspective, it is important to plan explicitly the career and training paths of relatives in the business. Moreover, as would have to be the case for nonfamily employees as well, career paths for relatives would have to mesh with the organization's overall goals. Any relative working in the firm whose interests and needs fail to mesh with the organization's goals would have to reconsider his or her employment in the business. From an ownership point of view, these individuals would be entitled, as members of the owning group, to claim a share of the family assets to invest in pursuing their professional objectives outside of the firm. The size of their share of family assets would, of course be determined by family and not by business principles.

Selected Bibliography

To my knowledge, one of the most complete sources on family firms to date is Pat Alcorn's *Success and Survival in the Family-Owned Business* (McGraw-Hill, 1982). This work is geared to a managerial audience and covers a broad range of issues from entrepreneurship to succession. Other classics in family businesses include: Harry Levinson's "Conflicts that Plague Family Businesses" (*Harvard Business Review*, March-April 1971); "Transferring Power in the Family Business" by Louis B. Barnes and Simon A. Hirshon (*Harvard Business Review*, July-August 1976).

Readers who might be interested in a more theoretical treatment of the conflicts generated by institutional overlap are directed to Robert K. Merton's classic, *Sociological Ambivalence and Other Essays* (The Free Press, 1976). Another classic sociological work that deals with the nature and consequences of structural conflicts is *Organizational*

Stress: Studies in Role Conflict and Ambiguity by Robert L. Kahn, Donald M. Wolfe, Robert P. Quinn, J. Diedrick Snoek, and Robert A. Rosenthal. (John Wiley and Sons, 1964).

Other relevant articles in the social/psychological literature include: M. S. Clark's and J. Mills's "Interpersonal Attraction in Exchange and Communal Relationships" (*Journal of Personality and Social Psychology*, January 1976), M. Deutsch's "Equity, Equality and Need: What Determines Which Value will be Used as the Basis of Distributive Justice?" (*Journal of Social Issues*, Justice Motive in Social Behavior Issue, Volume 31, Number 3, 1975), and C. C. Peterson, "Distributive Justice Within and Outside the Family" (*Journal of Psychology*, May 1975).

Chapter 6

Boards of Directors in the Family Firm

Owners of family businesses usually cherish their independence. Often, the last thing they want to do is share information with outsiders or justify their actions and decisions. Yet to improve family business's chances for survival and success, creating a meaningful board of directors containing respected outsiders is a widely offered prescription from those who work extensively with family businesses.

The planning essential for long-term success can be stimulated and guided by outsiders selected for their particular expertise and overall business acumen. They can provide invaluable contacts. Perhaps most importantly, the board helps with thorny questions related to succession.

Introduction

Conclusions based on research presented in this article show that small business owner/managers who don't plan penalize their business' sales, profitability and productivity. To effectively plan, however, smaller business should take advantage of outsiders to facilitate strategic planning. The study concludes that small businesses should incorporate outsiders into their planning and strategic decision making on a regular, repetitive basis.

The Importance of "Outsiders" in Small Firm Strategic Planning
1982

By Richard B. Robinson, Jr.

Small firm owner/managers do not engage in systematic planning. Planning in the small firm is: (1) often done on an ad hoc, problem basis (Golde, 1964); (2) frequently only a mental activity of the owner/manager (Still, 1974); (3) informal, sporadic, and closed (Still, 1974); and (4) often relying on advice from random acquaintances with less skill and/or less experience than the owner himself (Rice & Hamilton, 1979).

Although small business owners avoid planning, numerous authors extol the virtues and benefits planning would bring to the small firm (Gilmore, 1971; Steiner, 1967; Still, 1974). Limited empirical evidence is available to support these contentions (Chicha & Julien, 1979; Gasse, 1979; Potts, 1977; Trow, 1961).

Key Component: The Outsider

A considerable body of prescriptive literature has evolved in small business planning that emphasizes the important role of "outsiders" in improving the effectiveness of strategic planning in small firms. Unfortunately, only limited empirical evidence has been gathered to support such an idea. (Outsiders generally refer to consultants, lawyers, accountants, bankers, board of directors.)

Trombetta (1976) and Robinson (1979b) examine outsiders involved in small firm planning. Each author offers a case study of a small firm that utilized a consultant in its planning and strategy development. Both authors report a favorable response by the small firm manager, a thorough planning effort, and the adoption of actions that resulted in subsequent increased sales. Unfortunately, their conclusions are quite limited due to their single firm samples. Smith's (1978) dissertation looked at the effectiveness of one type of outsider planner—the Small Business Institute (SBI) program. Studying a stratified sample of 42 small firms receiving SBI assistance, Smith found that less than half of the clients gave favorable ratings to the value of SBI assistance. Yet, he also found that 60 percent of the firms implemented one or more of the SBI recommendations. Smith's study is of limited use, however, because "client's perception of SBI value" and "number of recommendations implemented" were the only effectiveness measures employed. Anderson's (1970) dissertation is another study tangentially addressing issues relative to the use of outside planners in small firms. Studying 75 small service firms, he found that 19 firms had Small Business Administration (SBA) loan guarantees and had utilized the management assistance officer (MAO) program of the SBA. Over half of these firms indicated that the SBA-MAO contributed nothing to the firm's success. Given the findings of Anderson (1970) and Smith (1978), Potts' (1977) dissertation might lead one to conclude that outside planners are potentially useful as long as they are not from the SBI or SBA-MAO. Potts compared successful and unsuccessful small businesses on their use of outside accounting services. Though both firms used such services, "successful firms made a significantly broader use of outside accounting services in a 'total planning activity'... had a more positive outlook towards such services... and placed greater importance upon these services" (1977, p.115). Again Potts' perceptual "effectiveness" measures restrict the extent to which definitive conclusions can be drawn.

A growing number of authors argue that outsiders are important participants in small firm strategic planning. Several reasons are offered. Golde (1964) suggests that most large corporations have full time planning staffs, but small firms cannot afford this luxury. Other authors offer this same argument (Buchele, 1965; Cohn & Lindberg, 1972; Krentzman & Samaras, 1960). They suggest outsiders as a remedy for this disadvantage. Still (1974) and Gilmore (1971) go further, suggesting that outsiders can improve the quality of decision making and the likelihood of repetitive use of systematic planning by small firms. In addition, they argue that planning interaction will cause small business managers to take planning seriously and become more motivated to allocate the time necessary. Buchele suggests that planning with "outsiders can get the small businessman away from day-to-day operations, thus allowing him the chance to plan" (1965, p.129).

Other authors suggest outsiders as a means to compensate for small firms managers' lack of planning skill. Sexton and Dahle argue that outsiders can supplement "limited entrepreneurial capacity...imperfect or insufficient information" presenting impediments to small firm planning (1976, p.164). Timmons, Smollen, and Dingee (1977) suggest that outside consultants can supplement inadequate skills in both the process of planning and the content of strategies. Timmons feels that outsiders can help difficult planning issues that concern family problems, difficult decisions, and trade-offs. Wheelwright (1971) reports that computer simulated consulting in strategic planning evokes more "creative and high payoff strategies" from small firm managers participating in a management development seminar.

Golde, one of the earliest proponents of using outsiders in small firm planning, makes the following observation:

Outside people may be very valuable aides to planning. Company directors, accountants, lawyers, bankers, or advertising agencies frequently prove helpful. In most cases, the help these people can provide is more in developing the planning approach than in actually doing major chunks of company planning. The cost of such outside help is likely to be minimal or nonexistent if these people are already servicing the company in some fashion. If more concrete help of a sizeable nature is required, it is always possible to call in an outside management consultant....Formal use of an outsider in planning has one other helpful effect...the (day-to-day) pressures on a small-company executive are immense, and the executive typically responds to the strongest pressures. An outside person can become the one who continually gives firm reminders that time must be spent on planning (1964, p.154).

Cohn and Lindberg (1972) surveyed 197 small and large firm executives about their perceptions of the critical difficulties in managing small versus large companies. Cohn and Lindberg found that although the skills, time, and staff necessary for planning are not major issues in large firms, they represent 98 percent of the planning-related management difficulties in small firms.

When these authors refer to outsiders, they discuss two basic types. Mainer (1968) and Buchele (1965) make reference to a board of directors for the firm. Following Golde's suggested "outside types of people" (1964, p.154), they perceived that small firms should include outside people with vested interest in the firm's performance in a board of directors role. Such people include primarily bankers, lawyers, and accountants with whom the firm does business.

Krentzman and Samaras (1960), while recognizing the importance of outside assistance in planning, apparently prefer consultants over the composition of a board of directors as previously described. They suggest:

The board of directors represents real resource....A well-informed, hard working, practical-minded outside board can be a precious asset, although...its members often do not have the time to help the manager in executing their good suggestions. Securing such a board is no easy task, of course, since they are rare among small firms....A firm's banker, lawyer, and accountant are often called on to serve in what is essentially a consulting capacity...but, except by circumstance, they lack the rounded view possessed by consultants...who are experienced in a range of problems....The executive of a small business is probably far better informed about the specifics of "his own industry" than are most advisors. What he needs is not only creative advice but on-the-job assistance in carrying out...resolution on immediate crisis situations and establishment of long-range planning techniques which will minimize future crises and maximize future opportunities... (1960, P.90).

Buchele supports consultants for small business planning. He suggests that consultants "often have insights that escape insiders, can see a possibility that the insiders cannot see...and offer realistic assessment of the firm's strengths and weaknesses" (1965, p.125).

The costs of such outsiders, whether directors or consultants, appears to be seen as prohibitive by many small firm managers (Krentzman & Samaras, 1960). Several authors see this perception as erroneous (Buchele, 1965; Drucker, 1977; "The Role of the Consultants," 1975). Nonetheless, given the strong support many advocates have offered for the potential of consultants to improve planning in small firms, increasing emphasis is being placed on government supported consulting assistance to small firms.

SBA sponsored programs received the most attention. These include the SBI, MAO, and Services Corps of Retired Executives (SCORE) programs. Studies by Anderson (1970) and Smith (1978) cast doubt on the ultimate effectiveness of the SBI and MAO approaches. The SBI program, using undergraduate students as consultants, was seen to be of more benefit to the student than to the small businessman. SBI and SCORE are both quite limited in resources and therefore lack the capacity to meet potential small business planning demands (Krentzman & Samaras, 1960). Anderson (1970) suggests that the MAO program places greater emphasis on policing SBA loans and loan guarantees than on management assistance. Fogel goes so far as to suggest that "the SBA could best help small businesses by helping them plan..not by giving them loan-guarantees" (1979, p. 9).

Small Business Development Center Program

Recognizing the need for staff specialists and planning consultants in small firms, as well as the hesitancy or inability of small firm owner/managers to procure such services through conventional sources, the Small Business Development Center (SBDC) program was inaugurated in 1977 on an experimental basis in eight states (Flewellen & Bramblett, 1978; 1979). These centers attempt to meet this outsider need more effectively by providing free, comprehensive managerial planning consultation to small businesses in a manner patterned after the Agricultural Extension Service (Flewellen & Bramblett, 1978). The SBDC programs are staffed by MBA students, Ph.D. students already holding the MBA, and full time professionals (holding the MBA). A major prerequisite at the University of Georgia SBDC is prior business experience in order to become a "staff consultant" (Flewellen & Bramblett, 1978; Robinson, 1979a). These staff consultants are available for "in-depth consulting....regarding the problems, critical decisions and planning...of the small firm manager" (Robinson, 1979a, p.124). SBDC staff consultants also engage in the transfer of specific information (for example, the types of business licenses that are needed for X business) and in continuing education seminars. The present study is concerned *only* with SBDC assistance of an in-depth nature with business owners or managers.

SBDC consultants assist the manager in analyzing and making strategic decisions regarding the client firm. Hofer and Schendel (1978) identify three major levels of strategy: corporate strategy, business strategy, and functional area strategy. For small firms, corporate and business level strategies are synonymous. Furthermore, in the small firm, the interdependence of business and functional area strategies is often inseparable when facing critical strategic problems. SBDC consultants consistently address a wide range of functional area problems or strategies (financial, marketing, personnel, control, etc.) in addition to the overriding business level strategy (for example, should a motel operator increase emphasis on his campground and gradually phase out the motel operation?) in their role as outsiders in the firm's strategic planning. In the aggregate, the range of problems or strategic issues addressed by SBDC consultants is broad. This is consistent with the idea that the content of strategic planning (or strategic management) in small firms must focus thoroughly on both business level and functional area strategy. Therefore, the assistance rendered by SBDC consultants in in-depth SBDC cases provides a logical operationalization of outsider-based, small firm strategic planning as it has been advanced in the literature.

Hypotheses

The overriding research question guiding this study asked: Is there a difference in the effectiveness of small firms engaging in outsider-based strategic planning (OBSP) and that of similar small firms that do not engage in such planning? The study compared the effectiveness of small firms that had engaged in OBSP (in-depth SBDC assistance) and two, small firm control groups that did not engage in OBSP. The experimental and control groups were compared over matching pre- and post-OBSP time periods. Two hypotheses were tested:

Hypothesis 1. *The profitability of small firms engaging in OBSP is not significantly different from a matched sample of small firms from RMA Annual Statement Studies (1978, 1979) during pre- and post-OBSP time periods.*

Hypothesis 2. *The change in effectiveness of small firms engaging in OBSP will not be significantly different from that experienced by a random sample of small firms in a bookkeeping service control group over matching pre- to post-OBSP time periods.*

Method

The focus of this study was to examine the impact of outsider-based, strategic planning on the effectiveness of small firms in an attempt to ascertain whether strategic planning, and particularly outsider-based strategic planning, is of value in the small firm. A firm was defined as small if it met each of the following restrictions.

1. less than 50 employees

2. less than $3 million in annual sales

3. independently owned and operated

Sample

The sample included 101 small firms that had received SBDC strategic planning consultation (outside-based strategic planning) and two control groups not engaging in outsider-based planning. The first control group was a matched sample of small firms from *RMA Annual Statement Studies* (1978). The firms in this control group were matched with SBDC sample firms by type of business (SIC code) and annual sales. The second control group was a random sample of 61 similar small firms from the files of a northeast Georgia bookkeeping service. Files were identified that were similar to the SBDC

Table 1. SBDC and Control Group Samples

Characreristic	Retail	Service	Manufacturer	Overall
Number in sample				
SBDC	48	40	13	101
RMA[a]	48	40	13	101
BKS[b]	31	30	–	61
Mean annual sales				
SBDC	$250,310	$181,730	$473,676	$251,904
RMA	$228,752	$152,451	$422,798	$225,710
BKS	$226,052	$118,594	–	$165,827
Mean number of employees				
SBDC	5.4	5.8	13.4	6.6
RMA	–	–	–	–
BKS	6.0	5.2	–	5.8

[a] RMA Annual Statement Studies (1978) sample.
[b] Northeast Georgia bookkeeping service sample.

sample by type of business (SIC code), annual sales, and number of employees. A random sample, every third folder, was selected. Table 1 provides a breakdown of the SBDC sample and the two control groups by type and characteristics of the firms.

Chi-square goodness of fit tests were used to examine the representativeness of the SBDC sample with the two control groups, the small business population in Georgia, and the small business population in the United States. Three dimensions of representativeness were examined: (1) percentage distribution of the three categories of firms, (2) percentage distribution of specific types of firms (by SIC code) within each category, and (3) mean/median annual sales and number of employees. The chi-squares ranged from 1.01 to 5.35, with none reaching significance at the .05 level. Therefore, a thorough pattern of representativeness was present

between the SBDC sample, the control groups, and the populations. This level of representativeness avoids what has been a major deficiency in previous policy research with small firms - a pervasive use of samples composed exclusively of manufacturing firms.

The SBDC sample and the two control group sample were compared on one additional dimension: profitability before engaging in outsider-based strategic planning. If pre-OBSP profitability was significantly lower in the OBSP group than in the control groups, then a subsequent finding of significantly higher improvement in OBSP firms' effectiveness might be attributable as much to normal recovery as to OBSP impact.

To compare the OBSP group with the RMA control group, net profit divided by sales was used as the measure of profitability. A correlated samples

310

Table 2. SBDC Versus RMA: Pre-OBSP Profitability

	Mean NPOS[a] %	t	df	p
SBDC	4.40	−.84	100	.41[b]
RMA	6.04			

[a] NPOS = net profit before taxes/total sales.
[b] No significant difference between SBDC firms and RMA firms on pre-OBSP profitability.

t-test was used to examine mean differences. The results are shown in Table 2. The pre-OBSP profitability of SBDC firms and RMA control group firms was not significantly different.

A similar procedure was followed to examine the pre-OBSP profitability of SBDC firms and BKS control group firms. Two measures of profitability were available in this case: net profit divided by sales (NPOS) and net profit plus owner compensation divided by sales - return on sales (ROS). A *t-test* was used to compare the SBDC and BKS means on each profitability measure. The results are provided in Table 3. The profitability of SBDC firms was not significantly different from the BKS firms during matching pre-OBSP time periods on either measure of profitability.

Table 3. SBDC Versus BKS: Pre-OBSP Profitability

	Mean NPOS[a] %	t	df	p
SBDC	7.18	−1.66	149	.11[c]
BKS	10.85			

	Mean ROS[b] %	t	df	p
SBDC	16.63	−1.39	143	.17[c]
BKS	20.52			

[a] NPOS = net profit before taxes/total sales.

[b] ROS = (net profit before taxes plus owner compensation)/total sales.

[c] No significant differences between SBDC firms and BKS firms on either measure of pre-OBSP profitability.

Operationalizing Outsider-Based Strategic Planning

SBDC strategic planning consulting, described earlier in this paper, provided the means to operationalize OBSP in this study. The OBSP firms (experimental group) engaged in in-depth SBDC consulting. The two control groups' firms did not engage in SBDC consulting.

A decision rule was employed to identify SBDC-served firms that had engaged in in-depth SBDC consulting (OBSP). To be included as an OBSP firm, the SBDC consulting (in that firm) had to meet each of the following criteria:

1. address business level strategy issues

2. include thorough analysis and decision making in two or more functional areas

3. involve 10 or more contact hours between client and consultant(s)

4. include three or more substantive, contact periods.

This decision rule reflects the basic characteristics of small firm strategic planning, particularly OBSP, identified earlier in the literature review.

Operationalizing Small Firm Effectiveness

The assessment of organizational effectiveness has received considerable attention in management literature. For a thorough, general summary of this literature, see Cunningham (1977). For a thorough summary relative to the small firm, see Robinson (1980a, 1980b). One major debate is between the use of organizational goals versus a systems approach to an accurate assessment of effectiveness. Another debate centers around the use of "hard"

measures (such as profit, sales, market share) versus "soft" measures (such as job satisfaction or social responsibility) in assessing effectiveness. One consistent theme in this literature is that organizational effectiveness is a multivariate phenomenon. In the present study, effectiveness generally was operationalized as a multivariate phenomenon. In the comparison of OBSP firms with RMA firms in Hypothesis 1, effectiveness was operationalized with only one measure: net profit before taxes divided by sales (profitability). A multivariate operationalization was not feasible due to the limited nature of Robert Morris Associates data (number of employees and owner compensation were not available). In Hypothesis 2, effectiveness was operationalized as a multivariate concept.

Table 4 presents the measures used to operationalize effectiveness in this study.

Growth, Profitability and Productivity. Friedlander and Pickle's (1968) in-depth study of small firms suggested that effectiveness as measured by improvement in profitability and growth in sales appears significantly associated with increased effectiveness as measured by satisfaction of community, customer, and employee needs. Studies by Alves (1978), Edmister (1970), and Gru (1973) support Friedlander and Pickle. Each found a measure of profitability, productivity, and a measure of change in sales to be the most significant components of discriminant equations between successful and unsuccessful small firms. Furthermore, all three studies concluded that return on sales was a more powerful measure of profitability than return on investment in small firms because specification of "investment" is inconsistent on small firm balance sheets.

312

Table 4. Operationalizing Organizational Effectiveness

Dimension of Effectiveness	Variable Used to Operationalize Each Dimension	Formula Employed to Measure Each Variable
Growth	Percentage increase (decrease) in total sales	$$\frac{\text{Total Sales for post-OBSP time period (adjusted for inflation)} \, [-] \, \text{Total sales for matching pre-OBSP time period}}{\text{Total sales for matching pre-OBSP time period}}$$
Profitability	(Hypothesis 1) Absolute increase in net profit before taxes/total sales (NPOS)	NPOS for post-OBSP time period $[-]$ NPOS for matching pre-OBSP time period
	(Hypothesis 2) Absolute increase in (net profit before taxes plus owner compensation)/total sales (return on sales-ROS)	ROS for post-OBSP time period $[-]$ ROS fo matching pre-OBSP time period
Productivity	Absolute increase in sales/employee	Sales/employee for post-OBSP (time period adjusted for inflation) $[-]$ Sales/employee for matching pre-OBSP time period
Employent	Percentage increase in the number of full-time equivalent employees (FTEs)	$$\frac{\text{Number of FTEs for post-OBSP time period} \, [-] \, \text{Number of FTEs for matching pre-OBSP time period}}{\text{Number of FTEs for matching pre-OBSP time period}}$$

Finally, each study employed sales per employee (total sales divided by number of employees) as a measure of productivity.

Social Responsibility. The small business sector of the economy creates more jobs than any other. Between 1969 and 1975, 14 million Americans joined the civilian work force and 9 million jobs were created. During that time there was no net increase in employment among the 1,000 largest U.S. corporations. Of the nine million

individuals in the new jobs, three million went to work for state and local governments, and the remaining six million went to work for small business (*Fact Book on Small Business,* 1979). Small business plays an important role in U.S. society as a source of employment. Therefore, increase in number of employees was used in this study to reflect the social responsibility dimension of small firm effectiveness.

Absolute Change Versus Percentage Change. The concern of this study was

Table 5. Results: Hypothesis 1

	Mean Sales	Mean NPBT[a]	Mean NPOS[b] %	t	df	p
Pre-OSBP time period						
OBSP firms	$252,724	$10,018	4.40	-.77	200	.44[c]
RMA firms	$225,710	$13,683	6.04			
Post-OBSP time period						
OBSP firms	$279,959	$24,636	8.79	2.31	200	.03[c]
RMA firms	$226,110	$13,877	6.09			

a Net profit before taxes over the time period in which total sales were generated.
b NPOS = (net profit before taxes)/total sales.
c Although the profitability (NPOS) of OBSP and RMA firms was not significantly different before OBSP, OBSP firms had a significantly (.05 level) higher profitability than RMA firms after engaging in OBSP ($p < .03$).

the comparative improvement in effectiveness over a specific time period between OBSP and non-OBSP firms. The four effectiveness measures were taken for matching pre-OBSP and post-OBSP time periods on all firms (with the impact of inflation on sales controlled for). The focus of analysis was the increase or decrease (change) in effectiveness (four measures) for OBSP and non-OBSP firms. Two effectiveness measures, sales and number of employees, were measured as "percentage change" from pre- to post-OBSP time periods in order to control for differences which might have been attributable to size if "absolute change" were used. For example, two firms (A and B) might experience an identical $100,000 increase in sales and an increase of 4 employees over the two time periods measured. However, if firm A had $200,000 in sales and 5 employees during the pre-OBSP time period while firm B had $1 million in sales and 45 employees, the relative accomplishment of firm A is considerably greater than firm B. The use of "percentage

change" controls for this size distortion in sales and number of employees. There is danger in the percentage change approach, however, if one group is predominated by very small firms (by sales) and the other by large (small) firms (again using sales). As reported earlier, this danger was examined via median sales and number of employees. No significant differences in the distribution of firms by sales or employees between the OBSP and non-OBSP groups existed.

Profitability (return on sales) and productivity (sales per employee) are ratios. The potential for distortion due to size differential does not exist. Therefore, absolute change was used to measure increase or decrease in these effectiveness measures.

Statistical Analysis

Hypothesis 1 was tested using the correlated sample *t-test*. Hypothesis 2 was tested using one-way multivariate analysis of variance (MANOVA) with Duncan's multiple range test as an a posteriori follow-up to isolate sources of overall differences (*Statistical Analysis System*, 1979).

Results

Hypothesis 1: Hypothesis 1 was rejected. The results of the test of this hypothesis are present in Table 5. Although the profitability of OBSP firms and RMA firms was not significantly different during the Pre-OBSP time period, the OBSP firms were significantly more profitable than RMA firms during the post-OBSP time period. Small firms that engaged in OBSP had a significantly higher increase in profitability (NPOS) than

did the matched sample of RMA firms. These findings were consistent in each of the three types of firms (retail, service, and manufacturing).

Hypothesis 2: Hypothesis 2 was rejected. The results of this hypothesis are presented in Table 6. Small firms engaging in OBSP had a significantly higher improvement in effectiveness than did the random sample of BKS firms. The Duncan's follow-up procedure found three sources (at the .05 level) of this overall significant difference: sales, profitability (ROS), and number of employees. These findings were consistent for both types of firms, although the differences were more pronounced in service firms.

Table 6. Results: Hypothesis 2

MANOVA: $F(4, 140) = 4.40$ $p = .002$
Duncan's Follow-up procedure:

	Sales[a]	ROS[b]	Employees[c]	Productivity[d]
Pre-OBSP time period				
OBSP mean	$270,764	16.23	5.82	$41,768
BKS mean	$290,197	20.52	5.83	$54,977
Post-OBSP time period				
OBSP mean	$297,955	17.76	6.40	$45,869
BKS mean	$296,910	18.21	6.12	$58,091
Change				
OBSP	29.1%	1.53	20.9%	$ 3,299
BKS	3.9%	−2.31	5.4%	$ 3,144
Significant difference[e]	SD@.05	SD@.05	SD@.05	NSD

[a] Total sales or revenue for matching pre- and post-OBSP time periods
[b] Return on sales = (net profit before taxes + owner compensation)/total sales.
[c] Number of full-time equivalent employees.
[d] Sales per employee over pre- and post-OBSP time periods.
[e] Using Duncan's New Multiple Range Test to isolate sources of overall difference found in the MANOVA procedure.

Discussion

The results of this study support the authors who have urged small businesses to utilize strategic planning. Small business owner/managers who continually "do not have enough time to plan" are penalizing their business' sales, profitability, and productivity. Indeed, this study would suggest that they are penalizing society by denying the potential for increased employment. In each hypothesis, small firms engaging in outsider-based strategic planning experienced significantly higher increases in effectiveness than did their control group counterparts not engaging in such planning. This appears to be the case whether the firms were retail, service, or manufacturing firms.

If small businesses are to utilize strategic planning as an effective management tool, a major necessity (based on this study) is the comprehensive inclusion of outsiders in the planning effort. Apparently, outside planning consultants supplement the owner's lack of planning orientation, skills, time allocation, and commitment. The tentative conclusion of this study is that small businesses should incorporate outsiders into their planning and strategic decision making on a regular, repetitive basis.

Strategic management/business policy theory and research has expanded considerably over the last fifteen years. Unfortunately, small firms have been basically ignored in this expansion. This study suggests small business to be a fertile area for policy research. Indeed, the role of outsiders suggests a specific difference in strategic planning in large versus small firms. A recent study found that "the degree of openness in long-range planning processes is directly related to the

degree of environmental complexity and instability for large firms, but inversely related for small firms" (Lindsay & Rue, 1980, p.402). Apparently firm size is a critical contingent variable in any evolving contingency approach to business policy. If so, the smaller end of this size contingency deserves considerably more attention in business policy research than has been given to date.

Several possible extensions of this research may be considered:

1. Is there a possibility that those business owners who choose to work with an outsider (or SBDC) have somewhat different qualities, such as openness to ideas or greater commitment to economic success? Though not specifically considered in this study, this condition may have some relationship with the decision to use an outsider, the nature of the relationship, and the subsequent impact.

2. Replication to confirm whether or not the outsider is an important aspect of strategic planning in small firms deserves further research.

3. What level of involvement should the outsider take? Determine what the content role of the outsider should be.

4. Is the use of outsiders (or the nature of their involvement) contingent on environmental circumstances, life cycle considerations, or other variables?

5. Determine whether different types of outsiders (such as SBDC, SBA, lawyers, accountants, consultants, business colleagues) are more effective. And is this continent on different factors or formats?

6. Determine at what point formal strategic planning emerges as an identifiable function in small business within different environmental circumstances

(Lindsay & Rue, 1980). Building on this suggestion by Lindsay and Rue:

a. At what point does the outsider become an important determinant of the emergence suggested?

b. If the outside planner expedites this emergence, is there a critical point(s) in the stages of development at which the payoff is greatest?

c. Is there a critical point(s) at which the outside planner should lessen or terminate involvement?

Efforts to develop a greater understanding of strategic management in small firms must be undertaken if a truly contingent approach to business policy is to be developed. Lindsay and Rue's suggestion that "small firms should be considered as a separate class in this and future related studies" (1980, p.402) is a positive, understated challenge to future policy research.

References

Alves, J. R. *The prediction of small business failure utilizing financial and non-financial data.* Unpublished doctoral dissertation, University of Massachusetts, 1978.

Anderson, D. C. *Factors contributing to the success of small service-type business.* Unpublished doctoral dissertation, Georgia State University, 1970.

Buchele, R. B. *Business policy in growing firms.* San Francisco: Chandler Publishing Company, 1965.

Chicha, J. & Julien, P. A. *The strategy of SMBs and their adaptation to change.* Trois-Rivieres, Quebec: Unviersity of Quebec at Trois-Rivieres, 1979.

Cohn, T. & Lindberg, R. A. *How management is different in small companies.* New York: American Management Association, 1972.

Cunningham, B. Approaches to the evaluation of organizational effectiveness. *Academy of Management Review,* 1977, 2, 463-474.

Drucker, P. F. Helping small businesses cope. *Wall Street Journal,* April 21, 1977, 30.

Edmister, R. O. *Financial ratios as predictors of small business failure.* Unpublished doctoral dissertation, Ohio State University, 1970.

Factbook on small business. Washington, D. C.: National Federation of Independent Business, 1979.

Flewellen, W. D., & Bramblett, L. R. The small business development center program in Georgia. *AACSB Bulletin,* Spring, 1978, 3-10.

Flewellen, W. D., & Bramblett, L. R. The small business development center act. Testimony before the senate select small business committee, United States Senate, 96th Congress, April 5, 1979.

Fogel, I. Importance of planning in small business. *Proceedings of the International Council on Small Business,* 1979, Quebec City, Canada, 20-1 to 20-9.

Freidlander, F., & Pickle, H. Components of effectiveness in small organizations. *Administrative Science Quarterly,* 1968, 13 (3), 289-304.

Gasse, Y. Management techniques and practice in small manufacturing firms. *Proceedings of the International Council on Small Business,* 1979., Quebec City, Canada, 16-1 to 16-15.

Gilmore, F. F. Formulating strategy in smaller companies. *Harvard Business Review,* 1971, 49 (2), 71-81.

Golde, R. A. Practical planning for small business. *Harvard Business Review,* 1964, 42 (3), 147-161.

Gru, L. G. *Financial ratios, multiple dicscriminant analysis, and the prediction of small corporate failure.* Unpublished doctoral dissertation, University of Minnesota, 1973.

Hofer, C. W., & Schendel, D. *Strategy formulation: Analytical concepts.* St. Paul, Minn.: West Publishing Co., 1978.

Krentzman, H. C. & Samaras, J. N. Can small business use consultants? *Harvard Business Review,* 1960, 38 (3), 57-64.

Lindsay, W. M., & Rue, L. W. Impact of the organization environment on the long-range planning process: A contingency view, *Academy of Management Journal,* 1980, 23, 385-404.

Mainer, R. The case of the stymied strategist. *Harvard Business Review,* 1968, 46 (2), 36-45.

Potts, A. J. *A study of the success and failure rates of small businesses and the use or non-use of accounting information.* Unpublished doctoral dissertation, George Washington University, 1977.

Rice, G. H. & Hamilton, R. E. *Decision theory and the small businessman.* College Station: Texas A & M University, 1979.

RMA annual statement studies. Philadelphia: Robert Morris Associates, 1978.

RMA annual statement studies. Philadelphia: Robert Morris Associates, 1979.

Robinson, R. B. Business information and consulting services: UGA-SBDC. Paper presented at the annual meeting of the Southwest SBI Association, Houston, 1979a, 127-138.

Robinson, R. B. Forecasting and small business: A study of the strategic planning process. *Journal of Small Business Management,* 1979b, 17(3), 19-27.

Robinson, R. B. *An empirical investigation of the impact of SBDC-strategic planning consultation upon the short-term effectiveness of small business in Georgia.* Unpublished doctoral dissertation, University of Georgia, 1980a.

Robinson, R. B. The measurement of organizational effectiveness for business policy research in small and growing firms. *Proceedings of the Southern Management Association Annual Meetings,* New Orleans, 1980b, 142-145.

The role of the consultant. *Viewpoint,* Fall, 1975, 3, 14-16.

Sexton, T. N. & Dahle, R. D. Factors affecting long-range planning in the small business firm. *Marquette Business Review,* 1976, 20(2), 158-165.

Smith, S. B. *The small business institute program: A study of its effectiveness.* Unpublished doctoral dissertation, University of Southern California, 1978.

Statistical analysis system. Raleigh, N.C.: SAS Institute, 1979.

Steiner, G. A. Approaches to long-range planning for small business. *California Management Review,* 1967, 10(3), 3-16.

Still, T. W. *An exploratory investigation of strategic planning behavior in small businesses.* Unpublished doctoral dissertation, Florida State University, 1974.

Timmons, J. A., Smollen, L. E., & Dingee, A. L. *New venture creation: A guide to small business development.*

Homewood, Ill.: Richard D. Irwin, 1977.

Trombetta, W. L. An empirical approach to marketing strategy for the small retailer. *Journal of Small Business Management*, 1976, 14(4), 55-59.

Trow, D. B. Executive succession in small companies. *Administrative Science Quarterly*, 1961, 6(3), 232-239.

Wheelwright, S. C. Strategic planning in the small business. *Business Horizons*, 1971, 14(3), 51-58.

Introduction

While a board of directors should help a CEO set objectives and policies, advise and counsel on important issues, elect officers and directors, and judge the CEO's performance and select his successor, CEOs generally fear the concept of a board. They crave freedom and dislike sharing information. They have no desire to be challenged or held accountable. That's why only one in twenty boards contains an objective outsider and only one in two hundred has a majority of objective outsiders. The author argues that a board can be a vital asset to a company if it is properly sought and managed. Specific advice in doing so is offered.

Finding and Using Outside Board Directors
1986

By R. Fulton MacDonald

The law in this country requires that a corporation has a Board of Directors. A corporation provides its founders — major stockholders — with three key abilities or characteristics:

1. Limited liability,

2. Preferential tax treatment,

3. Ability to raise capital (in special ways).

But a corporation is treated as a "legal person," with certain strict responsibilities — largely fiduciary. As a concept, the Board of Directors is charged with overseeing accountability. However, under limited liability provisions, in general, only the major stock holder/owner/manager is specifically accountable. In the case of the large public corporations, where ownership and management are separated, the Board is the formal agent on behalf of the stockholders.

What is the ideal? A Board should help the CEO:

• Set general objectives and management policies;

• Advise and counsel on important issues;

• Elect the corporate officers and fill Board vacancies;

• Judge CEO performance;

• Select a CEO successor.

In reality:

- Among public corporations: few of these tasks are done.

- In private companies: almost none.

Why? What is the problem? — Why such limited performance?!

The truth is that most CEOs fear the concept of a board. In small, privately held corporations, built by the owner/manager, the number one value — perceived and held to by almost all entrepreneurs — is *freedom*: being one's own boss.

That freedom, or flexibility, has often been very hard won. Fighting up the ladder of a new venture start is harrowing. Survival is the goal. Cash flow the focus. Friday's payroll the concern. The process almost forcibly builds a desire for, and appreciation of, *secrecy.*

One learns early that letting it out, being open with bankers, suppliers, customers, even employees can often backfire. Everyone gets nervous when they actually see how tight the financial situation is. If they know, they close in, to the detriment of the fledgling firm. So a new-venture CEO learns to be secretive, even alone — early.

Often, big public corporations are not too much different. It is not uncommon to see even very large firms run for the benefit of management, top management, rather than shareholders. The nature of inertia and diffuse ownership keeps the top teams in place, who merely vote other "team" players into their upper ranks. Business actions are often whimsical, not really well thought out. Emotions, and personal preferences, get involved.

Top management, having finally reached the top — with all of its power, perqs, and prestige, doesn't really want to be challenged. It likes its new found "freedom." And the drawbridge mentality goes into effect, shutting off outsiders or those who might threaten the newly achieved power (and freedom) position.

Boards of Directors — real, outside Boards — can, and should, challenge management, tactfully but clearly. That is one of a Board's true values. It is also a *threat.* For many top managements, finally on top — and treated like mini-royalty with aides, lieutenants, limousines, corporate planes, even hunting lodges and the like — being brought up short and reminded that they are not mini-Gods, but mere mortals, is just not pleasing. Let's face it: it is gratifying to be pampered and even worshiped a bit. After fighting so hard and so long, it is nice to enjoy the spoils — the perqs and unchallenged power of top office.

The fact is that very few Boards are truly objective outsiders.

Although Board of Directors' makeup varies greatly, most often it is heavily "inside," frequently including the firm's attorney, banker or investment banker; and if "outsiders" are included they are often persons with definite vested interests.

Inside Boards are generally "yes" men: who is really going to challenge the boss?! And, by definition, inside managers largely focus on short term scope and action, tactics: the current fiscal quarter's and year's revenues and profits.

"Stockholder" Boards focus on their own personal investment interests. Frequently, a small or privately held firm Board concentrates on issues of reinvestment/dividend splits/distribution of benefits. Family Boards are generally not professional managers, who

would have developed the business judgment that comes from years of responsible risk-taking.

Friends may or may not tell you the *truth*. Hopefully they love you. But in a company, a CEO needs business judgment: "no" tactfully given.

Most Boards are of little real value to the corporation. It is not surprising therefore that even large, public companies are caught by "surprise:" look at the failures of such as W.T. Grant, A & P, Food Fair (now reborn as Pantry Pride) – very few Boards are equipped to truly provide the value that they should: sound, experienced, objective business counsel. Board culture in our country is still deeply rooted to vested interests, protecting top management status quo, secrecy, and polite rubber-stamping.

Corporate culture is changing but only slowly. And the few "professional" outsiders often have severe conflicts of interest. It is estimated that only 1 out of 20 Boards has a real, objective outsider; only 1 out of 200 has a majority of outsider Board members. And as we have briefly reviewed, many of these outsiders are of questionable objective value.

When do you really need an objective, outside Board? When "Board" functions may not be properly addressed:

- Corporate & financial strategy review.

- Policies & plans implementation.

- Full formulation of the senior management team.

- Corporate controls, when they appear somewhat lacking.

- Employee and/or community relations, when there are signs of strain.

- And so on.

The principal value of an objective, outside Board is that it helps you, the CEO, perform *sharper* and thus more *effectively*. Focusing on both the present near-term targets, and the longer-view.

Recommendations;

1. Build an outside board.

2. Seek principally other risk-taking business builders and managers.

- Only business-building, risk-takers understand the "buck stops here" pressure and responsibility to balance people, money, and things.

- Most lawyers, accountants and the like, though of considerable value to the CEO as advisors, are by training experts in their (one) field. Staff is not line. Expert staff is not expert line (and vice-versa). The skills are very different. Further, these professional advisors often have conflicts of interest in truly challenging the person who pays their bills!

- Finding other business builders is not easy; but far more are present than you might realize.

- Just ask them. Though busy in their own companies, they will probably be flattered, and we all love to see other businesses in action.

3. *Approach the Board as an asset – build as a vital tool of the company.*

- As we have discussed, some CEOs fear Boards because they 'stir things up,' possibly challenging the use of funds (money is one of the most fundamental of all human sensitivities), and because Boards are viewed as 'necessary evils' – rarely approached with the view of making them positive forces.

Board composition and use will not change until CEO views change. Get over the hurdle! It is to your distinct advantage.

- Take the Board (concept) seriously. Once you pass the "fear" hurdle and view the Board as a key asset: solid counsel, outside perspective, the long view, allies in the lonely world of the top—you are truly *free*, not only as a Chief Executive but as an individual.

- Look to create a balanced Board. Think through your strengths, and relative weaknesses. Try to seek out people who complement, *add* what may not be your genius: Planning-thinking; As a safety-fuse (better inside than out); As big brothers (balancing the present, now, with continuity and the longer view).

4. *Identify appropriate new board candidates via your present professional technical advisory group; but recognize you probably already know the right candidates.*

- At first it may seem like these— ideal—Board candidates don't exist. Start the process through your professional advisory network— lawyer, accountant, banker, etc. Then stretch your thought to other managers who you may have long admired or respected for one reason or another. Consider, possibly, the use of a senior executive search firm to help fill the key spots.

- Chemistry—your comfort—of course is essential!

- The more confident, quietly assured, you are, the greater can be your "reach"—the more varied and "different" can be your Board composition.

- Introduce. Get on committees: audit, appraisal special ad-hoc.

- Compensate. Treat as professionals. Pay up front. Keep them informed and prepared (at least 3-4 days before meetings):

- Principal criteria in selection includes: people whose views the CEO can't "buy," men/women of clear integrity, possessing good judgment, problem solvers, action-oriented, understanding of risk-taking.

- Mix backgrounds; business affiliations, ages, expertise.

5. *Use the board for the long view. Keep management focus on the now.*

- A Board's real role is long term: planning reviews, succession, mergers/acquisitions/major growth steps, overall policy.

- Management should be focused primarily on generating near-term sales, profits, thwarting immediate competition, motivating employees now.

- A Board's job is management *review, not managing.*

- Most CEOs, particularly owner-builders, are *now* oriented. They have come up through the "survival" ranks.

- Boards aren't good for survival. They are not crisis-skilled nor focused. It is too immediate (A CEO needs a crash team to handle crisis).

- But Boards are extremely valuable to balance out the immediate view with regular, disciplined looks at and focus on the longer haul.

- The presence of a truly outside Board helps to sharpen the thinking and response of the CEO. And thus makes him much more effective at taking the right fork in the road — because the overall map has been looked at carefully. (Miss the big mistakes. Leave these for the ego-filled CEOs!).

- Hopefully, insiders add to the *quantitative* strength of a company: more sales of products X & Y, tighter profitability out of the existing resource structure, etc.

- Outside Boards can add measurably in *qualitative* strengths: increasing the firm's reputation; ability to deliver quality service and product; introduction of additional management techniques, etc.

- The CEO should recognize that good Board candidates — risk-taking, business builders, and men/women of integrity — are likely to be *very trustworthy and understanding* of what it takes for you, the CEO, to do your job — and to back you up, constructively.

Your hurdle is to *make* the tough decision: *to build a strong, objective Board.* It is a lot easier than building the corporation. But it can make the principal difference to long term growth, ultimate survival and the full realization of your asset-building goals. *It is good self-interest.*

Introduction

When CEOs of growing private companies reach the point when complexity and growth contain greater challenges than he can handle, many find it useful to create an independent working board of directors. Such directors can offer seasoned and objective guidance, an unbiased sounding board, specialized know-how or experience, or helpful contacts. The existence of the board forces the CEO to replace "seat-of-the-pants" management with a formalized planning process. When the leap from solo decision maker to accountability to an outside board is made, one gains a source of experience and creativity that greatly enriches the business.

Creating a Board of Directors: When Success Demands Too Much

1986

By Benjamin Benson

"(. . .no one) requires the formation of a working board. It only comes about if the owner-manager desires effective help to ensure the long-term viability of his company—and this requires outside directors who can stand up to the business owner's flak long enough to give him the advice, support and help he needs."

Léon A. Danco
Donald J. Jonovic

Outside Directors in the Family-Owned Business

"All those who disagree, please signify by saying, 'I resign!'" read the caption for a cartoon showing a company chairman at a board of directors meeting.

That scenario may not be very applicable to privately-owned companies, since, at most, such companies don't even bother having meetings. Boards of privately-owned companies normally consist of family members and the companies' lawyers, and usually exercise little of the authority vested in a board. The principal challenge to board members is to affix their signatures in the proper place to signify that a legally ordained meeting was held although the meeting never took place. It's just a formality to comply with legal requirements. Such boards have been referred to as "phantom boards."

Should it be any different? After all, the "boss" generally is the controlling stockholder. Why would he want an independent board of directors to which he would be accountable and who would question his operation of the business?

325

Many chief executive officers (CEOs) of developing privately-owned companies reach a point where the complexity of conducting business, coupled with the changes resulting from growth, strain his capacity to operate the business by himself. He had the vision to start the company, but now has encountered a new set of challenges and is no longer comfortable making all the decisions.

He relies on advice from outside sources, principally his accountant and lawyer; although both are generally valuable in assisting him with business decisions, their advice is limited to their particular disciplines. (In a survey recently conducted by Laventhol & Horwath, CEOs of privately-owned companies were asked, "If you were going to make an important business decision and wanted sound advice, who would you consult?" The predominant choice was the company's CPA, followed by the lawyer, business associate and banker.) It should be noted that many accounting firms have expanded their consulting capabilities far beyond traditional services and provide clients with a wide range of consulting services. One important distinction: These professionals provide advice, but do not establish policy or make decisions.

Many CEOs have found it beneficial to dispense with the phantom board of directors and to establish a truly independent working board. In the L&H survey, managers of privately-owned companies were asked if they had an independent board of directors. Less than one in five answered affirmatively, but this group believed overwhelmingly that such a board was valuable.

What are the Benefits?

Independent directors can provide the following benefits at low cost:

- Seasoned and objective guidance from successful business people.

- Possible contacts which may help the company in production, purchasing, sales or financing.

- An unbiased sounding board for family-owned business problems, such as succession.

- Specialized know-how not available internally.

Most importantly, the accountability of the CEO to an independent board forces him to conceptualize and formalize the planning process since he must "sell" his policies to the board of directors. This valuable process requires careful planning. The CEO must be in a position to defend his ideas when challenged by the board. It is, for him, an impetus to replace "seat of the pants" management with an organized planning process.

Who's Responsible for What?

The principal responsibilities of a board of directors are to establish corporate policy and oversee management performance.

The CEO is responsible for day-to-day operations and should submit policy issues for board determination. These include:

- Strategic planning for short- and long-term objectives, budgeting, marketing production and financial strategies, and organizational and human resource issues.

- Major corporate decisions, including acquisitions, mergers, possible sale of the business and major expenditures.

The monitoring of management performance is an important board responsibility, including management compensation and perquisites as well as plans for management succession. This can be a delicate issue since the CEO is usually a good friend of the board members, has invited the members to serve, and often has the power to dismiss them.

The board may also force the issues of organizational structure and management succession, which many CEOs are reluctant to face. This may involve sensitive family issues, such as compensation and authority of family members. The board may also provide unemotional and objective viewpoints in helping to resolve such issues.

The Key Emotional Issues

In publicly-owned businesses, the CEO is accountable to a board of directors which serves shareholders. CEOs of privately-owned businesses usually are accountable to no one. Many would not have it any other way.

Independent boards can only be effective when the CEO is emotionally secure and confident enough about his stewardship to voluntarily relinquish a degree of control to gain the benefits an outside board can provide. He must be convinced that the benefits of an independent board justify surrendering some control.

Unless he believes in this concept and is willing to submit to board recommendations, the independent board cannot succeed in helping to develop the business. This does not mean the CEO must relinquish all control. There may be times when he may find it necessary to exercise the prerogative of a major shareholder and make decisions contrary to the board. Board members will generally accept this, but they must believe that their opinions are valued and that their viewpoints have an impact on the business.

An effective working board should probe, challenge and offer recommendations in an atmosphere of mutual respect that is supportive rather than adversarial. This balancing act can only exist among mature people who are willing to subordinate their sensitivities to the good of the company. This means the CEO must terminate the aura of secrecy common to many privately-owned companies and be candid with the board. Most, if not all, of the skeletons must come out of the closet.

The board members have a final weapon if they believe that the CEO is not willing to accept direction. They can resign. They never asked for the job in the first place.

Who Needs Outside Directors?

Not every business is ready for an independent board. In addition to having the CEO's commitment to this management tool, various questions should be answered affirmatively before a business can be considered a prime candidate for an outside board:

• Is it a growing, maturing company rather than a one-man business?

• Is there enough substance to the business so that shareholder and operational issues can be distinguished from one another?

• Is the counsel to be gained from an independent board apt to complement or expand upon that received from existing professional advisers?

Many smaller companies operate very well as one-man businesses with the CEO making all the decisions. They neither seek nor would benefit from the disciplines and formality which an independent board would mandate. Others function well with an advisory committee comprised of the CPA, lawyer and other business associates. The vast majority have no formal advisory structure and merely call on professional advisers as needed.

Composition of the Board

There are no fixed rules about how large a board should be. One rule of thumb indicates that companies with a sales volume up to $50 million should not have more than five directors. Up to nine directors are considered appropriate for companies with sales up to $500 million. For companies with sales over $500 million, nine to 15 directors are considered sufficient.

The board should be built around the specific needs of the company, with members selected for the unique skills or experience they can bring to the business. If the company has production problems, a person experienced in this area should be considered. If a public issue is contemplated in the future, it may be helpful to have someone on the board who has been through the process. If the company is involved in international business or is considering entering the global marketplace, a person with international experience may help. Is there a proper balance of seasoned business advice, financial know-how, industry experience and marketing knowledge? Can you trust these people with the confidences you will share with them? Do they have track records of success? Do you trust their judgment? Will they ask hard questions and take a contrary view if the situation calls for it? Does the right personal chemistry exist between board members and the CEO? Will they have the time and commitment to attend meetings?

It is not necessary for an independent board to consist only of outside directors. Frequently, the CEO is chairman of the board with the responsibility for

organizing and presiding at meetings. The board may also include key officers of the company or family members whose presence can add to the deliberations. Everyone who sits on the board should be a contributing member; honorary positions should be discontinued. (Naturally, this may be difficult if the honorary position is held by the CEO's wife.) Tact, sometimes extreme tact, may be required.

Finding the Right Directors

Potential board members exist in every community. They consist of business owners and managers (both active and retired), educators and professional advisers, such as accountants, lawyers and bankers. To insure objectivity, board members should not include anyone who conducts business with the company. Many qualified people are challenged and flattered to serve on the board of a successful company and are willing to contribute their time, efforts and experience to a director's role. Some see this as an opportunity to enhance their own business capabilities through the experience gained as a board member. Frequently, if the chemistry is right, an atmosphere of camaraderie is attained and new close relationships are developed among board members. This can be enhanced by occasional company-sponsored social functions for board members.

Fees and Frequency of Meetings

Stimulation and challenge are the major reasons why busy and successful people accept board positions. Directors fees, while expected, are not a principal motivation.

There are no fixed rules about directors fees or frequency of meetings. According to *Small Business Report* (October 1985), a compensation guide for board members attending a four- to six-hour board meeting is:

Annual Sales	Minimum Compensation
Under $5M	$400
$5–15M	$500
Over $15M	$700

Directors fees should be a meaningful gesture of appreciation and recognition for the director's contributions, although there is no presumption that such fees compensate board members for the value of their contributions to the business. This is consistent with the psychology of why outside directors serve in the first place.

Frequency of meetings depends on the needs of the business. In the early stages, or if there are a multitude of major policy decisions to be made, four or more meetings a year may be advisable. In more mature situations, one or two meetings a year may suffice.

Directors Liability

Corporate directors have a fiduciary responsibility to the corporation and its shareholders. Inasmuch as the shareholders of privately-owned companies are frequently a small group who are active in management and well known to the directors, the possibility of being sued has not been of major concern to outside directors of privately-owned companies over the years. There are other circumstances such as fraud or negligence which expose directors to law suits by third parties, but such suits have been uncommon.

Traditionally, it has been possible to protect against law suits through the purchase of low-cost directors liability insurance. The proliferation of lawsuits against directors of large public corporations, however, has driven many insurers out of the business, and directors liability insurance is either unobtainable or very expensive.

Most business people who would be most competent to serve on an outside board are understandably reluctant to do so without adequate insurance to protect them from being sued in an increasingly litigious society. This is a serious obstacle in the trend toward outside directors serving in privately-owned companies.

Making It Work

Once an outside board has been assembled, here are some tips for the CEO to help make it effective:

• Treat the board members as if they represented shareholder control of the business, whether or not this is the case. Competent board members will not stay unless they believe their decisions carry weight.

• Define the board's functions, responsibility and authority in writing.

• Encourage board members to learn as much about the business as possible.

• Share your business problems. Remember, everybody has them. The board cannot help unless it knows about them.

• Prepare for board meetings. The agenda and all additional relevant information should be sent to each board member in advance.

• Prepare minutes for each meeting, summarizing action plans and timetables.

The entrepreneur/founder who is willing to make the giant leap from sole decision maker to accountability to others may find that an outside board provides a valuable source of unique business experience. It also can represent a more creative approach to a company's development, one that may profoundly affect the course of the business.

Introduction

Boards of family businesses should include carefully selected outsiders to provide accountability and to set company policy. Outside board members should be selected because of their particular expertise and their overall business acumen. They provide knowledge and perspective, but their purpose is not mediation of family disputes. Recruiting outsiders to the board lets family members better focus on their business.

Non-Family Board Members Can Offer New Perspectives for Family Businesses

1984

By Thomas Hubler and Stephen Swartz

John and Mary Smith's six-year-old manufacturing company had reached a critical stage. Their payroll had increased from five to 35 employees; their market share was growing and they saw opportunities for expansion in new product areas. But like most owners of small businesses, the Smiths were preoccupied with the day-to-day challenges of managing their enterprise. They had little time to even think about the expansion they knew would be required if they hoped to remain competitive in their field. They needed an astute assessment of trends in their market and some solid planning for hiring and promoting key employees to

new areas of responsibility. It seemed an almost overwhelming task, and in late-night discussions the Smiths weighed the pros and cons of moving their business into a new, more risk-laden phase.

Owners of small companies who face similar decisions often do one of two things; gear up quickly to take advantage of new opportunity, using the "shoot-from-the-hip" style characteristic of entrepreneurs – or decide they can't afford the time and money to make a well researched decision and let opportunity pass them by.

For the Smiths, however, neither approach was necessary. They brought a summary of their late-night discussions to their board of directors, asking each member to think through their company's options and make recommendations reflecting the individual members' expertise. Their ultimate decision to expand was a collective one — based on more than a hunch. In addition to solid accounting and legal advice from the professional advisors, they received a thorough evaluation of market trends and a reorganizational plan that would allow for growth with a conservative investment in new talent. The market assessment was provided by a retired executive the Smiths had recruited when they realized their own knowledge was limited to the narrow market segment they had been supplying, and the reorganization plan came from a vice president of a publicly held company that had undergone a number of transitions on its way to becoming a dominant force in its industry.

This experience confirmed for the Smiths the wisdom of expanding their board to include outside members. In doing so, they were deliberately counteracting the typical structure of family-business boards — a structure that makes them an under-tapped resource but potentially valuable resource for closely held businesses.

Typically, the board of directors of a family business includes the entrepreneur, his or her spouse, children active in the business and professional counsel — the company's lawyer, accountant and, occasionally, a banker or financial advisor. Many family-business boards also include family members who have ownership but are not directly involved in day-to-day operations, and some include employees involved in the management of the business. In most small companies, the underlying criteria for membership on the board is the relationship of each director to the entrepreneur rather than the skills, knowledge and

perspective that the individual brings to the corporation.

Family members who are not directly involved in the corporation often know little about the business itself. They are present because of their relationship to the entrepreneur, and often consider only the effect major decisions will have on their individual interests. Because they are usually dependent financially on the entrepreneur, they often follow his or her lead, rubber-stamping decisions with a "father knows best" rationale.

Employees who serve on their company's board face a similar dilemma: they also depend on the entrepreneur for the livelihood. In the business, their relationship is one of inequality, and it is difficult for them to challenge the founder on major *or* minor decisions. And although professional advisors — lawyers and accountants — bring some perspective to the business, they too have an interest in preserving their professional relationship and may see their role as one of support rather than challenge.

As a result, most family-business boards composed of the founder, family members, professional advisors and employees suffer from two major deficiencies: first, because they are close to the day-to-day operation of the business, they are often unable to distinguish between management and policy decisions; second — and even more important — they do not have the "clout" to hold the entrepreneur accountable.

A board of directors in any corporation, public or private, has two primary functions — to provide a structure for accountability and to set company policy. We have found that entrepreneurs are by nature difficult to hold accountable, and yet there is no successful business in which some form of accountability does not exist. For that reason we recommend broadening a family business board of directors to include outside members with particular knowledge and skills.

Who should those members be? We ask our family business clients to look carefully at their companies and to identify the areas of business management that are crucial to their success. If a business is people-intensive, for example, personnel management skill and human resources knowledge is essential. If a business depends on optimal use of capital, a member with broad financial experience can prove invaluable.

When the critical areas have been identified, a company can look to its local business community for people who have the skills it needs. Professional organizations, colleges and universities can provide leads. And organizations of retired executives are a great resource; their members welcome opportunities to use their talents and the experience they've acquired.

No matter how prospective board members are found, a business should look carefully at their reputation in the community, their track record and, most of all, their willingness to devote both time and energy to the task. Directors will be asked not only to attend meetings but to read and analyze information and to think through all decisions the board must make. The specific roles of outsiders will depend on their individual skills and knowledge. (A word of caution: the purpose of outside members is to provide accountability and perspective — not to serve as a buffer between family members. Outsiders who find themselves slipping into the intermediary's role should state clearly that it is not their purpose in serving.)

Although all corporations must by law have boards of directors, other business organizations can make use of outsiders' valuable perspective by establishing advisory boards. Community board members are often flattered to be asked and will willingly give of their time and knowledge. It is customary to pay directors for the time they spend; compensation varies with the number of meetings and the amount of responsibility required. Corporations should also provide directors' liability insurance that protects outside members.

Including outsiders on a family-business board of directors will enable family members to better focus on their business because they will be less likely to be distracted by non-business family issues. And enlisting outsider expertise will build in accountability — a critical factor in the success of any business.

Chapter 7

Family Business Growth

Among the challenges confronting family businesses is a tendency toward stagnation. Absent demands of public stockholders, family business owners can grow comfortable or even complacent in their economic niche. When the niche begins to close, however, change and growth are required for survival. Transgenerational entrepreneurial activity is required and can be seen in the example of M. Jacob & Sons where each of four generations has reinvented the family business.

To achieve growth, however, yet another family business paradox must be overcome. Entrepreneurship must be professionalized to be sustained—but professionalism must not destroy the entrepreneurial spirit.

Introduction

In this article, the authors discuss problems peculiar to family businesses, specifically focusing on management difficulties created by the "dual criteria" of family and business membership. To overcome these problems, they propose simultaneous application of a set of processes and applications derived from both organizational and family systems theories.

Adaptation, Survival, and Growth of the Family Business: An Integrated Systems Perspective
1980

By Peter Davis and Douglas Stern

Reprinted by permission of **Human Relations**, Vol. 34 (4), 1980. Copyright ©1981 Plenum Publishing Corp.; all rights reserved.

Family ownership and control are still significant in the majority of business enterprises in the United States. A high percentage of these companies face special problems particularly related to corporate development and transition from an entrepreneurial to a professional management structure. The dual criteria for corporate membership (family and professional competence) require special management efforts. Without these efforts, organizational rigidities develop which undermine the corporation's ability to function effectively. While the relevance of the interaction between family relationships and the working environment of organizational effectiveness has been recognized, family systems and organization approaches have never been simultaneously applied in the study of family-dominated businesses. In this paper we develop a scheme that is derived from principles of organizational and family-systems theory. We describe a set of processes and mechanisms that define and regulate the interaction between the business and family system. We show the applicability of these concepts to the study of adaptation and maladaptation in the family-dominated corporation.

In recent years, organizational research has yielded a rich set of alternatives as focal determinants of organizational structure and performance. Technology has been central. Environmental complexity and uncertainty have become prominent variables with the rise of the various contingency theories of organization. In some cases, mediating variables have been invoked to link primary technological and environmental characteristics with both structure and process. Analysis of control over uncertainty, its relationship to power, and the subsequent workings of power through interest group politics has proven a fruitful paradigm (Crozier, 1964; Pfeffer, 1972; Hickson and others, 1974). Bell (1973), Galbraith (1967), and Touraine (1971) have stressed the key relationship between technology, occupation and organizational power.

Within these various schemata, the role of the individual is viewed in the context of the whole, whether the whole be a group, substructure, or organization. With the emergence and subsequent dominance of the Weberian bureaucratic model, the individual, as an individual, has no significance apart from the functional contribution he makes to those organizational processes that are shaped by forces outside his control and generally outside his kin. Normative management practice tends to reinforce this state of affairs.

Members of the traditional human relations school and more recently the sociotechnical theorists have disputed this view, arguing for the centrality of human need and of the human relations that satisfy this need. Their arguments have focused descriptively on organizational performance deriving from an aggregate of individual behaviors, which are seen as adapting to both organizational pressures and individual requirements. The process of *human* adjustment leads to dysfunctional consequences that are adjusted through normative job redesign (Emery and Trist, 1960) or changes in interpersonal relations (Argyris, 1962).

Many human relations theorists thus accept the primacy of external determinants and look to human factors as perturbing elements and sources of dysfunctional behavior. The focus of their interventions is on coping and the adjustments of the individual or social group to the demands of organizational life.

To others, however, the primary determinants of technology, environment, and context do not inexorably specify the form and content of organization. They generate a force field with which the individuals as human actors must come to terms, always with an eye toward both organizational and individual survival and growth. In an important sense, the "human relations force field" and the "technological-environmental-contextual force field" codetermine the organizational outcome that emerges out of a relatively rich set of feasible and viable alternatives. The process of emergence to some is dialectical (Benson, 1977, p. 168): "The transformation of the social world is rooted in fundamental characteristics of human social life. People are continually constructing their social world. Through their interactions with each other social patterns are gradually built and eventually a set of institutional arrangements is established. Through continued interactions the arrangements variously contrasted are gradually modified or replaced."

The organizations is not in a "state of being" but a "state of becoming." However, the change process is not necessarily harmonious nor progressively adaptive in an evolutionary sense. "The organizational totality, as conceived dialectically, is characterized by ruptures, breaks, and inconsistencies in the social fabric" (Benson, 1977, p. 182).

The "ruptures, breaks, and inconsistencies" form the contradictions that may gradually generate alternatives to the established order or may, in contrast, destroy it.

In this paper, we will examine the process of change in a certain type of organization for which the dialectical view is particularly applicable. Our focus is on family businesses. A family firm as a firm operating in a business environment, is as influenced by the forces of technology, environmental complexity, and uncertainty as any other firm. But a family business must also contend with the business of the family. The emotional bond becomes a primary force and a focal point for organizational life. The intense personal and interpersonal issues generated from the role of the business as a context (or an arena) for acting out of the family agenda become powerful determinants of organizational structure and behavior. These issues are in every sense core to the family organization and cannot be conceptualized as subservient to external factors. Both external factors and family issues must be simultaneously accommodated to facilitate survival and growth.

The fragility of the family business in the contemporary business scene has been well documented. To many, the species is inherently flawed, and survival can be guaranteed through removal of the presence of the family. For example, Levinson (1971, p. 98) argues, "The wisest course for any business, family or nonfamily, is to move to professional management as quickly as possible."

Yet, despite such arguments, the family remains as *the* predominant form of business organization. As Hershon (1975) points out, there are roughly one million registered corporations in the United States; of these, 980,000 are privately owned family businesses. While the proportion of corporations under family control declines with corporate size, the much proclaimed conversion toward managerial (nonfamily) control of big business has been greatly overstated. According to Birch's calculations (1972, p. 101), "Over 42% of the largest publicly held corporations are probably under family control with another 17% placed in the 'possibly family' category. If the large privately owned firms were included, the number of family-controlled businesses would be even greater." A list of such private family-controlled businesses would include such corporate giants as Cargill, Bechtel, Continental Grain, Deering, Milliken, Hearst and Mars.

This obviously suggests that successful adaptations of the family firm to the business environment have been made and continue to be made. The family business as a *family* activity remains as a viable, legitimate entity and a continuing, significant organizational alternative.

In this paper we will examine the process of adaptation that allows so many family firms to survive and grow and the process of maladaptation that makes survival and growth so difficult.

Primary Adaptation

The distinct but interacting family and organizational agenda are central to an analysis of the family business. On the one hand, we can examine the behavior of the firm as a task-oriented business. This establishes those characteristics of the organization which are given meaning, credibility, and legitimacy in terms of their contribution to overall profitmaking performance. On the other hand, we can examine the basic assumptions governing behavior in the family business which are derived primarily from the emotional relationships which constitute the family process.

The process of accommodating the requirements of the family system to those of the task environment (and vice versa) can be represented as shown in

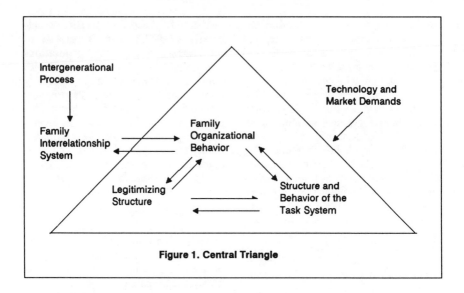

Figure 1. Central Triangle

Figure 1. Let us consider the central triangle first. Major decisions in the family firm will generally have meaning and significance within *both* the family and corporate systems.

In one company the decision was made by the CEO to promote his second son to the Presidency of a division (Division A) leaving the oldest son in another part of the company (Division B) with no responsibility and ill-defined prospects. Division A had to learn how to operate from an arm's-length relationship with the CEO as the second son struggled to establish his identity in his new role. Division B had to deal with the increased ambiguity surrounding the oldest son. The family had to adjust to the strengthening of one coalition (father-second son), the weakening of another (father-oldest son), and increased sibling rivalry. The decision also had the effect of publicly confirming the nature of the internal family coalitional structure leading to difficulties with some intimates outside the family.

As a consequence, the family business must struggle to establish sets of values, norms and principles which generate behavior which is jointly adapted to the needs of both the family and task systems. In contemporary society, the norms of the task system are highly developed and internalized, outside of any particular organizational context (Whyte, 1956; Riesman, 1950). These norms include standards of professionalism and equity, which the family firm may be unable to meet. For example, equitable rewards for performance may not be delivered as family members may be promoted at the expense of others. Basic contradictions may develop which may, in turn, threaten survival of the firm. As a response, the firm must struggle to establish a legitimizing structure of norms and values. This structure is often part truth and part fiction, but is sufficiently genuine to allow people to "buy into it" and legitimize their behavior. This legitimizing framework forms the third apex of the central triangle of determinants of the developmental process.

Moving out from the central triangle, the needs of the task system change with changes in technology and markets. New organizational structures may be required. New types of specialization and knowledge must be developed. New lines of business may be started as existing products enter the mature phase of the product life cycle. Many families controlling family businesses find it difficult to accommodate to these changing technological and environmental demands. Some are unable to face the family and organizational adjustments required, and they arrest the evolutionary process, often with disastrous consequences. Others may use the clearly *focused* and clearly *exogenous* nature of these external trends as a pivot for internal changes.

One entrepreneur heading a medium-sized company has brought several of his children into the business. The oldest son has been with the company for seven years. He had been given a series of tasks all of which were either extraordinarily ambitious or hopelessly vague. His inevitable failure at these tasks exacerbated the development of a posture of learned helplessness on his part. This posture was mirrored in the CEO's inability to come to grips with the issue, and an unhappy stalemate developed. Recently several events took place which led to a prolonged and sustained effort to redefine the relationship. For over a year core issues related to the son's role and his eventual succession were dealt with indirectly. Finally a meeting was arranged to discuss these issues in the presence of an outsider. The CEO began with a long, rather disorganized monologue on the changing nature of the business scene and the need for organizations to adapt and remain innovative. His uncoached intuitive strategy was to bring the outside forces into focus, then to say "look, it's a new world out there and we can redefine our relationship within this new world." He then appointed his son to a new position which had earlier been defined as essential to cope with increasing complexity in the supply area, and laid out a training program for his development.

Just as there are forces which initially impact on the task system and are then accommodated in the central triangle, there are forces which work their way in, primarily through the family system. Marriage, divorce, death and family succession (in the broadest sense of the mantle being passed to the next generation) are major influences. With subsequent generations, shifts in the fortunes of the different branches of the family due to external business factors may become important. Many issues, such as the aging of the founding entrepreneur and the imminence of his children's succession, are of such transcendence that they form a basic deep structural theme in family life. The anxiety associated with the issue and the form in which it is expressed will vary over time. It will typically come into focus around nodal birthdays (30 or 40 for the children, 60 or 65 for the father) and will be worked out within the business. Consider the statement by Stanley Marcus of Neiman-Marcus.

341

Probably the single greatest disappointment in my business career was the failure of my father, on his own initiative, to name me as president prior to my fortieth birthday.

Such external influences provide the grist for the mill. The family business will respond in a variety of ways, some adaptive and some maladaptive. The capability of generating responses which are adaptive to a particular problem, which increase the capability to respond adaptively in the future, and which reduce the "noxiousness" of external influences, become crucial to the survival and growth of the family business. The problem of seeking modes of operation jointly adapted to both sets of influence is a complex and dynamic one, which is usually addressed implicitly and intuitively. However, there are certain patterns in successful adaptation. Awareness of these patterns can often help both family and nonfamily members of the firm to place their own situation in context. It can facilitate a proactive approach in which the corporation shapes its own future, and is less and less trapped in a debilitating reactive mode, all energies dedicated to putting out the fires raised by the extraordinary array of threatening issues to which the family business is so vulnerable.

The Process of Adaptation

There are four major interrelated components that are critical to the process of adaptation in the family business:

1. The maintenance of an *appropriate boundary* between the emotional issues in the family and the tasks required for successful development and operation of the business.

2. The development of *processes and mechanisms* that enable the family to

contain and resolve its own emotional issues.

3. The development of *task structures and processes* which are adapted to the requirements of the business environment and which are not dependent on the resolution of unresolved family issues for successful performance.

4. The development of a *valid legitimizing structure* which maintains organizational cohesiveness.

We will consider each of these.

Intersystem Boundary Regulation

An intersystem boundary divides one system from another. If we imagine a space of behaviors normally taking place in and around a family business a key intersystem boundary would place one set of behaviors in one significance framework and another set into another such framework. There are many levels and types of significance frameworks relevant to the family business. We started out with two broad frameworks earlier. There are (1) family process, and (2) task requirements.

Thus, "My brother threw his coffee cup at me for the third time this month" probably has greater significance for family process than the task requirement framework. Similarly, "We have decided to establish a marketing department" under most circumstances would have no significance for family process. Certain decisions or behaviors are boundary spanning, having major significance for both systems. For example, "My brother and I cannot agree on an appropriate acquisitions policy after father retires."

Each of these broad significance frameworks may be further subdivided. For example, family process may be broken down into: (1) the succession framework (who is going to take over the business); and (2) the positional regard framework (who is going to be whose pet within the family).

The task system may be broken down in a variety of ways. We might distinguish: (1) issues of authority; (2) issues of competence; and (3) objective issues (to be dealt with by the "facts").

Successful adaptation of the family business requires the progressive development of boundaries which are (1) appropriate, (2) clear but not overly rigid, and (3) consistent.

Appropriate Boundaries

Appropriate boundaries allow problems and issues to be placed in a framework which facilitates their resolution. A basic condition for effective organizational functioning is the maintenance of appropriate boundaries between emotional issues in the family and the tasks required for the successful development and operation of the business. Inappropriate boundaries not only constrain the development of adaptive processes within each system, they also create conflict within the family and grossly impair management performance. For example, the tendency of nonfamily members to see family issues as motivating even the most straightforward and "businesslike" of decisions may frustrate the change efforts by family CEOs.

In one division, a reorganization of top management, suggested by an outside consultant as a means of improving performance through the provision of an improved capability to deal with key environmental factors, was interpreted by the nonfamily divisional president as a part of a family succession strategy, was resisted and was eventually sabotaged.

The appropriate definition of a given boundary becomes a sensitive issue. Consider the response of Henry Ford II to a question posed by *Business Week*:

How are you going to adjust to the idea of being retired? [*Business Week*]. That I don't know. That's one of the things that McKinsey and Co. tried to lay out for me, and I said: "Well, now you handle your business and I'll handle mine!" I said: "You just forget about it. I can't tell you, and I don't know." [Henry Ford II]

Clear Boundaries

Clear boundaries must evolve to allow problems and issues to be placed in any framework at all. This is a necessary precursor to the development of a general capability to face real issues and work toward their resolution. Boundaries will generally be rather inflexible or slack. However, boundaries which are at one extreme too rigid or at the other too loose and ill defined lead to dysfunctional behavior. Overly rigid boundaries do not allow adaptation as conditions change.

The assessment of the relative functionality of any given boundary or set of boundaries is a contextual problem. Any evaluation must consider the developmental state of the business as well as the maturational level of the family. Boundaries that seem to be functional at one point in time may appear to be grossly dysfunctional at another. Indeed, the nature of family agenda and its influence on the business changes from one generation to the next. An overly rigid boundary may stifle an adequate response to these changes (as we would argue is the case with the Ford quotation above).

An overly diffuse boundary is equally problematical. Too often in family businesses, problems and issues form an undifferentiated mess to those who participate. They cannot begin to relate to succession issues as succession issues, tasks issues as task issues, and joint issues as joint issues. As a result they are incapacitated as problem solvers, and are subject to high undifferentiated and unfocused anxiety. This inevitably leads to a search for outlets and intensely symptomatic behavior.

Consistent Boundaries

Consistent boundaries place similar issues in the same significance framework, or identify the same issues with a specific framework as the issues reoccur over time. Consistent boundaries also maintain consistent levels of clarity and diffuseness in distinguishing the principal systems.

In practice, it is useful to look at the consistency problems faced by family businesses in a dialectical context. A diffuse boundary in one domain is often associated with a rigid boundary in another. For example, it is common to see a situation in which family membership rather than demonstrated competence is the criteria for attaining key management titles within the firm. Thus, highly capable nonfamily professionals are prohibited from assuming a major role in directing the company. This situation may be seen as one in which the boundary between family and nonfamily managers is excessively rigid. An extreme concomitant of this phenomenon is one in which the transfer of family wealth is made contingent on the younger generation joining the firm. In this case, the boundary between rights of family membership and

the family member's obligation to the firm is an excessively diffuse one.

This regulation, whether implicit or explicit, forces the participation on the part of the children regardless of the level of fit between their interests and competencies and the needs of the business. The children resent the process and often act out their hostility by underfunctioning at work. Nonfamily members are often drawn into these conflicts. They assuage the intergenerational tensions by taking up the slack and masking the children's inadequate performance.

This process is often an insidious one. The children feel blocked and unable to develop personal and professional identities. Key nonfamily managers are placed under excessive emotional strain; and the otherwise aggressive CEO, sensing something askew, feels helpless to act.

The problems raised by boundaries which are in one respect too rigid, and in another respect too diffuse, are graphically illustrated in the relationship of the senior nonfamily managers (the "old guard") to the entrepreneur. The entrepreneur invariably surrounds himself with a loyal cadre of top management, usually made up of those few trusted individuals who have been with him from the start. Those are the people who have picked up the pieces, covered up mistakes and held things together over the years. Their stature within the corporation has grown as the corporation has grown but they have always lived in a reflected limelight. They are generally safe, steady, somewhat passive individuals tied to the entrepreneur through an intense mutual dependency. The intensity and permanence of the relationship joins them to the entrepreneur as members of a second family. Feelings of loyalty, trust, betrayal, and jealousy are prominent emotions.

The inner circle exists like a second family. In the absence of a catastrophic break up they form the permanent core of the organization. Like the family, they are tied by intense personal bonds, show little objectivity in assessing interpersonal relationships, and when the chips are down can be fiercely loyal to each other, often at great personal expense. The boundaries between this central organizational and the real family is in this sense ill-defined. Yet in other aspects the boundary is extremely rigidly defined. The central cadre will be explicitly excluded from both ownership and influence in the determination of succession. The business is after all a family business and as one family owner put it at the end of a debate with his core staff: "Whose marbles are they, anyway?" The core team is therefore in, but where it matters most, it is out. It is like being asked into the house but not being invited for dinner.

There is thus a vicarious association with the success of the firm which is confirmed through status and through an intimacy with the entrepreneur which nearly enables them to "think for him" and be a part of him. At the same time there is exclusion and denial of the rights of membership. This gives rise to undercurrents of bitterness and not infrequently acts of mutual sabotage.

In extreme cases the ill-defined nature of the relationship with the central core leads to a loss of self-identity of core members and disorganized behavior patterns. To what do they owe their position? How do they value themselves? Hence, how do they protect themselves? How do they value their competence since they have never been assessed on the basis of competence anyway. Could they get an equivalent job elsewhere? In most cases their prospects would be, at best, doubtful.

An important psychological principle of group process is that dysfunctional relations among a subgroup of an intimate system cannot be contained within the subgroup but will spread out to the natural boundaries of the group. This dysfunction at the top cascades its way down through the organization. The intense and highly adverse effects may reach the lowest levels of the organization. Consider the following illustration.

A member of the central core, unsure about his position and in a dependent yet resentful relationship with the founding entrepreneur establishes a structure in the division he manages so intricate and intertwined in its confusion that only he can keep it together, and operating in a reasonably effective manner. Management at the second level becomes tightly enmeshed. Jobs are ill-defined, as are responsibilities. When members of the group are pressed to define who is responsible for a given task they reply, "we can work it out together." Faced with such ill-defined roles, management at this level, in an attempt to legitimize and protect its position, develops a posture that "what really counts in this company is selling." Top management devotes a considerable amount of its time to selling, hanging on tenaciously to its own accounts. Through selling, members of this group entrench their positions. But as a consequence they have no time for management and become competitive with the sales force. The sales force in turn becomes resentful and isolated from the perceived workings of the division. This leads to disaffection and high turnover. The pattern of behavior develops out of and coexists with the dysfunction at the top. It is furthermore ultrastable and resists efforts at change so long as that dysfunction persists.

Emotional Containment

Successful adaptation of the family business requires that the family *as a family* develop internal processes which facilitate the containment, confrontation and resolution of family problems. Chronic dysfunction within the family, which its members are unable or unwilling to address, invariably "spill-over" into the business and may threaten survival of the firm.

During the initial inception of the firm, business activity often has a significant impact on family process. The entrepreneur's prodigious drive and his success at building a business often provide a number of stabilizing functions for the family. It can lend a cohesive structure to an otherwise disorganized set of familiar relationships. The business often gainfully employs wayward brothers, cousins, and even parents. Volatile emotional issues that might otherwise lead to conflictual behavior or defensive distancing may be dwarfed or subdued by a super task orientation that promotes cohesion around business concerns. Indeed, a myriad of urgent business demands can lend a form of legitimization to the avoidance of family relational issues (e.g., marital tensions).

As the business matures and assumes a stable identity of its own, the relationship between the family and the firm presents new forms of challenges and problems. One of the most formidable

obstacles of the stability and growth of the firm is the problem of succession. Unresolved emotional concerns that were tabled for years often emerge around this issue.

For the founding entrepreneur, the corporation is his product and in a very real sense, a part of him. The intense involvement of the entrepreneur, at one time vital to the development of the enterprise, can seriously constrain the business's ability to grow. Indeed, the literature suggests that few entrepreneurs are able to sufficiently restructure their lives to provide alternative outlets and support bases to allow for a successful transition to the next generation. The entrepreneur's ambivalence about redefining his relationship with the company presents special problems for the children. While his children often equate responsible adult functioning with their ability to make a substantive contribution to the business, they feel blocked by their father's unrelenting grip on the company. It is not uncommon to see a situation in which the entrepreneur plays one son against the other to keep each one in line. As a result sibling rivalry is exacerbated.

More generally, issues regarding succession can create major rifts within the family. Power struggles around relatives attaining key positions in the company are often fed by the shared assumption that being closed out of the business is tantamount to being cut off from the family. It is often the case that unresolved difficulties between the founder and his children remain unresolved even after he formally retires from the company. The founder leaves but symbolically remains. His "message" is to be carried on generating an ideological and procedural straightjacket for the future ("This is the way we have always done things in this company"). The sons are never able to effectively deal with each other. Conflicts are denied through stultifying pseudomutual relationships, or through excessive distancing (e.g., arranging schedules that prohibit interaction). The former results in chronic managerial indecisiveness. The latter results in a split organization — one that is incapable of developing a functionally integrated corporate structure.

As the transitions take place from generation to generation the rules of succession often become clearer and more established as an integral part of family tradition. The incumbent may hold on too long, or the son may be incompetent, but the extended family forms an envelope around the central core and has at its disposal the mechanisms for managing difficult transitions, constraining excesses or compensating for the inadequacy of its representatives.

The development of (1) broadly accepted rules of transition and (2) a social structure among the extended kinship system which internalizes family values and regulates and mediates conflict is a sign of healthy development of the family's relationship to the business.

The Development of Appropriate Task Structures

The development of task structures and processes which are adapted to the needs of the business environment and which are not dependent on the resolution of unresolved and uncontained family issues for successful performance is often a crucial determinant of survival. Its importance is obviously dependent on the extent and impact of these unresolved issues. Some families are simply lucky. They happen to have moved into a line of business which does not place such rigid demands on the

organization that the idiosyncracies of the family firm become a crippling obstacle. Others have an innate sense of what the family and the business environment can bear and move to a position of joint organizational adaptation.

In cases where substantive family issues remain chronic and unresolved there are a number of desirable organizational attributes which help maintain the firm.

Decoupling of the Production Unit

Many businesses, particularly those operating in mature, well-established markets, can function effectively without placing great demands on their management structure. Provided that the operational core is adequately supported and attention is paid to the necessary routine details, the organization can survive for extended periods without a highly proficient or innovative management group. One of the great talents of the founding entrepreneur often lies in his understanding of the basic operating requirements for success in the business. The development of superior practices in manufacturing or selling, or whatever the core activities might be, would have established the firm in the first place. If these practices can be maintained, survival will be assured unless there are major changes in, for example, technology or market preferences.

High Organization Slack

Organizational slack provides a buffer with which to absorb the variances raised by family issues. Businesses which are less competitive, which are operating in slowly growing markets and which generate high gross margins on sales often allow significant slack to be generated. This slack can then be used to employ the extra staff required to compensate for incompetent family members, absorb the cost of mistakes, or pay additional compensation to key but disgruntled nonfamily management.

Organizational Divisibility

It is often advantageous to manage a family business which can be divided along lines which mirror the lines of conflict within the family system. For example, if the business is run by siblings with strong unresolved differences (perhaps deriving from the first generation) a conglomerate type of structure with easily decomposable spheres of influence will minimize the opportunities for conflict and stalemate.

In general, the less the corporation must function with high-level professional management operating under immediate demands to produce and to integrate their work with others at the highest levels of the corporation, the more easily deviances will be absorbed. The more the corporation can coast on an established position and the less it must proactively plan for its future, the better it will be able to absorb the indecisiveness and confusion flowing out of structural difficulties within the core family system.

The Development of Valid Legitimizing Structures

Valid legitimizing structures are important for the preservation of organizational health. They play a vital role in the maintenance of the self-respect of organizational members. In addition, these structures help to cover over a sense of being exploited if not by the family itself, at least by the pernicious aspects of its agenda. Of course, not all the consequences of family ownership are negative. A great many family businesses are much more human places to

work than the stereotypical professional organization. There are high levels of concern and caring for the needs of employees as individuals. The family business acts positively as a family looking after its own. Such an atmosphere, when it exists, goes a long way toward the legitimization of participation.

Other aspects of the family business may be carefully cultivated as legitimizing factors. The legend of the founding entrepreneur may often serve as a symbolic distillation of espoused norms and values with which employees may readily identify. Traditions, and even traditional practices which may have derived from nothing more than a quirk of some family member in an earlier generation, have an immediacy and a tangibility through their association with the folklore of the family. Family folklore and mythology seems to be a key ingredient in the maintenance of cohesion and continuity.

Valid approaches to legitimization accept the inherent weaknesses of the family business and develop the counterstrengths. By placing the weaknesses in a positive framework, they legitimize them. Invalid approaches deny the weaknesses, and generally lead to postures with no more than surface content. Over-emphasis on the role of professionalism and participation of nonfamily members, denying the inherent deficiencies of the family business for the nonfamily members, often proves of short-lived convenience. This can be destructive of those positive value systems which are essential for organizational maintenance in times of stress and high anxiety. People do not know what to believe in once the legitimizing structure has proven to be false, which inevitably, in the long run, it must be.

Without the existence of a legitimizing structure there is intense pressure on the family to produce one. Denial of the basic problems often leads to the promotion of values which are fake and which cannot be sustained. Recognition of this by members of the corporation often leads to demoralization and attempts at patchwork solutions which do not recognize the basic contradictions. Eventually the firm which survives learns how to simultaneously accept the inherent strengths and weaknesses and develop a framework from the contradictions that exist. Such a framework better allows everyone in the corporation to cope. This can only be done with maturity and in the framework of a basically healthy family system.

This struggle for legitimization is an ongoing part of life in the family business. It absorbs considerable energy from all levels of the organization. The following extract from a statement of organizational objectives produced by top management in one large family business illustrates the problem.

The singular, most distinguishing characteristic of the corporation is the reciprocal identification with the family. It is an element which, for us, defied quantification or organization. It involves not only what the family wants, but what the corporation needs.

We do not believe this element of our corporate psyche vitiates in any way the validity of our findings. However, this significant element is not fully addressed on our recommendations, and we believe it needs to be and can probably be best addressed on an evolutionary basis.

The search for a complete, unified, coherent legitimizing framework is a hopeless one. These are deep-seated contradictions built into the family business which defy resolution. In this sense addressing the issues on an "evolutionary basis" is an important process. At best the family business can hope to develop a partial framework which provides enough common ground to support basic organizational coherence. Beyond that, issues have to be addressed as they arise and resolved in the best way possible.

As these issues are addressed tradeoffs must be surfaced or if they are nonexistent, developed. Thus the excessive power of family members may be compensated for by the lack of bureaucracy in the decision making process; and the lack of potential for upward mobility may be compensated for by the rewards for loyalty to the firm.

The partial framework that emerges becomes the "corporate philosophy." Unfortunately the difficulty in addressing issues one by one encourages the emergence of a "philosophy" which is overextensively applied and overly rigid in its application. This may have serious maladaptive consequences. However, even a modest philosophy will take on a life of its own, and over time become a determinant of organizational behavior independent of the specific needs of the family and task systems.

Conclusion

We see these four issues — boundary definition, emotional containment, task system adjustment, and the legitimizing process — as essential components of successful adaptation of the family business. Typically family businesses grow out of the initiative of the founding entrepreneur. As organizations they are held together by their focus on the single individual, by his dedication of purpose and the energy he devotes to the business. Once that drive is spent, the organization is susceptible to the effects of severe maladaptation. The energy of the corporate staff turns inward and is dissipated by fruitless internal activity symptomatic of that maladaptation. The company can only react to its environment and cannot in any significant sense create its own future.

We have found that over a period of time if the key actors in the corporation begin to address the four issues we have discussed, and confront the root factors behind the corporate maladaptation, it becomes increasingly possible for the corporation to plan proactively, master its relationship with its environment, and pull itself out of the mess it is in through a bootstrap operation.

Our broader point has been that family organizations pose special problems which have not been adequately addressed by classic management theory. In contrast to the "ideal" image of the organization as a rational, performance-oriented system, the family business represents a system that is organized around a set of highly charged affective relationships. The family firm represents a case in which two otherwise distinct social units are highly integrated. Under such conditions the effect of family-system variables cannot be ignored.

On the contrary, the characteristic histories, as well as the characteristic difficulties of such firms, can only be understood by careful analysis of the family system. The challenge for the interventionist is to develop an operational scheme that differentiates family dynamics from business operations. In order to be effective he must appreciate the key linkage points between the two systems and the nature of the differen-

tial processes that result in adaptive and maladaptive organizational behavior.

Once the key dimensions affecting adaptation of the family business have been developed, they can be used both for the diagnosis of particular cases and as a guide to the intervention process. In a following paper we discuss the implications for intervention and the ways in which adaptation and growth may be facilitated by outside consultants.

References

Argyris, C. *Interpersonal competence and organization effectiveness*. Homewood: Irwin Press, 1962.

Bell, D. III. *The coming of post-industrial society: A venture in social forecasting*. New York: Basic Books, 1973.

Benson, J. K. Organizations: A dialectic view. *Administrative Science Quarterly*, 1977, 22(1).

Boszormenyl-Nagy, I., & Spark, G. *Invisible loyalties*. New York: Harper and Row, 1973.

Birch, P. H. *The managerial revolution reassessed*. Lexington, Mass.: Lexington Books, 1972.

Crozier, M. *The bureaucratic phenomenon*. Chicago: University of Chicago Press, 1964.

Emery, F. E., & Trist, E. L. *Sociotechnical systems*. In *Proceedings, Management Science Models and Techniques, Vol. 2, 6th Annual International Meeting of the Institute of Management Science*. Oxford: Pergamon Press, 1960.

Galbraith, J. K. *The new industrial state*. Boston: Houghton-Mifflin, 1967.

Hershon, S. *The problems of succession in family business*, doctoral dissertation, Harvard University, 1975.

Hickson, D. J., Hinings, D. R., Lee, C.A., Schnuck, R. E., & Dennings, J. M. A strategic contingencies' theory of intraorganizational power. *The Administrative Science Quarterly*, 1974, 19, 22-44.

Levinson, H. Conflicts that plague family business. *Harvard Business Review*, 1971, March-April, 90-98.

Pfeffer, J. Size and composition of corporate boards of directors: The organization and its environment. *The Administrative Science Quarterly*, 1972, 18, 349-364.

Riesman, D. *The lonely crowd*. New Haven: Yale University Press, 1950.

Rioch, M.J. The work of Wilfred Bion on groups. In Clifford J. Sager and Helen Singer Kaplan (Eds.), *Progress in group and family therapy*, New York: Bruner/Maazel, 1972, p. 21.

Touraiane, A. *The post-industrial society* (L. F. X. Mayhew, trans.). New York: Random House, 1971.

Whyte, W. H. *The organization man*. New York: Simon and Schuster, 1956.

Wynne, L., Rychoff, J., Day, H., & Hirsch, S. Pseudomutuality in the family relations of schizophrenics. *Psychiatry*, 1958, 21, 205-220.

Introduction

To keep a family business healthy across several generations, owners must arrest the normal process of product life cycle decline by implementing management practices to support growth and transgenerational entrepreneurial activity. Through strategic exploration, organizational development, financial restructuring and behavioral change, the stage can be set for renewal and growth. Changes in reward or information systems, diversification or specialization in business where in-house expertise already exists or other approaches can stimulate necessary regeneration. The article provides numerous examples and cases, as well as useful guides to creating organizational cultures that support interpreneurship, financial restructuring options, overcoming barriers to interpreneurship.

Managerial Practices That Support Interpreneurship and Continued Growth

1988

By Ernesto J. Poza

Reprinted from **Family Business Review**, Winter 1988, Vol. 1, No. 4. San Francisco: Jossey-Bass, Inc., 1988. Used with permission of the publisher; all rights reserved.

A bottle manufacturer and distributor in Detroit has been revitalized by every single generation. Its founder built a business around the recycling of glass bottles in the late 1800s, when bottles were handblown and expensive. The second generation entered the business in 1915, and by the early 1920s it was distributing bottles to the largest beverage manufacturers and bottlers in the United States.

When the third generation of family entrepreneurs took over the business, they added plastic bottles to the line, because plastic bottles were rapidly gaining favor with bottlers. One generation later, this venture had become old hat and relatively unprofitable, so in the early 1980s the fourth generation decided to go directly to retail customers with new plastic bottles. A division was formed to support the pursuit of this vision. Today, the new division sells plant misters to K-Marts, nurseries, and drug store chains nationwide (Posner, 1985).

How did this company make its vision of growth and regeneration happen? This article reviews the management practices that help to implement changes that support growth and entrepreneurial activity across generations of managers and owners. These managerial practices are the bricks and mortar with which families build organizations that will last beyond a lifetime. This article considers strategic exploration by family and firm, organizational change and development approaches, financial restructuring, and behavioral changes in the family system. These measures set the stage for renewal and growth. Specific interventions, such as the implementation of business teams, changes in reward and information systems, and diversification or specialization in businesses where technology and market

knowledge already exist in-house, can then stimulate interpreneurship and appropriate business growth. Figure One outlines the steps to build interpreneurship into a business.

The practices and interventions considered in this article are the result of some years of consultation to family businesses and many more years of observing the risks of decline that such businesses face. On several occasions, interventions have been no more than informed experiments aimed at finding a way of reversing decline and regenerating the business. The discussion is also grounded in the existing

Figure 1. Creating the Culture That Supports Interpreneurship

Setting the Stage	Identifying and Managing Barriers to Change	Specific Interventions	Outcomes
Strategic exploration	Absence of growth vision	Specialization	Profitability
		Diversification	Growth
Organizational change and development	Distance from customers, employees operations, and the competition	Entrepreneurial approximations	Family harmony
Financial restructuring	Nervous money and short-term focus	Task and business teams	
Family system change	Large overheads and perception of high social (image) risk	Reward system changes	
		Information systems	
	Obsession with data and logic	Family venture capital company	
		Ownership equity structures	
	Inappropriate boundaries between management, owners, and the intrepreneur	Human resource policies and practices	

literature on family business and entrepreneurship and in the author's experience in organizational development and strategic management consultation.

Interpreneuring: The Concept

A business can be said to be interpreneuring when it organizes for and supports a revitalization of the business just prior to or during the tenure of the next generation. The motive for interpreneurship can be growth, leadership, fun, profit, or the perpetuation of important personal or family values. The word interpreneurship is derived from entrepreneurship. Much as intrapreneurship refers to in-house entrepreneurial activity (Pinchot, 1985), interpreneurship refers to intergenerational entrepreneurial activity.

Instead of pursuing growth and interpreneurship, many family businesses find themselves at the end of the founder's career with large cash reserves and assets but no stakes in the future of the business or the family. The founding entrepreneur who is interested in interpreneuring chooses to pursue growth rather than to address the later years through traditional estate and succession planning — or avoiding such planning. By funding a family venture capital firm or through joint ventures with other firms, the founder supports entrepreneurial activity by the second generation and beyond.

Peter Drucker (1985, p. 170) asserts that he knows of "no business that continued to remain entrepreneurial beyond the founder's departure, unless the founder has built into the organization the policies and practices of entrepreneurial management. If these are lacking, the business becomes timid and backward within a few years at the very latest." Drucker compares Walt

Disney Productions and McDonald's with companies that built entrepreneurship into their structure: "Within a few years after the death[s] of these founders, [McDonald's and Walt Disney Productions] had become stodgy, backward-looking, timid, and defensive." In contrast, says Drucker, Procter and Gamble and Johnson and Johnson, who put the appropriate policies, practices and structures into place, "continue to be innovators and entrepreneurial leaders decade after decade, irrespective of changes in chief executives or economic conditions."

Setting the Stage for Interpreneurship and Continued Growth

Setting the stage for interpreneurship usually includes changes in strategy, organization, business finances, and the family. for example, after a careful study of its marketplace and a thorough review of its organization, a well-known consumer technology retail chain in the Midwest, here called Midwest Electronics, embarked on a transformation aimed at revitalizing the business. The second-generation brothers envisioned a new position in the marketplace for the company. They restructured the organization to support increased customer orientation in the stores, and they made changes in their sibling behavior to increase the effectiveness of their shift toward greater customer orientation at headquarters.

The need for these changes was far from obvious to the brothers; they were too close to the problem to see it. But the eldest, the current president, was not getting what he wanted from the organization either in advertising copy or in product availability at the stores. The two younger siblings headed advertising and merchandising. The president

Figure 2. Financial Restructuring Options

Financial Restructuring Technique	What It Is
Real Estate Trust	A trust made up of a variety of real estate holdings. Although the tax benefits of trusts have been severely limited by recent tax laws, they can still provide an equitable distribution of the estate for family members not active in the business.
Preferred Stock Recapitalization	The creation of a higher-dividend-yielding stock with preferential redemption rights to replace some of the common stock issues. It allows for increased income to a founding generation, for example, while giving voting control via the common to the next generation.
Stock Swap	Similar in nature to the preferred stock recapitalization but involving exchanges of different classes of stock, some higher-yielding, others with capital gain appreciation potential.
Buy-Sell Agreement	An agreement between parties, often parents and offspring or siblings, to buy each other out under certain conditions and at a certain price. Often funded by life insurance in the event of the death of one party.
Private Annuity	An arrangement between the heir or heirs to a family business and the parents by which the children issue an annuity providing regular interest income to the parents in exchange for operating control of the business.
Installment Sale	Partial sale of stock over several years aimed at transferring control.
Limited Partnership	Provides siblings with a claim to a distinct portion of the assets while the general partner retains control. Often, the earlier generation can provide developmental and collegial opportunities for the next generation.
Holding Company or Capital Corporation	A portfolio of assets contained in a constellation of corporations, each with its own stock, and an ownership relationship with the "holding" or capital corporation.

called in a consultant to conduct an organizational review of the operation.

After much discussion and a significant amount of shuttle diplomacy on the part of the consultant, a consensus emerged about the need to change the organizational structure and the roles and responsibilities of the brothers. These changes, it was hoped, would help to change sibling behaviors that were causing frustration and disharmony in the family and in the business.

Midwest Electronics developed a new mission and positioning statement that focused the business on value-added customer service, following the strategic redirection called for by a recent customer study. At the same time, Midwest Electronics regionalized retail operations. This move removed one layer of headquarters retail staff and made it possible for store managers, who in the past had drowned in paperwork, to emphasize sales and customer service activities. Finally, they gave overall responsibility for retail stores to the very able and motivated younger brother. He had previously been second-guessing every decision made by the nonfamily retail operations manager.

In their changes of strategy, organization, and family behavior, the brothers have purposefully taken steps to bring about changes in both the family and the firm that support growth and interpreneurship.

Strategic Exploration. Management initiatives concerning strategy are often led by a successor to the founder/entrepreneur who acts as strategy czar. Through this managerial approach, a business can focus on its mission, examine its strengths and weaknesses relative to the competition, and map its future accordingly. Strategic analysis and planning tap the future orientation of the next generation and sometimes increase the entrepreneurial propensity of the founder. However, even an entrepreneurial and intuitive founder can have difficulties supporting or participating in a strategic planning process if the process is forced upon him by an aggressive, forward-looking second generation. It is important for the second generation to be sensitive to the needs of the founder at this late stage of his life (Lansberg, 1988). Framing the interpreneurial effort as a natural progression that builds on the founder's legacy and acknowledges the contribution that the founder has made can ease the transition to the next phase of growth.

Organizational Change and Development. Changes in strategy are often accompanied by changes in structure and vice versa. In growth-seeking businesses, the objective in changing the structure is to provide the various

product, business, technology, or geographic units with sufficient autonomy that they can operate with plenty of exposure to the competitive environment. The intent is to have new ventures operate as if in a free-market environment. Some of these innovative organizational approaches also help to institutionalize the process of growth.

In family-owned businesses, structural reorganization can also be aimed at developing managerial skills in successors and at reducing conflicts between potential successors (often siblings) or between founder and successor. The firm is split into separate functional areas, divisions, or geographical regions, each of which is headed by different family (and perhaps some nonfamily) managers.

But, there is more to organization than structure. Some firms have created new communication and coordination mechanisms, such as quarterly business review meetings for the family. Other businesses have emphasized management development for owners and other members of the organization. And, a family business can negotiate role changes that allow greater differentiation among roles within the business and the family. In family firms, differentiation between family and business roles is essential.

Other organizational development approaches used to promote continued growth include steering committees, asset boards, outside boards of directors, in-house management education for family members, the hiring of nonfamily professionals to complement and educate family members, and venture review boards that evaluate the interpreneurial plans of the next generation.

Financial Restructuring. Financial reorganization is perhaps the approach most often used to set the stage for new ventures in the family business. It has the clearest tax and economic consequences. Its popularity may also be due to the fact that, in contrast to other forms of business and family consultation, legal and accounting expertise have been relatively accessible to family firms. Figure Two summarizes the financial restructuring techniques now available: real estate trusts, preferred stock recapitalizations, stock swaps, buy-sell agreements protected by life insurance policies, private annuities, installment sales, limited partnerships, and multiple corporations with a holding company or family capital corporation model. While these techniques are still allowed under current tax legislation, recent changes in the law make expert tax advice necessary. In several instances, the time required for full implementation has been extended. This requirement has the effect of lengthening the founder's planning lead time. New tax legislation continues to provide strong incentives for employee ownership, and it has spurred the use of employee stock ownership plans (ESOPs) as an ownership succession mechanism.

Family System Change. A family in business shares the culture of the family and the culture of the firm. By *culture*, we mean the pattern of basic assumptions, values, symbols, and perspectives that underlies behavior (Schein, 1985). The basic cultural patterns in the organization center on the nature of leadership — paternalistic, laissez-faire participative, or professional — and they are heavily influenced in first generation firms by the personality of the founder (Dyer, 1986). Cultural patterns in the family can be characterized as patriarchal, collaborative, or conflicted (Dyer, 1986). The combination of the cultural patterns of the firm, the

family, and the board of directors creates a powerful dynamic that has significant consequences for the business' ability to be interpreneuring. The absence of consensus on what constitutes a desirable future or on how to get there can subject the business to prolonged periods of paralysis in which no interpreneurial activity is possible.

Family culture can also determine the extent of differentiation among family members: between parents and offspring and among the siblings. For example, a son or daughter may face a hard struggle in establishing his or her own leadership style and world view while working under the shadow of a parent who is also a boss. To the extent that principles of equality overshadow each individual's unique abilities and strengths, individuation and role differentiation among siblings may be difficult to achieve. These obstacles, in turn, often blunt the interpreneurial potential of next-generation family members, because they make it difficult for an individual to harness his or her energy and creativity.

Before we review managerial practices that weave interpreneurship into the fabric of an organization, let us examine the barriers to interpreneurship.

Barriers to Interpreneurship and Continued Growth

Most obstacles to interpreneurship can be labeled bureaucratic in nature. Bureaucracy, or the natural hardening of organizational arteries that comes with age, plays a part in slowing down growth. Unhealthy family dynamics and inappropriate managerial practices and organizational structures also put on the brakes. This section examines some barriers to interpreneurship.

Absence of a Growth Vision. Most entrepreneurs feel impelled by forces that they themselves often do not understand. Some call it heart; others call it passion or a crazy obsession. If nether the preceding nor the following generation in an organization has a vision of long-term growth, the possibility of interpreneurship is very slim.

Distance from Customers, Employees, Operations, and the Competition. Family businesses like Mars, Kings Supermarkets, and Kollmorgen stay close to their customers by engaging with them on new product ideas, product enhancements, and related opportunities. Von Hippel (1982) was the first to document the use of this practice; he called it the *customer-active paradigm.* In much the same way, companies committed to interpreneurship avoid anything that distances people within the organization, be it reserved parking spaces, titles, walls, privileged information, or "silver spoons." Families committed to interpreneurship are obsessive about communications and promote the personal growth and professional development of family members and nonfamily managers and employees.

Nervous Money and Short-Term Focus. Patience and timing are important skills whenever money is invested. New strategic directions are quite fragile until they take root and develop their own momentum and a critical mass of support. It takes time and money to regenerate the vitality of any business. Creating a venture capital arm and reorganizing the company into separate growing and mature divisions can help to overcome the obstacles imposed by nervous money and a short-term focus.

Large Overheads. The previous generation of owners or managers should not spare the interpreneur the pain of creating something new. Limiting the funding accorded to any new venture promotes creative "scrounging" or "bootlegging" by the interpreneur, replicates external market conditions, and sharpens the focus of the interpreneur's creative process. However, constricted funding also means that the interpreneur's project area should be shielded from the burden of the mature corporation's overhead expenses. Just as the entrepreneur usually starts in a low-overhead, inexpensive, and inelegant office space, the interpreneur should be allowed the freedom to start with a minimum of previous financial commitments. For similar reasons, the interpreneurial area should be minimally staffed, especially in regard to support personnel; in this way, it imitates the start-up situation of a firm composed of peer professions.

Perception of High Social (Image) Risk. While Exxon is not a family business, it provides a good example of the barriers to entrepreneurial activity posed by external perceptions. When Exxon changed the name of Jersey Enterprises to Exxon Enterprises, entrepreneurial employees felt both the constraints and the social pressure to perform in ways acceptable to Exxon. In his study of entrepreneurial management, Howard Stevenson (1985) of the Harvard Business School found the increased weight of what he called "social contracts" bearing down on managers in ways that prevented full consideration of opportunities. Trusteeship of resources and constituencies takes priority over adventurousness. Families in business are often highly visible in their own communities and need to create boundaries that allow them to free up time and resources to enable them to experiment without high social risk. Locating new businesses in different cities and giving them different names can help in this respect.

Obsession with Data and Logic. Computers have made the bias toward data and logic increasingly easy to pursue. The quantity and sophistication of financial software and the misuse of fashionable statistical process control methods throughout the entire business. Interpreneurs need the freedom to follow their hunches. Since control is probably still vital to the established segments of the business, it may be appropriate to cordon off an area for the interpreneurs that is not as controlled as the rest of the business.

Inappropriate Boundaries Between Management, Owners, and Interpreneur. It is difficult for people who wear different hats in different settings to be perceived appropriately in each setting. Is John the successor treated as John the son or as John the aggressive interpreneur? And, how can preconceptions and their accompanying role expectations be managed? When the boundaries between family and business are unclear, the family relationships may seem to be threatened by interpreneurial changes in the business.

Joseph Schumpeter (1934), an early writer in entrepreneurship, described entrepreneurship as the process of "creative destruction." The difficult destruction that is needed within a business to create something better is even harder to accomplish when the business system is entwined with a family system. A brother who is the chief executive of the family business may have to balance the task of interpreneuring with managing the shifts in his relationship to a younger brother who works in the business that occur as the business is reorganized. Executing the responsibilities of an interpreneur while meeting relationship expectations or psychological contracts based on the son role can create serious dilemmas. Such dilemmas can paralyze individuals

and bring interpreneurial activity to a halt.

Interventions Aimed at Increasing Interpreneurship and Promoting Growth

After setting the stage, recognizing existing barriers, and considering necessary changes in strategy, organization, finances, and the family, owners have to intervene directly in these areas. Interpreneurship requires overcoming the barriers listed earlier and shaping the systems and structures that will institutionalize the process of renewing or revitalizing the business. Figure Three relates requirements to interventions that can be used in the process of creating an interpreneurial culture. This section discusses the interventions outlined in Figure Three.

Diversification or Specialization. Unless the original market niche is growing, a growth strategy often requires diversification or further specialization. A must for successful diversification is knowledge of the market and the product and manufacturing process technology involved. A policy of every growth-seeking entrepreneurial organization should be to "stick to its knitting," or commit only to ventures in which the company has accumulated knowledge about a kind of customer or a technology. Ideally, the company has accumulated knowledge about both.

Many studies have explored diversification, its outcomes, and the conditions under which it is most likely to be successful. Unrelated diversification or diversification into businesses or industries not related to the initial core business is generally riskier. Research on diversification (Rumelt, 1982; Roberts, 1985) clearly shows that diversification that sticks to its knitting pays off. Most diversification outside

Figure 3. Creating an Interpreneurial Culture

	Requirements	Interventions
Strategy	Knowledge of product and manufacturing process technology	Specialization
	Knowledge of market	Diversification
	Overcoming absence of growth vision	Entrepreneurial approximations
Organization	Role differentiation and separation between family and business and between owners and managers	Task and business teams
	Focused structures	Reward systems
	Communication and problem solving	
	Overcoming distance from customers and employees	
Finance	Creating an information-rich decision-making environment	Information systems
	Funding of new ventures	Family venture capital company
	Overcoming obsession with data and the "nervous money" syndrome	
Family	Equity structures that support "focused" organization structure and a distinction between active and inactive owners	Ownership equity structures
	Commitment and sense of ownership by nonfamily employees	Human resource policies and practices
	Overcoming inappropriate roles and boundaries between founder, family and business	
	Overcoming perception of high social risk	

the products, manufacturing processes, and markets that a firm knows well fails.

But, the risks of unrelated diversification have been exaggerated, because owners and managers in search of growth have often behaved like bankers or venture capitalists, not like obsessed entrepreneurs. Putting sweat equity into something that you care enough about to support financially, on a shoestring, is very different from investing in a diversified portfolio of stocks.

Several rules based on this research should help diversification efforts: First, do not diversify unless you have to in order to grow or preserve the profitability of the business or to offer interpreneurial opportunities to a promising next generation. Second, do not think of acquisitions, mergers, or new ventures unless the profit margins in the new businesses are at least as good as they are in the business in which you are already engaged. Third, if you are going to diversify via equity positions, mergers, or acquisitions, distinguish between investing and committing to growth through new ventures. A company that spent several million dollars in twelve companies through the early 1980s had returns exceeding $200 million in cash and stock but not a single profitable major new business unit.

Fourth, do not diversify quickly into an area of business whose market or technology are alien to your firm. The batting average is good only when you know both, and it drops as you steer farther away from your company's area of expertise. An insurance company lost a lot of money when it diversified into construction. The son of the company's founder developed a new interest in construction as a result of managing a construction project for the company. Father and son colluded on this ill-fated diversification move for different reasons. The founder wanted to give the son a territory in which the son could pursue his own interests without interfering with the founder's domain, while the son was driven by the need to differentiate himself from his father. In the absence of product, manufacturing process, and market knowledge, venture capital investments, joint ventures, or licenses are better interpreneurial strategies.

Fifth, set up a competent venture review board. Many of the benefits of diversification observed in conglomerates may be due to the supervision provided by top management with

strategic oversight responsibility to a unit of a larger corporation (Lauenstein, 1985). While units of conglomerates must justify their decisions to higher-ups, family businesses often lack supervision by outside authorities.

Sixth, specialization is another very viable strategy, especially if you find most of your profits coming from only one or two of your product lines. While this strategy seldom leads to growth in the volume of sales, it often results in increased profitability and focus, a great foundation for renewed growth. Specialization typically cashes in on customers' needs for higher quality and customer service even if higher prices are the result. This is well-known strategic territory for many family businesses.

A final word of caution: Venturing into new businesses is, obviously, not an easy task. The casualty rate is high. But, the guidelines provided here should help. To summarize the advice just given on diversification:

- Do not diversify unless you have to

- Do not acquire, merge, or venture except for better profit margins

- Distinguish between passive investments and active business ventures

- Stay with familiar markets and technologies

- Set up a competent venture review board

- Consider specializing in a high-quality, high-service niche

- Remember that new ventures are risky.

Entrepreneurial Approximations. Perhaps least found and yet quite promising for interpreneuring and continued growth are the formation of venture capital firms (such as the Rockefellers' Venrock), the formation of new ventures divisions within businesses (often headed by successors), and the creation of ownership and reward systems that encourage long-term growth of the firm.

American Research and Engineering, a family business in Chicago, has set up a trust to enable the next generations to engage in entrepreneurial activity. Recognizing that the family business is often shaped by the personality of its founder and that it may therefore prove a poor fit for the succeeding generation, the founder created a venture trust. The trust, guided by the family philosophy "You get out of life what you put in," enables any child in the family to be funded in a business venture of his or her own choosing. The individual must present a business plan for review by a board of family members, who decide whether or not to fund it. If the plan is accepted, the interpreneurial family member receives the start-up funds in exchange for 49 percent of the shares of the company.

With 51 percent of the shares, the interpreneur owns the company and returns to the family trust a dollar for every dollar of profit that the new company retains. This return helps to fund children, cousins, nieces or nephews down the road (Liataud, 1983). Changes in tax laws make the counsel of expert advisors acquainted with the particular situation a requirement in implementing funds of this sort.

Another excellent example of the creation of an entrepreneurial approximation is that of Mars, Inc. The founder, Frank Mars, made arrangements for his son, Forrest Mars, to start a new business in England. Forrest traveled abroad with several thousand dollars of family venture capital and the recipe for

Milky Way, which in England became the Mars Bar. The European company grew at a very fast pace and in 1964 bought out its American counterpart.

One study (Biggadike, 1979) found that it takes an average of eight years for a corporate venture to reach profitability and about ten to twelve years before its return on investment (ROI) equals that of mainstream business activities. However, when independent entrepreneurs start businesses, they reach profitability in four years (Weiss, 1981). The contrast between these two studies points to two things: the need for medium- to long-term financial support of any new venture sponsored by a business or family and the need for better entrepreneurial structures within established companies (Drucker, 1985).

Forming joint ventures with other entrepreneurial businesses, where financial support of the other firm's more promising research and development is exchanged for stock or licensing agreements, is another interpreneurial strategy.

The family's ability to assess the quality of investments and its willingness to invest in them for the long term are critical to its ability to sponsor new ventures. Some families will never be able to act as venture capital firms for the next generation. But, many more could than currently do if they would commit to a vision of growth and interpreneurship during the high profitability years of the family business.

Task and Business Teams. Another organizational innovation that supports continued growth is task and business teams. Organized around a particular task or business unit — for example, new product development or business for a particular major customer — such teams are composed of representatives of various departments and top management as needed. Planning, doing, and reviewing are all responsibilities of these teams. Usually embedded in the context of a functional organization, they help a firm to become more responsive to change, more adaptable to rapid growth, and more efficient in the deployment of human resources.

An Ohio firm started these cross-functional teams along customer lines. Its concern was that rapid growth would lead to deterioration in product quality, on-time delivery, and manufacturing cost control. With a production manager acting as a team leader and a team composed of representatives from engineering, finance, quality assurance, personnel, purchasing, and distribution, the firm has significantly improved on-time delivery and shortened order-to-delivery cycles. These improvements have reduced the amount of cash tied up in work in process. The plants now operate with a strong customer focus. Top management periodically meets with the team to review accomplishments and do what it can to support continued improvement.

Still experimenting with interpreneurship and undergoing the test of time is Kollmorgen Corporation, a $350-million family business headquartered in Stamford, Connecticut. Bob Swigget, its chairman of the board, believes that in order to achieve innovation and growth a company must maintain a "free-market environment for every individual in the company" (Kollmorgen Corporation, no date). That way, he argues, "each employee is exposed to the risks and rewards of the market." He or she succeeds or fails on the basis of skills and abilities in meeting this responsibility. And, Kollmorgen believes that the best way of encouraging such entrepreneurial commitment is

to break a company into small, autonomous product or profit center teams.

Kollmorgen found its vision of the future operating within its own confines — in the Proto (for *prototype*) Department. The Proto Department was a thirty-five member unit that could turn around an order for a new type of circuit board in one to three weeks. It generally took six to ten weeks for other departments to produce a new board. The Proto Department was also the most profitable unit of the company. Nevertheless, it took top management several years to realize that this small renegade department had all the components of what is now the Kollmorgen philosophy: small groups of committed individuals acting autonomously to serve the customer, often innovatively, and the resultant payoff in profitability and growth.

Kollmorgen's compounded rate of growth between 1974 and 1984 was a staggering 18 percent. Since then, in perhaps the worst electronics industry recession in twenty years, the company's profit margins have narrowed, and its growth has slowed. But, Kollmorgen intends to continue to grow, if at a slower rate, and to produce a 20 percent return on equity for its shareholders. While other families in business could develop and promote a vision like that of Kollmorgen, family interests and desires need to complement the aspirations that have been set for the business. As a result of these other interests, rates of growth may not be as aggressive. Marriott, another family-controlled business, has also been able to maintain annual revenue growth rates at about 20 percent.

Reward Systems. Pay is a strong incentive for risk taking and growth. This is particularly true in family businesses where career opportunities for non-family members may be limited. Thus, to support the growth strategy that Kollmorgen managers had set for themselves, a new bonus plan was set up. This plan was to be driven by return on net assets (RONA). RONA also gave individuals throughout the company a handy way of keeping score. Individuals in a division that had a reasonably good year would end up with a bonus amounting to 15 percent to 20 percent of their gross annual salary. Within six months of implementation, receivables and inventories had been reduced by $11 million. On the long road to growth and continued entrepreneurship, significant short-term improvements were also evident. Kollmorgen shows that long-term business growth and short-term effectiveness go together.

Information Systems. Keeping up-to-date measures of company performance, when coupled with dividing the large enterprise into small business units, provides timely information to every employee about inventories, costs, customer wants, and competitor moves. This contact with the market creates an information-rich decision-making environment in which strategies and decisions are constantly updated and tested on the basis of new information.

Knowing the competition is particularly important in guiding growth and inter-preneurship, because competitive information may contain the seeds of opportunities available to the business. At the Detroit bottle manufacturer and distributor mentioned at the beginning of this article, the thirty-year-old fourth-generation president of the plastic bottles division frequently comes into the office with samples or cardboard displays of new product ideas. Combing through product show

and hardware and discount store shelves daily, he begins his days back at the office by laying out competitive product information for all to see. He tells everybody what is going on in the marketplace, what customers are thinking, and what new products he is considering. This practice has particular value for family-owned businesses. Because of the close attachments of family life, a family business may focus predominantly on internal indicators and ignore, deny, or minimize external information that has serious implications for market competitiveness.

Ownership Equity Structures. The family capital corporation model mentioned earlier is a particularly attractive ownership structure because it can accommodate the needs and preferences of different individual owners. This financial structure can contain all the assets of the family, both active business interests and passive assets (such as real estate and stocks in public companies). Issuing several classes of preferred and common stock can help different owners to achieve their objectives without disrupting the continuity of the active business. For instance, Class A preferred stock could be nonvoting, low par value, with a high dividend preference and liquidation preference after Class B preferred—perfect for a nonmanaging owner. Class B preferred could then have liquidation preference over all stock classes, dividend preference after Class A, and voting rights that lapse at death, and be convertible to common stock. The common stock could have voting rights and receive all capital appreciation and possible future control.

A number of entrepreneurial privately held and family-owned businesses have chosen to distribute some equity to employees in the conviction that the best way of getting people to behave like owners is to make them owners. After all, it is the family's "real" ownership of a business that is often discussed as a competitive advantage of tenacious family businesses with their long-term perspective (Ward, 1987).

A study of American Business Conference companies (Clifford and Cavanaugh, 1985) revealed that, in the best-performing of these mid-size companies (as measured by sales growth, return on equity, assets, and jobs created), 31 percent of the stock was owned by employees themselves. In contrast, less than four percent of the equity in the larger pool of *Forbes* 100 companies is employee owned.

Another study of companies with stock ownership plans (Conte and Tannenbaum, 1978) found a statistical correlation between employee ownership and profitability. Other things being equal, the greater the equity the employees owned, the greater the company's degree of profitability.

Human Resource Policies. There are a variety of other ways of increasing psychological ownership and commitment to growth among employees. Human resource policies that demonstrate caring, recognize individual differences, and promote respect and dignity, when coupled with management that supports its people with the right tools, raw materials, and information, promote high involvement and behavior that resembles that of proprietors. Some of the innovations in manufacturing organizations over the last twenty years support this claim (Poza and Markus, 1980; Poza, 1983). Gain-sharing and profit-sharing bonus plans that financially reinforce the attitude that "we are in this together" also help to create a sense of commitment that resembles that of equity ownership (Lawler, 1981).

The Politics of Survival for Interpreneurs

The founder of a graphic design and media services firm is transforming the company into an employee-owned organization as it moves to the hands of a second generation in order to preserve the high quality of its designs and services beyond the first generation. A high-commitment, peer-based professional organization is the founder's legacy to the next generation. And, his son has been an active codesigner of the entire transformation and regeneration of the business.

Today, this company relies on project teams led by team leaders for its creative tasks. The overall management of the business depends on weekly management team meetings and a series of management committees: finance, personnel, and marketing. These committees report to the Member Group, as the management team is called. A board of directors, which includes two outsiders, meets twice a year to review the firm's financial performance, provide management advice, review the firm's annual budget and financial goals, and monitor its strategic direction.

One way in which interpreneurs have achieved major breakthroughs is by starting small with broad goals, proceeding slowly and experimentally, and shying away from the spotlight in the early stages. There are good reasons for this pattern of success.

Politicians and strategic managers know that one way of minimizing early resistance to change is by keeping the vision broad. A broad vision makes it difficult for others to polarize around details. A broad vision encourages those who join to elaborate and shape the details, and it allows room for mistakes. With time, the number of new adherents and the objective results provide the critical mass that enables the new idea to withstand the opposition.

Interpreneurs and their advisers need to keep the new idea or new venture simple and small: Conceive of it as a series of successive approximations to the interpreneur's total vision. Clearly define, bound, and structure the new venture unit. Keep it separate from the rest of the company, preferably as a small team of peers in a simple, inexpensive setting (the classic garage, basement, or trailer). Dare to venture only on the basis of need. Make sure that others see the need for higher profit margins or that they have a quest, an obsession; get an "angel" for the venture. Recognize that both money and sponsorship are key. And, keep commitments flexible or negotiate agreements that prevent premature evaluation and undue pressure for early positive results.

A Case Example

S. C. Johnson and Son, Inc. is now stimulating growth after years of lethargy. This two-billion-dollar consumer products giant, best known for its Johnson Wax line of products, is being run by a fifty-nine-year-old member of the fourth generation, Samuel C. Johnson, chairman and chief executive officer. Johnson is currently stimulating growth through a series of new policies, structures, and practices all aimed at promoting interpreneurship by the fifth generation. Within the last several years, Samuel C. Johnson has instituted a matrix organizational structure to promote interdepartmental cooperation between such functions as manufacturing, marketing, and finance. He has also created four business teams: personal care, home care, specialty chemicals, and insecticides. The purpose here is to promote responsibility and other behaviors akin to those of owners and to reduce the bureaucratic layers of management.

Johnson Wax has overhauled the compensation system to promote pay for performance, a concept quite alien to this traditionally paternalistic company. To improve knowledge of technology, it has increased the R&D budget and hired a new chief scientific officer. Finally, Samuel C. Johnson recruited and hired his son S. Curtis Johnson III to head a venture capital unit that is investing in both related and unrelated businesses.

All this change making to facilitate interpreneuring comes out of a recognition that growth and innovation must be supported at a critical juncture for the company. Samuel C. Johnson's father had recognized a similar need a generation ago when he backed S. C. Johnson's idea for a new business unit, the Raid line of insecticides. It is currently one of the company's most profitable product lines.

This recommitment to growth and interpreneurship appears well timed both for the business and for the family. In the late 1970s, as a result of diversifying too far afield from what Johnson managers knew best — personal and home care products — the firm suffered financial losses from a string of acquisitions in the leisure and recreational equipment business. Recoiling from this and several other market blunders, S. C. Johnson and Son, Inc. headed for protected waters — core businesses in which it had technical and marketing expertise — only to find that more aggressive competition had moved in. Lethargy had resulted in uncompetitive production costs and higher prices on the shelves, which caused profit margins to erode and market share to decline.

On the family front, we find a fifth generation whose members had gone through college and were ready to make a contribution without knowing what context they could make it in. But, with Samuel C. in his fifties and S. Curtis and other members of the fifth generation in their late twenties or early thirties, the probabilities of enlisting the next generation for continued entrepreneurship are, psychologically speaking, the best they will ever be (Davis, 1983).

Time will judge the effectiveness of this case of interpreneurship, yet many of the elements are present: changes in organization that promote greater autonomy and free-market dynamics, including the use of business teams; changes in reward systems; additions to the company's knowledge of technology and markets; new information systems; and a venture capital led by an entrepreneur at heart, S. Curtis Johnson. The entrepreneurial fifth-generation Johnson admits he likes the freedom to explore opportunities that is built into his job. This ability to explore and commit, with passion, to new opportunities is at the heart of interpreneurship and continued growth.

Summary

Strategic exploration and planning by family and firm, organizational change and development, financial restructuring, stock ownership, and behavioral changes in the family system all set the stage for interpreneurship and continued growth. Task of business teams, changes in reward and information systems, diversification or specialization in areas where knowledge of technology and markets already exists, and in-house entrepreneurial approximations are interventions that support interpreneurship and continued business growth. While the evidence is not yet

extensive, comprehensive and consistent use of several of these interventions appears to be effective in stimulating interpreneurship.

The choice of interpreneurship practices ill have to be guided by the business and family cultures as well as the firm's technical and marketing expertise. Many entrepreneurs and interpreneurial families, particularly those involved in highly successful businesses, have so much of their identity and social status defined by the original product, service, or market served that choosing to expand in new directions creates extreme tension and discomfort. Much more than money is at stake. The choice will also depend on the degree to which the firm has already used interpreneurial structures, policies, and practices, on its financial status, and on general economic conditions. Interpreneuring is most likely to succeed when the business possesses a culture that is well suited to the ambiguity and risk taking of entrepreneurial activity; management supports the new venture with structures, policies, and practices that separate the young venture from the old businesses and shelter it from corporate burdens (such as high overheads) that it cannot carry; those who commit financial resources to the new venture take a long-term investment perspective; and the family culture supports new ventures.

This article can do no more than provide a glimpse of a powerful set of growth opportunities available to family businesses everywhere. The author is aware of at least a dozen experiments in interpreneuring now under way in the United States and Latin America. Research aimed at determining the patterns of success and identifying the sources of difficulties and failure is badly needed.

References

Biggadike, H. R. "The Risky Business of Diversification." *Harvard Business Review*, 1979, 57 (3), 103-111.

Clifford, D., and Cavanaugh, R. *The Winning Performance: How American Mid-size Companies Succeed.* Toronto: Bantam Books, 1985.

Conte, M., and Tannenbaum, A. "Employee-Owned Companies: Is the Difference Measurable?" *Monthly Labor Review*, 1978, 101 (7), 23-28.

Davis, P. "Realizing the Potential of the Family Business." *Organizational Dynamics*, Summer 1983, 12 (1), 47-56.

Drucker, P. *Innovation and Entrepreneurship.* New York: Harper & Row, 1985.

Dyer, W. G., Jr. *Cultural Change in Family Firms: Anticipating and Managing Business and Family Transitions.* San Francisco: Jossey-Bass, 1986.

Kollmorgen Corporation. Company philosophy statement, no date.

Lansberg, I. "The Succession Conspiracy." *Family Business Review*, 1988, 1 (2), 119-143.

Lauenstein, M. C. "SMR Forum: Diversification the Hidden Explanation of Success." *Sloan Management Review*, 1985, 27 (1).

Lawler, E. E. *Pay and Organization Development.* Reading, Mass.: Addison-Wesley, 1981.

Liataud, J. "Entrepreneurship and the Family." *Loyola Business Review*, 1983, 4 (1), 9-12.

Pinchot, G. *Intrapreneurship: Why You Don't Have to Leave the Corporation to Become an Entrepreneur.* New York: Harper & Row, 1985.

Posner, B. G. "The 100-Year-Old Start-Up." *Inc.*, September 1985, pp. 79-85.

Poza, E. "Twelve Actions to Strong U.S. Factories." *Sloan Management Review*, 1983, 25 (1), 27-38.

Poza, E., and Markus, M. L. "Success Story: The Team Approach to Work Restructuring." *Organizational Dynamics*, Winter 1980, 8 (3), 2-25.

Roberts, E. B., and Berry, C. A. "Entering New Businesses: Selecting Strategies for Success." *Sloan Management Review*, 1985, 26 (3), 3-17.

Rumelt, R. P. "Diversification Strategy and Profitability." *Strategic Management Journal*, 1982, 3, 359-369.

Schein, E. H. *Organizational Culture and Leadership: A Dynamic View.* San Francisco: Jossey-Bass, 1985.

Schumpeter, J. A. *The Theory of Economic Development.* Cambridge, Mass.: Harvard University Press, 1934.

Stevenson, H. H. "A New Paradigm for Entrepreneurial Management." In J. J. Kokao and H. H. Stevenson (eds.), *Entrepreneurship: What It Is and How to Teach It.* Boston: Harvard Business School, 1985.

Von Hippel, E. "Get New Products from Customers." *Harvard Business Review*, 1982, 60 (2), 117-122.

Ward, J. L. *Keeping the Family Business Healthy: How to Plan for Continuing Growth, Profitability, and Family Leadership.* San Francisco: Jossey-Bass, 1987.

Weiss, L. A. "Start-Up Businesses: A Comparison of Performances." *Sloan Management Review*, 1981, 23 (1), 37-53.

Introduction

M. Jacob & Sons, founded in 1882, has survived for four generations because each generation reinvented the family business. Founded as a dealer in used bottles and transformed into a distributor for glass bottle manufacturers, the company next became a supplier of plastic bottles to businesses. In its fourth generation, M. Jacob & Sons supplies specialized plastic containers to retailers for resale.

Third-generation chief executive Marty Jacob involved his son Joel in the business at an early age. The father explained to his son that he was welcomed in the business if he could contribute, but that he should make his own career decision. Joel developed a genuine liking for the business and a sense of family tradition. He then prepared himself through education and experience to join the firm. In time, Joel's new ideas and enthusiasm were contagious. A new business was born within the old one, assuring the firm's survival for another generation.

"The 100-Year-Old Start-Up"
1984

By Bruce G. Posner

In June 1982, when Joel Jacob was barely a year out of college, he took off on a three-month tour, the likes of which no one in his family's business had ever seen. Early each morning, he would climb into his Pontiac J2000, check the map, and begin another day of cold calling throughout Detroit on the smallest-volume customers, some of whom hadn't laid eyes on an M. Jacob & Sons salesman for many years. But now that Joel had come into the company—a 97-year-old distributor of bottles and plastic containers run by his father, Marty Jacob—he intended to shake away the cobwebs. The last thing he wanted was to become infected by his father's gloom.

At least 10 or 12 times a day, Joel would march through a customer's door with his catalogs, introducing himself as Joel Jacob from "the bottle company," the company his great-grandfather started. Outgoing, intense, always in motion, he would ask about the businesses: What did they make? How did they use the bottles and jars they bought from M. Jacob & Sons? Customers would often invite their young visitor to tour the premises, which was the part Joel liked best. He learned, for example, how one customer used plastic vials for storing artificial eyeballs, another used plastic bottles to apply glue to the seams of man-made reservoirs, and a third used the same bottles to squeeze oil into outdoor clocks. He was impressed by their ingenuity—but he didn't find much new business.

Then, around mid-August, he took a flier: He stopped in at the world headquarters of K-mart Corp., in Troy, Mich. For some reason, just sitting in the huge, plant-filled lobby, watching as hundreds of salespeople from all over the world milled around waiting to sell their wares, got his adrenaline flowing. He called his father on a pay phone to report on where he was.

What on *earth*, asked Marty Jacob, did he think he was doing *there*?

Joel reminded Marty that on one level, the world's largest discount retailer (1984 sales of $18.6 billion) was just another small customer of M. Jacob & Sons, buying around $40 worth of one-quart bottles a year to hold ink in the corporate print shop. But what if they could supply retail merchandise for K mart stores, like the vendors in the lobby? Wouldn't that be a new way to approach the bottle business?

As he left the building, Joel asked the receptionist for a list of buyers. A few weeks and many phone calls later, he was back for an appointment. No, he told the buyer, his company had never done business with a retailer of any kind —but it *did* supply the plastic bottles to the companies that made K mart's brand of suntan lotion, shampoo, and mouthwash, and it had never let them down. No company in the United States, he added firmly, knew bottles better than M. Jacob & Sons.

In November, the first order came through: K mart wanted 3,300 plastic bottles equipped with trigger sprayers, for sale in the lawn and garden departments of its Midwestern stores. Less than two years later—before Joel's 26th birthday—he was running a new

division that was shipping millions of units to retailers nationwide. And he had a hundred-year-old company acting like a start-up again.

It was a major change of direction, the kind most businesses never attempt—or, if they do, fail to pull off. Yet this wasn't the first time M. Jacob & Sons had been through such a transformation. Indeed, the company had reinvented itself at least twice before Joel even appeared on the scene.

The company was started by Joel's great-grandfather, an enterprising Russian-born Jew named Max Jacob who came to the United States in 1882 and soon settled in Detroit. In those days, bottles were handblown and expensive, and Max sensed that he could make a living by collecting used bottles door-to-door, then reselling them to local breweries and other large users. He cultivated friendships with brewery foremen at the city's downtown saloons, securing their goodwill and loyalty. As the business grew, Max took on more and more people—employing 40 at one point. There were many bottle peddlers in Detroit at the turn of the century, just as there were in other big cities. But Max Jacob outmaneuvered them all, becoming the city's undisputed king of used bottles.

By 1915, Max's sons were entering the company—and soon, they were reinventing it for the first time.

New technology had begun to make cheaper, mass-produced bottles widely available. So in the early 1920's — while continuing to collect and resell old bottles—the Jacob brothers struck up relationships with the nation's leading bottle manufacturers, serving as a distributor between the manufacturers and dozens of local beverage companies. William, the eldest son, was a salesman; Sam spent a few years driving the horse-drawn delivery wagon; and Ben, Joel's grandfather, was the family bookkeeper and cashier.

The Jacobs eventually developed customers throughout the state of Michigan. At the same time, they built a reputation for reliability and product expertise — advising businesses on which types of bottles and jars worked best in which kinds of settings. By the late 1940's when young Marty Jacob arrived on the scene, M. Jacob & Sons was a solid family company with sales of around $1 million, providing millions of bottles each year to Detroit-area makers of industrial cleaners, health and beauty aids, and pharmaceuticals — easily the biggest bottle jobber between New York City and Chicago. The hope was that the company would continue to grow.

And grow it did, modestly for 10 years or so—but then the growth stopped. More and more breweries and beverage companies went out of business, bought their bottles from other distributors, or began using aluminum cans. Sales volume, which had increased to around $6 million in the decade after World War II, began falling, eventually dropping by more than 50%. The older Jacobs, who were in their seventies, didn't fully appreciate the problem. But 33-year-old Marty, who had a wife and three children to support, most certainly did.

It really hit him, Marty recalls, at the company's 75th anniversary party, in April 1960. He remembers standing in his tuxedo in the Latin Quarter, a grand old Detroit supper club from the Roaring Twenties, surrounded by more than 500 friends and customers who had come to honor M. Jacob & Sons. And he remembers thinking, as the music played, that the most familiar faces —

executives from the Stroh Brewery Co. and Pfeiffer Brewing Co., and soft-drink bottlers like Faygo Beverages Inc. and Vernors, Inc. — represented the company's past. Where its future was, he didn't know.

The answer, and the key to the company's second major transformation, was that quintessential '60's word, "plastics."

Unlike bottle distributors elsewhere, which had major reservations about the impact of plastic on their profit margins, M. Jacob & Sons embraced plastic containers with the same enthusiasm it had shown for new glass bottles in the '20s. Marty's father, Ben Jacob, made the decision, and Marty (along with a cousin, Elaine Jacob, and Bob Stieler, a young salesman who joined the company in 1956) implemented it. "We couldn't afford to be proud," he explains. "If we didn't sell plastic, someone else would do it for us."

In this third incarnation, the company began representing a host of new suppliers. It expanded operations into the western half of the state, attracting such major new accounts as Amway Corp., the giant direct-sales company, which began buying a variety of plastic bottles and tubes for its home and personal-care products. By the late 1960's, plastic was a bigger portion of the company's overall volume than glass, and the preplastic slump was a distant memory.

By 1977, M. Jacob & Sons was selling nearly $20 million worth of bottles to Michigan companies — but Marty's outlook was starting to turn bearish again. The state's economy was declining with the fortunes of the auto industry, and Marty, who had taken over as president in 1966, kept an informal tally of the plants that closed and the customers

371

that moved south. Unit sales fell off, and profits shrank. "There was so much bad news," he recalls. "We'd keep asking each other who in Michigan we weren't selling to. We couldn't come up with *anybody*."

If only he could diversify—yet that seemed much easier said than done. During the '70s, Marty had considered wholesaling paper products, but found the field overcrowded. For a while, the company tried selling metal cans, abandoning the idea when it discovered how much new expertise its sales force would need to be effective.

Marty was desperate to reinvent the business one more time. "I can remember even talking about *shoelaces*," he says. He needed good ideas, and he didn't know where he was going to get them.

As it turned out, he only had to look across the breakfast table.

Marty didn't see his 23-year-old son as an idea-generator at first. He was more concerned with making sure Joel came into the business by a less demoralizing route than the one he himself had followed. But because of that concern— intentionally or not—he helped give Joel a fresh perspective on the bottle trade.

When Marty had joined the company 36 years before, no one was looking to him for bold ideas about how to breathe life into M. Jacob & Sons. He was expected to save his breath for loading and unloading trucks and railroad cars. Instead of going to college, as Joel did, he served briefly in the Army, then came home at the end of 1945 and went to work for his father and uncles. Because he lacked experience, they thought he should start at the bottom, where his efforts were needed.

He was happy to have the job, but he didn't look forward to coming to work in the mornings. "They didn't treat me like a boss's son," he says, "but like another insect working under a foreman." Marty's older brother had gone into the furniture business, and his cousins had become doctors, lawyers, and architects. There were plenty of days when he could understand why they did.

Only when a job became available was he given a chance to move ahead. He was placed in charge of shipping, then purchasing, and used his new positions to learn the finer points of managing the warehouse—how long it took to order from each supplier, and thousands of details about products. Finally, after being nearly invisible for eight years, his elders moved him into sales. "It was out of the blue," he says. "They asked me if I had white shirts and ties and a couple of suits."

So when Joel began to talk about working at M. Jacob & Sons, Marty wondered if it would be right for him. He still regretted his own decision at times. And he had known other sons of bosses who had gone to work for their fathers out of a sense of obligation; some couldn't *wait* to sell their companies after their parents died.

"I wanted him to search his soul," Marty says. "I told him that if he wanted to do something else—to be a doctor or a lawyer, or go off to the mountains and collect rocks — he wasn't going to break any hearts...I said if he came in, it would be neat, but he had to have *something* worth paying for—something that the company needed, that was marketable. Because if he couldn't add value, it wouldn't make much sense for him to be here. He'd be disappointed. And when the boss's son comes along and doesn't know anything, he's the boss's idiot son as far as everyone else is concerned."

What's more, Marty explained, there would be no guarantees about the future. "For him to succeed me as president, he'd have to show what he could do. It wasn't enough that his name was Joel Jacob, because he wouldn't just be working for me, but also for the cousins and the widowed aunts. They owned the business, too."

Joel listened, but he didn't have any of his father's doubts. He had prepared to work at M. Jacob & Sons — and no place else — from the time he was a small boy. Although his two older sisters showed no interest in the company, he was fascinated by the family tradition. "I felt like I was part of it," he says. "The company was founded just 20 years after the Civil War. Max Jacob died in 1945, but I felt like I *knew* him."

When Joel was 13, he went with his father to his first meeting of the National Association of Container Distributors, in Bermuda. His grandfather was one of the founders of the group, and its members included descendants of other bottle families from all over the country. Everyone expected that Joel would be bored by the business meetings and end up spending his time in the swimming pool. But he stayed close by, listening to hours of presentations and taking a genuine liking to the bottle clan.

His interest never waned, even when he went off to college. At Michigan State University, Joel studied business and took courses in packaging engineering. Marty always refused him summer jobs in the warehouse or as a shipping clerk ("We *had* people who could sweep floors and stuff envelopes," the elder Jacob explains). But one year, Joel was allowed to paint the warehouse

("because we didn't have anybody who could do that"), and he proved he could get a job done on time. He spent his senior year at Arizona State University, seeking out a bottle distributor in Phoenix for part-time work. And although he loved Arizona, he headed back to Detroit a few weeks after he graduated, ready to show his father what he could do.

Joel wasn't given specific responsibilities, so he spent the first several months watching how the business worked. He sat next to Frank Buchanan, the purchasing vice-president, in the large center office that was filled with desks. When Buchanan got on the telephone with a supplier or a customer, Joel would listen in to the conversation, and he remembers how nervous he was when one day, the vice-president turned a call over to him. An aggressive buyer from Ford Motor Co. ordered 1,000 eight-ounce plastic bottles with closures, then said he assumed that freight was included in the quoted price. "I didn't know, so I signaled to Frank," Joel recalls. "And Frank whispered, 'They pay.'"

The more he learned, the more he wanted to try things on his own. So the following summer, he headed off on his whirlwind tour of the customers. He brought his catalogs wherever he went, and talked bottles to anyone who would listen. He met hundreds of people, hurried through dozens of submarine sandwiches, and wrote orders here and there, mostly small ones. In the process, he visited nearly every K mart around — and had a break-through idea that months of office brainstorming might never have produced.

Wandering through the stores, he noticed the empty spray bottles K mart sold for watering plants..Joel was struck by the poor quality of the printing on them—the letters were often smudged —and by the fact that the bottles were frequently out of stock. Why not deliver a better one, at a better price? He knew the best suppliers; M. Jacob & Sons had been buying from them for years. What did it matter that the Jacobs had never sold to mass merchandisers before? If they succeeded, Joel told his skeptical father, there was no telling how far they could go. "The best way to kill enthusiasm is to tell a kid it won't work," says Marty, "even if you know it won't." So he told Joel to give it a try.

His pitch worked at K mart, and it worked at Frank's Nursery, a Detroit-based garden supply chain, as well. Both agreed to test Joel, and he bent over backward to service the accounts and learn as much as he could about his new customers. He contracted to have the sprayer and plastic bottles screwed together at a facility just minutes from his office, so he could keep tabs on any problems. And he built a sizable stockpile of spray bottles in case he got some lucky breaks. Sure enough, K mart called one day—one of its other suppliers had messed up—and Joel sent a truckload of sprayers to Atlanta within 24 hours.

In the meantime, realizing that he knew very little about his new business—and seeing that no one inside M. Jacob & Sons could help—he hit the road to learn about the retailing world.

In January 1983, he went to the National Housewares Show in Chicago. He wanted to see how different types of companies presented themselves to the buyers. All day long, he walked up and down aisles in the sprawling McCormick Place complex, collecting brochures, taking pictures, and sniffing for ideas. He came back with about 50 pounds of trade magazines and a new name for his branch of the company. It

should be called Sprayco, he told his father, so retailing people could remember it; M. Jacob & Sons was too cumbersome a name to promote. He hired an artist to design a logo—a bottle with mist coming out of the nozzle—and began putting it on everything in sight.

He entered a Cleveland marathon sponsored by Revco Drug Store Inc., because it would give him an excuse to talk with the Revco buyers again and, Joel says, because "I knew it would make an impression." It did. "I limped around the office for several days, but we got the business."

In the spring of 1984, Joel flew to Greenville, N.C., the home of an M. Jacob & Sons supplier called Empire Brushes Inc. He had taken a liking to Empire's 37-year-old president, Joe Gantz, at the Chicago housewares show; now he wanted to see what he could learn from Gantz's company. How did Empire manage its relationships with customers and sales representatives? How did it structure pricing policies and prepare for trade shows? He spent hours with Empire's top marketing people, and talked with Gantz long into the night. Gantz warned Joel not to move too fast, stressing the importance of a quality image. "Don't oversell what you can do." he warned, "or you might not get another chance."

A few months later, Joel flew to New York City to see Jerry Kearns, that year's president of the National Housewares Manufacturers Association. A major supplier to M. Jacob & Sons, Kearn's company, APL Inc., also sold products to retailers directly, and Joel wanted to tap into Kearn's experience. He brought along an introductory offer he had just printed up: 13 spray bottles for the price of 12. Kearns, with 35 years in business, studied the price sheet and shook his head. "He said it looked cheap," Joel recalls. "He said, 'Throw away those sheets and just give them 8% off their opening orders and one reorder at the same price.' How was I supposed to know? I had never done it before." Kearns coached Joel on the fundamentals of packaging and displaying. He gave him ideas for setting up a national sales organization, passing along the names of some of the better representatives he had worked with. And he spoke about basic values—not burning bridges, playing it straight, shipping on time. On the plane home, Joel's head was spinning with new ideas.

In August 1984, he ran an ad in *Hardware Retailing* ("100-year-old company seeks experienced representatives for new product line of plant and garden sprayers") and spent $15,000 putting together a booth for the National Hardware & Lawn & Garden Show in Chicago. After four days, more than 90 rep firms had stopped by booth 9042. "It was exhausting—I lost my voice," Joel says. "I didn't stop talking for the whole show." He took the resumes back to Detroit, and within 10 days, Sprayco had a network of sales representatives across the country, including Alaska and Hawaii.

Two months later, he was back in Chicago at another National Housewares show. Although exhibit space had been filled for weeks, Joel asked Jerry Kearns to help him out, and he ended up with a tiny, 10-foot basement booth in a back alley of the McCormick Place annex. By the third day, he was exhausted, but he was in the booth at eight in the morning, giving a pep talk to his new reps over coffee and doughnuts. Already, they had orders for spray bottles from more than 40 retailers, and Joel showed them his new line of travel containers-plastic toothbrush holders, soap dishes, and little bottles for carrying lotions and shampoo. All day, he refused to sit down ("you can't afford to look tired, because it turns people off"). And when he did take breaks, he would slip his red exhibitor's badge into his jacket pocket ("if anyone knows you're an exhibitor, they're not going to spend their time with you") and wander the aisles in search of still more new ideas.

Today, Joel Jacob works out of a small, windowless office neatly lined with enlarged photographs of generations of Jacob men and their delivery vehicles. All but one wall, that is, which is plastered with pages ripped from trade magazines—lists of the top 100 discounters, the top 50 drug chains, even the top 30 "deep discounters," with names like Rock Bottom and Get It For Less. This year, Joel says, Sprayco will ship several million units of product to about 150 customers. Retailers are buying both the spray bottles and the new line of travel accessories, which are offered in clear plastic bags with printed bar codes, ready for display at checkout counters coast-to-coast. More than 70% of the orders are coming from the sales reps, who can call Sprayco directly on a special toll-free number.

All of this has transpired in less than three years—and just two new people have been added to the company payroll, which now totals 24. "Every day," Joel says, "we're shipping all the new orders with the same people, the same warehouse, the same accounting departments."

Sprayco still contributes no more than 10% of overall sales to M. Jacob & Sons, but it may soon be the tail wagging the company dog. "A lot of 100-year-old companies really *look* like they're 100 years old," Joel says. "But my goal is to build on all our experience. I want to become an important source of a lot of quality products, not just bottles. I'd like to dominate a whole category, like a Rubbermaid."

"A few years ago," says David Levine, M. Jacob & Sons' controller for the past 20 years, "you used to have a pretty clear sense of what was coming up around here. Things were on such an even keel....Accounts either got bigger or they got smaller." But Joel's arrival changed many of the company's old rhythms. "Almost every day," notes sales service administrator Lila Starck, "he comes into the office with new samples or new cardboard displays. He'll lay them out and tell everybody what's going on and what he's thinking about. It's been like watching the birth of a nation."

Marty's hands-off approach to Joel's training has clearly paid off. The son's brainchild has become the business within the business that the father was searching for; and once again, M. Jacobs & Sons is being reborn. But the changes have come so quickly that the older man sometimes feels he has lost control. He speaks of Joel's energy with a voice full of pride — and just a tinge of regret.

"I'd look at what he was doing and I wouldn't understand it," Marty says. "He'd talk about how we were gonna do this and then we were gonna do that. I used to tell him he couldn't buy groceries with his 'we're gonnas.'...It's one of those cases of the son teaching the father-for the good of the company.

"People say, 'Wow, you've got your son in the business. You can sit back and take it easy.' Well, I used to think the same thing — how nice it would be to get together for breakfast. But, you know, we don't do that much anymore. I get so drained from all that enthusiasm, I feel like I need a shower and a change of clothes."

Chapter 8

Psychological Issues

Given the complications of family relationships being played out in a business structure, psychological dimensions are basic to family business systems. Articles in this section deal with the application of psychological therapy to family firms. The psychological problems that business families can confront range from the stress associated with passing the business to the next generation to substance abuse by family members. Ultimately, how and how well families cope depends on the family paradigms — the core beliefs through which family members experience their world.

Introduction

In this interview with **OD Practitioner,** *Will McWhinney discusses his development as a family business therapist. He explains the conceptual background of family business therapy and then details how he applied the process in a particular case.*

Interview: Will McWhinney — Family Business Therapy for Family Business

1984

By Ray Weil

ODP: You are excited about consulting to family-run firms. Off the beaten path, isn't it?

McWhinney: I would say so when you consider that family business has been almost completely ignored...by the business schools, for instance.

ODP: Why shouldn't they ignore it?

McWhinney: They account for 90 percent of all U.S. corporations.

ODP: Small potatoes, aren't they?

McWhinney: You mean Getty Oil? Some of them are pretty big. But look at them collectively. Family-owned businesses hold 40 percent of the productive assets of this country and nearly half the productive capacity. Some of them *are* small, but a surprising number are among the top businesses in the nation. But don't overlook the small ones.

ODP: Why not?

McWhinney: Taken together, big and small, they're a prime source of innovation in product and service. And they do long-range planning naturally...20 years ahead. At least the healthier ones do. If they're not screwed up, they're extremely good at human relations because they start with the ethos of family caring.

ODP: As a sector of the American economy, are they growing or shrinking?

McWhinney: I don't have that number. I can tell you that they are the highest-saving group in our society, consuming the least amount of earned income, pouring back large sums into capitalization...40 to 60 percent...sometimes more. If the American economy is going to flourish again, I believe it will

379

be because of these firms, not the massive, deadening business bureaucracies.

ODP: What's it like to consult for them?

McWhinney: It is demanding as hell, but very satisfying. When you help a family-owned company to straighten itself out, you can expect it to stay that way for a long time...because the *people* stay. It's not like a division of a big corporation where you may have helped to bring about a momentous change only to see a new general manager – off on his personal power trip – scuttle the achievement of years simply because he arrived on the scene, arrived with fixed pre-conceptions and no grasp of the division's history or even its balance sheet. *That's* discouraging!

ODP: What do your students and colleagues [at the Fielding Institute] say when you raise the subject of family business?

McWhinney: For the most part they say it's messy and they back off.

ODP: Is it messy?

McWhinney: Well it's complicated...certainly. You really must get to know the individuals you're dealing with. You can't treat them statistically as you might a group of managers or engineers in a large corporation. You're also dealing with a system beyond the individual, the *family* system.

ODP: I completely failed to make the obvious connection of family systems therapy to *family* business.

McWhinney: Finally, there's the *business* system. Needless to say, all three – the individual, family and business systems – are all bound up with one another.

ODP: So how do you go about untangling them?

McWhinney: One source of conceptual help comes from people who have been studying the normal phases of human development, including the later years. All the earlier development work, as you know, concerned children and adolescents. So first there's the strand of work about individual life-cycle transitions. Next, the study of stages of family development is inching ahead. The details of transition vary from one family to another but the basic sequence of development is common to families in a given culture. Finally, Larry Greiner did some fine work in marking out the evolutionary transitions of an entrepreneurial business. So we have these three maps of development as a framework against which to look at a family-managed business and to deploy the methods of family systems therapy, and these can be quite powerful.

And then, of course, there's general business consulting.

ODP: Which I suppose is necessary too.

McWhinney: In this work you're always dealing with the top. Therefore business issues – like the accounting system – have to be dealt with as part and parcel of individual and family issues. I worked with one family that just couldn't get a quarterly financial statement out of the computer, try as they might. There was nothing wrong with the computer or their technical skill in using it.

ODP: I can see why practitioners may be reticent to follow you. They would need a double education...at least.

McWhinney: A few of them have said that. It seems to me we have to learn to deal with higher levels of complexity.

ODP: I'm told that family therapists prefer to work in pairs because the action is mercurial and two pairs of eyes are quicker than one.

McWhinney: And also because a single therapist is likely to get hooked. I had to bow out of consulting for one firm because their problems were too similar to my own. I couldn't help them.

I'd strongly recommend working in pairs. I haven't, but I'm always on the lookout for a partner.

ODP: Is there a way to cut it so that a general business consultant and a family therapist work together?

McWhinney: I don't see how. Dick Beckhard and Elaine Kepner, his wife, who is a family therapist, say they do that: she does the therapy while Dick handles the business side of consulting. Well, Beckhard is not exactly your run-of-the-mill general business consultant, is he? I doubt if it really works that simply. But at the present time, I feel one needs a single systems viewpoint to fully integrate family therapy and business design work. Having to orchestrate two specialists' ideas while they are on the firing line is difficult.

ODP: You remarked that family firms are good at human relations.

McWhinney: They're fundamentally paternalistic, which we usually consider a negative. While there's much more of a family feeling, much more caring, it usually entails dependency relationships. They're likely to look after their employees, but not systematically.

However, it's the consultant's job to nudge them out of their paternalism and into a learning environment. After all, a healthy family does not set out to *keep* its children but to develop them into autonomous human beings. I believe that I have been successful in helping several family firms to conceive of themselves as learning enterprises in which people are treated like children in the best sense of the word. "You are here to be developed and to grow in your skills so that you may make a maximum contribution to your family. Or, if something outside beckons and you want to leave, go with our blessing."

ODP: You're known for your work in open systems. Is there a connection?

McWhinney: The reason I fell into family business therapy was *because* of my open systems work...where the participants made use of both their personal histories *and* their work lives. I became aware that I was dealing with the same factors as in family systems therapy, but without the dynamic of family history. So a simple broadening from personal to family to company put me on my way.

ODP: Can you give me a better idea of what you actually do as a family business consultant?

McWhinney: One of the preliminary steps of family therapy is to examine the background of a family through its family tree.

ODP: Genealogy?

McWhinney: Exactly. I aid the family in constructing a genogram for two or three generations. It stimulates them tremendously. And it is surprisingly predictive as you begin to understand the relationship to the parents...women to mothers, sons to fathers...two or three generations back.

ODP: In what way?

McWhinney: For example, we're often caught up in childhood behavior until the parent dies. If you're 70 years old and your parents are 95, you are still hooked to them in a child-parent relationship. As soon as they die, you are free to change. I know a middle-aged woman who responded to her mother's very fashion-conscious dress by affecting a peasant style for herself. Soon after the mother died, the woman switched her entire wardrobe toward her mother's style.

Also, we are sometimes trapped in a pattern of behavior that persists until we come to the same age at which the parent died. It appears to be happening to me. In the last couple of years, I've begun to interest myself in trusts...beginning when I was 52. Intriguing! My father, who was a trust officer in a bank, died at 52. Now I know how *I* got into it.

ODP: And you thought you were a free man.

McWhinney: It shows how the family tree clues you in on ways that the family may respond to crisis. I've been studying the milestones of crisis in family business, what brings them up and what kind of support will help a family business to weather the crises. And so in the genograms I look at early leadership patterns, more mature leadership patterns, and patterns of delegation. By learning about the family, maybe I'll be able to predict if the firm will innovate, seek outside capital, make crucial decisions in a timely manner or not.

ODP: I'm skeptical of all prediction in human affairs.

McWhinney: Well, I don't want to overstate that. How about things to watch for? Take such a thing as birth order, for example. First sons are apt to oppose their fathers. They seldom get through the basic conflict with the old man until they're 40 years old. They keep saying: "Dad, I'm as good as you are." Often they become aggressive towards their fathers, which in the long run means they are trapped into doing exactly what he did, only better. Or sometimes their fathers destroy them.

Over and over, first sons prove to be ineffective, at least during the lives of their fathers, after which they may break free. Second sons—and here the records go back to the Middle Ages—tend to be humanistically oriented. In traditional primogeniture societies, the first son inherited the property, the second son entered the church. Today, second sons are still more likely to become academics or artists than first sons. And second sons are almost always less potent as leaders. Years ago, I did a study in the Forest Service and discovered that engineers were dominantly first sons and foresters second and third. Third sons turn out to be most like their fathers because they've had the benefit of escaping their fathers' mistakes in raising their elder brothers. In some Eastern cultures, later sons were the prime inheritors. First son became a warrior, second son a priest, third son took over the farm...because he was best able to manage it.

ODP: I'm thinking of Lear's daughter, Cordelia. Most like him.

McWhinney: It's true of women as well, although most of the evidence we have concerns men. My eldest sister was so caught up by our father's career that she became the first woman bank president in the U.S. He had died before he made president.

People say family business consulting is messy. I don't. The same junk is kicking around in any organizational setting...in publicly-held corporations, too...except there's not way for a consultant to have direct access to it as you do in a family tree...That is, in the family firm you can use a more systematic (albeit complex) approach.

ODP: I certainly see how you can use a family history.

McWhinney: I get a good view of childhood background and they get to learn more about themselves and about the dynamics of their family. As you work on the family tree, someone cries out: "My God! My grandfather did it, my father did it, and here am I doing it again!" And they laugh. Discovering that their conduct has been determined gives them a sense of freedom. They can begin to make conscious choices as we do during reality therapy or analytic therapy. And so that fits my purpose, which is to help each family member to individuate.

ODP: What I need now is a case.

McWhinney: Here's a mother, two sons, and a cousin who is her contemporary. The firm was founded by the grandfather, now deceased, and continued by the father, who died a decade ago. You could say that the mother was a dowager queen, the eldest son was crown prince, and the cousin the regent.

Mother was president by inheritance. The prince ran a staff function and drew a good salary, but he was spending a lot of time with a psychotherapist and was utterly lacking in self-confidence.

The regent, who had entered the firm at the same time as the father but never came into a share of the ownership, was now executive vice-president. He seemed to me afraid of making decisions, a fact which kept the company from growing. He had survived a heart attack several years earlier.

The younger son looked to be a lost soul. He had moved to Boston and involved himself in an unfortunate partnership in publishing. He got by on handouts from his mother.

The mother came in to work every day and worried about the business. But she had no special gift for it and wasn't very effective.

ODP: What were *you* after in this situation?

McWhinney: I liked them all. I wanted to unsnarl the tangle, help them unkink their lives and get that business out of its rut. Also, I wanted to do something to rebalance the scales of family justice.

ODP: Justice?

McWhinney: Let me come to that. The mother heard of me through a mutual friend. On first contact she said she desperately wanted some sort of help with the family. She knew I wasn't a family therapist. I'm a business professor, or that's how I was described to her. But she had formed the impression that I would work on the family as well as on the business.

ODP: She didn't separate the two?

McWhinney: Didn't see the distinction. And she was right. They were all one. Well, we met once. Then the regent put his foot down. He opposed my becoming a consultant to the firm. Said it would destroy the prince. What he may also have had in mind was closer to home. So nothing happened for eight months, then she called again, said things had got even worse and that they just had to have help.

I began by interviewing each member of the family. Brought the younger son back to town for the purpose and then regularly to get him involved. The regent would talk to me only in his own office. He was very reserved at first.

At last I got the four of them together off-site for several long meetings. You should have heard the yelling! Three of them going at once. The regent didn't join in only because he feared for his heart. In the meetings we began to make good progress on the genogram as well as personal and corporate histories.

Now they were ready to allow the controller of the firm, who was not a family member, to join us in future meetings. He was the remaining significant power figure and couldn't be left out. Because they had always been so secretive, this was a revolution. It soon became evident that he already knew all the family secrets. So they dropped all that nonsense.

Then I began to work back and forth between family issues and business issues, not separately, not in separate rooms at separate times, but using business issues to flush out and define the structure of family conflicts.

ODP: An example?

McWhinney: Central issue. Mother complained that the prince was draining the company for his personal needs. How much? I wanted to know. Well, it seems he had no budget and she had no readily available numbers to back up her worry. But the controller was there and *he* knew. Turned out that the draw was much less serious than she thought.

So I asked her: "What are you getting at your son for? What are you after?" She answered: "I can't trust him." And I said: "How about setting up a budget for him instead of complaining that he's grandiose?" So we explored to find out

why there was no budget and no budget control in this case and others. Love, money, jealousy and justice had all got mixed together.

Then I asked: "Why do you drag out decisions in this company?" Why? Ten years ago, someone had made a bookkeeping error and their checks began to bounce. They were not going to let that happen again. So they kept a lot of money sitting in the bank to protect them against the possibility of damage to their reputation.

Clearly what was needed was better cash control. Needless to say, the controller had always known it, but he was afraid to interfere in family matters. Noting the controller's hesitation, each male member of the family found words to reveal his own customary reluctance to press mother into action.

Each one of these issues would reflect back onto the other. "Why don't we have better personnel policies?" It turned out that grandfather had been a tyrant. Until he died at 80, he never let go of control. Never even allowed his son even *nominal* leadership until a few years before the end. The father had died four years after *his* father. Destroyed by the entrepreneurial parent. Classic case.

The personnel policies were certainly strange. As I've said, they were used to being close-mouthed about any and all information so nobody could figure out even how to schedule vacations. No policy on vacations, wages, promotions. Nobody ever received a written evaluation of his or her performance...all because of grandpa's paranoia. So now we were able to do something about personnel policies.

And decisions were now beginning to be made. They began to invest heavily in a new plant, computerization, and in the upgrading of responsibility of all employees—and this in the middle of a severe recession— in order to be ready to grow when the economy turned up. They focused on long-term profitability. Now that the recession is ebbing, they're doing very nicely.

ODP: What about the cousin, the regent?

McWhinney: We persuaded him to enroll in a retirement planning program at the university. You see, the family was keeping him on because they feared that he would go to his grave six months after he left. He had nothing in his life except the company. That's all changed now. He's having a very good time in Palm Springs. Rarely bothers to call.

ODP: What became of the younger son?

McWhinney: You recall that he and a partner were struggling along in a little publishing venture from which the son had netted only $2500 during the prior year. The family hadn't given a thought to distribution of any capital. The elder commanded all the assets and drew a good salary. It was ridiculous! Although the money belonged to the mother, it made no sense for the younger son to wait until she died to benefit from his inheritance.

ODP: Justice.

McWhinney: You bet. It's central in working with families. But it made no sense either to give him half the capital. He never thought he was worth anything and he wouldn't have known how to use it. Besides, nobody was offering.

I said: "Of course you should have a share which would allow you to build a

publishing division and to live decently." I saw that the prince was unhappy so I turned to him: "By what right should you draw $80,000 a year and have four or five million in capital to play with while he lives on family handouts?...Just because you're four years older?"

He was furious. "What the hell has it got to do with you?"

"You are an employee as well as a brother."

"We can't drain money from the business," he said.

"What's the matter?" I said. "Aren't you taking home enough money?"

A dangerous confrontation. Eventually, the mother came to see that under cover of trying to protect her sons and the business she was really keeping them dependent. That's not a new story, is it?...abbreviated as it is. Everyone had understood what was going on but no one would say a word about how unfair it was. Now we could treat it openly.

We sat down together and started to lay out a reasonable operating budget for a new publishing division that might have a chance. Obviously, this called for business consulting skills. We had to deal with the younger son's guilt about taking anything out of the old family business because he was so worthless. Now family therapy consulting skills.

ODP: How's the publisher doing?

McWhinney: In 18 months he's gained national recognition and the last quarter's sales are running 25 percent above forecast. My concern now is that the younger son will eclipse the elder.

ODP: So it was getting some capital to use that really helped him?

McWhinney: Yes, of course, the money. And his own ability. And some new-found courage. And I hope it had something to do with my stance toward him and the family...that nobody was to blame for anything, that our job together was to find out how to make things work. And the prince knew that I wasn't blaming him either, although he certainly felt guilty about his personal problems and the various messes he had made. He saw that I genuinely cared for him as a person. That didn't mean he was my best friend but that I, as a compassionate human being, cared about him.

ODP: Tell me how you worked with the prince.

McWhinney: First I had to untangle mother and son without myself becoming a father-surrogate. We put an answering machine in the mother's house so she wouldn't have to answer his angry calls at all hours of the day and night. Naturally she forgot to turn the machine on...The entanglement was becoming blatant.

I set up some paradoxical rules for interaction. Since they persisted in talking to each other on the telephone, I required that they phone each other every day and tell each other what he or she was doing wrong. Soon they began to regard this ritual as dumb and they let me know it. "Of course it's dumb!" I said. Next, we stopped all calling. Within days, their anxiety had become so great that they would invent emergencies. I reminded her of the agreement.

"Why can't I talk to my own son?"

"You may talk to your son if you want to, but you told me that you didn't want to talk to him."

They began to explore the games they played to bait each other. It became obvious to them that they used anger as a way of calling for love. Now they stop themselves from their angry exchanges by reminding each other of the thousand dollars they spent on two answering machines that they never used. And they laugh.

ODP: Who is running the company now?

McWhinney: The eldest son.

ODP: How's the prince doing?

McWhinney: In control. He threw me out finally...very politely and nicely...as I had been goading him to do. Finally he said: *I'm* in charge here!" It was always a delicate relationship.

ODP: So the king is finished with you.

McWhinney: I'm on the Board of Directors and I attend quarterly meetings, but as a consultant I've done all I can.

ODP: You look pleased.

McWhinney: You bet. There can be no success unless there is individuation. The family ties are strong but now there are four adults leading independent lives.

ODP: It's time you told me how the mother weaned herself away from the firm.

McWhinney: Well, she had to let go just as I did. She's an attractive, creative woman of 60 with immense drive. She stopped going to work every day and finally we gave away her office. In cutting the cord she became depressed, going into mourning for the life she had shared with her husband, a postponed mourning. It was tough on her for some months.

One dream she had always had was to run a kind of literary or artistic salon...like Gertrude Stein. She has a lot of personal charm and many accomplished friends and the skills to carry it off. But she sabotaged every start she made because of her emotional entanglement with her sons. Now she is free to develop on her own.

Recently she learned of a wandering professor of philosophy and social activist who shared the same wishes. He wanted to open a conversational coffee house in L.A. It looked to me that she might join in priming the conversational pump, bringing in an initial cultured following, and putting up a piece of the ante.

ODP: Is that the new coffee house* in Venice I just read about in the paper? On Washington Boulevard?

McWhinney: Drop in. Wish them luck. Try the cheesecake for sure.

*Gunter's Cafe, 1009 Washington Blvd., Venice, California

Introduction

Five strategies for coping with the stress created by the intergenerational transfer of the family farm were identified in a population of midwestern families. These strategies were then associated with measures of psychological well being and perceived ease in making the farm transfer decision. Parents had higher psychological well being than their children, even though fathers reported the transfer decision to be somewhat more difficult that did sons. Use of family discussion was positively associated with personal well being for fathers. Daughters-in-law were especially lacking in effective coping strategies.

Coping Strategies Associated with Intergenerational Transfer of the Family Farm
1985

By Candyce S. Russell, Charles L. Griffin,
Catherine Scott Flinchbaugh, Michael J. Martin,
and Raymond B. Atilano

Reprinted with permission from **Rural Sociology**, Vol. 50, No. 3, Fall 1985. Copyright © 1985 Rural Sociological Society; all rights reserved.

Farm families routinely cope with high levels of stress caused by the dual demands of work and family life. Members must work together in an interdependent fashion because they experience an overlap in the physical space used for work and domestic life, and they must cope also with relative isolation from contacts and activities off the farm (Rosenblatt *et al.*, 1978).

Additional stressors include seasonal variations in work demands and income, infrequent days off, high accident rates (Rosenblatt and Anderson, 1981),

and economic vulnerability (Rosenblatt and Keller, 1983). Added to these is the stress of transferring the farm as the older generation retires. This shift in control from one generation to the next is both a business and family issue. The younger generation may be striving for self respect, autonomy, and a greater share of responsibility, while the older generation is striving to maintain control of decision making and respect for past accomplishments (Rosenblatt and Anderson, 1981).

The study reported here focuses on the coping strategies used by farm families during the process of deciding how to transfer the farm from one generation to the next. Data were collected from parents, the sons who were receiving the farm, and the sons' wives.

Literature Review

The McCubbin *et al.* (1980) review of family stress research over the last decade raises the challenge to learn more about the nature of critical transitions in the family system. Of particular interest is the role of family resources, including coping strategies, social support, and family problem solving, which lead to successful negotiation of critical transition points. Research efforts to date have primarily focused on the coping repertoires of three populations: military families, who cope with varying periods of separation (Hill, 1949; McCubbin and Lester, 1977; McCubbin *et al.*, 1976); corporate business wives, coping with repeated short-term separation (Boss *et al.*, 1979); and families, who cope with chronic illness (McCubbin *et al.* 1982). The stress that is encountered when intergenerational farm transfer occurs offers another unique population for extending the understanding of family adaptation to stressful normative events in the developmental life cycle. This transfer process involves critical role changes and task realignments, which are expectable at certain points in the family life cycle. Yet, this remains an under-researched topic of special importance to farm families and those professionals working with farm families (Hedlund and Berkowitz, 1979).

McCubbin (1979) directs us to consider coping as an *active* process of adaptation, and therefore involves variables which may be "taught" to families under stress. Much of the literature has followed Hill's (1949) classic ABC-X formulation of family stress research. Here, major attention has been given to

(1) identification of family stressors and the "pileup" of stressors, (2) assessment of family resources, (3) the family's perception or definition of the event, and (4) the role of the social network as a family resource and mediator of stress. Only a handful of researchers have attempted to shed light on the reasons why some families are better able to adjust and manage chronic stressors than others.

McCubbin (1979) has identified several coping strategies common to wives who cope with their husbands' occupationally induced separations. These include expressing feelings, reducing anxiety through alcohol or drugs, maintaining family ties, belief in God, establishing independence and self sufficiency, building interpersonal relationships, living up to the employer's expectations, and keeping active in hobbies. Pearlin and Schooler (1978) have done similar work in identifying the structure of coping among individuals facing marital, parental, and occupation-related stressors. These personal coping styles include self reliance, controlled reflection, positive comparisons, negotiation, selective ignoring and optimistic faith. While farm families are coping with high levels of togetherness rather than repeated separations (as in the McCubbin work), certain coping strategies (such as belief in God, expression of feelings, advice seeking) reappear in the work of Pearlin and Schooler and may be of more general applicability, including intergenerational farm transfer.

The Stress of Intergenerational Farm Transfer

Most farm families desire to bring members of the next generation into the business in some manner leading to a transfer of ownership (Bratton and Berkowitz, 1976; Hedlund and Berkowitz, 1979b). Titus *et al.* (1979) suggest that family disputes over inheritance cases are more common among farm families because beneficiaries may need to maintain the estate intact in order to maintain profitability, and emotional bonds to the land may be very strong. Inheritance serves as a vital entry point into farming for persons who are likely to be heavily socialized toward agriculture as a career. Bratton and Berkowitz (1976) report intergenerational assistance to beginning farmers in 15 of 21 families in their sample, emphasizing the complexity and variety of transfers that were found. For these reasons, intergenerational transfer of the family farm has been reported as a major stressor in the lives of farming families (Hedlund and Berkowitz, 1979b; Rosenblatt and Anderson, 1981, Rosenblatt *et al.*, 1978; Titus *et al.*, 1979). Hedlund and Berkowitz (1979b) report intergenerational transfer "problems" in 75 percent of their sample, although only 30 percent met their definition of "stressful" as "resulting in dysfunctional task or interpersonal performance."

The intergenerational transfer of the farm brings together numerous "critical role transitions" (Hill and Joy, 1979) within a unique economic and social context. Interpersonal friction may arise as the family attempts to accommodate a younger generation and phase out the older. The younger generation may be striving for feelings of self-respect, autonomy, and a fair share of responsibility, while the older generation may be striving to maintain decision making, psychic and physical territory, and the respect merited by greater experience and by precedence and investment in the enterprise (Rosenblatt and Anderson, 1981) as they near retirement. Other potential

difficulties relate to sibling rivalry and competition, which are reported as stressful in 20 percent of the Hedlund and Berkowitz (1979b) sample.

Wives of both generations report role stress as they attempt to mediate conflict. Hedlund and Berkowitz (1979b) find stresses relating to the wife in 60 percent of their sample, leading them to suspect that wives often attempt to play a peacemaker role. Interestingly, when open conflict is reported within the marriage or between siblings, the wife's role stress is lower (Hedlund and Berkowitz, 1979a). Kohl (1976) suggests that wives fill a powerful "switchboard" position. Barnes and Hershon (1976) also document this sort of coping strategy in family businesses where the wife plays an important "bridging" role between father and son in helping a transition to occur. Though stressful for the wife, this "switchboard" or "bridging" role may be a useful way of organizing in families where communication between father and children is not open. Berkowitz and Perkins (1984) find that husband support is an important factor in the amount of stress experienced by their wives. Therefore, if the wife feels supported by her complex role in the family, her own stress level is likely to be lower.

Additional literature highlights the importance of open communication in families involved in intergenerational farm transfer. Communication which is "open and free" ... [and where] feelings, opinions, and ideas of all family members are heard and understood" (Hedlund and Berkowitz, 1979b:240) is frequently mentioned as a mediating factor. Bratton and Berkowitz (1976:9) report that families who are able to achieve intergenerational continuity "were able to communicate about needs, desires, and future possibilities.

They could talk about options without making the children feel obligated to stay on the farm." Openness of the communication and decision-making style appear to be related to level of stress. Hedlund and Berkowitz (1979b) report a significant relationship between shared decision making and lower marital and intergenerational stress. Furthermore, in issues surrounding inheritance, Rosenblatt and Anderson (1981) and Titus *et al.* (1979) report that the likelihood of bitter feelings and conflict is lower when the disposition of property is clearly discussed in advance with all involved parties.

Several sources suggest that farm families may be likely to use distancing as a coping mechanism. Distancing may be accomplished by family members working off the farm, living off the farm, or expanding the operation (Rosenblatt and Anderson, 1981). For instance, farm wives in the Hedlund and Berkowitz (1979b) sample who reported low levels of stress had strong involvements outside the farm. In both the Boss *et al.* (1979) study of corporate executive wives' coping patterns in response to routine separation averaging eight months in military families, the wife's response of establishing independence and self-sufficiency emerged as a basic coping strategy.

The role of social support networks has received much attention in the family stress literature as another major variable affecting families' abilities to manage stress. Cobb (1976) defines social support as information that communicates an esteem, understanding, and belonging. Social support may also include information about problem solving and new social contacts who may help. The importance of developing and maintaining supportive relationships with the community

emerges as a major predictor of successful adaptation to stress (McCubbin, 1979). However, little attention has been given in farm family literature to the possible function of community support networks, perhaps, because of the perception of the relative isolation of farm families.

The present study is designed to identify the coping strategies that are associated with managing stress produced by the transfer of the family farm from one generation to the next. It builds upon the literature reviewed above by assessing the effectiveness of those coping strategies that have previously been associated with occupationally and/or family-induced stress. More specifically, the research investigates the "B" or "resource" factor in Hill's (1949) ABC-X model by exploring resources that families use to keep the disruptive effects of intergenerational farm transfer to a minimum. Furthermore, the specific coping strategies identified as resources represent the three categories of coping behaviors McCubbin (1979) identified in his integration of individual coping behaviors into family stress theory. These are: (1) management of family stability and individual anxiety, (2) procurement of social support, and (3) direct attack upon the stressor event through individual and collective family effort.

Method

Sample Selection

The sampling frame includes families where an intergenerational transfer decision has been made within the last five years. The transfer was between the parent generation and child generation, and at least one of the children was 18 years of age or older. Furthermore, farming was the primary occupation of the donor generation at the time of the

Table 1. Terminal five-factor solution (varimax rotation) on coping strategies (N = 390)

Factor I[a]	Factor II[b]	Factor III[c]	Factor IV[d]	Factor V[e]	Item
0.40340	0.14367	0.20678	0.16370	-0.08147	Purchasing nearby land
0.35838	0.11172	0.18455	0.16717	0.09564	Specializing in a particular aspect of farm operation
0.53212	0.01045	-0.02555	-0.00844	0.09314	Membership in American Ag. Movement
0.45920	0.05548	0.04839	0.09970	0.02486	Membership in National Farm Organization
0.54615	0.13679	0.03693	0.11818	0.05419	Membership in Wheat Growers Association
0.68584	0.03166	0.04687	0.20172	0.02755	Membership in Kansas Livestock Assoc.
0.14837	0.76776	0.15778	0.11471	-0.05844	Talking with my children (parents) about the Farm Transfer Decision
0.19570	0.81430	0.15986	0.13132	0.04564	Discussing management of the farm with my children (parents)
0.04430	0.53279	0.16136	0.20587	0.09339	Discussing retirement needs and goals with my children (parents)
0.14786	0.19729	0.62403	0.12431	0.02090	Believing in God
0.14786	0.20883	0.77419	0.09559	0.09570	Telling myself I have many things to be thankful for
0.07294	0.05378	0.48511	0.05936	0.14256	Keeping problems to myself
-0.02185	0.04989	0.48529	0.13744	0.08517	Becoming more involved in activities off the farm
0.10254	0.19613	0.08356	0.68975	0.23760	Consulting Extension Agents
0.14701	0.17506	0.12163	0.66140	-0.00101	Attending Estate Planning Workshops
0.19191	0.07760	0.11807	0.50212	-0.01079	Membership in Farm Management Association
0.29361	0.04660	0.21764	0.42730	0.00450	Membership in Farm Bureau
0.01211	-0.05064	0.15349	0.10018	0.64615	Allowing myself to become angry
0.17256	0.11920	0.14467	0.01301	0.70128	Getting angry at the whole economy

[a] Factor I = farm management, mean = 9.09, SD = 14.64. Eigenvalue = 4.05466; 50.6% of variance. Alpha = 0.66.
[b] Factor II = discussion, mean = 8.39, SD = 6.19. Eigenvalue = 1.25051; 15.6% of variance. Alpha = 0.78.
[c] Factor III = individual coping, mean = 11.46, SD = 8.00. Eigenvalue = 1.11930; 14.0% of variance. Alpha = 0.71.
[d] Factor IV = professionals, mean = 7.22; SD = 9.50. Eigenvalue = 0.82021; 10.2% of variance. Alpha = 0.71.
[e] Factor V = expression of anger, mean = 2.71, SD = 5.00. Eigenvalue = 0.76260; 9.5% of variance. Alpha = 0.65.

Table 2. Use of coping strategy by family position in weighted scores*

	Fathers (N = 86)	Mothers (N = 91)	Sons (N = 89)	Daughters-in-law (N = 73)	Overall x
Farm management	2.00	1.57	2.32	1.79	1.92
Discussion	5.08	5.20	5.06	3.52	4.72
Individual coping	4.95	5.33	5.27	5.27	5.21
Professionals	3.33	3.36	3.15	2.42	3.07
Expression of anger	2.10	2.31	3.30	2.91	2.67

*Scores were weighted, based on number of items in each scale: Farm management (1.0,) Discussion (2.0), Individual coping (1.5), Professionals (1.5), Expression of anger (3.0). The reader should note that these are not standard scores and therefore should not be used to compare any one individual's score to group means.

transfer decision. Finally, at least one member of the donor generation was still alive.

In order to represent the state of Kansas as adequately as possible, ten counties from each of the five geographic regions of the state (Northwest, Southwest, South Central, Northeast, and Southeast areas) were randomly selected. Agriculture professionals provided names of families they believed met the screening criteria. From these names, families were randomly selected and contacted by telephone to determine their eligibility, to secure their cooperation, and to generate names and addresses of children in the receiving generation.

One hundred fifty-seven eligible families were contacted. Of these, 113 (72 percent) were unwilling to participate.

Respondents Compared with Nonrespondents

Completed questionnaires were received from 81.9 percent of the parents, 81.3 percent of the children and 75 percent of their spouses. Phone follow-ups were done with nonrespondents to get reasons for nonreturn and responses to a few crucial questions,

including perceived ease of transfer. With phone follow-ups, the response rates were 95.4 percent, 92.8 percent, and 90.2 percent for parents, children, and spouses, respectively.

The most frequent reason given for not returning the questionnaire was "didn't get around to it," followed by low perceived relevance of the questionnaire for self. Daughters-in-law who did not return questionnaires reported significantly more difficulty with the farm transfer decision than did their mail-responding counterparts (F = 2.38; 7,371 d.f.; p .05). In most respects, however, nonrespondents did not differ from respondents in background or in their perceptions of the farm transfer decision.

Sample Description

The analyses are limited to those families where a son who was receiver of the farm was also on the farm. This selection procedure maximizes the homogeneity of the receiving group since fewer females than males were receivers, and receivers who lived off the farm were usually involved in nonfarm occupations as well. The daughters-in-law included in the analyses were married to the sons targeted for analysis and thus were also living on the farm. The analyses are based, then, on 86 fathers, 91 mothers, 89 sons, and 73 daughter-in-law, representing 92 intergenerational families. Each of the five demographic areas of the state was represented in the sample, with each region representing between 15 and 25 percent of the total. If each region were equally represented, its share would have been 20 percent of the total.

The parents were typically about 60 years of age with a high school education or an additional year of college or vocational training. The sons averaged 31 years of age (range 20 to 53) with two and one-half years of education beyond high school. The daughters-in-law averaged 30 years of age (range 18 to 48) and had two to six years of education beyond high school.

The predominant farm structures were "individual ownership" (31 percent) and "corporation" (24 percent). Other structures included "informal partnership" (18 percent), "legal partnership" (12 percent), a "combination of the above" (8 percent), or "other" (8 percent). The average farm size was 1,989 acres (range 130 to 12,000), devoted to pasture and/or crops. Typically, the farm had been in the family for three generations.

Instrumentation

Thirty-five items representing methods of handling stress created by the farm transfer issue were factor analyzed in order to identify statistically independent coping strategies. Relevant items from the McCubbin *et al.* (1981) Family Coping Inventory (FCI) and Pearlin and Schooler's (1978) Occupational Coping Responses were adapted and included in the original pool of 35 items together with additional items specific to the farm transfer experience.

Included in these items was information on membership in farm organizations, attendance at estate-planning workshops, specialization in a particular aspect of the farm operation, involvement in activities off the farm, open discussion of competition between two or more family members, discussion of parents' retirement needs and goals with the children, and parents making it clear to children that their choice of occupation is their own decision. The items adapted from the McCubbin *et al.* (1981) and Pearlin and Schooler (1978) inventories were more general ones, including areas of social support, emotional expression, faith, positive comparison, negotiation, learning new behaviors, ignoring, escape, and isolation. The original 35 items are available upon request from the first author. Respondents checked each item as "not used," "not helpful," "minimally helpful," "moderately helpful," or "very helpful." The factor analysis was based on degree of helpfulness, which could range from one to four. Three hundred and ninety questionnaires from the total sample of farm families, including siblings of the sons targeted for further analysis were used for the factor analysis.

The terminal five-factor orthogonal solution with varimax rotation (see Table 1) revealed the following coping strategies: a Farm Management factor, which includes membership in farm organizations, Discussion, Individual Coping, Use of Professionals, and Expression of Anger. The scales ranged from two to six items, with internal consistencies ranging from 0.65 to 0.78. The items falling within each style together with their factor loadings are listed in Table 1. Personal well being was assessed by the Campbell *et al.* (1976) Index of Well Being. This is a nine-item semantic differential scale composed of

Table 3. Perceived helpfulness of coping strategy by family position in

	Fathers (N = 86)	Mothers (N = 91)	Sons (N = 89)	Daughters-in-laws (N = 73)	Overall x
Farm management	5.51	4.03	5.91	4.39	4.96
Discussion	16.42	17.00	14.84	9.74	14.50
Individual coping	15.21	16.64	14.22	14.75	15.21
Professionals	9.50	9.54	7.76	5.81	8.15
Expression of anger	3.24	3.81	4.98	5.16	4.30

*Scores were weighted, based on number of items in each scale: Farm management (1.0), Discussion (2.0), Individual coping (1.5), Professionals (1.5), Expression of anger (3.0). The reader should note that these are not standard scores and therefore should not be used to compare any one individual's score to group means.

general affect and life satisfaction items with a reported internal consistency of .89 (Campbell et al., 1976:50). This is the scale used by the Institute for Social Research in its series of cross-national studies of adult well being. It distinguishes between employed and unemployed segments of the population and between divorced and married adults (Campbell et al., 1976-51). Campbell and his associates (1976) report a correlation of .26 with their measure of "fears and worries" (p. 58) and .35 with their Index of Personal Competence (p.60).

Perceived ease of making the transfer decision was measured with a single Likert-type item: "How easy was it for you to handle the farm transfer decision?" Responses ranged from "very difficult" to "very easy." The item was significantly correlated with reported life satisfaction (r = .20, p .007) and with satisfaction with farming lifestyle (r = .22, p .003).

Research Questions

The data were analyzed separately for four groups: fathers, mothers, sons who were to receive the farm and were also living on the farm, and their wives. The following research questions were

addressed: (1) Which coping strategies are reported to be most helpful? (2) Which coping strategies are used most? (3) Are there significant differences in use of coping strategy according to family position? (4) Is the use of coping strategies associated with personal well being and perceived ease of making the transfer decision?

Results

Use of Coping Strategy by Family Position

Each item in each coping factor was scored as either "used" or "not used." However, since the number of items per scale ranged from two to six, weighted scores are displayed in Table 2 in order to cancel the effect of unequal number of items per scale.

The two coping strategies reported to be used most were Individual coping and Discussion. This was true regardless of family position. Expression of Anger was the next most frequently used coping strategy among daughters-in-law, while Use of Professionals was the third most frequently used style among fathers and mothers. Farm Management was reported as a coping strategy by more males than by females.

Table 4. Perceived helpfulness of coping strategy by family position in weighted scores*

	Fathers (N = 86)		Mothers (N = 91)		Sons (N = 89)		Daughters-in-law (N = 73)	
	Well being	Perceived ease	Well being	Perceived ease	Well being	Perceived ease	Well being	Perceived ease
Farm management	.03	−.11	.11	−.10	.05	−.15	−.11	.01
Discussion	.23*	−.22	.06	−.14	−.06	−.15	−.11	−.14
Individual coping	−.02	−.14	−.02	−.09	−.07	−.04	−.16	−.15
Professionals	.16	.09	.01	−.24*	−.15	−.21*	−.25*	−.03
Expression of anger	−.20*	−.30**	−.17	−.12	−.35***	−.15	−.29**	−.06

* = Significant at .05 level.
** = Significant at .01 level.
*** = Significant at .001 level.

Scheffe's test (Winer, 1971) of multiple comparisons was used to assess the significance of differences at the .05 level in use of the five coping strategies by the four groups included in the sample. Daughters-in-law reported using Discussion (F = 18.30; 3,327 d.f.; p .01) significantly less than all other family members. Daughters-in-law also consulted Professionals (F = 3.79; 3,319 d.f.; p .01) significantly less than either parent. Mothers reported significantly less use of Farm Management (F = 3.48; 3,310 d.f.; p .05) strategies than did sons, while sons used Expression of Anger (F = 4.41; 3,327 d.f.; p .01) significantly more than their fathers did.

Helpfulness of Coping Strategy by Family Position

As with scores on the use of coping strategies, scores for perceived usefulness were weighted in order to cancel the effect of an unequal number of items per scale. The two styles reported to be most helpful, regardless of family position, were Discussion and Individual Coping. Expression of Anger was reported to be the least helpful coping style, except for daughters-in-law, while Use of Professionals and Farm Management were intermediate in helpfulness (see Table 3).

Mothers reported use of Individual Coping to be significantly more helpful than was true for sons (F = 4.38; 3,327 d.f.; p .01). Fathers, mothers, and sons reported Discussion to be significantly more helpful than did daughters-in-law (F = 21.47; 3,327 d.f.; p .001). Daughters-in-law also found Professionals to be significantly less helpful than either parents (F = 5.73; 3,319 d.f.; p .001). Finally, mothers reported Farm Management strategies to be significantly less helpful than was true for sons (F = 3.61; 3,310 d.f.; p .01).

Relationship of Coping Strategies to Personal Well Being and Ease of Transfer

Table 4 displays correlations between the use of each coping style and the dependent variables of personal well being as measured by the Campbell *et al.* (1976) scale and perceived ease of making the farm transfer decision.

Among fathers, Discussion was significantly related to well being (r = .23, p .05) but was negatively associated with perceived ease (r = -.22, p .05). Also among fathers, Expression of Anger was associated with low levels of well being (r = -.20, p .05) and with reports that the transfer decision was a difficult one (low ease) (r = -.30, p .01).

Among mothers, perceived ease was negatively associated with Use of Professionals (r = -.24, p .05). Use of Professionals was also used by sons when the farm transfer decision was perceived to be difficult (r = -.21, p .05). In addition, sons who used Expression of Anger as a coping strategy were significantly more likely to score low on personal well being (r = -.35, p .001). Daughters-in-law who used Professionals and Expression of Anger as coping strategies were also likely to score lower on personal well being (r = -.25, p .05 and r = -.29, p .01, respectively).

Discussion

In reviewing the frequency and perceived usefulness of each of the five coping strategies identified in this population, it is striking that they are generally ordered in a sequence reflective of the basic values of rural America: self reliance (Individual Coping), family (Discussion), and then community (Professionals). However, sons and daughters-in-law are more likely to use Expression of Anger before using Farm Management strategies or turning to the community for professional consultation. Both members of the younger generation appear to turn to Expression of Anger in the face of limited power vis-a-vis the parent generation.

In this population, the mothers and daughters-in-law present an interesting contrast. If we can apply the results of earlier research to this group of farm families, the women in the older generation may be highly involved in the transfer as "bridges" between father and son (Barnes and Hershon, 1976) and as mediators of conflict (Hedlund and Berkowitz, 1979b). The younger women, who have married into the family more recently, may hold the least involved family positions, and they certainly were the least likely to report themselves as having a "great deal of influence" on the transfer decision (F = 62.24; 3,328 d.f.; p .001). Given their position of low influence, it is not surprising that the daughters-in-law present a profile of coping strategies where use of Individual Coping is primary. As a relative newcomer to the family and possibly even to farming, the daughter-in-law may not be aware of, accepted by, or comfortable with established agricultural support systems. Furthermore, if the daughters-in-law perceive themselves as having less influence on the transfer decision than others, it is not surprising that they are significantly less likely to consult farm professionals or even engage in family discussion around the transfer issue . . . or to find them helpful when these strategies are attempted.

Low influence, however, does not mean low involvement. To whom the farm is transferred, by what means, and the timing of that transfer may be of great importance to the daughter-in-law. While the younger women reported using fewer coping strategies than others and reported some strategies to be less helpful when they were used, both sons and daughters-in-law scored significantly lower than the parent generation on our measure of personal well being (F = 11.81; 3,335 d.f.; p .001).

This suggests that daughters-in-law may occupy an especially vulnerable position; one that is highly stressed, but one with relatively more limited access to or familiarity with coping strategies and social support.

Openness of discussion within the family has been highlighted in the literature as an important predictor of success in making inter-generational farm transfers (e.g., Bratton and Berkowitz, 1976). In our research, the Discussion coping strategy was significantly associated with reports of personal well being for fathers, though *negatively* associated with perceived ease of making the transfer decision. At least two interpretations of these data are possible. First, fathers faced with especially difficult transfer decisions may use Discussion in such a way as to support personal well being when they are under stress. Second, those fathers with high levels of personal well being may be the ones who dare to open up Discussion despite the difficulty of the issue. Either way, it is important to point out that fathers rank Discussion number one in the hierarchy of helpfulness of coping strategies. Furthermore, while others rank family Discussion high in helpfulness, fathers are the only ones for whom this coping strategy is significantly associated with personal well being.

It appears from these data that use of the five coping strategies by other family members reveals more about their stress than about their well being. Mothers who seek Professionals are low on perceived ease. Among sons, consultation with Professionals is also significantly negatively associated with ease of the transfer decision. The more difficult the transfer, the more they consult. However, these efforts are only reported to be moderately helpful, ranking below the helpfulness of family

Discussion and Individual Coping. Those sons who report Expression of Anger as a coping strategy are significantly more likely to report low levels of perceived personal well being, and this coping strategy appears at the bottom of the list so far as helpfulness is concerned. Daughters-in-law with low levels of perceived well being are significantly more likely to use Expression of Anger and consultation with Professionals as coping strategies, both of which are ranked midway in their list of strategy helpfulness.

In sum, the receiving generation appears to be more stressed than the parent generation, probably because they have less control in the situation and are less well supplied with helpful coping strategies. This is particularly true of daughters-in-law. It is somewhat surprising that distancing through nonfarm involvement was not identified as a coping strategy among these families. This may be because of the strong emotional tie family members feel to the land. A pattern of expressing anger was used by some, though it was generally one of the least helpful of the strategies respondents reported using. Following the thinking of Rosenblatt and Anderson (1981), one might speculate that if family members were to use distancing through nonfarm involvement, they might use Expression of Anger less often as a coping strategy and perhaps would experience less stress and perceive greater personal well being.

Implications

The findings of this study would appear to be particularly helpful to persons attempting to aid farm families through this stressful transition period. Interventions that would encourage families to engage in open discussion between both generations (particularly the daughter-in-law) might be useful. This type of approach might help the receiving generation to feel that they have some control over the situation, ease the stress level, and contribute to their overall feelings of well being. Within the donor generation, the wife might be the most likely person to serve a "bridging" function by suggesting that the family discuss the intergenerational transfer as a complete unit, excluding no one. Another approach to helping families through this transition period might include an attempt to strengthen the coping styles of the individual family members. Family members who are able to deal with their own stress may be able to assist each other through the stressful period and avoid the "pile up" of stressors within the family.

Professionals such as attorneys, farm management organizations, and estate planners need to be aware that critical psychosocial transitions are occurring within the farm family at the same time that economic transitions are occurring within the farm business. One approach that is commonly used from a business standpoint to reduce the uncertainty of the intergenerational transfer is incorporation. Salamon and Markan (1984), however, have suggested that incorporation may succeed in reducing the amount of role ambiguity in the farm family but may also be a tool to exploit or enforce authority over the younger generation and thereby increase their stress level. In our sample, sons involved in corporations and partnerships are somewhat more likely to perceive the transfer decision as difficult than those involved in individual ownership (X = .88; 2 d.f.; p .06). This relationship just misses the traditional .05 alpha level but supports Salamon and Markan's position and is worth investigating in future research.

Psychologists and family therapists working with farm families need to be sensitive to the unique implications of the joint business-family nature of the family farm and the stress that is created as a result, particularly around the intergenerational farm transfer issue. Future research needs to focus specifically on successful intervention strategies for working with families who are experiencing difficulty with intergenerational transfer decisions.

References

Barnes, L.B., and S. A. Hershon, 1976, "Transferring Power in the Family Business." *Harvard Business Review*, 54 (July-August): 105-14.

Berkowitz, A. D., and H. W. Perkins, 1984, "Stress Among Farm Women: Work and Family as Interacting Systems." *Journal of Marriage and the Family*, 46 (February): 161-66.

Boss, P.G., H. I. McCubbin, and G. Lester, 1979, "The Corporate Executive Wife's Coping Patterns in Response to Routine Husband-Father Absence." *Family Process* 18 (March): 79-86.

Bratton, C. A., and A., D. Berkowitz, 1976, "International Transfer of the Farm Business." *New York's Food and Life Sciences Quarterly* 9 (April-June): 7-9.

Campbell, A., P.E. Converse, and W. L. Rodgers, 1976, *The Quality of American Life*. New York: Russell Sage Foundation.

Cobb, S., 1976, "Social Support as a Moderator of Life Stress." *Psychosomatic Medicine*, 38 (September-October):300-14.

Hedlund, D., and A. Berkowitz, 1979a, "Farm Family Research in Perspective: 1965-1977." Ithaca, New York: Cornell

University Agricultural Experiment Station, *Rural Sociology Bulletin 79*.

Hedlund, D., and A. Berkowitz, 1979b, "The Incidence of Social-Psychological Stress in Farm Families." *International Journal of Sociology of the Family*, 9 (July-December): 233-43.

Hill, R., 1949, Families Under Stress. New York: Harper and Row.

Hill, R., and C. Joy, 1979, "Conceptualizing and Operationalizing Category Systems for Phasing of Family Development." Unpublished Manuscript, University of Minnesota.

Kohl. S. B., 1976, *Working Together: Women and Family in Southwestern Saskatchewan*. Toronto: Holt, Rinehart and Winston of Canada.

McCubbin, H.I., 1979, "Integrating Coping Behavior in Family Stress Theory." *Journal of Marriage and the Family* 41 (May): 237-44.

McCubbin, H., and G. Lester, 1977, "Family Adaptability: Coping Behaviors in the Management of the Dual Stressors of Family Separation and Reunion." Paper Presented at the Military Family Research Conference, San Diego, California.

McCubbin, H., B. Dahl, G. Lester, D. Benson, and M. Robertson, 1976, "Coping Repertoires of Families Adapting to Prolonged War-Induced Separations." *Journal of Marriage and the Family*, 38 (August): 461-71.

McCubbin, H., C. Joy, A. Cauble, J. Comeau, J. Patterson, and R. Needle, 1980, "Family Stress and Coping: A Decade Review." *Journal of Marriage and the Family*, 42 (November): 855-71.

McCubbin, H. I., R. S. Nevin, A. E. Cauble, A. Larson, J. K. Comeau, and J. M. Patterson, 1982, "Families Coping with Chronic Illness: The Case of Cerebral Palsy." Pp. 169-88 in H. I. McCubbin, A. E. Cauble, and J. M. Patterson (eds.), *Family Stress, Coping, and Social Support*. Springfield, Illinois: Charles C. Thomas.

McCubbin, H., and J. Patterson with A. E. Cauble, A. Larsen, J. K. Comeau, and D. A. Skinner, 1981, "Systematic Assessment of Family Stress, Resources and Coping: Tools for Research, Education, and Clinical Intervention." St. Paul, Minnesota: University of Minnesota, Department of Family Social Science.

Pearlin, L., and S. Schooler, 1978, "The Structure of Coping." *Journal of Health and Social Behavior*, 19 (1): 2-21.

Rosenblatt, P., and R. Anderson, 1981, Interaction in Farm Families: Tension and Stress." Pp. 147-65 in R. Coward and W. Smith, Jr., (eds.), *The Family in Rural Society*. Boulder, Colorado: Westview Press.

Rosenblatt, P. D., and L. O. Keller, 1983, "Economic Vulnerability of Significant Attributes of Farming to Family Interaction." *International Journal of Sociology of the Family* 8 (January-June): 89-99.

Salamon, S., and K. K. Markan, 1984, "Incorporation and the Family Farm." *Journal of Marriage and the Family*, 46 (February): 167-78.

Titus, S., P. Rosenblatt, and R. Anderson, 1979, "Family Conflict Over Inheritance of Property." *The Family Coordinator*, 2 (July): 337-46.

Winer, J. B., 1971, *Statistical Principles in Experimental Design*. New York: McGraw-Hill.

Introduction

Addictive behavior, no matter the substance, is often embedded in the family. It is rare for substance abuse to appear in only one member of a family or in one generation. This reality, combined with the destructiveness of drug abuse on any business, calls attention to the compounded effects of drug abuse in family firms. David Bork suggests that families must support those seeking to overcome their addictive behavior.

Drug Abuse in the Family Business
1986

By David Bork

Reprinted by permission of **Nation's Business**, December 1986. Copyright ©1986 U.S. Chamber of Commerce; all rights reserved.

Drug abuse in any business is destructive and complicated, but in a family business, it is even more devastating. Alcohol and other drugs can be a family's biggest competitor for profits and business longevity. And the problem is compounded because of the close personal relationships and the perceived stigma of admitting a problem within the family's ranks.

The Beser family owned a chain of specialty retail shops. Richard Beser resented his "take-charge" brother, Edward, and retaliated by becoming drunk at all family functions. When Edward was chosen as the father's successor in the business, it was the final blow to Richard's ego, and he moved his family to another state. His father, depressed about the break in the family, had a stroke.

The family members blamed Richard and cut off communication with him. Further, he was denied revenues from the company, both by his father's will and by his brother. Soon after, Richard died in an auto accident, but his wife and other family members were never certain he had not committed suicide.

Charles Harwood indulged in both alcohol and marijuana as a college student. When he joined his father's manufacturing firm, his drinking problem became increasingly severe.

But Harwood's father ignored the obvious symptoms and never referred to them. Louis Harwood had always used alcohol as a relaxant and as a business-social tool. He had many three-martini lunches and sometimes imbibed heavily after hours. If he occasionally took a day off to "rest," no one regarded it as a recuperative period from anything except overwork.

401

The names and businesses here are fictitious, but they are based on cases that are very real: As the Harwood case suggests, addictive behavior, no matter the substance, is often embedded in the family. It is rare for substance abuse to appear in only one member of a family.

Often family members tend unwittingly to keep an addicted family member in a dependent position, to infantilize him, to see him as weak and to encourage him to escape frustrations rather than overcome them. In this way, families act in collusion to perpetuate substance use. This collusion may take the form of only token concern with alcoholism or even active support of the drinking behavior.

As damaging as the addiction problem may be, recovery may present a threat to other family members, friends and associates. Focus must be placed on the entire social system that supports and derives rewards from the addictive behavior. Treatment is often based on "unlearning" destructive behavior and altering patterns that reinforce the addiction. Within the family, such change involves major shifts in power allocation and reward systems and demands new forms of communication.

The recovering "problem carrier" may want to reoccupy the powerful, influential roles that are now occupied by others. If Richard Beser had not been an alcoholic, he might have been a serious contender for the succession — and thus a threat to his brother's position.

Had Louis Harwood admitted his son's drinking problem, he would have had to examine his own drinking patterns. Thus, others in a family may even encourage the addiction in order to ensure the status quo.

Some families are able to face what must be done, however.

Foster Ellison, his wife and two other partners ran a rapidly expanding telecommunications business. Ellison's college reputation as a heavy, but not problem, drinker followed him into business, where major sales agreements were negotiated in the warmth of good restaurants and mellow wines. Long periods of work and growing conflicts among the partners resulted in a serious attack of hypertension for Ellison.

His wife dealt with the disability by increasing his life insurance — not by insisting that he alter his lifestyle. Startled by this pragmatic attitude, Ellison sought medical advice, which included a rigid diet, shorter work hours, and an end to both smoking and drinking.

Three brothers — Johnny, Pat, and Sam Moser — continued the "booze and build" tradition of their hard-working father and grandfather when they joined the family construction business. They added two new substances, cocaine and marijuana. When Pat began to make major, costly mistakes, Johnny and Sam discovered he had a drug problem that siphoned off more than they "allowed" for drug and alcohol use.

One day Johnny was almost killed in a job-related accident. He was hospitalized for several months, which forcibly dried him out and gave him a long time to think. He resolved to stop drinking, and his decision to stop led Pat and Sam to do the same.

The one thing that kept the brothers on their new path was the support they gave each other. None wanted to see the other two fail. All went into treatment, and they encouraged employees with addiction problems to do so, even paying for their treatment when necessary.

Several years later, the Moser business was not only clean of abusive substances but headed toward its highest profits ever.

Families need to support those who seek to untangle themselves from addictive behavior. In the end, a family in business needs to ask itself if what it has built is in danger of being destroyed by substance abuse.

Introduction

Presented originally as a Distinguished Psychiatrist Lecture at the 1980 annual meeting of the American Psychiatric Association, this article discusses the existence and impact of "family paradigms." A "family paradigm" is the set of core assumptions, convictions or beliefs that a family holds about its environment and which shape its members' experience and perception. Reiss maintains that a family's health depends on conserving its paradigm . While family paradigms can persist across generations, they can break down at times of great family stress. At such times families will evolve new rules and more explicitly deal with family members. Such circumstances represent a crossroads where the family can move toward disintegration or where the family is opened to outside influences which can help the family to heal and revitalize itself.

The Working Family: A Researcher's View of Health in the Household

1982

By David Reiss, M.D.

Reprinted by permission of **American Journal of Psychiatry**, November 1982, 139:11, pp.1412-1420. Copyright © 1982 American Psychiatric Association; all rights reserved.

A brief description of two families will help me begin my discussion of the working family.

The first family is the Ingalls, immortalized in an autobiographical series by one of its children, Laura[1]. In the family was a father who was known simply as "Pa." He was a Jack-of-all-trades. There were also Ma, endlessly resourceful, and three mischievous daughters, Mary, Laura, and Carrie. The Ingalls were part of the great migration that moved westward after the passage of the Homestead Act. Pa was restless and always searching for uncharted roads and open spaces. Indeed, the dominant theme in the life of this family was their isolation from others and the inner strength they summoned during crisis after crisis as they moved from Wisconsin, to Kansas, to Minnesota, and finally to the Dakota Territory. One move was to a one-room dugout home on the banks of Plum Creek in Minnesota. The Ingalls would be living underground in a strange and dark room dug out of a small hill. Alongside was the swirling and treacherous Plum Creek. Laura described how the family turned their shared exploration of this new territory into a game.

Ma was the first to show uneasiness about the family's new home. In

404

response, Laura and Pa—with much enjoyment in the task and each other—went off to cut a few willow branches for what was to be, temporarily, a bed. This bed was clearly more symbolic than real. In the following days it was the creek that had to be explored. It had deep spots and rapids in which adults, let alone small children, could easily drown. To master this, the parents took their three girls swimming in a safe spot, but near the rapids. As each child swam out a bit too far, Pa played at dunking her and—through laughter—made clear the consequences of carelessness. While the family remained on its banks, Plum Creek became transformed into a respected and cherished core of its daily life.

The second family lived in my neighborhood when I was a boy. I will call them the Ivanovs. The family consisted of a husband—a businessman—a wife, who taught piano, and her maiden sister, who edited children's books. They were all in their 70's when I knew them as a child. They had been members of the minor Russian nobility and had fled their homeland during the revolution. They lived in an aging apartment building whose corridors were garishly lit by unshielded fluorescent lights. I remember how immediately different things seemed as soon as I entered their apartment. Everything was dark and heavy. The windows were all but covered by red satin drapes brought from Russia. Ornately colored glass lamps, also from Russia, were in every corner. The walls were covered by dark, embroidered Russian fabric. Pictures of Russian composers were hung everywhere. Because I was young and because I was interested in music I was one of the few neighbors who regularly was allowed into this dark museum of Russian history. The talk between the three old people was often of music and sometimes of Russia. Interspersed were politely contemptuous complaints about their present circumstances: the dirty building, the noisy streets, or the city crowds.

There are many ways to contrast and compare these two families. Research conducted by my colleagues and me during the last 16 years has led me to focus on one approach in particular. Both families found themselves in an ambiguous and uncertain situation. The Ingalls were alone on a vast prairie and the Ivanovs were in a country and city that seemed enduringly strange and disordered in comparison with their memory of prerevolutionary Russia. Both families were alike in sensing some potential danger of difficulty in the ambiguous setting. Where they differed most strikingly was in the hidden potentials or possibilities they sensed in their immediate world. The Ingalls grasped the possibility of mastery through learning by direct experience. Thus, the children were directly exposed to the hazards of Plum Creek as a way of mastering them. The Ivanovs' preoccupation was with the past. The potential in their environment was the possibility of its connection to their past. Their love of music—particularly the darkly sentimental Romantic music of Russia and Eastern Europe at the turn of the century—pervaded their life. Also, they sought out emigres with a history similar to their own. Their American friends were picked with an eye toward status; they were picked, as I remember, because in some way they were members of an American nobility of some sort or they had the breeding to appreciate and recognize nobility when they saw it.

Both families had an unshakable set of assumptions about the fundamental nature of the social and physical world beneath these images of the environment. The Ingalls believed the world operated according to principles that they could discover through ingenuity and direct experience. No matter how many misfortunes befell them, and there were many, they seemed to draw something from them. They were able to take on new challenges in the belief they had learned something about the world and themselves. For the Ivanovs the world did not have the same fascination and discoverability. Rather, their world was organized with reference to their own history. These two views or beliefs were not, I think, modifiable by experience. Indeed, they shaped, for each family, what experience was sought. For the Ingalls their central beliefs set their focus on their habitat and what it offered for survival and satisfaction. For the Ivanovs their core beliefs heightened their sensitivity to the events and people that connected the present to their own past.

I have found in the work of T. S. Kuhn a useful metaphor for characterizing these underlying beliefs of family life: I refer to them as *family paradigms*. Briefly a family paradigm is a set of core assumptions, convictions, or beliefs each family holds about its environment; these assumptions guide the family to sample certain segments of its world and ignore others. The evidence I and others have collected so far suggests that the life of each family is organized by an enduring paradigm which emerges in the course of family development. As I will describe later in this paper, I believe that family paradigms can undergo profound alteration at times of severe family disorganization but otherwise persist for years and even for several generations. They are difficult to assess directly. They are manifest, however, in the fleeting fantasies and expectations shared by all members of the family and, even more important, in the routine action patterns of their daily lives.

Further, I believe that whatever arguments and tension pervade the family, all members agree on the fundamental family paradigm. In the Ingalls — as in many families of the Great Plains — there was often tension about moving on or staying put. Pa appeared to be the restless one, wanting always to move on to the next wilderness. Ma was more conservative, or so it appeared. She wanted the comfort of staying put. Recall her insistence on a symbolic bed on her first night in the dugout. But the difference in the Ingalls family — as in many families — was more apparent then real. All members longed for the past, for stability (recall the pleasure with which Laura and Pa fetched the willows, supposedly just for Ma's benefit). All members also longed for the adventure and excitement of discovery and exploration.

The concept of family paradigm will be my point of departure for discussing the working family; what characterizes its health and its disorder. I hope to show that the concept of paradigm permits us to recognize a wide variety of healthy working families; it also helps us to conceptualize some forms, at least, of family disorder and — perhaps more important — may alert us to important self-healing powers within the family, ways in which the family — without our professional intervention — may right itself at times of crisis.

Some Evidence for the Family Paradigm

The keystone of our group's research program on the family paradigm has been the laboratory study of family problem solving, where we have developed a large set of new techniques. Conceptually, however, our work build on a foundation laid by several others, particularly Kluckhohn and Strodtbeck[2], Bion[3], Hess and Handel,[4] and Wynne and associates[5].

A core hypothesis of our work is that a family's paradigm becomes clearly manifest in a special type of family problem-solving task. One task we have used in many studies requires the family members to sit separately in booths. Their individual task is to sort a deck of cards that have series of letters on them into piles. Many families recognize that the cards can be grouped together according to the sequential pattern of the letters. For example, PMSMSVK can be grouped with PMSMSMSMSVK, and PMSFK can be grouped with PMSSSSSFK. In some phases of the task they can talk with one another on a telephone-like-hookup; in others they work alone.

Virtually every family in our testing situation is at first, puzzled. Our description of the study—its aims and procedures—as well as the laboratory instructions are clear enough. But every family seems to ask us, in its own way, "Why are you doing this to us? What do these games really tell you about our family?" At the core, our subject families face the same central interpretive challenge as did the Ingalls and the Ivanovs: What are the hidden potentials and possibilities in this strange situation? During all the years we have used procedures of this kind, it has been our impression that a family's approach to solving puzzles of this kind depends heavily on its own interpretation of what we, as a research staff, are really up to. No matter what we tell our families, they make their own determination and then seem to listen to only those parts of the explicit experimental instructions which fit with this determination. Some families, of course, believe what we tell them and follow our

experimental instructions to the T. But this also is an active, interpretive process on their part. They have determined we can be trusted, whether or not we actually deserve such trust. The most crucial point here is that I believe we can infer, with great precision, a family's view of us by objective and quantitative measures of their problem-solving performance.

Families' performances in the card-sorting procedure differ along three distinct dimensions. A family high on *configuration* shows distinct improvement from the first phase of the task, when members work alone, to the second phase, when they work together. In other words, their work together helps them see patterns and organization in the cards that they could not recognize as individuals. At the other extreme are low-configuration families where members' performance deteriorates from the initial, individual phase to the second, family phase. In these families, joint work interferes with members' capacity to recognize patterns; family interaction blurs or obscures the organization inherent in the cards. It is likely that the Ingalls family would have shown high-configuration performance and the Ivanovs low-configuration performance. Our hypothesis is that high-configuration families are not simply more skillful at problem solving that are low-configuration families. Rather, high-configuration families see the problem as soluble from the very start. Low-configuration families feel we have given them an insoluble problem. I will return to this hypothesis later.

A second way in which families differ is the degree to which the efforts of each individual member are integrated into a common strategy during the part of the task when the family works together. We call this dimension *coordination*.

Members in high-coordination families are careful to pay attention to what the others are doing. There is often much discussion, serious attempts to reconcile differing views, and – as a consequence – each member's actual solution is similar or identical to that of other members in his family. In contrast, in low-coordination families, there is little integration of each member's efforts. At the extreme, they hardly talk to each other and each member seems unaware of what the others are thinking or doing. It is likely that the Ingalls and Ivanovs would have shown high coordination, but for very different reasons. The Ingalls felt that mastery comes through cooperative use of their own family's inner resources. The Ivanovs felt the past can be kept alive through shared reminiscence.

In the card-sorting procedure, families differ in yet a third way we call *closure*. Some families pick a solution early in the family portion of the task and stick with it through thick or thin. Other families seem willing to change their system in the light of new data. We have hypothesized that early-closure families attach priority to their own traditions and past, very much like the Ivanovs. In effect, the world is divided into categories shaped by the family's immersion in its own history. Delayed-closure families see each experience as novel and unrelated to them and their past. They search for what is unique in each new setting. We might be tempted to regard the Ingalls as a delayed-closure family, but the family's need for a familiar piece of furniture gives a hint of the important though subordinate role of tradition in that family.

Thus, in our most-used problem-solving setting, three dimensions distinguish family performance; configuration, coordination, and closure. We have

found, in a large number of clinical and nonclinical samples, that these dimensions are uncorrelated.[6, 7] Thus a family can be high on any one and low or high on the other two. I am proposing that these three dimensions assess characteristics of the family's underlying paradigm: a set of fundamental assumptions each family holds about the world which guide its understanding of action in that world. I will summarize some lines of research my colleagues and I have pursued during the last decade that support this proposal.

First, we have asked a rather limited question. Does a family's problem-solving performance really reflect its approach to interpreting its experiential world? Perhaps problem-solving performance reflects such mundane variables as intelligence, problem-solving skills, or social class, or more interesting – though tangential – variables such as the perceptual style or personality traits of individual members. In a long series of detailed studies, Sheriff, Salzman, Oliveri, Costell, and I[8-14] could find no evidence that variables of this kind influenced a family's performance on the card-sorting task. (Data on perceptual style and personality traits are, as yet, unpublished.) We therefore turned to more direct tests of the relationship of family problem solving to the family's approach to interpreting its experiential world.

To date we have complete three studies. In one, Oliveri and I asked family groups to place a series of small felt figures – a family of two parents and two children, two strangers, and some geometric forms – on a large felt board.[15] Previous data for individuals and families had suggested this technique as a useful probe of subjects' experience of themselves in relation to the outside world. [16-20] We compared our families' performance on the card-sorting task with their performance on the figure-placement procedure.

As anticipated, high-configuration families showed evidence of feelings of comfort and mastery in relationship to the outside world. For example, they were apt to bring strangers close to the family or to include them within their midst. Low-configuration families not only kept strangers at a distance but arranged the family figures in conventional arrangements. These arrangements suggested that low-configuration families were having difficultly responding to familiar aspects of their environment as well as portraying novel aspects of themselves. Also as anticipated, delayed-closure families showed evidence of being intrigued and engaged in the unique and novel aspects of their outside world. For example, these families, in contrast to early-closure families, frequently included the inanimate objects within the family, often inventively arranging them into toys or furnishings.

My associates and I[21] worked on a second direct assessment of the relationship between a family's problem-solving style and how it views its world. We studied families who were members of a multiple-family group that met for an hour weekly as part of an inpatient adolescent treatment program. We were interested in how our subject families perceived and understood the other families in the group and, more particularly, whether we could predict how one family perceived another from its performance on our card sort. Our measurement procedure required the family to sort and talk about photographs of other family members in the group. We asked them to pick the families they knew the best, pick the members of each of these families who were most like one

another, and pick one adjective or descriptor that best described this similarity. We were able to measure quite precisely, for each family tested, how attentive to each other they were in discussing and elaborating their image of each of the other families.

As anticipated, members in high-coordination families showed a great deal of attentiveness of this kind. More particularly, this procedure allowed us to measure how the family evolved and organized a system or set of concepts for judging and understanding other families. If a family has a coherent and organized set of ideas about other families, then it is capable of making fine discriminations between families, relating one family to another and developing explanations, for itself, about how other families operate. A well-developed conceptual framework, then, reflects a sensitive engagement by the subject family in the observation and understanding of other families. As expected, high-configuration families showed the more complex and developed conceptual framework, whereas low-configuration families had no such system.

In a third study, my associates and used a Q-sort procedure to measure how families perceived or experienced the ward setting of an adolescent inpatient treatment program to which one of their children had been admitted.[12] Here again we found our card sort could predict how a family experienced an important segment of its social world. High-configuration families, for example, developed subtle and sophisticated images of the ward setting, images that were similar to their images of other families.

The data we have presented support the notion that our problem-solving procedures do measure the family's more general orientation toward and sensitivity to its social world—its paradigm. We can now ask a more pertinent question: How does our measurement and understanding of the family paradigm help us to think about and assess health in the working family? I believe that one contribution of the paradigm concept to the discussion of family health is that it refers to an underlying structure that shapes or modulates a variety of more surface family behaviors. I believe this structure can, in the short term, shape or modulate a family's responses to the stresses of daily living, as it did for the Ingalls in their dugout. It can also, in the longer term, determine the family's ties and relationships with its social community: its kin and neighborhood as well as institutions such as schools, hospitals, and places of employment. Thus, a variety of surface manifestations of family health or disorder might be explained parsimoniously by a strength or weakness in this central organizing structure. We must ask, however, whether there is any evidence that the family paradigm does exert this kind of control over family affairs.

My associates and I[21] recently completed two studies exploring this question. In the first, Oliveri and I asked each member of our subject families to name members of their extended family who were important to them in some way. [22] We were interested in three aspects of these relationships. First, we were interested in the number of family members our subject families listed as important to them. We reasoned that families who felt a large number of members were important were opening themselves up to diversity of experience. Thus, we expected delayed-closure families to score high here. The results confirmed this expectation.

Second, we were interested in relationships between those members of the extended family which our subjects selected as important to them. Almost all families picked members from both the maternal and paternal wings. We had a particular interest in whether there were relationships between the members selected from each wing. If so, the selected extended family would function as a large, unified social world—just the kind that we would expect our high-coordination families to shape and encourage. But highly connected superfamilies, as the work of Bott[23] and others[24] has shown, can exert strong influence and control on the nuclear families that are their members. This would be particularly true if every member of the nuclear family felt tied to the same subset of relatives in the superfamily. Because low-configuration families feel controlled and shaped by forces outside themselves, we would expect them to form just this kind of shared relationship with a tightly knit superfamily. Indeed, we found that members in high-coordination families selected interconnected family networks and members in low-configuration families jointly selected the same members of this superfamily.

This study, however, has several important limitations. First, it is a study of preferences of families for important segments of their social community. It is not a direct assessment of their actual interaction with that community. Second, we studied our subject families' problem-solving styles and their extended family relationships at a single point in time, long after these relationships had formed. Therefore, we cannot know whether a family's problem-solving style preceded and, quite possibly, caused its pattern of extended family relationships, or whether the reverse was true. In order to deal with these two difficulties, Costell and I designed a study in which we could directly observe the development of our subject families' relationships with a broader social community and predict this development by assessing the families' problem-solving style *before* those relationships developed.[11] As in the family-perception procedure, we measured each family's connection to the multiple-family group. Several findings suggested that the family's paradigm directly, shaped this relationship. For example, high-coordination families become engaged in the group; this was indicated by their interaction patterns and the feelings other families had about them. This pattern is similar to the high-coordination families' reports of their relationships with extended families. In addition, families with low scores on both configuration and coordination, indicating they felt pessimistic about their power to accomplish anything as a group, were the least engaged in the group and at greatest risk for dropping out altogether.

Conservation and Collapse of the Family Paradigm

I suggest that a family's health depends on the conservation of its paradigm. Family disorder occurs when the paradigm collapses. We can understand health and illness in family life by exploring mechanisms that conserve the family paradigm and those stresses which disrupt these conserving mechanisms. My basic hypothesis here is that certain ordinary and routine family interaction behavior serves a special conservative function and that any stress which interrupts these critical family routines can bring on collapse of the paradigm and serious family disorder. (A more detailed account of the theory of family paradigm and of the family mechanisms that conserve it over time has been published elsewhere[25].)

The work of Steinglass,[26] Bossard and Boll,[27] Wolin and associates,[28, 29] Kantor and Lehr,[30] Howell,[31] and Bermann[32] suggests that there are two types of family routine which conserve the family paradigm. The first type may be called *pattern regulators*. These are a series of highly routinized behavior patterns in every family which have two primary functions. First, they regulate space: the spatial relationships between the family and the outside world and within the family itself. We have seen evidence of these in the Ivanovs: the care with which they patrolled their own boundaries and kept themselves relatively distant from their workaday world. In contrast, the patterns of playful exploration in the Ingalls engaged the family fully in their immediate world. These pattern regulators perpetuated shared feelings of mastery or, in our term, the high configuration of their paradigm. A second function of pattern regulators is to control the family's experience of time. Once again, the Ivanovs had a number of highly repetitive patterns that served to establish their overriding ties to their own past. Recall, for example, their finicky selection of friends and their conversations always toned by complaints about the shabbiness of their present world. In our terms, these pattern regulators conserved the early-closure character of their paradigm. In all families, these highly routinized patterns occur on a daily basis and are so familiar that the families are usually unaware of the patterns. Further, the patterns need not be engaged in by all family members simultaneously.

In sharp contrast are another group of family behaviors we have called *ceremonials*. These are usually episodic and engaged in by most or all of the family together. Not only is the family explicitly conscious of these patterns but also the patterns are often so engrossing as to, for the moment, blot out everything else from awareness. Moreover, in contrast to pattern regulators, they are deeply symbolic — almost every gesture carries some special meaning for the family. These ceremonials often endure for years and may even span several generations. For example, Ma Ingalls — like her mother before her — carefully saved buttons. As a special treat the buttons would be brought out from their careful storage place and placed on a thread to make a "button-string," a special present for very important occasions such as Christmas. The whole family engaged with intense delight in this ceremony, which jointly expressed the family's ties to their past and their own sense of themselves as a group carefully conserving their most precious resources for special moments when they matter the most. It was clearly this characteristic of the Ingalls which helped them face with optimism the enormous trials of life on the Great Plains.

Ceremonials preserve what Wolin and associates called the *family identity* — its central and shared concepts of itself as a group. For example, in the O'Hara family the father and three sons, for more than 30 years, would briefly arm-wrestle as a ceremonial form of greeting when any of the four returned home after a prolonged absence. Mother, taking a background position, would somewhat cautiously applaud the mock combat. This ceremonial consecrated the tough, adventuresome image of itself the family wished to maintain. Indeed, father's father had been among the first to strike oil in Pennsylvania after years of frustrating failure, and father himself had been a daring, muck-raking journalist in the deep South. The ceremonial also gently denigrated mother by making her a passive and peripheral audience. In fact, the family wished to exclude from its identity the long history of depression and suicide in mother's family.

I am proposing that pattern regulators and ceremonials play complementary roles in conserving the family's paradigm. Ceremonials consecrate some aspects of the family's past and denigrate others to shape a family's sense of itself. Pattern regulators, in subliminal fashion, convert this subjective identity into the family's shared conviction in the reality of this vision of the outside world. If this is true, then it follows that a major disruption in either or both will constitute a major family stress and place the family's paradigm in jeopardy. Briefly, a broad variety of stressor events can severely alter or curtail the family's ordinary patterns of behavior. In broad terms, these events can be divided as external or internal to the family. External events include those which impinge simultaneously on a large community of families, such as natural disasters and economic crises, and those which strike individual families, such as serious physical illness. Internal events also may be divided into two categories: those which arise in the course of ordinary family development — such as the birth of a child, children leaving the family for school or marriage, retirement, or death of older members — and those which are not expected in normal family development — such as marital crises and psychiatric disturbances in individual family members.

It is possible to represent a range of a family's response to stresses of this kind as a series of stages. In each stage the family attempts to restore the ordinary routines of its daily life and with such restoration to strengthen the integrating function of its paradigm. However, if these efforts cannot succeed, the family is in danger of going on to a more serious stage of disorder. I will talk about the collapse of a family paradigm very schematically, as if it occurred in three delineated stages. However, this is a vastly oversimplified scaffolding for more detailed theoretical and empirical work. Informed, in particular, by the work of Kantor and Lehr,[30] I refer to these stages as *the emergence of rules,. the explicit family,* and *rebellion and action.*

The Emergence of Rules

We have defined a family stress or event as one that has a profound impact on the routines of daily living in the family—particularly the ceremonials and pattern regulators. Although the nature of the event may vary—from death of a member to the family's traveling in a strange country—the family's initial responses to the stress have a single central feature. The family must, in some explicit way, rearrange its ordinary patterns of action to accommodate the new event. In some families these rearrangements are explicit and carefully designed. In other families they are haphazard or implicit and partially concealed. In either case, these rearrangements burden each family member with additional imperatives or requirements; therefore, following Ford and Herrick (unpublished 1972 paper), we refer to them as rules.

All rules developed when a family is in an early stage of crisis probably have two objectives: adaptation and constraint. Rules can permit a family to come to grips with the stress. Consider, for example, the James family. It consists of two parents, a daughter, Marilyn, age 16, and a son, age 10. When they were traveling in a foreign country, where only the daughter knew the language, they developed a simple rule: "Each time we deal with an official,

Marilyn must be with us." This simple rule allowed the family to adapt to an unfamiliar and potentially difficult situation.

A rule of a different quality was formulated in the Michaels family. This was a well-do-do family consisting of a father, mother, father's mother, and two boys 9 and 11 years old. The father was killed in an automobile crash. After the period of acute grief, several rules began to emerge. The first was motivated by the family's heightened fear that yet another member would be killed in some sort of accident. "Neither child is allowed to go out of the house unless accompanied by an adult."

Under optimum circumstances family ceremonials and pattern regulators give the family a lively, vivid, and meaningful sense of their world, although, as we have seen, this shared experience can be radically different from one family to another. When these fundamental family routines are altered, the family is decentered: it begins to focus more on its own processes as objects of regard than on the world in which it lives. When Marilyn's family was at home, in a familiar neighborhood and country, all members engaged equally in every aspect of their community. The basic style of the family was shared exploration of the many facets of their own country. When abroad, this typical pattern was partially blocked by a language barrier, but the family provided a rule that accorded special status to Marilyn; this rule served as an ad hoc strut until the stress was over.

In the Michaels family, the father had been an enormously successful businessman and was able to place his family in the highest stratum of society in a large, cosmopolitan city. To affirm their sense of removal from the ordinary strain of city living, the family purchased a penthouse apartment, reached by special elevator, on top of one of the city's tallest buildings. Father's death threatened to destroy the family's position of privilege. The first rule—still directed at keeping the family aloof from the stresses of city living (danger to the children in this case)—was an understandable outgrowth of the family's patrician outlook. Nonetheless, it involved a decentering away from the family's Olympian conception of the city beneath them to a preoccupation with itself: the adults were preoccupied with the potentially dangerous behavior of the children and the children with the constraining behavior of the adults.

The Explicit Family

Marilyn's family developed one or two more explicit rules to guide them in their travels, but, as might be expected, these disappeared on their return home. Their temporary, problem-solving qualities were fully apparent. In the Michaels family the case was different. The recovery of both adults from their grief was slow. Aside from tension between them they remained depressed or, more accurately, drained and without energy. A second rule was soon developed: "Everyone in the house should make his or her own breakfast." So far these two rules were not in conflict. However, as the days wore on the second was generalized to another one: "The children should not make demands on the adults for anything." Here the potential conflict became serious. If a child was not to go out alone but also could not make a demand on an adult, then a child could go out only if the adult initiated the idea. This meant that the children were even further constrained and the adults, implicitly or explicitly, had to monitor the children or feel burdened by their more incessant requests. From a series of

simple rules—rules that began to become stringent and internally inconsistent—emerged a fabric of constraints and burdens nobody in the family wanted and no one felt responsible for. It became a daily occurrence for each individual to feel the family was a burden and for no one to recognize his or her role in creating that burden. Each person felt the family as external, as pressing down from outside. This was clearly a reversal of a family functioning under the guidance of a coherent paradigm. When the paradigm is coherent, the family's processes are in the background, shaping—in ineffable and subliminal ways—the family's meaningful sense of location in an experiential world. At this level of disorganization the family has become an explicit, bounded thing external to all its individuals.

Just as the stage of family rules provides an opportunity for family reorganization and self-healing, so does the state of the explicit family. The emergence of rules can, as it did with Marilyn's family, constitute the basis of an adaptive strategy. The emergence of the explicit family begins a process whereby each individual partitions himself off from his family. This is an illusory partition, of course, because each member is projecting aspects of himself onto a reified entity he terms "my family." Nonetheless, this illusory partition frees each individual for action. As we will see in the next stage, some of this action may be destructive but some of it may be constructive in crucial ways.

Rebellion and Action

This stage is a continuation and exaggeration of the last, but it is more grotesque and dangerous. Each member has participated in the creation of an illusory family, which takes on its own vivid reality. It is illusory because many members are disowning it as if they had no part in its creation, but a few others may be taking it within themselves, holding themselves fully responsible for its major characteristics. The family is not just explicit but is experienced, in some sense, by all members as tyrannical. The usual mode of experiencing at this stage, however, is not for each member to feel the family as a whole is a tyrant. Often one spouse will feel the other has become an oppressive burden. Usually the least accepted part of one spouse projects the least accepted aspects of himself onto the other in what Wynne[33] called the "trading of dissociations." A similar process from parent to child has been delineated as "projective identification" by Zinner and Shapiro.[34] Often an individual or subgroup in the family will be scapegoated and hounded out of the family.

For example, consider Fred and Ann at the end of two years of marriage. Each came from a family where the issues of aggressions and passivity remained problems that could never be entirely embraced, worked through, and regulated by an implicit paradigm. Indeed, Fred's family encouraged aggressive behavior on the basis of the implicit assumption that people who did not assert themselves would get nothing. By contrast, Ann's family encouraged passivity on the assumption that aggression was always potentially dangerous to others. During their first months of marriage, the new couple built a somewhat tenuous fabric of implicit conventions around the issue of aggressions and passivity. Manifestly, Fred became the "aggressive one" and Ann the "passive one." Suddenly, Ann's mother — still a young woman — suffered a severe and totally disabling stroke, leaving her permanently paralyzed and unable to utter or understand speech. Fred and Ann each felt a fleeting but intense and unspoken experience of guilt: Fred had a sense that somehow the stroke was a consequence of his aggressivity, and Ann felt that their passive inadequacy was to blame. In the months following the stroke, the marriage began to deteriorate. Fred began to find Ann too passive, depending too much on him. He felt both drained and furiously frustrated and began to verbally and then physically attack her. At the same time Ann became preoccupied with an image of Fred as aggressive and dangerous and secretly feared he would kill someone. In an effort to restrain her own anger she began to offer certain rules. "Look," she said, "each time we're angry let's not say anything. Let's go off by ourselves and try to cool down." Soon more rules were suggested. Explicit schedules were aimed at getting Ann to take more responsibility, and others were aimed at forestalling the potentially murderous effect of Fred's anger. Fred and Ann both came to feel trapped and overwhelmed by an engulfing, unproviding "marriage" for which each blamed the other. Neither individual could recognize his or her own contribution to the edifice. Each sought to escape it or — more dangerously — to destroy it. The explicit, opaque, and constraining rules — that last vestige of family order and cohesiveness — were defied, circumvented, unilaterally enforced, and capriciously modified.

Two major possibilities seem to lie before a family at this stage. Perhaps the more expectable one is that the family continues to disintegrate. A scapegoated child may be extruded and a marital couple may break up. What is perhaps more interesting, however, is the possibility for self-healing at this stage. I believe that some families reaching this crisis point can make major qualitative changes. At this point the family is particularly open to new outside influences. These experiences may include a fresh and novel involvement with large segments of their social world, leading ultimately, to new visions of the possibilities inherent in that world. Or outside influences may enter the family through new relations with outside individuals. The deepening crisis has, in effect, opened the family in this way. The old paradigm is in tatters. As the family's ceremonials and more routine patterns have been disrupted, its sense of itself and of the cardinal realities of its world has weakened. Members are no longer integrated with one another in the subtle and implicit task of reaffirming family convictions and maintaining the family's usual distance or closeness to the outside world. Members shift more radically from feeling a part of the family to feeling enclosed in the outside world itself. In this unstable state individuals may attempt quick alliances with other who are brought into the family in an effort to produce some change.[35] Indeed, Fred and Ann sought marital therapy, or, more precisely, Ann sought out a therapist to take her side against Fred.

The outsiders who are drawn into the family at this point may be people whom the family has known more peripherally for some time or they may be total strangers, such as therapists. They may also be, in some sense, family members themselves. Quite often substantial portions of the personal skills, resources, and imagination of its members have never been integrated into the life of the family. These portions of each individual, in a sense, are outsiders to the family but may enter into the family for the first time during this phase of crisis. For example, a family was thrown into crisis by the severe medical illness of a teenager while the family was camping in a remote area. The father, who in this family had always been a self-effacing, boyish prankster, rose to the occasion in ways no one in the family had ever seen or thought possible. He became serious, mature, comforting, wise, and extremely effective in organizing the family's return to a more settled area. He continued in this role for the long months of his daughter's recovery and rarely returned to his former, more puckish role. Indeed, everyone in this family not only took each other more seriously but had an enriched sense of their effectiveness as a group.

It is my belief that families at this stage actively draw in outsiders rather than leave the initiative up to the outsiders themselves. I think many family therapists will agree that they are often drawn into families with a force so strong that they can lose a sense of their own moorings. The strength of this pull is some indication, I believe, of the force still left in the family that it can harness to foster its own recovery. More speculatively, I propose that family crisis serves a positive function in the life of every family. Though filled with risk, it ultimately opens the family to new experience, altering its sense of itself and the outside world and thereby transforming a paradigm that may have guided it for years or even generations.

Conclusions

In conclusion, let me reflect on this brief sketch of family health and disorder. First, it has attempted to indicate the rich variety among families. In this model both the Ingalls and Ivanovs are seen as healthy in very different ways. Implicit here has been the idea that a healthy family is one which is integrated by an implicit paradigm affording each member a sense of conviction about the possibilities inherent in the social and inanimate world. My proposal is different from some other recent concepts of family health which argue that all healthy families are alike.[36] Second, this sketch has attempted to define family disorder by considering malfunctioning in the family *qua* family. This contrasts with many approaches in use today that define family disorder according to the level of disturbance of its individuals-for example, "families of schizophrenics" or "multiproblem families." Third, it has attempted to define a sequential process of family disorganization that pictures the family as first becoming overorganized and then disintegrating in the face of enduring stress, a view supported by the recent work of Lewis[37] and his group. Fourth, it has made an effort to identify the self-healing potential in family disorder, or, to put it another way, to conceive of family crisis and recovery as intrinsic parts of family life and as being necessary for family adaptation and change.

References

1. Wilder L : *On the Banks of Plum Creek.* New York, Harper & Row, 1953

2. Kluckhohn FR. Strodtbeck FL: *Varieties in the basic values of family systems, in A Modern Introduction to the Family.* Edited by Bell NW, Vogel EF, Glencoe, I. Free Press, 1960

3.Bion W: *Experience in Groups.* New York, Basic Books, 1959

4. Hess RD, Handel G: *Family Worlds,* Chicago, University of Chicago Press, 1959

5. Wynne LC, Ryckoff IM, Day J, et al: Pseudo-mutuality in the family relations of schizophrenics. Psychiatry 21-205-222, 1958

6. Reiss D: Individual thinking and family interaction, V: proposals for the contrasting character of experiential sensitivity and expressive form in families, J Nerv Ment Dis 151:187-202, 1970

7. Reiss D: Varieties of consensual experience, M: dimensions of a family's experience of its environment, Fam Process 10:28-35, 1971

8. Oliveri ME, Reiss D: A theory-based empirical classification of family problem-solving behavior. Fam Process 20: 409-418, 1981

9. Reiss D: Intimacy and problem solving: an automated procedure for testing a theory of consensual experience in families. Arch Gen Psychiatry 25:442-255, 1971

10. Reiss D, Salzman C: The resilience of family process: effect of secobarbital. Arch Gen Psychiatry 28:425-433, 1973

11. Reiss D, Costell R, Jones C, et al: The family meets the hospital: a laboratory forecast of the encounter. Arch Gen Psychiatry 37:141-154, 19980

12. Costell R, Reiss D, Berkman H, et al: The family meets the hospital: predicting the family's perception of the treatment program from its problem solving style. Arch Gen Psychiatry (in press)

13. Reiss D: Individual thinking and family interaction, II: a study of pattern recognition and hypothesis testing in families of normals, character disorders and schizophrenics. IJ Psychiatr Res 5:193-211, 1967

14. Reiss D: Varieties of consensual experience, III: contrast between families of normals, delinquents and schizophrenics. J Nerv Men + Dis 152:73-95, 1971

15. Oliveri ME, Reiss D: Families' schemata of social relationships. Fam Process (in press)

16. Madanes C, Dukes J, Harbin H: Family ties of heroin addicts. Arch Gen Psychiatry 37:889-894, 1980

17. Kuethe JL: Social schemas. J Abnorm Soc Psychol 64:31-38, 1962

18. Kuethe JL: Pervasive influence of social schemata. J Abnorm Soc Psychol 68:248-254, 1964

19. Kuethe JL: Social schemas and the reconstruction of social object displays from memory. J Abnorm Soc Psychol 65:71-74, 1962

20. Higgins J, Peterson JC, Dolby LL: Social adjustment and familial schemata. J Abnorm Soc Psychol 74:296-299, 1969

21. Reiss D, Costell R, Berkman H, et al: How one family perceives another: the relationship between social constructions and problem solving style. Fam Process 19:239-256, 1980

22. Oliveri ME, Reiss D: The structure of families' ties to their kin: the shaping role of social constructions. Journal of Marriage and the Family (in press)

23. Bott E: *Family and Social Network.* New York, Free Press, 1957.

24. Turner C: Conjugal roles and social networks: a re-examination of an hypothesis. Human Relations 20: 121-130, 1967

25. Reiss D: *The Family's Construction of Reality.* Cambridge, Mass. Harvard University Press, 1980

26. Steinglass PJ: The alcoholic family at home: patterns of interaction in dry, wet and traditional stages of alcoholism. Arch Gen Psychiatry (in press)

27. Bossard JHS, Boll ES: Ritual in Family Living, Philadelphia, University of Pennsylvania Press, 1950

28. Wolin SJ, Bennett LA, Noonan DL: Family rituals and the recurrence of alcoholism over generations. Am J Psychiatry 126:589-593, 1979

29. Wolin SJ, Bennett LA, Noonan DL, et al: Disrupted family rituals: a factor in the intergenerational transmission of alcoholism, J Stud Alcohol 41:199-214, 1980

30. Kantor D, Lehr W: *Inside the Family, San Francisco, Jossey-Bass, 1975*

31. Howell JT: *Hard Living on Clay Street*, New York, Anchor Books, 1973

32. Wynne LC: *Some indications and contraindications for exploratory family therapy, in Intensive Family Therapy.* Edited by Boszormenyi-Nagy I, Framo JL. New York, Harper & Row, 1965

34. Zinner J, Shapiro R: Projective identification as a mode of perception and behavior in families of adolescents. Int J Psychoanal 53:523-530, 1972

35. Gelles RJ: *The Violent Home: A Study of Physical Aggression Between Husbands and Wives, Beverly Hills, Calif.* Sage Publications, 1972

36. Olson D, Sprekle D, Russell D: Circumplex model of marital and family systems, I: cohesion and adaptability dimensions, family types, and clinical applications. Fam Process 18:3-28, 1979

37. Lewis JM: *The family matrix in health and disease, in The Family: Evaluation and Treatment.* Edited by Hofling CK, Lewis JM. New York, Brunner/Mazel, 1980

Chapter 9

Change and Conflict in Family Businesses

Nothing is constant in life but change and the only thing that is everywhere the same is that there are differences. The inevitable realities of changes and differences lead to inevitable conflicts in family businesses.

This section explores changes experienced during the life cycles of family firms. To an extent these changes can be managed, but at other times changes or differences lead to unavoidable conflict. Rivalries develop. Differences provoke animosity because consistency was anticipated.

Methods are available to render conflict less destructive. Sometimes these methods can be reduced to rules. In other cases attention to how individual goals work with family goals and a real commitment to information-sharing can help to resolve conflict — sometimes before it begins.

Introduction

Although family-owned firms constitute a large portion of corporate America, they face unique problems that are rarely discussed. In this paper, the authors outline key issues that they feel an owner of a family-owned firm must address to avoid losing control of the business. They also make suggestions for those families who want to retain control of their companies through succeeding generations.

Managing Change in the Family Firm: Issues and Strategies

1983

By Richard Beckhard and
W. Gibb Dyer, Jr.

Reprinted from **Sloan Management Review**, Spring 1983, Vol. 25, pp. 59-65, Copyright ©1983 **Sloan Management Review** Association; all rights reserved.

The success of a business depends on its ability to maintain stability while managing change in the face of internal and external pressures. Although all organizations have some difficulty adapting to changing conditions, one type of organization, the family-owned and managed business, presents a number of unique issues and problems. The interdependency between ownership and management in these firms creates forces which tend to make executive and strategic decisions more complex and more subjective.

Although well over 90 percent of all corporations (and many of the largest public corporations) in the U.S. are family owned or controlled, the average life expectancy of such organizations is only twenty-four years, and only three out of ten family firms survive into the second generation.[1] Of the 70 percent that do not survive into the second generation, many could survive if only the owner managers better understood the key issues involved in managing change and if they were better equipped with some change strategies to handle the process of adaptation and continuity more effectively.

In this paper we will examine some of the issues, "trigger events," and resistances that are involved in managing change in family-owned firms. We will also present a framework for managing the change process, apply the framework to a specific case, and draw some guidelines for family firm owner/managers.

Key Issues in Managing Family Firms

There are a number of key issues that leaders of family businesses should address. Failure to understand and

421

manage these issues, particularly during transition periods, often results in conflicts that are destructive to both firm and family, and may contribute to the high mortality rate of family-owned firms. These key issues are:

- Ownership continuity or change;

- Executive leadership continuity or change;

- Power and asset distribution;

- The role of the firm in society.

1. *Ownership Continuity or Change.* The first critical issue concerns the degree to which the family is, or wants to remain, involved in the ownership of the firm. While founders usually want very much to continue family ownership, this may not be true of their wives or second generation family members. Thus, some questions that typically arise are:

- How important is maintaining the family business as an asset?

- How will ownership of the firm be distributed among the family now and in the future?

- Does the family wish to have the family name identified with the business in the future?

Family members often differ from the founder in their answers to these questions, and conflict frequently results.

2. *Executive Leadership Continuity or Change.* A related issue concerns the family's involvement in the management of the business. While some families remove themselves from management and become absentee owners, others prefer to be actively involved in managing the firm. Any change in the family's degree of involvement in the management of the business is likely to be resisted by certain family members, and even the nonfamily employees. When leadership succession is imminent, the owner/manager's family and nonfamily professionals are often in conflict with each other over this issue.

3. *Power and Asset Distribution.* This is one of the most complicated issues for the founder and his family. Most family members want their "fair share" of the firm's wealth and the power that comes from it, but the way the stock is allocated and the way management and board positions are assigned within the family can create a variety of conflicts. Moreover, the needs of nonfamily employees must also be considered. Estate planning, the setting up of trusts, etc., are concomitant issues that must be addressed.

4. *The Role of the Firm in Society.* We found that some families hold widely divergent views concerning the role of the firm in society. Some family members may see the firm as a means of benefiting society and, therefore, they may wish to use the firm's assets to provide educational, cultural, and employment opportunities for employees and of members of the broader society. Others, however, may see the firm merely as an economic asset whose role is to provide income for family members. Still other family members and nonfamily professionals who manage the business may want to use the company's profits to increase the firm's growth. The potential for conflict here is, of course, enormous.

Trigger Events and Destabilization

When a major change in the firm occurs, it has a profound impact on the relationships between family members, and family and professional managers. The entire "system" becomes unstable, causing previously predictable behaviors to become unpredictable. Conditions that "trigger" such behaviors are:

A decision by the founder/leader to step down;

The death of the founder/leader or some other significant family member;

The entry of a family member (or failure of a family member to enter) into the firm or a new position;

A decision to merge or sell the business;

Significant growth or decline in profitability.

When one or more of these trigger events occur, all too often the "solutions" that the founder, his family, and the nonfamily employees thought were sufficient to deal with the issues presented earlier are no longer valid given the new state of affairs. They simply do not work in the new mosaic of roles and relationships precipitated by these events. Consequently there is usually a sense of loss of power by second generation family members, and new questions about leadership arise. Potential owner/managers may have to reevaluate their careers as well as nonfamily members. Although during this time major changes take place, the conflicts and resistances in both the firm and the family make managing change a difficult task.

Resistance to Change in Family Firms

Family firms are often led by a strong founder or other family leader who has a certain management style, a set of values, and a vision for the firm that are usually difficult to change because they are so ingrained. Indeed, it is the unique set of personality traits and skills of the founder that has led to the firm's initial success. As a result, the founder may be reluctant to try out new behaviors. We often hear founders say, "My style has always worked in the past. I'm successful. Why should I change?" Founders may also resist planning for any changes that affect their role because of reluctance to face their own mortality. As one founder described it:

"The basic dilemma is that succession planning by a founder is really, in a way, digging your own grave. It's preparing for your own death, and it's very difficult to make contact with the concept of death emotionally . . . It is a kind of 'seppuku,' the hara-kiri that Japanese commit . . . [It's like] putting a dagger to your belly . . . and having someone behind you cut off your head . . . That analogy sounds dramatic, but emotionally it's close to it. You're ripping yourself apart— your power, your significance, your leadership, your father role, your chief executive role, and your founder role . . ."

Thus resistance by the founder/leader is often the major stumbling block in planning for change in family firms.

Further problems may occur because of the history of familial relationships outside of the business. Often old sibling rivalries and jealousies reemerge, and conflicts between fathers and sons, husbands and wives, or the in-laws develop during transitions which create resistances to change. The source of the conflict usually goes undetected because its origin is found in events that occurred in the family many years earlier. Thus, recognizing the source of resistance and conflict is often difficult because it comes in so many disguises.

Another difficulty often encountered has to do with the organization norms, values, and traditions that are closely linked with the family owners. We have found in some firms, for example, employees whose sense of identity and security is closely linked with the culture of the owning family, and particularly the founder. Any attempt to change this relationship may well be resisted by the key employees.

Managing Change

To cope with the conflicts and resistances that accompany major changes in family firms, as well as to minimize their potential negative effects on family members, nonfamily executives, and many other constituencies, requires careful analysis and planning. As there is usually no precedent for managing a complex change such as leadership succession, founders often have no framework for managing the process. As a result, they are forced to proceed by best guess.

The help founders/leaders manage such changes, we present below a framework that can and has been applied successfully in a number of family-owned enterprises. It contains three basic steps:

1. *Defining the Future State.* This involves developing a scenario for what the total system—both firm and family—will look like after the change has taken place.

2. *Determining the Present State.* This step includes:

• Defining the cluster of change problems that must be managed;

• Identifying the key players whose support is necessary for the change to take place successfully;

• Determining the attitudes of the key players toward the change and their capabilities for change; and

• Outlining the relationships between the key players.

3. *Determining the Transition State.* This step involves action planning and should incorporate the types of activities necessary for the change to occur; the kinds of structures needed to make the transition; the level of commitment needed from the key players; and strategies for generating commitment.

By presenting an actual case study of a family-owned business, we will attempt to describe how this framework can be applied.

A Case Study

A food manufacturing company with sales of $400 million was founded thirty-seven years ago by a bright, aggressive entrepreneur. Until recently the company has been very successful as a result of excellent and aggressive marketing, and high technical innovation in processed foods, microwave specials, take-out suppers, etc.

The founder has been CEO for the lifetime of the company. One of his sons is in the business and the founder hopes that eventually the son will succeed him as CEO. His other son is in unrelated work, and has no interest in the business at present. There are two daughters who are both married, one has children. One son-in-law is a financial consultant to the company; he would like a full-time executive role in the business.

The viability of the business is highly dependent on the quality of some key executives in the firm; a technical "genius" and the executive vice president, an excellent all-around businessman who had been the number two executive for ten years. The founder is now sixty-three years old. For several years he has been planning to move away from actively directing the business at age sixty-five. He is hoping that his son will replace him.

In the last two years the business environment has "gone crazy." Executive management is faced with unprecedented challenges. The son, who has been a competent senior executive, has not responded with great imagination or initiative to the changing circumstances. On the other hand, the executive vice president has shown real leadership and imagination. The founder is experiencing some real doubts about whether his son is "ready" to take over. The executive vice president, who is fifty-five years old, clearly could do the job, and the founder is leaning toward making him CEO for at least five years after he (the founder) moves out to become nonexecutive chairman in two years.

The founder has been in general good health, although recently he is experiencing chronic high blood pressure. His doctors have warned that he should seriously consider "slowing down." Recently he has made a definite, though still private, decision that he will step down from CEO in two years. He has told only his wife of this decision. She is delighted and is looking forward to their son succeeding as chief executive.

With the business in potential trouble, the founder, however, wonders whether he can trust anyone to take over. He sees a number of problems regarding the executive succession issue:

- If he puts the most ready and competent person—the executive vice president—into the job, it will send a message to the employees, customers, and suppliers that his son is not going to be the "natural successor."

- His wife will be disappointed and, perhaps, angry. She does not particularly like the executive vice president.

- The son will, at best, be deeply disappointed. How will he respond?

- The son-in-law will be angry. Why was he not considered?

- The other key professionals will have mixed feelings; their chances for top management positions will be minimized or closed as a result of their ages. Family executive management will now not be a given as they had previously thought. How will they feel about working for a nonowner?

- Other key family members may feel a loss of control over some of their assets.

The founder also has several important values that he wants to protect:

Controlling ownership must stay in the family.

Family members must have opportunities in the business if they want them.

The business must remain an entity; that is, it is not to be merged or sold.

Reliable return on investment is a priority over growth on past income.

Quality must remain a mark of identification with the company.

The founder also wants to be sure that family members collaborate as owners. Moreover, he wants the family to stay together and to minimize family conflicts. Toward achieving these ends, the founder has, in consultation with legal advisors, set up an "estate" that specifies that:

Fifty percent of his holdings (85 percent of total shares of the company) will go to his wife;

Equal shares of the other 50 percent will go to his wife and their four children. (The children will get 10 percent each and the wife will end up with 60 percent.)

At his wife's death, her 60 percent will be divided equally among the four children. None of them can sell their shares except to each other;

Only a unanimous "shareholder" vote can dispose of the business;

They will (as a family) stay out of direct management of the business except for those who are full-time in the management group.

Other questions facing the founder are:

How should he finalize the decision on executive succession?

What linkages are needed between owners and business board members?

Should there be an "active" board of directors for the firm? Who should be on it?

Who should appoint future executives from the family?

How should family make joint decisions?

Who should be told what when?

In this particular case, we can see that the founder's decision to step down as CEO "triggers" a number of key issues and creates a number of dilemmas.

Conflict concerning the issues of ownership, management, distribution of assets, and the role of the firm is likely. Moreover, there will probably be strong resistances to the change, both from inside and outside the family.

Determining the Nature of the Future State

If we apply the three step process described earlier for managing change to this situation, the founder could begin by developing a picture of the organization after the change to new leadership. He will need two scenarios:

1. A picture of what it will look like two years from now with a new CEO and himself as chairman of the board; and

2. A picture depicting what the firm will be like when he retires as chairman five years from now.

By engaging in this process of "scenario building," the founder should be able to describe the nature of the relationships and relative power between family members outside the business, family members managing the business, and the nonfamily professionals. He also should be able to describe the key decision processes to be used after the change. After determining the nature of the future state, the founder can then move on to the next steps in the process.

Analyzing the Present State

To diagnose the present state, the founder should begin by analyzing the current conditions in the firm, the family, and the ownership/governance structure. By examining the present state and relating it to the desired future state, the constellation of key changes and their priorities begins to emerge. In this particular case, they are:

Change in executive leadership;

Change in governance;

Change in "philosophy" from having family members as CEOs to using competence as the criterion for advancement;

Change in succession pattern in firm and its effect on key professional managers;

Change in ownership status (after founder transfers his shares);

Change in power relationships (mother might be majority owner with son in key position in the business);

Change in rules for selecting board members, chief executives, key professionals (all previously centralized in founder);

Change in ownership-management relationship (if family stock is owned by several individuals);

Change in ownership rules; can individual family shareholders sell their stock? Can some subset of family owners sell the company?

Change in perceptions of the character of the business from personal, founder-centered family business to more professionally managed, family-controlled enterprise;

Change in career and life plans for family members in second and third generations;

Change in decision-making pattern. The family now participates more in making decisions.

From all of these changes, the founder might feel that four or five of them demand early action.

If failure to make these changes is to be avoided, the founder must next identify the key people or groups that must be committed to carrying out such changes. This should be a small number of people. In this case, the key people might be the wife, the son in the business, the executive vice president, the technical genius, one or two other key managers, and perhaps an outside person, such as the president of the firm's bank. It would probably not include the son-in-law or the son not in the business. Although consulting them at some point would be advisable to make sure that they do not feel left out entirely, it is not essential to have them involved at this stage.

The founder also needs to think through both the present attitudes and abilities of the key actors to play their roles in the change. For example, given that the wife would probably be very upset if a nonfamily CEO were selected, the founder must be prepared to work out that problem. If the founder is around to manage the transition to professional management, this problem is easier to work through; however, the founder might not be present and, therefore, preparations should be made to assure communication and cooperation between the key individuals during this period.

At this stage, it is also important that the founder look at the key people in relation to one another. For new roles and relationships to be learned and established, communication between the key parties is imperative. For example, if the executive vice president and the founder's son are unable to communicate, a mechanism should be set up to assure communication during the period when their new roles are being learned and negotiated.

Managing Leadership Transition

As the founder begins to plan for the transition in leadership, he will first need to determine the kinds of activities that must be carried out to make the change effort a success, in this case, the founder might engage in the following activities:

- Analyze the leadership competence of both family and nonfamily managers;

- Communicate with key people regarding his (the founder's) decision and, in some cases, make joint decisions;

- Examine the various types of trust and stock arrangements available;

- Determine what kinds of activities can and should be left to third generation family members;

- Explore the kinds of activities he (the founder) might want to engage in after retirement.

After outlining the major activities, structures can now be put in place to manage the transition. The key structures that will need to be implemented in the next five years are:

A new board of directors;

A new system for allocating and defining board and CEO responsibility;

An asset or family stock management group to coordinate family-owner positions. This group is separate from the board of directors;

A system for representing the family's interests on the board of directors;

An executive council of key managers to assure continuity of quality products, maintain strategies, etc.

Obtaining the necessary commitment from the key players is also essential during the transition period. In this case, the commitment of the executive vice president and the key technical genius to stay for some years is imperative. The son's commitment to stay is also important. It is also necessary to have someone in the family committed to be on the board of directors to represent the family after the founder leaves. Whoever is chosen, his or her commitment to the overall plan is essential. Finally, developing a strategy to gain such a commitment for key individuals within the time requirements of each stage of the change is important.

Conclusion

Family-owned firms—when the firm and family leadership are in the same person or persons—make unique and identifiable demands on such leaders that are different from the demands of executive leaders in public corporations. When significant change in family businesses (i.e., selling the business or changing top leadership) is indicated, the central executives must concern themselves *explicitly* with both the *immediate* and *long-term* impact on the firm, the family owners, the key family members, and the professional managers in the business.

The management of such change is not just an economic optimization process. Methods must be found for dealing with both the family and the firm as separate entities as well as with all their interdependencies.

Through our study of family-owned firms, we have devised systematic steps for managing change which we feel can significantly help decision makers of such businesses. As previously discussed, these steps include:

Diagnosing the present state of the firm;

Designing an executive succession plan;

Developing structures, plans, and methods for managing transitional periods when management is changing hands;

Designing explicit strategies for obtaining and monitoring commitment and "ownership" of change.

If these steps are followed, we think family owners can control the massive information needed to avoid major "disasters" for their firms and/or families during the leadership change period. However, it is crucial that they pay particular attention to the following concerns:

The economic viability of the firm;

The reputation of the firm;

The continuity of key executives;

The confidence in future top management;

The relationship of key family members;

The dynamics of the family under stress during the transition period;

The roles and relationships of spouse, children, in-laws, and grandchildren.

In summary, to the extent that family-owned businesses are able to identify the key issues they face regarding managing change and management continuity, we believe they can overcome their unique problems and continue to operate effectively and profitably in corporate America.

1 See: P. B. Alcorn, *Success and Survival in the Family Owned Business* (New York: McGraw-Hill, 1982); and R. Poe, "The SOB's," *Across the Board,* May 1980, pp. 23-33.

Introduction

It is always difficult to move from small entrepreneurships to large management structures. But a family-operated firm may have twice the difficulties, as family interrelationships complicate the changes. This examination of such complications describes methods of overcoming growth problems in family businesses including redefining management, focusing on the family and engaging in strategic planning.

Life-Cycle Changes in Small Family Businesses

1983

By Richard B. Peiser and Leland M. Wooten

Reprinted from **Business Horizons**, May/June 1983. Copyright ©1983 the Foundation for the School of Business at Indiana University. Used with permission.

Every successful small business must sooner or later face the problems of growth and expansion. Where family businesses are concerned, normal growth problems are compounded by the difficulties of separating family relationships from business decisions.

One of the crucial tests of a successful small business is its ability to make the transition from the entrepreneurial stage to the administrative stage in its development. This transition frequently occurs in family businesses by transition from the first generation to the next — a transition which many family businesses do not survive. In this article, we examine the process of managing life-cycle changes, both in the firm and in the family, so as to provide growth and development beyond the state of entrepreneurship.

The Project-Oriented Family Firm

The types of small businesses discussed in this article have several common features. First, a family is deeply involved in the affairs of the business, having in most cases founded it. Most of the firms which survive as long as the second generation of both the family and the enterprise have come to grips with problems of growth, purpose, personal conflict, succession, and a whole host of family issues ranging from the mundane to the bizarre.

A second characteristic of the firms discussed here is that they are in the process of transition, both in the firm and in the family. Businesses go through life-cycles; so do the families playing the dominant roles in managing these firms. It is this overlap of family life-cycles on top of business life-cycles

430

that provides a central issue in making a successful transition.

A third characteristic of these small businesses is their project-oriented nature. While family businesses are found in every industry, they are particularly important in a number of project-oriented industries such as real estate, construction, and various consulting services. Day-to-day activities are centered around individual projects rather than around continuous activities such as manufacturing or retailing. Often, they are firms in easy-entry and easy-exit industries because the time frame of management is short-term and project-oriented.

The project nature of these firms offers some opportunity for smoothing the problems of transition between generations because it provides a way to give the second generation experience and responsibility. However, it also adds another difficulty to the transition—namely, the ease with which project-oriented firms can be divided. If transition difficulties become too severe, one solution is to divide the firm up among the family members. Because this represents a reasonable possibility, the transition from the founding generation to the next is more complicated than in nonproject-oriented family business.

Firm and Family Life Cycles

A number of typologies have been used to describe the various stages of a firm's life cycle.[1] One such typology describes three stages of evolution for a small business: survival—the firm's founding stage in which it struggles to stay alive; success—a period in which the growing company breaks out of resource process; and take-off—a period in which the company evolves toward a big organization. All three of these stages come under Henry Mintzberg's category of a "simple structure."[2] The life-cycle crisis frequently comes at a point when the firm is in the "success" stage. As Churchill and Lewis describe, in the success stage the company may either prepare for growth or may decline as the owner begins to disengage himself.

Paralleling the firm's life cycle is the life cycle of its owners. In family businesses, the life-cycle of the founding member or founding generation has particular significance because of the need for successful transition of power from the founding generation to the next. This transition is complicated by the very spirit that often makes the firm successful in the first place, the entrepreneurial spirit of its founders.

This entrepreneurial spirit creates particular problems for the passing of power between generations: "For the entrepreneur, the business is essentially an extension of himself, a medium of personal gratification and achievement above all."[3] If the firm is to survive, he must find a way to disengage himself. However, the multifaceted aspects of family relationships—father-son, brother-brother, mother-child—may make the process of disengagement more perilous than it would be for the founder in a non-family business.

The life-cycle crisis often occurs at the time when the second generation has developed enough expertise to assume major responsibility in the general management of the firm but the first generation is not prepared to share that responsibility. While this point may occur during any of the three firm life-cycle stages, it typically occurs during the second stage when the firm has reached a plateau of success. What happens at the crisis point is crucial, because it determines whether a successful transition is made to the second generation. If the founding generation cannot relinquish sufficient responsibility, then the second generation may break away from the family business. Of course, the original firm may survive, but not in the form which its founders envisioned, and not in a form which perpetuates the family's fortunes with the firm.

The timing of the second generation's involvement may be crucial to the occurrence or severity of the type of life-cycle crisis described here. The second generation may acquire the needed experience to run the business at a time when the founding generation is ready to step down or to become more involved in outside activities such as public service. If so, then the life-cycle crisis may not be severe and a relatively smooth transition is apt to occur.

More often, however, timing is not optimal, and many pressures occur which threaten to pull the firm apart. Consider the following case:

> Jim, a developer who has built a number of buildings in his community over the last ten years, is in his late forties. He is one of the leaders in the community and has devoted an increasing amount of his time to community activities. In so doing, he has slowed his development activities and is spending more time managing his current holdings and less time working on new ventures.

Jim's son, Junior, entered the business five years ago and has worked in all areas of the firm, from construction to leasing and management. Junior is eager to pursue new, innovative multi-use projects, but Jim is reluctant to undertake major new commitments.

Jim's firm is in a life-cycle phase that parallels his own. His energies are being concentrated outside the business, and the business is in a holding pattern. Whether the business enters a success-growth phase instead of a success-decline stage depends on whether Jim is able to turn over responsibility to his son and on whether Jim is willing to let Junior initiate projects and incur risks that Jim no longer would undertake on his own. If Jim does not, then the business may continue in a holding pattern while Junior becomes increasingly frustrated, or Junior may simply give up and go elsewhere.

As the principals in a family business age, their needs and goals change. The first generation tends to become more conservative, but their need for stability and for holding on to what they already have runs directly counter to the needs of the second generation who want their turn to prove themselves. In non-family businesses, this presents less of a problem because the business management tends to revolve around more people, and the transfer of power from one principal to the next does not involve the same sort of conflicts formed by family familiarity.

When Goals Collide

The life-cycle crisis is frequently precipitated when goals of the founding generation and those of the second generation collide. Goal congruency exists when the personal goals of each individual are consistent with the business goals of the firm and when the personal and business goals of each individual are consistent with those of the others. This does not mean that every member of the family must share all the business goals of each family member. What it does require, however, is that a level of understanding and tolerance exist in the organization such that diversity becomes a strength rather than a seedbed for conflict.

In the early stages of a firm's development, goal congruency is rather high, giving the firm a sense of what it wants to accomplish in the future. In fact, goal congruency is seldom a problem at this stage, and any failure of the firm is more probably caused by misjudgment of the entrepreneur rather than by the lack of goal congruency.

Lack of goal congruency comes later in the life of the firm, after the firm has achieved a measure of success. The problem can appear in several forms. The founder's interests may move in directions away from the firm, and what is best for the founder may cease to be what is best for the firm. At this point, many non-family businesses move in the direction of professional management. In family business, as other family members become ready for general management, goal congruency not only becomes a problem between each family member and the firm, but also between the family members themselves. In other words, family members must share the same general goals for the firm. Furthermore, if authority is shared, they must agree in how the firm should best proceed toward those goals.

In the example above, the energy level of the first generation was declining as Jim spent more time in community activities. As a result, the firm was in a holding pattern, sustaining past levels of activity but generally static in terms of growth. The second generation (or younger brother) enters the firm and develops the competence and expertise to take over the firm's leadership at a time when the first generation's goals are changing. A crisis occurs when the disparate goals of the two generations create conflicts. The firm can either begin a new phase of growth with the second generation taking leadership, or it can decline as existing projects wind down, or it can dissolve with each generation going its separate way.

External business pressures such as prosperity or recession may significantly contribute both to the timing of the life-cycle crisis and to its outcome. Recession may force the firm to narrow its scope at a time when the second generation is eager to expand. Despite the reduction in economic prospects, a declining economy may hold the firm together as opportunities outside the firm are reduced. On the other hand, a vibrant economy may bring the life-cycle crisis to a head as the second generation sees opportunities for growth that the first generation would prefer to pass over.

Symptoms of the Life-Cycle Crisis

The absence of goal congruence frequently shows itself in many small ways, irritating family members and distorting the purpose of the organization. The focus of the family members changes from a strategic perspective to one of managing minutia. When more and more time is being spent making decisions, and when the firm is being pulled in different directions by the family, it is time to stand back and take stock of where the firm is and where it is going. But this is especially difficult to do in family firms where relationships developed over a lifetime make open communication cumbersome.

A number of symptoms of the life-cycle crisis, shown in Figure 1, signal the growth of a situation which could easily become a very serious developmental crisis for the firm.

Consider the following case, in which the facts have been changed only slightly, involving the interaction of three brothers.

Three brothers run a successful apartment construction business. The two eldest, John and Paul, founded the business and have built it up over ten years. The third brother, Richie, is eight years younger than Paul.

Richie has been in the business three years and wants to try building an office building. John and Paul are satisfied with what the firm is doing now. They do not feel that Richie has enough experience to build an office building, and

Figure 1. Symptoms of a Life-Cycle Crisis

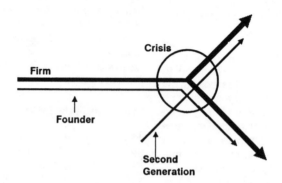

- **increased levels of interpersonal conflict, leading to a belittling of each other's goals.**

- **attention to short-term profits rather than long-term goals.**

- **ill-defined management procedures emphasizing the short term.**

- **no defined process for integrating new family members.**

- **no career plans, offering the younger generation no enticement.**

- **failure to tap available financial resources from the external environment**

- **difficulty in valuing diverse contributions of family members to the firm, using conformity to avoid the strengths of diversity.**

- **leveling off of growth and/or profits, probably an indicator of a lack of shared long-term goals.**

F igure 2. Critical Issues of Goal Congruency

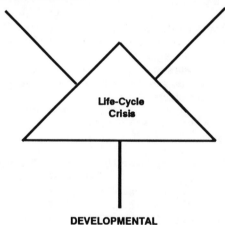

MANAGEMENT ISSUES

FAMILY ISSUES

Faulty project
management

Family interaction and its
effect on firm

Poorly defined
responsibilities

No conflict resolution
process

Poorly defined
accountability

Lack of financial
controls

Perception-reality gap: Self
perception vs. other's
perception of family member
contributions

Day-to-day detail
displacing broader
management perspective

Changing personal and
professional goals

Life-Cycle
Crisis

DEVELOPMENTAL
STAGE

- increasing reluctance to be innovative, a classic risk-avoidance posture.

- failure to exploit the reputation of the firm for developing new business—a withdrawal strategy.

- increasing difficulty in making consensus decisions, a key indicator showing the lack of goal congruence.

they are upset with his work habits. Richie likes to party at night and come to work at 9:30 or 10:00, although he tends to work late.

Paul is upset with both John and Richie because he feels that he is doing more work than the others. The eldest brother, John, spends almost one-half of his time as president of the local Apartment Builders Association.

The brothers own equal shares of the business. To equalize their time, Paul suggested some time ago, and the other brothers agreed, that each of them should start keeping a time card. However, Paul is the only one doing so, and he is getting more frustrated and upset every day.

The three brothers are caught up in "fire-fighting" activities of running a business. Each brother is at a different stage of his personal life cycle, and a lack of goal congruency is causing them to lose sight of strategic issues and to focus instead on daily minutia and the irritating work habits of the others.

Their firm has enjoyed a history of success, but activity has leveled off. Whether they enter a growth stage or a decline stage depends on their ability to deal successfully with the life-cycle crisis. The business is primarily a reflection of the needs of the three brothers. However, their needs are different, and Richie's position as the "baby in the family" makes it difficult for him to achieve equal status with the other brothers. Typically, each brother feels he is carrying an unfair share of the total workload.

This firm is encountering many of the problems shown in Figure 1 which are symptomatic of a life-cycle crisis. The indicators obviously point to the need for change and suggest some type of intervention in the day-to-day activities of the firm. Before the intervention takes place, however, the managers of the firm should have a clear picture of the exact nature of the issues they are facing. These issues, shown in Figure 2 are essentially threefold in scope.

Management Issues. These usually provide the first indicators of the life-cycle crisis. In the early years of the firm, management issues did not pose problems because the entrepreneur-founder simply made all the important decisions. With more family members in management, responsibilities and accountabilities are often ill-defined. For example, in the case described above, the three brothers had divided authority along functional lines so that each brother was involved at some point in every project, and all important decisions (and most minor ones) were made collectively. If a project fell behind schedule, the brothers blamed one another for the delay. A first step in the clean-up process may be a careful delineation of responsibility and accountability, one that makes responsibility clear and identifies success or failure with each individual.

This redefinition of responsibility is designed to replace the old system, a personalized authority system of the entrepreneurial stage. When the second generation (or younger brothers) becomes involved, some mechanism is needed to let them be successful on their own. At the same time, some mechanism is needed to reduce the personalized authority of the first generation, characterized by their over-involvement in every project. A more formal project management structure provides the appropriate mechanism to produce the required changes in behavior and responsibility. Yet once the cleanup process begins, it will inevitably lead to the emergence of a second set of issues, that of new family roles.

New Family Roles. Many small businesses have the luxury of dealing with the goal congruency crisis without the complicating aspects of family involvement. Not so here. Family involvement gives a personal quality to the crisis since the family itself must change as the firm enters a new stage of development. This can be especially hard since family roles are conditioned by a lifetime of family interaction. Suddenly, younger brothers or children must be met on equal terms — a transition which may be easier said than done. Perceptions of one another, as well as of one's own capabilities, must often be changed, but it can be difficult for family members to interact on the basis of job performance rather than prior family relationships. Conflict resolution may be necessary as may be matching each member's aspirations for his or her life-cycle to organizational goals.

Development Stage. This involves the joint evolution of the firm and the family. The resolution of strategic management issues requires that the changing nature of family roles be recognized at the same time. It is virtually an impossible task in most situations of this type to begin a process of extrapolating the firm into the future if the key members of the organization have not begun to grapple with the task of linking changes in the family with changes in the firm.

Assuming that the members of the firm recognize the symptoms of a life-cycle crisis, what can be done to resolve the problems flowing from these issues, and more importantly, what about the resolution of the life-cycle crisis itself?

Resolving the Crisis

The issues point to the need for some type of intervention into the day-to-day activities of the firm. In most cases a third party outside the organization or an outside board member could best manage the processes of confronting the problems at hand and defining a new direction. Businesses get mired down by the conflicts within the family; not often will someone within the firm be objective enough to stand back and examine the problems without bias. Consultants are not always clothed in time-honored virtues in the eyes of the small business community, but some form of outside intervention is strongly recommended. What, then, is the role of the outside intervener?

Information may not be as widely shared in a family as some would think. For example, entrepreneurs often keep in their heads most of the information about certain problems and management procedures, and particularly about future personal and professional goals. As the organization begins to expand, this becomes both an untenable and a deeply imbedded source of conflict. Therefore, the primary goal of the intervention and background data collection will be to create a public forum in which the key members of the organization can wrestle with issues and solve problems. In the schema defined here, data should be collected in the following ways:

1. In-depth interviews should be conducted with key members of the organization.

2. Organizational-profile instruments can develop perceptions about such things as organization structure, leadership characteristics, or problem-solving styles.

3. Each key member of the organization should list what he or she sees as the problems,

challenges, and future directions of the firm.

Once data are collected, the consultant or outside board member must exercise influence in the feedback process. He must be able to demonstrate expertise in three areas of concern to small family business: conflict resolution, response to management problems, and strategic planning. While the latter two functions are traditional management consultant skills, the first function, conflict resolution, may seem to the family members far more important than the development of a business plan.

Conflict resolution begins with the in-depth interviews. If conflicts exist, the consultant can easily draw out the nature or source of the conflict since it will probably be foremost on the minds of the participants. Sometimes conflict may be resolved simply by opening up new lines of communication. However, it may be rooted in misperceptions of one another or of one's own capabilities, or in the problems of goal congruency mentioned earlier. The process resembles that in family counseling, so there is no magic formula guaranteeing success.

Assuming that major conflicts are resolved, the next step is interpreting the data and feeding it back to the participants, in this case according to the scheme suggested in Figure 2. The goal is to engage the key members of the firm in responding to issues raised, and more importantly, in solving the management problems.

The third step involves strategic planning. The consultant must help the organization develop a procedure which allows the wheels of the firm to turn more smoothly. This planning phase requires linking the short-term strengths of the firm to its potential for long-term growth. An action agenda is drawn up and individuals commit their energies to the task of pointing the organization in new directions. In this stage, new risks will be taken but managed in a different way.

This important activity can be structured by an action agenda, a type of planning process in reverse. The normal procedure followed in planning for change is to go from the general to the specific—that is, to think first about broad goals before reaching any commitment to action. However, in the crisis depicted in this article, a slow movement away from a rather stagnant situation is necessary. As such, a few simple refinements in the management system of the firm are an appropriate first step, allowing the organization to regain a sense of direction and movement. With this in mind, the following steps are recommended:

1. **Redefine project management.** As we noted, one of the characteristics of these firms is a project-oriented nature. Yet the management structure is often organized along functional rather than project lines to keep the entrepreneur the only one with the "big picture." If several family members function as equals, as in the case cited, there is a tendency toward management by consensus. Functional organization (finance, sales, production, and so forth) gives every family member responsibility while making it harder to divide up the firm. Of course, if the consensus breaks down, so does the management.

As a first step in refining the management system, everyone in the organization should be aware of the various current projects. Second, as a management team, family members should define a set of objectives committing individuals to short-term performance goals. These objectives should be measurable, time bound, specific, and realistic. This is not a rigid system of management by objectives, but rather a simple attempt to involve the key decision makers in the process of defining and evaluating performance. Therefore, the third step is to define check points around which evaluation can be assessed. Individuals should accept responsibilities for project objectives suited to their abilities, and be evaluated on the basis of accomplishment of those objectives. Such a more formal, yet still flexible, system of managing the day-to-day affairs of the business makes job performance more explicit by giving those responsible for successful projects credit and by pinpointing responsibility for failure.

It should be noted that members of the family may be averse to true project management for two reasons: first, because it does clarify success and failure; and second, because it may simplify breaking up the firm along project lines if the life-cycle crisis remains unresolved. Nevertheless, if a principal source of conflict is the perception of unequal workloads and unequal contributions to the firm, then objective measurement of contribution is an essential step in reducing conflict and improving decision making.

2. Focus the family upon itself in both an affective and rational manner. The emotional aspect of a family business can be an important dimension of its success. The family business may in fact have a built-in advantage little explored in the literature and probably little appreciated by the family members themselves. In short, the conflict resolution process described above is not merely designed for encouraging people to bury the hatchet; rather, it is a critical procedure whereby the family can again focus on the subjective feelings, emotions, and intuitions which bond the family together and form an important organizational rationale for staying together rather than being a divisive force.

Secondly, the focus shifts to the rational aspects of family contributions to the firm. With the data collected around family issues, the firm can deal with the thorny issues of perceived work loads, career goals, and personal goals. It should be no surprise to any family business that these perceptions and goals change over time. In fact, if they don't, then the firm has another indicator of the loss of dynamism and another piece of data suggesting the future may be beyond the evolutionary capabilities of the firm. Therefore, the firm must begin to look beyond the dominant roles played by each family member in the past to developing a more sophisticated notion of diverse career paths and contributions. Indeed, the perception of some family members that others are not contributing as much to the firm's success as they did in the past is a major source of conflict. One can never lose sight of the traditional key functions in the organization, such as project management or sales, but one must also never fail to accept new roles and functions as the organization and the family evolve into different stages of development.

Everyone need not perform the same function, such as project manager, in order to have contributed equal value to the firm. Once again, a diverse approach to contributions and rewards is absolutely critical. The cost/benefit evaluation of activities may suggest that some activities are more important than others. The family needs to rethink how it has valued certain activities in the past. If in the past, projects were virtually found on the doorstep of the organization, in the future the function of bringing new projects into the firm might be elevated to a new importance. This part of the action agenda should aim at a redefinition of both the affective and rational contributions of the family so they can rediscover those bonds which will help them confront the next stage of development. To complete this process, the action agenda must next look at strategic plans for the future.

3. **Make strategic plans.** The strategic planning process goes beyond the daily routines of the firm and looks at critical issues in the future. Once the firm has "cleaned up" its management procedures so that decisions are again being made, and once the family issues are being addressed, then it is time to look ahead. In doing so, those plotting the future should answer a number of questions.

• What is the current strategy? What are the problems with this current strategy? Is the company having difficulty implementing the current strategy? Is the current strategy no longer valid? Does it lack competitive advantage? Does it fail to exploit the firm's distinctive competencies?

• What are some alternative strategies? Which ones are acceptable? How do present competencies limit alternative strategies? Which alternatives offer the best competitive advantages? Which ones minimize the creation of new problems?

• Which new strategies are most appropriate? What are the long-term implications of these new strategies? What new skills are needed?

• What are the implications of these new strategies on family participation in the business? How will responsibilities be shared with non-members who will have a larger role

in the firm? What value will be attached to the diverse roles which will be played by various members of the family? How will consultive management procedures be different from the paternalistic ones of the past?

We have tried to add to the literature on small businesses by taking a contextual approach — that is, small businesses are varied, with a rich diversity of problems and potential contributions to our economic well-being. We have discussed the life-cycle crisis unique in one kind of firm — the project-oriented family business.

What makes the life-cycle crisis so important is that it may be the most critical test to the family business's survival once the early stages of the firm's growth are past. The heart of the crisis is the interrelationship between the personal life-cycles of the family members with respect to one another and to the life-cycle of the firm.

While the life-cycle crisis may range widely in terms of its severity, we believe that it is a crisis that is faced sooner or later by virtually all family businesses. By recognizing that it is a common malady, with common symptoms and cures, we hope that more family businesses may pass successfully through the crisis and into a new success-growth stage.

1. Neil C. Churchill and Virginia Lewis, "A Typology of Small Businesses: Hypothesis and Preliminary Study," Southern Methodist University, *Working Paper 82-103*,1982. See also Larry E. Greiner, "Evolution and Revolution as Organizations Grow," *Harvard Business Review*, July-August 1972: pp. 37-46.

2. Henry Mintzberg, "Organization Design: Fashion of Fit?" *Harvard Business Review*, January-February 1981: pp. 103-116. Mintzberg's other

categories—machine bureaucracy, professional bureaucracy, divisionalized form, and adhocracy—all describe larger firms with some form of post-entrepreneurial structure.

3. Harry Levinson, "Conflicts That Plague Family Businesses," *Harvard Business Review*, March-April 1971: pp. 90-98.

Introduction

The job of operating a family-owned company is often grievously complicated by friction arising from rivalries involving a father and his son, brothers, or other family members who hold positions in the business, or at least derive income from it. Unless the principals face up to their feelings of hostility, the author says the business will suffer and may even die. He offers advice on how relatives can learn to live with their peculiar situation, but the only real solution is developing professional management.

Conflicts That Plague
Family Businesses
1971

By Harry Levinson

In U. S. business, the most successful executives are often men who have built their own companies. Ironically, their very success frequently brings to them and members of their families personal problems of an intensity rarely encountered by professional managers. And these problems make family businesses possibly the most difficult to operate.[1]

It is obvious common sense that when managerial decisions are influenced by feelings about and responsibilities toward relatives in the business, when nepotism exerts a negative influence, and when a company is run more to honor a family tradition than for its own needs and purposes, there is likely to be trouble.

However, the problems of family businesses go considerably deeper than these issues. In this article I shall examine some of the more difficult underlying psychological elements in operating these businesses and suggest some ways of coping with them.

They Start With the Founder

The difficulties of the family business begin with the founder. Usually he is an entrepreneur for whom the business has at least three important meanings:

1. The entrepreneur characteristically has unresolved conflicts with his father, research evidence indicates. He is therefore uncomfortable when being supervised, and starts his own business both to outdo his father and to escape

the authority and rivalry of more powerful figures.[2]

2. An entrepreneur's business is simultaneously his "baby" and his "mistress."
Those who work with him and for him
are characteristically his instruments in
the process of shaping the organization.

If any among them aspires to be other
than a device for the founder — that is, if
he wants to acquire power for himself —
he is soon likely to find himself on the
outside looking in. This is the reason
why so many organizations decline
when their founders age or die.

3. For the entrepreneur, the business is
essentially an extension of himself, a
medium for his personal gratification
and achievement above all. And if he is
concerned about what happens to his
business after he passes on, that concern usually takes the form of thinking
of the kind of monument he will leave
behind.

The fundamental psychological conflict
in family businesses is rivalry, compounded by feelings of guilt, when more
than one family member is involved.
The rivalry may be felt by the founder
— even though no relatives are in the
business — when he unconsciously sen-
ses (justifiably or not) that subordinates
are threatening to remove him from his
center of power. Consider this actual
case:

An entrepreneur, whose organization
makes scientific equipment and bears
his name, has built a sizable enterprise
in international markets. He has said
that he wants his company to be noted
all over the world for contributing to
society.

He has attracted many young men with
the promise of rapid promotions, but he
guarantees their failure by giving them
assignments and then turning them

loose without adequate organizational
support. He intrudes into the young
men's decision making, but he counter-
balances this behavior with paternalistic devices. (His company has more
benefits than any other I have known.)

This technique makes his subordinates
angry at him for what he has done, then
angry at themselves for being hostile to
such a kind man. Ultimately, it makes
them feel utterly inadequate. He can
get people to take responsibility and
move up into executive positions, but
his behavior has made certain that he
will never have a rival.

The conflicts created by rivalries among
family members — between fathers and
sons, among brothers, and between executives and other relatives — have a
chronically abrasive effect on the principals. Those family members in the
business must face up to the impact that
these relationships exert and must learn
to deal with them, not only for their own
emotional health but for the welfare of
the business.

I shall consider in turn the father-son
rivalry, the brother-brother rivalry, and
other family relationships.

Father-Son Rivalry

As I have indicated, for the founder the
business is an instrument, an extension
of himself. So he has great difficulty
giving up his baby, his mistress, his instrument, his source of social power, or
whatever else the business may mean to
him. Characteristically, he has great
difficulty delegating authority and he
also refuses to retire despite repeated
promises to do so.

This behavior has certain implications
for father-son relationships. While he
consciously wishes to pass his business
on to his son and also wants him to

attain his place in the sun, unconsciously the father feels that to yield the business would be to lose his masculinity.

At the same time, and also unconsciously, he needs to continue to demonstrate his own competence. That is, he must constantly reassure himself that he alone is competent to make "his" organization succeed. Unconsciously the father does not want his son to win, take away his combination baby and mistress, and displace him from his summit position.

These conflicting emotions cause the father to behave inexplicably in a contradictory manner, leading those close to him to think that while on the one hand he wants the business to succeed, on the other hand he is determined to make it fail.

The son's feelings of rivalry are a reflection of his father's. The son naturally seeks increasing responsibility commensurate with his growing maturity, and the freedom to act responsibly on his own. But he is frustrated by his father's intrusions, his broken promises of retirement, and his self-aggrandizement.

The son resents being kept in an infantile role—always the little boy in his father's eyes—with the accompanying contempt, condescension, and lack of confidence that in such a situation frequently characterize the father's attitude. He resents, too, remaining dependent on his father for his income level and, as often, for title, office, promotion, and the other usual perquisites of an executive. The father's erratic and unpredictable behavior in these matters makes this dependency more unpalatable.

I have observed a number of such men who, even as company presidents, are still being victimized by their fathers who remain chairmen of the board and chief executive officers.

'Why Don't You Let Me Grow Up?'

Characteristically, fathers and sons, particularly the latter, are terribly torn by these conflicts; the father looks on the son as ungrateful and unappreciative, and the son feels both hostile to his father and guilty for his hostility.

The father bears the feeling that the son never will be man enough to run the business, but he tries to hide that feeling from his son. The son yearns for his chance to run it and waits impatiently but still loyally in the wings—often for years beyond the age when others in nonfamily organizations normally take executive responsibility—for his place on the stage.

If the pressures become so severe for him that he thinks of leaving, he feels disloyal but at the same time fears losing the opportunity that would be his if he could only wait a little longer.

He defers his anticipated gratification and pleasure, but, with each postponement, his anger, disappointment, frustration, and tension mount. Here is a typical situation I know of:

Matthew Anderson, a man who founded a reclaimed-metals business, has two sons. John, the elder, is his logical successor, but Anderson has given him little freedom to act independently, pointing out that, despite limited education, he (the father) has built the business and intuitively knows more about how to make it successful.

Though he has told John that he wants him to be a partner, he treats John more like a flunky than an executive, let alone a successor. He pays the elder son a small salary, always with the excuse that he should not expect more because someday he will inherit the business.

444

He grants minimal raises sporadically, never recognizing John's need to support his family in a style fitting his position in the company.

When John once protested and demanded both more responsibility and more income, his father gave Henry, the second son, a vice presidential title and a higher income. When Henry asked for greater freedom and responsibility, Anderson turned back to John and made him president (in name only). The father, as chairman of the board and chief executive officer, continued to second-guess John, excluded Henry from conferences (which of course increased John's feelings of guilt), and told John that Henry was "no good" and could not run the business.

Later, when John sought to develop new aspects of the business to avoid the fluctuations of the metals market, his father vetoed these ideas, saying, "This is what we know, and this is what we're are going to do." He failed to see the possible destructive effects of market cycles on fixed overhead costs and the potential inroads of plastics and other cheaper materials on the reclaimed-metals business.

The upshot was that profits declined and the business became more vulnerable to both domestic and foreign (particularly Japanese) competition. When John argued with his father about this, he got the response: "What do you know? You're still green. I went through the Depression." Once again Anderson turned to Henry—making the black sheep white, and vice versa.

Angered, John decided to quit the business, but his mother said, "You can't leave your father; he needs you." Anderson accused him of being ungrateful, but he also offered to retire, as

he had promised to do several times before.

Despite his pain, John could not free himself from his father. (Only an ingrate would desert his father, he told himself.) Also John knew that if he departed, he could not go into competition with his father, because that would destroy him. But John shrank from entering an unfamiliar business.

Nevertheless, from time to time John has explored other opportunities while remaining in the business. But each time his father has undercut him. For instance, John once wanted to borrow money for a venture, but Anderson told the bankers that his son was not responsible.

Now, when John is middle-aged, he and his father are still battling. In effect John is asking, "Why don't you let me grow up?" and his father is answering, "I'm the only man around here. You must stay here and be my boy."

'He's Destroying the Business'

The son also has intense rivalry feelings, of course. These, too, can result in fierce competition with his father and hostile rejection of him, or abject dependence on him. Sometimes the competition can lead to a manipulative alignment with the mother against him. Consider this actual case:

Bill Margate, a recent business school graduate, knew that he would go into his father's electronic components business. But he decided that first he should get experience elsewhere, so he spent four years with a large manufacturing company. From his education and experience, he became aware of how unsophisticated his father was about running the business and set about showing the senior Margate how a business should be professionally managed.

Margate can do no right in Bill's eyes, at least not according to the books which he has read but which his father has never heard of. Bill frequently criticizes his father, showing how ignorant he is. When Margate calls his son "green," Bill retorts, "I've forgotten more about managing a business than you'll ever know."

Bill's mother is also involved in the business; she has been at her husband's side for many years, though their relationship is less than the best. Mrs. Margate dotes on her son and complains about him to her husband, and she encourages Bill in his attacks on his father. When Bill undertook several ventures that floundered, she excused the failures as being caused by his father's interference.

But whenever the father-son battle reaches a peak, Mrs. Margate shifts allegiance and stands behind her husband. So the senior Margate has an ally when the chips are down, at the price of a constant beating until he gets to that point.

The struggle for the business has remained a stand-off. But as the elder Margate has grown older, his son's attacks have begun to tell on him. Bill has urged him to take long Florida vacations, but Margate refuses because he fears what would happen when his back is turned. For the same reason, he does not permit Bill to sign checks for the company.

Now Margate has become senile, and Bill's criticism of him continues, even in public. "He's destroying the business," Bill will say.

However, Bill cannot act appropriately to remove his father (even though he is

now incompetent) because of his guilt feelings about his incessant attacks. That would destroy his father, literally, and he cannot bring himself to do it.

'The Old Man Really Built It'

The problem for the son becomes especially acute when and if he does take over. Often the father has become obsolete in his managerial conceptions. The organization may have grown beyond one man's capacity to control it effectively. That man may have been a star whose imagination, creativity, or drive are almost impossible to duplicate. He may also have been a charismatic figure with whom employees and even the public identified.

Whatever the combination of factors, the son is likely to have to take over an organization with many weaknesses hidden behind the powerful facade of the departed leader. For these reasons many businesses, at the end of their founders' tenure, fall apart, are pirated, or are merged into another organization.

The Ford Motor Company, at the demise of Henry Ford, was a case in point; a completely new management had to be brought in. Henry Ford II was faced with the uncomfortable task of having to regenerate a company that appeared to have the potential for continued success, but which, according to some, could easily have gone bankrupt.

While the son is acting to repair the organizational weaknesses left by his father, he is subject to the criticism of those persons who, envious of his position, are waiting for him to stumble. They "know" that he is not as good as his father. If he does less well than his father, regardless of whether there are unfavorable economic conditions or other causes, he is subject to the charge of having thrown away an opportunity that others could have capitalized on.

The scion cannot win. If he takes over a successful enterprise, and even if he makes it much more successful than anyone could have imagined, nevertheless the onlookers stimulate his feelings of inadequacy. They say, "What did you expect? After all, look what he started with." To illustrate:

Tom Schlesinger, the president of a restaurant chain, inherited the business after his father had built a profitable regional network of outlets with a widely known name—a model for the industry.

Tom has expanded it into nearly a national operation. He has done this with astute methods of finance that allow great flexibility, and with effective control methods that maintain meal quality and at the same time minimize waste. By any standards he has made an important contribution to the business.

But those who remember his father cannot see what Tom has done because the aura of his father still remains. They tend to minimize Tom's contribution with such observations as, "Well, you know, the old man really built that business."

Tom cannot change the attitude of those who knew his father, and he feels it is important to keep lauding his father's accomplishments in order to present a solid family image to employees, customers, and the community. But he is frustrated because he has no way of getting the world to see how well he has done.

Brother-Brother Rivalry

The father-son rivalry is matched in intensity by the brother-brother rivalry. Their competition may be exacerbated by the father if he tries to play the sons off against each other or has decided that one should wear his mantle, as I showed previously. (In my experience, the greatest difficulties of this kind occur when there are only two brothers in the organization.)

The problem is further complicated if their mother and their wives are also directly or indirectly involved in the business. Mothers have their favorites—regardless of what they say—and each wife, of course, has a stake in her husband's position. He can become a foil for his wife's fantasies and ambition.

The rivalry between brothers for their father's approval, which began in childhood, continues into adult life. It can reach such an intensity that it colors every management decision and magnifies the jockeying for power that goes on in all organizations. Consider this situation:

Arthur, five years older than his sibling, is president, and Warren is an operating vice president, of the medium-sized retailing organization which they inherited. To anyone who cares to listen, each maintains that he can get along very well without the other.

Arthur insists that Warren is not smart, not as good a businessman as he; that his judgment is bad; and that even if given the chance, he would be unable to manage the business.

Warren asserts that when the two were growing up, Arthur considered him to be a competitor, but for his part, he (Warren) did not care to compete because he was younger and smaller. Warren says that he cannot understand why his older brother has always acted as if they were rivals, and adds, "I just want a chance to do my thing. If he'd only let me alone with responsibility!

But he acts as if the world would fall apart if I had that chance."

Every staff meeting and meeting of the board (which includes nonfamily members) becomes a battle between the brothers. Associates, employees, and friends back off because they decline to take sides. The operation of the organization has been turned into a continuous family conflict.

The Elder . . .

Ordinarily, the elder brother succeeds his father. But this custom reaffirms the belief of the younger brother (or brothers) that the oldest is indeed the favorite. In any event, the older brother often has a condescending attitude toward the younger. In their earliest years the older is larger, physically stronger, more competent, and more knowledgeable than the younger merely because of the difference in age, as in the case I just cited.

Only in rare instances does the younger brother have the opportunity to match the skills, competence, and experience of the elder until they reach adulthood. By that time the nature of this relationship is so well established that the older brother has difficulty regarding the younger one as adequate and competent.

Moreover, the eldest child is earlier and longer in contact with the parents, and their control efforts fall more heavily on him. Consequently, older children tend to develop stronger consciences, drive themselves harder, expect more of themselves, and control themselves more rigidly than younger ones. Being already, therefore, a harsh judge of himself, the eldest is likely to be an even harsher judge of his younger siblings.

. . . And the Younger

The younger brother attempts to compensate for the effects of this childhood relationship and his older brother's efforts to control him by trying to carve out a place in the business that is his own. This he guards with great zeal, keeping the older brother out so he can demonstrate to himself, his brother, and others that he is indeed competent and has his own piece of the action for which he is independently responsible.

If the brothers own equal shares in the organization and both are members of the board, as is frequently the case, the problems are compounded. On the board they can argue policy from equally strong positions. However, when they return to operations in which one is subordinate to the other, the subordinate one, usually the junior brother, finds it extremely difficult to think of himself in a subservient role.

The younger one usually is unable to surmount this problem in their mutual relationship. He tends to be less confident than his brother and considers himself to be at a permanent disadvantage, always overcontrolled, always unheeded. Since the older brother views the younger one as being less able, he becomes involved in self-fulfilling prophecies. Distrusting his younger brother, he is likely to overcontrol him, give him less opportunity for freedom and responsibility—which in turn make for maturity and growth—and likely to reject all signs of the younger brother's increasing competence.

If for some reason the younger brother displaces the older one, and particularly if the latter becomes subordinate to him, the younger brother is faced with feelings of guilt for having attacked the elder and usurped what so often is accepted as the senior brother's rightful role.

Intrafamily Friction

The problems of the father and brothers extend to other relatives when they, too, become involved in the business. In some families it is expected that all who wish to join the company will have places there. This can have devastating effects, particularly if the jobs are sinecures.

The chief executive of a family business naturally feels a heavy responsibility for the family fortunes. If he does not produce a profit, the effect on what he considers to be his image in the financial markets may mean less to him than the income reduction which members of his family will suffer. So he is vulnerable to backbiting from persons whom he knows only too well and whom he cannot dismiss as faceless. Consider this case:

Three brothers started a knitting business. Only one of the brothers had sons, and only one of those sons stayed in the business; he eventually became president. The stock is held by the family. Two widowed aunts, his mother, his female cousins (one of whom was already widowed), and his brother, a practicing architect, depend on the business for significant income.

When business is off, the women complain. If the president wants to buy more equipment, they resist. If they hear complaints from employees or merchant friends, they make these complaints known at family gatherings. The president is never free from the vixens who are constantly criticizing and second-guessing him.

Perhaps more critical for the health of the business are the factional divisions that spring up in the organization as associates and subordinates choose the family members with whom they want to be identified. (Often, however, those

who take sides discover that in a crisis the family unites against "outsiders," including their partisans, who are then viewed as trying to divide the family.)

If the nonfamily employees or board members decide not to become involved in a family fight and withdraw from relations with its members until the conflict is resolved, the work of the organization may be paralyzed. Worse yet, the dispute may eventually embroil the entire organization, resulting in conflicts at the lower levels, as employees try to cope with the quarrels thrust on them.

Now the business has become a battleground that produces casualties but no peace. Such internecine warfare constitutes a tremendous barrier to communication and frustrates adequate planning and rational decision making.

A business in which numerous members of the family of varying ages and relationships are involved often becomes painfully disrupted around issues of empires and succession. Its units tend to become family-member territories and therefore poorly integrated organizationally, if at all.

As for succession, the dominant or patriarchal leader may fully expect to pass on the mantle of leadership to other, elder relatives in their turn. He may even promise them leadership roles, particularly if he has had to develop a coalition to support his position.

But for both realistic and irrational reasons he may well come to feel that none of the family members is capable of filling the role. He cannot very well disclose his decision, however, without stirring conflict, and he cannot bring in outside managers without betraying his relatives or reneging on his promises.

On the other hand, he fears what would happen if he died without having designated a successor.

He may decide that the only way out is to sell the business (at least each relative will then get his fair share). But that solution is costly—it signifies not only the loss of the business as a means of employment, but also the betrayal of a tradition and, inevitably, the dissolution of close family ties that have been maintained through the medium of the business.

Facing Up To It

What can be done about these problems?

Most entrepreneurial fathers seem unable to resolve their dilemma themselves. They tend to be rigid and righteous, finding it difficult to understand that there is another, equally valid point of view which they can accept without becoming weaklings. Well-meaning outsiders who try to help the father see the effects of his behavior and think seriously about succession usually find themselves rejected. Then they lose whatever beneficial influence they may have had on him.

Several approaches have worked well. In some instances, sons have told their fathers that they recognize how important it is to the father to run his own business, but it is just as important for them to have the opportunity to "do their own thing." They then establish small new ventures either under the corporate umbrella or outside it, without deserting their father.

In a variant of this approach, a father who heads a retail operation opened a store in a different community for each of his sons. They do their buying together, with appropriate variations for each community, and maintain a

common name and format, but each son runs his own operation while the father continues to run his.

In still another situation, the father merged his company into a larger one. Each of his two sons then became president of a subsidiary, and the father started a new venture while serving as a policy guide to his sons.

The Son's Role

Whether such alternatives can work depends in part on how the son conducts himself. He must be honest with himself and consider his paternal relationship candidly. He must take steps like these:

• He must ask himself why he chose to go into the family business. Most sons say it is because of the opportunity and the feelings of guilt if they had not done so. Often, however, the basic reason is that a powerful father has helped make his son dependent on him, and so his son is reluctant to strike out on his own.

He rationalizes his reluctance on the basis of opportunity and guilt. Struggling with his own dependency, he is more likely to continue to fight his father in the business because he is still trying to escape his father's control.

• Having examined this issue, and recognizing whatever validity it may have for him, the son must realize how often his own feelings of rivalry and anger get in his way. The more intense the rivalry, the more determinedly he seeks to push his father from his throne and the more aggressively the latter must defend himself. The son must therefore refrain from attack.

• He must quietly and with dignity, as a mature man, apprise his father of the realities—that he needs an area of freedom and an independent medium to develop skills and responsibilities. He can do so within the company framework or, if that is not feasible, outside it. In his own self-interest, as well as the company's, he must be certain that he gets the opportunity.

- He must not allow himself to be played off against his brother, and he must not allow his guilt to be manipulated. By the same token, he himself must become involved with others in manipulation.

- He must honestly recognize and respect his father's achievement and competence. To build a business is no mean task, and usually the father still has useful skills and knowledge. Furthermore, the son should recognize the powerful psychological meaning of the business to his father and not expect him to be rational about his relationship to it.

If the son is still unable to make choices about what he wants to do, then, despite his pain and his father's reluctance to seek help, he himself must do so. Only he can take the initiative to relieve his anguish. Here is an example of how a group of sons has taken the initiative:

In Boston, a group calling itself SOB's (Sons of the Boss) has been formed to encourage men in that position to talk over common problems and share solutions. After educating themselves about the psychological dimensions of their situation, the group will make it a practice from time to time to invite their fathers as a group to discuss their problems openly. Then fathers and sons will get together separately.

This procedure may enable fathers and sons to realize that their particular problems are not unique to themselves,

and to obtain support from those in a similar predicament.

Another approach for a son would be to ask his father to read this article and then discuss it privately with a neutral third party of their choice, to develop a perspective on their feelings and behavior. Having done so, a father is then in a better position to talk with his son, in the presence of the third party.

The third person must use his good offices to subdue recrimination. At the same time he must foster the father's expression of his fears over losing control, being unneeded, and suffering rejection, as well as the son's concerns about being overcontrolled, infantilized, and exploited.

If meeting with the third party fails to help, the next step is consultation with a psychologist or psychiatrist. There are rare instances, usually when conflict becomes severe, in which father and son are willing to go to a professional together or separately. In such cases it is often possible for the father to begin to make compromises, learn to understand his and his son's motivations, and work out with him newly defined, more compatible roles. Usually, however, such an effort requires continued supportive work by the professional and strong desire on the part of both men to resolve their differences.

If all these measures fail, those who work with patriarchs must learn to tolerate their situation until the opportunity arises for a change.

Fraternal Spirit

With respect to the brother-brother conflict, it is important for brothers to see that in their relationship they recapitulate ancient rivalries, and to perceive clearly the psychological posture each assumes toward the other.

Once they understand these two issues, they must talk together about them. They should try to discuss freely the fears, worries, anger, and disappointments caused by each other. They should also be able to talk about their affection for each other.

Since there is love and hate in all relationships, theirs cannot, by definition, be pure. They should not feel guilty about their anger with each other, but they do need to talk it out. Having done that, they then must consider how they can divide the tasks in the organization so that each will have a chance to acquire and demonstrate competence and work in a complementary relationship with the other.

A brother cannot easily be subordinate at one level and equal on another. If a brother is an operating executive subordinate to the other, he gets into difficulty when he tries to be an equal on the board of directors. If more than one brother is on the board, then only one, as a rule, should be an operating executive. Of course, such rules are unnecessary if the brothers work well together.

If the brothers still cannot resolve their conflicts, then it becomes necessary to seek professional aid. If that does not help, they should consider being in separate organizations. In such a case, the big problem is the guilt feelings which the departing brother is likely to have for deserting the other and the family business.

Toward Professional Management

Where there are multiple and complex family relationships and obligations in a company, and particularly problems about succession, the best solution is a transcendent one. The family members should form a trust, taking all the relatives out of business operations while enabling them to continue to act in concert as a family.

The trust could allot financial support to every member who desires it to develop new business ventures on behalf of the family, thus providing a business interest that replaces the previous operating activity. This also helps maintain family cohesion and preserve the family's leadership role in the community.

In general, the wisest course for any business, family or nonfamily, is to move to professional management as quickly as possible. Every business must define its overriding purpose for being, from which it derives its objectives. Within this planning framework, the business must have a system for appraising the degree to which it and its components are achieving the goals that have been set.

All organizations need to rear subordinates in a systematic manner, thus creating the basic condition for their own regeneration. I know of no family business capable of sustaining regeneration over the long term solely through the medium of its own family members.

Where there is conflict, or inadequately rationalized territories, members of the family should move up and out of operations as quickly as possible into policy positions. Such movement recognizes the reality of ownership but does not confuse ownership with management.

It also opens the opportunity for professionally trained managers to succeed to major operating roles, instead of having to go to other organizations as soon as they are ready for major responsibility. The more competitive the business situation, the more imperative such a succession pattern is.

More than others, the family members need to have their own outside activities from which they can derive gratification equal to what they can obtain in the company. Otherwise they will be unable to let go and will continue to be barriers to others. Moreover, they will make it difficult to recruit and develop young persons with leadership potential who, as they mature, will see the inevitable barriers.

A number of family businesses have handled these issues wisely and have become highly professional in their management. The Dayton-Hudson Corporation and E. I. du Pont de Nemours are examples. Family members in both organizations must compete for advancement on the same terms as nonfamily managers. This practice is reinforced, at least at Dayton-Hudson, by a thorough performance appraisal system which includes appraisal of the chairman and president by a committee of the board.

Concluding Note

It is very difficult to cope with the problems of the family business. That does not mean, however, that one should merely endure them. There is no point in stewing in anger and guilt, since chronic irritation is only self-flagellation. It solves no problems; it only increases anger and hostility and paves the way for explosion, recrimination, and impaired relations.

The family member can do something about such problems, as he can with any other. If reasonable steps to solve the problems do not work and he continues to feel bound to the organization, his problem is largely psychological. To free himself to make choices about what he wants to do, he must talk his feelings out with his rival in the organization, which is best done in the presence of a neutral third person. Sometimes professional help is necessary.

This will reduce sufficiently the intensity of the emotions generated by the problem, so that he can see possible alternatives more clearly and make choices more freely. That is better than the years of agitation that usually accompany such problems, unless of course the rival needs to expiate his guilt by continuing to punish himself. In that case, it is his problem and not necessarily that of the family business.

1. For two thoughtful views of the subject, see Robert G. Donnelley, "The Family Businesses," *Harvard Business Review*, July-August 1964, p. 93; and Seymour Tilles, "Survival Strategies for Family Firms," *European Business*, April 1970, p. 9.

2. See Orvin F. Collins, David G. Moore, and Darab B. Unwalla, *The Enterprising Man* (East Lansing, Michigan State University Bureau of Business Research, 1964).

Introduction

This article is about differences among family members in business together, the problems such differences can cause and how such problems can be dealt with. The root of problems, suggest the authors, is the desire for others to be like oneself. Confronted with the problems wrought by differences, people tend to avoid conflict, complain to other or fail to communicate effectively. Suggestions for solutions include: stop blaming the other guy, commit to doing something, get outside help, learn listening and feedback skills, learn problems solving and negotiating skills, devote some concentrated time to the effort, and recognize the despite your efforts, failure is a real possibility.

All in the Family: Why Can't He Be More Like Me?
1982

By Peter Wylie and Mardy Grothe

This is an article about what it's like to be a father or son in a family-owned business. It's also a story about being in a relationship with another human being who's *different* from you. It's about the problems these differences can cause and about how *you* probably tackle these problems. And finally it's about what's needed to help fathers and sons deal more effectively with these kinds of problems.

To help make our story as interesting and relevant as possible, you might even read the article along with your father or son. Or at least have him read it when you're finished.

The Source of the Problem

Now take this person you've spent so many years with and start thinking a little bit about how the two of you are different. For example, you might tend to be a real striver whereas he is more relaxed about his work. He might tend to be a decisive person who like to move quickly, while you are more cautious. Or you may be sort of broad-brush in your approach to things, while he may be rather detail-oriented. Reserved/outgoing. Demanding/low-key. Laid-back/worrier...

Now it's perfectly natural for the two of you to be different in these and many

454

other ways. Every human being is unique. That's not the problem. The problem is the way you *see* each other's differences.

Now think for a moment about some of his major traits and how they've bothered you. Think about the times when your stomach muscles tightened or your blood pressure rose after he said or did something that upset you. Write down your thoughts. After you've done that, write down some of the things he might say about you.

By now, we hope you'll see that the trouble isn't that you're different from each other. The trouble is that you both find it hard to understand why the other guy can't see and do things *your* way. Somewhere down inside, maybe not right on the surface, each of you keeps asking: *"Why can't he be more like me?"* And that's the root of the problem. Believing the other guy should be more like you is the cause of most flareups in both professional and personal relationships. Whether or not he should be more like you, he's not going to be more like you. Not in any fundamental way. He's always going to be more like himself.

But if you're like most of us, you don't give up hope. You keep persisting, keep hoping he'll change. And when he doesn't, you start getting frustrated and confused. Or resentful and angry. And all these feelings help drastically reduce your working effectiveness.

Common Pitfalls

From our personal experience as partners and from helping father-and-son teams in family-owned businesses, we'd bet that the two of you tackle your problems with each other by doing at least one of these things:

1. You avoid dealing with the problem.

2. You complain to somebody else about the problem.

3. If you do sit down to discuss the problem, you find you can't communicate effectively.

Let's talk a little about each of these three tendencies, why you do them and what makes them so bad.

1. Avoiding the Problem

This is typical of a lot of relationships. Husbands and wives often avoid their problems for years. Friends, even pretty good ones, do it too. Avoiding the problem doesn't necessarily mean you don't talk to your father or you son. In fact, you may do a lot of talking with each other. But what you don't do is talk about the important things, the "touchy" subjects that really bother you. Why? We've heard lots of reasons: (a) "He's pretty sensitive—I don't want to hurt his feelings"; (b) "I'm not sure how he'd react. It could make things a lot worse"; (c) "Now's not a good time. Let's not upset the apple cart." But what's the *real* reason? "I'm scared! Even the thought of sitting down to talk about it makes me nervous."

Unfortunately, being scared, as understandable as it is, isn't a good reason for avoiding these problems. *Not* dealing with your problems won't make them go away. If anything, they're going to get worse.

2. Complaining to Somebody Else

This is something all of us do from time to time. We unburden our frustrations about a person on other people. We complain to our spouses about how difficult the guy is to work with. We corner our friends at cocktail parties and bend their ears about how unreasonable he is.

We even do it on airplanes with complete strangers.

Why do we complain about fathers or sons to people outside the relationship?

Several reasons:

- It's easier to talk to somebody else about him. Going to him directly would make you nervous, anxious and uncomfortable.

- You usually get some sympathy. People say nice things like, "Oh, I can imagine how frustrating that must be for you. I don't see how you put up with him."

- You can fool yourself into thinking that you're really doing something about the problem. After all, you usually feel pretty good after a "venting" session.

But complaining doesn't get the job done. You eventually become an annoyance, a pain in the neck to the people you complain to. More important, you're wasting your time talking to the wrong person. Sooner or later, you've got to go to the source, if the problems between the two of you are going to get solved. You've just got to sit down face-to-face, eyeball-to-eyeball and get things out on the table.

3. Not Communicating Effectively

So let's say you screw up your courage, sit down and confront your father or son with the fact that you've both got to do some things differently to improve your relationship. He agrees and says, "let's talk about it." One guy starts out being the "talker" and the other guy starts out being the "listener." But as soon as the talker says something the listener disagrees with or that makes him nervous—boom! The two of you immediately get quagmired in an argument, and then neither listens to what

the other is saying. All you do is prepare your counter-argument while the other guy is talking. And you get absolutely nowhere. The problem doesn't get solved. It may even get worse because now you're both more pessimistic than ever about being able to sit down and really talk the thing out.

"Well," you say, "avoiding the problem doesn't seem to make much sense. Complaining also doesn't do much good. But when we sit down to talk about it, we don't make much progress. What do I do?"

What to Do

Let's say you and your father or your son are having some of the kinds of problems described above. And you'd like to do something to resolve them. Here are a few suggestions:

- Stop blaming the other guy. Don't lay all the responsibility for the problem on him and the way he is. You're part of the problem too. And *both* of you will have to be part of the solution.

- Make a commitment to do something about the problem. Say to yourself, "It doesn't have to be this way. I'm going to do something to improve the situation. I'm not going to cheat myself out of enjoying my life and my work one more minute!" Try to get the same commitment from him.

- Agree to get some outside help. If the two of you were married, you might get into marriage counseling. Find a sensitive and skilled person to help you resolve your differences. There aren't many people around who do this sort of thing, but you'll find somebody if you look hard enough.

- You've got to learn how to communicate effectively with each other. And this will take a lot of hard work. Most people would rather talk than listen when they're upset about something. You've got to learn how to draw the other guy out, to get him to talk fully and freely, especially when he's saying something you disagree with or that makes you nervous. You've got to learn how to give him feedback so that your message has a good chance of being heard. You'll probably need some help learning these valuable listening and presenting skills.

- You've got to learn some problem-solving and negotiating skills to go beyond the resolution of differences. You need to learn how to capitalize on your differences, not agonize over them. By coming up with solutions you can both live with, you can create a relationship where the two of you are more than just the sum of your parts.

- You've got to be willing to devote some concentrated time to these efforts. Problems between fathers and sons in family-owned businesses don't arise overnight. They're often years in the making. You may want to get off to an isolated spot for several days (with outside help) to get the issues out on the table and learn some skills and techniques to resolve the problems you've been experiencing. Continuing with regular follow-up sessions to keep the momentum going and intercept potential new problems is also a good idea.

- You've got to accept the possibility that all of these efforts may not work. There's a good chance that you'll be able to forge an effective and enjoyable working relationship if you follow these suggestions. But you may fail. You may discover that the best course is for one of you to leave the business, as painful and complicated as that might be. But you'll decide to do that knowing you gave it your best shot. And you'll vastly reduce the amount of acrimony and pain that usually accompanies such a decision.

Introduction

When the author's husband went to work for her father, everyone suffered. Then she discovered 16 rules for making a family business run smoothly.

How to Keep Families from Feuding
1982

By Margaret Crane

I will never forget that hot, muggy day in the summer of 1980 when my husband came home and announced he had marched boldly into my father's office and resigned.

Anger and disbelief were my first reactions. But I wasn't surprised: Trouble between my father and my husband had been brewing for almost six years. For all this time, I had been living in the middle of an emotional tug-of-war that is all too typical of what happens in family businesses.

The strain began when my father, Joseph Rothberg, finally decided he needed a successor to carry on our St. Louis-based wholesale wine-and-spirits business. My father had no heir apparent and at first considered selling out. Then it occurred to him to invite my husband, Nolan, to join the family company. Without much discussion, the two men agreed to work together—

and then spent six years feuding with each other.

For my father, a self-made man who grew up as part of a generation dedicated to the values of sacrifice and hard work, learning to share any authority in the company he created was difficult. For 32 years he had pushed, prodded, and nurtured his Manhattan Distributing Co. to make it grow and prosper. When the company first opened its doors in 1950, it was one of 22 St. Louis-area liquor wholesalers, with a staff of 10, one spirit line, and annual gross sales of $300,000. Today, Manhattan has become the third-largest independent wine-and-spirits house in Missouri, and has 90 employees, more than 40 lines, and annual gross sales approaching $30 million.

Over the years, the business had become my father's alter ego. He had learned to manage every aspect of the business by himself. But now that Manhattan had become a much larger operation, it was becoming clear to all of us that management changes were needed.

458

So in walked my husband, a son-in-law, who represented those changes. Unlike my father, Nolan was the product of a more leisure-oriented generation. He had spent 10 years working for large corporations, and his motives for entering the family business were varied — security, economic stability, a chance to get ahead faster. He was anxious to succeed, but was not as willing as my father to devote his entire life to the business. Moreover, Nolan was in a hurry to learn everything he could, at times displaying little patience and coming across as brash and too assertive.

To avoid confrontations, my father soon became isolated at the top. He made decisions in a vacuum, and rarely talked to Nolan about goals, job responsibilities, or the industry itself. As the situation grew worse, I could see my husband becoming irritable, cynical, depressed. He did not know how to approach my father to talk about the problem, and never felt quite confident about his role in the company and his authority to make the changes he felt were necessary.

Both tried to draw my mother and me into the battle, but we refused to take sides. I felt a lot of the stresses personally. When there were disagreements, I constantly had to fight the urge to get involved. This became my toughest challenge.

I knew for my own sanity I would have to take action without getting visibly involved in their battle. I decided to learn all I could about family business relationships, but didn't know where to begin.

I was lucky. One night at a cocktail party, I overheard a friend who works for his father in the construction business commenting, "I'll never have any say in our business unless they carry my father out feet first." He went on to mention his membership in an organization called Sons of Bosses, which had helped him in dealing with the situation.

I discovered that the St. Louis chapter of SOB is one of the largest and strongest in the country, so I contacted the local SOB founder, Marc Boguslaw, to find some answers. I also attended a lecture by SOB founder Gerry Slavin.

My first discovery was that there is a subtle difference between a son and a son-in-law (or a daughter and a daughter-in-law) in a family business. A son often has a tough time because his father knows him too well to be dispassionate about the son's actions and mistakes. With every decision that involves passing on responsibility, a father often cannot help thinking of his son at least partly as a child rather than an adult.

A son-in-law, by contrast, comes into a family firm with a clean slate. He is accepted as an adult. But he is still a stranger and his father-in-law may perceive him as an opportunist who walks into a role he did not work to earn.

As I talked with SOB members about their own experiences with family businesses, I began to see that my father and husband had done a lot of things wrong. And when the big blowup finally occurred — over my father's cancellation of a wine order my husband had placed — my shock was tempered by a good deal of understanding of the emotional strain both men had endured.

In fact, my husband's resignation became the turning point in his relationship with my father. For the first time, the two of them had let their real feelings show, and were talking about the reasons for friction. My father conceded that he had acted hastily, and asked my husband to stay on. It took a few months, but after that incident, he and Nolan began to communicate and show some real respect for each other.

We all began to think more about how to make a difficult relationship work better. Ultimately, we realized there are some simple, practical rules that anyone who brings a family member into his business should follow.

Rule 1. *Deal objectively with a son or son-in-law's qualifications.* We learned this rule the hard way, because failure to follow it plagued us for six years. Nolan brought to his new job a solid background in promotion and marketing as a division manager for Capitol Records and Warner Communications for 10 years. But his particular experience and skills weren't ideal qualifications for his new financial and management responsibilities. He knew absolutely nothing about the liquor industry, and needed training—which my father wasn't willing to supply.

The two of them should have talked in advance about how Nolan would learn the things he needed to know. Would my husband start at the bottom and learn every aspect of the business on his own? Would he rely on middle management to train him? Would he start at the top and learn from observing my father in action? In the end, the answer turned out to be a combination of all three methods. This uncertainty caused a lot of wasted effort and bruised feelings.

Rule 2. *A son or son-in-law should acquire practical experience elsewhere.* This allows the junior family member to grow and mature away from home and will give him a different perspective on how a company is best organized and managed.

Rule 3. *Clearly define responsibilities.* It was not until shortly after Nolan began working at Manhattan that he realized how really reluctant my father was to share his position and power in the company. When he saw that his job was so loosely defined, Nolan quickly began to figure out the tasks my father did not like to do, and focused his efforts on doing those things better, or at least as well. He also created his own job function and title, initially calling himself "general manager," and started to work with the sales staff and key outside accounts. But he could never feel fully confident about his authority, or be sure he was doing the right job.

Rule 4. *Divide responsibilities.* To avoid future power struggles, we learned, it is also a good idea to assign each family member a job that he does best. Nolan is most effective in sales and is an excellent manager of people. My father excels in finance and purchasing. Yet the two never sat down and divided their roles accordingly. As a result, each fought for his own bit of turf, and their functions constantly overlapped.

Rule 5. *Establish working hours in advance.* Are you expected to work 9 to 5? Are you supposed to be the first to arrive and the last to leave? Are there busy seasons with extended hours? How much travel does the job entail? When my father was building his business, he worked long, hard hours, and felt this kind of dedication was necessary for success. My husband, who is a well-organized, no-nonsense manager, believes in working hard, but also likes to devote time to family and has many outside interests. In my research with SOB and in talking to other sons and sons-in-law, I have discovered one hard-and-fast rule about hours. Those going into a family firm must be prepared to work harder, longer hours in the first five years than they have ever worked in their lives.

Rule 6. *Find out who reports to whom.* This might include some discussion of the attitude of employees who have been with the firm for some time. Discuss with your father or father-in-law how you will be introduced to these employees and in what way you will be working with them. When my husband began, he did not have a staff of his own. So he created one. He initially tried to establish a good working relationship with all employees. But because his role was vague, many veteran employees felt threatened by my husband's presence, until they grew to trust and respect him.

Rule 7. *Plan office space and equipment carefully.* A former meeting room, which is attached to my father's office, serves as my husband's office. The proximity of the two offices has been auspicious. My husband is in the center of the action, and has been privy to important meetings, phone conversations, and various business transactions from which he might have been excluded otherwise.

Rule 8. *Introduce the son or son-in-law to key outside people.* This significantly helps to build the heir apparent's credibility, but my father overlooked this responsibility most of the time. As a result, Nolan had to take it upon himself to develop a relationship with the company's bankers, accountants, suppliers, insurance agents, union managers, and attorneys. This often put tremendous pressure on him, since my father was not available to provide background information or support. For example, Nolan was forced to learn about union management when employees started to come to him with grievances. Afraid he would mishandle situations without knowing union rules

thoroughly, he had to work exceptionally hard to keep in touch with union executives.

Rule 9. *Discuss salary and perks in advance.* When negotiating salaries, it is vital to talk about raises and bonuses, expenses, and amenities such as cars, insurance, and vacation time. After he began, Nolan discovered that my father does not believe in taking vacations unless they are business-related. Nolan, however, feels vacations are an important time to get away from business to clear his mind. It took him a couple of years before he felt comfortable taking time off for himself.

Rule 10. *Fight issues, not emotions.* This is the most important rule my husband has learned. For example, almost two years ago, when the time seemed ripe for expansion, my husband was determined to make my father see the importance of entering the wine market by forming a separate wholesale wine company. After plotting and pushing, he got the okay. But this was the beginning of almost daily confrontations. He and my father began to fight over people hired and money being spent. If they had discussed plans for company expansion rationally, before my husband began working for my father, much of this could have been resolved.

Rule 11. *A son or son-in-law, to be effective, should be free to do things his own way.* He cannot be intimidated by what others might think. For example, I consider my husband's biggest contribution to our family business to be simply his ability to pick good people, then staying out of their way. But this is the antithesis of my father's approach. Just months after my husband began work, he realized that to handle the direction in which the business was growing, it was impossible for one man to continue to manage everything. The company had to departmentalize, and it had to hire good managers who could make their own decisions. So my husband began hiring new people and firing those who had become obsolete. His approach risked upheaval, but it paid off.

Rule 12. *Define the roles of other family members in the business.* Right now my husband is the only second-generation family member in the business. Regardless, it is important for any son or son-in-law to discuss the possibility of other relatives coming into the firm in the future. One of my husband's friends works in a third-generation family business with 10 relatives. There are few problems. Ownership is concentrated in one able successor and the rest of the family has divided the responsibilities into mutually exclusive territories.

Rule 13. *Work together on estate planning.* A son or son-in-law should be apprised of all legal estate planning and should be included in any meetings that relate to this.

Rule 14. *A son or son-in-law must begin to learn on his own.* My father is one of the most highly respected and established leaders in the liquor industry and my husband has learned a great deal from observing him. Yet any effective manager has to go further and take courses, attend seminars to improve business management skills and make use of videotapes and other teaching aids.

Rule 15. *After a year or so, arrange a long vacation for the boss.* It is important for a father or father-in-law to see that the business will not fall apart or go bankrupt without him around. This was the hardest rule for us to deal with. My husband had been urging my father for several years to take an extended vacation, which he finally did about two years ago. He went to Europe and, for perhaps the first time in his life, really relaxed and ignored the business.

Rule 16. *Establish a family council.* We have found this is an excellent way to communicate and to air any problems or differences that might otherwise be overlooked or ignored if they had to be discussed during the business week.

I have discovered one additional principle. Time is on the side of the son or son-in-law, if he can wait long enough to get to do what he wants. But it is not worth the years of aggravation to reach this point when problems may be worked out in advance.

It has been six years and my father is just now slowly beginning to back out of certain areas of the business, giving my husband more control and autonomy. Although he will never completely let go, my father now sincerely wants to let my husband have the reins when they are both ready.

As for my husband, today he is exactly where he wants to be as president of a newly formed subsidiary wine company (Allied Wine) and as executive vice-president of the parent company, on the leading edge of a fast-growing wine and spirits operation. With good people and resources behind him, he can now get more personally involved in the corporate finances and in making creative decisions.

Sales are increasing rapidly. We are acquiring new lines on a regular basis. And most important, suppliers feel safe with Manhattan and Allied because they are solid, family-owned and family-operated companies.

Introduction

Estate plans are frequently put together without the slightest thought as to the survivors and, once the estate owner has left the scene, it is the survivors who must live with what has been done. As a result, more of the professional executors time is spent on people problems and human relations work than on tax and legal matters. This is especially true when a family business is involved in the estate.

The Importance of Human Relations in Estate Administration

1975

By Gerald L. Gaffner

Not much attention has been paid to the psychology of either estate planning or administration. I'm afraid that we have buried that aspect because it borders on the mystical, the unquantifiable or the occult. It is far easier to prepare orderly charts and graphs and comparative figures of taxation rather than analyze the characteristics of those who will live under the terms of these charts and graphs. It is far easier to acclimate them to the abstractions of the plan than to the realities. Yet, when that plan is activated, it is for the most part irrevocable and its terms are applied not just to assets but to human beings and their emotions. Loss of a loved one is never an easy experience but such a loss aggravated by poor people planning can be painful.

The simple truth is that the estate plans are frequently put together without the slightest thought to survivors — only the figures. This may be satisfactory to the client who asked you to participate in the plan, but once he has left the scene, it is the survivor or survivors who must live with what has been done, and, all too often, attempt to comprehend and appreciate it. The planner has a duty to consider the implications for the survivors; and to point these implications out to the estate owner who may be so mesmerized by the tax savings that he can't see the family implications.

I will not dwell on the psychological aspect of enticing a client into estate planning. The estate owner is not the subject of my remarks.

However, one of the psychological problems of the estate owner is the inability to articulate plans and envision problems which can develop at death.

It is this inability which I believe receives short attention in the planning stage and which can cause the most problems in administration, particularly where that inability relates to the elicitation of personal data about the family. It is difficult enough to ask for confidential financial information but it is exceedingly awkward to delve into personal relationships. However, the availability of that information and the reasoning it contains is most helpful to the Estate Administrator in his later work.

In this short span of time, one cannot fully discuss all of the planning stage human relationships, psychological and communications problems which will someday be factors in the Estate Administration. There are three areas which stand out in my mind as paramount considerations for the gathering of information and the preparation of the survivors.

Two of these areas are rather specific but are surrounded by nebulous inquiries. They are, "Will the widow or a child be named as a co-executor?" "How will the family business be handled?" and, finally, the more indefinable of the three, "Has the plan really been communicated to the survivors?"

The majority of the professional executor's time, at least in my experience, is usually spent with "people problems" and not with actual tax and legal questions. I believe that a far greater portion of the executor's total time commitment is devoted to human relations work rather than to technicalities or in explanation of technicalities.

A further generalization is that it is usually a widow who consumes the major portion of that time. It, therefore, seems to follow that she should consume in most instances as much or more time than the estate owner in the planning stage.

Time after time, the widow and children are completely excluded from the planning process. There may be reasons for the exclusion. There are families where the wife is completely unprepared to handle financial matters and no degree of training or reeducation will increase her capabilities. However, the planner should make a studied decision about that possible fact with the estate owner. The husband should be probed in detail about his wife's abilities and temperament and those of his children. When they are included in planning, I believe the planner must be specific about the events which will occur after the husband's death.

Why do they need to know? After all, it is supposedly in their best interests, isn't it? I can only empathize by saying that I know how resentful I am when plans are made for my "benefit" and I am not included. I am naturally resentful or at least suspicious of the end product. That is sometimes the attitude of the unconsulted child and wife after death.

This lack of involvement can be a problem for the corporate executor. An attorney could not have stated the problem more eloquently when he said: "How do you deal with a lady who suddenly finds herself to be a widow involved with an estate handled by a bank she neither likes nor wants, sitting with a young trust officer she neither likes nor wants?" Reflection about his statement told me that a widow can have that reaction. Indeed, I have had a few who have admitted later on in administration that they had experienced a desperate feeling after suddenly finding themselves at the mercy of a corporate executor, not really knowing those who were to help them and completely

uninstructed about the events beginning to unfold. It is this desperate feeling, sometimes a sensation of being
trapped, which must be dispelled quickly or you will suddenly hear her saying
that all their family property has been
given away, tied up in trust, or, that half
the estate was given away to the
children, and on and on.

All widows and even some children,
whether average, brilliant, or dull need
the privilege of consultation about the
estate plan. If they are to be involved
with a corporate executor, they need to
be taken to the trust department for a
personal visit. It is highly advisable that
they meet and have an acquaintance
with everyone in the estate planning
team.

Use of Explanatory Letter

Some of the planners in our area summarize the estate plan for the major
parties with a letter after the plan is
prepared. These are most helpful. We
incorporate them into our permanent
probate file when they are available
after the death of the estate owner.

Near the end of the planning process or
at its end, I strongly urge that the estate
owner draft a simple letter explaining
his plan to his family and the executor.
It will help him clarify the plan and his
thoughts and it will later help his family
in understanding his plan. Such a letter
should be written with care and
reviewed by his attorney. However, it
can cover many instructions not stated
in the will.

Such a letter is helpful when the wife
and/or prime beneficiaries have been
involved in planning but they are ten
times as helpful where one or more of
those people have not been involved. I
see such a letter as precatory in nature.
Including statements of wishes and

intentions can make a considerable difference in post-mortem human relations and communications. It becomes
a personal expression of intent
separated from the legalese of the formal document. There are numerous
areas in which such letters could be
utilized. The uses will be apparent from
the facts as you are able to discern them
in the planning stage. Let me mention
a few possibilities.

It seems to me that the most frequently
misunderstood will provision is the two-
trust marital residuary split. In most
instances, the wife is the Number One
beneficiary and the split was made for
tax reasons. All too frequently, the
widow considers the second trust a dis-
inheritance, a taboo source of funds to
which she should not look to for assistance. Even with great insistence she
would rather do without than look to the
"children's money." Often, no explanation was given to the children about the
residuary trust. Immediate inquiries
begin to flow in about distributions from
their share and such a concept of the
trusts may be true. In either case, if the
decedent were to outline his understanding of how it works, it would help.
Let me suggest a few possible clauses
for such a letter.

For instance, "I have set up two trusts
for the maximum tax advantage. I do
not mean by this arrangement to
diminish the main purpose of my
trust — the care of Mary. I have left the
benefit of all of the income to her and
much of the principal. I have provided
the authority for the trustee to make
encroachments for the children and to
use income for their benefit. I hope that
they will make no requests for funds
except in extreme need and that they
will meet their ordinary needs from
their own endeavors and not think of
this as a new bank account."

The elderly are sometimes offended by arrangements of deceased children for trusts, so possibly this message: "I hope, Mother and Dad, that neither of you will consider this trust as evidence of a lack of confidence in you. I know that time may have its effects on you in later years. I have thought long and hard of how I can care for you if something happens to me. This trust gives me great relief and I hope that you will understand that it is the best gift which I could conceive of for your sake."

Or, where you have a family business: "Son, over the years you and I have talked a great deal about your running the company. As you know, I don't believe you should do it. I have given your mother and the bank the power to sell it as they see fit. Don't pressure your mother to let you try your hand at it. You are a great house painter and I think that is where your future lies."

Such letters can lend color and humanity to what has become a rather cold and calculated process and they can constitute a warm message of intent more persuasive in a personal situation than the cold prose of a will.

Selecting an Executor

Selection of executors or an executor is important. An end product of the involvement of the wife and other beneficiaries in the planning process is the decision whether a wife should be named as a co-executor or not or possibly a child. If she is amply involved, it should become apparent whether a wife's services would be wise to use or not. She may be perfectly qualified in one type of an estate but not another. It may be that a son, not the mother, is the logical choice. The very involvement of either of them in the planning process with a detailed study of what happens in an estate may be enough to convince them that, in any event, they should not

serve. On the other hand, a wife formerly considered by her husband to be less than a mental giant may suddenly display hidden qualities.

The selection of any executor should be made on a basis other than the necessity to keep that person better informed. Communication and information are essential to Estate Administration, no matter whether a vital party is a co-executor or not - giving them official status does not usually increase that information and can endanger decisions which need to be completed timely. The determination of a person's capabilities may sometimes be better directed not at what they should do, but at what they should not do.

Where There is a Family Business

The existence of a closely held corporation or a family business is an important factor in whether to use a wife as an executor or co-executor. Where no plans have been made to dispose of the company or to provide for successor management, it is debatable whether management will exist at all. As a corporate executor, we would like to think that we can be all things to all people. We cannot. And, with very few exceptions, we cannot step in and manage a business. You're left with the choice of selling or finding successor management. Certainly, that business owner would not have walked into the trust department and asked me or any other officer if we would open up shop tomorrow, since he was no longer going to be there. And, that should not be the result of his death.

The situation can be worse with a widow as a co-executor. A widow who is not at all prepared for business or the business of death, and who is acting as a co-executor finds herself in a precarious position where such a business exists.

The unprepared widow sometimes is effectively crippled by the sudden blow of death for several months. Some decisions can wait – a business cannot. Those decisions begin almost the day after the death. If the problem is not engaged, competition moves in, suppliers begin to pull back, old customers, drawn mainly by the husband, find the overtures of competitors hard to resist, key employees get fidgety and some search for other jobs while debtors payments slow down.

Unprepared, the widow may find herself simply wrapped in a cloak of indecision which is one of the most pervasive and numbing of psychological disturbances. Worse yet, her decisions, in spite of all supplications to measure the potential dangers involved, will be based on emotion. She may see the business as a monument to the efforts of her husband or she may suddenly suffer from visions of grandeur about assuming the management responsibilities herself.

Importance of Communication

It is during the initial six months of administration that so many of the very important decisions are made. Draining off vital time for needless post-mortem psychological preparation only derogates from the time required for critical decisions and impairs flexibility.

Generally, Estate Administration breaks down into eight categories: (1) Information gathering for later purposes; (2) Asset marshalling; (3) Debt payment; (4) Receivables collection; (5) Tax preparation (6) Liquidity requirements; (7) Asset distribution in accordance with the will and applicable laws; and (8) People and communication.

Although time-consuming and sometimes embellished with thorny

problems, the first seven are relatively easy, were it not for the eighth all pervasive area of people and communication. People require and demand, as they should, an understanding of what you are doing in the first seven duties and that is a communications problem.

As in estate planning, it is necessary to get off on the right foot in Estate Administration. Some of the attorneys with whom we work make a practice of writing a letter at the beginning of the estate which summarizes for the key beneficiaries the terms of the will and trusts. This is a very helpful practice for the beneficiaries and the executors.

Communication is a human relations must. Our first major effort at communicating the technical details is to provide an estate folder for permanent use by the key beneficiaries, widow and co-executors. The folder contains a chronological checklist of 139 items normally followed in administration. It also contains a brief summary letter which concisely states what will occur during the administration of the estate. The major purpose is to give them a road map of where the estate is going and more importantly, when we expect to get there. I know how anxious I get on an unfamiliar road heading toward a specific destination. I constantly check the map to see where I am. To many in the administrative process, there is that constant question.

To each person having such a folder, as well as the attorney, we send copies of all our important correspondence. For those with the folder, this type of communication is for information, and it avoids misunderstandings at a later date. There is another factor. In the practice of law, we noticed that the most crestfallen clients leaving our office were those who had nothing in hand to show for the bill they had paid, even though valuable services had been delivered. Your correspondence and major documents are all evidence of the work you have done. Copies are relatively easy to provide. At the end of an estate, or of estate planning, a complete folder of the important papers is documentation of having received more than just a bill.

In the final paragraph of our initial summary letter we indicate to the recipient that we have been in the Estate Administration business so long that we are unable to anticipate all of the questions which may bother them. We urge beneficiaries to let us know unhesitatingly what their questions are, no matter how trivial. We ask that they make generous use of the telephone and personal visits.

This critical use of communications is vital, not just to transmit technical explanation, but in the development of confidence. Communication develops the necessary underlying base of confidence.

The type of communications depends on the beneficiary. There are a variety of personalities among the survivors which may require the estate administrator to be a bit of a chameleon. Certainly not changeable in his basic integrity and philosophy, but adaptable to the variations or personalities which he faces.

The businessman-survivor often presents no problem. But, the survivors are usually the widows, elderly and uninformed who have no familiarity with business practices. They can be exasperating in their slowness to grasp and because of their constant repetition of questions. Yet, their confidence is won only by patient, unpatronizing understanding of their situation. This is merely old-fashioned parlor talk,

getting to know one another and establishing the ever sought after individuality. If a person finds this type of dialogue excruciatingly slow and dreary, either in planning or administration, then possibly they would be better suited to some other endeavor with more mentally stimulating contacts.

In planning and administration, some time spent on parlor conversation, particularly with the widow, and getting to know one another can certainly ease the technical jobs later on. Quite frankly, it creates good will which creates favorable word of mouth which is, after all, the best form of new business. Beneficiaries must receive attention. And that attention should be accorded in reasonable amounts even if it means having to move on a dead run to meet your schedules after they leave. They deserve your undivided attention.

We are in a sense, nothing more than "time and advice" merchants. We have to be aware of how those irreplaceable commodities are used, what they cost and how to more efficiently utilize them. We see a lot about office economics and cost accounting. I certainly don't disagree with time savings procedures and time keeping. However, I do believe that saving time simply for greater volume is not the sole reason for doing it. Some of that newly found time must be allocated and devoted to better people relations in planning and administration or one of the most important points in saving time will have been lost.

Some Keys to Good Estate Communication

There is a list of items which I think are some of the necessary but not all of the possible keys to good estate communications and the building of confidence. Following are a few points I have found helpful in planning and administration:

1. Return your calls the same day they are received if at all possible. A small problem unanswered has a habit of becoming a big problem. One of C. Northcote Parkinson's laws of human behavior is that an overheated mind can discharge excess heat only by transfer of heat to a cooler mind, which is usually you. Particularly, the widows and elderly with time on their hands will dwell on a problem and magnify it.

2. Professionals understand messages from one another when delivered by secretaries. Beneficiaries don't always and they can soon get the idea that you don't really care too much.

3. When you hold an important meeting with several people, summarize it in a letter for the parties. it is amazing how several people can sit through the same meeting and hear a different conversation. The fact of the matter is that we usually hear what we thought was important to ourselves. Certainly, a verbal summary before the meeting is concluded is in order.

4. When you can't finish a job on a promised date, take the initiative in communicating that inability. Your candid admission will be appreciated, and your honesty noted.

5. If you have committed an error requiring corrective steps, admit it and proceed. If they have been treated properly in the first place, the beneficiary will be forgiving. But, too many errors and you might as well transfer the account because you will have lost their confidence in your technical ability. Again, your honesty and integrity will be appreciated.

6. When you have material to transmit which you feel will raise questions and you have nervous recipients, don't mail it so that it is received on the weekend and they are unable to contact you. By Monday, Parkinson's overheated mind theory is in full force and effect.

7. Never assume in your discussions and communications that anything is routine. It may be to you but it isn't to them. And, they will sometimes resent explanations that it is routine.

8. Establish a pattern, especially in the beginning of an estate, of calling beneficiaries for no reason but to check on them.

9. Do considerably more listening than talking.

10. Never underestimate the fuzzy technical questions of the so-called uninformed. We have discovered new approaches as a result of their questions on more than one occasion.

11. All of us need to couch our responses in non-technical layman's language.

12. Customers and clients want communications about their business to be confidential. I have heard, to my surprise, from several but not necessarily reliable sources that the folklore of the feminine bridge table classifies bankers and lawyers particularly as gossips.

In that same vein, let me add this aside. Several of my estate planning colleagues have commented about how easily a well thought out estate plan can be torn apart by the off-hand remark of another, usually a person who has had no part in developing the plan.

This same type of "free advice" can create difficulties in Estate Administration. I urge each of you to condition the parties in planning so that they will have the confidence in the people who will administer and will not rely on idle gossip.

Bridging the gap between estate planning and Estate Administration should not be difficult. After all, will maturity is only the natural extension of planning. By sharpening our focus in the planning stage on the fact that these events are not abstract but real and by educating those who will participate in the Estate Administration, we may find there is no gap at all. I do urge that, at some point in planning we stop for a minute and forget law and taxes and insurance and ask where do the people fit in.

Estate Administration is the implementation of the design developed in estate planning, however rudimentary or sophisticated. People, and communication to people, in the post mortem situation are the most difficult problems of Estate Administration. Planners and administrators can ease those problems by involving all essential parties in the planning and administrative states as early as possible and in detail. Summaries by the planners, administrators, and even the estate owner at critical stages keep the whole design in focus. Generous doses of patience and understanding with the untrained, elderly and confused ease the communication process.

Scott L. Probasco, Jr., vice chairman of our Board of Directors, tells a story that helps clarify for me our relationship with estate beneficiaries and those for whom we plan.

Scotty, as we all know him, was flying in his personal airplane near Atlanta on his way to Florida. He hates the Atlanta air traffic. He called air control and asked for traffic advice. Air control came back and said they were too busy to handle his request. Scotty shot back at them: "Am I up here because you are down there or are you down there because I'm up here?" Air control came back, "Roger, will handle."

Estate Planning/Estate Administration — we're there only because people are there, on a flight plan, requesting advice — for the entire flight.

Chapter 10

Family Relations

What makes family businesses different from other businesses is the inclusion of family and the relational bonds among family members. This section explores family relationships as a component of family business systems and deals with constructively managing those relationships. Productive family relationships begin with the recognition and tolerance of differences among family members.

Rather than viewing family matters as disruptions of rational business practice, a more systemic, coevolutionary perspective offers greater understanding and insight. The integration of family and business cultures plays a powerful role in the satisfaction experienced by family members from their involvement in the family business.

Families place restraints on their businesses which affect business strategy and can cause conflicts in the family/business relationship. How such conflicts are managed depends in part on the manager's power base and interpersonal skills. However, if the family has developed consensus around its goals and values and explicitly recognized its commitment to the family and the business, the environment of family relations can be positively affected.

Introduction

One of two sons of a family business owner, unlike his brother the author chose not to enter his father's firm, pursuing instead a career in education. His poem recognizes the differences between the two boys, and celebrates the unique contributions each can make to the family.

To My Brother
1987

By Craig E. Aronoff

Reprinted by permission of the author from **Loyola Business Forum**, 1987. Copyright ©1987.

We are of one seed
and both in one meadow stand —
two trees, strong, yet
growing apart so that neither
robs the other of the sun.
Still, our branches touch
and our roots intertwine.

We are of one seed
yet my wood is hard,
yours soft —
I am oak,
you are pine
and as you cannot produce an acorn,
I cannot grow cones —
you have needles, evergreen,
and I have leaves,
ever turning and dying.

And as winds blow,
you will bend and I will stand —
yet come storm,
I would likely be the first
to break.

And in the winter of my life
when I am gaunt and bare,
your greenness will be standing
against the skies that for me are
cloudy gray. . .

And in summer,
when I
in full foliage bloom,
you will stand drooped, parched
and dry brown
in my sunlight.

And when we grow old,
when the axeman comes to hew us
down
and cuts us into logs to burn in his
hearth,
it will be I who burns brighter,
hotter, longer. . .
but you will longer resist the flame
and you will smoke and as you burn,
you will emit a perfume
for those who are warmed
by your consumption.

Yet, we are of one seed and
we stand in one meadow.

473

Introduction

Decision-makers in family firms can find themselves with "no win" choices within business decisions damage kinship bonds or when by honoring family bonds, the business suffers. Tightly interwoven strands of family and firm may not be disentangled without seriously disrupting one or both systems. The article deals with the mutually interactive development of family and business systems, particularly stressing the function and organization of the family system.

The Family and the Firm: A Coevolutionary Perspective
1983

By Elaine Kepner

If they base their decisions on what the firm needs, kinship bonds may be disrupted and damaged; if they choose to honor family bonds, the business is likely to suffer.

The unique nature of the family-owned firm has presented dilemmas and frustrations to those who manage, work in, and consult with such firms. Organizational theorists have found it difficult to apply their task-oriented, competency-based models to a business in which the boundaries between task and kinship considerations overlap. Practitioners who work with such organizations find that the types of interventions successful in other situations are likely to rejected or to be found inadequate in dealing with the particular complexities involved. Founders are called on to make choices that put them in "no win" double-bind situations.

The Unique Problems of the Family Firm

What can be done to understand this unique form of organization and respond to the types of crises that seem to be inherent in it? Early practitioners in the art of working with family firms attempted to identify the primary sources of the problems that plague them from a linear-causal perspective. The most salient causes identified include the nature of the entrepreneurial personality, disturbances in the father-son relationship, nepotism, and the influence of family dynamics on executive and management decisions.

Recently, new perspectives based on an "open systems" approach have emerged. While they differ in may respects from each other, the various perspectives all regard the family and firm as sub-systems of a mega-system in which boundary conditions are overly diffuse and permeable, resulting in a high degree of mutual influence that is dysfunctional when viewed from the firm's perspective. Intervention strategies are designed to strengthen and regulate the boundary conditions of each system to prevent spillover of family agendas into executive and management decisions.

However, a view of the family firm as a total system has yet to be fully developed. All of the literature on the family-owned business has been written from the firm's perspective. Although it does acknowledge that family dynamics intrude on the rational functioning if the business, little or no attention has been given to that other part of this complex system: the family as a system. The firm's perspective is structured by its primary consideration: the adaptation and effective functioning of the business. Yet this view fails to take into account the fact that the tightly interwoven strands of family and firm may not be disentangled without seriously disrupting one or both systems. The firm's dualistic perspective focuses on one system at the price of the other. One gets the impression that the family is still something of a scapegoat in the family-firm system. This dualism ultimately sets the family and the firm at loggerheads with each other.

An alternative view of the family firm would transform this dualistic view into a comprehensive one that would violate neither family nor firm as systems. From a systems perspective one cannot consider the family firm without assuming that the behavior of any one part of a system will influence and be influenced by all other parts of the system. The family may act upon and influence the firm but, at the same time, it is influenced by the communications it receives from the firm.

When the maintenance of the family's integrity and cohesiveness is a consideration, as the chief executive often makes it, we need to begin to ask a different set of questions. For example:

• What is the nature of the interactive relationship between the family and the firm?

• How do events in one subsystem affect the other, leading to a crisis in the system as a whole?

• Given the interpenetration of these sub-systems, how can one go about unraveling the complex of intertwined strands so that the fabric of each system is not irreparably damaged?

This article attempts to expose the complexity of relational patterns between the firm and the family, and within the family itself. The ecology of the family firm as a whole system cannot be comprehended unless the more neglected half of the system is, for the moment, placed in the foreground.

The Coevolution of Family and Firm

At the founding stage of the family firm, those in each of the respective systems perceive the other as being distinct, separate, and well-bounded. The relationship between family and firm is not considered problematic. The founder usually creates and develops the enterprise at the same time that he or she creates a marriage and has a family. The founder is not trying to build a family business but is driven by a need to actualize an idea or set of values, with a preference for controlling the destiny

475

of that which is created. The spouse is usually occupied with developing skills as parent and homemaker, and as the creator of a social and extended-family network. The mission of each of these systems is sufficiently different and compelling that the illusion of separateness can be maintained for many years, even though each subsystem is developing a force field of its own with respect to the other.

The purpose of the business is to make money. Even though people development may be a widely held value, the firm must produce goods and/or services at a profit, or it cannot survive. This goal is explicit and commonly understood. To support this, the firm develops structure, processes, and control mechanisms on the basis of "rationally" derived management models or empirically tested practices, which are also explicitly labeled. Whatever the model, authority and responsibility are distributed hierarchically; there is a clear division of labor and function, and activities are coordinated in a planned manner. Because an organization is fundamentally a pattern of roles and a blueprint for their coordination, it exists independently of particular people and can survive in spite of 100 percent turnover of membership.

On the other hand, a family is in the business of caring for and developing people; its boundaries are sustained by face-to-face contact, and membership in that system is by blood, not through criteria of competence. How a particular family interprets its goals and carries them out is highly variable, depending on culture, social class, values, and personal idiosyncracies. But both the goals and the manner in which the family operationalizes them are rarely explicitly labeled. Instead, it is necessary to infer norms, operating procedures, roles, and decision-making

processes from the family's behaviors and communication patterns. Furthermore, such tangible criteria as profit-and-loss statements give a business a decided barometer of its success. The criteria used to measure success in a family are loose and intangible terms, such as the level of each member's self-esteem, the members' ability to function as responsible and autonomous human beings in an age-appropriate manner and, finally, the experience of affectional ties and a sense of loyalty upon which the system as a whole depends.

Let us now focus on the family as a system before elaborating further on the co-evolution of family and firm and the interactive effects of one upon the other.

The Family System

In this section, I will be providing a context for understanding family systems in general, their purpose as satisfiers of certain universal human needs, the way they are organized to perform their functions, and the cultural dimensions by which they regulate themselves and their development. Under each of these topics, I will describe the ways in which the family's organization and culture are influenced by its relationship with a firm.

The family is a social system endorsed by law and custom to take care of its members' needs. The glue that holds it together through the vicissitudes of its life-cycle transitions and the intricate, complicated interpersonal linkages are the emotional bondings and affectionate ties that develop between and among its members, as well as a sense of responsibility and loyalty to the family as a system.

The family functions as a whole system. Actions of one family member affect and influence the actions of all other members and the system as an entity. For example, the wife who wants to return to school or to her former career introduces shifts that affect the homeostasis of the system. All members will feel the impact. If this shift is supported and maintained, the system's rules and norms will change, and other individuals will experience the stress of new norms as they take on different responsibilities and roles. If this shift is not supported, the system becomes dysfunctional in terms of its purpose; one or more family members will carry the symptoms of dysfunction – in this case, probably the couple in terms of an increased emotional distance between husband and wife.

Purpose of the Family

In addition to providing for the economic security of its members, the family must satisfy deep social and emotional needs for belonging, affection, and intimacy, and it must provide a sense of identity that includes experiencing one's self as a source of influence and power.

Belonging needs. All of us need to feel that we belong to and can be accepted as a member of a group. To be included gives us a sense of our self-worth.

Intimacy needs. Intimate attachments are not based on one's dependency needs alone. Instead, they are predicated on valuing and cherishing the other for who the person is, rather than for what the person could or should be. This attachment can be depended on over time and through changing circumstances; it survives through periods of conflict and separation. What the family provides, as not other institution can, is an orderly access to intimacy.

Identity and autonomy needs. Just as we are drawn toward others to share and to connect, so do we need to pull apart and differentiate ourselves from the herd. It is through separating that we find out who we are: our identity is a process of distinguishing ourselves from everyone else. We discover our unique qualities, capabilities, and values by experiencing our differences. To do this, we must be able to say "no," to exert influence on others and the flow of events that sometimes threaten to engulf us, and to feel that we have the power to make our own choices and to take responsibility for their consequences.

This inherent rhythm that pulls people together and pushes them apart is a polarity that every family must manage. If there is too much individuation, with each person doing his or her own thing, the system suffers. On the other hand, too much unity and merging causes the individual to become so enmeshed in the family that he or she cannot separate and become an autonomous and competent adult.

The Organization of the Family

To satisfy and manage the needs of belonging, intimacy, and identity, the family organizes itself by dividing labor and allocating responsibility into different parts, or subsystems. The obvious categories are the couple, the parents, and the children. Each of these subsystems performs certain specialized functions for the family, and each of them maintains a boundary between itself and the other subsystems.

The *spouse subsystem* has a two-fold function: to meet the personal and interpersonal needs of the husband and wife and to carry the leadership dimension for the system as a whole. It must maintain certain separate activities and privacy boundaries to differentiate itself from the rest of the system. As a policy-making body, it decides on such things as the way family resources will be used, where and when family members will go on vacation, who will manage the finances, how the family will relate to their in-laws, who will be included in the extended family and social network, how aging parents will be cared for, and so forth.

As soon as they marry, couples begin to work out the rules about who is to take charge of which area and under what circumstances. There are three basic modes of relating with respect to leadership in the spouse system: symmetrical, complementary, and reciprocal.

A *symmetrical relationship* is a competitive one in which each spouse needs to prove to the other that he or she is just as good, powerful, skillful, and intelligent as the other. It is a relationship in which each one is simultaneously indicating a wish to determine the rules and to have equal control. A status struggle begins, and once such a behavioral sequence starts it often spreads and becomes pervasive.

A *complementary relationship* is one in which one spouse is in charge of certain areas while the other spouse has different areas of control. Traditionally, roles and responsibilities were differentiated along gender line: The husband, who provided the major financial income, made the decisions involving allocation of resources; the wife ran the household as she wished, disciplined and supervised the children, and spent whatever funds she deemed necessary to care for the family. However, today's age of affluence and egalitarian values has led to a general loosening of the traditional role definitions and to increasingly complex marital relationships.

Today, the mode of many marriages is a *reciprocal relationship* in which spouses alternate between symmetrical and complementary modes of relating, depending on the nature of the situation to be managed and their respective talents and resources.

The *parenting subsystem* evolves as the couple have children and begin to raise a family. As parents, the couple work out ways of managing the education and upbringing of their children. Whether or not they discuss these matters and consciously decide how they will do this, their behavioral interactions with the children determine the way in which conflicts among the siblings will be managed and the way in which attention, nurturance, support, and limit setting will be handled for each child.

The *sibling subsystem* is a peer learning group. Siblings relate to each other for mutual support, and for some caretaking and care-giving functions. It is the environment in which social and educational skills and competencies are acquired; it is also the arena in which competitiveness and assertiveness are developed and sometimes honed to a fine edge as they compete for the love, attention, and approval of their parents. Their existence as a subsystem provides a sense of mission for the parents and can be a transformative and transpersonal developmental experience for the parents.

Triangling

When spouses are unable to meet each others needs for affection and companionship or unable to resolve the inevitable differences and conflicts between them, they may make an alliance with one or more of the children and draw that child into the spouse subsystem as a third member. The child becomes overly involved or enmeshed with that parent, and the usual generational boundaries are breached. Such triangles develop in a number of ways:

The parent becomes the child's protector, and the child becomes the parent's protector. Sometimes the parent may draw one child in for support in a conflict with the other marital partner; thus the child may become either (1) a judge or advocate in the spouse system or (2) the scapegoat of the system by being the symptom bearer (getting ill, failing in school, or engaging in delinquent behavior). This forces the parents to align themselves with each other to deal with the "sick child."

Other sets of people or entities that are outside the nuclear family may be "triangles" into the spouse subsystem. These may not be physically present, but they exist in the hearts and heads of one or both of the spouses. These may be one or more members of the family or origin, one or both spouses' careers, or the family business. In a first-generation family business, the interloper may be the founder's "kitchen cabinet," people who are like a second family to him or her. As one founding entrepreneur labeled it after analyzing a dream he had after a consultation on succession, "I realized that my trusted and valuable colleagues in the firm are my symbolic 'mistress.'" For the family involved with a firm, the business may be experienced as a shadowy but nonetheless potent third party to their family life.

Dimensions of Family Culture

According to Edgar Schein, "culture" is a human invention; it is a way of perceiving and thinking—of judging, evaluating, and feeling; it is a way of acting in relation to others and a way of doing things and solving problems. Culture deals with the problems of internal integration and social survival and, as such, it tends to be passed on as a preferred set of solutions to successive generations. The pattern of culture that has been adopted or inherited serves to reduce anxiety by providing a set of guidelines as a basis for action; it gives purpose, value, and meaning to what might otherwise be experienced as overwhelming or confusing events. Families develop rules to enforce their culture; these rules are usually covert, but can be inferred from behavior and communications.

Families can be described in cultural terms by the way in which they manage differences and conflicts, individuation, emotional expressiveness, the congruence of their perception of reality, and separation and loss.

Management of Conflicts

Management of conflicts refers to the way in which a family system deals with differences between and among its members. Some differences are preferences, the resolution of which is arrived at by a process of "give and take." Other differences may be profound. Difference in values and in perceptions about the system's goals and purposes are not so easily resolved. They may be dilemmas that must be managed rather than problems that can be solved. Some families believe that differences are dangerous. They suppress acknowledgement of them and discourage attempts by anyone in the system to bring them into awareness. But these conflicts do not go away; they simply go underground and are expressed indirectly through simple withdrawal or through passive-aggressive behavior.

The spouse relationship usually prescribes the way in which differences will be managed in the family system. Symmetrical couple relationships are likely to produce families in which differences are expressed spontaneously, continually, and in an escalating fashion—without benefit of a direct encounter and conflict negotiation about the differences. These relationships breed a "no-win" situation. Complementary families, in which parental roles are well differentiated and the leadership styles is authoritarian, tend to apply rigid rules about what is right and wrong and reject influences that would compromise these rules. Reciprocal families would be more likely to listen to different points of view, encourage discussion and negotiation, and try to come to a resolution that, if not perfect, can be lived with. They are also likely to have some healing mechanisms or rituals that validate the person and support their self-esteem during and after the battles.

Obviously, the way differences are managed affects the kind of influence that people can wield and their individual sense of power as an influencer.

Individuation

Individuation may be nonacceptable, tolerated, or encouraged in families. Pressure may be brought to bear so that everyone thinks and feels alike, and differentiation is actively discouraged. In families where nondifferentiation is extreme, the identity of one person becomes fused or enmeshed with that of another; parent-child relationships are symbiotic, and each cannot, or will not, get along without the other. A little further along the continuum are families that permit a type of individuation that is consistent with the rules, range, and norms of their culture. Criticisms of deviant behavior are frequent, either by discrediting, blaming, or scapegoating (that is, seeing the problem as a fault or basic inadequacy in the individual). In other families a high degree of individuation and autonomy is fostered, and children are listened to and have

appropriate influence on family decisions.

Emotional Expressiveness

Feelings and emotions are some of the resources that we, as human beings, are born with and develop. They give us information about what makes us feel good, how we want to relate to others, and what we want to do with our lives. Feelings enable us to be affectionate, to say no or yes, to be empathetic, and to care for others as well as ourselves. Some family cultures are based on the assumption that feelings are unreliable, embarrassing, and not to be trusted, so that the members never learn to accurately label and differentiate between one set of feelings and another. The expression of feeling is either very subdued, inhibited, or ritualistic. Some families are more comfortable with the expression of negative feelings and the quality of their empathy is somewhat strained. By contrast, some family cultures can encompass and value both negative and positive feelings, and encourage the expression of feelings that are appropriate to the context. Negative emotions are accepted as information, and the members are quick to pick up the feelings of others and to approach problems with directness and with a lack of defensiveness.

Acceptance of Change, Separation, and Loss

A number of critical transition periods in the family life cycle, beginning with the marriage, impact on the family as a system; the birth of the first child; the early years of raising and educating the children; management of teenagers struggling to be autonomous and free, the process of becoming a launching center for the next generation while maintaining a supportive home base, maintenance of ties with children and grandchildren, revitalization of the marriage in the middle years, and adjustment to age and retirement. Each of these transitions is marked by progressive increases in the degree of separation, and the feelings of loss that the separation entails may be painfully intense during certain transition periods.

In families, major transitions occur every five to seven years; so within a given time period, it has had more practice in managing transitions than have such larger social systems as organizations, whose life cycle spans a longer time frame. The capacity to accept separation and loss — to grieve and then let go and move on — is at the heart of the skill repertoire needed for healthy family adaptation. In a sense, a competent family of origin "self-destructs," and families vary in their ability to deal with this. However, whatever the degree of competency the family has developed to deal with separation and loss, the stress is compounded when transitions in the family life cycle coincide with transition crises in the life cycle of the firm. At these times (for example, during the succession-planning process) each system is concerned about maintaining the integrity of its own system boundaries and is more resistant to differentiation and separation. The major symptoms of dysfunction in the family/firm relationship are likely to occur during the periods of simultaneous transition stress in each of the systems.

Perception of Reality and Family Myths

Families' cultures are based on certain beliefs and assumptions that create a matrix of shared meaning and a perception of reality that is experienced by all system members. This can be influenced, for example, by parental attitudes about the meaning of life.

Some parents take their children as they are and go with the flow of their unique developmental process. The meaning the child makes out of this is that life is a fluid dance; errors in form and performance are part of living and the dancer can trust his or her own feelings and perceptions to take him or her through the next series of steps. Other parents, who feel that there are things one does to guarantee success in life, mold their offspring to fit a particular pattern; if life is a dance, it is a highly formalized waltz. This child's view of reality is that there is a fixed path one must tread, that there are right and wrong "steps" to make, and that one must discern the correct moves to make.

Among the many facets of a family's shared perceptions, two stand out as significant: the myths held by a family and the way these myths become fixed and unchanging. Family myths are a set of well-integrated beliefs; they form the group's inner image of itself, allowing a positive perception to be maintained despite flagrant evidence to the contrary. Take, for example, parents who have had a relatively easy time raising young children; they still see themselves as a happy, untroubled family even though one adolescent son has a drinking problem and the daughter has just run away from home for the fourth time. Family myths also refer to fixed-role perceptions, as illustrated by the family members who continue to treat the eldest daughter, who was a rebellious child, as the "bad, irresponsible child," even though she has earned a Ph.D. and raised a family. The child who was the "late bloomer" is still seen as a slow learner by the family despite later success in academia and business.

Family myths are often internalized by the individuals involved; although they are distortions of present reality and needs, they continue to operate in the roles these individuals play out in their adult lives, including those they take in the family firm. The eldest son who has been the responsible child becomes the guardian of the family assets; the aggressive one in the family takes over the business.

The Firm's Effects on the Family

The particular way in which the family's cultural dynamics are influenced by their relationship with a firm will vary depending on such factors as the management model adopted by the firm (which may be a royalist, competency-base, or mixed model), the clarity with which boundaries and opportunities presented by the firm to family members are communicated, and the particular family culture that develops independent of the firm's influences. Given these qualifications, there are certain influences the firm will have on the family dynamics because the firm is a part of the psychological if not the actual environment of the family. It is always a "third party" that is carried around in the minds of people in the family system. The health of both the individual and the system is affected more by how it manages and adapts to forces that impinge on it rather than by what it has to manage. The conditions I will be describing do not necessarily produce unmanageable stress; they simply represent a different set of dilemmas for the families involved in a firm situation.

I would like to look at some of the interactions within the family and between family and firm that affect the family as a whole system — its subsystems and the family culture. These family dynamics then bleed over into the firm and back to the family in a circular, cybernetic pattern.

Effects on the Family System

The family as a system derives some of its sense of belonging, influence, and social identity from being related to a successful enterprise and a successful entrepreneur. This is a mixed blessing because certain costs and consequences — for example, a heavy social and travel calendar in the service of the firm — may put time and energy constraints on the intimate relationships in the system. The family may feel responsible for protecting and projecting their image of being a well-functioning and cohesive family, and masking or ignoring the ordinary conflicts and strains of family life.

The effects of this are illustrated by the reminiscences of a 32-year-old founder's son in the business for five years:

> Growing up in this family was like being a member of a royal family. A lot of people knew me and treated me well just because my father had an important business in the community. It had its good points, though — I always knew what I could do when I grew up, and I had a lot of advantages other kids didn't have, like trips to Europe every summer and the best bike on the block. But my parents made a federal case out of every mistake I made. When I goofed off at school or got into some minor scrapes as a teenager, they'd blast me about what that would do to the family's image in the community. Well, "Blast the business," I thought at that time. Now that I'm in the business and slated to take over when Dad retires, I worry about whether I'll ever be able to fit into the old

482

man's shoes. It's a bit more than I expected or bargained for.

Effects on Spouse and Parenting Subsystems

The social demands of the business may seriously intrude on the energy and time available to the couple for time alone. In the traditional family business in which the founder is the male head of the family, the typical family relational pattern is a "complementary one"; he is in charge of the economic security for the family, and she is in charge of the home, child rearing, and social and community responsibilities. Basically the wife accommodates to support the husband's demanding career. While this life structure may be eminently satisfying to many women, it does constrain and limit her choices. Many younger wives today find this situation not entirely satisfactory. But it is difficult to push they system's existing boundaries when the financial and social benefits that flow from the business through the husband are so pleasurable. And it is an onerous task to move into a more challenging stance when the husband is such an important authority figure in the family system and is, moreover, perceived by those who are outside the family as such a powerful and important person.

For the father in such families, the dilemmas are also painful and exhausting. Whether the message is given directly or indirectly by the parents, by the time the children are grown up and enter the business as second-generation leaders, they know they will inherit the business assets in some way. Along with the firm's executives, they experience themselves as stakeholders in the business. They have a special interest in how the business will be managed and/or the way in which the assets will be distributed, and perhaps they confuse the differences between management and ownership—possibly because they have seen their father, the first generation founder, being successful in both roles. In any event, the children's attempts to exert influence on father as they come into the business, or as he is getting ready to retire, may make him appear more resistant to retirement than ever.

As one owner said:

> I didn't develop this business to create a safe nest for my family. I was simply carrying out my mission in the world—creating an extension of myself and my values. Of course, I'm very pleased that I will leave my wife and children with an assured income because they will inherit the stock ownership. But now I'm getting ready to retire and I find myself feeling resentful toward my children because they take for granted what I fought for and finally achieved. They and the executives in the business, whom I also brought up, so to speak, are squabbling about "their" rights! Sometimes I want to shout "A plague on both your houses" and sell this damn thing to the highest bidder!

Effects on Sibling Subsystems

It is universal and normal phenomenon for children to compete with each other for preferential treatment from parents. From the child's perspective, there are always inequities and injustices, some of them inherent in their birth order. Younger children envy the capabilities and privileges enjoyed by the older ones; the older ones resent that the younger ones are babied and allowed "to get away with murder." Female children resent the roles and rewards conferred on their brothers, and frequently vice versa. Middle children, sandwiched between their siblings, have their own axes to grind. All of them try to compete for the love, care, approval, and attention of the parents, no matter how hard they try to be fair.

Sibling rivalries begin as soon as the second child is born into a family, and frequently these hostilities continue throughout their lives. During adolescence, however, as the children begin to leave home, they bond with peer groups and develop outside love relationships, and the rivalries begin to dissipate. As the children separate from the family of origin and establish lives and careers of their own, they may even begin to regard their siblings as people for whom they have some real fondness. In a family firm, on the other hand, it is easy to transfer childhood feuds into the business arena. Furthermore, the roles and rewards conferred by the father on the children who come into the business are experienced as symbols of the father's love, regard, and preference "which exacerbates the original rivalries even further.

From a normal developmental perspective, the father-son relationship is fraught with ambivalences on both sides, and is a difficult one to manage. Usually the son both (1) identifies with father and wants to be like him and (2) competes with him for the mother's attention. When the son enters the business and the father becomes his supervisor, the problems are compounded.

One owner of a successful business of his own and the son of an entrepreneurial founder tells this somewhat poignant story.

I'm the son of a founder, but I went out on my own after working for Dad for eight years; I'm happy to report that I now own a thriving business of my own. I just couldn't take it anymore – working in Dad's business. It was ruining me and tearing the two of us farther apart. Now my sons are in college and I've already told them there will be no place for them in my business. It's hard enough to build a decent father-son relationship, and it just gets too damned complicated when father becomes boss or teacher. My sons, of course, think I'm just being arbitrary and stingy. I guess you just can't win in a situation like this.

If one of the sons becomes the wife's favorite, she may promote him for leadership in the firm – which further alienates father from son. This will be acted out as the father introduces and manages the son's career in the firm.

The father-daughter relationship and the daughter's development is also more complicated than usual. Family businesses usually operate on the principle of primo-geniture; the mantle of leadership is passed on to the males in the family – usually to the first-born son. With some rare exceptions, the daughters are not considered in the line for succession. Growing up in such a situation creates subtle but powerful reinforcements for already existing cultural stereotypes.

Sometimes the father is ambivalent about the role of daughters in the business – a situation that creates a double-bind situation for the daughters. The case of an empire-building entrepreneur illustrates the rebound effects of this on the firm, the daughter, and the family. Father had encouraged her to major in economics in college and to earn a master's degree in business administration. Because she demonstrated competence in the business as a vice-president in charge of financial planning for six years, she expected to be chosen as one of the inner circle in the succession plans. Her father died unexpectedly one month after her younger brother, the heir apparent, had graduated from college. She relates:

> The succession plan my father left turned over the leadership to my brother and a small group of non-family professionals, with no mention or provision for me at all. I felt betrayed and humiliated by my father. I've always been very close to my brother but now I can't look him in the eye without wanting to scream. I'm sorely tempted to cash in my stock — although I know that would create havoc with the business right now — and go to work for one of our competitors!

Daughters who do not choose to enter the business may fall back on the time-honored option for women of exerting their influence vicariously — for example, by promoting their husbands' career in the family business to protect their interests. When conflict develops between her husband and father, or her husband and her brothers, she finds herself in a dilemma. She may be forced to choose between loyalty to her own nuclear family and her family of origin. Daughters who do enter the business, on the other hand, must deal with the usual array of subtle and overt resistance in what has been a predominantly male domain, with the added burden of being the boss's daughter.

Effects of the Family System's Cultural Dimensions

Of the five separate but interrelated family culture dimensions previously discussed, the ones most likely to be influenced by the family's relationship to the firm are those dealing with management of conflict, individuation, and perception of reality.

Management of Conflict

Willingness to acknowledge difference and appreciate deviance from cultural norms varies, of course, from family to family, but the pressure on a family-firm family to maintain an image of cohesiveness may suppress family conflicts. Furthermore, the economic interdependence between family and firm makes it difficult for people to tell each other when their needs for belonging, influence, and intimacy are not being met. Although the business may be perceived as an intrusive "third party" in the family's life, it is problematic to bite the hand that feeds you. Furthermore, the family frequently views father as a powerful or heroic larger-than-life figure. The children may find the normal testing of authority boundaries as too threatening. With these factors operating in the system, the family may not provide itself with an opportunity to learn healthy conflict negotiation skills or to develop healing rituals and mechanisms.

Individuation

Individuation may be harder for family members to achieve; at least it will be a different process than that of the average person, whose psychological dependence on the family diminishes when he or she becomes economically independent and establishes a career outside the boundaries of family influence. Sons of founders usually find it more difficult to test out and gain a sense of their own competency under their father's shadow. Whatever their role in the family firm, they are simply more visible than others. They are being appraised as a replacement for father, and their "mistakes" are being judged by different criteria than executives. Because of family myths about father and firm, many sons burden themselves with the belief that they must be "just like Dad" to be a successful leader in the business. In reality, they are entering a business that is in a new and different stage in its developmental life cycle, a period in which the business is becoming more differentiated and structured. New control mechanisms and integrating and executive functions are required to manage a more complex enterprise; whatever the son's role in the business, it will not be as encompassing as that of the father.

Perception of Reality

Knowledge about the external environment — the "real world" — may be expanded for the family through their contacts with people and events that cross into the boundaries of family life through the father and the firm. However, their perception of reality is influenced by their identification with the firm as a source of social power and prestige, and they may develop a bloated sense of their own importance. Furthermore, the firm's myths and culture may be different from those of the family even though father is central to both systems. Family members entering the firm may go through a period of culture shock and resocialization to adapt to the firm's myths and culture.

As we have seen, myths are perpetuated by "time binding," a way of denying the passage of time. While such denial alleviates pain, it can lead only to denial of other realities and eventually to dysfunctional symptoms. The succession issue is one that tests the ability of the family system to deal with the pain of loss, separation, and change in the inevitable process of growth and development, aging, and death. Obviously, change is inevitable with the passage of time. The distress it creates also opens up the possibility of wisdom, which comes with acknowledgement and acceptance.

The Process of Change

All change in living systems involves a conflict between two opposing tendencies: the pull to remain the same and defend the status quo and the push to change its processes and structures and move on to a new level of differentiation and integration. Maintenance of the status quo is comfortable; it is supported by well established, semi-automatic, and dependable behavior patterns requiring minimal effort and low risk. Change, on the other hand, is energizing but challenging. Because there is always the risk of failure, change is experienced both as a danger and as an opportunity and thus is approached with ambivalence. Equilibrium is destabilized and, temporarily, the system seems to regress or function in a less than optimal fashion. Transitions involve new and different problems that must be solved and new skills that must be learned. Some of the previously adaptive attitudes, beliefs, and behaviors must be given up before a new gestalt or configuration can emerge.

Some of the changes associated with the developmental life cycle of the family in relationship with the firm are first-order changes — that is, they are responses to minor fluctuations and do not require any major changes in the ground rules by which the family operates. For example, both firm and family make only minor shifts when the eldest son is employed in the firm during summer vacations. Some changes are second-order changes, requiring a major shift in orientation and expectations and the creation of new boundaries and rules. Two such second-order crises occur for the family when the firm's organization develops in size and complexity and outsiders or professional managers are brought in, or when company stock is placed on the public market.

Anyone who tries to answer the question, "What can be done to reduce the tension and uproar that can occur between the family and the firm at these critical times?" is bound to sound simplistic and prescriptive in a situation that requires a profound appreciation for the singularity and uniqueness of the families and the firm in their interactional relationship with each other. However, there are some concepts that can serve as guidelines in developing preventive interventions that might head off some of the more serious problems.

Information

The first of these concepts has to do with information. In social systems, information is a type of energy that leads to reduction of uncertainty. Lack of information leads to uncertainty, and uncertainty is a fertile breeding ground for projections and political maneuvers.

To avoid human beings' natural tendency to fill in the information vacuum with illusions and false expectations, the founder can prevent the tensions between family and firm from developing into serious symptoms by communicating his or her thoughts or decisions as early as possible to the family and the firm on these issues:

Who will be considered for what roles int he firm: Sons? Daughters? In-laws?

What are the criteria of competence required for positions in the firm, and what are the criteria used to assess this competence?

How will the inherited assets be distributed and managed?

The founder can do this by informing them, persuading them, consulting with them, or collaborating with them in the decisions that lead to a resolution of these questions. Formal or informal mechanisms can be evolved in the family's life to learn about the business and to develop an informed understanding of the whole system of which they are a part and on which they depend.

Awareness

The second of these guideline concepts has to do with awareness. Utilizing the leadership of the spouse subsystem, the family as a system can become aware of the additional layers of complexity with which they must all deal in being matrixed with a firm. This awareness itself may be curative. They can pay more attention to the satisfactions for belonging, identity, and intimacy in the family system and build protective boundaries to prevent encroachment by the firm. If the family can develop an appreciation for difference, divergence, and conflict and understand its members' needs for influence or participation, they will be able to create processes and mechanisms to inform, influence, negotiate, and heal. If access to information about what is happening in the firm is not contingent on being a member of the firm, some of the problems arising between firm and family may be alleviated.

Selected Bibliography

The author is indebted to the growing body of literature on the theory and practice of family therapy for the concepts expressed in this paper. Notable sources are the following: Lynn Hoffman's *Foundations of Family*

Therapy (Basic Books, Inc. 1981); William Lederer's and Don Jackson's *The Mirages of Marriage* (W. W. Norton & Company, 1968); *No Single Thread: Psychological Health in Family Systems*, edited by Jerry M. Lewis (Brunner/Mazel, 1976). Two papers on the coevolutionary perspective have been particularly useful; Penny Penn's "Circular Questioning" *Family Process,* September 1982), and Lynn Hoffman's " A Co-evolutionary Framework for Systemic Family Therapy," which is chapter 2 of *Family Diagnosis and Assessment* (Aspen Publishing Company, 1982).

Acknowledgments

Acknowledgments are also due to the author's colleagues on the organization and systems development program at the Gestalt Institute of Cleveland for the opportunity to collaborate with them in the mind-stretching process of reframing Gestalt and Systems theory, to her dear friend and family cotherapist, the late Dr. William S. Warner, and to Richard Beckhard with whom she has co-consulted in working with family-firm clients. Appreciation is also given to the members of the family-firm families who shared their personal dilemmas and thereby contributed immeasurably to her understanding of the family perspective in these complex systems.

Introduction

Families and businesses develop structures and cultures. In a family business these cultures overlap and reflect each other. The founding generation of a family firm should establish ground rules and define the integration of their two cultures. Satisfaction with involvement in the family business is related to the fit between family and business values. Subsequent generations must redefine family business culture to adapt to changing times. Adaptation is stimulated when family business systems are forced to deal with crises, often beginning around seemingly minor issues with major consequences. An example illustrates the cultural evolution of a complex family-business system.

Building Successful, Enterprising Families

1983

By Susan Golden, Ph.D.

Reprinted by permission of **Loyola Business Forum.**, Summer, 1983, Vol. 4, No. 1, pp. 22-23. Copyright ©1983 Loyola Business Forum; all rights reserved.

What's satisfying about being a family member of a family business? What makes it work for you? What's your definition of being a successful family business?

As a family therapist accustomed to meeting families when they are in trouble, I am better at seeing pitfalls than windfalls. Interviewing family business members has given me an appreciation of the rich variety of the kinds of successful family businesses at different stages of development. Just as each family has its own organization and 'culture' developed across generations, businesses also develop an organizational structure and culture.

When an organization is a family business, the two cultures overlap and reflect back on each other. There is an exchange back and forth. The task of the first generation of a family business is to set the ground rules and define the integration of these two cultures.

Family businesses are special cultures because they share a fundamental belief in the interdependence of family members, stressing and valuing family connectedness. As a result the action and perceptions of one member can have enormous implications for other family members. The task of the founder is to develop a stable and coherent ideology for the business that will enable the family to work together to build the business.

Satisfaction with being an on-going part of the business is often related to the level of fit between family values and the nature of the business. A book manufacturer described his satisfaction with his career in his fourth generation family business as related to the fact that he sees it as a clean business, where he values the product, meets and works with interesting, diverse and bright people. This contrasts with the satisfaction expressed by a second generation owner of a scrap metal business. He commented that his family has always been good at making do, making the most of things. They enjoy working with messes and turning them into something constructive and lucrative, and find the industry fits with their enjoyment of a lot of conflict and the intensity which is part of the process.

These themes are then integrated into the family culture, its definition of itself. The choice of the kind of business that the family founds amounts to the selection of a work environment that the family will seek to control, and that will, in turn, greatly influence the environment of the family. Subsequent generations must eventually redefine the culture of the family business for it to continue to successfully adapt to changing times.

Interviewing family business families, I have been struck by the centrality of the family culture in determining the business' vulnerabilities and strengths. Davis and Stern from the Wharton School describe the importance for family businesses of establishing a valid legitimizing structure; a set of values, norms and principles which generate behavior, which is jointly adapted to the needs of both the family and the business task system. Another term for this is the family business's paradigm.

Crises can serve an adaptive role in the development of this legitimizing structure or paradigm in the family business.

A crisis presents an opportunity to restore family cohesion and to revise the rules of the family culture, shifting the definition of what the family and business are about in response to the changing needs and stages of development. If these changes are adaptive, and new family business rules emerge, the family and business can be strengthened. Obviously crises can also result in loss of all kinds. The family paradigm in the well functioning family is shaped by the crisis it encounters. The seeds of the paradigm are evident in the family business founder's story of "how we came to be, who we are and what we are about." The first revision is evident in the story of the business' first crisis, as family and business goals begin to shift in response to actual experience working together. It is modified as new solutions to the challenge of perpetuating the family business emerge. The paradigm provides cohesion, differentiates this business from other businesses, reaffirms values, provides directions, goals and priorities.

In successful family businesses there exists:

1. a fit between the task of the business and the paradigm of the originating family.

2. a paradigm which contains rules for how things are done here, guidelines for dealing with crisis, with conflict between future growth versus a maintenance approach, as well as for continued belonging (who we are, what we can be, the kind of business and people we are).

There are rules about trust and mistrust which determine the role of outsiders, spouses, non-family employees, and rules for screening and bringing in new ideas, allowing for subsequent maximization of good fit for outsiders brought into the system. There are rules for handling differences, areas of conflict and risk-taking and finally, the paradigm contains the seeds of the model of succession that will work for the family (based on family precedents for separation and differentiation).

The following example illustrates a small second generation business's use of a crisis to lay the groundwork for movement to the next developmental stage. This service business was founded as a mom and pop shop with the husband running production and his wife doing the books, controlling the money. The family had eight children, six sons.

At the time of interviewing, the father had been semi-retired for four years because of a stroke. The mother still ran the books and was the conduit for information on the business to her husband. The three oldest sons then drew up a legal partnership agreement that established rules based on fairness and performance that would enable the younger siblings to qualify for partnership.

The evolution of this document was consistent with the family goal of staying together, and shared value of fairness, and the ethos that any family member who wants to and works hard, can join the business. However, this document was developed with the expectation that the business could potentially expand to meet the needs of all family members, supporting three to eight families. While the business tripled in size in four years, it was unclear whether it would have the capacity to expand eight-fold to accommodate the family goal of keeping everybody in the business.

At the time of the founding, the goal of the business was to simply provide a living for the family. By the second generation the goal had become to keep the family working together as a team, particularly the sons. The family values of working hard, staying together, mutual responsibility, pride in quality teamwork and fairness were central to the development of the second generation's horizontal structure. The questions they faced in this generation were: How do you earn your place? Can you be your own person? Can the business support this expanded family?

Minor crises do not always generate minor consequences. Revision of the family paradigm often begin around seemingly small issues, preparing the way for work on major changes and differences. While many of the sons and their wives were entering the parenthood years, the mother who controlled the money in the business and her oldest daughter who worked in the office, experienced their minor disagreements and tensions escalate into a major family blow-up. There was a great deal of conflict in this usually low-conflict family, pressure to take sides, and ultimately the lining up of all family members and their spouses on either the mother's side or the daughter's side. Finally, the daughter decided to leave the company, the first family member to leave. Her husband stayed on as an employee.

The crisis over the daughter served to clarify aspects of the family ethos, and lay groundwork for several important upcoming family issues: 1)the conflict between the family need to perpetuate connection and all continuing to work together, with the business's need for disconnection, (i.e. acknowledge increased competition for scarce resources, worry that the payroll wouldn't be able to support all family members, raising the possibility of either restructuring or splintering), and 2) the issue of succession, who would take over the mother's role.

The crisis outcome reaffirmed: that it is possible to leave the business by rehearsing a leave-taking crisis with a less central family figure, the oldest daughter; and that the succession issue was premature. The father was ill and out, but the mother was still central and the sons would side with her.

The crisis was an impetus to revise the goal of the business of keeping the brothers working as a team. It fostered decisions which served to differentiate more clearly separate spheres of control for the brothers, reducing the threat of too much increased conflict by simmering down areas of greater competition. Also, shortly after the crisis, the brothers decided that the middle son would take over the task of working more closely with the mother, gradually taking over the books and beginning for the computerization of more company functions.

The brothers then worked together to develop plans for expansion, use of new technologies to broaden the base of the business, and made two decisions which served to create a healthier distance between them. One brother began to set up out of town contracts. The group also decided to build an addition to their office space that would provide more privacy and separate offices for the first time.

The work out of town perpetuated another crisis when it coincided with the birth of a new baby in the family and there was a period of increased tension with the wives. Through the crisis the wives formed a stronger coalition, advocating for their needs, pressing for more home involvement and structured, predictable vacations for their spouses. This surfaced issues to differentiate more clearly points of conflict between the business's needs and the differing needs of the individual nuclear family units.

Some of the signs of well functioning on the part of the family were their ability to use the crisis to reaffirm basic family values and an ethos of balancing the needs of the business, the extended family and individual family units; and their ability to use the crisis to develop adaptive strategies for innovation and expansion, hence, family and business survival; and finally, their ability to begin to surface the upcoming issues of some brothers or sisters leaving the business, of the mother's movement out of the business and out of her role as information link to father, and of differential role expectations.

The family was able to begin to recognize and legitimate the wives' roles by helping the sons establish clearer boundaries from their family of origin and the business. They were able to begin to air conflict and establish rules as they entered a stage requiring greater conflict and differing visions of the future.

The family's areas of vulnerability seemed to be the possibility that they might be distracted from key conflictual issues by creating tension and false fights between the wives, and that the younger, unmarried family members would choose spouses that challenged the rules of the system and wanted more involvement. Thus far, the brothers had chosen wives with independent professions who did not want to be part of the business, and could buffer financial crises when the company had trouble meeting payroll.

Introduction

The interaction of constraints placed by families on their businesses and the competitive requirements of the business is the central issue affecting family business strategy. Strategic issues related to family constraints include financing, risk, resource procurement and allocation, reward systems and the purpose/scope of the business. When family constraints and business requirements conflict, the family/business relationship becomes a part of the decision making process.

Managing the family/business relationship is a critical aspect of success in family businesses. Formulating and implementing strategies requires sensitivity to family constraints. Constraints can be treated as a variable, however, depending on the manager's power base and interpersonal skills. The ability of family and non-family managers to assess accurately their business and family power bases will go a long way in guiding their behavior.

Balancing the "Family" and the "Business" in Family Business
1984

By Phyllis G. Holland and William R. Boulton

Like an aging relative who complains of innumerable ills but lives on and on, family business, characterized as small, inbred, backward, and riddled with nepotism, perseveres and prospers. Family businesses may be large (Gallo, Mars), growing (Flowers Industries), or small (McIlhenny & Sons of Tabasco sauce fame); they may be national or international in scope, or the local firm we think of most often.

Family businesses, as opposed to small or privately-held businesses, have the following characteristics:

- The founder or a family member is the president or chief executive officer.

- Members of the founder's family are employed by the company.

- Members of the founder's family can, if they agree, decide issues brought to a shareholder vote.

- Managers accept the designation of their firm as a family business.

The family's association with a business presents unique problems and challenges for the strategist. Although these challenges are related to the general strategic problems of managing external and internal relationships, it is the balance between "internal" and

493

"external" influences on the family business which requires examination and discussion.

Consideration of research on family business and observation and conversation with managers in family businesses have led us to conclude that the monolithic concept of "family business" does not adequately describe the complexity of the institution as it exists currently. Although there is widespread agreement that family business exists as an institution, the organization so identified may range from a mom-and-pop company to a large corporation. It may be owned and managed by a combination of family and nonfamily individuals or managed solely by siblings or other related individuals.

Our investigation of family businesses (see box) has led us to propose a theory of family business evolution from entrepreneurial to post-family

(see Figure 1) relationships. We distinguish four structures of relationships between the family as an institution and the business organization. These evolving relationships are referred to as family-business relationships. These four relationship structures contrast with the single concept of family business.

Strategic Implications of the Family-Business Relationship

In the family business an important component of the general management task is the management of the family and professional relationships which crisscross the board room, the executive suite, and the dinner table.

Mismanagement of these relationships can have a variety of consequences:

- Disgruntled managers form new, competing businesses.

Figure 1. Structures of the Family-Business Relationship

Structure	Initiated by	Relationship characterized by	Focus on relationship
I. Prefamily	Founding of business	Concentration of power in single individual	Survival, succession
II. Family	Entry of relative of founder or sole owner/manager into management and/or ownership	Power dispersed among several individuals based on family connection	Resource acquisition
III. Adaptive Family	Sale of stock to nonfamily members	Power based on management position and stock ownership	Performance
IV. Postfamily	Liquidation of family stock holdings	Power based on ability to function in the new organization	Adjustments

- Disgruntled managers launch battles for control.

- Competitors can identify patterns of management decisions.

- Opportunities are missed; risks are ignored.

- Subterranean warfare wears out the organization and causes the best people to leave.

When family relationships are properly managed, however, the results are positive:

- Organizations become more cohesive.

- Resources (both human and financial) become readily available.

- Strategists take a long-term view.

These results are not dependent on whether the company, is publicly or privately held or on the size of the company, but rather on how the family-business relationship is managed. Strategists in the family business must concern themselves with two aspects of the family business relationship:

- Determinants of the content of the decisions, and

- Role of the strategist in the decision process.

Determinants of Decision Content

The managers of family businesses in our sample frequently made strategic and operating decisions which had little family significance or provoked little family interest. These decisions might be significant to the business, but they did not trigger any family-business interaction. However, some decisions that were no more significant to the business might trigger upheavals in the relationship. We found it important in understanding the family-business

---

Research into the Family Business Relationship

The research which produced the findings reported here included a general investigation into the nature of the family-business relationship followed by a more focused consideration of the relationship in specific companies. Discussions were held with individuals connected with family businesses in various ways which might be characterized as participants (family and nonfamily managers, family members) and observers (representatives of lending institutions, stockbroker, industry association executive). Specific companies included in the second phase of the research ranged in size from three employees and $250,000 in sales to more than 7,000 employees and annual sales of over $350 million. Firms were in the first, second, third, or fourth generation of family management. Two had recently discontinued the family association with the business. The research included both publicly and privately held firms and included firms with a wide variety of performance records.

The variety of the sample allowed us to examine family businesses in which the family had varying terms of tenure; firms with poor, moderate, and good performance; and firms of different sizes and different ownership patterns. All firms were engaged in some form of food processing and had similar operating problems and environmental challenges.

---

relationship to understand the distinctions between these decisions. In-depth interviews allowed us to examine decisions from multiple perspectives and provided some insight into the background and context in which decisions were being made.

We found that each family-business relationship could be described in terms of the constraints which the family placed on the business and the business' requirements for survival. We found that managers (whether family members or not) had flexibility to

Figure 2. Strategic Family Constraints

Constraint	Expressed As	Company
Capital structure	"My Daddy didn't build this business for me to lose it to the bank. We do not borrow money."	small, privately held
Risk	"The fortunes of this family are tied to the stock of this company. They are very careful."	large, publicly held
Allocation of resources	"A west-coast facility would save us in shipping but the family wants all production here so I dropped the idea."	small, privately held
Procurement of resources	"The family provides top management. A [family member] will always be president."	small, privately held
Purpose/scope	"We go with what interests us; we can do that since we own the company."	small, privately held
Reward system	"My title doesn't reflect what I do. Only family members are officers."	small, privately held

handle business requirements as long as they operated within family constraints. However, when events precipitated a conflict between family constraints and business requirements, the family-business relationship itself had to be included as part of the negotiation and decision process. Three possible outcomes in this conflict included:

- Revision of the constraints so that business requirements could be met.

- Ignoring the business requirements so that constraints could be honored.

- Adjusting the family-business relationship so that the constraints no longer applied.

Periodic conflicts between family constraints and business requirements affect the ability of the organization to interact with its environment, and require that the family-business relationship be managed.

Interaction with Environment

Family constraints vary across businesses and vary in strategic importance. Strategic constraints included (see Figure 2) procurement of financing, attitudes toward risk, allocation of resources, procurement of resources, reward systems, and purpose/scope of business.

Figure 3. Managerial Orientation as a Function of Family and Business Power of the Individual Manager

Power in the Family

		High	Low
Power in the Business	High	Action	Negotiation
	Low	Counseling	Mediation

A company which is growing, operating in a volatile environment, of competing in an evolving industry is likely to confront challenges to family constraints. Formulating and implementing strategies will require cognizance of the constraints and how the content of strategic decisions will meet or conflict with constraints. If constraints are firmly held, compliance with he constraints may require sacrificing the business requirements or changing the family-business relationship itself. Attacking the problem of changing the relationship may be more fruitful in some instances than arguing over the constraints. When constraints can't be changed, we frequently observe the family selling its interest in a business.

The Strategist's Role in the Decision Process

Managing in the family business environment depends heavily on the manager's position and power in the organization. A manager derives power from his or her position in the business and in the family. Business-related power must often depend on one's position in the management hierarchy (where higher positions confer greater power), stock ownership (where larger percentages of ownership confer greater power), and experience in the business. Family-related power generally comes from family seniority or from one's ability to influence senior members of the family. The nature of a manager's power base will determine the freedom with which he or she can adjust family constraints to meet the competitive requirements of the business. The source of a manager's power base also dictates the kinds of skills he or she will need in managing the family-business relationship.

For those who derive power from both the family and the business, managing the family-business relationship may be no more difficult than carrying out his or her daily job. However, managers with limited powers require political, diplomatic, and interpersonal skills if they expect to adjust family constraints or meet the competitive requirements of the business. To identify critical management skills, Figure 3 suggests four management strategies: action, negotiation, counseling, and mediation. Each management strategy relates to one's level of power in the business and in the family.

Action Management

The manager who derives power from both the family and the business may be the object of envy to those managers in more ambiguous situations. Often such a manager is the owner/operator of a small business or the chief executive and largest stockholder of a larger business. She or he may also be the senior member of a family in which no one stockholder has a larger share of stock. Such a manager has significant decision making freedom and can easily "turn thought into action."

Action managers must be especially conscious of their own priorities since adjustments to family constraints and competitive requirements can be influenced by their personal objectives. The commitment of action managers to their own objectives and their assessments of the need for making adjustments determines what actions they will take.

Action managers must develop skills for implementing strategic and operating decisions. In smaller firms the action manager may directly implement strategy while in larger firms, the implementation of strategy will require appropriate organization and management systems as well as strong leadership. One danger that action managers must face is their tendency to view the business as an extension of themselves rather than as a separate entity. This tendency can result in a failure to provide for succession or to make adaptations in the relationship.

Negotiation Management

When managers have relatively high power in the business but relatively low power in the family, they must depend on negotiation skills. Like action managers, they will be judged on the firm's performance and on their ability to make and implement strategic decisions. When family constraints conflict with the competitive requirements of the business, they do not have the action manager's power to adjust family constraints. Instead, they must rely on their political skills to achieve those same ends. The fact that negotiation managers have power in the business gives them a base from which to deal with powerful family members who depend on their expertise in operating the business. Because of their business clout, negotiation managers can afford these occasional confrontations.

Problems for negotiation managers come with increasingly frequent confrontations between family members and the management team. Since both are operating from positions of power, political maneuverings may subvert the decision process completely.

Counseling Management

Family members in the business may find themselves with low business-based power for several reasons. They may be one of several subordinates with limited powers. They may even be the appointed successor to a strong leader who never quite steps down. In the opposite situation, counseling managers may still be in the business but may have delegated so much authority to their successors that they have effectively transferred their business power. However, counseling managers still have a good deal of power in the family due either to their seniority or experience,

498

or both, even though they have abdicated much of their business power. Counseling managers may have much to offer in advice and consultation, but their best contribution to the family-business relationship will be to use their influence to smooth the way for the adjustments which others will make.

The acceptance of this counseling role may involve a change of style which is difficult for some individuals and impossible for others. Those who have developed skills in implementation and bargaining may not be able to take a lesser role. The danger is that managers with declining power in the business will continue to act as if nothing has changes, thus hindering the development of implementation and bargaining skills by other managers.

Mediation Management

Managers who find themselves with little power in either the business or the family are in the most precarious position of all in attempting to manage the family-business relationship. Considerable interpersonal skill is essential when dealing from a low power position in both family and business. The ability to generate support will depend on the personal competence of these managers and the ability to communicate that competence in their dealings with individuals of power.

Assessing Managerial Power: A Concluding Remark

The ability of managers to assess their own power base accurately will go a long way in guiding their behavior. Power in the family is largely dependent on the structure of the family. Seniority is very important, and the oldest brother, uncle, or cousin is likely to have more influence with younger members to the family than their stock holdings

might imply. A father retains influence over children through a lifetime of interactions. Sex also determines family power; most firms are male-dominated. Women involved in businesses we've explored had nonmanagerial positions and did not actively influence the family in business matters.

In addition to sex and age, family power also accrues to those family members whose experience and expertise in the firm contribute to the enforcement of family constraints. Former managers who have retired or who have gone on to other jobs are likely to have more power in the family than members who have little knowledge of the business. By the same token, family members who have experience and expertise in any business have more power than those who have no business experience at all.

Power in the business stems from the position of the manager in the managerial hierarchy and from the experience and expertise which the manager brings to this position. It is not usually possible to assess the power which a manager in a family business wields by simply looking at the organization chart. Family managers tend to make informal arrangements among themselves concerning division of power and the organization chart does little to reflect these arrangements. In one firm, the manager insisted that his father was the most powerful person in the business even though he had neither a managerial position nor stock in the business. The nonfamily manager in the family business must develop a tolerance for sporadic second-guessing of his or her decisions while at the same time working to prevent those circumstances from becoming dysfunctional to the family-business relationship.

The ability to change family constraints and decide which techniques to use depends on a manager's power base in the firm and in the family. Managers in a family business must consider their positions in relation to the family as well as their role in the business. In family businesses, this consideration becomes critical since, no matter how competent managers are, they cannot do their job if they cannot function in their position in the family business.

Introduction

Families with businesses need mission statements for their families as well as businesses. The family mission statement is a document that lays out your family's goal of working together as a family in business, spells out the benefits and pledges the family to the goal. It is hammered out through discussion, clarifying areas of consensus and conflict. Concerns are aired and discussed at a family meeting. If the business is seen as worth the family's commitment, write it down. The process can energize the family for years to come.

A Family Needs a Mission Statement
1987

By John L. Ward and
 Laurel S. Sorenson

Why does succession have to be so painful?

Can our sons and daughters work together?

Will our family business last?

These questions worry every family business. They come down to one issue: Is it worth it?

In times of doubt, it's helpful to open the desk drawer and take out a piece of paper that says "Yes! It is worth it," and goes on to say why.

This piece of paper is a *family mission statement.* Separate from the business mission statement, it lays out your goal—your dream, really—of working together as a family in business. It spells out the benefits. And it pledges your family to make the dream come true.

To be sure, coming up with such a statement isn't easy. Sometimes, even deciding to stay together in business is difficult. Uncomfortable questions must be asked—and answered—to make that happen. When should the business pass from one generation to the next? Who is welcome in the business? What qualifications must they have? What compensation do they deserve? What titles should be bestowed? How should ownership be distributed? What returns do owners deserve? How shall business decisions be made?

Any of these issues may spark a debate that will threaten your dream. Yet if your family has a commitment, you have a much better chance of resolving the debate than a family without it. A mission generates enthusiasm. It encourages solutions. And it diverts squabbles into more productive channels.

"Energies once devoted to sibling rivalry are now put to better use," says a manufacturer of specialty-meat products, who last year spent 16 hours over six months with his wife and four children (three work in the company) to develop the family's mission statement. "We now have a common understanding of the commitment we must have to the business. And we know what each of us can expect in return."

Preparing your mission statement means, first of all, getting the family together after hours in a conference room, the family den or even a vacation retreat. The setting doesn't matter, as long as the atmosphere is casual and the time is not constrained.

The leader of the discussion might begin by summing up the uncomfortable questions outlined above. "Family businesses inevitably have these tensions," he might add. "So this has got to be something we really want to do. Otherwise, it's not worth it. So do we want to do it? And if so, why?"

You can expect family members to exchange nervous glances. A few throats will be cleared. Then comments will start to surface.

Some will be uncertain: "It's a lot of responsibility. I'm not sure I can work for Dad. What if fighting about the business tears the family apart?"

Others will be more positive: "I want to work for myself. Let's keep it alive for the kids. I think it's great working together as a family."

Airing concerns might take more than one meeting. But eventually, your family will arrive at a consensus. Then—if the answer is yes—you can set your

dream down in a short document that everyone can refer to in the months ahead.

The specialty-meat manufacturer, for example, took just two sentences to summarize the family's decision. "We have a mutual commitment and obligation to family security and development. Perpetuating the family business will encourage independence and opportunity for self-actualization for all employees—family and non-family alike."

One of the best family mission statements we've seen comes from a family that has been in the newspaper business for three generations. Five sets of parents and all their children met on three Saturdays over the course of a year at a local hotel.

Sticky issues that they examined ranged from developing retirement programs for parents to equalizing voting control among the families. Yet, they decided, strong emotional ties to the paper and to their hometown made the work worth the effort. Two "children" (in their 30s) volunteered to draft the decision as a letter between the generations.

"To our parents," the one-page epistle began. "We resolve to keep our company in the family as long as possible. We ask you to hand down a precious legacy. It's not money. It's not fancy cars and fat salaries. It's an opportunity to maintain a tradition of journalistic excellence.

"You have instilled in us a tremendous pride in our business and in our family. It's because of this pride that we ask you to entrust us with this valuable inheritance."

The signatures of 19 of the younger generation lay below the last line.

You don't have to be a professional writer to get your point across. If your family agrees the business is worth the effort, just say so, in a brief letter to yourselves. Explain why. Then ask everyone to sign.

And keep in mind that it won't work to copy some other family's statement.

The process you go through in coming to agreement on your own is more important than the words you finally commit to paper, because if usually draws family members closer together. Once you've agreed to a mission statement, you'll find that it gives you energy and hope for years to come.

Chapter 11

Women in the Family Firm

Women are becoming more involved in the business side of family business. Increasingly they move into executive roles in family firms. Special issues confront women assuming leadership roles, not the least of which are the positive and negative aspects of such responsibility on the women involved. While additional potential successors can further complicate succession planning, women may bring special skills to the firm. Socialized nurturing skills can be translated into management skills. Daughters are better than sons at avoiding intense rivalries and power struggles with father. A woman's involvement is not always a matter of choice, however. Many a woman has stepped into a dead husband's role. A woman married to the family firm's founder should be prepared for her contingent role.

Introduction

Background, environment and family/business interaction are key issues in understanding women's traditional roles in family businesses. The authors suggest that women who seek to develop greater advancement potential within family businesses should engage in both networking and career planning.

Women in Family Business: An Untapped Resource
1985

By Amy Lyman, Ph.D.,
   Matilde Salganicoff, Ph.D. and
   Barbara Hollander, Ph.D.

Reprinted by permission of **SAM Advanced Management Journal**, Winter 1985. Copyright ©1985 SAM Advanced Management Journal; all rights reserved.

"My father started the family business twenty years ago. I've always helped out — offered suggestions, done a lot of the bookkeeping, designed an inventory control system—but my position has never been formalized. I have a title but it doesn't reflect all of the different things that I do."

"We started our own business five years ago. We wanted to spend more time with each other and be able to set our own hours. I find that most of the business decisions are made by both of us, but I still carry most of the family responsibilities. My husband doesn't see it as his place to contribute."

"I love owning my own business and my husband is very supportive of my work —always. Now that we are thinking about who will succeed us we're faced with some tough decisions. Two of our children work with us now, our daughters. Our son isn't interested and I think that's good because he's not right for the business. But my husband is upset that his son won't carry on the family tradition. I think our business will do very well with our daughters in control."

These statements are characteristic of those made by many women who work in family business, and they represent the kinds of frustrations they encounter. The unique problems and rewards that affect women in family business are slowly but surely coming to light, and women are discussing them openly. They are exchanging information with other mothers and daughters and extended family members who find themselves in similar situations. These women, who are committed to seeing that both their businesses and families remain strong, have acknowledged the presence of the family business in almost every aspect of their lives. They are now in the process of understanding what this presence means.

The advantages of family businesses are many. They provide a supportive environment flexible work hours, committed employees, and they encourage personal responsibility. But they can also bring added stress and strain to family relationships. Saying "no" to the boss could mean saying "no" to your husband, and playing hooky from work could be the topic of conversation at the dinner table. Competition among family members may be keen with salaries and job performance used as measures of worth. How well a woman manages these kinds of complications may well determine her success in fulfilling her roles in both the family and the business.

Several sets of issues have been identified as key to developing an understanding of the situation of women in family business. Although these sets overlap, they may be roughly labeled as background and environment, family and business, and networking and career planning. The boundaries between these categories are by no means distinct, but they provide a useful framework for examining the issues faced by women in family run businesses.

Background and Environment

Although family businesses vary widely in form, they share common background characteristics that define the environment within which family and business interactions occur.

A family business is one whose strategic policy is determined by a majority of the family members. The long-term direction and character of the firm are established through family priorities, either voted on through the use of proxys or stated by the founder and her or his family members.

Some form of family influence is almost always present. The family may influence the business directly by maintaining control of the management process, but control is not always actively exercised. Passive influence may take the shape of a strong business charter, or it may come from the electrifying presence of the founder of the business — who may visit but not have a direct responsibility for daily business operations. Or there may be a portrait of the founder displayed in the office, with a suitable motto encouraging hard work and family loyalty. Whether this inspires fear or awe, it serves as a reminder of the founder's guiding principles.

Cultural traditions that place women and men in different social positions, with gender-based definitions of work and family responsibilities, play a large part in establishing the work environment. That environment is defined by everything from the portrayal of women in the mass media to the historical dominance of women's family roles over business ones. The essential roles that women have played in the economic development of our country are now being documented and it is dawning on many that women have always worked, though they have not always received recognition for the variety of their responsibilities. In *Women Have Always Worked*, by Alice Kessler-Harris, documentation of the work performed by women includes such tasks as plowing fields, pitching and baling hay, general household maintenance and equipment repair, family business budget management, inventory control, etc.

Kessler-Harris' book is one example of the changes that are now occurring in our perceptions of traditional role boundaries. Family business members must be in tune with such changes in our values and perceptions if they are to ensure the survival of their family business.

Family and Business

Members of family businesses may try to keep family and business responsibilities separate, but that works only up to a point. To ignore the reality that family and business affect each other is to invite trouble. Disgruntled employees are a problem for any business, but when those employees sit around the same dinner table the stresses of poor planning take an even higher toll.

Historically, family business configurations have focused on the male founder and his heirs. Business plans were thought to be etched in stone even though successive generations may have wanted to adapt the business to new market needs. Mothers, wives, daughters and female in-laws have often been represented in family trees but without job titles and salaries next to their names. The strength of traditional family roles, both within society and within individual families, kept women's business contributions from being acknowledged.

In accordance with this, many women in family business take on the role of passive tradition bearers. As caretakers for family members they are in the perfect position to hear about family concerns such as Uncle Stanley's distrust of the accountant or daughter Sarah's plans for the future of the business, both of which could be important pieces of information that will affect the business. These women may know the business inside and out, but they must overcome their concerns about stepping over role boundaries in order to take an active role and put their information to good use. By keeping the information inside, they deprive the business of the benefits of their knowledge.

To succeed in a family business a woman must make sure that she has the necessary skills and knowledge to be an asset to the business, and that she is willing to make a commitment to help the enterprise succeed. She must confront traditional notions of what women should and should not do as she attempts to gain support from family members and other employees. Mothers of successful daughters may feel that their role as homemaker is being challenged through the daughter's pursuit of a business career, or siblings may have difficulty recognizing each other's successes at work — especially if the sister is more successful than the brother. It is important to understand that women in family business, just like men, are reflecting neither the family nor the business, but are trying to fit both into their lives.

As one woman in a family business said, "A life of shrimp salad and tennis was the ideal I was encouraged to seek, but a business career is very challenging. I am still ambivalent at times, but now it is easier to see myself as a business woman than when I first started working." This feeling of ambivalence is characteristic of the either/or bind with which women struggle as they try to see themselves as both family members and business people.

Within families the issue of succession can be a thorny problem, and in fact, many family businesses fail because no clear plan for passing on the enterprise is ever established. Recently it has become more popular to consider women as successors, and "and daughter" has even begun to appear on business cards and shop signs alongside of "and son." Members of the extended family also need to be considered as family members whose personal and work roles are involved in the success of the business.

Evidence suggests that in many industries family businesses are initially more successful than non-family ones, but that they have a lower survival rate after the first generation. Poor planning and a failure to develop the potential of family members contribute to this low survival rate. Developing a business plan that addresses family concerns such as child care, career development, and includes wives, mothers, daughters and female in-laws in current and future business decisions can help ensure the success of the family enterprise.

Networking and Career Planning

Women facing the pressures of family business life often think that they are the only ones in the predicament. They are unaware that many other women face conflicts involving family and business needs. At times it may seem as if they could use the talents of a juggler as they attempt to fulfill the dual responsibilities of family and career, especially the balancing of child rearing with career development. It can be difficult to get other family members to fully appreciate that while a woman may be a wife, mother, daughter or female in-law, she may also be the vice president for operations.

To successfully cope with this situation, and to successfully develop their careers, women need to develop networks with other women in family business. Such groups are still few and far between. Through networking, women

can get in touch with other women who have been able to deal constructively with the competing interests of families and careers, and come up with ways to deal with their own particular situation.

Establishing networks of women in family business will help establish role model and mentor relationships so that women can actively encourage each other to seek fuller participation in their family businesses. Just knowing that someone else has managed to balance childrearing with a business career — and has remained sane, for most of the time — can provide much needed encouragement. By sharing information, women can adapt family management strategies that have been tested in different settings to their own needs. Also, friends and acquaintances who can discuss the issues of family business can bring to life for women the realization that concerns about family business careers are legitimate and widespread.

Like any successful business person, a woman in a family business must take the time to evaluate her skills and plan a career carefully and conscientiously. Networks can help with this by putting women in touch with other women in family business. But women can also find support within their own families. Family members can encourage their pursuit of meaningful work in the business, and exposure to a variety of opportunities can be helpful especially when the opportunities are available on the basis of skill and not solely due to family position.

The development of a woman's strengths and talents through her work can ease some of the tension associated with changing roles. But she must know that there are opportunities for her personal and professional development within the business in order for her commitment to remain high. For many women, pursuing a business degree or apprenticeship appear to be impossible tasks.

There may not be any ready cash for tuition since all assets are tied up in the business. But overlooking valuable resources can spell disaster for any business, and women are currently an underdeveloped resource in many family businesses.

Adopting an approach to family business planning that includes career development for family members can be regenerative for the business. Once women are considered in the succession line for example, sons of founder's who have been groomed to take over the business, whether they want to or not, might now be able to pursue their secret career desires. Other family members will also have the freedom to pursue careers in other fields without feeling guilty about breaking up the business.

And women who had been forced to consider other professions or careers can now think seriously about a position of responsibility in the family business.

Within families, members should discuss the different position each person holds, and plan to take advantage of each persons' skills, talents, and interests. Women may still face the ambivalence involved in making the switch from a life of shrimp salad and tennis to the pursuit of a business career, but they should receive opportunities and support within their family businesses to do this. As women work with other family members to ensure that their needs are met and that their strengths are incorporated into the family business, the question of what a woman's proper role in the family business is will be answered. And the answer will reflect each woman's skills and career goals, not her gender.

Introduction

Women are increasingly being viewed as viable and valued partners in the family business. They bring special skills to the workplace. Relationships between daughter and parents differ from those of sons and parents. But with more family members in the business, management becomes more complicated. More extensive communication and planning are required.

"Odd Couples" in the Family-Owned Business
1988

By Mary Dana Korman and
Thomas M. Hubler

In 1978, Dana Oehrlein was in high school when her family, in a humorous yet welcoming gesture, re-lettered their residential trash hauling truck from OEHRLEIN & SONS to OEHRLEIN & SONS & Daughter.

"The 'and Daughter' was done in small curly-Q letters. I was so surprised when I saw it," Dana recalled.

"I soon began working part-time at the family business, during my senior year of high school in 1981, and then became full-time after high school. Now the lettering is all the same size on all our trucks. Our business has quadrupled in the last five years and changed a great deal. We recently sold the residential hauling business and we now concentrate only on commercial work.

Many people say they try us because of the mention of me in our name."

Dana is the bookkeeper and communications hub for Oehrlein and Sons and Daughter which also employs her three brothers, her husband, and four other employees in addition to her parents who now work part-time. "I think our business is good," she says, "because I never lie to people. If we can't do a job today, I say, 'It will be 3 o'clock tomorrow when we can get there.' People like that because I don't over-promise. They've come to associate us with honesty and dependability."

Dana's mother held this same job for 30 years, "But she did it out of our house," Dana says, "and still took care of four children. She also got very little credit for all her hard work."

As the Oehrlein story illustrates, the family-owned business in America has undergone some significant transformations as women are increasingly being viewed as viable and valued partners. In the past they were invited, often out of necessity, to "join" the business as traffic managers or bookkeepers and usually worked from home or part time to fill in behind the scenes.

The conscious involvement of both sexes in the American family-owned business has paved the way for a complete examination of how gender differences affect this very fragile American institution.

The gender combinations in family-owned businesses seem endless because death, retirement, marriage and divorce result in a varied assortment of individuals who end up in families and in business together.

Gender Differences

Men and women simply have different frames of reference and bring somewhat different skills to the workplace. An acceptance of this idea combined with a desire to capitalize on these male/female differences is crucial to the success of any family-owned business where different family members interact.

Generally, women are communicators and peacemakers at work and at home. Traditionally they have been more compliant and less independent than men. Competition has not been stressed. In their formative years, most girls in our society are not taught "How to be Feminine and Operate a Business." Women successful in business often run a high risk of being called "too tough." Critics may say, "She acts just like a man."

Conversely, men have been more competitive and task-oriented. They tend to be more aggressive and less able to recognize and express feelings. When in their formative years, most boys in our society are prepared for being "in charge." A man who is successful in business is regarded as shrewd and hardworking, not criticized for his competency.

Both kinds of skills and competency wind up being useful differences in business and provide balance. Increasingly women included in the "real" responsibility of business management enrich and expand the possible perspectives.

Children

As parents, owners of a family-owned business are not only raising their next generation but are also rearing a second generation CEO, managing editor or president. Consequently, routine parent/child dynamics in other families become double-edged dilemmas for the family which owns and operates a business.

All children, as they mature, need to pull away from their parents to establish their own identities and this pulling away tends to set up competition with their parents. Intense competition can result if a child wants to be very dissimilar from a parent. Simultaneously, however, children can experience a natural pull toward their parents. A child encounters numerous problems trying to become his or her own person while working or being groomed to work in the shadow of a parent. Offspring in a business struggle to separate and emancipate while having the office next door and being introduced as "Sam's son."

Furthermore, second and third generation children in the family-owned business may be better educated than their parents or, from observation, may have fresher, bolder business ideas. They may forget to value wisdom and the experience of learning the hard way, adding to tension with their parents. Their energy and enthusiasm for risk and innovation may come at the time when the "old man" is slowing down and is ready to coast. But these children are likely to be caught—either in being reluctant to outperform their parents or in not being encouraged to do so.

Father/Son

Bill, Sr. and Bill, Jr. at a printing company in the midwest have typical father/son difficulties. Bill, Sr. wanted his children to be better off than he was. Simultaneously, he didn't want them to get things too easily and fail to understand the value of hard work.

Bill, Jr. was college educated when he started in the family-owned business and he harbored a fear, along with his aggressive ideas about how to change the business, of running away with the business, leaving Dad behind.

Bill, Sr. started his son out pushing a broom which made it very difficult for Bill, Jr. to prove his worth. Consequently, "Dad" retained visibility and power and his son stayed in the background.

Eventually Bill, Jr. climbed up in the company but older employees continued to go to his father with questions that were within Bill, Jr.'s purview. Bill, Jr. was repeatedly referred to as "Bill's son" even away from the office at the bank and at social clubs. Creating his own area of expertise and authority became a never-ending tension between father and son.

Men often find closeness with each other by doing tasks together whereas women often bond by emotional sharing. The father/son business relationship may fall short when it comes to confronting personal issues, such as, disappointments, needs and concerns.

Take the situation of Bill, Jr. whose anger and frustration increased over the years. He was able to work out tangible compensation issues and partnership agreements with his father. However, he was unable to sit down and hammer out the ground rules necessary to fully manage their professional/personal relationship which often interfered with their ability to resolve conflict and do business together.

Father/Daughter

Every cultural stereotype gets in the way when "Daddy's little girl" goes to work for him. Protectiveness of the father for his daughter, a tendency to downplay the usefulness of her brain power, and a reluctance to let the intellectual side of the business give way to the more interpersonal considerations she may have, all play a part.

The biggest problem in this family combination has to do with the early unconscious exclusion of girls from the family business. By age 2 many girls are already being given negative messages about their abilities and interest in the family-owned business. These messages may be so well accepted that daughters may not even think of the family-owned business as a possibility.

By the time she graduates from high school or college, if a daughter wants "in" major problems can exist and conflict may get unleashed. It is hard for her to get others to comprehend the seriousness of her interest. Father, especially, may fail to see her viability as a business partner.

Should she join her father in business, a daughter's major obstacle is getting recognition for competency—similar to her male counterpart. She will also have to struggle with not being well regarded except in traditional or supportive roles. However, the daughter may be more adept at "talking things out".

Mother/Son

Here we have a different kind of role reversal. Mother is expected to be a homemaker and is often a peacemaker between her husband and son. However, it is not assumed she can be her son's supervisor in business.

The most common mother/son family business relationship occurs when father dies, leaving the family-owned business to his wife. She is likely unprepared and anxious because her role, up to now, has been largely more traditional. If she has worked in the business she may have not been a decision maker. Now the task of being an owner/operator is awesome and the alternative, of being dependent on her son, is no better.

Mother often has the hardest time of all being regarded as a key business player. Comfortable with the nurturer role, a woman in this position in a resort business became the caretaker of all the employees thereby failing to fully define herself in the business because she made all her employees into surrogate children. It is hard to make tough decisions while seeing yourself as responsible for the emotional well-being of others.

In a mother/son relationship, the son can assert himself because the mother may find it harder to take risks and will solicit her son's help to do so. Conflicts easily arise over ownership and management prerogatives.

Mother/Daughter

A woman and three daughters inherited a trucking firm when the husband/father died suddenly. One of the daughters wanted to sell out and pursue a career away from the family-owned business. Mother not only insisted that they all work together but she also wanted them to all be in the business with equal authority. Without a chain of command, the four of them fought incessantly.

In this case the mother was focused on relationships – wanting to keep the family together – and so she lost sight of the business needs.

Finally, the mother set about to make it possible for the one daughter to leave the business and she, herself, took a stronger hand in its management.

The irony of the mother/daughter relationship is now that it is acceptable for a woman to choose a business career, a mother and daughter frequently witness the deterioration of an otherwise healthy relationship when they begin working together.

In a restaurant and motel business where the daughter was in law school, her father, the Chief Executive Officer, died and his widow took over in his position. Formerly, the mother and daughter were supportive of each other regarding father and the business. The daughter came home to be the chief operating officer, and as such they became combatants with on-the-job differences to work out, each with her own way to do things.

In this case the mother typically had feelings of incompetency, particularly when she contrasted herself with her daughter who had a considerable amount of business acumen and training. But as the senior member of the family, it was hard to take a back seat.

In personal dealings, the daughter returned to her previously supportive relationship with her mother. But at the office she eventually learned to say "No" to her mother at key times and in appropriate ways.

Sister/Sister

In sister work relationships there is sometimes a healthy support for each other although there can also be feelings of professional jealousy to deal with that are just as intense as in the brother/brother combination. Each has mixed messages to deal with — messages that go way back and say, "Get a college education but don't use it," "Stay feminine," or "Don't be assertive." Sometimes misunderstanding can seem disastrous if the sisters are accustomed to a supportive and close relationship. However, in this relationship there is often a shared understanding of what it means to "do it all" — to manage a career and a family.

Brother/Brother

In brother work relationships, competitiveness is both a source of energy and a destructive ingredient. Male family members in business together tend to be socially and emotionally separate. They bind together solely around their work, sometimes to the detriment of putting their individual, personal attributes to good use in the business. In addition, issues of compensation and performance evaluation can become areas of tension.

After they have been in business together for a few years, men usually have a huge pile of unfinished issues which they have failed to address and which are hampering day to day operations.

In-Laws

The in-law issue is a decidedly sexist one. When a son marries there is rarely a threat to the business. Acceptance of his spouse does not usually include a business role.

On the other hand, when a daughter marries the new son-in-law is looked over as family as well as business material.

An interesting in-law case involved two sisters who inherited a family-owned business. One married a man with an MBA degree and he was instantly viewed as heir apparent to the business. The other sister remained unmarried. Neither daughter was considered for management positions. This dynamic resulted in many business problems, hurt feelings and ownership issues.

Parent/Child Solutions

All children have to go through a process of emancipation from their families in order to mature. This issue is even more critical in the family-owned business where a child can be concerned about being his or her own person while working under the authority of mother or father.

In order to let children individuate themselves, many families with businesses now encourage them to work elsewhere before joining the family-owned business. In this way offspring can verify and experiment with their own personal and work styles in someone else's business. They can prove themselves to themselves as well as to their parents.

Parents, too, can work to maintain a separate/equalness while on the job with a child. When a son is called "Charlie's Kid" at age 50, how can he act with authority? Taking a child around and introducing him or her as a department manager, for example, and recognizing the child as such in day-to-day practice can alleviate the most common problem afflicting families when two generations work together.

Rules for Both Sexes

To keep sex differences within the family from harming the operations of the business, consider the following:

1. Communicate often and openly. Set and keep meeting times to discuss *tasks* and separate times to discuss *process*. Consider both to be important.

2. Keep small grievances from growing into irreconcilable difficulties. Practice being open and fair with the concerns of all family members in the business.

3. Define and address differing agenda. Father wants to retire at age 60 and take some profits out of the business. His son wants the profits for an expansion of the business. This conflict can be worked out so as to save the business *and* the family.

4. Recognize and devise ways to handle unequal workloads. Mother is CEO but her MBA daughter actually runs the business. Other family members want equal salaries and profits but they put in fewer hours and have less responsibility. Compensation and profit sharing must be established with the knowledge and understanding of all employed family members.

5. Business relationships mature over time and require work like any other relationship. Just because you got along well with your father at home doesn't mean that you'll get along well with him at the office.

6. Outside, professional consulting expertise is a good way to resolve an impasse or to set agenda. Outsiders, with no vested interest, will make the business a priority and will point out problem areas in a way that facilitates their solution.

7. Working with a family member who is also a member of the opposite sex is a good way to gain varied business insights. Recognize and capitalize on gender differences.

Seventy percent of American family-owned businesses fail to survive into a second generation and sex and equality issues play a big part in this failure rate.

Imagine a family with a business run by the father where there are three children, two boys and a girl. Over time many personal combinations are possible for running the business. If the family is committed to having the business survive, then talent and competence in all family members need to be given consideration to maximize the future of the business.

There are still many estates which leave the family business to the sons and leave other real estate, personal valuables such as jewelry, and trusts to the daughters. While some sons are interested in going back and redistributing their shares of the business to achieve more equity and relieve hurts, this kind of planning ruins many other businesses and family relationships.

A family-owned business relationship should be a long term commitment for family members. Yet all the role expectations we have in the family, combined with a few extra in the business, enter into this union to potentially disrupt it. Development of ground rules, adjustments and improvements in the relationship are worth investing with a lot of time, energy and communication.

Introduction

Successful women in family-owned and operated businesses learn to exercise power by translating their socialized skills as nurturers in the family into management skills in the family business. An experienced family business consultant outlines five important steps employed by these pathfinders. A case study illustrates an important issue in family business: women are customarily perceived in traditional roles and not as future CEOs.

Like Father, Like Daughter: A New Vision for Family Business
1988

By Carol Eve Goodman, MSW

Reprinted by permission of **Vision/Action**. June, 1988, Vol. 7, No. 4. Copyright © 1988 by Seabrook Institute; all rights reserved.

From the first day Tom Logan saw his twins in their bassinets at the hospital, he dreamed that Tom Jr. would someday inherit Logan Motors. His dream for Thomasina was that she would marry the right man and make Tom Sr. a proud grandfather.

Tom started Logan Cadillac in 1955 when he returned from the Korean War. It was a way to support the family, pay for the house, and provide for his retirement. He never envisioned owning the largest Cadillac Agency on the West Coast. The business became a source of great personal satisfaction and a reflection of his own values of superior business ethics and service. As the employer of over 100 mechanics, salesmen, and bookkeepers, Tom Sr. felt an obligation to pass on the business

that supported all these families. Tom Sr. had a strong relationship with his employees. He was godfather to over thirty children, and the company barbecue was indeed a "family affair." So Tom Sr. envisioned the business as a trust and a commitment to all his family.

When Tom Jr. entered law school, his dad saw it as a training ground for Tom Jr. taking over Logan Cadillac. What better way could there be to prepare to be CEO? He championed the idea, and father and son prepared for the eventual transition. Tom Jr. worked in the business during the summers. He was respected and well liked by his fellow employees.

The news that young Tom wanted to pursue a career in criminal law came as quite a shock to his father. Rather dramatically, he grabbed his chest as if he had been stabbed and began gasping for air. Fortunately, a cardiac surgeon was on the show-room floor shopping for a new car when 60-year-old Logan had a massive heart attack.

"I was a fool, a shortsighted, opinionated fool," Tom Sr. admits now, years later. "All I thought about was myself. When my son told me of his choice to pursue his dream, I thought he had betrayed me. Why did I build Logan Motors? All my sacrifice for naught. What should I do? Sell it out to the highest bidder and get a payout?"

The truth was he did have alternatives. For years he had thought that Logan Motors was no place for a woman. Most importantly, how could his daughter fulfill his dream of rearing all his grandchildren and still run a large company?

It is this logic, in part, that is responsible for the fact that no more than 39 percent of all American family businesses succeed to the second generation. "Fifty percent of potential successors are daughters," says Donald Jonovic of Family Business Management Services in Cleveland. "If only five percent of actual successors were daughters, it would be a significant improvement."

As in the case of the Logan family, the bias toward the son starts early. The son views the business as his birthright, and many times does not take the trouble to earn his place.

As a single parent, Tom Sr. often brought his children to his "shop." They spent many hours at Logan Motors. Tom Jr. loved to hang out in the service department. By day's end he was covered with grease. He once proudly announced that he had assisted with four lubes and singlehandedly rotated the tires on his father's car. Bill Forst, the shop foreman, instructed and mentored Tom Jr. and kept an eye on him. Thomasina, on the other hand,

preferred playing with the women in the bookkeeping department. They helped her choose a wardrobe for her favorite doll. Sophie Belanger, the office manager, became Thomasina's confidante and de facto step-mother.

During their teens the children's interest in spending time at Logan Motors developed in opposite directions. Tom Jr. was hired as a part-time service technician, while Thomasina visited occasionally to have lunch with Sophie. Tom Sr. was pleased with his children's progress. He encouraged his son's interest in the business and accepted Thomasina's more peripheral interest. Tom Sr. took his son to sales meetings and conferences, while Thomasina remained at home with the housekeeper. And so dad sowed his message early on by rewarding his son with trips and positive reinforcement and protecting his daughter from the trials and pressures of the business world.

In many cases, when a daughter like Thomasina comes into the business, it is after she has proven herself in other arenas. She has had to work harder to prove herself. And women have inherent talents that make them superior managers. According to Mathilde Salganoff, Ph.D., a Philadelphia family-business consultant and therapist who runs workshops for women in family businesses at the Wharton School of Business: "Women are taught to be more nurturing, more attuned to emotional needs, and are socialized to express more concern with helping the family . . . Women generally go into the business to help the family, and secondarily to develop a career. But most sons don't go in primarily to help their fathers or their families — it's simply not their central theme."

Thomasina graduated from UC Berkeley with a degree in Fine Arts. She worked as a secretary for the San Francisco Symphony and eventually became its Public Relations Director. She excelled in communications and fund raising. "I always loved and respected Dad," Thomasina smiles proudly as she sits behind her oak desk at Logan Motors. "But you know when Mom died, Tom Jr. and I were six years old. Tommy was interested in football, but somehow I fell into the role as the family nurturer."

"When Dad finally accepted the reality that his son would not step into his shoes, his first thought was to sell outright," Thomasina added. "At the time I was ready for a change in my career." A friend of Tom Sr.'s strongly suggested the need for consultation with a family business specialist. He began to realize the possibility that his daughter had the managerial skills needed to operate Logan Motors.

Interviewing successful women in family businesses like Thomasina, I discovered how they learn to exercise power as managers and family members. Successful women discover their skills in the home can be translated into leadership skills at work.

They follow the following five steps:

- Step One: Assessing Family and Business Needs.

Women know where they are in the life developmental cycle and are able to evaluate how their personal family, and business needs mesh or conflict. Women are brutally honest with themselves regarding the conflict between personal time commitments and business responsibilities. Thomasina was not ready to accept the CEO position in her twenties due to her professional commitments and goals outside the

family business, but when she turned thirty-two she was developmentally ready for larger responsibilities and remuneration.

- Step Two: Tuning in to Key Relationships.

Women look at their own behavior patterns and inventory their responses toward men and women at home and in business. They are able to smooth out conflicts. They are able to employ both their feminine and masculine natures, rather than aspiring to become 'one of the guys,' or overcompensating for being a woman. They learn the importance of leadership skills, of empowerment and motivation, instead of 'position power.' Thomasina placed key loyal employees in positions of power and delegated authority. She took the position of a female CEO/daughter of the founder, yet refused the 'queen bee' role.

- Step Three: Assessing Risk-Taking, Power Plays and Competition

Women have a clear idea about the importance of taking risks, achieving power, and competing. They are comfortable with each role. These roles are often not part of the female socialization process, which emphasizes nurturance, following, passivity, and non-assertive behavior. They learn to walk the tightrope between passivity and assertiveness without becoming 'one of the guys.' Thomasina was determined to lead the company without behaving like a female Tom Sr.

- Step Four: Developing a Mentor and Support System.

Women usually choose a male mentor (father, uncle, male loyal employee), as there are fewer female mentors available. They are able to sustain long-term supportive relationships with men and women who offer guidance and support. Thomasina viewed Sophie as her mentor and mother figure. She understood the need for mentorship, especially since her mother and father were not available in that capacity.

- *Step Five: Developing an Individual, Family, and Family Business Strategic Plan.*

Women start planning individual goals early and utilize these planning skills in the business. They develop a collective vision of how the family and the business work together. These women conceptualize their roles clearly, unraveling the mixed messages of earlier expectations of themselves, and develop great clarity of purpose. Thomasina planned to achieve outside the family business prior to participating. Although she was not sure of her eventual role in the family business, she became aware of her business interests and wanted to pursue them. Once in the business, she proceeded to develop a business plan that incorporated her ideals, financial goals, and differing levels of family participation.

It was not easy for Thomasina to shift gears. "It's a long way between the Symphony and the showroom, but not so far as I thought: people are people," she mused. When Thomasina, always a good communicator, decided to accept her father's offer to be CEO of Logan Motors, her father said: "We both sat down and made two lists. We did that separately. One list was Thomasina's strong points vis-a-vis Logan Motors, and the other was her weaknesses." "And then I went to work," she continued. "I knew nothing about cars, so that meant learning and it meant

delegating more authority. We immediately put Bill Forst into a managerial position and gave him a percentage of the business."

Thomasina realized the potential of women as a growing force in automobile consumerism. She instituted an ad campaign based on a survey she conducted to identify what women wanted in the car they drove. High on the list was safety: it was a much higher priority for women than men. And the most salient safety features in a car are size and engineering, two strong points of a Cadillac. The campaign proved a huge success. Thomasina, in an effort to appeal to this growing segment of business, began to hire women in the sales division and placed Sophie in charge of their training.

And so Logan Motors continued to grow under the watchful eye of Thomasina. Tom Sr. is a part-time consultant to the sales staff and teaches fly casting at the extended education department of a nearby community college. "I was some kind of nut," he says, as he bounces his three year old grandson, Timothy, on his knee "I never thought of ever wondering how my son would solve the problems of running Logan Motors and raising a family, but it sure was something I thought Thomasina probably could not do. Well, she sure showed me. And look here." The proud grandfather opened his wallet and showed me pictures of all eight of his grandchildren. "These two are Tom Jr.'s and guess what? He somehow manages to run a successful law practice and be a good dad ... "

Introduction

Daughters assuming leadership of family firms share high levels of self-esteem, realistic ideas about their futures and a strong desire to control those futures. While they were not typically groomed for succession, they are strongly motivated to work with their fathers.

The lack of specific grooming can be a plus when it permits the development of general leadership skills. Because women are rarely considered heirs apparent, they avoid the pressures, rivalries and power struggles that can occur between fathers and sons. Two case studies are given.

Why Certain Women Outdistance Brothers in a Family Business

1984

By Sandra Pesmen

Step aside, boys, a new breed of executive sister is taking charge.

For generations, girls uncomplainingly took ballet and piano lessons while their brothers took the family businesses.

But a new kind of daughter is emerging in Chicago-area entrepreneurial families — one who wasn't groomed to go into the business but who decided to join because of a close relationship with her father.

The movement of women into Chicago family-business board rooms isn't brand-new.

"We could tell something was happening during the last four years when we began getting women members and had to change our names from Sons of Bosses to Family Business Council," concedes a spokesman for that Chicago organization.

The Center for Family Business, a national organization with headquarters in Cleveland, estimates that 500 women are currently running family businesses in the United States. The organization's programs to train successors, who used to be exclusively male, have been averaging 43 percent female enrollment in the past two years.

These assertive, executive daughters share a high level of self-esteem, realistic ideas about their futures and a strong

522

desire to take charge of those futures themselves.

But new studies suggest that the most important factors are contradictory. These women weren't groomed for their jobs but were drawn in by the desire to work with the fathers they unabashedly admit they love very much.

Helena Lopata, author and director of Loyola University's Center for the Comparative Study of Social Roles, says such a woman often makes a better corporate officer than her brothers simply because she wasn't groomed for the job from childhood.

"A *Women's Managerial Study* done in the 1970s clearly shows that women who climb to the top of corporations were encouraged to do other things in their youth," Ms. Lopata notes. "Because of that diversification, they became generalists, something that's necessary for top management.

"The boys in the family, on the other hand, are usually trained to work in the family warehouse or factory from childhood, and become specialists because they know only about that business."

In that situation, Ms. Lopata adds, it's difficult for a son to develop the general communication skills necessary for supervision beyond middle-management level.

Desire for Nearness

John Ward, the Ralph Marotta Professor of Free Enterprise at Loyola University and a specialist in family business research, points to the strength of a daughter's desire to be near her father.

"Men go into the family business because they're expected to," he says. "Also, they know they have a better

chance of success there, and they want to help the family. Women usually want those things, too, but when I ask them about it, they just say they want to work with their fathers."

He adds that because women are rarely considered heirs apparent, they also avoid the pressures, competition, rivalry and power struggles that can cause friction between entrepreneurs and their sons.

"It makes me believe that there is certainly a special love between most men and their daughters," he suggests.

Ms. Lopata adds that she often talks with entrepreneurs who worry about what's going to happen to their businesses when they retire or die. They usually complain that their sons don't want to join them because they studied to be professionals or they started their own businesses.

"So I always ask, 'How about your daughters?' and they usually answer, 'Oh no. One daughter is married to a doctor, and the other's husband is incompetent.' It never occurs to most of them that the daughter herself might be a candidate."

But two Chicago entrepreneurs did lure their daughters to follow in their footsteps. In both cases, the women have been very successful and are being groomed to eventually head their companies.

Marilyn Kelly, 31, is now vice president of Kelly Flour, a $5-million company founded by her grandfather and run by her father, Donald M. Kelly, 69.

A Phi Beta Kappa in college, Ms. Kelly successfully took over the management of two different film companies after graduating.

"I loved running companies," she says. "After I'd been doing it in California a couple of years for someone else's family business, I realized I had all the responsibility and made all the decisions, but had none of the authority. So, when I came home at Christmas in 1979, I approached my father about joining his company."

The following summer, in the airport in New York after a family vacation, he told her, "You've been in California two years and you've not married yet, so it's time you came home. I have no one in line to follow me in the business. I've got seven brokers, and I'll pay you so much to come back and run the place."

She grins. "I told him, 'Let's put it all in writing.' and he sent me a handwritten letter outlining my responsibilities. He also wrote, 'And I promise you a rose garden right beside the soya tanks' (tanks behind the plant that hold flour)."

In somewhat the same way, 36-year-old Kay Sisson became secretary-treasurer and office manager of the $8 million Midway Supply Co. in Zion. The company is a wholesaler of heating and air conditioning equipment supplies, founded by Ms. Sisson's 62-year-old father, Grant Sisson.

After a pleasant childhood during which her father was her role model, Ms. Sisson majored in speech in college, worked in the theater and later married and moved to California.

But by 1973, her marriage was in trouble and she was living in a community working as a waitress. When Ms. Sisson returned to Chicago for the Christmas holidays that year, her father mentioned that he didn't know what he was going to do with his business.

Discovering a New World

"I'd started taking business courses in junior college – like retailing, accounting and finance – and I loved them," she remembers. "It was like discovering a whole new world.

"And here was my dad talking about how he didn't know what to do since the eldest of my brothers was then studying to be a minister, my sister was marrying a doctor and my youngest brother was in grade school. I thought about it more, and decided to come back."

Interestingly, there are several parallels in these women's lives – and much of what they have experienced jibes with the experts' observations.

For example, both women have brothers who also are associated with the family business in affiliated roles. Both women love their mothers and get along well with them, but never wanted to emulate their lifestyles.

Warm Relationships

Most important, Ms. Kelly and Ms. Sisson also say they enjoy "special" warm, loving relationships with their fathers that enhance their working relationships.

Ms. Kelly recalls that after her father had worked for her grandfather for several years, he started his own company in the basement of their home, which later merged with the family business.

"I was the youngest of three children and I know I was always closest to my father," she says. "In fact, the others remind me that I was the only one who wasn't afraid to talk back to him.

"I was only 9, 10 and 11 years old when he had his office at home, and I used to run down there after school to keep him company. Now that I look back, I know

I just wanted to be with him. I didn't think about that at the time."

Ms. Sisson, the eldest child in a family of two girls and two boys, remembers that she became particularly close to her father after her sister was born. "I was four, and I remember being really angry when she turned out to be a girl because my parents had talked so much about wanting a son.

"I think I made the decision in my head that I was going to be just as good as a son. I was always a good student and a very good athlete partly to please my parents."

Both women can cite company improvements since their arrival in the corporate offices.

"When I joined the company, it was taking in $2 million or $3 million and had a very loose structure," notes Ms. Sisson. "I came back to be the office manager. We had—and still have—a vice-president of marketing and sales who is not a family member. He's always been more controls and formal line-oriented than my father was, and a lot of what I've helped do is bridge the gap between him and my father. I've also developed a data processing department and written all the programs for it."

Ms. Kelly spends most of her time streamlining operations. "My first project was to bring in some young blood. The average age of our brokers was 70," she recalls.

Gauging Reactions

And how do men in these corporations react to women bosses?

"Nobody knew I was coming, so there was some condescension," Ms. Kelly says. "They called me 'Honey' and 'Dear' at first. I think some people in the plant thought, 'Who the hell is she and what does she know?'

"Now, we all work very well together, and I know the men in the plant call me 'the boss lady' behind my back."

She also admits there has been some bewilderment at some of her new ideas.

For example, late last year, plant foreman Sam Vergara turned 30. Ms. Kelly decided to surprise everyone with a friendly little party in the front office, an unprecedented move.

She ordered a cake and told everyone to come in after lunch—without saying why. The men kept stopping her in the hall, saying they didn't ordinarily come up there and asking what she wanted.

"When they did come in and I lit the candles and the secretaries helped me sing 'Happy Birthday,' everyone was visibly relieved," she remembers.

"Then I found out the only time they'd ever been up front was when my father caught them drinking in the plant, called them into his office and fired everyone. He hired them back the next day, but it scared them enough so they were afraid that I'd invited them up to fire them again."

Ms. Sisson also is confident that her being a woman hasn't hurt her company.

"There are 40 people on the payroll and maybe some of them have some feelings about my being a woman," she concedes. "But when the four people who manage this company sit down together, we exchange ideas. And for those four individuals, it doesn't matter that one is a woman and three are men.

"That's the way it's coming through to me . . . that I came through."

Introduction

Widows are a tremendous force in family businesses, but they often need more knowledge and preparation for the responsibilities that may be thrust upon them. The spouse of a family business owner needs to be involved in succession planning, not underrate her skills and get good advice. Wives are often better than their husbands at bringing children into the family business. A "Spouse Survival List" will help family businesses prepare for the possibility of the spouse's death.

When Widows Take Charge
1988

By Sharon Nelton

Reprinted by permission of **Nation's Business**, December, 1988. Copyright ©1988 U.S. Chamber of Commerce; all rights reserved.

If she had it to do all over again, says Seona T. Baldwin, she would become more involved in her husband's business earlier and would ask more questions.

But she doesn't have it to do all over again. George Baldwin died in an automobile accident in 1981, and two years later she stepped in to run Baldwin Sanitary Service, Inc., the Portland, Ore., trash-collection company that her husband had founded in 1971. She knew little about the business, and she thought her involvement in it would be only temporary. She has been running it ever since.

Widows "are a tremendous force in the survival and growth of family businesses," says Matilde Salganicoff of the Family Business Consultancy in Philadelphia.

At first a widow may take over a business to preserve its founder's vision or because it offers the best livelihood for her family. Or she may see herself as the caretaker of the business until it can be passed to the next generation.

Joyce Signer, in Corvallis, Ore., owns Signer Motors, Inc., a General Motors dealership that her husband was buying when he died of a heart attack in 1970. Signer, then a housewife and former schoolteacher, used to tell herself, "If I can just keep this until my son is out of college and old enough to take over!" Her son was 19, and she also had two younger daughters to support.

In Detroit, Helen Keene McKenna's leadership of McKenna Industries was described in a 1956 story under the headline, "Fulfills Her Late Husband's Dreams." Three years earlier, after her husband, Patrick, was killed in an automobile accident, she took over the company he had founded in 1952. "I wanted to do it for him," says McKenna. At the time of her husband's death, her daughter was 14 and her son was 8. The company, now in Troy, Mich., makes production models for the automobile, aircraft and aerospace industries.

Rosemary S. Garbett, president of Los Tios Mexican Restaurants in Houston, was a 40-year-old housewife with four teenage children when her husband accidentally shot and killed himself in 1976. Garbett learned she could get only $800,000 – half the book value – for the three struggling restaurants he left behind and that she would have to pay off debts out of that. So she decided that keeping the restaurants and making them go would offer her family a better livelihood than living off the interest from the money she would get by selling the business.

Women are often the "supporters and enhancers" of their husbands while the men are still alive, says Salganicoff, but they are more assertive and aggressive after they become widows. Under their leadership, she adds, the businesses often flourish because these women, though generally conservative, are open to new ideas. And they often come to realize that they are no longer running the businesses for their husbands or even for their children.

"That wonderful business I was saving for my son is still mine, and my son is a Buick dealer in Fremont, Calif.," Signer said recently at a family-business conference at Oregon State University.

McKenna Industries had five employees when Helen McKenna took over. She still says she doesn't know how to read a blueprint, but the business today comprises five companies, employs 150 and does $11 million in sales annually. Son Mike is now president and CEO, but McKenna stays on as chairman.

"When I took over the business, I was scared and had no confidence at all in my ability to do anything," recalls Rosemary Garbett. Her husband had occasionally "allowed" her to be a cashier at the restaurants, she says. But she also had done the bookkeeping. "I knew how every dollar was being spent. I knew every debt and how it was or was not being paid."

She began to tighten controls to keep money from flowing out the door. She instituted other measures, such as centralized purchasing to hold down costs, and a centralized kitchen to assure product quality and consistency in all the restaurants.

"The original debt-ridden three Los Tios restaurants have grown to 10 successful, debt-free restaurants," says Garbett. She employs 375 people and has increased the company's annual sales to over $7 million from $2.5 million. The once-frightened homemaker has twice been honored by the city of Houston with a "Rosemary Garbett Day."

Taking over the businesses wasn't easy for any of these women. Baldwin gave up an 18-year telephone-company career to run Baldwin Sanitary Service, and she did so only after a buy-sell agreement transferring ownership to an employee fell through, and efforts to find a manager failed. The company was losing money when she took charge, but she turned it around.

Some of Los Tios' key employees quit to work for competitors, and a bank that had done business with the firm for years refused Garbett a loan. But what really put steel in her spine were the put-downs she got from people who thought she couldn't succeed. Creditors, suppliers and landlords feared they wouldn't get paid, and Garbett heard comments such as, "If she doesn't sell, we'll have to eat a lot of enchiladas to get our money back."

Joyce Signer found that her husband's will was one of her biggest obstacles. It provided that the business be sold and the proceeds go to a trust, a plan that might have been practical had she not decided she wanted to run the business herself. She had to go to court to have the will set aside.

Yet a widow may find encouragement to step in and run her late husband's company. It was a family friend who first suggested to Signer that she could take over the business. And while Mc-Kenna found that some purchasing agents didn't want to deal with her in what was then an all-male field, she encountered many more who went out of their way to help.

Most family-business owners are men, and women tend to outlive men by about seven years. So it makes sense for a woman to consider ahead of time what will happen to the business after her husband dies. Experts on family businesses offer these tips:

Do succession planning, but don't lock yourself in — or out. Many wives do not realize, until they become widows, that running a business will be their best choice. She would not have been her husband's choice of a successor, says Signer. And if he had had a buy-sell agreement arranging for someone else to buy the company upon his death, she would not have the business today. "Keep all your options open," she advises.

Think of yourself, adds Jane Siebler, assistant professor of management at Oregon State. She urges wives to consider not only the founder's dreams for a business but their own dreams as well. And when it comes to determining who should succeed the owner, Siebler suggests, a wife should consider herself as a choice.

Don't underrate your skills. Widows who succeed at running the family business are often self-effacing, says Salganicoff. "They will say, 'I was lucky. I had good support. My brother-in-law helped me. My lawyer was great.'" They call on a lot of resources, says Salganicoff, not recognizing "that to get adequate help is a sign of mature management."

Garbett says she became a success "by transferring the homemaker's rules to business . . . A mother who manages a household with a tight budget and raises a family, while saving a little and paying off creditors, can do what I've done."

Be prepared to seek advice, but also be prepared to go against it. When Garbett decided not to sell Los Tios, she did so against the recommendations of her accountant and her lawyer. Siebler says, "If your intuition is telling you one thing and your advisers are telling you another, you can trust your instincts."

Get involved in the business early. Seona Baldwin advises women to discuss the business with their husbands and to ask questions if their husbands are "open-minded enough" to share information.

The presence of wives working in a family firm helps guarantee the continuity of the business and makes it easier for children to gain access to it, according to Salganicoff.

Husbands often are ambivalent about having children in the business, and older men may feel they are in competition with the younger generation. But women, she says, really want the children in the business.

So Salganicoff urges wives to become actively involved in the company. "It's good for their husbands, it's good for the business, and it's good for the family."

Preparing to Step in
After Your Spouse

If your husband or wife is a business owner and dies or becomes disabled, the survival of the business may depend on your having vital information.

The following is excerpted from the "Spouse Survival List," prepared by the Family Business Program at Oregon State University. Have your spouse fill out the information, and go over it together to make sure you understand every detail.

For a copy of OSU's complete checklist of information that a spouse should know, send your name and address to: Spouse Survival List, Family Business Program, College of Business, Oregon State University, Corvallis, Ore. 97331, or call (503) 754-3326.

Date:_____

Owner'sfull
name:_____

Birth
date:_____

Social Security Num-
ber:_____

Full family business name (list additional family businesses as appropriate):_____
_____
_____

Address:_____

Office
Telephone:_____

Fax num-
ber:_____

First employee to be
phoned:_____

Important Documents
Attorney's
name:_____

Office
telephone:_____

Home
telephone:_____

Do you have a will? When was it last updated?
Location of
will:_____

What are the essential terms of your will____
_____
_____

Is there any kind of buy/sell agreement for the
firm?_____

Will your ownership in the business be trans-
ferred to me? If not, how much can I expect to receive for your share of the business?_____

How and
when?_____

Is there any legal documentation that would help establish the value of the business?
_____
_____

Accountant's
name:_____

Office
telephone:_____

Is the business financially sound? What kinds of financial commitments have been made on behalf of the business?_____
_____

Does the accountant have personal financial statements for us? If so, for what time period?_____

Where are our most recent tax returns filed?_____
_____

Banker's
name:_____

Office
telephone:_____

Bank account numbers and locations:

Personal checking:_____

Personal savings:_____

Business checking:_____

Other:_____

What type of estate-planning mechanisms do you have in force?_____
_____

Will I have access to cash at the bank? At the business? Whom should I contact?_____
_____

Insurance and Retirement
Insurance
agent(s):_____

Office
telephone(s):_____

Type of
coverage:_____

Do you have key man life insurance? If so, how much? Who is the beneficiary?_____
_____

Do you have long-term disability insurance? If so, for how long?_____
_____

Are you eligible for full Social Security? What other type of retirement plan do you have?_____
_____
_____

Other Investments
What other investments do we have besides our family business(es)?_____
_____
_____

Obituary and Funeral
What media should we notify?_____

What one special request would you like to make regarding your funeral?_____
_____

Leadership Succession
If you have identified a successor for yourself, who is it? What should he/she be told at this time?_____
_____

If you have not identified a successor, is there anyone within the business who could run it on an interim basis?_____
_____
_____

Whom, among the employees, do you most trust me to confide in and to ask for advice?
_____

The least?_____

Strategies
What is the greatest opportunity you are facing?_____
_____
_____

The greatest
risk?_____
_____
_____

What deals are in the making?_____
_____
_____

Have you entertained any buyout offers? If so, from whom?_____
_____
_____

Last Words
If you had the opportunity to give me some advice, what would it be?_____
_____
_____
_____
_____

Copyright ©1988, Family Business Program, Oregon State University.

Chapter 12

The Younger Generation

To survive as a family business, business families must produce heirs with appropriate values, skills and motivations and who view active participation in the business as a meaningful life's work. Then the relationship between parents and children must survive the normal pressures of maturation plus the difficulties of working together.

This section deals with the dilemmas confronting the younger generation working and considering working in the family business. The decision to enter the business is a crucial one — both from the perspective of the younger generation's considerations and for the parents' who want to attract their children's real commitment to the business. Once the decision to join the business has been made, a strategy for gaining legitimacy and credibility still must be developed.

Introduction

This **Wall Street Journal** *article recognizes and explores the plight of SOBs — sons of bosses. The difficulties of working with and for parents grow from issues including personalities, emotions, behavior, appearance and authority. Since these and other matters are often interactive, the problems can be exceedingly complex. The article discusses an SOB convention created to make fathers aware of the need to expose heirs to all important aspects of the business in the process of preparing them to run the business.*

You Have Problems? Consider the Plight of the Nation's SOBs...

1975

> — *Their Lives Are So Wretched That They Are Organizing To Cope and Commiserate*

By Everett Groseclose

Richard Pocker of New York is a self-proclaimed SOB who doesn't mind telling it like it is.

"Listen," he declares. "I love my dad. He's a terrific guy. But the business wasn't big enough for both of us. I wanted him out. So about a year ago, I sent him on a vacation to Europe. While he was there, I called him up on the phone and told him he was fired, that he was out of a job. Wham! That was it. There wasn't much he could do about it."

Sound brutal? Perhaps. But keep in mind that Mr. Pocker is an SOB. And

not just your average, run-of-the-mill SOB. He's an accomplished SOB. What's more, he wears the title with pride.

You see, the way Mr. Pocker and a number of other young men and women use the term these days, it isn't shorthand for the common insult. Instead, it means "son of a boss." And to those in the know, it implies a whole specialized world of management, a hypersensitive, emotion-filled world of conflicting wills, bruised egos and rivalries.

It's the world of the father-son relationship and what happens when dad brings junior into the family business.

Like Sharing a Mistress

As Harry Levinson, a psychologist who has studied father-son relationships in family-held firms, has put it, "When a son is brought into the business, the father has all the problems of a man who introduces his rival to his mistress."

The principal reason, he says, is that most men who run their own firms are intensely competitive entrepreneurs, as opposed to professional managers who can run any number of companies without becoming emotionally involved. But for the entrepreneur, says Mr. Levinson, the business "comes to define his position in life." Thus, when a son comes into the firm, an entrepreneur may view his offspring as a threat, a potential embarrassment or merely as someone to be tolerated to keep peace in the family. Only rarely is a son welcomed and given a free rein, says Mr. Levinson.

Such difficulties between fathers and their heirs led to the founding six years ago of an organization known of Sons of Bosses International. With chapters now in 12 states, the group is made up mostly of young men who have taken over control of the family business or are in line to one day get the job. Daughters of bosses (DOSs), sons-in-law (SLOBs) and other family members headed for the top slot are also admitted as SOB members.

"The key thing that all SOBs have in common is that we're all trying to solve the problems that we have working with and for our fathers. Believe me, that's not easy," says Gerald D. Slavin, a lanky 30-year-old who founded the SOBs after he got together with some like-minded friends in a Boston restaurant "to moan about how awful we were being treated." These days, with more maturity, most SOB chapters also have begun to delve into more mature problems, such as estate and tax planning, purchase and sale agreements, hiring and firing.

Commiserating on Miseries

But the core of the organization is still the father-son relationship, and there is still a lot of moaning because, to hear SOBs tell it, the life of an SOB is anything but easy. Moreover, because personalities, emotions, behavior, appearance and the whole question of authority are involved, the problems of most SOBs are exceedingly complex and varied. Thus, among SOBs, there are always plenty of experiences to be shared and lessons to be learned.

Consider, for instance, the trials of Mr. Pocker, the New Yorker who fired his father. About two years ago, when he was graduated from college with a degree in psychology, he says, "it was just natural" that he go into the family picture-framing and print business, known as J. Pocker & Son Inc. "After all, I had worked for my dad after school and every summer since I was 10," Mr. Pocker says.

But soon the two men began to differ on many points—how frames should be made, how employees should be handled, how to deal with customers and the like. With tensions steadily mounting, Mr. Pocker says he dispatched his father on that fateful European vacation and seized power, along with his younger sister, Robin, who now is a full partner.

He got more than he bargained for. "I came in with my own philosophy, that you can be sweet, kind and loving with employees," he says. "Well, you can be— and the business will go straight to hell. I learned pretty fast that people want to have direction, to be dealt with fairly and evenly, but not sweetly."

But his biggest problem, he says, continued to be his father. "For six months after I took over, every time I would look up, there he would be," adds the younger Mr. Pocker. "He would have called up one of his old associates and made an appointment to meet them here at the store."

The elder Mr. Pocker pleads guilty to his son's charges and much more. "The business was my whole life. It hurt like hell to give it up," says Marvin Pocker, in recounting how he felt when his son dropped the ax. He adds, however, that he soon realized "the ego trip was over. I had done it. There was nothing more to prove."

Actually, the elder Mr. Pocker didn't resist as stiffly as most other bosses probably would if their sons tried to swing the ax. The reason for the elder Mr. Pocker's restraint: In 1954, he had fired his own father, who founded the firm 50 years ago.

"Well, I didn't exactly fire him," explains Marvin Pocker. "I just made his life such hell that he finally quit. I would argue and fight with him about everything until he finally gave up."

Marvin Pocker adds that he not only desperately wanted control of the business, he also wanted to protect the health of his father, who had suffered a heart attack. Of the firing, he says, "My dad resented it like hell. He never even came back for a visit. I wouldn't want it to be that way with Dickie and me."

Invasion of Privacy

Mr. Slavin, who founded the SOBs, had a much different problem when he joined his father's stainless-steel distribution business. "At first, my office was right outside my dad's office. Hell, he always knew who I was talking to and what I was saying. He knew what time

I came to work, what time I went to the bathroom and when I went home." A move across the building helped ease the tension, he says, but there were still many differences. The most acute one had to do with a seemingly trivial matter — working hours.

There's just no way in the world my father and I could ever agree on hours," says Mr. Slavin. "The way he see it, he opens for business at eight in the morning, so that's what time I should be there. Well, there's just no way I'm going to be in that early. Maybe by nine or nine-thirty, but never by eight." Their solution to their differences was to form a second company, a maker and seller of packaged metal stock for use in manufacturing. In effect, the two companies do business in related fields, but under different top management and operating under dissimilar policies. On the problems of SOBs in general, Mr. Slavin adds, "The question of why they work is usually very important to SOBs, because many fathers and sons work for different reasons. The fathers are working so the business will grow, so they'll have more work to do. But the sons are working so that they won't have to work so much. There's a big difference."

Most SOBs agree that once they have decided to go into the family business, the most difficult problem revolves around how much authority, if any, the father is willing to yield. In many cases where the answer is none, a parting of the ways is often inevitable. SOBs note, however that it's usually the son who departs.

Division of Labor

By far the most common approach when sons enter the business is some division of responsibility. Dave Landsberger, whose family owns Bel-Arts Products, a maker of laboratory

535

and scientific products in Pequannock, N.J., says that before he started to work at Bel-Arts more than three years ago he sat down with his father and they "decided on very definite limits to start with." At first, he says, he did almost every lowly job in the company. Later came added duties. He is currently responsible for Bel-Art's advertising and marketing. He's also beginning to try his hand at some personnel functions.

How did old-line employees at Bel-Arts react when the owner's son began? "Well, a couple of my dad's chief lieutenants were resentful and worried," Mr. Landsberger says. Their fear, of course, was that he would soon have their job, he says. "It became a question of my taking them aside and saying bluntly, 'Listen, you dummy, I don't want your job. I want to be your boss.'"

Indeed, for many SOBs, it is a question of biding their time and behaving themselves while father continues to run the show. Fred H. Lewis, a 32-year-old SOB who has worked since 1966 at the family agency, Lewis Advertising Inc., in Newark, N.J., says that at first he believed that because he was the son of the boss and already knew something about advertising, he would have freedom and power and his father's blessing to wheel and deal.

"Basically, there was a problem from the beginning," he says. "I wanted my own image. I wanted to dress different, act different, sell different. I wanted to do everything different than my father was doing it. I thought it was possible to do social good with advertising." he says.

Matter of Life-Style

Not many months ago, the younger Mr. Lewis says, the simmering conflict in his family began to boil over. "I guess I was really saying that I wanted to take the big plunge. I wanted to manage the whole thing. I wanted to be the boss," he says. The conflict over the direction of the business, he adds, "lasted six or eight months" and included a "whole series of meetings, some of them real shouting matches," with his father.

Eventually, he says, he began to understand. His father wasn't about to yield. "I also began to look around and see that he had a point," the younger Mr. Lewis says. He adds: "I could actually see that my long hair and my dressing style were having an influence on my selling to accounts." Thus, among other things, he "began to take a softer line," had his collar-length hair trimmed and left his mod clothing in the closet. How does he view his father now? "Well, he's the boss. No question about that," he says.

Once he enters the family firm, according to Mr. Slavin of Boston, an SOB may find himself locked in. Immediately, he says, an SOB is sure to have trouble landing a job in a field he knows anything about. "No competitor in his right mind is going to hire him, because the competitor thinks to himself, well, two years with me and he'll learn the names of all my customers and all my trade secrets, and then it's back to the family firm. There's no way a competitor is going to open himself up to that sort of thing."

Mr. Slavin adds that the SOB organization is trying especially to make fathers be more aware that they need to expose their heirs to all important aspects of the business, to prepare them to run the business. If they instead keep absolute power in their own hands, he says, "here you are, one day the vice president in charge of the company picnic—and zap! Two days after the funeral, you're running the business.

The organization is also working to improve the public image of SOBs. Most meetings are devoted to a speaker, usually the son of a boss who is successfully managing the family company and is therefore considered an "accomplished" SOB. But the meatiest sessions are devoted to a discussion by members of "their mutual problems with their fathers." Referring to the second type of meetings, Mr. Slavin says: "A lot of people look at us as a bunch of kids who have been given the gift horse and then get together once a month to bitch about his breath."

Introduction

Deciding whether to join the family firm can be an agonizing experience. This article raises the important questions that a young person should ask while making that decision, provides advice from leading experts and cites experiences of those who elected to join the family business.

Shaky About Joining the Family Firm?

1983

By Sharon Nelton

Doris Mattus Hurley, 42, president of Haagen-Dazs Franchise, Inc., the nationwide chain of ice cream "dipping" stores based in Englewood Cliffs, N.J., was in her early 30s before she did it in 1974.

But Terry Squibb, 30, purchasing and inventory control manager of Welders Supply Inc., of Dallas, did it as soon as he got out of college.

So did Edward R. Schwinn, Jr., 34, president of the Schwinn Bicycle Company in Chicago.

What they did was join the family business. And although, as Schwinn warns, being a member of a family business is "not a piece of cake," the three are satisfied with their decisions. "Everyone is working together for a common goal, the success of the company, because it's *ours*," says Schwinn, whose great-grandfather started the firm in 1895.

Deciding whether or not to join a family firm can be an agonizing experience. Often children are tormented by feelings of disloyalty when they turn their backs on the business. Many parents feel betrayed or rejected when their children decide to do something else. One tough-minded Iowa company president admits that when his son finally decided to join the family firm, "I sat down and cried like a baby."

There are an estimated 12 million family-held businesses in the United States. Most experts agree that only 30 percent or so survive into the second generation as family firms; less than 15 percent make it into the third. Some are merged or acquired, and some simply go out of business.

Whatever a company's fate, employees are affected. According to Léon A. Danco, who heads the Center for Family Business, a consulting firm in Cleveland, a whole town may be hurt by heirs' inability or reluctance to continue a large family enterprise.

538

Furthermore, the younger generation can be vital to the quality of management in a family firm, observes Peter Davis, director of the Wharton Applied Research Center at the University of Pennsylvania. It is often difficult for smaller companies to attract top-rate managers, he explains, and young family members are frequently brighter and abler than management the company can attract from outside.

Among the points a young person must consider in making the decision, experts generally agree, are these:

- Do you *really* want to join the family firm? Would you enjoy it? ("The world doesn't need a reluctant heir," says Danco.)

- Are you prepared to join it? Do you have the education? Experience from another company?

- What alternatives do you have?

- Can you work with your parents or other relatives in the company? (Says Schwinn: "We are a tight, loving family. We all like each other. It makes it a good deal easier. If you don't have those basics, you are not going to have a happy time.")

- Are you interested in the company's products or services? If not, are there other aspects of the business such as marketing or management that offer excitement?

- Are you comfortable with inherited wealth? (Not all family businesses result in wealth for the younger generation, but many do.)

- If you were eventually to take over the company, would you have the energy and commitment required?

For some heirs, joining a family business brings unexpected rewards, such as a strengthened bond with one's parents. Doris Hurley had little interest in joining Haagen-Dazs Ice Cream, founded by her parents, Reuben and Rose Mattus. Before her children were born, she worked in the office, and she had had enough of that.

After she thought her children were old enough, she went to work as a sales representative for another company. When she was offered a promotion a year later, her father made a more attractive bid, and she accepted. Not long after, she convinced him she should launch the franchise operation, which now numbers over 260 stores.

(The Pillsbury Company acquired the Haagen-Dazs companies earlier this year, but family members retain the top management positions. They include Kevin Hurley, who is president of Haagen-Dazs Ice Cream and who became Doris' husband three years ago.)

"As a child, you don't necessarily understand what is going on when you have parents who are completely dedicated to their business," says Doris Hurley. Because she had an opportunity to become part of the business, she says, resentments she felt as a girl have been dispelled, and she has a great deal more understanding of the sacrifices her parents made in building the company. She admits it can be emotionally difficult for family members to work together. But, she says, "our extraordinary feelings about the business and the product override any other consideration we have."

Just as hard as deciding to join the business is sticking with it. Welders' Terry Squibb admits to a period of unhappiness when there was just not enough communication between him and his brother, Randy, the firm's sales manager, and their father, Charley.

"My dad had told us he was going to retire in 1985," recalls Squibb. "I didn't think I was being prepared to take over. I wasn't sure he would teach us what we needed to learn." There was uneasiness between the brothers about who would succeed their father and how the stock would be shared.

The Squibbs got help. All three have attended seminars and programs at Danco's center. Terry Squibb also underwent aptitude testing that boosted his confidence by showing him how good he is at paper work and by indicating talents—like a potential for selling—that he did not know he had. His father listened to a taped analysis of the test and, Terry says, "we had a starting point." Now, he reports, the two of them can talk to each other without getting angry within 10 minutes.

Charley Squibb still plans to retire in 1985, but he is no longer leaving his sons in the dark. He has laid out a stock transfer plan for the next 12 years that will result in the brothers' having a 50-50 partnership in the firm.

Once in the company, some young people cannot get up the courage to leave it, even if that would be best. Compounding their unease may be doubts they have about themselves—Could I really make it on my own?—and the stigma that often goes with being an heir. In some circles, heirs are said to belong to the "golden sperm club."

Indeed, notes Danco, some heirs have great difficulty dealing with wealth because they associate it with evil.

"Why are you hung up on the fact that you are inheriting money?" Danco asks young people who attend his seminars. He tells them that they should learn to handle wealth just as they might handle other unearned privileges, like health,

good looks, athletic ability or being born in the United States. "Accept that you are privileged," he counsels, "and work like a dog to be worthy of it. You have to make a contribution."

But he adds: "If you can't be comfortable in the family business because of hang-ups, don't go into it."

People love to talk about the problems of being in family businesses, observes John Messervey, executive director of the National Family Business Council in Chicago. He illustrates with a chance encounter:

He was sitting in the anteroom of an auto repair shop while his car was being serviced. Also waiting was a young man who turned out to be the son of a sausage manufacturer whose company did $100 million or so a year in sales. The stranger began to unburden himself and finally lamented, "I don't want to make sausage the rest of my life!"

Messervey warns that a son's or daughter's decision to join the family firm carries heavy emotional freight, bound up as it is with their relationship with their parents. Unless the heirs understand what they are getting into, the decision could lead to disappointment and disillusionment that threaten not only the parent-child relationship but also the business. When the going gets tough for an heir or the family, it is time, Messervey says, to get professional help from a clinical psychologist specializing in family business issues.

One such specialist is Matilde Salganicoff in Philadelphia. In addition to her private practice, she is on the staff of the University of Pennsylvania Center for the Study of Adult Development.

"Unfortunately," she says, "Most of the people I work with remain in the family firm out of inertia or because they're afraid to go into the outside world. It's not a thought-out decision."

The main thing she says, is for the young person to know what he or she wants to do. And that can be extremely difficult if parents are pressing a son or daughter to go into the business.

Salganicoff advises young people to work outside the family business before they make a final decision. Outside experience will prove they can make it on their own; they need not be nagged by lingering doubts. It will also help them gain credibility with the family firm's employees. And they will learn things that they would not learn otherwise. "It's like going to a different country," Salganicoff says. "You always come back enriched."

Other ways to help determine what one really wants to do include a lot of talking about the issue with family and friends, reading and taking courses. Salganicoff also suggests simply making a list of what one likes to do best and what one likes to do least.

"The essence of the whole process is not to betray yourself," she says. "Do what you really like to do."

She cautions both parents and children not to close the door. If the young person chooses the company initially, he should have the freedom to leave later. If he at first decides against the company, he should be allowed to change his mind.

Another major issue for the young person, she says, is the need to become independent. Everyone must gain independence no matter where he or she works, but it is more difficult to do so in a business where the owner is one's parent. For the offspring, she explains, it is like being an adolescent again. The parent may send double messages: "Be

dependent but independent" or "Be creative but consult me first."

A young person may join the family firm because it offers an easy way to get employment in a tough job market, according to Léon Danco. "Add to that the potential for getting paid more than the going market rate, and you have a heavily baited hook. It looks like guaranteed security."

Danco warns, however, that "if an heir joins a family business with anything other then competent hard work and a sense of teamwork in mind, sooner or later he or she is going to get badly burned." The heir who does not make a contribution will be resented by those who do. Failing to attain a key management position, he may eventually have to live with the insecurity of having his fate in someone else's hands.

There are also wrong reasons for staying out of the business, Danco points out. Inability to get along with Dad (or Mom) tops the list. Danco urges young people to understand that the experiences the parent is going through "teaching a successor and preparing for retirement" are new to him and that he may be just as confused as his offspring.

If joining the firm is attractive in most other ways, making the attempt to get along is worthwhile, Danco says.

With all the stigma and challenges and family conflict, why stick it out in the family business? Opportunity for self-employment is the No. 1 reason, according to preliminary research conducted jointly by John L. Ward, professor of management at Loyola University in Chicago, and Donald J. Jonovic of the Business Succession Resource Center in Cleveland. Family expectations, an opportunity to share interests and commitments with loved ones and a sense of belonging are among other reasons cited.

Salganicoff points out that a family business offers an opportunity to be creative, even though the young person may not have the challenges of starting and building an enterprise, as his parents did. The heirs, she says, "are not condemned to do the same thing that was already done in the business" in style, process or products. There's flexibility." Adds Danco: "The real fun of business lies in preparing for the future, in planning for change, adapting to conditions, moving a company toward its full potential," often in directions significantly different from its present products or services." Too few entrepreneurs, he contends, convey the fun and joy of business to their children.

Introduction

The best way to attract children into the family business is to create an inviting atmosphere which maintains freedom of choice. The child should feel welcome in the business but understand that the choice to participate is his or hers. Assure that the child hears the positive aspects of the business as well as its problems. Involve the children by taking them along on business trips, giving them part-time jobs and introducing them at the office. Make clear rules specifying conditions for preparation and communicate them clearly and early.

Bringing The Kids Into Your Business

1988

By John L. Ward and
Laurel Sorenson

Sidney Taylor did not expect all his sons to join the family business. Yet today, Scott, Jeff and Bruce work for the Cole Taylor Financial Group, a bank holding company based in Wheeling, Ill. So does his daughter's husband, Daniel Bleil.

This turn of events is still somewhat mysterious to Taylor, 64, who says he did little to accomplish his secret hope that his children would love banking and join him in it.

"I didn't push," explains Taylor, chairman and CEO of the company. "I wanted them to do what made them happy." The excitement of the changing financial industry, he adds, was probably the chief allure.

Taylor may be too modest. Granting his children freedom to choose careers outside the family business — coupled with his own enthusiasm for the industry — was the best that Taylor could have done to achieve the dream of many family-business parents: bringing children into the company.

Like Taylor, you can create an atmosphere that results in a child truly wanting to join the family firm. It's critical, for instance, to let offspring know that though they are free to choose another career, they are also welcome to choose the business. You can convey this message gently in conversation — or perhaps in a family letter — without imposing obligation.

Key ideas are:

- The child is welcome.

- His or her participation in the business is voluntary.

543

- The outcome will be supported, no matter what the choice.

A conversation might go something like this:

"Your mom and I would love to have you in the family business. Of course, it's completely up to you, and it may be too early for you to know. But we want you to know you would be welcome. And we will endorse whatever decision you make."

Making the business sound like a special, exciting place is also important. At home, try discussing the joys of your job instead of only airing complaints. At work, introduce young ones to the office. Offer part-time jobs to school-aged children. Consider taking them to trade shows or on business trips.

Frances Todd Stewart, president of Kerr-Hays Co., a small specialty manufacturer headquartered in Ligonier, Pa., remembers going with her father to visit suppliers and the company's plastics factory in Hong Kong. "Dad always made business fun," she says. "He taught us the world was a place of opportunity." As a result, she eagerly joined the company at age 22.

Finally, it's important to make rules for your children's participation so they will know what they must do to earn a place in the company. Rules answer key questions, such as:

How old must I be to join?

Do I need education or outside experience?

Should I apply for a vacant post or will you create a job for me?

If I leave the company, may I return?

Rules may be oral or written, rigid or flexible. One Midwest floral retailer with more than 80 employees has only one rule for family participation: "We'll move 'em in and move 'em up as fast as we can." But a Southern commercial printing house that employs more than 100 people won't permit family members to work for the company unless they hold a master's degree in business from one of a few specified schools.

No matter their content, the rules need to be communicated and fairly enforced. This prevents misunderstandings that not only drive children away from the business but cause deep rifts within the family.

Taking steps to welcome children doesn't guarantee that your sons and daughters will come into the company. But such measures significantly increase the chances.

Introduction

How does the next generation earn legitimacy in the family firm? How do offspring gain credibility? This report on interviews with 30 family business executives suggests that to succeed, boss's children should: 1) Start early with summer jobs; 2) demonstrate competence by sound handling of day-to-day work and decisions; 3) take time—five to ten years—to gain thorough knowledge of all aspects of the business. Alternatively, next generation executives sometimes gain credibility through innovative behavior that improved current operations. Even in cases where innovators' actions hastened executive credibility, however, the groundwork was laid with experience gained through day-to-day work. Exploring the advantages and disadvantages of low-level vs. delayed entry strategies, the authors point out the risks involved in the approach usually advocated by family business experts.

Entry of the Next Generation: Strategic Challenge for Family Business

1988

By Jeffrey A. Barach, Joseph Gantisky,
James A. Carson, and Benjamin A. Doochin

Planning for the integration of the younger generation into the family firm is an issue of strategic importance, although offering challenges and finding a place for younger family members, or adjusting the organization to the new generation's inputs and demands are issues not usually included as goals for sound business planning.[1] In fact, business theorists generally point out the drawbacks of constraining business decisions by any criteria other than profit. While arguments can be made

both for and against nepotism,[2] Harry Levinson, who has written thoughtfully about family businesses, notes:

It is obvious common sense that when managerial decisions are influenced by feelings about and responsibilities toward relatives in the business, when nepotism exerts a negative influence, and when a company is run more to honor a family tradition than for its own needs and purposes, there is likely to be trouble.[3]

For owner-manager firms, successful integration of offspring into the firm is almost always an issue. As one family business owner said:

> I started this firm to gain freedom and security not available elsewhere. The success I have had is something I would like to pass on to my children. I hope they come into the firm, but they must have the patience to learn the business before they take over.

Patience is a two-way street. To succeed in transferring the business to their offspring, family business CEOs must be ready to adjust the organization to the skills, perspectives, and values of the next generation as part of the implementation of strategy. The successful integration of new family members is a goal for many family firms as important as profit targets, business niches, and other determinants of the firm's business policy. Incorporating new family members into the firm, however, is complicated by the blurring of the boundaries between the family and the family business.[4]

Strategy for the owner-managed firm requires that economic success be achieved in a context that includes presently and prospectively employed family members. Owner/managers have often changed their organization's structure to reflect the needs of children entering the business. For example, entrepreneurial firms have been structured to provide territories for siblings in the firm; and separate divisions have been started in some firms to give offspring a place to thrive under the family banner.[5] It can sometimes be beneficial to split the original firm into a family of enterprises in order to achieve the twin goals of family continuity and financial success.

Owner/managers of family businesses face the dual challenges of rearing children who want to join the family business and to shape a work environment where the young person can "earn legitimacy": the confidence and ability to make significant contributions and the trust of others.

The purpose of this article is to report the results of interviews with executives in family businesses in order to explore ways in which the introduction of family members can be accomplished successfully. In this context, "success" refers to favorable outcomes for both the family members and the firm. The focus of the analysis is on how the next generation achieves a position of power within the firm, not necessarily on replacement of the older generation. This process is termed "earning legitimacy."

Background

Earning Legitimacy

The present article reviews the literature on entry strategies and presents results from interviews with 30 family business executives. The interviews focused on strategies for gaining credibility once the family offspring entered the firm. These can be classified as career paths which are primarily innovative or non-innovative. The various career strategies were examined in the light of the situation that prevailed in the firm.

Early writing described legitimacy as based on such factors as tradition, attitudes about the propriety of a particular order, or a rational belief in a particular social structure.[6] Legitimacy, for purposes of this article, has both tangible and intangible elements, most of which must be present before legitimacy can be said to be achieved. Both the boss and scion must feel the scion has executive status. The scion must feel that he or she plans an important role in the firm, and not only the boss (whether father, mother, or relative), but other family members, employees and significant others must see the scion as having earned rather than inherited the responsibility and respect of his or her position. This legitimacy is demonstrated to the potential successor by the actions of others.

Literature Review

Many writers have suggested strategies for the younger generation's entry into the family firm. Most agree that children should work elsewhere early in their careers.[7] Some writers have pointed out that entry into the family business via summer or low-level jobs is less than ideal in creating the image of a competent leader in the eyes of other employees, customers, and other groups significant to the transition. Yet 80 to 90 percent of family members do enter the firm through summer jobs or low-level employment.

Sathe advised managers in general to be aware of the level of acceptance and credibility they enjoy in the organization, with acceptance defined as "the extent to which others perceive one believes and behaves as prescribed by the culture," and credibility as "the perception of others in the organization of his or her ability and intention to deliver valued results."[8] Sathe feels that long-term success may be determined by the level of acceptance and credibility the scion has achieved. He concludes that acceptance and credibility are achieved independently of each other, but neither alone is sufficient for success.

Credibility can be the key to legitimacy. If the older and younger generations are not willing to accept each other, and if they do not recognize each others' abilities, then successful entry to the firm may be impossible. Credibility is

therefore crucial to successful integration into the firm. Without credibility, the potential successor cannot attain legitimacy (see exhibit 1).

Christensen has noted that:

> The newcomer must be able to prove his ability to the other executives and win their confidence. In their eyes, at least, he is on trial. Although he has legal authority of the name and future ownership, [of the firm] he must earn the real respect of his associates. The father can appoint the son to the office, but he cannot force acceptance by the organization.[9]

How a family member enters the firm affects credibility, and therefore the attainment of legitimacy. Donald Jonovic proposes these rules:

> 1. The child should work elsewhere and act as if he or she did not have the family firm to fall back on.
>
> 2. He or she should be treated like any other employee, instead of as the heir to the company throne.[10]

This rationale for working outside the family firm is justified, Jonovic says, because "an entry-level successor is not just a new employee in the office. He is the next vice-president or the next president. What would be normal mistakes for anybody else will be looked upon as signs of incompetence."

Most successors join the family firm upon completing their education. MBAs who come from families which own businesses usually say they don't intend to join the family firm when they graduate, but when they get their degrees, most do go on to work for the family firm at some point.[11] (Jonovic

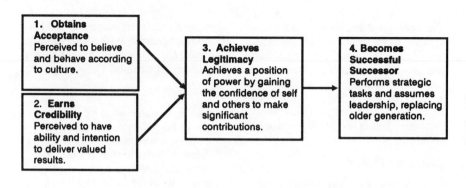

Exhibit 1
Succession in the Family Business

notes that almost 85 percent of all successors go to work for the family firm immediately after graduation.)[12]

Tagiuri and Davis counsel delay in entering the family firm due to the stressful period of the life-cycle which the CEO may be experiencing, pointing out that as the successor is finishing college, the parent may be in his or her early forties – a time when many business owners (and others) evaluate their accomplishments and look to the future. When business owners enter their fifties, they have generally weathered this crisis and are better able to teach the successor about the management of the business.[13]

There are strategic reasons for determining the timing of both entry into the firm and succession to power. Barnes and Hershon show how strategic changes can facilitate succession.[14] Well-planned strategic changes can also create a place for the next generation. The timing of strategic events can pressure an offspring into the firm or allow time for broader experience. A variety of reasons are offered for why the potential successor should delay his or her entry into the family firm. The basis for most is that the delay permits a gain in outside experience and objective recognition. But there are problems with the "outside entry" thesis. One is that expertise developed elsewhere may be less valuable in the family business than in other locations; it may conflict with existing resources and/or the power structure of the family business; or it may not be needed at all at the time of entering the family business. (Later, however that expertise could provide management flexibility in the face of strategic challenges.)

It would appear, however, that summer and low-level jobs can often be a viable strategy for entering family firms – one which can work when the potential successor can develop relevant expertise in a fashion consistent with the culture, resources, and priorities of the firm.

By entering the family firm through summer jobs and low-level employment, credibility can be achieved in the eyes of those important to the success of the new entrant. This manner of entry can also provide the successor with knowledge of the firm's operations which helps generate a feeling of confidence and respect.

A summary of the advantages and disadvantages of two common entry strategies (low-level and delayed entry) is depicted in exhibit 2.

Sample and Method

Family executives in thirty family businesses were questioned at length on their ideas about optimal succession strategies and about their own succession. Since the selection was necessarily based on accessibility and willingness to cooperate, the sample cannot be considered random. However, the businesses represented a wide cross-section of firm types and sizes. Nine had fewer than 50 employees; eleven had between 50 and 200, and eight had over 200. Annual sales ranged from under $10 million to more than $50 million. The businesses were equally

Low-Level Entry Strategy	
Advantages	Disadvantages
1. Intimate familiarity with the nature of the business and employees is acquired. 2. Skills specifically required by the business are developed 3. Exposure to others in the business facilitates acceptance and the achievement of credibility.	1. Conflict results when owner has difficulty in teaching or relinquishing control to successor 2. Normal mistakes tend to be viewed as incompetence in the successor. 3. Knowledge of the environment is limited and risks of inbreeding are incurred.
Delayed Entry Strategy	
Advantages	Disadvantages
1. Successor's skills are judged with greater objectivity. 2. Development of self-confidence and growth independent of familial influence are achieved. 3. Outside success established credibility and serves as a basis for accepting the successor as a competent executive. 4. Perspective of the business environment is broadened.	1. Specific expertise and understanding of organization's key success factors and culture may be lacking. 2. Set patterns of outside activity may conflict with those prevailing in the family firm. 3. Resentment may result when successors are advanced ahead of long-term employees

Exhibit 2

Comparison of Entry Strategies for Succession in Family Business

divided between those in second generation of leadership and those which were moving into the third.

There is a natural bias in the sample toward success, since only those family members who had made a successful transition into the business and those businesses which had successfully weathered the transition have survived to give the interviews. No data are available from this study on businesses which failed.

The interviews were designed to yield insight into the following four propositions:

Proposition I: Summer and low-level jobs are viable ways for future managers to begin learning the business and earning respect.

Proposition II: Most successful managers and entrants advocate a non-innovative career path, earning legitimacy by "learning the ropes and not rocking the boat," except in uncertain situations.

Proposition III: In times of transition or uncertainty, innovative behavior may be a means of bypassing the slow path to credibility.

Proposition IV: Prior, successful non-innovative behavior may place the entrant in a position to innovate successfully.

Results

● Start Early

Of those offspring who joined the firm after having summer jobs, most felt that they were received favorably by employees. Furthermore, they showed strong agreement on how to start a successor in the business (even among those who themselves entered through management positions). They agreed that they would introduce their heirs via summer jobs, a finding which supports Proposition I.

Several successors who began their involvement with the family firm in summer jobs felt they gained valuable insight into the basic operation of the firm that could not be gained in management position. As one stated: "Washing grease off nuts and bolts didn't teach me much, but I learned a lot about the mentality of the people who worked on production lines that way."

● Slow and Steady Wins the Race

Ninety percent of the interviewees advocated a succession strategy whereby the newcomer earns credibility "by having the necessary experience to do the job better than anyone who could be hired." All agreed that the potential successor should "demonstrate competence," and 92 percent agreed that the potential successor should "earn spurs." Nine to one, respondents advocated sound handling of day-to-day work and decisions, rather than innovative behavior, as a proper means of gaining credibility.

● Time to Credibility

There were differences in the time taken to achieve credibility. The average, in the judgment of interviewees, was five years (for those who followed the non-innovative path); two years for those using innovative behavior. But these differences did not depend on prior outside work experience—the average for those with and without prior experience was the same—four years. In some instances, however, the process can take longer, as observed by one who entered the firm as its chief executive: "It takes about ten years before employees defer to your knowledge instead of your position." The point made was that it may take a very long period before the successor gains thorough knowledge of all aspects of the business.

● The Innovators

A minority of next-generation executives attained credibility through innovative behavior early in their careers with the family firm. Two who did innovate told of experiences that support the proposition that innovative behavior may be a good means of establishing credibility in times of change. One executive who joined the firm during a time of adversity said, "No one knew what was going on. I applied cost accounting stuff I learned in school, just basic things. It made me look like a star. From then on Dad listened to me; everyone listened to me." Another executive implemented simple marketing techniques which saved a major unit of the family firm.

There are pitfalls in attempting to be innovative before credibility is well established, but the executives who achieved credibility through initial innovative behavior brought something to the firm which improved current operations. It is probably easier to do this during times of high flexibility, when the firm can afford to pursue new ideas, or during times of turbulence, when change is necessary.

● Earning the "Right to Innovate"

In the interviews, the executives were asked, "Did you have a critical incident or turning point in your career?" This was asked immediately after asking how credibility was achieved. One respondent captured the tone of all participants. After stating that he had gained credibility through day-to-day work, he described a critical incident in

his career. "I worked on all the background for the introduction of a new product line. Suddenly I became the expert on what no one else knew about. But I never would have been given the project if I had not proven myself in the past." This statement demonstrates the feeling among many successful successors that experience gained through day-to-day work prepares the way to grasp opportunities for innovation, supporting Proposition IV.

Discussion and Conclusions

The data base was not sufficient to draw any conclusions about management-level entrants, but data for those entering through summer and low-level employment were sufficient to permit some inferences.

Most future successors join the family firm immediately after completing their education. One viable strategy is to use summer and low-level jobs as methods of entry. Most writers in the field argue for the rarer course of external employment after school and prior to working for the family firm, a course which has value for numerous reasons. In many cases, the young person may not feel a sense of personal accomplishment or self-confidence in a family environment, and thus should start out independently. Non-family firms may provide more objective opportunity and judgment of a young person's achievement. Experience in other companies can also provide a broader perspective on business and develop capacity to adapt to radical environmental change. Furthermore, achievement on the outside can win the entrant credibility and respect when joining the family firm.

What is not considered by advocates of this course, however, is that the young family member entering from the outside and transferring credibility can also make mistakes. These mistakes may be damaging for an outsider not yet familiar with the intricate operations and relations of the firm. After a brief honeymoon, he or she may fail to develop a support system among managers and employees. To regain credibility after a mistake is more difficult than building it day by day. For this reason, early exposure to the family business may be as critical for those coming into the firm after outside experience as for those who enter just after college.

The successor with experience from summer and low-level jobs has had the opportunity to become familiar with the business and its workers, and to build a central network within the ongoing organization. One family firm executive stated: "Everyone who intends to enter the family business should get some early experience from that business. You need to know what's going on and you learn by being there."

The real importance of succession strategies is their impact on the strategic planning of the firm. The founder must determine whether or not his or her children will play a role in the firm. If the answer is "no," arrangements should be made to hire professional management or sell the business. If the answer is "yes," one must determine how to arrange for the entry of the younger generation. This article does not argue for the desirability of one entry strategy over the other in specific cases. Such decisions as how to bring family members into the firm must be made by weighing the numerous and complex criteria which affect the likelihood of success in each instance.

But it can be argued that succeeding generations can achieve legitimacy in family firms by rising through summer and low-level jobs, as well as by gaining credentials outside the firm.

Whichever entry strategy is used, an early introduction to the firm through low-level and summer jobs may be desirable by giving successors a valuable working knowledge of the firm.

CEOs of family firms and their successors can benefit from thoughtful career planning for the next generation, because goals of both the firm and the individual are involved. Care given to the career path of the next generation is an essential part of the implementation strategy of family firms.

1. D. M. Ambrose, "Transfer of the Family-Owned Business," *Journal of Small Business Management*, (January 1983), pp. 49-56.

2. D. W. Erwing, "Is Nepotism So Bad?" *Harvard Business Review*, (January/February, 1965), pp. 22-40 and 156-160.

3. H. Levinson, "Conflicts That Plague Family Businesses," *Harvard Business Review* (March/April 1971), pp. 90-98.

4. For a more thorough discussion of familial factors in business, see the following: P. Davis and D. Stern, "Adaption, Survival, and Growth of the Family Business: An Integrated Systems Perspective," *Human Relations*, vol. 34 no. 4 (1980), pp. 207-224; W. G. Dyer, Jr., *Cultural Change in Family Firms: Anticipating and Managing Business and Family Transitions* (San Francisco: Jossey Bass, 1986); P. G. Holland and W. R. Boulton, "Balancing the 'Family' and 'Business' in Family Business," *Business Horizons*, Vol. 27, no. 2 (1984), pp. 16-21; and E. Kepner, "The Family and the Firm: A Coevolutionary Perspective," *Organizational Dynamics*, vol. 49, no. 2 (1983), pp. 57-70.

5. J. A. Barach, "Is There a Cure for the Paralyzed Family Board?" *Sloan Management Review* (Fall 1984), pp. 3-12.

6. J. P. R. French, Jr., and B. Raven, "The Bases of Social Power," *Studies in Social Power*, ed. D. Cartwright (Ann Arbor: University of Michigan, 1959); Max Weber, *On Charisma and Institution Building*, (Chicago: The University of Chicago Press, 1986).

7. See, for example, Renato Tagiuri and John Davis, "Life Stages and Father-Son Work Relationships," *Working Paper 9-784-026* (Boston: Division of Research, Harvard Business School, 1984); Léon Danco, *Beyond Survival*, 5th ed. (Cleveland: The University Press, 1979); and "A Lot of Enterprise Is Staying in the Family These Days," *Business Week* (July 1, 1985), pp. 62-63.

8. V. Sathe, *Culture and Related Corporate Realities* (Homewood, Ill.: R. D. Irwin, Inc., 1985), pp. 264-261.

9. R. C. Christensen, *Management Success in Small and Growing Enterprises* (New York: Arno Press, 1979), p. 182.

10. Donald Jonovic, *The Second Generation Boss* (Cleveland: The University Press, 1982), pp. 113-115.

11. W. Kiechel, "How to Relate to Nepotism," *Fortune* (Feb. 6, 1984), pp. 143-144.

12. Jonovic, *The Second Generation Boss*, p. 99.

13. Tagiuri and Davis, "Life Stages and Father-Son Work Relationships."

14. L. B. Barnes and S. A. Hershon, "Transferring Power in the Family Business," *Harvard Business Review* (July/August 1976), pp. 105-114.

Chapter 13

Raising Rich Kids

Much of the conflict between generations in the family business is engendered by disparities of values and differences in developmental experiences. While a business's founder may be a star graduate of the school of hard knocks, his or her children may have enjoyed the benefits of the silver spoon.

Articles in this section encourage viewing "the silver spoon syndrome" as the result more of processes at work in family business systems than from intentional revolt. These processes can be more effectively managed if the family can properly diagnose the malady and combat its negative dimensions, and if parents know how to deal with the impact of wealth on children.

Introduction

A universal disparity in values exists around the use of time and money between first and second generations in family businesses. This "silver spoon syndrome" is a prime source of conflict. To combat the syndrome, have children work elsewhere before joining the family business and set clear guidelines and evaluation criteria upon entry.

Silver Spoon Syndrome
1987

By Barbara S. Hollander

A common saying in the world of family business is "shirt sleeves to shirt sleeves in three generations." The generalized scenario is that the first generation makes it, the second generation spends it, and the third generation buries it.

As I have worked with family business members over time, this old saw has been both proven and disproven. However, what seems universal is the seeming disparity in values around the use of time and money between the first and second generation members in a family firm. This seems to emerge as a prime source of conflict between founder and successor.

Folklore blames the successor — pointing to lack of healthy work ethic, commitment, twisted values, and the generalized "born with a silver spoon in the mouth" syndrome. Indeed, I often see behaviors which reinforce these notions.

However, the damning of the second generation needs to be looked at as an outcropping of a process rather than an intentional revolt.

What I often see in the family-held corporation that contributes to the "silver spoon syndrome" is the seeming inability of the founder to take a stand where it counts. Undoubtedly, there is most often ample advice about car allowances, paper clips, what color tie to wear, how often to call Mom or Grandma. What I often don't see are guidelines and ground rules around expectations for performance, feedback, mentoring, training, and career development goals.

The lack of these all important guidelines seems to be traceable to a common dynamic. Often, the "old man" as we affectionately call the founder, was an absentee father. This became and continues as an issue in the family. The founder has been blamed repeatedly for lack of attention to family matters, particularly as the children were growing up. Mom was the disciplinarian.

The entry of the second generation into the business may indeed be the first time that the founder is primarily responsible for discipline or guidance. Often, founders feel guilty about their previous absenteeism. To compensate, they offer free rein to the entrant. I call this the "nosing around" training program. The next generation is invited to sniff around and identify an area where they would like to work. Little guidance and few ground rules are established at the outset. The next generation often flounders as a result.

Another aspect of the reluctance of the founder to take a stand on the big issues often has to do with Mom. The demands of the founding of the business (in second generation businesses, at this point in time, most founders have been males) have left his spouse with most of the home responsibilities. She has learned to focus on them as intently as he has learned to focus on the business. Taking on junior, therefore, often seems to mean taking on Mom, who is often highly invested in the progress and success of the next generation, and may have some different ideas about the management of the offspring.

In the face of these powerful forces, the founder backs off. The next generation swims around in the business often without direction and therefore accomplishment. The founder complains about shortcomings and the successor feels less and less competent. The cycle escalates to the point where the successor develops a "what the hell" attitude, the onset of the "silver spoon" syndrome.

How to Break the Cycle

Some antidotes to this cycle are the following:

1. The successor spends the first few years of his/her career working outside the family business, perhaps in a related field.

2. Upon entry, guidelines, ground rules, expectations are established based on acceptable business practices, and all key parties are informed, including Mom.

3. A mentoring relationship is established and encouraged. The mentor may be a key person in the business, not in line for succession.

4. Periodic evaluation and discussion of progress about business performance and working relationships is scheduled.

5. Criteria for being a "good son or daughter" are distinguished from criteria for being an effective manager.

Introduction

A psychological disease afflicts many who inherit wealth. Characterized by lack of motivation, low self-esteem and loneliness, the author of this article calls it "affluenza." It results in those who have the opportunity to live "the good life" to do so without purpose or enthusiasm. Worse, it too frequently results in drug abuse, divorce or even suicide. Psychologists estimate that as many as 80 percent of heirs have problems with their inherited wealth.

Affluenza
1987

By Robert Farago

Carl contemplated the plunging Alpine slope. One little push and the sole inheritor of an $8-million stock portfolio would be flying down an endless carpet of hip-deep snow. Carl would then be free—free from the aimlessness, the doubt, and the failed relationships that had plagued him since he graduated from Harvard University in 1977. The fact that the ski slope was strictly off-limits—a well-known avalanche hazard—only added to the appeal.

"I had a real death wish," Carl admits. "I'd never come to terms with who I was or what I wanted from life. My net worth was somehow always more important than my self-worth."

In a very real sense, Carl was not alone on that mountaintop. Every day thousands of young inheritors face identical problems: lack of motivation, low self-esteem, and loneliness. Society might callously dismiss them with a sarcastic comment such as "poor little rich kids," but these young men and women often face serious—sometimes life-threatening—psychological trauma. Carl was not the first troubled inheritor to risk his life for a moment of escape. Nor is he likely to be the last.

There is an epidemic of profound unhappiness among young inheritors. Lurid media stories about rich kids' drug abuse, violence, and perversion reveal but the most obvious evidence of their deep troubles. Spend some time in any one of 100 affluent U.S. suburbs from Long Island to Bel Air. Talk to middle-aged parents. Soon you'll hear strikingly similar stories about children who drift from job to job, marriage to marriage—kids who live the "good life" without apparent purpose or enthusiasm. This condition is as socially pervasive as it is individually devastating. Yet it's also treatable and

559

preventable. Thanks to those who are addressing the problems of inherited wealth, "it" now has a name: affluenza.

"About four out of five (heirs) have problems with major inherited wealth," claims psychologist John Levy. "The problems are essentially inevitable."

Levy, director of San Francisco's Carl G. Jung Institute, is also an independent consultant on inherited wealth; he has spent five years investigating the psychology of inheritance. Levy began his study at the urging of a father who was worried about his offspring's unhappiness. Suspecting that his children's generous inheritance somehow caused their depression, the concerned parent paid Levy $20,000 to study the wider implications of inherited wealth. After talking with money managers, psychologists, psychiatrists, and more than 30 Bay area inheritors, Levy compiled his findings in "Coping with Inherited Wealth," an unpublished article.

Levy's research indicates that inheritance is a mixed blessing. Inherited wealth often buys children a reprieve from the aggravations of earning a weekly paycheck. It opens up a world of fulfilling, non-commercial career possibilities — everything from painting to public service. Yet unearned money can also shield inheritors from the financial and emotional challenges that are critical to developing self-confidence and maturity. Using their bankroll as a cushion against hardship, emotionally immature inheritors simply walk away from careers and relationships that require serious commitment. As a result, they often feel bored, lonely, and listless.

"If I had to boil it down, these inheritors lack self-esteem," Levy says. "You have to meet challenges to feel good about

yourself. If you have a lot of inherited money, you're never quite sure if you could exist without it."

Simply put, affluenza stems from too much, too soon. John Sedgewick, author of *Rich Kids*, compares the stress experienced by poorly adjusted inheritors to an overwhelming Christmas.

"It's like coming downstairs Christmas morning and instead of finding a few presents, suddenly facing a whole roomful," he says. "To say the least, it's very unsettling."

Many Americans dream of such a bounty or of a distant relative suddenly leaving them a large fortune. They imagine a life of leisure — a life free from everyday struggle and toil. What they fail to consider is the barrage of emotional, moral, and financial questions inheritance brings with it. Jennifer's experience is typical.

"When I turned 18, I got a call from my trust officer," she recalls. "In these nice somber tones he quietly informed me that I was now worth $2 million. I said, oh, that's great. No one in my family had ever discussed money with me, so it just wasn't real.

"Suddenly I had to make all these decisions. Should I work 9 to 5? Should I work for money? Who controls my money? What are all these papers they want me to sign? What kind of investments do I want to make? How much do I spend? Where do I live?

"Then the deeper issues surfaced. Should I tell my friends? Who do I trust? Do I deserve this money? For years I had no idea what to do."

Compounding the problem, less-affluent people and the media view inheritors' psychological stress with little or no sympathy. "Most people believe that if they only had enough money they would live in a state of constant bliss," Levy explains.

"They tend to respond disdainfully to any suffering by the affluent, particularly if these people didn't earn their fortunes," he says. "For the inheritors that means they feel badly and think they shouldn't feel this way."

The contagious respiratory disease influenza got its name because it was believed to be influenced by the stars. Abandoning superstitious astrology in favor of rational analysis was the first step to devising a cure. So, too, inheritors often view their unearned money as being "heaven-sent" — the fruits of a divine birth lottery — and thus feel that the attendant problems are inescapable.

For affluenza-stricken inheritors who are willing to take a good look at themselves and for parents who don't want their money to ruin their children's lives, professional help is available. A growing cadre of therapists and money managers is sensitive to the problems inheritors face and is skilled at finding solutions. Locating a sympathetic listener who is familiar with the problems of inherited wealth is the first step to recovery.

"The first thing to do," counsels San Francisco psychologist, author, and teacher Judy Barber, "is to articulate the problem so a therapist can understand. Say: 'I need someone who's willing to talk to me about practical reality as well as symbolic meaning.'

"Many psychologists say money is symbolic and ignore practical realties," she says. "They don't want to consider budgets, taxes, or wills. They don't understand trusts or the mechanics of inherited wealth."

Inheritors face two sets of overlapping issues: financial and psychological. Separating the two may not only be impractical, but undesirable. Says Barber: "I had a woman client — a teacher in her mid-30s. She received a large portfolio from her father that included substantial holdings in nuclear power plants. Her father didn't approve of her academic lifestyle and she didn't approve of the nuclear stocks.

"She wanted to invest in something she loved: oriental rugs. But guilt and a sense that the money wasn't really hers prevented her from acting.

"After counseling she decided to confront her father first. Eventually," Barber continues, "she made more money in oriental rugs than she had with the stocks. In the end their relationship improved."

When a donating parent or grandparent is still alive, such issues of control can arise. As Jennifer discovered, however, even independently controlled inheritance brings family relationships sharply into focus. Frequently major inherited wealth arrives after a parent's or grandparent's death — the culmination of a lifetime of work. When trying to administer what they consider "my family's money," inheritors can feel guilty or just plain incompetent. Therapists need to consider an inheritor's family relationships as well as their financial experience or, more commonly, lack of experience.

Inheritors who are reasonably secure with the circumstances of their inheritance still may need money advice that is tailored to their emotional needs. Even therapists like Barber, who specializes in the psychology of money, don't recommend particular investments or investment strategies. That task falls to money managers, financial planners, and trust officers. However, all too often these professionals fail to consider their clients' state of mind. The result: confrontation, miscommunication, apathy—in short, more affluenza.

Lawrence A. Krause, owner of a San Francisco-based personal financial planning service, maintains that inheriting money forces heirs to assume responsibilities they may not be ready to handle, which in turn creates anxiety. Unless inheritors' financial advisers are sensitive to the often-hidden psychological motivations of their clients, financial advice falls on deaf or uncooperative ears.

"Sooner or later most people who inherit money they're not used to become insecure," Krause says. "I had one client who was earning about $50,000 a year. One day he inherited $2 million. When he became a client, he had a very hard time writing checks for $100,000 or $200,000. That would aggravate some financial planners, but they have to realize that if a client has a $50,000-a-year mentality, he needs to mature into the million-dollar mentality. It's not easy."

San Francisco tax attorney David L. Gibson concurs: "Sometimes inheritors put off issues of inheritance. They don't file tax returns, pretending the responsibility doesn't exist. I kept seeing clients who'd get things fixed up, then go right back and get them messed up again. I began to understand that these problems came from unresolved emotional questions. My background and training as a tax lawyer didn't prepare me for dealing with the emotional issues around money."

The success of Victoria Felton-Collins' financial planning service is proof that inheritors want money managers with training in psychology. Says Collins, a psychologist and a certified Financial Planner: "My counseling background helps me understand what my clients' goals really are. Then I can help translate those goals into a financial strategy."

Most money managers are problem solvers who focus on the bottom line. It's no surprise then that they have trouble dealing with inheritors who have ambivalent feelings about money. In order to shake the affluenza paralysis, inheritors must learn not to assume that financial advisers are better qualified than they are to make the final investment decisions.

Inheritors must begin by examining their own values and taking control. Obviously they have a better chance of finding a cure for their malady if they establish a relationship of mutual respect with a sensitive financial professional.

Collins recommends inheritors interview three or four planners to find one with whom they can develop a sense of security. This, she says, is "one of the best investments an inheritor can make."

Inheritors who start actively managing their money soon find they need a whole new set of skills in order to communicate with their advisers. On one level they're unaccustomed to the jargon of the investment world. On a deeper level, like Barber's client, they confront for the first time the ethical questions raised by having wealth. Acquiring the communication skills and exploring their investment options often lead inheritors to the emotional support necessary to overcome affluenza.

More than a dozen ethical-investment foundations are administered nationwide. Philadelphia's Bread and Roses Community Fund, New York City's

North Star Fund, San Francisco's Vanguard Public Foundation, and Boston's Haymarket People's Fund are examples of progressive groups that advise inheritors. They work with inheritors to stimulate social change through the support of grass roots organizations, environmental groups, and community causes. The groups also provide peer support and workshops that focus on their members' emotional needs.

"It's easier to call for investment information than to call and say, 'I'm having trouble dealing with my wealth,'" says inheritor Paul Haible, coordinator of Vanguard. "It's not easy to admit your problems with money when the whole society is set up to perpetuate wealth. But isolation is a real problem. When inheritors come in they look around and say, 'Wow, a whole group of people I can talk to.'"

Curing affluenza is not just a matter of determining that it's OK to be rich. Inheritors must also confront the implications of having money—emotional, financial, and moral. If inherited wealth makes some people feel guilty, inheritors must address these feelings in order to live a happier life. Progressive funds demonstrate that society can benefit from inheritors who work to cure their affluenza.

"For an inheritor with a social conscience, guilt is an appropriate response," says Haymarket development coordinator Hillary Smith. "But at what point does the guilt become immobilization? Haymarket helps people become unstuck, to take responsibility and control of their lives. At the same time we help people who weren't born with as many advantages."

In addition to its grants, newsletters, and referral service, San Francisco's Women's Foundation runs a Managing Inherited Wealth program. At a series of monthly meetings, attending female inheritors choose two discussion topics. The topics are evenly split between technical and emotional issues. On a typical evening inheritors might choose Mutual Funds or Money and Relationships and Comparing Tax Strategies or Your Contribution to Social Change. Throughout emphasis is on empowerment—the need for women to take control of their lives and their money.

Affluenza can be cured. Unfortunately, only a small percentage of inheritors are willing or able to examine their unhappiness. The rest drift along, waiting and hoping for their lives to take direction. For parents that's a very disturbing image. Money managers, psychologists, and other experts agree, however, that there's nothing intractable about affluenza; there's a great deal parents can do to spare their children this unenviable fate. Most of it, of course, is common sense.

"Money is like sex to most people," says Levy. "It's something dirty they don't discuss in front of the kids. Parents need to prepare children to be inheritors. They need to tell kids about money from an early age."

Greg, like Jennifer, grew up disoriented. "I never even knew where the money came from until I was a teenager," he says. "I mean, my dad put on a suit and tie and went downtown, but I never knew where or what he did. Whenever my family needed money he just wrote a check. When I came into my inheritance it was like joining this club—except I didn't know the rules."

If Greg's parents didn't give him the skills he needed later in life, at least they were there to offer support. Many inheritors report an appalling lack of parenting. From his research for *Rich Kids*, Sedgewick is convinced that absentee parenthood is a major cause of affluenza. "If kids are being fobbed off with money or servants, it's going to really mess them up," he says. "Your psychological development is completely wound up in your parents. Parents need to spend quality time with their kids."

Then there is the money itself. Today, many wealthy parents are giving children their inheritance later, are spreading payments over a long period of time, and are reducing the size of the inheritance to a more sane, manageable amount; the rest usually goes to charity. These parents want their children to have certain important advantages — a house to live in, private education for their children — but not so many advantages that they won't find challenging work. They recognize that too much of a good thing — an overwhelming Christmas — is no good at all.

One millionaire father, a man who worked his way up from the streets of Brooklyn to the top level of a *Fortune* 500 company, puts it this way: "No way I want my kids to have to go through what I did. But I'm not giving them a Ferrari or trips to Club Med every other week, and I'm not leaving them the kind of money that buys those things. If they want that kind of extra, that's fine; let them earn it on their own.

"My responsibility is to keep them sane and happy. For that they need two things: love and some kind of job that makes them feel useful."

Affluenza may not be the scourge of the Western world. Yet realizing that there are psychological ramifications of wealth and that there is a limit to money's benefits is critical to understanding a productive economy. Irradicating affluenza — and saving the Carls of this world from an ugly and untimely end — mandates that everyone involved contemplate the true nature of money and how it affects their lives and the lives of those around them. As the committed inheritors at Vanguard and Bread and Roses will tell you, that kind of thinking is the first step to creating a better world for everyone.

Introduction

One of the greatest dilemmas facing successful business families is dealing with the impact of wealth on children. As megabillionaire Curtis Carlson puts it "How the hell do we keep our money from destroying our kids?" When FORTUNE Surveyed 30 multibillionaires, 20 percent planned to give their children minimal inheritances and half plan to leave as much to charity as to heirs. Many successful people fear that large inheritances will allow offspring to do nothing with their lives. Psychologists suggest that many wealthy children have little self-respect because they can't take much satisfaction from their accomplishments. Of course, not passing money to your children can also cause problems and resentment, particularly when the decision not to give is based on parental disapproval rather than understood principle.

When the legacy is a family business, estate planning is especially difficult. Keeping the business whole, in family hands and successful is very difficult. Strategies used by Chicago's Crown family and Colorado's Coors are presented.

Should You Leave It All To The Children?

1986

By Richard I. Kirkland Jr.

Warren Buffett, 56, the chairman and guiding genius of Berkshire Hathaway, the phenomenally successful holding company, is worth at least $1.5 billion. But don't bother being jealous of his three children. Buffett does not believe that it is wise to bequeath great wealth and plans to give most of his money to his charitable foundation.

Having put his two sons and a daughter through college, the Omaha investor contents himself with giving them several thousand dollars each at Christmas. Beyond that, says daughter Susan, 33, "If I write my dad a check for $20, he cashes it."

Buffett is not cutting his children out of his fortune because they are wastrels or wantons or refuse to go into the family business — the traditional reasons rich parents withhold money. Says he: "My kids are going to carve out their own place in this world, and they know I'm for them whatever they want to do." But he believes that setting up his heirs with "a lifetime supply of food stamps just because they came out of the right womb" can be "harmful" for them and is "an antisocial act." To him the perfect amount to leave children is "enough money so that they would feel they could do anything, but not so much that they could do nothing." For a college graduate, Buffett reckons "a few hundred thousand dollars" sounds about right.

How much *should* you leave the kids? Agonizing over that question is a peculiarly American obsession. In much of the world custom and law dictate that children, unless they have committed some heinous crime, automatically receive most of the parents' wealth when they die. Only Britain and her former colonies — common-law countries all — give property owners the freedom to leave their children whatever they want.

And nowhere is the feeling about inherited wealth so ambivalent as in the U.S. No country so readily celebrates the self-made man; no culture is more suspicious that the silver spoon contains something vaguely narcotic. Says Curtis L. Carlson, 72, the Minnesota travel and real estate magnate (Radisson Hotel Corp., TGI Friday's restaurants, and the Ask Mr. Foster travel agency), who has a net worth of $700 million and two married daughters: "There's nothing people like me worry about more — how the hell do we keep our money from destroying our kids?"

Certainly nowhere else in the world do so many parents enjoy the privilege of grappling with this dilemma. The Federal Reserve Board estimates that some 1.3 million U.S. households enjoy a net worth of at least $1 million. The vast majority of millionaires inherited their wealth or built it on a business they founded Plenty of corporate careerists

have also racked up seven-figure estates by taking advantage of profit-sharing and pension plans. But concern for how best to provide for the offspring is not exclusive to the millionaires' club. Estate planning is fast becoming a major concern of the middle class.

Whatever their misgivings about inheritance, most Americans — rich, poor, or somewhere in between — keep the bulk of their estates in the family. Once formed, the chain of inherited wealth is rarely broken — until the money runs out. It has pretty much run out for some of the great names of U.S. business: the Dodges, Reynoldses, and Vanderbilts. The sons of Texas oil tycoon H. L. Hunt, whose fortune was once estimated at $8 billion, have just filed for bankruptcy protection for the family's corporate jewel, Placid Oil Co.

Of 30 multimillionaires recently surveyed by *Fortune,* six say their children will be better off with only minimal inheritances. Almost half plan to leave at least as much to charity as to their heirs. In an area where almost no research exists, Alexander Sanger, a partner with the law firm White and Case, New York, offers a revealing statistic. Of 20 wills Sanger has drawn up for newly-wealthy parents with net worths of $1 million or more, 16 left at least half their estates to charity. Of 12 comparable old-money estates, only one gave so much away.

Old money tends to keep its wealth in the family. "After a generation or more, inheritance becomes a stewardship kind of thing," says Alexander Forger, head of estate law at the New York firm Milbank Tweed Hadley & McCloy. Sometimes, as in the case of one of the firm's clients, the Rockefeller family, the progenitor already fattened some foundation with a big endowment years ago.

Even inheritors who want to give their money away feel duty-bound to pass on some of their wealth to their children. George Pillsbury Jr., 37, a scion of the Midwestern baking family, inherited more than $1 million while still in college. He has spent his adult life building and bankrolling a network of foundations that tap young inheritors for a variety of liberal causes. "Robin Hood was Right," declares one foundation pamphlet. Pillsbury believes in "much, much higher" inheritance taxes. Yet despite his politics, he says "it seems unfair" not to leave his two young children at least a few hundred thousand dollars.

Why shouldn't parents leave it all to the children? Newspaper headlines shriek the more lurid reasons — drugs, derangement, even murder. In July a Pennsylvania judge ruled Lewis du Pont Smith, 29, heir to $1.5 million of the du Pont fortune, "mentally incompetent" to manage his affairs; Smith had been handing over thousands of dollars to political extremist Lyndon H. LaRouche Jr. This month a Florida judge sentenced Steven Benson, 35, heir to a $10-million tobacco fortune, to 72 years in prison for killing his mother and her adopted son with a car bomb.

What usually troubles successful entrepreneurs and executives, however, is the mundane but far more likely prospect that large inheritances will encourage their offspring to do nothing useful with their lives. They worry that Commodore Vanderbilt's grandson William, heir to some $60 million in 1885, was right when he declared that "inherited wealth . . . is as certain death to ambition as cocaine is to morality." (An indifferent businessman and dedicated bon vivant, William suffered a fatal heart attack at a fashionable French race track in 1920.) Says centimillionaire Curt Carlson: "I know one extremely wealthy Minnesota family that has 63 heirs in the fourth generation, and none is gainfully employed. I think that's terrible."

One self-made multimillionaire wants to ensure that his heirs are leading productive lives before they get a share of his estate. He has set up trusts for each of his children — a sound estate-planning practice even for middle-income families. None of the trusts pays a penny until the child turns 30. Until then, the entrepreneur says, he expects his sons and daughters, all still under 30, to "live on the salaries that young adults who are college graduates can make." The terms of his trusts also allow him or his executors to withhold the kids' patrimony in certain situations. Says he: "I believe you've got to be doing right, or you don't get anything. If I end up with a 30-year-old who's not worth a plugged nickel, all his money goes to my personal foundation."

Encouraging rich children to be self-supporting can be good for them. John L. Levy, executive director of the C. G. Jung Institute of San Francisco, has spent the past five years studying the effects of inherited wealth on 30 families. He concludes that many wealthy children experience "considerable suffering and deprivation" because they have little self-respect. "It's hard for them to take much satisfaction in their accomplishments since they always suspect that their successes are at least partly the result of the wealth and position they inherited."

To let children grow up free of their parents' long shadows is the main reason rich individuals choose to withhold or limit their legacies. New Yorker Eugene Lang, 67, for example, built a fortune of more than $50 million by founding REFAC Technology Development Corp., a high-tech licensing company. Lang paid for the education of his three children and after college handed each "a nominal sum" — he won't say how much. Since then he has given them nothing but encouragment. Says Lang: "To me inheritance dilutes the motivation that most young people have to fulfill the best that is in them. I want to give my kids the tremendous satisfaction of making it on their own." Now in their 30s, his children are a lawyer, an actor and an investment analyst. They will get nothing from their father's estate. Lang plans to provide "adequate security" for his wife and bequeath the rest to a charitable foundation. He has already given away more than $25 million to hospitals, colleges, and a scholarship program for Harlem schoolchildren.

Californian Gordon Moore, 57, who co-founded semiconductor maker Intel and is worth $200 million, agrees that "children ought to have a sense of accomplishment for what they've done." Moore set up small trusts for his two sons when they were young — "the sort of thing that let my older boy make a down payment on the house" — but does not plan to do much more. He expects to leave "almost everything" to charity.

Still, the urge to heap most of the wealth upon the family continues to be powerful. "I'd rather give my money to my kids than do anything else with it," says Jackson T. Stephens, 63, chairman of Stephens Inc. of Little Rock, Arkansas, the largest investment bank outside New York. "If my heirs want to clip coupons, that'll be their business. I can't control the future, and I'm not going to worry a whole bunch." Stephens, who has four children, and his older brother Wilton, who also has four children, share a net worth of at least $500 million.

Some entrepreneurs and their heirs argue that rather than being a disincentive to work, an inheritance can give a child a target to outstrip. "I feel I've got to make my mark equal or better than my father," said Warren Stephens, 29, Jackson's son. California real estate developer M. Larry Lawrence, 60, who has three children and a fortune worth more than $200 million, concurs. Says he, "If the children have been brought up right, they end up attempting to outdo the parents."

Inevitably those who hand on their wealth see proper upbringing as the ultimate safeguard against potential problems. Says Katherine Graham, 69, chief executive of the Washington Post Co. and head of a family whose fortune totals some $350 million: "My instinct would be to just pass the money on and hope that in doing so you also pass on your values — how to use it, the life to lead, the standards to have."

Besides, some rich individuals argue, not giving it to the children can cause problems too. Says one: "If you're the child and you see your father with all this dough and you get some but not much, I just can't help thinking resentment will enter in." Susan Buffett, who works in Washington as an administrative assistant to the editor of *U.S. News & World Report* and is married to a public interest lawyer, admits her father's position is tough to live with. "My dad is one of the most honest, principled, good guys I know," she says. "And I basically agree with him. But it's sort of strange when you know most parents want to buy things for their kids and all you need is a small sum of money — to fix up the kitchen, not to go to the beach for six months. He won't give it to us on principle. All my life my father has been teaching us. Well, I feel I've learned the lesson. At a certain point you can stop."

Parents who disinherit not on principle but because they disapprove of their young heir's behavior might face a troubling prospect — they might be making a mistake. Just days before committing suicide in 1963, R. E. Turner Jr., the father of maverick television mogul Ted Turner, arranged a quick sale of his Atlanta billboard business to Curt Carlson. Recalls Carlson, who had no idea that the elder Turner was planning to kill himself: "He told me he wanted to have some money to leave his wife when he died, but that everything he had was tied up in his business. He said he was sure if Ted got his hands on the business, he would run it into the ground." Within days of Turner's death, Carlson got a call from his widow, Florence, and a visit from Ted, then 24. Says Carlson, "His mother wanted Ted to have the business back, and Ted, who can be very convincing, talked about how this was his one chance to get going in life." Persuaded, he sold the business back to Ted, who has been going fast ever since.

Estate planning is particularly tough when the legacy is a family business. Most entrepreneurs do not plan to sell out, as R. E. Turner did, but try to keep the business in the family. Says Curt Carlson, whose privately held Carlson Cos. brought in revenues of more than $3 billion last year: "You think of your company as your own baby. You hate to think of someone buying it and then the name is gone."

But leaving it to the children will not guarantee that the business stays in family hands. Because of fraternal fights, the Bingham family's Louisville newspaper and broadcasting empire went up for sale last January. Destructive squabbles are most likely to break out when family members try to sell company stock to outsiders, an act viewed as disloyal by those desperate to

keep control. In St. Louis the heirs of legendary Joseph Pulitzer staged a noisy row this year over the attempted sale of some Pulitzer Publishing Co. stock. The family members who wanted to sell backed a takeover bid by Alfred Taubman, a Detroit-based real estate developer. Chairman Joseph Pulitzer Jr., his half brother and a cousin struck a deal to buy out the dissidents' shares at three times the pre-feud price. Taubman is still fighting in the courts.

Chicago centimillionaire Lester Crown, 61, worries that mercenary motives among family members could one day force the breakup of his very private business empire. The Crowns' holdings range from building materials, hotels, and real estate to 23 percent of General Dynamics, one of the largest U.S. defense contractors. Over the years, says Lester, he and his father, Henry, 90, have "always treated our operations as a common pot." They have handed out voting shares and limited partnerships in the various businesses to Lester's uncles, cousins, brothers, nieces, and nephews, as well as his seven children. Lester predicts that "one of these days we're going to get hit in the back of the head because we did this." If he could do it over again, he would still give the family "the ability to enjoy the good life" by setting up a single trust to pay out a guaranteed income to everyone. But he would make sure that control of the companies was "retained by those who operate the business."

The Coors family of Colorado has kept its brewery bubbling with just such an arrangement since 1969. All the company's voting stock sits in a trust, whose trustees can only be family members active in the business. Says Bill Coors, 70, chairman of Adolph Coors Co. and grandson of the founder: "We've minimized family feuds by concentrating control in the hands of those most dedicated to preserving the family values."

Warren Buffett argues that most proprietors should forget trying to keep the management of their beloved companies in the family; he assumes current nonfamily management will continue running Berkshire Hathaway after he is gone. He grants that occasionally an heir may be the most suitable candidate to manage a company but believes the odds are against it. Says Buffett: "Would anyone say the best way to pick a championship Olympic team is to select the sons and daughters of those who won 20 years ago? Giving someone a favored position just because his old man accomplished something is a crazy way for a society to compete."

Buffett especially admires how fellow Omaha businessman Peter Kiewit solved his legacy problem. Kiewit arranged his affairs so that when he died in 1979 his 40 percent stake in the family's enormously successful construction company was sold to employees. The proceeds from the sale then went to a charitable foundation that he had established to promote education and social services in Nebraska. Kiewit left approximately three percent of his $186-million estate to his widow, his son, Peter Jr., 60, and other relatives. Peter, a successful Phoenix lawyer, was surprised by the $1.5-million legacy he received at age 53. Says he, "I was raised to expect nothing, and supported myself all my life. In the end, I think my father was saying from the grave that he approved."

For wealthy parents, and even for those with more modest estates, the question of how much to leave the kids is a highly subjective matter. But here are a few points worth keeping in mind.

- Don't play hide-and-seek.

Forget locking your will away in mystery like some 19th-century miser. Bring the family finances into the daylight, so the children will know what they are getting and where it came from, and will have some idea of how to hold on to it. They should also, of course, know if they are not getting anything. For example George Pillsbury knew that he would get more than $1 million when he turned 21 – "It's tough to be unaware of your wealth when you have a brand name," he says. But many of his friends had no idea what was coming to them. "A lot of them were shocked," he recalls, and some had trouble coping with their new fortunes.

John Train, whose investment firm claims to be the largest in New York City serving rich families, recommends that talks about money, like those about sex, begin as early as possible. These can evolve into full-scale sessions on the family finances. Lester Crown is a big booster of this idea: "We started when the kids were young and put the dollar signs in as they got older."

Former Treasury Secretary William Simon, who has made tens of millions in leveraged buyouts since leaving Washington, says that at one of his family's regular meetings, his seven children had to read and discuss 19th-century steel magnate Andrew Carnegie's essay "The Gospel of Wealth." (Carnegie argued that by giving away their great fortunes, rich men would produce "an ideal state in which the surplus wealth of the few will become, in the best sense, the property of the many.")

Though the children of Eugene Lang will not share in his estate, they and Lang's wife are trustees of his private foundation and join in deciding where to give. Says Lang: "In a way they're spending their inheritance with me here and now and getting a lot of satisfaction and joy from it."

No amount of family talk will guarantee that the children will not turn out like Tommy Manville, the asbestos heir who went through 13 marriages and millions of dollars, or Huntington Hartford of the A&P fortune, who has lost a reported $90 million in a lifetime of bad business deals. But it should help.

• Shelve the silver spoon.

Psychiatrists say the lack of work experience not only alienates heirs from humanity, but also contributes to insecurity about their ability to survive without their inheritance. H. Ross Perot, 56, the Texas billionaire who founded Electronic Data Systems, a computer services company, and sold it to General Motors, puts it this way: "If your kids grow up living in fairyland thinking they're princes and princesses, you're going to curse their lives."

T. Boone Pickens Jr., chairman of Mesa Petroleum and worth tens of millions of dollars, remembers his middle-class upbringing as "the best a boy could have." When he graduated from college, Pickens thought his father, a buyer of oil leases for Phillips Petroleum, might give him $500 or so. Instead, all he got was "good luck." Pickens plans to leave at least half his estate to charity; he has arranged what he considers small trusts for his five children and three stepchildren. Says he: "If you don't watch out, you can set up a situation where a child never has the pleasure of bringing home a paycheck."

• Don't be afraid to experiment.

Robert D. Rogers, chief executive officer of Texas Industries, a manufacturer of cement and steel, swears by a Texas-sized version of every parent's

basic financial training tool — the allowance. At 18, each of his three children began receiving annual stipends that covered living expenses and then some — college costs, clothing, travel. The youngsters were not accountable for the money, but if it ran out, tough luck. As an incentive to save, the children could claim whatever remained when they reached 25. "My oldest son ran through his first year's income in nine months and had to go to work," recalls Rogers, who credits a Texas Instruments co-founder, Eugene McDermott, with the idea. Young Rogers never ran out again. If you are going to leave money to your children, a generous living allowance should give you a good idea what they will do with it.

Parents who want to encourage their offspring to work, and provide them a little extra money besides, can create incentive income trusts designed to match or double the child's salary. The trusts also can be set up to pay out principal if a child achieves some objective, such as attaining tenure at a university or even holding down a steady job.

• Give later rather than sooner.

Most estate advisors now agree that 21, the age of majority, is too early for most children to reap a windfall. Warns John Train: "Very large sums handed over to children who have done nothing to deserve them almost inevitably tend to corrupt them." Ross Perot, as usual, is more blunt: "Anybody who gives kids a lot of money at 21 doesn't have much sense." Bill Simon suggests that "sensible parents" put a reasonable amount in a trust that only starts paying interest at, say, 35, and then allows access to principal in two installments at 40 and 45. What's a reasonable amount? Says Simon: "Everybody has to define that for himself."

- Trust in God and take short views.

It's 2075. Do you know who your great-great-grandchildren are? Do you really care? Louis Auchincloss, the novelist, estate lawyer, and scion of one of America's most prominent families, believes the "dynastic impulse" is on the wane in America. "When I came out of law school, people were always deeply concerned about their great-grandchildren," he says. "Not now." That may be no bad thing; the U.S. is littered with indolent people who were ruined by trusts set up by adoring grandparents.

Besides, Congress has tightened tax loopholes that encourage generation-skipping trusts. If you want to ensure some accountability among your heirs, you might consider Ross Perot's advice to make bequests one generation at a time. Says he: "Let your children decided how much to give their children."

- Don't live and die in Louisiana.

The Bayou State adheres to the Napoleonic Code, which requires forced heirship: A single child is entitled to one-quarter of any estate, two or more children split half. If you want to give more, that's no problem. If you want to disinherit, Baton Rouge lawyer Gerald Le Van says the state recognizes a few reasons as valid — attempted assault against the parent, conviction for a felony, and a debatable rule, just passed by the legislature last session, "failure to communicate for two years without just cause." If you want to give it all to charity, Le Van advises moving to another state.

- Put child-rearing before estate planning.

Child psychoanalyst Roy Grinker Jr. worked with the children of the very rich for 15 years. Often the problem in wealthy households, he says, is that parents pay too little attention to their children's upbringing. "Rather than give rich parents money advice, I would give them child-rearing advice," says Grinker. "I would say, 'Pay attention to your kids, spend some time with your kids, love your kids.'" Warren Buffett cheerfully agrees: "Love is the greatest advantage a parent can give."

Chapter 14

Consulting to Family Business

A special breed of consultants, thoroughly understanding both business and family processes, now offers their services to family firms. This section explores who these consultants are, the problems they confront and their approaches to family business systems.

The type of family firm a consultant works with does much to determine the circumstances that will be confronted. In any case, consultants would do well to question the perspective of any family business participant. Consultants should work to clarify purposes, roles, expectations and norms, helping members to find common ground and manage differences.

While intervention can be helpful in resolving challenges confronting family businesses, the consultants and their employers are warned not to overestimate the probability of success.

Introduction

There are three kinds of family firms: traditional, conflictful and entrepreneurial. Traditional companies are long-established, well structured, paternalistic organizations. Their problems involved suppressed generational differences. Conflictful organizations maintain family cohesion, but suffer major disagreements about business strategy and power. Entrepreneurial companies remain dominated by their founders and are the most difficult to deal with.

Consultants who work with family businesses must realize that they are often contacted by family members in pain but with little power. The deep complexities of family businesses must be recognized. Assumptions about the validity of any individual's perspective, commitment to the family, or the probability of successful outcomes should be made very carefully.

Consulting With Family Businesses: What to Look For, What to Look Out For

1983

By Harry Levinson

Reprinted by permission of **Organizational Dynamics**, Summer, 1983. Copyright ©1983 American Management Association; all rights reserved.

It's safe to say that no two family businesses are alike. Yet the consultant called to intervene when problems strike such firms should be aware of the broad categories into which these firms fall. (He or she should of course be aware of much more as well—but first things first.)

Kinds of Family Organizations

There are three kinds of family organizations: family traditional, family conflictful, and entrepreneurial. Let's take a look at each in turn; first let's examine family traditional organizations.

Family Traditional

These companies are long established, usually over several generations and, in business terms, are going along quite well. They usually have a good reputation for customer service or product quality. They have a planned continuity in the sense that it is taken for granted by both parents and offspring that the sons (and now, sometimes, daughters) will follow the fathers. They anticipate continuing to be in the same business. Customarily they are not caught up in pressure for rapid expansion, but rather anticipate slow and steady growth, usually as a product of their reputation. Growth is from within.

These are essentially quiet organizations. People don't say much about them or hear much about them. They tend to be heavily paternalistic in their orientation. The problems that arise from time to time are likely to be intergenerational and handled with refined self-control. There may be professional managers between given fathers and sons if the age gap between them is too large; often a major problem has to do with the fate and future of those managers. In many cases, the chief executive had to wait many years for his own role before his father retired.

Family members usually have significant influence in their local communities because most such organizations tend to be in relatively small communities. For estate reasons many of these organizations have disappeared into larger acquirers.

Consultation with such organizations may frequently involve dealing with suppressed generational differences, particularly an effort of the young to initiate change in managerial practice. Issues of succession usually are quite clear, with younger sons assuming in turn the roles in which they are preceded by older sons. At times other family members are brought in, usually sons-in-law, and they take their respective places in the organization, though ordinarily not as successors to top management.

The consultation process in such organizations is usually a sporadic one. That is, people will call upon the consultant to help them cope with specific problems, often of selection or of dealing with loyal employees about whom major decisions now have to be made or

dealing with individual clinical-type problems or sometimes conflicts between two major employees. Rarely are group process activities entertained because of the turbulence they stir up, unless one of the sons, having succeeded his father, becomes enamored of something in which he has participated. Referral for professional help for family members through the consultant is also rare. They usually take care of such problems on their own.

Family Conflictful

The second kind of family organization follows from the first. Family cohesion is maintained and there is an effort to sustain a certain kind of tradition, but major conflicts arise, usually out of differences of opinion about the direction in which the business ought to go and sometimes over power. Faced with potential product obsolescence or with declining markets, the older and more established family members want to intensify their efforts to continue to do more of the same. Others, seeing certain handwriting on the wall, are unable to sustain their interest in or commitment to that course of action and want to pursue another. A split in the family usually follows along these two lines. That split is exacerbated if the family business is headed by one or more brothers who are also split along those lines and each in turn is supporting his own dominant son. Yet a consultation with such organizations usually fails because the split is so wide and each position is based on different sets of rigidly held assumptions. More often than not, the outcome of that kind of conflict is the sale of the organization.

Entrepreneurial

The third kind of family organization, the one that features the most difficulty, is that in which the entrepreneur who started it continues his leadership or is followed by one or more sons whose leadership efforts are going less well. In such situations, family feuds are precipitated, family conflicts are engendered and maintained, and family bitterness is endemic. After the founding father has left the scene, problems in such organizations are compounded by the growing number of children, grandchildren, and even great-grandchildren who continue to enter the business or, alternatively, who ultimately want their inheritance in cash.

Entrepreneurial family businesses are the most difficult of all to deal with, whether as an employee, a family member, or an outside consultant. The two major psychological reasons lie in the unique psychodynamics of the entrepreneurial founder and in the fact that historical family rivalries, which under other circumstances would ordinarily be dissipated in work roles removed from the family, are perpetuated in the family business.

The family business that grows beyond the Mom and Pop grocery store does so because of the entrepreneur's drive. That drive arises out of a characteristic interpersonal configuration — specifically the rivalry between father and son, which is most acute in the period from three to six years of age of the child, and which Freud referred to as the Oedipus complex. Ideally, that rivalry is resolved when the son, recognizing that he cannot compete with father for mother's attention and affection, identifies with the father on the assumption that if he cannot have mother but becomes like father, he will get somebody like mother. That identification makes for the "chip off the old block" phenomenon.

However, the identification process is not always as smooth as the ideal.

Sometimes the rivalry is perpetuated, either because the son believes that mother indeed prefers him to father or that he can still win the battle. That unresolved rivalry becomes unconscious. It is usually reflected in intense, angry competitiveness, with the father and subsequently others, which then leads the son to create his own business and, in effect, marry it. His business becomes symbolically his spouse, his child, his instrument for attaining personal and social power, and his device for mastery. Entrepreneurship is predominantly a male phenomenon, for though many women have started businesses, few have built them to significant size.

The rivalry phenomenon also reflects itself in a low self-image because, symbolically, the son is competing from an infantile position and must become all-powerful to defeat the surrogate enemy. The perpetual anger results from the repression of the unresolved conflict. It is that anger that fuels the intense drive to achieve, the dogged persistence to stick with the project against all odds, the unrelenting competitiveness, the need to overcontrol, and the inability to give up when it is time to yield the reins. Entrepreneurs are angry, determined men.

Though an entrepreneur may build an organization to even massive proportions, it is characterized by one dominant feature: There is great difficulty in establishing succession. The entrepreneur can tolerate no rivals and promptly slaps them down or ejects them when they become threatening to him. Henry Ford II, for all practical purposes an entrepreneur because he rebuilt the Ford company, fired Lee Iacocca when Iacocca came too close to the throne.

Characteristically, the entrepreneur is also paternalistic. He usually seeks to obtain the loyalty of his followers by being a "good father," by being beneficent and caring. Their affection enhances his self-image. However, his underlying motto is, "Look how good I am to you. Why don't you do what I tell you to do?" He wants the loyalty and fealty of all who work for him and he wants them all to serve him and his purpose, that purpose usually being to fulfill his own ego-ideal aspirations. Thus he manufactures guilt and makes detachment difficult.

All this is magnified in the family business. The father wants the sons, particularly, to serve him and to allow him to remain the head of the business as long as he possibly can. In my experience, only a very few fathers have stepped aside before they were compelled to do so. The father often communicates to the sons that he is building the business for them, that it is going to be theirs, that they should not be demanding of either appropriate salary or power because they are going to get it all anyway in due time. Nor should they leave the father and the business, because it is self-evident that he has been good to them and is going to give them so much. Thus they are manipulated into a continuously ambivalent position of wanting to become their own persons with mature adult independence on the one hand, and the wish to take advantage of what they are being offered on the other. If they leave, seemingly they will be ungrateful. If they threaten to depose the father or demand to share his power, then they will indeed destroy him. If they don't do as he says, then they are disloyal and unappreciative sons.

This problem is further complicated by the fact that not all of the sons are equally competent (and sometimes this applies to other relatives, too). Yet there must be a place in the business for each of them and each must be treated not on the basis of competence, but on the basis of position as a relative in the family. Those who are less competent are not subject to adequate supervision by the more competent — because, after all, they are presumably equal relatives — nor can they be fired, because family is family and blood is thicker than water. The family is never free of the business; all conversation and relationships seem to be built around it. Nor is the business ever free of the family. Neither can escape the other.

What They Do Before the Consultant Comes

There are only two conditions under which these issues can be resolved, and both have to do with the degree of pain felt by the eldest or dominant son in the relationship with the father. Usually because of the issues of guilt described above, the son is caught in a double bind. If he leaves, his guilt is exacerbated. If he doesn't, he runs the risk of being stamped out and losing his own momentum. Usually, in such cases, if the pain is severe enough for that son, he will seek clinical help and resolve the conflict. If the pain is not severe enough, then he will continue to rock back and forth in the perennial bind, feeling guilt no matter which way he turns and unable to move anything or take any action. In some instances, psychotherapy relieves the guilt sufficiently so that the son can indeed take over the business in which the father, usually because of age, has had to move into an advisory role In such a case, the son must disregard the repetitive attacks of the father. Usually he is strong enough to do so only for having had outside psychotherapeutic help. He then must go about running the business as it should be run, rather than as his father thinks it ought to be.

One such father brought along an assistant with an array of charts to the consulting session to demonstrate the ways in which his son was causing the business to function ineffectively. Asked simply to talk about his feelings concerning his son and the business, the father could not do so—he could only attack in the way he was attacking. Actually, the son was handling the situation quite well by keeping his father at arm's length, appeasing him, cajoling him, and having him close by so that he could see that the business wasn't falling apart; nevertheless, it was a continuous battle until the father died.

Double Bind

Sometimes the situation is painfully threatening and tragic, as in the case of a man and wife who had built a profitable business and asked their son and his wife to take it over. The son, a business school graduate, had been employed by another company—but he responded to his father's entreaties and returned. However, the father and mother retained the controlling stock. The father became increasingly senile and unable to respond to the needs and decisions of the business—yet he kept forestalling the son's wish and need to control. He would not put his stock in a trust or in any other way make it possible for appropriate decisions to be reached. Complicating matters, he was being pursued by a predatory potential buyer whose efforts threatened the son's position. Yet the father would not hear the problems or advice of the son, because he felt that the son was trying to take his company away from him. The mother, always loyal to her husband, would not vote her stock against the father.

The son was faced with a choice between (1) leaving and (2) staying with the business and continuing to build it, while continually running a risk that it might be swept from under him. There was nothing he could do to cope effectively with the situation. To leave would be to let his father down; to stay would be not only to run great risk, but also to dissipate the years—which, if devoted to his own or another business, would have enabled him to attain much greater success. The guilt feelings were too powerful. He stayed.

Frequently in entrepreneurial situations involving two or more sons the eldest brother is beaten down by a dominating father. As a result, he is not in a position to take over by the principle of primogeniture. The next younger son then takes over when the father dies or becomes unable to function. However, that younger son cannot have the support of the older son, nor can he fire him. The younger son must nevertheless direct the older son or assume responsibilities that the older son cannot assume. Even so, the older son demands his just due of income and position. He is unwilling to be in a secondary role, yet simultaneously is unwilling or unable to assume the leadership role.

If there are other sons, usually they have positioned themselves to have perquisites and powers of various kinds, having been assigned to managerial roles regardless of their competence. None wants to give up his perks or position. Sometimes each is also maintaining a foothold in order that his sons may come into the business on an equal footing with the sons of all of his brothers. Furthermore, none wants to be bought out; few have other occupational options open to them, and certainly not at incomes they draw from the business. Their position in the community, their stature, their role of power in the organization all hinge on their staying in the jobs that they have maintained for themselves. There is then an internal equilibrium that is difficult to disrupt despite the discomfort that it causes for some of the family members.

Water: Sometimes Thicker Than Blood

Usually, a consultant is sought by one of the younger sons to help alleviate the chronic pain of such a situation. But the consultant confronts the fact that no one wants to yield; no one sees enough of a problem to require interference by an outsider except the person who called the consultant; and no one wants any of the others to become more powerful, more adequate than he. Each has at least a negative vote that keeps the whole system from functioning as well as it might, though each cannot do what is required to enable it to function at maximum effectiveness. If, under such circumstances, the business must be sold for estate reasons, the antagonism of the respective brothers is translated into the behavior that would have taken place before had not the business held them together. They become separated from each other and lost touch with each other. Blood is not thicker than water except as a cliche with which to inhibit action.

This example illustrates another phenomenon. The most difficult problem in family business consultation is the fact that the key figure in that system does not have sufficient pain to want to change. Usually, the consultation is sought by one person of lesser power in the system — one who is experiencing pain and seeking a way to reach the entrepreneurial power or the person of greatest authority. (In the illustrative case above the younger son called for help.) The authoritative person ordinarily sees no problem or feels that he can manage it, or resents the intrusion of the outsider and the brashness of the family member who invited the consultant in.

Sons and Brothers

The power problem among sons is compounded if the elder son, as is typical of elder sons when they haven't been beaten down, is the more orderly, compulsive, aggressive, and intellectual. Usually, this eldest son wants to maintain tight control and high standards. The second son, who more often wants to be liked, thinks the former is being too controlling. The elder son thinks the younger is too easy-going and not a sharp enough businessman. If there is a third son, frequently he is dragging along behind unless he has a unique talent or ability that enables him to assure the success of the older ones.

When brothers who have maintained and even expanded an effective family business leave their business to their respective sons, in turn, because of death, frequently the brothers' rivalry is displaced onto the sons and they in turn jockey for position for their own sons. This problem becomes more acute if one son is dominant either because of competence or because of primogeniture. In a case of the competent son, the less competent ones may then begin to act out against the values of family and organization. This acting out may range from becoming playboys to carrying on various other irresponsible escapades that reflect on the company and the family reputation.

If the family succession is a matter of primogeniture, and particularly held in place by the senior brother of the two or more elder ones, there tends to be a seething rebellion underneath. The respective cousins are held in place by the force of their fathers, but underneath each is waiting to overthrow that senior person held in place by his dominant father. Each is waiting to go his or her own way when free of this kind of pressure. Most have already lost interest in the business, if they had any to start with, and seek only their portion of the inheritance. That means that the commitment to the organization is significantly limited to the dying brothers and those few people closer to the top who are jockeying for power. In such situations, again, the organization usually is ultimately sold because the power issues cannot be resolved.

In situations like this, the consultant faces the fact that people compelled to be together by their stake in the business really don't want to be, and the intensity of their anger with each other and their disappointment in each other, which has usually been going on for years, makes it difficult for him or her to find appropriate leverage. As in the case of the senile parent, it is not unusual for problems to be of clinical proportions.

In one instance, for example, the elder of two brothers had started the business and had scrounged under the most difficult of circumstances not only to build the business, but also to send his younger brother through college. The younger brother's professional training contributed significantly to the growth and development of the business, but the fact that he had had such training and, in effect, had had an opportunity created by the older brother, left the older brother feeling that the younger was insufficiently grateful and that he, despite his lack of college education, knew more about how to operate the business than the younger. The younger, with great patience, tried to recognize the elder's efforts and express appreciation for the

opportunities the elder had given him. However, he could not bring to bear what he had learned professionally without incurring the elder's wrath. The hassle between them produced severe chronic conflict that carried over into their family relationships.

Finally, the wife of the younger brother asked for consultation. The two brothers appeared for consultation for three successive sessions. When it became clear to the elder that he was the problem in the sense that as he had become more paranoid and hostile as he had grown older, he withdrew from the consultation. The younger brother could not leave the elder, who had done so much for him, nor could he do so for fear that the business would collapse without his technical input. Yet the cost of staying was high and he would not himself seek individual therapy to enable him either to stay or to decide to leave.

One factor that may compound such problems occurs when one brother or another has a woman friend on the side. Sometimes these are long-standing situations with implied or expressed promises of divorce and marriage. Such situations ultimately blow up and make for great family conflict within the family of that brother. That conflict, in turn, reflects on the others, who begin to take sides and become angry about the reflection on the family. If sons of the couple having difficulty are in the family business, they too become split and that further upsets the equilibrium.

A Danger for the Family

The kind of consultant called in may pose a danger for the family. In one case, for example, two brothers were battling vigorously and had been battling for many years — yet they declined to follow advice that they seek professional psychotherapeutic help with some of their problems. Instead, they found a consultant with some background in group dynamics who offered himself as a trainer. That consultant quickly exacerbated the guilt of both brothers and encouraged them to bring their wives to their meetings, which they did. As the conflict he stimulated between the brothers mounted in intensity, their respective wives applauded the consultant—because he encouraged them to go at each other publicly, and each had been waiting for a long time for her husband to attack the other. To make a long story short, the consultant became the Rasputin of that organization; ultimately, no decision was made in it without consulting him. He developed a following of sycophants and a list of enemies; the latter were gradually eliminated from the organization. But when the business turned out to be less profitable than before, the brothers were compelled to bring in a professional manager who promptly threw the consultant out.

Daughters and Widows

In some situations, the sons are pushed aside for the daughter. Given their psychological history, fathers rarely have rivalry problems with daughters. One way for a father to deal with this situation is to define the sons as incompetent and to push them aside. That puts the daughter, who is usually younger anyway, in the position of supervising her brothers and, in effect, taking charge of them. For brothers who are probably already emasculated, this increases the intensity of their feelings of dependency, rivalry, and helplessness. Unlikely to succeed in the organization, they become a continuous burden.

That kind of problem usually will not be solved by consultation because both the father and the daughter want things to be as they are and the sons are too powerless to do anything about them. Sometimes the daughter is able to marry a person who in turn takes over the managerial responsibilities of the business. This usually happens when the sons have chosen to leave the business and pursue their careers in other directions, usually more successful ones than those represented in the business.

Situations in which one of an association of brothers dies, his wife takes over his role, and his son is in the business can become very disruptive. Usually the widow has inherited the husband's share and automatically sides with her son in business discussions. She will hear nothing of his inefficiencies or ineffectiveness and takes a fixed position reinforcing his. That creates severe managerial problems, particularly if a group of brothers (and perhaps others) are still involved, one among them being the senior or managing partner. In such situations the wiser course is for the family group to become a formal stock-owning partnership, then evolve a board of directors to manage the business and hire professional management.

If the family manages to stick together through three generations, usually the proliferation of family members by the third generation is such that few have specific interest in the business other than for income purposes. It is difficult to mobilize them to come to some agreement for appropriate decision making and, when professional managers have taken over, they usually have great difficulty maintaining coalitions of family members to accomplish their tasks. If the family members remain actively involved, their relationships are frequently contaminated by the pressures of spouses, each jockeying for position and particularly for advantages for their children.

Three Options

In most instances family members have three options. In some businesses each family member can have his or her own operation. In the Newhouse newspaper chain, for example, the family has bought a new newspaper or radio station or TV station for each eligible member. Given their independent activity, they are able to accept the counsel of senior members. Another version of this is a chain of independently owned department stores in the Midwest. Family members do their buying together, but each manages his own operation. That business has been eminently successful for all of them.

Failing such an arrangement, either family members have to leave the organization or the organization must be sold. Usually, the history of conflict has been so long and so severe by the time a consultant is called in that the problem is refractory to consultation.

Intervention

These examples illustrate the fact that only rarely, perhaps in one incident out of each ten approaches, is a consultation process in a family business consummated. It is extremely difficult to get people in a family business to buckle down to the work of resolving the conflicts and problems in that business. The problems for which consultation is sought are rarely amenable to successful consultative effort. Careful diagnostic assessment is required, lest the consultant find himself or herself entangled in a complex network of alliances and hostilities.

If a family is willing to accept a consultant and if therefore a consultant has entered into a family business, it probably will be wiser for that person to interview each of the people separately and at some length to get a sense of the family dynamics, the business problems, and the fears and anxieties of each of the participants. In the process, the consultant ideally will be establishing a degree of trust and rapport with each participant individually. When the consultant has established enough information and enough trust, he or she then is in a position to bring the respective family members together in a group, then ideally to summarize his or her findings anonymously and ask what they want to do about the problem.

In such circumstances, the consultant becomes the trusted "other" who enables the family to mobilize itself to deal with its problems. Ideally, each trusts the consultant (to varying degrees), though the family members may not trust each other. That continued trust is the basis for getting family members to agree on at least some of the major steps they must take. Those who do not like each other do not have to learn to do so; indeed, in most cases they will not. Nevertheless, they do have to learn to work together in their common interest.

The consultant who enters into consultation with a family business must recognize that he or she is entering an old battleground. What is to be learned and dealt with is not merely a matter of contemporary differences. Many of them are unconscious and go back for an almost literal lifetime. Understanding this, however, the consultant who maintains a focus on the contemporary problem-solving efforts of the organization, particularly around issues that threaten the livelihood or succession of the younger family members, may be able to sustain the working relationship long enough to help solve the problems.

Summary

In summary, consultants should be wary of consultation with family businesses. Here's some other advice for consultants, with implicit interest of course to family members and others who work with them.

1. Expect contact by people who have pain but no power, and expect only one out of ten of those contacts to turn into a more formal consultation activity.

2. Recognize the deep complexities of the family business, the multiple rivalries, the difficulties of family secrets, and the displacements of hostilities from generation to generation; be especially careful about establishing individual trusting ties before trying to bring the family together, as in a family therapy model.

3. Recognize that many of the people caught up in the conflict have only minimal commitment to each other, to the family, and to the organization; they are held together by some expected gain for their own children or because they can't give up an advantage they already have. This makes it difficult to establish a sense of common purpose, except in the narrowest sense.

4. Weigh family ties carefully. A sufficiently intense wish on the part of the family to remain together as a family with a strong sense of family pride is an optimum condition for inviting them to consider how to go about resolving some of their differences. Where commitments are weak, it may be wiser to appeal to methods that should loosen the painful tie that bind the family members together and allow them to go their respective ways free of those burdens.

5. The Gordian knot in such situations is usually the pain of the single dominant son, who most often can resolve that pain only with psychotherapeutic help. With that, it may be possible also to bring son and father — or sons and father — together to resolve some of their other differences, but as long as one or more of the sons is in a double-bind situation, movement is unlikely.

6. Don't be overoptimistic about your chances for success. It is easier for the family members to split and run than to sit together to resolve their problems. In most instances there are many outside distractions and not enough centripetal force to hold them together for problem-solving efforts. Issues of intense rivalry over years cannot be surmounted unless somehow the consultant finds leverage that makes it most important for all involved to resolve the problems at hand.

7. Don't be disappointed if you fail.

Introduction

Consulting to family business involves working with the family as a system, clarifying purposes, roles, expectations, and norms, before it can resolve the problems of the business and its future. This article explores the major areas of family systems consultation to members of a family business. A particular focus highlights the problems of different norms and expectations in the family and the business, and passing control of the business to the next generation.

Consulting To The Family In Business
1988

By Dennis T. Jaffe, Ph.D.

I. Introduction/Overview

Behind the impersonal facade of many of the world's businesses lie the complex, richly textured relationships, visions, dreams, and struggles of a family seeking immortality and security through the generations. In the tortured succession of the Richards and Henrys of Shakespeare's plays and in the 19th century corporate families such as the Rothschilds, behind nearly half of the *Fortune* 500 companies the family dramas play out while the company may be held hostage, waiting for the outcome.

It has been estimated that over 90 percent of all businesses and nearly half the GNP is controlled by the family businesses. Half the companies in the *US News* 100 — the largest fortunes and controlling ownership of companies — are families, and 35 of the 100 hold top management in the companies they own. In addition, many families who no longer manage the business they founded have special classes of stock that keep them in control. Smaller family businesses use these same methods to maintain ownership and control, and to keep their stamp on their business.

Family businesses represent the best and the worst of business. At best, a family business is freed of the pressures for short-term profits. It often has the foresight and power to take a long view, thereby saving and reinvesting capital and seeing the business as a legacy for heirs. Unlike the entrepreneurial business, founded on a single person's vision, the family business, when founded by two or more caring family members, tends to extend that caring, family feeling to loyal, long-term employees.

However, there is a downside to family business as well. Often, it will endure mediocrity due to a feeling of obligation to family members. It can be hard for professional management teams or new ideas to take root. The founder can be autocratic as well as paternalistic. The family business owner may have little time for the family at home. Non-working spouses may feel lonely or left out and resent the business.

Family conflicts or splits can paralyze business. The tragedy of the Bingham family, where the father/owner of a three generation family newspaper made the decision to sell it because his son and heir could not work out his relationship with his two sisters who held large blocks of stock, shows what can happen when a family can not separate its personal issues from running the business. Other examples in recent times are the family feuds between father and son over the ownership of Mel's Diner; the matriarch of the Sebastiani family firing her eldest son and installing her second son as his replacement; the public bloodletting in the Guccis, and the recent public couple conflict that divided Esprit.

To really understand these businesses we need to understand the aspirations, relationships, and interconnections within the family and address such questions as: is the business run to make a profit, or is it run to provide a place for the founders' children to work and grow? How can a business problem be kept from erupting into an old family argument, split along sex or generational lines? Who shall be the heir apparent, and what can be done about the hurt feelings of the others? Can you fire a family member? How does a son supervise an employee who changed his diapers 22 years ago? Is the Hallmark family tradition of no layoffs and support for employees who have been with the company for generations themselves more important than the bottom line?

Consultants specializing in family business have begun to address these issues and develop tools and theory to make sense of them. Knowledge of both organizational behavior and family systems is crucial. A normal crisis in one system can have difficult consequences in the other system. The consultant helps the family business members see themselves as both a family and a business system, and helps them grow and develop in each domain.

Systems theory teaches that when a problem cannot be resolved at one level of the system it must be addressed at another level. The problems of the business cannot be addressed by looking at the business alone; the intervention must start with the family. Here are some examples.

II. Issues in Family Business

Family Norms vs. Business Needs. Brothers David and Leon Warshaw started a manufacturing business forty years ago. Their sons all grew up in the business, visiting often and working there as soon as they were able. It made their family instantly recognizable in the community and, as the business grew, around the country. There was a family rule that "the business was for everyone, and everyone was expected to work there."

When David's three sons and Leon's two finished college and entered the company, the nature of the business was starting to change. Competitors were emerging and more specialized manufacturing and marketing tools were needed. Leon, who handled marketing, was more in tune with what was needed and increasingly took the leadership role, although the brothers were nominally equal. As the sons entered the business the ad hoc nature of its organization frustrated them. Cousins and brothers fell all over each other. A younger cousin was expected to teach the business to his elder, just arrived from business school. The family business norms—"there is room for everybody," "we're all equal," and "we'll take it one step at a time,"—were being tested by the new generation.

The business was suffocating, not for business reasons but because it had to be a container for every child in the family. An OD consultant might have tried to carve out more explicit roles and create better management coordination and supervision. However, to do this would have proved difficult because such changes conflicted with the family's norms. Family authority structures are generational: to try to have lines of authority between siblings or cousins just won't work.

Tensions appeared between David's traditionalism and Leon's vision. Furthermore, Leon's oldest son, Ray, was not very aggressive or far-seeing, while David's second son, Andy, had all the skills to be natural heir to Leon. What you might imagine happened: the two families began to feud. Cousins began to fight and to stop talking to each other. "I won't take orders from him," became the refrain. A personal dispute between Ray and Andy, unrelated to the business, further polarized the two families. As revenues declined for three years Leon began to consider the unthinkable: sell the business. Instead, he sought consultation.

Consultation began with interviews of each family member to probe for family issues as well as to explore how each person saw the business and his role in it. Each of the sons had very different needs, expectations, and perspectives;

yet all were treated alike in the business. A weekend retreat at Leon's home was a powerful experience. In a generation of close, loving, warm relating, they had never sat down and shared their visions of the business and how they might fit so many sons into it.

At the Warshaw factory there was reluctance to evaluate the performance of the sons, to choose leadership, and perhaps to suggest that some heirs leave. The non-family managers saw all this but found it hard to bring such issues up, seeing the family as a closed, united front.

In addition, Leon and David found it hard to discuss their difference: Leon was the sparkplug of expansion, while David felt more comfortable with a smaller, less leveraged company. Some sons were in each camp.

Many families try to maintain harmony by not discussing issues that may raise conflict. That may work within a family, but it rarely works in business.

At the retreat everyone agreed to meet one day a month for a year to sort things out. The process was difficult, but they created a Family Business plan, including some clear guidelines and expectations for the next generation. The plan outlined how the skills of the heirs would be assessed and developed. It clarified their commitment (with David's agreement) to growth, and acknowledged the likelihood that they may seek merger or acquisition with a larger company in their industry. During the process two heirs decided to work elsewhere, and the family found it could maintain its closeness even without working in the same factory. They also created an outside Board of Advisors, which included two key non-family managers, to bring new ideas and help the family focus on strategic and organizational issues. Each son was paired with a non-family senior manager as a mentor, and the sons were given clear responsibilities. They got a chance to develop, and outside managers got a clearer sense that while family management would continue, competence and accountability would prevail in decisions.

Perpetuating the family-owned business is, first, a family issue. If the family does not have a plan and does not take the time to meet regularly about their commitment to the future and how they want things to be, the business can be severely stressed and decline, because their unwillingness to make choices can paralyze or undermine the business' chance to make it. Often when family members come together like this, it is the first time an heir hears the full story of the business. The personal history of a family business is very special, because it is the story of a family and its way of making its mark in the world.

Succession Crises. Today, facing new competitive pressures, many family businesses face a crisis: will family heirs or outside management take the business into the second generation, or, like most family businesses, will they close down, sell out, or fold up? The average span of a family business is 23 years. Only a third of family businesses make it to the second generation. The shift from entrepreneur to management team is not easy, and becomes more complex when the entrepreneur is dad or mom. Underlying this is the question "When will they hand over the reins and move out of control?"

Such is the drama of the family business. Some fathers never leave. One fiftyish CEO son reports that this year his 85-year-old father finally dropped out of the company's everyday affairs. The reason: he is going on his honeymoon!

In this case, the third generation is not interested in the business, so preparations have been made to sell it. This CEO is glad his children have found other careers. He feels that the family business has been a form of slavery for them.

Another service business had a slightly different problem. Rick Wilson, the talented son of Wilson Financial's chairman, was always the golden boy and heir apparent. He received his MBA and spent three years with a large investment bank in New York. Rick entered the company and began to work alongside his father, who had inherited the business from his father. Dad at 50 was planning retirement, but Rick, itching for authority and wanting to make his mark, was frustrated. After 7 years a large company offered Rick a division presidency, and he found himself attracted by the offer. He went to his father and said he was going to take the job.

His father listened and said he could see Rick's reasons. The next week the Board voted to make Rick President and he stayed. He thought things would change, but they didn't. Like many heirs, he had responsibility without authority. Again he felt himself wanting to withdraw. Dad had difficulty listening to Rick. He had waited for his own father to retire and had assumed Rick would as well. Also, like many people in their late 50's, he wanted to consolidate the business and insure his own future. His entrepreneurial energy was low, while Rick wanted to move into new markets and take advantage of some opportunities he saw. The old way vs. the new is the drama in many family businesses.

A consultant was hired to help with a family planning process, followed by decisions about how to accomplish the transition. In several talks the father and son saw that their value differences had to do with their various life stages. The father agreed to a more limited role, overseeing investment opportunities with some of his long-term clients. He purchased another small business in order to let go without retiring. Rick was allowed to run the business.

A family business needs at least two separate business plans. First, there needs to be a plan for the family—its goals, values, commitment to the business, and plans for how family members will participate. If that is clear, people inside and outside the family will know where they stand. Second, there is a need for a clear business plan.

Men and Women. Increasingly today, the single entrepreneur is being replaced by the entrepreneurial couple who decide to extend their relationship to work. They bring their energy, but also their unresolved couple issues, into the workplace. One wife who ran a restaurant kept hearing about her husband's difficulty in supervising employees in the kitchen. She felt she had to protect him, but her protective behavior insured he would keep creating the problem. Another couple had a personal relationship characterized by very little division of labor. Each one would do a little of everything, but they had difficulty checking in or coordinating activities. Their business was run on the same ad hoc basis, and the pair began to be confused, overwhelmed, and angry at each other. They simply could not clarify their roles and responsibilities. Until they did the business remained chaotic. It is important that the relationship issues of role clarification, communication, and handling of conflict be addressed in business by couples.

In planning the future of the family business, the role of family members who are not managers, but own shares of the business is crucial. For example, many spouses feel left out or excluded, and indeed, many family businesses explicitly exclude them from management or ownership roles. They may seek influence indirectly. Spouses of founders often feel the business is their husband's mistress. And divorce can not only tear apart a family, but can force a sale or result in other business decisions that would not otherwise be made. Each of these issues needs to mediated and resolved.

III. Guidelines For A Healthy Family Business

In conducting research into the qualities of a healthy family business, I have designed a Family Business Assessment Inventory that looks at six key factors for family business effectiveness. The inventory helps family business members assess themselves and compare their perceptions among themselves. For each area I will discuss some of the ways that family businesses might improve their health:

- 1. Clear and Explicit Mission, Vision, and Purpose.

Tell the history and vision between generations. The family's history is the business, and children need to know the whole story. The vision of the founder needs to be shared, and there needs to be room to expand to include the dreams and new values of the children.

Have a continuously updated strategic business plan. Create a well-formulated strategic plan and circulate it. Look at goals and values as a family as well as in business. Include the future direction as a reality, just as you incorporate and share the stories of the past.

● 2. Clear Communication and Conflict Resolution.

Meet as a whole family. In most family businesses, the business is the vehicle for the family to thrive and express itself. Every few months members of the core family or families, including spouses and children in and out of the business, need to get together to talk about where things are now and where they are going.

Talk openly about differences and conflicts; practice forgiveness. The greatest pain in families comes when a conflict causes a rift and people become estranged, or the business suffers. Prepare to act as a mediator to help open up and resolve conflicts. Don't let them simmer underground. Also, prepare each family member to broaden their point of view and listen to their relatives and managers.

● 3. Clear Procedures and Expectations for How Family Members Participate in the Business.

Talk about career paths and preparing to enter the business. Don't make the future an implied or avoided subject. Talk about plans and help each heir learn their future role and apprentice inside and outside the business. Help everyone to learn the business, especially its organization and finances. Talk about different capabilities among children. While rivalries are inevitable, try to find places for each man and woman to grow inside or outside the business. Notice the roles of wives and husbands who marry into the business. They may feel excluded or have difficulty making their contribution. Be aware of any bias toward men or women.

● 4. Willingness to Listen to Outside Advisors and Managers.

Create a Board of Advisors. Families can be dreadfully shortsighted and narrow. Enlarge a family business' adaptability, no matter how small it is, by having a formal or informal group of advisors who meet periodically to reflect on business decisions and offer the kind of advice that sometimes even a spouse won't tel you.

Develop a management team outside the family to bring in skills that family members don't have. Professional management, technical skills, and experienced employees are the cornerstone of every small or medium sized business. Make sure the family is not so narrowly self-serving that it forgets to validate, promote, offer opportunities, and compensate fairly the key employees outside the family. Consider profit sharing and distribution of ownership.

● 5. Guidelines and a Plan for Generational succession.

Recognize that the next generation needs different leadership. The skills of the founder may not be what the business needs today. The business usually needs new skills in its leadership and may be forced to take a new direction. Help the family to allow the business to grow and change, while trying to retain and strengthen the core values that made the business special to the founder.

● 6. Ability to Spend Time and Have Fun Outside the Business.

Non-Business Family Time. A family needs to spend time outside the business, take time to build personal relationships, care about personal health, and have a life that is more than just business.

IV. Conclusions

Family businesses have unique problems that stem from their origins in the family system, with its deeply entrenched values, norms, and relationships. The addition of the family dimension to organization development consultation enables us to work with and solve problems of family business that might otherwise be intractable, confusing, or obscure. By exploring and making the family system explicit and planning together for the future of the business, consultants can lead even a very stuck and conflicted family business to a new stage of growth and effectiveness.

Special thanks are due to Carol Goodman of the Family Firm Network for the ideas expressed in this article.

Introduction

This article provides a good inventory of the business and family challenges that can confront a family business. The consultant to the family business is offered insights into certain peculiarities of family/business systems. A case demonstrating the role of the consultant in solving business and family problems is presented.

Consulting to the Family Business
1987

By Jacqueline Babicky

Reprinted by permission of **Journal of Management Consulting**, 1987, Vol. 3 (4). Copyright ©1987 Institute of Management Consultants; all rights reserved.

Family business is the kind of small business started by one or a few individuals who had an idea, worked hard to develop it, and achieved, usually with limited capital, growth while maintaining majority ownership of the enterprise. To succeed, the founder/entrepreneur has to have a great deal of energy, drive, motivation, and the proper temperament, as well has persistence, dedication, and a realistic view of himself and the world. All in all, it's not easy.

Closely held or family businesses account for nearly 95 percent of the businesses and 40 percent of the jobs in the United States. Yet these businesses, despite their importance in the American economy, have a high failure rate. The small family business can be a risky undertaking because of competition and high costs. To succeed it needs a wide diversity of talents, abilities, and management skills, as well as liquidity, working capital, planning, and financing.

The family-owned business must overcome a myriad of technical problems such as:

Start-up costs,

Financing,

Product development,

Market penetration,

Employee training and hiring,

Delegation and systems,

Goal setting and budgets,

Outside agency requirements,

Equity and ownership.

In addition, family-owned business faces another set of problems resulting from the very basis of its existence, the family relationship. For discussion purposes, family can be construed to include the close personal relationships that develop between non-family owners of a small enterprise during the years of building the company.

One of the motivating factors in starting a small business is for the founder to provide security, self-direction, and safety for himself and his family. He envisions an enterprise that will give him satisfaction, will provide a good living for himself and his family, will support his children into their adulthood, and will then provide for his own retirement. Often he sees his children coming into the business as one of his great lifetime achievements and a measurement of his success.

Dreams Can Be Nightmares

On the other hand, having the family in the business creates numerous opportunities for conflict and dissension. The basic causes of conflict in the family business are the different needs of individual family members. Often, unreal assumptions are made about the family members' abilities and wants. If conflict becomes severe, the business will flounder. Conflict can be dealt with if there is no sudden change in the company. However, a crisis such as a death, a strike, a change in competition, or a recession can cause the conflict to surface and paralyze the company just at the moment when cooperation and positive action are most crucial to its survival.

Some of the specific causes of conflict in the family business are:

- The children are expected to learn too fast. Since the business has been a part of their entire lives, it is assumed they have already learned how to operate it.

- The children become impatient with the parent's methods and want to experiment with new ideas and modern techniques which the parent resists.

- The owner has worked hard and is satisfied with his achievements; the children want growth and excitement.

- The owner wants to sell and retire; the children, having never worked anywhere else, are afraid to lose their jobs.

- The owner does not know how to handle a child he sees as incompetent. He neither wants to give the child responsibility nor wants to have to carry him.

- The owner/parent may be angry at his child's domestic relationship, i.e., marriage or divorce.

- The business may not be able to support the children's families comfortably. After years of supporting the original founder well, there may now be too many people for the business to support, but none of the children will give up their high standard of living.

- The parent can be jealous of the child, his youth, education, benefits, all the things the parent worked so hard to provide.

- The parent may be unable or unwilling to recognize the child's ability.

- The children may hold inappropriate jobs relative to their ability. They can be named executives and managers because of their familial relationship, yet lack the talent or training to direct the organization.

- The children may not be interested in carrying on the business, whereby the parent feels he has built the business for no purpose.

- As the children marry and in-laws become involved, jealousies and rivalries can develop.

- Those family members inside the company have a different perception of the strength and wealth of the business from those outside the business.

- Ownership may be concentrated in family members outside the business, while jobs in the business are held by other family members.

- Key employees may not stay because they have no chance at promotion or equity when family members are involved.

- Employees can be confused as to who is in charge, the manager or the family member.

- Some family members may wish to sell, while others want to maintain family ownership and continuity.

All businesses have political conflicts and internal maneuvering for power, recognition, and pay. In the family business the consultant must additionally be aware of the potential parent-child, brother-sister conflicts that may be years, even generations old. The wounds from childhood events and episodes can still be festering. Siblings may still be maneuvering for parent approval and competitive advantage, wasting energy that should go into job performance.

In a family business, the consultant will often find these characteristics:

- All the players are not "on the board." That is, very important and influential decision makers may not actually work in the business; the consultant may have to spend substantial time and do much creative listening before he finds out who they are.

- All the players may not even be alive. Children and spouse may still be operating under the directives and influence of a founder who died some time ago.

- The family relationships are longstanding and may have solidified into destructive patterns years ago. If so, the pattern will not be changed with all the logic in the world. Instead, the situation will have to be changed.

- There can be strong emotional undercurrents. There are society taboos and "shoulds" about family behavior. If these "shoulds " are not being met, there can be anger, guilt, and resentments.

- There can be highly emotionally—charged words and situations that bring reactions the consultant never anticipated because he did not know the family history or the background.

- On the other hand, there can be the positive side of all these statements. Much care, strength-giving, and respect may exist because of the family relationship.

If the family acts as a team, they are almost unbeatable. If the family is self-destructive, no one can keep it together. The best course then becomes to find a way to save the business and get the family out of it while they can still salvage some assets and some tangible reward for their efforts.

To discuss theses characteristics more fully, let's examine a recent consulting case involving a family business.

Bad Times Hit a Good Business

The client was a popular restaurant ("XYZ") in a resort town. "XYZ" was founded 25 years ago by Father and Mother. Four years ago Father died, and since then Mother, Son 1 ("Al") and Son 2 ("Bob") had been running the restaurant.

In earlier years "XYZ" was so profitable and self-sustaining that the family was able to leave it for several months every year and spend winter in the sun.

Sales began steadily declining several years ago, while costs were rising. Many new restaurants opened in the area, and "XYZ" had competition for the first time in its history. No one changed the business operation to meet these challenges. The local economy began suffering from a long, severe recession. This volatile combination of events sent "XYZ" into a severe cash crunch: bills went unpaid and sales declined further. The consultants were finally called in when the IRS filed a lien to collect substantial unpaid withholding taxes.

The client had hired an accounting firm for many years, who had acted primarily as bookkeepers. Although company personnel completed a daily sales report, made the bank deposits, and wrote checks, they had no daily, weekly, or monthly operating data. The accountants compiled a monthly sales journal, produced the payroll, created a general ledger and a cash basis financial statement. However, the statements were four months behind and, being on a cash basis, they did not show approximately $60,000 of unrecorded accounts payable to suppliers and vendors. No one at "XYZ" had any idea where the business actually stood, what the monthly expenses totaled, or their breakeven point.

Morale was low among employees as they had neither clear job descriptions nor clear areas of responsibility and lines of authority. The brothers, "Al" and "Bob," fought with each other in front of the employees and gave conflicting instructions. Mother also got into the fray and often gave employees yet another set of orders. There were "armed camps" of employees and even vendors supporting one brother or the other.

Because "XYZ" was such a painful battleground for the family, they all abandoned it. Mother, 68, decided she was tired and ready to retire, so she began to schedule herself to work only when she saw fit and then could not be counted on to appear.

"Al" and his wife decided to open a second restaurant four miles away. This second restaurant ("ABC") had a beautiful location and "Al" planned to build it as an exclusive gourmet restaurant. "Bob" and his wife originally invest in "ABC" with "Al," but a year after "ABC" opened, "Al" and "Bob" realized that because of their different temperaments and lifestyles they could not work together. "Al" had agreed to buy out "Bob's" interest, but "Bob" had received no payments. "Bob" was very nervous since he was still a guarantor on the loan originally taken to buy "ABC." "ABC" was also in severe financial trouble. It owed past payroll taxes, had had no statements for six months, and was beginning to bounce checks. Expenses were out of control and the mortgage unpaid.

After leaving "ABC," "Bob" and his wife opened a gift shop in a nearby town. Literally, no one in the family was running "XYZ."

Family Counseling Necessary

This case is typical of many family consulting engagements. On the surface were a series of large financial and accounting problems, but these problems could never be solved until the family conflict was resolved and some agreements were successfully negotiated among the family members. Therefore, two consulting engagements went on simultaneously: one of financial technical advice and planning and the other involving the negotiation and conflict resolution skills of the consultant.

It was important that the consultant recognize the real source of this business's problem. The lack of money, as critical as it had become, was only a symptom of the underlying family and planning issues. If not resolved, these would stand in the way of solving the business problems. Over a six-month period, the consultant performed several technical functions for each restaurant:

(1) He brought the accounting up to date so everyone knew exactly where the business stood. The accounting is the critical reporting system that shows what the business is actually doing.

(2) Using history as a guide, the next year's operating budget was created. In a crisis situation, the first question the consultant must answer is can the business be profitable? If a plan resulting in profit cannot be created, the business should close or be sold before all the equity is dissipated.

The budget process is a tool used to involve everyone in planning the future. Preparing the budget allows the consultant to access all records and all departments of the business. Each manager should be interviewed, as they can help the consultant quickly identify the problems of the business.

The budget process also helps the managers and owners agree on goals. A survival budget will include severe cutbacks in many expenses. If managers are involved in the budget process, those affected by the cuts know that the

most reasonable choice went into the plan, not an arbitrary or emotional choice made by someone else.

(3) With help from the consultant, the client communicated with all creditors. The unsecured vendors were informed that in order to survive the company was going through a reorganization. Among the prime points in the reorganization plan, gaining vendor support was paramount.

(4) In the course of communicating with the bank, a secured creditor whose loan was in default, the bank let it be known that it would entertain a proposal to refinance the loan if a property appraisal would support it. The bank would base the loan on a formula using fixed asset value combined with annual sales. "XYZ" was able to meet both requirements.

(5) A nationally acclaimed cook and restauranteur was hired to consult on food menus, preparation, and kitchen training for both restaurants.

(6) The family was able to recognize that "XYZ" would not be successful unless "ABC" also became successful. When the financial information became available, it was clear that "XYZ's" cash flow problem was the result of "ABC" having been capitalized with "XYZ" funds. In effect, "XYZ" had "borrowed" $150,000 from the IRS and the State and, in turn, "loaned" it to "ABC." "XYZ" could not afford to write off this "loan."

(7) The cash plans and budgets were presented to the taxing authorities who allowed "XYZ" sixty days to negotiate new long-term financing. Their proviso was that tax payments for current payroll be kept current during the grace period. The refinancing was achieved,

the taxes were paid, and a year later "XYZ" was profitable.

Time to Get Personal

While these technical issues were addressed, the consultant began working on the underlying problem — family conflict. The consultant called meetings of the entire family. "Al" avoided three of these meetings before his curiosity overcame his suspicions and he attended a session. The past performance, the current situation, and the projections were presented to the family. For the first time, all family members were apprised as to the exact financial situation including:

–lack of statements,

–cash shortage,

–employee attitudes,

–amount of unpaid bills,

–debt owed to taxing authorities,

–liability of the family members.

The cash flow and budget projections were presented to the family showing them that "XYZ" could be profitable if certain assumptions were met and strict budgets maintained. The family was then helped to see and evaluate their choices in the business crisis. Their choices were:

A. Do nothing, let the creditors take control. There were only two secured creditors, the bank with the long-term real estate loan, payments were ninety days past due, and the IRS who had issued a collection/closure demand notice. If the secured creditors took control, they would seize and sell assets. Liquidation would probably produce enough cash to pay off the secured debt, but nothing would be left over for the family or the unsecured creditors.

B. Do enough to hold the company together until a buyer could be found. The history of the company, combined with its location, would probably, given enough time, enable the company to find an outsider who would pay enough cash for it to pay off the secured creditors, compromise with the unsecured creditors, and leave some minimal payment for the family.

C. Take a long-term approach to the problem. Develop the systems and budgets to get "XYZ" healthy and running. When the business was healthy, "Al" would buy out the ownership interest of the rest of the family. Perform the same functions to get "ABC" healthy.

None of these choices would be pleasant or easy. Choices A and B would result in both companies going out of business. Each family member's role in each solution was discussed. The family agreed unanimously on choice C.

The goal setting and agreement process is critical. Any solution to the problems of a business cannot be the one advocated or chosen by the consultant. The end goal must be the client's. If the consultant tries to superimpose his own goals, the project will fail. Reaching any goal will always be difficult, and the client will have to solve problems and make sacrifices that he did not foresee at the time the goal was set. If the stated goal is not the client's goal, he will not support the transitions and changes required to succeed, nor will he display the tenacity required when the process becomes difficult.

The goal setting result is also critical. Now the consultant has an anticipated end against which every idea, every program, and every change proposed can be evaluated relative to whether it will help the client move closer to his goal.

The consultant's role becomes that of a facilitator. The consultant has a tool by which to make the participants accountable. It is not a matter of the consultant imposing his will on the client, it is a matter of the consultant helping the client evaluate choices relative to how well they help progress towards the goal. There is a subtle yet critical importance here that is basic to the consultant's future action and relationship with the client.

As objective facilitator, the consultant's comments, criticisms, and directions are not perceived by the client as emotional statements or personal criticisms. Instead, they can be perceived as his objective evaluations of choices relative to the client's own needs and desires. The client continues to choose.

Setting Up Targets

The process followed was one of needs assessment followed by goal setting. The goals were then translated into objectives. Needs assessment is the process of identifying the gap between current results and results that should be obtained:

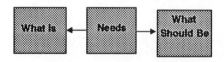

The consultant is a vital force in this process, listening to participants at all levels throughout the company and identifying both sides of the needs assessment formula — *What is* and *What. should be*. It is often the first job of the consultant to identify what is really happening. The next step is to meet with the decision makers and express to them his perception of the current situation. Once everyone can agree on *What Is* the current situation, the consultant can point out several alternative courses of action depending on various possible choices of *What Should Be.*

The needs cannot be determined nor goals set nor objectives developed until the family members or business owners have agreed on what should be. A goal is the general statement of intended results. The agreement on an overall end goal comes first. Once that goal is set, there are in fact many other subordinate objectives that "should be." Therefore, the consultant and the family business owner must focus on needs, identifying, agreeing upon, prioritizing, then selecting for resolution. Needs are prioritized by asking two questions: What will it cost to meet the need? What will it cost to ignore the need?

The means of achieving those needs can then be determined, by exploring alternative courses of action, by listening carefully to what the business owner believes will work, and by discussing the problems fully with those concerned with carrying out any solution.

Next a formal statement of objectives should be created. It includes the results to be obtained, what will display the results, the criteria to measure the results, and the conditions under which the results will be measured.

At each step along the way, the consultant must get agreement of the parties involved and work to reconcile differences between them. The differences can be the result of the parties' differences in experience, perception, or frame of reference.

In our case, the process worked as various family members and employees took on different responsibilities. Their objectives were expressed as budgeted sales targets, as a cash requirements plan that eliminated overdrafts, and as budgeted labor and food costs. To measure these objectives, all the accounting and financial reporting was brought in-house and up to date. The previously unrecorded liabilities were recorded on the books.

"Bob" was given the job of keeping a daily running cash balance, of paying all bills, negotiating with vendors, and making certain that payroll and taxes were covered before a single paycheck was issued.

The general manager was shown how to schedule labor on a cost basis. He and "Al" created a daily sales projection. The goal was to maintain loaded labor cost as 28 percent of sales. He became aware daily, even hourly, of sales and developed a system by which to control the cost of labor. He began to send people home or call them in as needed. This was a new concept at "XYZ" and employees who could no longer get enough full-time hours in the slow winter months quit. By attrition, the client was able to develop a small well-trained core staff plus a quickly available call-in list for surges and unexpected rushes.

The food cost was reviewed daily. With vendors and purveyors on COD, the tendency to over-buy and store went away; there was no spare cash to purchase food inventory if payroll and other fixed obligations were to be met. This daily review also forced the kitchen manager to become involved in the sales projection process.

"Al's" objectives were to streamline systems at both restaurants by combining the purchasing, hiring, training, and bookkeeping functions. He was also to control the kitchen and labor costs at

"ABC" and negotiate with their secured creditors.

The consultant's objectives were to create the information systems that would allow management to quickly identify future needs and current position. In order to be able to see the differences between what is and what should be, it is imperative to know what is.

Daily reports were created. The reports told the manager:

–daily sales total,

–daily sales by cost center,

–cash deposited in the bank, ending cash balance,

–labor costs, total dollars and percentage of sales,

–food costs, total dollars and percentage of sales,

–number of customers served,

–average dollars per customer,

–menu items ordered,

–liquor consumed,

–weather,

–unusual events.

Monthly reports created were the financial statements, cash flow statement, monthly sales and cash projection, last month's actual results compared to planned results.

"ABC" was in more trouble than "XYZ" and had no long history to draw upon. Recovery here was slower and more difficult. Finally, the two businesses were merged and, with the help of the food consultant, "ABC" began to earn its reputation as an outstanding gourmet restaurant. However, "XYZ" had to continue to finance "ABC" for another two years.

What Really Improved?

Why would all this work now, when it wouldn't work before? What had changed?

First, for the first time, all family members had agreed on a goal. Now there was a direction that did not involve emotional judgments as: who was right, who was best, who handled people better. The consultant's job became one of using the family's stated goals as the basis to negotiate the family conflict.

Second, the family not only agreed upon a leader, but they agreed to let him lead. In any business there must be a clearly identified leader who interacts with the management team. The consultant's job was to support "Al" as the leader, while creating the communications and reporting system for him to use. There are some very basic human requirements for any leader to use to achieve results. The leader, to keep the business successful, must be one who:

–can get others to want to do things,

–can give people goals and a sense of direction,

–can help people see their work as important so that they in turn will want to be part of the overall business operation.

To achieve these ends, some techniques the leader will use are:

–he keeps his people informed and involved,

–he delegates, giving others responsibility,

–he uses recognition to motivate people,

–he gets everyone's ideas before making major decisions,

–he shows appreciation for their efforts (often just saying thank you),

–he watches how he delivers his message (the leader has lots of impact and people are sensitive to him),

–he makes certain his criticism is of employees' methods and not of their motives,

–he criticizes in private, praises in public.

Third, the family in fact negotiated a contract between all members active in the business. The result of the negotiation was to give each one what he most wanted from "XYZ."

Mother agreed that she really wanted to retire, that she really wanted relief from the day-to-day responsibilities, that she really wanted "Al" to be able to buy the business. Mother also agreed that "Al" and "Bob" would never work well together, that there were old resentments between them, and that she was willing to give "Al" an opportunity to bring the company into line with the plan. Her agreement was that she would be allowed to fire "Al" after ninety days if no demonstrable progress had been made. She agreed that, in her mind, acceptable progress could be defined as a gross profit margin of 30 percent. She stepped back, named what she would accept as results, and agreed not to interfere with "Al's" methods.

"Al" agreed that he really wanted to be the owner/leader. He agreed that he would concentrate his efforts at "XYZ" as well as "ABC" if he was allowed to work his way, with his people. He agreed that 30 percent gross profit was a reasonable goal. He agreed he would keep his mother apprised of his actions, but she was not to interfere as long as he reported his decisions to her.

"Bob" agreed he wanted out of the business. He agreed he would handle the money until "Al's" buy-out could be arranged. He also agreed that he would not make management decisions. "Al" agreed he would listen to comments and suggestions from "Bob," but that he was not required to follow them. If his ideas were not adopted, "Bob" agreed, he would not try to install his ideas anyway by giving conflicting direction to the employees.

Because they now had a negotiated contract, the family members were able to discuss issues, not emotional situations or personalities. The business could move forward.

Where Father Had Failed

There are some other lessons in this case for consultants to the family-owned business. In retrospect, Father should have planned for the succession of ownership. Father took it for granted that, because his sons had always been in the business, they would be successful at running it. In reality, Father was a one-man show and never shared any decision-making responsibility with anyone. He did it all and continually fine-tuned the organization without letting anyone know what he was doing or on what basis he was making his decisions. The successor should have been trained to know exactly what it took to make the business run. Instead, because Father appeared to do it so effortlessly, everyone assumed the business could run itself.

There should have been an annual valuation of the company and a price set on the stock. A buy-sell agreement should have been in place with an agreement as to the price the son would pay.

Father had never allowed "Al" to be the leader. When Father died, everyone stepped in to run parts of the company. Each person was critical of the others' performance and no one had full authority over all operations.

There was no plan for maintaining key employees. There was no designation made by Father that "Al" was to be his successor.

The family business needs a plan to either sell out or succeed to another generation. The business owner should discuss and consider his choices and move to position the company to fulfill either goal. If the owner does not strategically plan for the future, the future will be that which is planned by others.

Peculiar Challenges in Family Dealings

On a broader base, it should be clear that there are numerous consulting opportunities in the family business. The family business is almost by definition short of some of the talents, skills, and abilities that it takes to make and keep a business successful. The consultant can fill these gaps on a short-term basis: bring wide experience to the business, share the expertise acquired from work with many clients, and not be a long-term cost commitment to the organization.

In family businesses, there are external factors which can have immediate negative impact. These include government regulation, labor problems, and material scarcity, and they can adversely affect the company while the owner can exercise almost no control over them. One of the challenges for the family business is to remain flexible enough to meet and adapt to the changes brought about by external factors.

The business can never assume that good times will last.

In the family business the consultant has numerous opportunities for service. There is the need for market review and analysis, product planning, employee and human resources review, cost studies, feasibility studies, goal setting, operational review, and updating financial and accounting data.

It is usual, however, that the consultant will not be hired until the business has a major problem. Therefore, to succeed as a consultant to family business, the consultant needs to hone his people skills. One reason why the consultant finds family business difficult is that the money problem that causes the entrepreneur to hire a consultant is usually a manifestation of not only the technical problem the business is experiencing, but also of a people problem—a family relationship problem that the consultant is going to have to address. It is almost universal that under every technical problem there exists a human problem that must be included in the technical solution.

The people problems will involve motivation, trust, recognition, job satisfaction, training, leadership, responsibility, competence, and succession of ownership.

The consultant must guide the business owner to the underlying problem, then help him identify it, recognize its causes, and help him find and implement solutions. Often the identification of the real problem is more difficult than the solution. Often the family-owned business will not ask for help until it is too late. As part of his engagement, the consultant must either find and effect meaningful family relationships or propose a transfer of ownership. The consultant must assume that what is best for the business is best for the family.

Consulting must be temporary. The consultant is not a substitute for the family business owners' own management team. The consultant must aim to work himself out the door, for despite all the benefits and direction the consultant can provide, the ultimate responsibility for the success or failure of the business depends on the family business owner developing a competent management team and solving family relationship problems.

Introduction

Family owned businesses are unique and complex, with family and business issues invariably intertwined. Liebowitz presents the premise that it is often useful to assume that a family member's decision to enter the family business is intended as a positive attempt to resolve long-standing family issues that may not otherwise or easily be resolvable. Numerous case examples are presented to illustrate this theme, and suggestions as well as a point of view for consultation are offered.

Resolving Conflict in the Family Owned Business

1986

By Bernard Liebowitz

Reprinted by permission of **Consultation,** Fall 1986, Vol. 5, No. 3. Copyright ©1986, **Human Sciences Press**; all rights reserved.

The family owned business (FOB) is part of the fabric of the American work ethic. Threaded throughout is the tradition of hard work and self-support. In addition to this heritage, FOBs also share many of the same economic and psychological advantages all entrepreneurial businesses potentially enjoy, including quick responsiveness to the marketplace, lack of bureaucracy, and close employee identification with the company and its products.

Despite the generally appealing picture this may conjure up, FOBs have more often been condemned, blamed, cursed, and ridiculed. They are, for instance, often sources of: (1) employment and financial security for otherwise unemployable offspring and relatives, (2) constant criticism and tension between founder(s) and their relatives in the business, and (3) unsolvable family disputes. Indeed, outsiders often view the FOB as grossly inefficient, and ambitious and talented outsiders avoid employment with a family business.

Given the potential for serious problems in FOBs, it is not surprising that they have become a fertile area for consultants. Unfortunately, from my perspective, most interventions focus on either identifying the family member responsible for the current business crisis or attempting to undo past business wrongs, thereby avoiding the notion that family and business are invariably intertwined and that family emotional issues (not often immediately apparent) must also be resolved. This paper offers some preliminary guidance to the consultant for resolving conflicts in family owned businesses.

Entering the Den

A basic assumption underlying this paper is that the entrepreneurial business, be it family-owned, closely-held, or partnership, is a different breed than the publicly held firm. There are many characteristics held in common, but essential differences.

An *uncommon* interpretation of the attraction FOBs hold for relatives is that forming or entering an already-established FOB is intended as a positive attempt by them to resolve long-standing family emotional issues seen by relatives as not otherwise resolvable, that the surge of subterranean emotions and conflict surrounding these issues is most apparent when succession is being considered and implemented, and that how the succession process as well as the business progresses is one of the best measures of how well family issues are being resolved. This is not to say that other motives for entering the FOB do not exist. However, alongside and prompting these other motives lies the desire of offspring, siblings, in-laws, and parents, in varying combinations, to resolve long-standing family conflicts.

Sometimes the psychological issues and conflicts are fairly conscious. For example, it may be the goal of a parent to give an aimless-appearing son or daughter a last chance, "but this time I won't let my wife (or husband) interfere or baby him/her!" often, the threads of family and business are intertwined in such a way that the family emotional issues are not immediately apparent, e.g., the refusal of a parent to agree to the new marketing plan conceived by the offspring may have been only partially based on its merits. It may have been that the plan was too creative, adding weight to the ever-raging

argument about whether the offspring was ready to become president. Many times the psychological issues are so denied or hidden that the business is allowed to deteriorate, requiring bankers, friends, creditors, stockholders, etc., to intervene.

However, regardless of the degree of awareness involved or of the interwoven character of business and personal issues in any particular FOB, I choose to make the assumption that a family members' motivation to enter a FOB is a positive attempt to resolve a family issue. The business decisions made to ensure its viability become a powerful and dramatic medium for resolution. During the process of succession the FOB becomes the stage for these enactments.

Not all FOBs produce the kind of overt conflict and turmoil that will be detailed here. This does not mean that the thesis is true only for a narrow spectrum of the FOB population. The many that do function successfully both as a business and family are engaged in an ongoing process of resolution well before succession is raised. In fact, the process for them begins at the moment an entrepreneurial business is designated as a FOB by the introduction of relatives. These are the FOBs that are open to external sources of information (e.g., outside boards of directors, consultants, advisors, etc.). They are the ones that involve the entire management team in planning, as opposed to reserving this task solely for the founder. These are the businesses continually learning about themselves.

For these companies conflict is a signal that it is time to make changes in the business and/or the family, and the only question is how to implement them. Problem-laden FOBs may acknowledge the buildup of conflict, but view it as unnecessary, "bad", as evidence of greed or disloyalty"anything but the occasion for planning and change. For these businesses, conflict is to be resolved in the same old way, only more so.

There is another group of FOBs that do not put their emotional upheavals on display, but also do not resolve family issues. They leave the process of resolution to the next generation. Typical of these families is the presence of a founder/father who dies at age eighty while still sitting in the president's chair. A son, usually about sixty or so, finally becomes president while his brother continues as vice-president. These prototypical brothers and their children are the ones who have to confront the family issues that have been contained in cold storage.

A Strategy for Consultants

One implication of attributing positive motivations to family members entering a FOB is that consulting to FOBs entails helping the family work through and resolve long-standing emotional issues as a family. This approach is clearly in contrast to most theorists dealing with the FOB.

Barach (1984) suggests that the "cure" for the paralyzed family business is for individual family members to grow and go their own ways either by separating from the FOB or by heading up different businesses (as the result of diversification) under the auspices of the original firm. However, it is not clear how either approach helps. Family members can "leave," but the problems back at the FOB will still persist. Diversification simply compounds the problems, albeit on a grander scale. In other words, a warring father-offspring will continue to war even while in different businesses (under the same financial auspices) in different cities.

Also, many FOBs cannot afford the luxury of diversification as a solution.

Levinson's (1971) position is that the unique psychodynamics of the founder and the historical family rivalries, which would otherwise not persist, perpetuate family business tension. Conflicts emerging in the FOB are reflections of individual psychopathology and require individual therapy to resolve. A consultant in one case failed in his assignment *ipso facto*, according to Levinson, because of engaging several brothers and their wives in the consulting process rather than supporting a referral to a psychotherapist.

Levinson assumes that individual psychotherapy provides an answer for the FOB. A major criticism of this approach is that therapy becomes an instrument for passing judgment by identifying the one in therapy as the problem. The "problem" is thus seen as "in the individual." Levinson simply overlooks family dynamics entirely, dismisses group dynamics cavalierly, and promotes the consultant to the role of judge.

Danco (1978) takes the position that the success of the FOB requires the planning for the parent relinquishing authority to a heir. Were an emotional problem in succession to occur, it is attributed either to the inability of the parent to hand over control or the incompetence of the heir to assume control. Danco's task as consultant is to make a Solomonic decision about which is which, similar to Levinson's position.

None of the authors cited above consider that the emotional upheaval frequently exhibited by FOBs serves a function. Its occurrence is a negative by-product of individual psychopathology and only rarely, if ever, is an expression of a family system issue.

Neither the solution offered by Barach, the psychodynamic view of Levinson, nor the role of the consultant as perceived by Danco, add to our understanding of the persistence and ubiquity of the FOB.

The particular role the consultant assumes simultaneously reveals and hides certain features of the client situation, be it individual or marital therapy, business consultation, or family business assistance. The criteria for consultant role selection, to the degree the consultant is conscious of them, evolve around what works for him or her. Since the writer is also subject to this bias, the following comments should be considered in that context.

My basic stance is that a family member blaming one or more relatives is an utterly useless exercise. Also futile are attempts to undo the ill effects of the past and to right past wrongs; there is either no end to the amount of retribution sought by the supposedly wronged party, or else a new cast of "wronged" characters will be created.

A new frame of reference has to be introduced, one that is future-oriented and goal-directed and that channels psychological conflicts into viable economic goals. Instead of, "why do you favor one son over the other?", the question becomes, "If you were to favor your other son now, how would things be different?" "What would occur if you and your brother stopped fighting now?" replaces "Why did you start competing so viciously as kids?" Even the apparently most self-destructive behavior ("I may be cutting off my nose to spite my face, but at least my brother will be begging out on the street with a tin cup!") can be dealt with similarly; e.g., "What then would happen with you

not having a nose or a source of income, though feeling satisfied?"

A second fundamental refrain is that everyone in the family, and not only those in the business, are assumed to be involved in the problem. This includes the brother who teaches at the university, the sister married to a physician, and especially the mother who is volunteer-of-the-year at the hospital.

The Players

This section provides some basic principles for consultants seeking to understand and work with the dynamics of family relationships and their impact on FOBs. The vignettes, from actual case experiences, demonstrate the need to "move" beyond the visible business issues when consulting with an FOB.

The Help Seekers

Principle 1: *The person (or persons) in the family who wants to initiate the process of resolution is the one who stands to lose the most if something is not done or a decision is not made, and also to gain the most if something is done. It is crucial that both gain and loss be explored.*

The loss may assume different forms. The person in the family acknowledging the problem might be the founding father afraid of alienating one son if he makes his daughter the president. He can no longer delay making the decision since the bank may not extend the loan necessary for the business's growth. Or, it might be the son who no longer can wait for promises to be fulfilled. He has been offered an attractive position at a large corporation and the offer has a short lifespan. If he stays, his bargaining position with his father might weaken and the chances of resolving their emotional issues might decrease. On the other hand, becoming ensconced in a responsible and lucrative corporate role might shatter any hopes of resolution. Or, we may deal with a daughter not in the business but caught in the conflict between her father and husband (who works in the business) seeking relief by insisting that a consultant be introduced. Otherwise, she might be forced to choose sides, thereby losing a husband or a father. Or it might be the mother wants to stop being referee for the free-for-alls between her husband and daughter. She knows that her husband cannot continue to run the business and that her daughter is better equipped. However, she fears that a retired president would become a depressed husband hanging around her to the point of distraction.

The family member who wants the ostensible problem to be resolved is frequently dissuaded by others and/or becomes frustrated in the process of seeking help. As the family begin to discuss the problem, all too often the underlying and long-standing family issue threatens to emerge. Buried family secrets (e.g., who loved whom the most, living down past sexual escapades, etc.) and myths (e.g., that father really was a tough and shrewd businessman who built the business without help or advice from anyone) begin to flutter as the window is opened. Unspoken resentments are stirred. The veil over incompetence is pulled back. The delicate threads of family and business can appear to unravel as attempts are made to resolve the problem. It is usually at this point where consultants not trained in family dynamics pull back and suggest that one or more individuals seek psychotherapy, or suggest "quick business fixes" that all will accept. Unfortunately, both only delay the inevitable—the need to uncover and deal with the real agendas.

The Founder's Marriage

Principle 2: *The most significant influence on the family problems and their successful resolution is the marriage relationship of founder and spouse.*

Usually there is little or no mention of spouse (most often, mother) when the FOB gets together to discuss their problems. All too often mother, her role, and her marriage to father are part of the hidden agenda, the family secret that is too explosive to reveal. A long-standing fear experienced by family members is that their marriage is too fragile to be questioned. It is felt almost better to continue the family than to resolve it by discussing the marriage and the spouse's role in it. Yet, business decisions and the marriage are undoubtedly intertwined in the fabric of the family business and, often, right on the edge of the tear.

The following vignette illustrates how vivid this process can be and at what price discussion of the marriage relationship is avoided despite its blaring influence on business.

The employees in one FOB would repeatedly complain to the owner's son about the extreme amount of stress they experienced in the office. The employees worked in close physical proximity to one another and to father, mother, and son. Mother would scream at anyone whenever she was upset or felt challenged by someone. As father was reluctant to take issue with mother on any topic that he thought might upset her, they only rarely discussed business. Even this, however, could not prevent their sniping at each other. The son half-heartedly attempted changes in the office in order to reduce stress and inefficient management practices.

The son saw his life-long task in the family as being a mediator between his parents, thereby softening their conflict and acting as a buffer between his parents and staff. He knew they could and would disagree about anything on principle alone. And, he also knew that the business could not bear much longer the burden of their fighting.

He complained that employees were weighing him down with their complaints of stress. They were also constantly asking him to make the simplest of decisions; otherwise, they feared their work would be the occasion for another encounter with mother or for another disagreement between the parents.

Why didn't the son simply tell his mother that her yelling was bad for business, advise father to get mother out of the office, or suggest to both that they both leave and allow him to run the show? The son was afraid that pursuing any of these options would result in the immediate dissolution of their marriage and of the business. Better to suffer the ulcer and related stomach problems.

What allowed the FOB in the next vignette to resolve the ostensible problem, succession, was the mere suggestion to include mother in the consulting efforts.

Tom and Herb were in charge of different departments in a large firm founded by their father. Their older divorced sister was not active in the business, but she and her children were being supported by the parents. The younger son, Tom, was the father's confidante. Herb had joined the family business within the last three years after having earned his MBA and worked at a large company in an unrelated field. Succession had recently been brought up by Herb who had flatly stated that,

unless he were made president, he would leave the business. Tom's reservations about this proposal were that, if Herb were made president, he wanted to be sure that decisions would nevertheless be a joint endeavor.

It was apparent that Tom was father's choice to succeed him. In his opinion Herb's ideas were too "radical," "impractical," and "impulsive." Besides, he wasn't sure that either son wouldn't run the business into the ground. The financial future of his wife, daughter, and himself in retirement might be at risk.

After establishing that Herb's opinions and suggestions warranted at least a hearing, it was suggested that perhaps the next meeting be with the mother present. Although this suggestion was hurriedly set aside, that meeting marked the beginning of a series of steps rapidly taken to resolve the problem of succession, to everyone's satisfaction.

What was there about the suggestion to include mother that put the process into motion? Until Herb had joined the business, there was little family cohesion. The daughter had been a source of worry throughout her life, and mother was constantly in attendance. Meanwhile, Tom and father had been forming a team, while Herb working in the corporate world became an outsider (or, simply remained one by not going into the FOB). Herb's entrance into the business can been seen in retrospect as his attempt not only to bring together the two halves and himself, but to make contact with father in a way he never had before. Herb's attitude was that he knew best what was best for both family and business. In a sense he did, but this put him into direct conflict with father. The split in the family was emphatically denied by father and Tom. Father emphasized how he and his wife had treated their sons equally and without disagreement. The very presence of mother in the consultation would have shattered this myth, might have opened up how in fact the parents had been split, and would have most likely disclosed other issues that the family preferred to conceal. Rapidly resolving the matter of succession had the intended effect. An important byproduct was that father and Herb had to spend more time together to iron out business-related details. They had to draw closer for perhaps the first time in their experience. Herb no longer needed to make shocking statements about ". . . going down the drain unless we do . . ." such and such in the business. As he had the decision-making power he required, the presentation of his ideas became less dramatic, and his father could listen without dismissing them immediately. Another way of stating this is that Herb needed and wanted his father's respect and a sense of family cohesion, but did not know that the way to secure it was by involving mother directly, in contrast to confronting father over every issue big or small.

Parents and Offspring

Principle 3: *Parent-son conflicts often suggest a theme of exiting from under the parent's authority and becoming one's own independent person.*

Very often the first question, whether verbalized or unspoken, asked about a FOB is: how do the parent and son(s) or daughter(s) get along? When the FOB is characterized as inefficient, the analysis often revolves around the parent-offspring conflicts that frequently prevent adequate management, planning, and decision-making. A question that highlights the paradoxical nature of these themes is whether one

can be simultaneously independent and eligible to inherit. Resolving this paradox is the key to resolving the conflicts.

Nick, after being in a large and successful FOB for approximately five years, had begun to disagree with his father rather frequently. Father announced, "My wife and I have never disagreed with each other and that's how I want my son and I to work together in business!" Even seeking a consultant had become a point of contention between them until the father had agreed to have one enter the picture. The content of their recent arguments was not the crucial matter. It was simply the fact they disagreed and, lately, too frequently.

"What would happen if you two could never agree on decision X?" the consultant asked. Father's reply was that they would grow to become antagonists and one or the other would have to leave the business. "And what would happen if you still couldn't agree, but didn't become antagonists and no one left the business?" Father said, "I wouldn't be able to stand the tension!"

As the father continued to pursue what "not being able to stand the tension" meant for him, the son sat with his mouth and eyes wide opened, shocked into rigidity. As he later explained, this had been the first time he could recall ever seeing his father uncertain. The revelation for him was how much he, the son, had adopted a lifestyle of also agreeing with the world to preserve the peace, even in the face of his better judgment. In fact, one reason he had decided to enter the business was to learn how his father could preserve his equanimity, as he himself had enormous trouble controlling a tendency towards being argumentative.

The problem for Nick and his father, as it is in many FOBs, was disagreement over disagreeing. The family theme was that one does not openly disagree with others, especially family. But, how is this rule even possible to follow? Nick, in entering the business to be near his father, was preparing for that time when he could disagree with his father, feel that it was right to do so, and begin to deal with the world differently than father. He had to learn once and for all whether conflict was good, bad, or in between. He learned that "it depends." The involvement of a consultant was necessary to bring out this insight.

Principle 4: *Not retiring leaves open, often painfully, the undiscussable wound of unfilled ambition among offspring.*

In many FOBs the theme of "dying in the saddle" voiced by the founder is prominent: "What would I do with myself if I weren't working?" Indeed, it is a fact that many founders die within a two-year period following retirement, though physical health had never been in question earlier. Retirement is not a necessity, nor a good thing in and of itself.

Jack wanted his father to retire and enjoy the wealth he had acquired. Father insisted otherwise. At age 70 he was a vital man who enjoyed his work, his wife, and his hobbies. What was it, then, that prevented a creative solution to Jack's ambition and father's desire to remain active in the business? What fueled their fighting?

Jack had defined a criterion by which he would know he had escaped father's mantle: a two-fold increase in sales under his sole management. Father's presence in the business meant for Jack that the glory accompanying such a sales increase, or any success for that matter, would never be clearly his. In fact father somehow had managed to turn Jack's past innovations into his, the father's, doings. This had a been a lifelong pattern between the two and a source of intense bitterness. It appeared that mother had supported this pattern out of deference to father, and had ambivalently encouraged her son to do likewise. Jack had entered the family business to settle this issue, and even more dramatically, to do so on father's territory.

Jack agreed that being president wasn't his main concern, but rather being able to call his accomplishments his own was. Father's criterion for claiming or not claiming glory was whether he himself had tried something and succeed, or failed. Confirmation for this was that Jack's success in college had never been claimed by father as his own success. Since father had flunked out of several universities, it wouldn't have been part of father's style to claim glory. Thus, father would not be able to claim victory were Jack to open up an entirely new sales territory after he, father, had tried and failed.

It became clear to Jack what he had to do. A year later he had, in fact, opened up the new territory. Father had not intimated or implied that it was because of his involvement that the territory was being successfully tapped and Jack's insistence on father's retirement had receded in importance. Needless to say, father had begun spending even less time in the office and had invited Jack to take over more of his former responsibilities.

Principle 5: *Parents often avoid honest appraisals of offspring for fear of "hurting them" or causing other problems.*

A very common occurrence when succession is on the agenda is a parent expressing a lack of faith in the ability of his/her offspring and heirs to manage the business. Often the parent is seen as reluctant to give up control. However, just as often, or rather parallel in these instances, is the unwillingness of the offspring to insist upon appraisal of their abilities and a definitive succession plan that corresponds to the evaluations. It's as if the parent should "come through" for them. Many times parents delay their appraisal because they fear hurting one or more of their heirs. An unfortunate consequence is that it may be too late for the heir to obtain employment elsewhere"too late in the sense of being too old to change careers or get a suitable job elsewhere. The results may be threats, lawsuits, appeals to the rest of the family, and loyalty splits in both the family and the business. Throughout their association in the FOB, both father and offspring appear to have been in a silent conspiracy not to allow underlying conflict to emerge and be resolved, even though when they started, each had hoped there would be a resolution that would satisfy everyone.

Frequently founders never had intended to pass the FOB on to their offspring, although making vague promises to the contrary. The offspring's competence may never have been tested; he/she may not have been adequately prepared to move up.

Father, when asked, refused to increase the stock ownership of his son, Bruce, who had been in the FOB for several years. His reason was that Bruce was still a "babe in the woods," unseasoned and inexperienced. When asked to give specific examples of his objections, the father found it very difficult. In fact, he had been spending a good part of the year in Florida, leaving the day-to-day management to his son.

Bruce had left a previous career upon his father's invitation to join him, and had been promised a full partnership and buy-out option when he proved himself. Neither promise was in writing, nor had the meaning of "proving himself" been discussed.

For Bruce at this point, the issue was whether he wanted to continue a pattern of guessing about father's intentions and consequently never being sure of where he stood with father, or whether he wanted to take a proactive stance to satisfy his needs. In opting for the latter, Bruce announced to his father that he had secured a management position at another company and was giving a month's notice, whereupon father offered to increase his salary if he would stay. Bruce maintained his stance and left the FOB.

Bruce's unfinished psychological task in dealing with father has been waiting for him to "come through" for him. The invitation to enter the FOB seemed to be that signal that "this time father would be different." Throughout his life Bruce had experienced father making promises to him and then breaking them. From father's point of view, the promises he had made to Bruce were at the instigation of and under pressure from his wife. Even father's invitation to Bruce to join the business had been extended to appease his wife. It was as if father saw Bruce as mother's son and, to keep peace at home, would accede to her demands on Bruce's behalf, resentfully and half-heartedly. Bruce feared that, were he to pin father down to a yes or no, this pattern of conflict between father and mother might be exposed. He gradually became aware of having tried to hide this pattern throughout his life. His perpetual hope that father would "come through" served to protect him from seeing his parents' unhappy marriage.

As it happened, father had no intention of giving over the business; he had been prepared to sell it all along.

Siblings

Principle 6: *Sibling relationship patterns are likely to continue and even become intensified, in a highly interdependent working relationship.*

Frequently the creation of an FOB occurs when several relatives decide to form a business. Quite often the relatives are two siblings who, in creating the company, attempt to resolve issues in their personal relationships. One type of relationship is seen in the two playing out the roles of rescuer and rescued, of protector and protected, of the overadequate and the underadequate siblings.

Joe and Mike, two brothers, fought as soon as they began their venture. But, then, they expected to fight; they had been doing so ever since they could remember. Their business was still in its formative stages and, though exceedingly successful, could abort because of their conflict. The pattern of their behavior was that Mike would make impulsive, dramatic and often creative moves that committed Joe, the older brother, to a course of action he was never sure was appropriate and that obligated him to rescue Mike. This entailed fulfilling promises made, following up on necessary details, and the like. Their fights occurred after each such pattern of events, and stopped each time Joe threatened to leave the FOB. The most serious and recent episode preceded Joe's telephone call requesting consultation.

What would happen if Joe left the FOB? His dilemma, as it turned out, was twofold. Not only was he concerned about his ability as an entrepreneur, but he also would feel that he had failed to protect his brother, a role in life he had assumed early on. Mike's behavior had been screening Joe's lack of confidence. Mike had been the adventurous and daring son throughout his life, getting into scrapes as a youngster and into trouble as a businessman. Joe tagged along, vicariously reaping the benefits and then rescuing Mike when necessary. During their youth their parents would argue between themselves about Mike, praising Joe for his levelheadedness and holding him up as a model for Mike to emulate. However, they hadn't know what to do with Mike except to pray that Joe would be around to rescue him.

Though aware of this pattern, Joe nevertheless became a partner with his brother. Why? To paraphrase Joe, he was hoping that in business, with money on the line, Mike would at last change and free him from the role of rescuer, that the hard cruel world of business would wake Mike up, and that then he might be free to discover his own capabilities.

What would happen were Joe to assume the initiative and aggressively take a course of action that committed Mike, a tack contrary to their previous pattern? As Joe was prompted to propose the most outlandish business schemes he could think of, Mike objected more and more, toning down Joe's ideas, offering alternative suggestions"in brief, acting the responsible businessman.

It wasn't that Mike lacked a sense of self-restraint or self-criticism. With Joe around he just didn't feel the need to exercise it. As Joe became more daring and creative in his thinking, Mike had to begin putting the brakes on his brother. The younger brother was no fool! If Joe wanted Mike to act responsibly, Joe would have to become more adventurous and depend on his brother to come to the rescue.

A second type of relationship is encountered when two brothers, while forming a business, attempt to clarify their lifelong competitiveness.

Nat, the eldest, had always been Dad's son, and everyone knew that Steve was Mom's. They had competed over toys as kids, over girls and in sports as teenagers, and for grades in college. Retrospectively, one can see that they had gone into business together to settle finally who was top dog. Going into separate businesses would not have done it.

Their current competitiveness, however, prevented their making a crucial decision about an acquisition that potentially could solidify their market position, or, given the economy at the time, bankrupt them.

The following scenario was posed to them. "Assume that you both got along very well in business and were very effective as partners. Your parents found out that this was occurring after all the years of rivalry and competition. How would they feel? What would they think? What would then change for them?"

After the expected jokes ("Dad would have a stroke" and "Mom would serve you your favorite meal one day a week for the rest of her life"), both brothers sadly recounted the many fights and arguments that characterized their parents' marriage. As they continued reliving these memories, they became more heated and argumentative with each other about which parent caused which fight and for what reason.

"And, what if it turned out that their conflictual marriage had no right or wrong on either side, that after recognizing this, they would miraculously stop fighting? What would then change for the two of you?"

This question stopped their arguing! It enabled them perhaps for the first time to experience their competitiveness as an extension of their parents' battle over who was right and who was wrong (about anything, but especially about which son was "better"). Nat and Steve had been acting as if, were they to agree or cooperate, they would be disloyal to that parent whose son they had become. Were their parents to stop fighting (as imagined by the brothers), there would be no reason for the brothers to continue competing as stridently as they had been.

An important aside in this regard is that the wives of the brothers had also become involved in this competitive struggle, thereby complicating the issues.

Principle 7: *A son-in-law is usually the pawn in the struggle between owner and daughter, always needing to prove himself.*

There are many different reasons a son-in-law is invited into a FOB. From the point of view of the owner, these include the preference for hiring an available family member rather than spending the time and money involved in searching for an outsider, the need for the special expertise the son-in-law has and the owner requires, the desire to perpetuate the business through the son-in-law in the absence of a blood relative who could or would take over, and the wish to make room for any family member who would want to enter the business. From the son-in-law's perspective, he may prefer the FOB because it is available, thereby avoiding the problems associated with job-seeking. He may accept an invitation to "save" a floundering FOB. His wife may have prevailed upon him to "keep it in the family." He may see the possibility of satisfying his ambitions earlier than expected. He may simply need employment.

A theme underlying these circumstances is that of giftedness and indebtedness, i.e., as the son-in-law is not blood-related, his being in the FOB is a gift. This theme is present even if the son-in-law is essential to the FOB. Giftedness is the package within which other themes are contained, though hidden: father not having to let go of his daughter, mother not wanting her daughter to move away, parents wanting to protect and provide, etc. In resolving the question of giftedness for himself, the son-in-law becomes a participant in family conflict resolution.

Jack's marriage to Edna was welcomed by her parents. It meant that Edna would be settling down after a career as an artist, which they had been supporting through liberal financing, and begin to raise a family. It was the first time the parents could remember feeling that Edna's rebelliousness was at an end and they could now have the relationship with her that until now had been denied them.

Because he had entered the FOB without a business background, Jack wondered what his future would be like there. His attempts to earn an MBA, to attend seminars, and to learn the business were discouraged by his father-in-law, or at least not encouraged. His suggestions and opinions were tolerated but had little functional impact. His father-in-law's basic attitude was that Jack was Edna's husband, not a potentially valuable partner. Jack's marriage was progressively suffering.

Whenever he talked about leaving the FOB, Edna angrily withdrew. She had become accustomed to the security the business offered.

A critical juncture occurred when Jack insisted that either the present sales force, his area of responsibility, be revamped in terms of personnel and accountability or else he would leave. Many months after winning this battle and proving his plan to be eminently successful, he announced that Edna and he were divorcing. Father needed to resolve the dilemma whether to retain an ex-son-in-law who had shown his value to the company, or fire him at the insistence of his wife and daughter.

"What would happen to your relationship with your wife and daughter were you to retain Jack?" Father related how he had always tried to appease his wife by giving in to her over the years. He was sure that one reason he worked such long hours was to escape an unhappy home life. He had agreed to take Jack into the business in the first place only because of his wife's insistence, not because he needed another employee. But Jack had grown in stature and had become a trusted and well respected vice-president in charge of sales. Were he to retain Jack in the business, his home life would be jeopardized. He would be forced to stand up to his wife in a way he had never attempted before. He did decide to retain Jack and to face the consequences.

What had been seen originally by the father as an opportunity to forge a relationship with his daughter evolved into a decision to stand up to his wife. It was not having made this very decision earlier that had prevented Edna from being the daughter her parents had wanted. She had all along felt ashamed of her father for his weakness and angry at mother for being so overbearing.

The entrance of Jack into the FOB set the stage for family conflict resolution in a way perhaps no other event could have done. If Jack had been given a gift, he returned it in full measure.

The outcome was not as successful for the business in several other similar situations. For one owner whose children were divorcing, the decision to fire the son-in-law and keep the peace at home was based on father deciding he really preferred the status quo, i.e., having a family life that did not intrude on his long-standing extra-marital relationship. The unspoken agreement between father and mother was that it could continue as long as mother got her way otherwise. In another situation the threat by his daughter never to speak to him again prevented the father from acting in the best interests of the FOB and the family. He settled for peace at any price, not understanding.

Summary

Horror stories about conflict in the FOB outweigh reports about successful FOBs. If, in fact, there are more conflict-laden FOBs than otherwise, why do family members choose to enter business together? Surely, easier and less bruising ways exist to earn a living. An underlying theme observed in FOBs that may provide an answer is that forming or entering an FOB is often intended as a positive attempt by the family member to resolve long-standing family issues that may not otherwise or easily be resolvable. These conflicts usually appear in full regalia and drama during the process of succession. The challenge to consultants entering the world of FOBs is to look beyond immediate business issues and accept the role of family dynamics in contributing to current business problems. By referring questions toward future impact, one can effect the emergence and consequent resolution of the real underlying issues.

References

Barach, J. A. (1984, Fall). "Is there a cure for the paralyzed family board?" *Sloan Management Review.* 26 (1), 3-12.

Danco, L. A. (1978). *Beyond Survival.* Cleveland: University Press, Inc.

Levinson, H. (1971). "Conflicts That Plague Family Businesses." *Harvard Business Review*, 49 (2), 90-98.

Chapter 15

Family Business in Society

Business and family as Western institutions have grown together such that family business is the root of society's wealth and innovation. This reality has not always been appreciated by economists and sociologists who have thought they recognized the end of family capitalism, when in fact it remains a potent force in both advanced and developing socioeconomic systems.

Placing family business in historical perspective shows how family firms shape and are shaped by the society in which they are embedded. Indeed, family firms are so much a part and product of their communities, that when new owners with different values take over a family firm, negative impacts are felt in terms of productivity, turnover and profitability.

Introduction

The family is the heart of economic activity, the motivating force of economic activity, the unit of learning economic activity, and the carrier of economic skills. Thus, it is not surprising that in a historical sense, business and the family as Western institutions grew together.

Michael Novak points out the family business is the root of American wealth and invention. Economists, he says, make a tremendous mistake when they use the individual as the unit of analysis. Looking at the family provides a better understanding of American economic life.

Business, Faith and the Family
1983

By Michael Novak

Reprinted by permission of **Loyola Business Forum**, Summer, 1983, Vol. 4, No. 1, pp. 6-8. Copyright ©1983, **Loyola Business Forum**; all rights reserved.

Business and the family grew together. Yesterday's 'new class' was the rise of the bourgeois family. This is the first theme I wish to introduce. Secondly, in order to understand why that happened and what it meant, you have to grasp the idea of the system which made both of those things possible. Specifically I will discuss those ideas in the 'new order' which opened up the path to community and to family life in a way the world had not known before. Finally, I will explain how the family functions with important roles in each of our systems — economic, political and moral.

First then, is the rise of the free family, of yesterday's new class. When I speak of the new class, I am picking up the contemporary argument about the emergence in the United States since WW II of a new class. The argument, to summarize, goes like this. In 1939, 900,000 students were in college, but in 1979, 13 million. In 1939 there wereabout 60,000 professors, in 1979 well over a million professors, laboratory technicians and assistants. This has come to be a substantial class of people. Now the scholars are the experts without whom nothing in the world of business or politics or religion can be done.

My father-in-law, who is a lawyer in Iowa, used to tell me at least twice a year as I was studying history and philosophy, "if you can't do it, teach it." That's a pretty good view of the way America was when he was growing up. People who did things were the movers and the shakers, and the people of ideas were ornaments. That is now reversed. Since WW II, the makers of ideas and symbols are the movers and shakers. Both in politics and in business, people who do things find it exceedingly hard to accomplish very practical things because the world of ideas won't let them.

When I speak of the rise of the new class, I mean the swollen elite. If you define an elite in terms of education, income and status, on all three accounts you must observe the growth. Now 15 percent of the American adult population has at least four years of college. In 1939 the average income of a surgeon or lawyer was $4,500. Only one out of 39 Americans paid an income tax, and the average tax paid was $25. Today a full 20 percent of the population by household earns over $30,000 yearly. What's a significant factor, comparatively speaking, is the large numbers with considerable disposable incomes. In terms of status, in the 1970 census 23 percent of the work force had status as managers or professionals in professions that didn't even exist as professions in 1939. Thus, there has come to be created through this new class, a whole different road to power, influence and wealth.

In most of recorded history there was in Europe and elsewhere, an economy based on land aristocracy. With very little industry to speak of and very little manufacturing, the economy was based on the land. There were few markets and nothing to buy in them. There were few roads. The wealthy, since they had land, raised lots of food. But there being no markets, they had no place to sell it. As a consequence, they raised armies. There was no point in investing in anything because there was nothing to manufacture. You lived from season to season, and off of the profits, built for glory.

By the 18th century a new point of view began emerging, with which to look at the aristocracy, the military and the clergy, other than from the position of subservience. There had begun to emerge a new class of artisans and craftsmen and makers of cheese and wine; persons who were no longer serfs.

With the emergence of the business class, constantly being strengthened as new businesses were added, there came to be a great restlessness for greater liberties. There came to be a hunger for political liberty. Why? Political systems characteristically allowed few liberties; they were tyrannical and they taxed you to death. Business people could predict nothing. So there was a move to seek free cities, republican cities in which the government would be elected. Rule would be based not only on birth and status, but on accomplishment, merit and suffrage — election.

A new class was emerging based on a new form of power and wealth with very new ideas, which came to be codified in the expression, "political economy." More and more citizens wanted to participate in making the decisions that affected their lives. It was at this time with the emergence of private property and its importance to the family, that individuals began to take two names. They began to be individualized or personified, and did not simply have a family name.

With the emergence of what was eventually called capitalism, a youngster was no longer imprisoned by birth. A youngster could become of a different politics, or a different religion, or a different art or craft or business. A youngster could forge an identity for himself or herself. This had never been possible before. Then came the movement of what we now know as individualization.

What I want to call your attention to even more dramatically, is the emergence of the family as the central vehicle of civilization. It was for one's children that people normally worked. The butcher can stand the blood all day and the baker can stand the heat all day, in almost all cases, not for himself, but for his family. If it weren't for his family, he wouldn't do it.

The very notion that there could be property had two implications. One, that the government could not intrude on you. It was a limitation upon government; that's the first meaning of property. That is why there is the saying "to every man, his home is his castle." When you owned your own home, by the rights of England, the King could not intrude without a warrant. You had a space which politics could not cross.

Also, owning property meant that you had a bond on the future. for the first time families had a future about which they needed to take responsibility. John Stuart Mill in his book *Political Economy* wrote in 1864, "We in our generation work far harder than our grandparents or ancestors because they lived for sustenance." People began to live for the future and to work harder in the present so if they themselves couldn't have something, their children would have it. The notion of property had both of these important differences to make; a limitation upon the state and the purchase of the future—both with foundations in the family.

What I mean by democratic capitalism and what the nation has always meant by it, is the system in which the political system plays a very active role. It was the political system that insisted on the Homestead Act, that insisted on the land grant colleges, that built the extension service which eventually provided rural electrification and the Federal

Highway Act. You can't imagine development without a very active political system, but the democratic capitalist idea for a political system is one that doesn't attempt to manage everything. We know what happens when governments manage; they've managed from the beginning of time. What's distinctive about the American idea of democratic capitalism is that government must be active and it must promote general welfare. It must promote manufacturing and industry, otherwise democracy will perish.

If we're all farmers without industry or manufacturing, we'll all have the same religion, the same views and we will form a moral majority which will deprive minorities of their rights in spiritual and intellectual matters. To break that up we must have a diversity of industry and commerce. If you multiply the sources of intellect throughout the country, you have a much richer intellectual, inventive life.

I want to conclude these ideas by pointing out that a capitalist and a democratic society is dependent upon a distinctive notion of community. Of all the communities which it builds and which it needs, the family is the most important.

Second, the most distinctive invention of this new civilization was not the individual, but the corporation—modeled on monastic law. The first transnational corporation was the Benedictines who made and sold wines and cheeses in multiple locations on a worldwide basis. The notion that this should be applied to the economic order was what was so novel. Two insights evolved; the economic task is too complicated for any one person and too protracted for any one generation. You need a forum which brings many people together, and which goes longer than anyone's lifetime. Thus in 1800 corporate law came to be formulated in the United States and there were more corporations here than in all of the world combined. We only had four million people, but we had far more corporations than any other nation.

Also, with the invention of the corporation, a new social instrument evolved, a new personality. Democratic capitalist people do not bring up their children to be rugged individualists. In my own case, we have a son and two daughters. In the case of my youngest daughter, by the time she was seven she had already belonged to more organizations, took part in more activities and went to more different group meetings than both my wife or I could drive her to. We don't bring up our kids to be rugged individualists ... We bring them up to be the most socially skillful people on earth. That degree of social skill is extraordinary. It is one of the fruits of democratic capitalist societies.

I come now to the third point I wanted to conclude on, namely the role of the family in all three systems. First, in the economic system, without the family there is no way of passing on those skills which make for a vital economy. When I was living on Long Island I met a young man who built a pizza parlor near the beach. Since there were already four other pizza parlors near there, I was curious as to how he had the courage to do that. He wasn't worried. His father had nine restaurants. He'd been taking inventory in these restaurants since he was nine years old. By the time he was 14 years old he had been in charge of some of them. He said he already planned to add 200 more square feet in August, and hoped by the time he was 35 years old to have four restaurants. Now my family isn't like that, we don't own businesses, I wouldn't know how to take inventory or go to banks and make

a proposition to them. In his family, those skills are obviously there, and they're going to be passed on from him to his sons and from them to the next generation. That family has an economic strength that's not comparable to that of other families.

Again, when some successful member of a family moves into a new city or area of life, that becomes an access for the entire family. If you have legal problems, there is cousin Joey, the lawyer. Every family member who blazes a trail into a new area becomes a source of family lure for anybody else in the family who is interested. Much more than we realize, the family is the heart of economic activity, the motivating force of economic activity. Much more than scholars notice, the family is the unit of learning of economic activity. It is the carrier of economic skills. Families that have a complex, subtle set of skills to pass on are way ahead of families who don't.

As a recent study of the American Jewish community over the last 100 years points out, the great tradition of owning your own business, which almost always means a family business, has been wide spread in the Jewish community. In Eastern Europe, Jews were not allowed to own land. They couldn't live as farmers or as peasants. What was their punishment there, became their salvation here. They came here almost all knowing a trade — tinkering, tailoring, baking, merchandising of one sort or another. When they came to the American culture, they already had a tremendous set of skills. This is also true of the Greeks, Italians, Armenians — again, families in very large numbers. Such families suffered much less during the depression than other families. Those who worked for the large companies suffered with those companies, as they are doing even today. They never got terribly far ahead because being paid wages, those wages would rise and fall with inflation. That's all they had. Whereas those who owned their own businesses were not only taking wages, but getting a capital accumulation as their businesses grew. It's not generally known, but the surest way to wealth in the United States is starting your own business. People who work for major corporations get large salaries, but those salaries are taxed at wage rate taxes. It's very hard to accumulate a fortune that way.

The root of wealth and invention in the United States is the family business. The passer-on of economic lure is the family. Almost every family in the United States can tell you stories of how when things got bad, so-in-so moved in with a cousin, brother or in-law. The family nourished them. Almost everybody can tell you stories about how their own income misstates their own economic situation. When their roof needed to be shingled, they had a cousin who did it. They have another cousin who's an electrician, another who sells cars. From each of these cousins they get a discount. So just from within the family they increase their annual income by $3,000 or $4,000 per year, just through attaining services from family members. Economists make a tremendous mistake when they approach economic reality as though the individual is the unit of analysis. If you take the family as the unit of analysis, you see a lot more of the reality of American economic life. You can't imagine a vital, growing capitalist system without those families.

Second, in the moral system, if I speak simply from experience about the role of the family, I would say it is above all, a learning of realism. If you don't like the truth, don't get married. Your spouse is going to tell you all those things about yourself that you don't want to hear. A spouse will even insist on naming your illusions, and refusing to be bound by them, will not allow you to live as you think proper, but as the spouse thinks is more realistic, more in touch with reality. The same thing is true with your children.

One reason I say this is because capitalism and democracy are systems for adults. Almost all other systems are systems for adolescents. They're systems of ideals. Socialism is for adolescents; it pictures a beautiful society in which people are equal and cooperative and fair. It is the way every adolescent would like the world to be. I tell my children every day that life is unfair and to get used to it.

I want to conclude on this note; small businesses in the United States, although not generally recognized, played a tremendous role in the great achievements of the last 10 years. We created 17 million new jobs in this country. The largest number of new jobs in one decade in all our history. And 80 percent of those jobs were created by small businesses, which in almost every case means family business.

When I talk about family business, I want to underline one of the things I mean, and that is—part of the capital for running that business is the contribution of each family member. In Washington, a family of six run a restaurant. All six members work at different hours at the counter, buy the food, prepare it, serve it, and clean up. They pay no salaries, they pay no social security tax on each employee which would normally cost a firm $2,000 + for each one. This family firm doesn't have to pay that. They have capitalized on the labor of the family. From that they have bought the restaurant where they are now working. From that they have bought the home where they are now living. From that they have bought the first for the oldest son. All from the labor of six members. This is an extraordinary achievement. It is the way an extraordinary number of businesses in the United States are started. Seven hundred thousand new businesses were started last year, and this is a record. The rate this year is running ahead of last year. A great many of these will fail, it's true. But the strength and inventiveness of where this country will be 20 years from now disproportionately depends upon these small businesses, and therefore disproportionately depends upon the families of the United States and their capacity for imagination, for invention and for work.

Introduction

In this early article, noted sociologist Daniel Bell recognizes the central role of the family in the capitalistic system. Modern society's loosening of the traditional relationship between property and family has led to a decline of "family capitalism." "Private productive property, especially in the U. S., is largely a fiction . . . " Bell writes.

While it is true that the American economy is no longer dominated by a small number of wealthy dynasties, Bell's contention that "the system of family control is finished" is belied by today's economic reality. While family businesses coexist with corporations not controlled by specific families, the renaissance in family business clearly shows Bell's conclusion in error. The article, nonetheless, is quite worthwhile for its analysis and as a product of its era.

The Break-up of Family Capitalism
1957

By Daniel Bell

Reprinted from **Partisan Review**, "Spring 1957, Vol. 24. by permission of the author. Copyright ©1957 by Daniel Bell; all rights reserved.

The story of the rise and fall of social classes in Western Society, as Pirenne and Schumpeter have pointed out, is that of the rise and fall of families. Without understanding that fact, as many American sociologists, accustomed to viewing class position in individualistic terms, have failed to do, one cannot understand the peculiar cohesiveness of dominant economic classes in the past, or the sources of the break-up of power in contemporary society today. A bold statement, perhaps, but one which the following sketch attempts to prove.

Capitalism is not only, as Marx saw it, an economic system with employer-worker relations and classes formed on strictly economic lines, but a social system wherein power has been transmitted through the family, and where the satisfactions of ownership lay, in part, in the family name by which the business enterprise was known. The social organization of the family rested on two institutions: property and the "dynastic" marriage. Property, sanctioned by law and reinforced by the coercive power of the state, meant power; the "dynastic" marriage was a means of conserving, and through inheritance laws of transmitting property and so preserving, as the case might be, the continuity of the family enterprise. Through the fusion of the two institutions, a class system was maintained: people met at the same social level, had similar educations mingled in specific milieux—in short, created a distinctive style of life.

The singular fact is that in the last seventy-five years the old relationship between the two institutions of property and family, which, Malthus maintained, represented the "fundamental laws" of society, has broken down. The specific reasons for this breakdown are too complex to describe here, but the process is clear. In bourgeois society, marriage was a means of keeping sex relations within bounds; in bourgeois marriage, as Denis de Rougemont wittily observed, every woman had a husband and desired a lover; the great Continental novels of the nineteenth century, Tolstoy's *Anna Karenina*, Flaubert's *Madame Bovary*, with their geometry of adultery, pointed up this paradox. The growth of romanticism, the high premium on individual attachment and free choice, the translation of passion into secular and carnal terms — all worked against the system of "dynastic" marriage. The emancipation of women meant, in one sense, the disappearance of one of the stable aspects of bourgeois society. If women could marry freely, crossing class lines if they so desired, then the economic enterprise with which the "dynastic" marriage was intertwined would lose some of its staying power.

But there are also reasons more indigenous to the nature of the economic system for the mode of family capitalism having given way. Some are general: the decline of the extended family or clan narrowed the choice of heirs competent to manage the enterprise; the increasing importance of professional techniques placed a high premium on skill rather than blood relationships. In the United States one can point to even more specific factors. The break-up of family capitalism came, roughly, around the turn of the century, when American industry, having over-extended itself, underwent a succession of crises. At this point, the bankers, with their control of the money and credit market, stepped in and reorganized and took control of many of the country's leading enterprises. The great mergers at the turn of the century, typified by the formation of United States Steel, marked the emergence of "finance capitalism" in this country.

By their intervention, the investment bankers, in effect, tore up the social roots of the capitalist order. By installing professional managers — with no proprietary stakes in the enterprise, therefore unable to pass along their power automatically to their sons, and accountable to outside controllers — the bankers effected a radical separation of property and family. The "young men from the provinces" passing through the classrooms of the Harvard Business School, now had an avenue by which to ascend to high social as well as economic positions. In time, however, the power of the bankers, too, declined as the managers became able, especially in the last twenty years, to detach themselves from financial controls, and win independent power in their enterprises. In some cases they were able to do this because they, the corporate organizers, were strong individuals; even more important was the enforced separation, by the New Deal measures, of investment and banking functions, which limited the investment bankers' control of the money market; but most important of all, perhaps was the fact that the tremendous growth of American corporations enabled them to finance their expansion from their own profits rather than by borrowing on the money market.

The breakdown of family capitalism may explain, in part, the "dynamic" nature of modern American capitalism, for the establishment of independent managerial controls has produced a new impetus and new incentives. Unable to withdraw enormous sums of wealth from their corporations, as, say, Andrew Carnegie did from his steel company, the chief status drives of the managers have been performance and growth. Such aims, combined with the changed tax laws, have stimulated a high and constant degree of reinvestment of profits. Whereas only 30 per cent of corporate profits in 1929 were reinvested, about 70 per cent of corporate profits in the postwar years were plowed back for expansion.

The fact that the new managers have lacked a class position buttressed by tradition has given rise to a need on their part for an ideology to justify their power and prestige. In no other capitalist order, as in the American, has this drive for an ideology been pressed so compulsively. In other orders it was less needed. Private property was always linked, philosophically, to a system of natural rights; thus property itself provided a moral justification. But private productive property, especially in the U. S. is largely a fiction, and rarely does one hear it invoked any longer as the moral source of the corporate executive's power. As we have had in the corporation the classic shift from ownership to managerial control, so, on the symbolic level, we have the shift from "private property" to "enterprise" as the justification of power. And, as with any ideology, the symbol itself sometimes becomes a propelling force, and "performance" for its own sake has become a driving motive of the American corporate head.

Sociologically, the break-up of family capitalism is linked to a series of shifts in power in Western society as a whole. No longer are there America's "Sixty Families" (or even France's "Two Hundred"). Family capitalism meant social and political as well as economic dominance: the leading family used to live in the "house on the hill." It does so no longer. Many middle-sized enterprises are still family owned, with son succeeding father (e. g., breweries), and many towns, like St. Louis and Cincinnati, still reveal the marks of the old dominance by families, but by and large the system of family control is finished. So much so that a classic study of American life like R. S. Lynd's *Middletown in Transition*, with its picture of the "X" family dominating the town, has in less than twenty years become completely outmoded.

Two "silent" revolutions in the relations between power and class position in modern society seem to be in process. One is a change in the *mode of access* to power insofar as inheritance alone is no longer all-determining; the other is a change in the *nature of powerholding* itself insofar as technical skill rather than property, and political position rather than wealth, have become the basis on which power is wielded.

The two "revolutions" proceed simultaneously. The chief consequence, politically, is the break-up of the "ruling class." A ruling class may be defined as a power-holding group which has both an established *community* of interest, and a *continuity* of interest. In effect, there is an "upper class" and a "ruling group." Being a member of the "upper class" (i.e., having differential privileges, and being able to pass those privileges along to one's designees) no longer means that one is a member of the ruling group, for rule is now based on other than the traditional criteria of property; the modern ruling groups are essentially coalitions, and the means of passing on the power they possess, or the institutionalization of any specific modes of access to power (the political route, or military advancement) is not yet fully demarked and established.

Introduction

While the nepotism and paternalism of family firms are sometimes viewed as detrimental to economic development, this paper maintains that such firms are important to the economic growth of low income countries. The family firm is well placed to take risks in developing and unstable economies. Under such circumstances, family firms' development of human resources, access to capital and provision of continuity and security cannot be matched by large publicly-owned or government enterprises.

This article is particularly interesting because it offers a multicultural perspective on the processes contained in family firms.

Family Firms and Economic Development

1968

By Burton Benedict

Reprinted by permission of the author and the **Southwestern Journal of Anthropology**, Vol. 24 (1), Spring 1968. Copyright **©Journal of Anthropological Research**. All rights reserved.

Where the family does play an important part in business it is often a reflection of the economic immaturity of the population, the absence of a tradition of impersonal service in industry and the unreliability of employees who have no kinship ties to the firm. Industrial development cannot be handicapped by inappropriate standards of economic morality (United Nations 1955:20).

Economic planners commonly assume that family firms are detrimental to economic development because they are based on nepotism and paternalism which foster inefficiency. Such a point

of view assumes that impersonal role relationships are necessary for economic development and that the major economic effort should come from the public sector. It maintains that the private sector must be controlled to fit in with this (United Nations 1951).

My investigations have led me to dispute this point of view. This paper contends that the private sector as represented by the family firm is an important growing point in the economics of low income countries. I do not claim that family firms are suitable for every sort of enterprise required by a developing economy but that for commerce, industry, and many types of financial activity they are extremely well-placed to assist economic growth because they combine a number of unique sociological and economic characteristics. This paper examines the sociological characteristics of the family firm. It attempts to isolate a number of variables and treat them diachronically with the development of the firm. The principal data are drawn from two family firms from East Africa, but material from Europe, India, the Lebanon, and Pakistan is also used.

I hypothesize that family firm organization is more important in the early stages of the growth of the firm than in the later stages. Indeed it seems likely that the role relationships in the firm must change qualitatively if the firm is to grow. At what stage the change occurs and how the transition is brought about are important problems for future fieldwork. On the economic side I shall attempt to show that the family firm is extremely well placed to take risks in a developing and perhaps not very stable economy, that is can make investments in the training of personnel which can hardly be matched by large private firms or by public sector agencies, that it is well placed for raising capital, and that it provides continuity and social security which can scarcely be matched by large private or public enterprises.

Sociological Aspects

In Parsonian terminology (1939, 1951) family roles have long been characterized as clustering around the particularistic pole of role relationships. The behavior of individuals playing such roles depends on *who* they are. An individual's father, for example, is set off from all other males by virtue of his particular relationship to that individual. Parsons has also characterized such roles as being functionally diffuse. They are not organized around one or a few specific functions, such as

the relationship between a customer and a shop assistant, but around a host of functions which are usually not very specifically defined. Gluckman (1955:18-19) has called these multiplex in that the social relationship "serves many interests." A further characteristic of such relationships is that they are affectively charged. The incumbents of such roles have strong positive or negative feelings about each other. Finally, such role relationships extend over a considerable span of time.

All these characteristics of particularistic role relationships are important in analyzing the family firm, but I wish at this stage to place emphasis on the last — the time span. It is the development of family role relationships over time which I feel is crucial in understanding the development of the family firm. In other words I do not wish to construct two static models, one of the family firm with its particularistic role relationships and the other of the impersonal business enterprise with its universalistic role relationships, and merely contrast them. This has some heuristic value, but it does not permit us to study process either to perceive how the family firm develops or to learn how it transforms itself from a family to a non-family business.

For this dynamic analysis I shall attempt to sue the concept of transaction as developed by Fredrik Barth (1966). Transactional analysis is based on reciprocity and the ideas of prestation and counter-prestation. In Barth's formulation each actor in a set of role relationships keeps a kind of mental ledger of value gained or lost in his relations with other actors. Each successive action affects that ledger and so affects subsequent choices of behavior. Each actor must make an assessment of whether he will gain or lose by a given action, and this means he must make some estimate of what alter's moves will be. "Many possible courses of action are ruled out because...an actor must expect that value lost will be greater than value gained" (Barth 1966:4), but this still leaves him a choice. The range of choice will depend on the situation. This is a kind of games analysis based on a somewhat Leachian notion (1954) of power as a chief motivating force in human actions. It is also a model of process as it depends on successive actions over time. Barth maintains that this type of analysis enables us to see the ways in which a variety of social forms are generated from a much simpler set of social forms. I think it is possible to start from any set and observe the generation of new forms. What is required is some definition of the status involved in terms of rights and expectations, which, of course, assumes an underlying set of values. It then becomes possible to see, through the observation of transactions between the incumbents of such statuses, the way in which new forms appear. I assume that these are not random (they cannot be because of underlying values and the assumption of gain or loss by a given form of behavior). They become patterned, but this does not mean that they are in a state of equilibrium. It is this feature of transactional analysis which represents an advance over equilibrium theories of social structure associated with Radcliffe-Brown(1952). In transactional analysis attention is focused on the individual actor. Instead of looking at the external sanctions which bring an individual actor back into line if he has transgressed the norms of a particular role, we look at the transaction itself in terms of gains or losses to the interacting actors. Thus attention is focused on forces internalized within the individual, at his range of choices in a given social transaction.

In applying this model to the family firm I shall be particularly concerned with family roles. I shall try to show how business roles are generated from these and how they change as the business develops. I must emphasize that my field data are inadequate, but I hope at least to set up a paradigm which may be applied in the field.

Father-Son Roles and the Generation of Trust and Confidence

In any family firm the relations between father and sons are of crucial importance. If confidence is not built up between them, the firm cannot grow. The son as a child is dependent upon his father for maintenance, instruction, affection, encouragement. He is continually making prestations of trust to the father, and these are reciprocated by counter-prestations of confidence in the son. In the family firm these prestations and counter-prestations are not simply confined to the domestic scene. Many of them take place in the context of the business. Indeed the business and domestic spheres overlap, as business matters are apt to be the major topic of conversation within the family. Very early the son is given such tasks as helping with the merchandise, opening the premises, or cleaning up. As the son grows older the father begins to give him more responsible tasks. At first these may be simple, such as carrying messages. The father here makes a prestation of trust in his son. The son makes a counter-prestation in delivering the message successfully. This permits the father to make greater prestations of trust in the son for carrying out more complex tasks. But the son has alternatives. He may go off to play instead of delivering the message. He has then failed to make a satisfactory counter-prestation to his father, whose trust in him will be diminished.

Even at the message-running level the bonds of trust between father and son can be vital to a business transaction. In one case in East Africa when an important meeting of the shareholders of a large enterprise was to be called, the manager sent his son with a form which each shareholder was required to sign, testifying that he would appear at the meeting. The boy travelled long distances and far into the night to obtain the required signatures. The corporation had a paid secretary, but such service could not be expected of him. There were not the same kinds of ties binding him to the service of the firm as bound the manager's son to his father.

By the time one of the sons of a firm in East Africa, which I shall call firm A, was 12 or 13 he spent 2 or 3 hours a day in his father's business in addition to attending school. He served customers and began to learn how to keep the books. The father made greater and greater prestations of trust in more and more aspects of the business, and the son made more and more counter-prestations. But a new pattern of relationships was also being engendered. The roles were not just those between father and son but between business manager and business associate. The content of the roles began to have more to do with business and less to do with family relationship. But there was always a range of choice for father and son. The father could make choices which would give his son more or less responsibility in the firm. The son could make choices accepting or rejecting the opportunities given him. One firm in East Africa was managed by a man with 7 sons. He failed to train his sons, who made choices outside the family business. The business failed to expand, and the sons dispersed to other areas. Thus it is of major importance for the family firm that there be transactions between

father and sons to generate patterns in the business sphere. If these transactions are successfully carried out, the sons (and often the daughters) have made very large commitments to the family enterprise before they are old enough to make significant alternative choices. A pattern of roles has been generated which can be seen, from the point of view of the firm, as a device for accumulating labor and capital, for the children are not paid salaries.

The Provision of Training

We have already seen how training in the family business is given to sons as they mature. In this way they come to know every aspect of the family business. For successful expansion specialized training is required. An outstanding characteristic of successful family firms is the amount they invest in the education of their members. This again can be regarded as a transaction The father invests a large sum in his son. The counter-prestation by the son not only involves the successful completion of his studies but also his return to the family firm to apply his expertise. Here we can see more clearly the fusion of family and economic obligations in the pattern of transactions. In firm A the father planned to divide his business into five shares. He began by giving 20% to his wife and retaining 80% himself. As each of his three sons attains the age of 21, he will receive 20% *provided he is still working for the family firm.* Thus, each son during his period of training has a potential interest in the firm, which becomes an actuality on his return to it. All money for the education of sons is withdrawn from the firm. The son is obligated to repay the cost of his education from his 20% of the firm's profits when he returns to it. If he does not return, he need not repay the money, but it is both his duty and in his interest to return. Apart from the purely financial aspects there are strong moral obligations to the family built up over many years. As one younger member of a family firm put it, "If I don't go back, my father will feel bad and my brother will say, 'See, he betrayed us.'" This pattern of investment in training is found in firm A. The eldest son was sent first to England and Germany and later to Japan for training. A daughter was trained in bookkeeping and typing, and she performed these duties for the firm until her marriage. The second and third sons were also sent to Japan for training as was the wife of the eldest son who was trained as a cosmetician. (The firm handles a line of cosmetics.) Two other young kinsmen were also sent to Japan for training, but, perhaps because the forces of obligation were not as strong, they failed to return to the business.

The investment in training, especially overseas training, by family firms presents an interesting contrast with similar investments by the governments of developing countries. Most such governments have scholarship schemes for sending promising students overseas, but they experience considerable difficulty in getting them back. This can be explained, at least partially, by transactional analysis.

The student makes prestations to the teacher by his mastery of the material which he is set to learn. The teacher makes counter-prestations by conferring or withholding good grades for the student's performance, not for his personal qualities. It does not alter the basic pattern if we start with the teacher making prestations of material to be learned by the student and the student reciprocating by mastering the material. The student has a range of choice which will generate various transactional patterns with the teacher and vice versa. The lack of a continuing relation over time means that there is a discreteness about the transactions. At the end of the course or the end of the year the relationship ends. There are no further prestations to be made. This contrasts with the transactional patterns between father and son described above. When the student has completed his education, which has been paid for by his father, he still has further counter-prestations to make to the father.

The student who wins a government scholarship does not feel that he has further counter-prestations to make, though governments attempt to make him feel this. But no transactional pattern has been built up between the student and the donor of the scholarship. The student feels he has made the final counter-prestation in the series by winning the scholarship. The verbs used are revealing. From the student's point of view he has "won" or "earned" his scholarship, but government officials speak of having "given" or "granted" such scholarships. If students, having received their training overseas, fail to return home, governments respond by attaching conditions to the scholarship to insure a return. Sometimes these are carrots in the form of a promise of a job; sometimes they are sticks, such as refusing to give a scholarship unless the student guarantees to return or forcing him or his family to pay back the cost of his overseas training if he fails to return. In the cases that I have encountered in Mauritius, the Seychelles, and England, the student does not feel a strong obligation to return. There is not the feeling of letting down people who had trusted him, a feeling which characterized the reactions of the young member of the family firm mentioned above. How could there be? There was no pattern of transactions between these students and *any individual* in their countries in which the scholarship itself was a significant prestation.

This transactional analysis, sketchy as it is, would seem to have some practical applications for developing countries. I do not think it is practical for governments to enter into the kind of transactional pattern with students which will insure their return, but something more personalized would help. More practical might be the encouragement of training through the family, perhaps by some form of subsidy through the family business. Of course, this will not be suitable for all kinds of training, but it is a possibility worth exploring. The discouragement of family enterprise, which is the policy of some governments of developing countries, would seem to operate against providing the country with trained personnel.

The Family Firm and the Structure of Authority

Sending sons and daughters away for training represents a great prestation of trust by the father, for he is investing an important part of his human capital as well as considerable financial resources. It also generates new transactional patterns affecting the structure of authority between a father and his children. The trained sons will bring new ideas into the business and will want a greater say in how it is run. This is a situation which is fraught with potential conflicts.

For daughters these conflicts do not arise. Although daughters accumulate equity in the family firm, they do not accumulate authority. Even the mother in Firm A, though she has a 20% interest, has no formal authority in the firm. Her interest is regarded by other members as an assurance that she will be supported when her husband dies. The most usual pattern for daughters in

family firms is marriage out. In this case they receive their equity in the form of a dowry, but they have no share in the business. Should a daughter's husband be brought into the business, it would be he, not his wife, who would exercise any authority in running the firm. The question of the type of family structure most suited to the development of the family firm is important but falls outside the scope of this article.

In the early stages of the development of the family firm the father holds almost complete authority, both in his role as father and as head of the firm. Indeed, as we have seen, there is no clear distinction between these two roles. The transactional pattern is one in which the father sets the tasks and the sons reciprocate by carrying them out. We have also seen how this pattern generates new patterns as the father entrusts more and more important tasks to the son and the son successfully carries them out. The pattern thus generated in a successful firm moves towards consultation. It also moves toward separation of the roles of father and manager, son and business associate. If the firm is to persist, the father must give more responsibility to the sons. But this is not just a matter of the father relinquishing power; it is also a matter of the son taking it. In firm A, a retail business, the father did not wish to sell radios, but the son by using a matrilateral kinship connection, procured three radios which he sold at a profit. In his transaction with his father he made a choice other than unquestioning obedience. The father also had a choice. He could continue to oppose his son's idea of selling radios, or he could acquiesce. In doing the latter he continued the generation of the new pattern of transactions between them. The son now had more authority in the firm. He wrote letters to obtain franchises. A greater equality, at least in a business context, characterized father-son relations.

Clearly this is a delicate stage in the growth of the family firm. Insistence by the father on an authoritarian role can break up the firm. Desai (1965:5) points to conflicts in the East African family firm when a person occupies a managerial role which is not compatible with his status in the family. There exist several ways of resolving this conflict. One method is to accord deference to the father, by structuring affairs so that he is seen to be the authority. Thus, in firm A it was the father who first went to Europe and Japan to investigate the possibilities of importing radios, at the urging of the son. Publicly he is seen to be the prime mover, even though in fact he may not be. Another way is for the father to take a prominent part in community affairs. This gives him such prestige, which reflects on the whole family, but also removes him from much of the day-to-day running of the business. This course has also been taken in firm A, where the father is the leader of the local Ismaili community. In a second East African firm, which I shall call firm B, we can see a variant of the process. When the father died, the 4 sons decided to remain associated in the family business. The youngest was by far the most enterprising, but family norms require deference to the elder brothers. When decisions are taken, they are taken in consultation with and in the name of the eldest brother, though in fact they are often initiated by the youngest brother. In this firm the youngest brother sent all 3 of the older brothers to Japan before he went himself, again publicly demonstrating their seniority. The second brother is now a member of his country's legislature, again showing the use of this avenue of activity.

These examples show how new transactional patterns are generated. The father in firm A recognizes the worth of his son. The elder brothers in firm B have increasingly turned to their youngest brother in business matters. The systems of prestation and counter-prestation are complex and protracted. Prestations of deference must be accorded to the elders, and these are returned by counter-prestations of confidence. Conflicts occur, and sometimes outside relatives or friends are called in to mediate, but a pattern emerges in which the elders can accept innovation from their juniors provided it is properly presented. It is in the interest of all parties to maintain amicable relations, both for the good of the family and the good of the firm.

Yet another way of resolving the conflict in authority roles is through opening branches of the business. This has occurred in both firms A and B. In firm A the eldest son now operated the branch of the family firm in Nairobi, where he is in complete charge. In firm B the youngest brother manages the firm's company in Dar-es-Salaam. This solution, however, carries a risk of dissolution. It is essential that the family firm members meet, especially when there are important decisions to be made. Both firms have evolved this procedure, but it results in generating a pattern of nearer equality between members. This pattern of development would appear to be very prevalent in family firms.

Similar patterns seem to have operated in the history of one of the best known family firms of Europe. Meyer Amschel Rothschild began to incorporate his children in the family firm when they were very young. The two eldest children, both daughters, were trained as bookkeepers, and the sons by the age of 20 were incorporated into the

business. (Corti 1928:23). Around 1796
Meyer Amschel entered into a deed of
partnership with his two eldest sons
(Corti 1928:24), in which profits and
losses were to be divided among them.
Later the two younger sons were included (Corti 1928:85-87). The parallel
with the system of shares for sons in firm
A is clear. As the Rothschild firm expanded, sons were placed in the capital
of Europe - London, Paris, Vienna, and
later Naples. One of the reasons for
sending Nathan Rothschild, the third
son, to London was that he "felt that his
elder brothers did not give him sufficient scope" (Corti 1928:26). A major
factor in the success of the firm was the
degree of communication which the
brothers maintained. Despite wars and
revolutions they managed to meet to
discuss major business innovations, and
the lines of communication which they
established frequently yielded them
great profits. Though we do not have
sufficient information, it appears that
the same conflicts and the same transactional patterns developed among the
Rothschilds in the late 18th and 19th
centuries as developed in firms A and B
in the 20th.

The Family Firm and Risk Taking

A member of a family firm in describing
another family firm attributed its lack of
success to the fact that there were not
enough sons. What are the advantages
of using family members in the firm?
One advantage is keeping information
about the firm and its operation secret.
Business secrets are family secrets.
This was clearly very important for the
Rothschilds, and their biographer
claims that the abundance of family
members "made it unnecessary for
Meyer Amschel to take strangers into
his business and let them into the
various secret and subtle moves of the
game" (Corti 1928:23). The confidence
built up among family members as well

as their own self-interest insures this. A
second advantage lies in the incentives
that family members have for putting
forth effort. Members of the family can
be expected to do more work and put in
more hours than paid employees.
Again this is built on the transactional
patterns among them. A third advantage rests in the use of liquid resources. The members of the firm, at least
in its early stages, usually live as a joint
family. Firm A's original premises were
both a residence and a place of business. The eldest son with his wife and
small children formed part of a joint
household with his parents, thus reducing expenditure. The consumption
level was kept low. Salaries and profits
were ploughed back for investment and
inventories, and father and son
withdrew only a small percentage of
their total salaries, just enough to take
care of family expenditures. All members of the firm, including woman and
children, performed some duties for the
firm, thus minimizing the expenditure
on hired labor. Besides achieving
economies of scale in family finances,
the family firm is able to generate capital and manpower resources for the
firm. This kind of arrangement could
not be matched by a firm employing
outsiders. It gives the family firm considerable advantages in the use of its
liquid resources. It also commits family
members further and further to the firm
as they invest more and more in it.
Should a son leave firm A, he is entitled
to his back salary; but it can be seen that
this might be crippling to the firm and
acts as a sanction against his leaving.

A fourth advantage of having family
members in the firm lies in the manner
in which they can make the most of new
business opportunities. In the early
stages the father himself takes the risk
on behalf of the firm. Later, after a
pattern of consultation has been

generated between father and sons, they are still able to move quickly to profit by a favorable situation. They are in constant communication. Their relations are built on trust. They are partners in the enterprise. They often have considerable advantages over large impersonal firms which must check with the home office or over public corporations which must consult a bureaucracy and call experts. Firm A, for example, was able to purchase a large consignment of radios when the opportunity arose without having to consult outsiders, by which time the opportunity might have been lost.

Over and over in the history of the House of Rothschild, we see the brothers making a relatively quick decision to take advantage of a change in events. The family firm is well placed to take risks. Of course, they are not always successful, but the flexibility which they exhibit often gives them an advantage over more bureaucratic organizations. I suggest that this is particularly important in conditions of economic and political instability. Again the Rothschilds are a classic case. The Napoleonic period in Europe was certainly one of political and economic instability. But this is also the case in many developing countries. Indeed it is just such conditions which make it so extremely difficult to secure foreign investment. The family firm operates within the country. It is tied to the country by residence as well as by kinship and friendship networks. I think a good case could be made for showing that such firms stimulate the economic growth of such countries not only in commerce but in many branches of manufacturing. The opposition of the governments of developing countries to such firms would seem to be short-sighted. In their examination of family firms in the

Lebanon, Khalaf and Shwayri (1966:68) conclude that "family firms have exerted a positive effect on industrialization." Papanek (1962) makes a similar point for Pakistan. The evidence needs to be collected and analyzed by anthropologists, sociologists, and economists It is a topic of major practical importance.

The Use of Wider Kinship Links

There would seem to be three ways in which kinship connections outside the domestic group can be used to develop the family firm: by obtaining financing, by making useful business connections, and by recruiting new personnel for the firm.

In the early stages of development before the credit-worthiness of the business has been established, it appears very common for financing to be sought through kinship connections. Thus, firm A probably received some of its initial financing from the wife's father. In firm B, which has interests in 15 businesses, the second brother's father-in-law supplied some capital and is a partner in some firms. In firm A the second daughter's husband belonged to an already established family firm, which went into partnership with firm A to open an office in Kampala. A merger is proposed of part of the business of firm A with that of firm B, which is matrilaterally linked to it. This is a further example of the use of kinship to expand and finance a growing business. When firm A began to look for dealers for its expanded line of products, the first two dealers were the father's sister's son and the father's sister's daughter's husband. They were assisted by being given favorable credit terms. They also, at the beginning, dealt exclusively in firm A's products.

As a number of the above examples illustrates, connections advantageous to the growth of the firm are often made through marriage. Nathan Rothschild, at the age of 29, married the daughter of a wealthy Jewish businessman who had emigrated to England from Amsterdam and with whom Nathan had already had business dealings. His wife's dowry was an important financial asset. Shortly afterwards his wife's sister, Judith Cohen, married Moses Montefiore, an extremely prominent and wealthy London businessman who became associated with the Rothschilds in a number of ventures (Corti 1928:111ff.). A large number of other cases of this kind could be cited from other parts of the world (see, for example, Lundberg 1937, chapter 1). The point should be made that these alliances are not mere business deals. The contracting families usually belong to the same social milieu and share common values, including allegiance to the family firm. Such marriages, therefore, serve both personal and business interests analogous to the way that family role relationships in the firm serve both family and business interests.

Kinship or membership in the same community or caste in East Africa can be used to obtain credits in terms of commodities purchased from big wholesale enterprises. Such credits are never fully paid back but are rotated as only part payments are made. Larger amounts of credit can be given to a family than to an individual, for the family can offer more security to an outsider. It should be remembered that all the members of the family share the "joint responsibility" of the debt, as there is no separation between household and business accounting and no separation between the private wealth of the family members and the property of the firm. The reason is that a family firm is considered to be an integral part of the organization of the family.

The fact that kinsmen can be used for financing and for making useful business connections again derives from the nature of the transactional pattern between them. Failure to lend or to repay not only alters a relation between business associates but one between kinsmen. Of course, this kind of dereliction sometimes occurs; but, when it does, pressures through other kinsmen are often brought to bear. Failure to cooperate with kinsmen often leads to a complete rupture of relations. The nature of the system of prestation and counter-prestation built up throughout the years affects such relations. As an example, the dissatisfaction of the founder of firm A with the share of the fish buying business he was getting from his brother led to his breaking away to found a firm of his own. If we trace the history of the relationship of the two brothers we can see some possible reasons for this. The founder of firm A was only 5 years old when his father died. He was much the youngest of his brothers. His older brother did not send him to school. He was not trusted by his older brother, who would not let him into the tobacco factory in which he had an interest. Thus the pattern was not one of a building up of trust and confidence but rather the opposite, and the younger brother broke away when he could.

Sons are vital to the family firm, especially in its early stages. A lack of sons in the first generation after the founder can be crippling and, even in the second generation, can be a serious handicap.

A large family, which to so many people is a cause of worry and anxiety, was in this case [the Rothschilds] a positive blessing as there was abundance of work for everybody....Since the number of available children increased in proportion as the business expanded, it was possible to keep all the confidential positions in the family (Corti 1928:23).

Where this abundance is lacking, attempts must be made to find other kinsmen to enter the firm. We have seen that the father in firm A sent two young kinsmen to Japan to train with his sons though they did not remain in the business on their return. The incorporation of sons-in-law is a common solution to this problem.

Firm B is now faced with this problem. Although 3 of the 4 brothers have sons, only the eldest son of the eldest brother is old enough to take an active part in the business. Yet with 15 companies firm B has a desperate need of personnel. Some have been obtained through affinal links: the third brother's wife's sister's husband is an important businessman; his sister's husband and the husband's brother both take an active part in the business, but clearly there are not enough kinsmen to run the enterprise.

The Incorporation of Outsiders

If a family firm is to grow, non-family members must be brought into it. There are a number of reasons for this. In the first place, sheer size means that there will not be enough family members to perform all the necessary tasks. As the firm spreads geographically, this problem becomes more acute. Secondly, the need for expertise and specialization of roles increases as the firm grows. The family cannot provide enough experts (though it can provide some as we have seen in firm A), and outside technicians or other specialists must be employed. Thirdly, the need for the financing of expansion involves the firm in extra-familial credit relationships with banks and financing companies.

These creditors, in a desire to protect their investments, will insist on certain patterns of business management and procedure which bring in outsiders. Fourthly, the firm becomes involved with many other firms as suppliers and customers; business arrangements will be entered into with such firms and may lead to a more impersonal organization of the family firm itself. Fifthly, as the firm becomes more successful, a number of family members may wish to pursue other careers in politics, the professions, or other businesses and so are lost to the firm. Sixthly, over the course of generations the transactional patterns between family members alter. Cousins are not as close as brothers, and even brothers operating in widely separated areas are less close than they were in the parental household. The original joint family breaks up, and new families evolve, bringing different sets of values and different transactional patterns.

The first non-family employee in firm A, apart from servants, office boys, and casual laborers, was an accountant whose principal job it was to deal with income tax returns. Here is a case in which expertise was essential but in which it would have been impractical and indeed wasteful to train a family member. The second outside employee was a salesman, necessary because the volume of business could not be handled by family members. The third non-family employee was hired to collect payments from customers who had made purchases on credit. Again, this is a time-consuming occupation which would have cut down business volume if a family member performed it. The fourth employee was a travelling salesman hired to increase business volume over an area greater than that which could be covered by family firm members. The fifth employee was a manager for one of the firm's stores. By this time the firm had two stores in the town in which it had started and was establishing a branch in Nairobi under the management of the eldest son. There were not enough family members to manage all these enterprises, as two sons were still being trained abroad. The sixth employee was a repairman, a technical expert needed to service the merchandise that the firm was selling. By 1966 there were 20 non-family employees in firm A, excluding servants, office boys, and casual laborers.

As the size of the firm grows, administrative tasks increase, and the father and his sons find themselves spending more time at these duties. A complaint the sons of firm A sometimes make about their father is that he is too willing to do the menial tasks of the firm — to rush forward to serve a customer, for instance. This, they maintain, is not an economical use of his time.

The introduction of non-family employees into the family firm alters the pattern of role relationships. Desai (1965:3) asserts that the introduction of an extra-familial partner or manager may give rise to conflict. He maintains that when a family member wishes to secede from the firm, he may bring in outside management to start the process of fission. I lack data on the effect of the introduction of outside employees, but it seems certain that a more impersonal transactional pattern develops between such employees and family firm members. It is also likely that the relations between family members themselves will alter, if it is borne in mind that outsiders are brought in with the expansion and geographical dispersion of the business.

Firm B represents a further stage of development than Firm A. It is a generation older, a good deal bigger, covers a greater diversity of products and services, and is more dispersed geographically than firm A. In the first place, we note that only 2 of the 15 companies are 100% owned by the 4 brothers. Five others are jointly owned with kinsmen; 2 are owned with kinsmen and non-kinsmen who are Ismailis; 1 by kinsmen, non-kinsmen Ismailis, and a foreign (Japanese) company; 4 others with non-kinsmen Ismailis; and 1 with non-Ismailis. This is a clear indication of the degree to which non-kin elements have entered. Moreover, there are indications that family loyalties do not take precedence over business considerations. When the younger brother moved to Dar-es-Salaam, he sold the majority interest in company number 8, which he had been managing, to 2 local Ismailis, only 1 of whom was a kinsman. Firm B has also shown willingness to acquire interests in firms in which there were no kinsmen. Many of its enterprises have been financed by local banks, and recently there have been attempts to raise capital overseas. Companies granting franchises, especially the Japanese, have insisted on certain criteria of performance. Partnerships with other companies have introduced standards of procedure which are not family oriented. These and similar considerations tend to alter transactional patterns. Transactions center about business performance and not family obligations. The fact that the 4 brothers are widely dispersed and pursue different careers also alters transactional patterns in the direction of business oriented transactions.

The incorporation of outsiders clearly benefits the economy as a whole. It provides additional employment and training which can generate new enterprises. It also shows how, as the firm develops, strictly business considerations begin to take precedence over family obligations. I do not possess sufficient data to analyze exactly what occurs during the phase of expansion; but it seems clear that if the firm is to grow and diversify it must introduce outsiders, and if it is to retain good outsiders they must be given responsibility and perhaps an interest in the firm. Some of the younger members of both firms A and B propose giving shares to capable outsiders. The recognition of this principle is well established in large American firms where stock incentive plans are the order of the day. If, in this phase of its growth, a family firm fails to bring in competent outsiders or insists on filling vacancies in the firm with relatives no matter what their competence, it seems likely that its expansion will be inhibited or even reversed. It is in this situation that nepotism and paternalism can operate against business success. The obligation to care for family members remains. If the firm grows enough and if family members are properly trained, this can operate to the advantage of the firm or at least by a neutral factor. I once discussed the matter with the manager of a very large London firm (a daughter's daughter's husband of the founder). He saw the firm functioning as an enormous balance wheel. He maintained that if he did not hang too many "nepots" (his word) at one place on the wheel it would continue to turn. Balance them around the wheel, and its rate of turning will not decrease. It may even accelerate. But if you put all the nepots in one place, e.g., in the head office, the wheel may grind to a halt.

Where family members are no longer active in the business but remain large shareholders, the effects of unprofitable nepotism may be reduced, for the non-active owners are interested in profits, not job opportunities. On the other hand such large shareholders can hold back the development of the business through lack of knowledge or interest in it and/or reluctance to interfere.

The Family Firm and the Minority Group Factor

The family members of firms A and B all belong to the Ismaili sect. The Rothschilds are Jews. How important is minority group status for the development of the family firm? My data does not permit me to give an unequivocal answer to this question. The family firms in Lebanon described by Khalaf and Shwayri (1966) do not appear to belong to any particular minority group —except that nearly every group in Lebanon could be called a minority. Family firms as they developed in the Untied States and Britain seem to come from many ethnic, religious, and national backgrounds. In Nigeria family firms are found among the Yoruba, one of the dominant categories of the population. But a difficulty arises in deciding what we mean by a minority in this context. Are we to follow Weber and define the minority as the group with the protestant ethic? Geertz seems to incline towards this view when he defines the businessmen of Modjokuto as a "socially well-demarcated entrepreneurial group" "set apart both by their social origins and their religious intensity" (1963:76,74), but I feel this involves us in a chicken-egg argument. The transactional patterns which are generated by business activities produce entrepreneurial values. We run the danger of attributing to every successful group of businessmen the elements of the protestant ethic and to find them lacking among the non-entrepreneurs.

There are certainly economic advantages in belonging to the Ismaili community (see Morris 1958). Ismailis have a number of useful organizations: a series of financial institutions which lend money to members, an advisory service which investigates business prospects for new ventures in which individual Ismailis are interested, various sorts of cooperatives, an excellent educational system, and a scheme which will enable every Ismaili in East Africa to own his own home. Of course, these projects must be financed, and Ismailis make large contributions to the community. Entering into business with another Ismaili involves less risk than dealings with a stranger because there are community sanctions. If an Ismaili businessman is going bankrupt, his Ismaili creditors meet and make some arrangement to bail him out and, of course, retrieve their own investments. If he goes to court and is declared bankrupt, nobody wins, because the court is apt to rule that he pay back his creditors as some very low figure per week. If he should go to court, he will be unlikely to be able to start in business again, as he will have lost the good will of the Ismaili community and will be unable to get financing.

Another factor which may strengthen the community sense of a minority is prejudice and discrimination directed against them. Corti (1928:23) maintains that this was an important factor in the case of the Rothschilds. As they were unable to have transactions with non-Jews, they mobilized support, at least in the early stages, among other Jewish businessmen. Yet this seems to require modification. Nathan Rothschild in London and James Rothschild in Paris, capitals in which there was relatively less anti-semitism, seemed to have a much easier time and become more quickly successful than did the eldest brother, Amschel Meyer Rothschild, in Frankfort, and the second brother, Solomon, in Vienna,

where Jews suffered restrictions as to residence and type of business in which they could engage. In Pakistan, which has experienced an extremely high rate of industrial growth, much of it through family firms, it is the trading experience of such firms rather than their minority status which appears to be crucial (Papanek 1962: 53,55). "The more significant of them (Memon, Chinioti) are Sunnis, the majority division among Muslims, and are distinguished primarily by geographic origin" (Papanek 1962:54). Kasdan's (1965) study of entrepreneurship among the Basques would seem to indicate that family structure and the transactional patterns generated among family members are more crucial variables than the minority factor.

My own guess would be that the minority factor is not crucial for the successful development of the family firm, though it may be a factor inducing some members of a population to enter certain types of business because other avenues of upward social mobility are closed to them. Once the business is started, however, it is the generation of roles within it which is crucial and can lead to its growth.

Summary

In this paper I have tried to indicate the importance of family firms for economic development particularly in economically underdeveloped countries. The use of family roles in a business context can generate maximum use of liquid resources and, where patterns of trust and confidence are built up, can provide efficient training for firm members and encourage the firm to embark on enterprise involving considerable risk with a good chance of success. These factors should make the governments of developing countries pause to consider whether it might not be good policy to encourage such firms. Because they are based on the family and thoroughly embedded in the culture of the country, they provide a form of organization which, with relative ease, can be activated for development.

Family firms appear to face two major crises in the course of their development. The first arises when the sons reach maturity and want to have more influence in the management of the firm. The second makes its appearance when the firm has grown to such an extent that outsiders must be incorporated. If these two crises are not met by an alteration in the pattern of relationships between firm members, the firm will be unlikely to expand and may even dissolve.

A great deal more work needs to be done on family firms. We have no intensive studies of the sociological characteristics of the family firm and changing patterns among members as the firm develops. We need to know what types of family structure are best suited for the development of family firms and what types of enterprises family firms can best engage in. A much closer examination of the factors making for success or failure of the family firm is required. This necessitates both historical analysis of family firms in a wide variety of societies and intensive field work on family firms in developing countries.

Bibliography

Barth, F. 1966 *Models of Social Organization*. Royal Anthropological Institute Occasional Paper no. 23.

Corti, E. C. 1928 *The Rise of the House of Rothschild*. New York: Grosset and Dunlap.

Desai, R. H. 1965 "The Family and Business Enterprise among the Asians in East Africa," in *East African Institute of Social Research Conference Papers,* January, 1965, Section C - Sociology and Anthropology, pp.1-6.

Geertz, C. 1964 *Peddlers and Princes*. Chicago: University of Chicago Press.

Gluckman, M. 1955 *The Judicial Process among the Barotse*. Manchester: Manchester University Press.

Kasdan, L. 1965 Family Structure, Migration and the Entrepreneur. *Comparative Studies in Society and History* 7:345-357.

Khalaf, S., and E. Shwayri 1966 Family Firms and Industrial Development: the Lebanese Case. *Economic Development and Cultural Change* 15:59-69.

Leach, E. R. 1954 *Political Systems of Highland Burma: A Study of Kachin Social Structure*. London: Bell

Lundberg, F. 1937 *America's 60 Families*. New York: Vanguard Press.

Morris. H. S. 1958 The Divine Kingship of the Aga Khan: a Study of Theocracy in East Africa. *Southwestern Journal of Anthropology* 14: 454-472.

Papanek, G. F. 1962 The Development of Entrepreneurship. *American Economic Review,* Papers and Proceedings, vol. 52, no. 2 (May, 1962), pp. 46-58.

Parsons, T. 1939 The Professions and Social Structure. *Social Forces* 17:457-467. Reprinted in *Essays in Sociological Theory, Pure and Applied*, pp. 185-199. Glencoe, Ill.: The Free Press, 1949.

1951 *The Social System*. Glencoe, Ill.: The Free Press.

Radcliffe-Brown, A. R. 1952 *Structure and Function in Primitive Society*. London: Cohen and West.

United Nations 1951 *Measures for the Economic Development of Under-Developed Countries.* New York: United Nations Department of Economic Affairs.

1955 *Processes and Problems of Industrialization in Underdeveloped Countries.* New York: United Nations Department of Social and Economic Affairs. The London School of Economic and Political Science London, England.

Introduction

How do dynastic families adapt to social and economic forces restricting attempts to transmit family wealth from one generation to the next?

A Historical Overview of Family Firms in the United States

1988

By Peter Dobkin Hall

Reprinted from **Family Business Review,** Spring 1988, Vol. 1, No. 1, pp. 51-68. San Francisco: Jossey-Bass, 1988. Used with permission of the publisher. All rights reserved.

Writing in the 1850s, the physician and novelist Oliver Wendell Holmes summed up the problems faced by Americans who hoped to pass their firms and fortunes intact to their children and grandchildren: "It is in the nature of large fortunes do diminish rapidly, when subdivided and distributed. A million is the unit of wealth, now and here in America. It splits into four handsome properties; each of these into four good inheritances; these, again, into scanty competencies for four ancient maidens, — with whom it is best that the family should die out, unless it can begin again as its great-grandfather did. Now a million is a kind of golden cheese, which represents in a compendious form the summer's growth of a fat meadow of craft or commerce; and as this kind of meadow rarely bears more than one crop, it is pretty certain that sons and grandsons will not get another golden cheese out of it, whether they

milk the same cows or turn in new ones. In other words, the millioncracy, considered in a large way, is not at all an affair of persons and families, but a perpetual fact of money with a variable human element" (Holmes, 1961 [1860], pp. 15-16).

Holmes knew what he was talking about, for he was heir to two venerable family dynasties. His mother's family, the Wendells, of Portsmouth, New Hampshire, had reaped the "fat meadow of craft and commerce" of the eighteenth-century West Indies trade. His father's family belonged to a New England Brahmin caste of clergymen and scholars.

Combining these two dynastic strands in a secular and industrial age, Holmes practiced medicine, taught at Harvard, and wrote for his own amusement. As a healer, he ministered to the bodies and minds of Boston's elite, who were struggling to run, pass on, and inherit family firms and fortunes. He distilled their experiences and distinctive outlook into popular poems, novels, and essays that, in a significant sense, gave voice to the critical problems faced by nineteenth-century Boston merchant families. Though pre-eminently concerned with Boston, which Holmes dubbed the "hub of the solar system" in one of his essays, Holmes's conception of the predicament faced by family dynasties in a democratic and capitalist society held true for the United States as a whole.

This paper will give a historically informed, multidisciplinary account of the obstacles to dynastic success in the United States and discuss some of the special means that families have used to surmount them. The following topics will be considered: the impact of the law of inheritance on family property, including its role in dividing and consolidating family interests; the impact of economic and technological processes on ties between families and firms; ideological and political obstacles to dynastic formation; the resolution of the conflict between dynasty and dominant democratic and meritocratic values; and the significance of the family firm and the dynastic process in American social and economic life. Although this paper deals with the past, the purpose is not historical. Rather, it is to provide a cultural framework that helps us to understand some of the problems that family business managers, advisers, consultants, and therapists face today.

The Law of Inheritance

When Alexis de Tocqueville visited the United States in the late 1820s, he wanted not only to observe how the world's first modern democracy worked but also to discover how it had become a democracy in the first place. As a French aristocrat, he was exquisitely sensitive to dynastic issues, which for centuries had shaped the

political and social life of Europe but which appeared to be entirely absent from the New World. Not only were Americans able to do without a titular aristocracy, they also lacked the sentimental and legal ties that bound European families of all classes to land, crafts, and occupations.

Tocqueville could easily understand how the patchwork character of early settlement, the heterogeneity of the colonists, and the privations of life on the frontier had prevented the establishment of feudalism and its apparatus of family succession. More puzzling was the failure of dynasty to establish itself—even in an informal way, based on wealth or political alliances—once the colonies had advanced beyond the stage of pioneering.

Tocqueville came to view the law of inheritance as the most important single factor shaping American life and character (1945 [1835], I, pp. 50-51): "When the legislator has once regulated the law of inheritance, he may rest from his labor ... When framed in a particular manner, this law unites, draws together, and vests property and power in a few hands; it causes an aristocracy, so to speak, to spring out of the ground. If formed on opposite principles, its action is still more rapid; it divides, distributes, and disperses both property and power. Alarmed by the rapidity of its progress, those who despair of arresting its motion endeavor at least to obstruct it by difficulties and impediments; they vainly seek to counteract its effect by contrary efforts; but it shatters and reduces to powder every obstacle, until we can no longer see anything but a moving and impalpable cloud of dust, which signals the coming of democracy." The division of estates broke up family holdings, transforming land from patrimony to commodity and family from corporate group to collections of autonomous individuals. Individualism and the ability to buy and sell property freely created the basis for the democratic state and a capitalist economy.

Americans were curiously ambivalent about the inheritance of property. As responsible citizens, virtually all Americans agreed that accumulation of vast fortunes was inimical to democracy, and for that reason they supported the passage of laws favoring the division of estates. However, as individuals, they continuously sought ways of passing their farms, firms, and fortunes on to the next generation intact. They devised a variety of adaptive strategies to counteract the erosion of family resources by the system of partible inheritance (Farber, 1972; Hall, 1982).

In the eighteenth century, kin-marriage was a basic means of preserving land, labor, skill, and capital from the inheritance system. Kin-marriage circumvented the partition of estates with elegant simplicity. Visualize a three-generation family: generation one consists of two grandparents, generation two of their four children and generation three of their eight grandchildren. In the normal process of estate partition, generation one's estate would be divided eight ways by the time it was distributed to generation three. However, if the grandchildren were encouraged to marry one another rather than nonfamily members, their one-eighth shares in their grandparental estates would be recombined. The number of divisions of the grandparent's estate would be reduced by half from eight to four.

Another method, sibling exchange, worked even more efficiently. It involved encouraging siblings in one family to marry siblings in another family. Imagine two business partners, each with four children. If each child married outside his or her family, the estates of the partners would be divided eight ways on their deaths. But, if the eight children of the partners married one another, the number of divisions would be reduced to four, and assuming that each couple produced two children, it would only increase to eight in the next generation. Sibling exchange had the particular virtue of both consolidating existing wealth and combining resources that had hitherto been separate.

Cousin-marriage, sibling exchange, the marriage of widows to their husband's brother, and delaying or preventing marriage were among the estate-preserving strategies in common use throughout the colonies by the early 1700s (Farber, 1972; Hall, 1982). The strategy used depended on the needs of the group using it. Farmers and artisans, whose primary interest was preserving land, labor, and skill, encouraged alliances between related male lines: Sons tended to marry the daughters of the father's brothers. Merchants, whose primary interest was increasing capital and extending commercial contacts, favored marriages linking previously unrelated males, such as sibling exchanges between the children of partners, and encouraged sons to marry the daughters of their mother's sisters, which tied the unrelated maternal uncle into the family. Having a widow marry her late husband's brother kept her dower right (one-third share) of his estate as well as the shares of his children within control of the paternal line. Preventing marriage, especially of daughters, assured that their share in their parents' estates would be distributed among their male siblings. This practice had much to do with the large number of unmarried women among elite New England families in the nineteenth century.

Dynasty and Democracy

The use of marriage for dynastic purposes was ultimately limited in its effectiveness. Kin-marriage slowed, but did not stop, the partible division of estates. As holdings became smaller, more effective means of keeping estates intact had to be devised. In any event, children in the post-Revolutionary era were less willing to allow their parents to dictate their marital choices. Under these circumstances, farmers and artisans increasingly left the "family place" or the craft to their younger sons as a trade-off for caring for parents in their old age (Waters, 1978). In more affluent families, older children were provided with educations, with apprenticeships in other crafts, or with farms in other places. Poorer families simply sent them off to seek their fortunes, a practice that had much to do with the growth of the free labor force in the first decades of the nineteenth century.

While farmers and artisans had little to lose by sending their children out to seek their fortunes, those who already possessed fortunes could not afford to take such risks. Each child remained a potential legatee. And, even if a child was disinherited, he or she could challenge a parental will with a fair hope of success. For purely instrumental reasons, elite families had an interest in reigning [sic] in their children. Beyond this, the social styles of the Enlightenment and the Romantic period promoted the sentimentalization of relations between parents and children. This sentimentalization produced emotional bonds that made it difficult for parents to allow their children to go their own way, and it sapped the desire

of children to do so. Finally, because wealthy Americans modeled themselves on their aristocratic European counterparts, they began to view themselves as family founders, as dynasts. The 1780 declaration of Massachusetts nouveau riche John Adams typified this sensibility (Smith, 1962, pp. 468-469): "I must study war, that my sons may have liberty to study mathematics and philosophy. My sons ought to study mathematics and philosophy, geography, natural history and naval architecture, navigation, commerce, and agriculture, in order to give their children a right to study painting, poetry, music, architecture, statuary, tapestry, and porcelain."

The urban merchants of the New Republic, rather than leaving their children to fate, turned to formal legal mechanisms to preserve their estates and to keep their children in dynastic orbits. Their wealth enabled them to be more sophisticated about the law and its uses. They rediscovered English law and introduced to America doctrines and practices that their forebears had left behind in the Old World or that had failed to develop when first brought here. One of the most important of these involved equity jurisprudence (Scott, 1939). In equity jurisprudence, it was possible for one person to hold legal title to a piece of property, while another was entitled to receive the benefits of it. This division of ownership and use was the basis for *trusts*. Trusts made it possible to keep capital intact for generations in the legal possession of a trustee; the earnings of that capital could be partibly divided among descendants, the holders of equitable title. Trusts, which could be set up between living persons, under wills, or as perpetual charitable endowments, opened new vistas for the founders of trading and industrial fortunes.

The Massachusetts merchants of the post-Revolutionary era spearheaded the legal innovations that would eventually be adopted everywhere, laying the foundation for dynasties of national significance (Hall, 1973; Marcus, 1983). The changes wrought by these men in the law of inheritance were not, notwithstanding John Adams's assertion, intended to create a European-style aristocracy. They appear to have understood that, in the American setting, the survival of family dynasties depended on continuing commercial, industrial, and financial eminence. This is evident in some of their key contributions to the law of trusts, particularly the introduction of the rule against perpetuities and the prudent man rule.

The rule against perpetuities had its roots in Tudor England. The rising middle class of the sixteenth century had feared that the use of trusts by the aristocracy and the monasteries would ultimately make it impossible to buy or sell property, thus strangling commerce. The English courts began to hand down decisions limiting the length of time that a trust could run before its principal ultimately "vested" in an individual. The basic rule, as handed down in 1682 in the Duke of Norfolk's Case, stated that the limitation on the duration of a trust was "a life or lives in being" at the time the trust took effect, plus twenty-one years, plus nine months (Newhall, 1942). This seemed to strike a reasonable balance between the desire of families to keep capital intact for two generations and the public good of freely circulating property. By the nineteenth century, however, elites on both sides of the Atlantic had become more dynastically minded. The phrase *life* or *lives in being*, which comprised the most flexible element in the formula, came to be stretched to the point

of absurdity: One will specifying the group to be all the lineal descendants of Queen Victoria living at the time the will was made was upheld by the British courts. This version of the rule was accepted in Massachusetts.

Although the rule against perpetuities strengthened trusts, it still conceded the ultimate necessity of freeing family property from testamentary restrictions. To this extent, it acknowledged the mandates of a triumphant capitalism as well as the extent to which all dynasties both sprang from and returned to the world of market relations.

The prudent man rule, which was enunciated by the Massachusetts courts in 1830, dealt with the investment of trust capital. Much as they wished their capital to be safe, the Massachusetts merchants also wanted it to be available for investment in the region's economic growth. When a group of beneficiaries sued a trustee for investing in the shares of manufacturing corporations, which the beneficiaries regarded as unsafe securities, the court, after reviewing all the possible ways in which money could be invested, declared that there was no perfectly safe investment vehicle. All that could be required of a trustee was that he be guided by the practice of "men of prudence" in managing their own affairs "in regard to the permanent disposition of their funds" (*Pickering's Reports*, 1830, p. 461). This decision had a twofold effect. First, it protected trustees from legal action by beneficiaries, thereby enabling them to pursue their dynastic purposes more effectively. Second, it made trust capital available for investment in the industrial economy. This enabled Massachusetts to lead the nation in industrial growth and to its role as an early center of investment banking.

A third feature of the Massachusetts trust doctrine was the development of charitable endowments. While such endowments dated from Puritan times, their establishment became tied in the early nineteenth century to the mercantile effort to conserve and consolidate family capital. Charitable endowments, whether held by organizations like Harvard College or free-standing like the Lowell Institute, served not only the long-term goal of preventing the division of estates but also the short-term goal of providing for the needs of children and grandchildren. The creation of charitable endowments was the most complex of the dynastic strategies used by Massachusetts families.

The basic business organization used by these families was the partnership firm, in which all members were related by blood or marriage. Before the Revolution, sons generally entered their father's firms and daughters married partners, reducing the erosion of operating capital caused by death and subsequent divisions of estates. Business practice began to change after independence. Freed from the restrictions of British mercantilism, merchants who once traded only with the West Indies and England now expanded to India, China, and Latin America. Such large scale trade was risky. It was also expensive, often requiring nonfamily capital. For these reasons, firms not only had to begin to admit unrelated partners, who brought their capital with them, but competence became more important than blood.

Responding to these changes in economic life, the merchants began to encourage vocational diversity. Those with an aptitude for business became businessmen; those without such an aptitude were encouraged to enter the law, medicine, or some other respectable occupation. Endowment trusts played a key role in this process. Endowing colleges and professional schools made alternatives to business careers more attractive by raising the status of the professions and by creating positions of influence for family members (Hall, 1973; Story, 1981). Endowments themselves constituted important pools of investment capital that were not only managed by family members of governing boards but also used in underwriting family businesses (White, 1955; Hall, 1973). Family involvement in the governance of endowed charitable corporations, usually via business members, perpetuated intergenerational control and authority and created arenas in which the competence of relatives and in-laws could be assessed.

In devising special means to overcome the centrifugal and individuating dynamic of the inheritance system, the Brahmins never forgot that they were, first and foremost, a business class whose pre-eminence depended on active participation in the new nation's exponentially growing economy. The portrayals of aristocratic disdain for commerce so favored by fictioneers mask the long traditions of managerial and entrepreneurial leadership maintained by some patrician families (Kolko, 1967). The genius of the institutional system devised by the Bostonians and adopted by other urban patriarchates lies in its capacity to sort family members for fitness, recruit and maritally coopt talented outsiders, and constantly produce "golden cheeses" by farming ever new "fat meadows of craft or commerce."

All Americans in the eighteenth and early nineteenth centuries struggled to keep farms, firms, and fortunes intact against the divisive force of the law of inheritance. Not only were some groups more successful than others, but the relative degrees of success profoundly shaped the emerging hierarchy of wealth, power, and influence (Hall, 1982).

Farmers fared worst. Although they were the most numerous group in the population, they became steadily more impoverished and powerless. Land holdings were often successfully preserved through such strategies as kin-marriage and leaving family farms to the youngest son. But, the price of success was enormous. Providing the other sons with apprenticeships and farms in new settlements cost money, which could be earned only by shifting away from self-sufficiency toward commercial agriculture and participation in markets over which the farmers had little control. The outmigration of all but the youngest sons meant that farm families lost invaluable human capital. The most ambitious went West or gravitated to the cities. What remained was the pathetic spectacle of ingrownness, isolation, and poverty so accurately depicted in novels like Wharton's *Ethan Frome* (1911).

The effectiveness of the adaptive strategies that artisan families used is more difficult to assess, because rapidly changing technology and the changing character of the markets played so important a role in shaping relations between family and productive enterprise. In highly skilled and highly capitalized occupations like printing, ties between family and craft were unusually long-lasting. For example, the Green family of Boston remained closely identified with the printing trade for more than five generations (Thomas, 1970). To maintain such enduring ties between family and craft required considerable geographical mobility, since colonial cities could not support an unlimited number of printers. To remain

printers, the Greens sent sons to establish shops in Connecticut, Nova Scotia, Maryland, and Virginia.

Other artisans chose to stay where they were, even if it meant altering their occupations. Such highly skilled artisans as silversmiths and cabinetmakers developed a specialized and cooperative division of labor. The woodworkers often became upholsterers, coachmakers, or japanners – all interdependent crafts. In a similar fashion, silversmiths became jewelers, engravers, or clock and instrument makers (Jobe and Kaye, 1984). A few craftsmen became entrepreneurs, moving out of production into financing and marketing the work of others.

Of the major occupational groups in early America, only the merchants succeeded in using the major adaptive strategies – occupational diversification and kin-marriage – to long-term advantage. But, their success in maintaining continuities of family, firm, and fortune depended on their ability to create unified institutional infrastructures that both collectivized their human and financial capital and served as a mechanism for coopting talented new blood. This was not possible everywhere. In cities like Boston, where institutional development was relatively integrated, elite families not only displayed remarkable continuity but remained economic leaders into the twentieth century. However, in New York and Philadelphia, many of the families that were prominent in the late eighteenth century were either swept away or left the great commercial and industrial achievements of the nineteenth century to more ambitions strivers (Baltzell, 1979).

The great industrial fortunes created in the decades after the Civil War were the substance of the final development of dynastic machinery in the United States. These fortunes presented their founders with unique problems, not only because of their enormous size but also because their creation coincided with the appearance of mass poverty and unemployment. For this reason, the final development in the legal machinery of dynastic formation was the charitable foundation, which combined features intended to maintain family control of wealth with socially concerned philanthropy. The emergence of foundations was also tied to the changing structure of family firms, which, as they increased their scale of operations and capital requirements, came to be incorporated enterprises. In this setting, ostensibly charitable foundations served as holding companies that removed control of the firm from the testamentary process, permitting division of income while at the same time perpetuating and formally collectivizing family and inheritance taxes, foundations also became a major means of tax avoidance (Hall, 1986).

For many wealthy families, philanthropy itself became an important occupational alternative involving both altruistic and self-interested components. The Rockefeller "family office" in Room 5600 at Rockefeller Plaza served as the nerve center for managing the family's assets, coordinating its public relations, and overseeing its numerous charitable interests (Collier and Horowitz, 1976). As family holdings diversified and as family members scattered occupationally and geographically, it also played a central role in sustaining the family identity and mission (Marcus, 1983).

We should not make too much of the ability of some families—the Rockefellers, the Du Ponts, the Cabots, and others—to resist the divisive dynamic of the inheritance system, because even

for the largest and most enduring family fortunes, each new generation presents the challenge of successful transmission. For example, it is by no means clear that the Rockefeller family will continue to exist in any dynastic sense a century from now. Collier and Horowitz (1976, p. 624) point out the problems posed when the number of heirs to a fortune increases from six siblings to twenty-two cousins: "Instead of *the* family, there will be five families—those of each of the male heirs of the Brothers. Long after the Brothers have died, their grandchildren—the fifth generation—will finally inherit the vestige of Senior's fortune, the '34 Trusts, which terminate by law when they reach maturity. The aging Cousins will no doubt worry over the impact this sudden wealth will have on their children and what it will portend for the Rockefellers and their concept of service. But by that time the sense in which this has been the most royal of America's families will have passed, and the question will be largely academic." As Tocqueville wrote a century and a half ago in the passage quoted earlier, the law of inheritance in the end "shatters and reduces to powder every obstacle" placed in its path.

From Firm to Fortune

The perpetuation of a fortune and the perpetuation of a family's ties to a particular business constitute distinct but overlapping issues. Because those who seek guidance from consultants and therapists are often closely tied to the enterprises from which they derived their wealth, it is tempting to focus exclusively on the ties between family and firm. However, doing this arbitrarily excludes those who have successfully diversified their interests beyond a particular enterprise but for whom family economic interests remain centrally important. What makes an activity a family enterprise is the degree of family involvement in the sources of family wealth, however diverse those sources may be.

Diversification, like partible inheritance, is tied to the fundamental dynamics of American economic life. As the inheritance system detached families from the land, it also detached artisans from their crafts. Profits rather than perfection became the artisan's goal, and earning profits – even survival itself – demanded continuous technological and organizational innovation. In this rapidly changing and intensely competitive environment, maintaining close ties to a single productive activity and retaining wealth became virtually incompatible. As the nineteenth-century industrial system grew more complex, success even in a single area"for example, steel"required the control of coal, ores, railroads, and construction companies, as survival increasingly hinged on strategic control of raw materials, market access, and markets themselves. To be sure, many small firms found niches for themselves, either by producing specialty products or by establishing client relationships with larger enterprises. But, over the longer term survival inevitably required the dissolution of ties between family and firm or, under special circumstances, the development of interrelated and interdependent clusters of enterprises, such as those created by the Du Ponts.

The changing scale of market activity also worked against family firms. Until the early nineteenth century, most markets were local, and most enterprises were familial. Economic activity was noncompetitive, and consumer choices were governed not by rational choice but by kinship and loyalty (Jobe and Kaye, 1984). The growth of translocal markets was accompanied by the growing use of money, which provided a standard for making rational economic choices. As market relations grew more impersonal, they also became more competitive, because successful firms depended increasingly on mechanical efficiency, the quality of decision making, and the rational division of labor.

Under these circumstances, the factors that had made family firms so vital a part of the colonial social and economic pattern became in many instances obstacles to their survival. As capital markets grew and as family firms began to compete with publicly held corporations, depending solely on the family for financing became a disadvantage. Resistance to employing nonrelatives and reluctance to promote newcomers to positions of responsibility deprived family firms of the talents and skills of these individuals, many of whom became commercial rivals. Unless family firms were fortunate enough to find a niche through control of resources and industrial processes, as did the anthracite coal operators and iron makers of northeastern Pennsylvania (Folsom, 1981), they found it increasingly difficult to succeed in the emerging national economy of the nineteenth century.

In the aggregate, such factors could affect the destinies of towns and cities as they struggled for market dominance in the heady antebellum economy. Nineteenth-century Boston, despite its reputation for Old Family exclusiveness, was remarkable for its ability to attract and provide places for the talented. As lesser cities came within its intellectual range, it drained off their wealth and talent, their promising authors, rising lawyers, large capitalists, and prettiest girls (Holmes, 1957 [1859]).

Where Boston succeeded, other cities failed. Middletown was the largest city in Connecticut in 1800, but its economic life was closely controlled by a small group of traditionally minded families. As early as 1806, a letter in the *Middlesex Gazette* (1806) complained of the unwillingness of "older and wealthier citizens" to "induce young men of property, industry, and enterprise to become inhabitants." Instead of attracting them, the writer noted, "they have actually been driven from the place." By 1860, Middletown had fallen from first in population to seventh, and, in spite of its strategic location on the Connecticut River, the industrial and commercial growth that had enriched the state's other cities largely passed it by.

Dynasty and the Polity

The third force that has persistently worked against family firms is political. In a certain sense, this is the most important force, since it is the political process that shapes the legal and tax environments so central to the survival of family firms. Political opposition to dynasticism is embedded in the earliest legal codes, and it has arisen episodically as a component of electoral appeals.

Partible inheritance was not introduced to the British colonies of North America in order to prevent the intergenerational transmission of farms and firms. On the contrary, its original purpose was to assure patriarchal and patrilineal continuities of authority and property. But, as extraordinary population growth severed the ties between families, land, and traditional occupations, it began to serve a contrary purpose.

In this setting, some families proved more adept than others at operating in the emerging market system, and the countryside witnessed the emergence of a class of landed entrepreneurs (Sweeney, 1984). In the towns and cities, the merchants benefited both from the rise of colonial markets and from the integration of these markets into an international mercantilist system. By the mid-eighteenth century, significant differences in economic and political interests had begun to divide American society. It was at this point that antidynastic political sentiments began to be voiced.

The revolutionary legislatures abolished entail, the English law that in some colonies had perpetually tied lands and families. Many legislatures also repealed the entire body of English common law and with it the statute of uses (the juridical basis of trusts) and the statute of charitable uses (the basis for endowment). As the propertied worked to form for-profit and not-for-profit corporations, they were opposed at every step of the way by their political enemies, who understood the dynastic implications and the larger political consequences of incorporation, private charity, and testamentary trusts (Hall, 1982).

Thomas Jefferson was the most eloquent spokesman for the populist, antidynastic "Virginia Doctrine." He opposed industrial and commercial development, describing market dependency as "a canker which soon eats to the heart of [a republic's] laws and constitution" (Koch, 1965, p. 393). More important, he believed that every generation should be free to work out its own destinies unencumbered by the past. "The earth belongs to the living," Jefferson declared, "the dead have neither power nor rights over it" (Koch, 1965, pp. 329-330). This position was the kernel of the Virginia Doctrine and the basis for antidynastic legislation and court decisions throughout the United States (Miller, 1961).

The Virginia Doctrine distorted the institutional and economic life of the early republic. In spite of its large population, the Jeffersonian South had few business corporations or cultural institutions. In contrast, Federalist New England possessed two thirds of the business corporations and most of the colleges in the United States (Davis, 1917). These institutional differences were paralleled by advances in economic development which were in turn closely tied to the use of testamentary and endowment trusts, the fundamental legal mechanisms of dynastic formation.

In the 1820s, Jacksonianism represented the final crystallization of antidynastic politics. This development was especially evident in states like New York, which enacted laws limiting the proportion of estates that could be left to charity, made the size of institutional endowments subject to the will of the legislature, and established governmental oversight of charitable organizations (Scott, 1951). Although the federal courts eased some of these strictures, antiaristocratic doctrines remained strong. As late as the 1880s, New York courts enforced the Jacksonian statutes against the trustees of Samuel J. Tilden, who had left the bulk of his fortune to establish the New York Public Library. Only a national outcry spearheaded by reformers concerned about the need for private wealth to serve the public good led to a change in the state's laws (Ames, 1913).

Antidynasticism was not the exclusive property of populist politicians. Social Darwinism influenced some founders of the great post-Civil War industrial fortunes to question the wisdom of passing on huge accumulations of wealth. Andrew Carnegie was the most outspoken of these. Proclaiming that he who dies rich dies disgraced, he became the greatest philanthropist of his generation. He advocated a progressive income tax and confiscatory inheritance laws (Carnegie, 1889). Carnegie was echoed by Boston legal scholar John Chipman Gray. In criticizing the legitimation of spendthrift trusts, Gray (1895, p. vi) denounced mechanisms through which the rich could "assure undisturbed possession of wealth to their children, however weak or wicked they may be."

Politically impelled opposition to dynasties and the institutions that produced them continued into this century. Efforts to obtain a federal charter for the Rockefeller Foundation in 1910 led to three years of congressional hearings, which ended only when Rockefeller withdrew from the battle. The New Deal's 1935 revision of the tax code was explicitly framed to "soak the rich." And, the Temporary National Economic Committee (TNEC) investigations conducted by Congress in the late 1930s devoted volumes both to the vast size and to the extraordinary influence of the nation's dynastic families. In 1969, a decade of enquiry into the charitable foundations led to changes in the federal tax code affecting self-dealing, excess business holdings, reinvestment of income, and public accountability. These changes came close to eliminating the usefulness of foundations as dynastic mechanisms (Andrews, 1968, 1970; Neilson, 1972, 1985).

Ambivalence

In Europe, aristocratic dynasties were protected by a special legal status. The law of inheritance required lands and titles to be passed undivided to the eldest son. Entail prevented the sale or seizure of dynastic property by nonfamily members, however indebted the family might be. In America, dynasties enjoyed no special standing. That they could exist at all was due to the adeptness of family founders and their successors in preserving and renewing their wealth and sense of special purpose—really the only things that set the so-called "great families" apart from the others. In the end, the survival of the great families depended on their ability to participate effectively in the capitalist economy and to defend their place in the democratic polity. Neither their own sense of special purpose nor their standing in the eyes of others exempted them from accountability to the marketplace. As one nineteenth-century dynast put it (Hall, 1892, p. 3), "No amount of good blood can make a fool other than he is, but family pride may stimulate a person of respectable origin and but limited capacity to exertions that will bring success in life."

The absence of special legal status meant that the children of dynastic families, like the children of lesser families, had to live in society and exert themselves in order to succeed. These were the only ways of assuring the survival of the dynasty. The rich could be exclusive, but only up to a point. The economic and political skills essential to dynastic survival could not be learned from private tutors; they could only be acquired in schools where merit, not manners, was the standard of excellence. The wealthy in America could not live idly when their self-interest required activity and engagement. They could not set themselves apart, either from society in general or from people like themselves, because the perpetuation of wealth was a matter of collective action to deploy political and economic resources.

However great a family's wealth and however compelling its sense of special destiny, no dynasty could be indifferent to the dominant democratic and meritocratic values of American society. Dynastic survival depended not only on institutional effectiveness in the marketplace but also on the ability of members, who as Americans were influenced by the dominant values, to reconcile the privileges of wealth with social expectations of individual achievement. Because a dynasty is ultimately an affair of persons, its continuation has depended less on its wealth than on the willingness of individuals in each succeeding generation to carry on the family mission. Individual responses to the conflict between dominant values and the family myth ultimately determine the fate of dynasties.

In dealing with this conflict between family and society, each child faces choices about how to use the family myth and the fortune that accompanies it. It can be a source of strength, a crippling burden, or an excuse for failure. The Adams family is a case in point. George Washington Adams (1801-1829), the son and grandson of presidents, lived a short and miserably failed life. He drowned himself in Long Island Sound when, during a psychotic break, he hallucinated that the engine of the steamship on which he was a passenger was speaking reproachfully in his father's voice (Nagel, 1983). In contrast, his brother Charles Francis (1807-1886) accepted both the assets and the liabilities of dynasty and built a brilliant career as a lawyer and diplomat in the mold of his forebears.

Eli Whitney, Jr. (1825-1895), son of the famous inventor and industrial pioneer, represented an interesting variation on this theme in which even children who forge successful careers and fulfill dynastic expectations remain incapable of valuing their achievements. Although his father died when Whitney was an infant, the son spent most of his life in the shadow of the great man's reputation. It was predetermined that he would take over management of the Whitney Armory, which his uncles operated during his minority. Whitney took over the firm shortly after graduating from Princeton. He was phenomenally successful in an intensely competitive industry. But, he was incapable of seeing himself as a success. Through the decade of the 1850s he kept a diary in which, between notes on spectacular transactions, he endlessly reiterated his sense of personal failure (Whitney, 1852-1860, p. 2): "July 9, 1852: I am very blue and possessed of a feeling of uncertainty as to my future business prospects and standing as a man ... I seem to have been continuously putting my hand to the plow and looking back all my life long. My mistakes in life have been many. I am called somewhat energetic but lack energy more than anything else." The tone of the diary begins to change when, in the late 1850s, Whitney becomes involved in the effort to organize the New Haven Water Company. Initially an outsider to the project, he eventually not only became its largest stockholder but built the waterworks itself. What began as an effort to secure a greater power source for his father's factory became in the end a means of creating his own identity as a person and as an entrepreneur. Only by making his work his own could he have a sense that it had any real value. At the same time, it is significant that his self-affirmation came not from rejecting the dynastic burden but from accepting it and building his own life on and beyond it.

As the wealthy in America coalesced into a class at the end of the nineteenth century, the conflict between dominant values and dynastic claims came increasingly to be institutionally mediated. This was no accident, for, as

the Holmes quote that began this paper suggests, dynastic families were becoming deeply concerned about their prospects for survival. After the Civil War, private education in America underwent a fundamental restructuring that was largely underwritten by dynastic families. Although they were motivated by the obvious need for an educational system appropriate to a national industrial economy, they were no less concerned with ensuring their own place in that new world.

The keystone of the new elite boarding schools and great private universities was an ethos of public service. This ethos not only legitimated the wealthy as a class but also created a matrix in which members of dynastic families could work to resolve the family-society conflict in a reasonably regulated way. Surrounded by people like themselves who were undergoing the same kinds of stresses, the sons and daughters who filled the prep schools played an especially important role in institutionalizing the intrapersonal struggle and guiding its resolution in socially productive directions. This development probably accounts for the fact that most dynastic families in America ended up accommodating the conflict between dynasty and democracy through public service and philanthropy rather than through exile or Bohemianism.

Conclusion

In spite of the social, economic, and political forces arrayed against them and in spite of individual ambivalence and family conflict, the dynastic process continues. It involves not only the heirs to great eighteenth- and nineteenth-century mercantile or industrial fortunes but any parent who, having succeeded in business, hopes to found a family and any child who faces a future in which expectations and resources garnered in the past have set him apart from his contemporaries.

Although social commentators, from Tocqueville in the nineteenth century through Weber and Parsons in the twentieth, have assured us that the future lay with impersonally and professionally managed bureaucratic enterprises, family firms and the dynastic processes that they often set in motion continue to play a dominant part in American life.

The persistence of family firms suggests that they are not merely holdovers or throwbacks. They can do things that more formally structured business organizations cannot. Proprietors accountable to themselves and their sense of family responsibility can act more flexibly and imaginatively than managers beholden to accountants and anonymous stockholders. The importance of family firms in the newspaper business is not a coincidence. Family control gives editors and publishers the independence of marketplace accountability that permits them to take unpopular or unprofitable stands. And, the family tie to the community makes these stands influential. Family firms have a capacity to make long-term investments and resist the pressure of financial analysts for short-term returns that currently bedevil many publicly held corporations.

The persistence of the family firm, together with evidence of the roles that it plays in industrial innovation, community leadership, and philanthropy, has important implications not only for therapists and management consultants but also for students of economic development and public policy. The larger social, technological, and political forces working against family firms have not been forces of nature but products of legislation and

jurisprudence. Investigating them may lead both to a clearer understanding of the dynamics of family firms and to changes that will alter those dynamics.

An earlier version of this paper was presented to the Family Business Conference, the Wharton School, University of Pennsylvania in October 1986. The research from which this paper was drawn has been supported by the American Council of Learned Societies, AT&T Foundation, the Ellis Phillips Foundation, Equitable Life Assurance Society of the United States, Exxon Education Foundation, General Electric Foundation, the Teagle Foundation, and the Program on Nonprofit Organizations, Yale University.

References

Ames, J. B. *Lectures on Legal History and Miscellaneous Legal Essays.* Cambridge, Mass.: Harvard University Press, 1913.

Andrews, F. E. *Patman and the Foundations: Review and Assessment.* New York: The Foundation Center, 1968.

Andrews, F. E. *Foundations and the Tax Reform Act of 1969.* New York: The Foundation Center, 1970.

Baltzell, E. D. *Puritan Boston and Quaker Philadelphia: Two Protestant Ethics and the Spirit of Class Authority and Leadership.* New York: Free Press, 1979.

Carnegie, A. "The Gospel of Wealth." *North American Review,* 1889, 148, 653-664, 149, 682-698.

Collier, P., and Horowitz, D. *The Rockefellers: An American Dynasty.* New York: New American Library, 1976.

Davis, J. S. *Essays in the Earlier History of American Corporations.* Cambridge, Mass.: Harvard University Press, 1917.

Farber, B. *Guardians of Virtue: Salem Families in 1800.* New York: St. Martins Press, 1972.

Folsom, B. W. *Urban Capitalists: Entrepreneurs and City Growth in Pennsylvania's Lackawanna and Lehigh Regions, 1800-1920.* Baltimore, Md.: Johns Hopkins University Press, 1981.

Gray, J. C. *Restraints on the Alienation of Property.* Boston: Boston Book Company, 1895.

Hall, P. D. "Family Structure and Class Consolidation Among the Boston Brahmins." Unpublished doctoral dissertation, Department of History, State University of New York, Stony Brook, 1973.

Hall, P. D. *The Organization of American Culture, 1700-1900: Institutions, Elites, and the Origins of American Nationality.* New York: New York University Press, 1982.

Hall, P. D. "An Historical Overview of the Private Nonprofit Sector." In W. W. Powell (ed.), *The Nonprofit Sector: A Research Handbook.* New Haven, Conn.: Yale University Press, 1986.

Hall, T. P. *Family Records of Theodore Parsons Hall and Alexandrine Louise Godfroy.* Detroit, Mich.: W. C. Heath, 1892.

Holmes, O. W. *Elsie Venner: A Romance of Destiny.* New York: Signet, 1957 [1859].

Holmes, O. W. *Autocrat of the Breakfast Table.* New York: Sagamore Press, 1961 [1860].

Jobe, B., and Kaye, M. *New England Furniture: The Colonial Era.* Boston: Houghton Mifflin, 1984.

Koch, A. *The American Enlightenment.* New York: George Braziller, 1965.

Kolko, G. "Brahmins and Businessmen." In B. Moore and K. Wolfe (eds.), *The Critical Spirit: Essays in Honor of Herbert Marcuse.* Boston: Beacon Press, 1967.

Marcus, G. "The Fiduciary Role in American Families and Their Institutional Legacy: From the Law of Trusts to Trusts in the Establishment." In G. Marcus (ed.), *Elites: Ethnographic Issues.* Albuquerque: University of New Mexico Press, 1983.

Middlesex Gazette (Middletown, Connecticut), May 16, 1806.

Miller, H. S. *The Legal Foundations of American Philanthropy.* Madison: State Historical Society of Wisconsin, 1961.

Nagel, P. C. *Descent from Glory: Four Generations of the Adams Family.* New York: Oxford University Press, 1983.

Neilson, W. *The Big Foundations.* New York: Columbia University Press, 1972.

Neilson, W. *The Golden Donors.* New York: Dutton, 1985.

Newhall, G. *Future Interests and the Rule Against Perpetuities in Massachusetts.* Boston: Hildreth, 1942.

Pickering's Reports, Boston, Mass.: 1830, 9, 461.

Scott, A. W. "Charitable Trusts in New York." *New York University Law Review*, 1951, 26 (2), 251-265.

Scott, A. W. *The Law of Trusts.* Boston: Little, Brown, 1939.

Smith, P. *John Adams.* Garden City, N. Y.: Doubleday, 1962.

Story, R. *The Forging of an Aristocracy: Harvard and Boston's Upper Class, 1800-1870.* Middletown, Conn.: Wesleyan University Press, 1981.

Sweeney, K. M. "Mansion People: Kinship, Class, and Architecture in the Mid-Eighteenth Century." *Winterthur Portfolio*, 1984 l9 (4), 231-255.

Thomas, I. *History of Printing in America, with a Biography of Printers and an Account of Newspapers*. Barre, Mass.: Imprint Society, 1970.

Tocqueville, A. de. *Democracy in America*. New York: Vintage Books, 1945 [1835].

Waters, J. "American Colonial Stem Families: Persisting European Patterns in the New World." Unpublished paper presented at the History Department Faculty Seminar, Wesleyan University, April 1978.

Wharton, E. *Ethan Frome*. New York: Scribners', 1911.

White, G. T. *History of the Massachusetts Hospital Life Insurance Company*. Cambridge, Mass.: Harvard University Press, 1955.

Whitney, E., Jr. "Business Diary. 1852-1860." Whitney Family Papers, Yale University Library, Box 11, Folder 173.

Introduction

When a family business is acquired by new owners, success will depend on whether the firm is managed in harmony with local culture. Through an extensive case study relationships between ownership, firm and community are explored.

Using a cultural perspective, this article investigates the proposition that family businesses acquired and managed in a manner that is at odds with the local culture will suffer, while firms that are acquired and managed in harmony with the local culture will have a higher level of morale and long-run productivity.

Family Firm and Community Culture
1988

By Joseph H. Astrachan

Reprinted from **Family Business Review**, Vol.I No. 3, 1988. San Francisco: Jossey-Bass, 1988. Used with permission of the publisher. All rights reserved.

Family Firm, Community Bureaucratic, and Urban Culture

Basic assumptions, which constitute the deepest level of culture, can be broken into five categories: humanity's relationship to nature, the nature of reality and truth, the nature of human nature, the nature of human activity, and the nature of human relationships (Schein, 1985; Parsons, 1951). The idea that bureaucracies are not like family firms is neither new nor controversial (Weber, 1947). Family firms often struggle to balance the cultural elements of families with the cultural elements of bureaucratic organizations (Lansberg, 1983). An analogue to the divergence of family firm and bureaucratic needs can be found in the tension that exists between communal and business needs in developing communities (Stein, 1973).

Figure 1 displays the five cultural categories with respect to family firms, bureaucracies, urban settings, and close community settings. Figure 1 shows that the only two combinations of firm and environment culture that appear to be wholly compatible are family firm with community culture and bureaucracy with urban culture. It should be noted that the description of bureaucratic culture explored here is consistent with what Walton (1985) defines as "control driven." It is not meant to be representative of emerging "commitment-driven" bureaucratic forms. While the long-term results are not yet in, such forms frequently attempt to integrate the cultural elements described here as communal with large corporate size and attendant diversity.

660

Figure 1. Cultural Archetypes

Category of Cultural Assumption	Community and Family Firm Culture	Urban and Bureaucratic Culture
Humanity's Relationship to Nature	Harmony with nature; emphasis on maintaining a delicate balance with nature	Domination of nature; even the bureaucratic form seeks to shape and control nature
The Nature of Reality and Truth	Testable truth is pragmatically defined	Truth is to be found in the next higher level of the hierarchy, in specialists who have expertise, and in "careful" analyses
	For firms, untestable truth is defined by founder or ownership	Highest form of truth is that which survives conflict and debate
	For communities, untestable truth is defined by a council of elders of the "town fathers"	
	Polychronic or diffuse sense of time: open and unlocked space	Time and space are rigidly defined and compartmentalized
The Nature of Human Nature	Basically good, trustworthy, capable of substantial development, responsible, and accountable unless proved otherwise	Capable of limited growth, untrustworthy, self-seeking, and greedy; can only individually be proved otherwise
The Nature of Human Activity	Reactive; little emphasis on specific or detailed planning	Always planning and forecasting for future activity; actions are evaluated on the basis of plans; most behavior is routinized; new behavior is made explicit prior to its implementation
	Highest-priority activities are those that benefit the collective	Highest-priority activities are those which benefit self
	Long-range time orientation	Short-range time orientation
The Nature of Human Relationships	Highly emotional, diffuse in nature, particularistic, sharing, cooperative, ascription and collectivity oriented	Emotionally neutral, specific in nature, impersonal, universalistic, achievement and self orientation

Note: The descriptions and assumptions in this figure are based on Ben-Prath, 1980; Bendix, 1956; Blood and Hulin, 1969; Braverman, 1974; Clark and Mills, 1979; Dyer, 1984; Etzioni, 1968; Gouldner, 1954; Hall, 1966; Hofstede, 1980; Merton, 1968; Milgram, 1970; Miller and Rice, 1967; Miklofsky, 1981; Parsons, 1951; Schein, 1985; Simmel, 1950; Taylor, 1947; Toennies, 1963; Weber, 1947.

Figure 1 is presented as an aid to understanding the case that follows; it considers forms of organization theoretically. As we well know, actual organizations may fit the idealized forms considered here only imperfectly. Further, the point is not the relative merits of one form over another. Rather, these assumptions are elaborated to gauge their consistency and degree of contradiction.

Railtown and the Quality Commodity Company

To study the relationship between family firm and community culture empirically, I was fortunate to be given access to Quality Commodity Company, a business located in America's Midwest. (Names and many of the details have been altered to protect the firm's identity.) The firm exists in a community of fewer than 10,000 people. When it was founded by the Alden family around the turn of the century, there was one other major employer in Railtown. After prospering as a family firm for over fifty years, the company was purchased by Corporal Industries, a large conglomerate. Approximately ten years later, Corporal Industries sold the business to its current owners, the Newcastle family. At the time I completed the fieldwork, the Newcastles had owned the firm for more than nine years. They are not related to the original owning family, and they had never lived in the surrounding community. Currently, Railtown has five large employers. Quality Commodity employs about 500 people and has sales of between $20 million and $50 million.

This interesting case provides a rich source for learning. It has many characteristics of the so-called natural experiment. The company and its community have essentially remained intact, because there have been no large emigrations to or immigrations from the community during the years covered by this investigation. This fact makes comparisons of the three ownership periods valid.

With the exception of the conglomerate's corporate headquarters, whose members declined to be interviewed, I talked with people at all levels of the firm. The interviewees included line personnel who had worked at least fifteen years in the firm, the current owning family, and the former chairman and chief executive officer (the founder's son) who had sold the firm to the conglomerate. Historical and archival data were collected to corroborate the interview material.

The case examination of the proposition that firm productivity and morale are closely related to the compatibility of company and community culture will occur in several steps. Each of the three eras in the Quality Commodity Company's history—Alden family, Corporal Industries, and Newcastle family—will be examined, and data relevant to the multiple culture categories will be provided. After the three time periods are compared in terms of culture, morale, and productivity, some implications for firms going through management changes and for organizations that are acquiring firms will be outlined.

Quality Commodity: The Early Years

Shortly after the turn of the century, the Quality Commodity Company settled in Railtown. The company began operations with the explicit intention of becoming the town's company. Its leaders publicly offered minority ownership interest in the company to the townspeople. As an article in the local newspaper stated, "It is the intention of the men at the head of this company to make it a substantial asset to the city of Railtown and the community and to only increase growth along the lines that experience has shown to be conservative....This is a local institution, and the stock should be owned and controlled int he community." To Mr. Alden, the company's founder, being the town's company meant both that the company's primary responsibilities lay with the town and that the town had a mutual responsibility toward the company. As the eighty-year-old unofficial historian of Railtown explained to me during an interview, "Mr Alden had the idea that not only should a company have a conscience about its people, but also the people should have one about the way they should handle their company. It was, I think Mr. Alden would say, a two-way street." During these early years, Quality Commodity shaped and reflected Railtown's community culture.

Mr. Alden's direction was congruent with beliefs already existing in Railtown. The community's traits, which came from its "notable fathers," included "having the good judgment to open the door when opportunity knocked," punctuality, honesty, trustworthiness, donating of self, teaching by example, and having a firm idea of right and wrong and making that idea understandable.

From its founding until the end of this first period, Quality Commodity had the express goal of slow and cautious growth. The desire was to maintain harmony with the community and citizens of Railtown. For example, Quality Commodity helped many employees to buy homes, and it gave annual picnics for the entire community. Neither firm nor town attempted to dominate its members. As an article in the local newspaper put it,

"For many years, the personnel policies of Quality Commodity carried out a 'one big family' concept. Group insurance, profit sharing, a liberal pension plan, and other benefits were set up for employees....Mr. Alden believed that business should be ruled by principles of integrity, fair treatment of employees, and the manufacture of a quality product." The wish to harmonize with employees is manifest in the company's early adoption of many liberal personnel policies. These policies included a five-day work week, company cafeterias, no time clocks, and seven-and-one-half-hour days with no reduction in pay.

As in many family firms and close communities, pragmatism was a high priority. Quality's early move into an automated manufacturing process was also a pragmatic decision. Initially, a line employee convinced Mr. Alden to try a small automation experiment in one small step of the manufacturing process. When this experiment was demonstrated to be successful, other parts of the line were automated. Quality Commodity occasionally suffered because of its trial-and-error method of decision making. Projects were cancelled when a series of trial-and-error experiments failed.

From the very start, Quality had an open sense of time and space. Few meetings were scheduled, and they occurred as needed. Although space was not abundant, it was open. Since its founding, the company had, on the average, added a new building more than once every five years.

Mr. Alden had strong beliefs about the good in people. As one interviewee phrased it, "Mr. Alden was a faithful human being; he had faith in things and in people." Born in Appalachia, Mr. Alden was self-educated, and he had worked on the family farm in his youth. Within the business, his beliefs about the developmental capacity of human beings were evident in his policy of promotion from within.

Every person from this first era whom I interviewed acknowledged that the highest-priority activities were those that ultimately benefited the firm and, through the firm, the community. A concrete example of Mr. Alden's altruism occurred during the depression: He used his own life insurance policy as collateral to borrow money to secure the payroll. During that period, employees worked without pay for company-issued scrip, which was honored in stores more than four towns away; employees could exchange the scrip for shares in the company. In the community, people were reported to have pulled together, not to have separated or left the town.

There was generally little precise advance planning. The earliest example of advance planning comes from the decision concerning the type of product that the firm would manufacture. The original plan was that the firm would produce a product that would compete in a new, fast-growing, yet increasingly congested market. When it finally began production, the company used a similar advanced technology to produce an entirely different (though not a new) item. The company's decision to enter this niche was a reaction to limited financial resources not to market research. There was no evidence in Railtown of community planning, even during the depression. Although activities related to survival during the depressions were not planned, they did involve the entire community, and they were usually initiated by the town's business leaders.

Perhaps because of the size of Railtown, people knew each other in many contexts. A retired employee informed me that "in the earlier days things were simplified because most of the people were local people, so you know a lot about them, their families, and their backgrounds."

People were generally treated independently and in a particularistic manner. One former manager said, "We tried to treat all the people based on what the person and the work called for." Particularism within the firm is evidenced by the firm's practice of allowing employees to arrange their own schedules in a manner that resembles what is now known as flex time. Everyone reported that, up until the end of this period, there had been a large degree of caring for individual people.

Cooperation was the rule in the company. One manager said, "We had real team work. You'd work with the guys using each other's ideas, and then we'd do the best job possible." If people on the line needed help, it was common for management to give assistance.

Ascription (rights and responsibilities based not on merit but on birth) was also accepted. The succession from first to second-generation Alden proceeded smoothly. The employees saw the succession from one generation to the next as a legitimate and necessary transfer of ownership and managerial responsibilities. No fighting for top positions was reported. One common comment was, "If I had children, I think that it'd be natural that they come into the business." When Mr. Alden's son came into the business, the employees sought to improve his skills and build cooperative relationships with him rather than challenging his right to the job. Only a few years after the junior

Alden joined the firm, he was asked to accept full responsibility for the company when his father suddenly died of a heart attack.

The Alden family reduced some of the tensions that can accompany a strict adherence to ascription by frowning on displays of class differences or other symbols that imply a separation between people. Family members worked to create a feeling that everyone was in the firm together for equal reward and for benefit to all. The Aldens lived in an average house. During the depression, even the Aldens did not buy clothing for more than eight years. They chose instead to save for times of greater despair and for others. Although the sale of the firm to Corporal Industries created millionaires in the town, as an article in a national newspaper reported, no displays of affluence could be found except in the "local banks' balance sheets."

The Aldens labored to create a powerful sense of community in both the Quality Commodity Company and Railtown. They encouraged their employees to participate in management and ownership of the company and in committees in town. The Aldens felt that people would be especially motivated to work by the feeling that they were working for themselves, their families, and their community. They believed that a sense of family benefitted everyone in Railtown. The Aldens' influence in the community was demonstrated by the view of many that they were one of the town's founding families, although they had arrived more than a generation after the town was founded.

Until shortly before the business was sold, Quality Commodity maintained its high level of morale and prosperity under the direction of Mr. Alden's son.

In the years preceding the sale, employees began to have doubts about the future of the company and its management. This short period of discontent was brought about by the declining health of the junior Alden. President for more than twenty-five years, the junior Alden had suffered at least one heart attack and was contending with a very painful and visible angina condition. Following his physician's advice, he withdrew from the business. It was speculated in town that his condition had been brought about by his own son, who had refused to take over the business and left Railtown to seek his fortune elsewhere.

Employees, who had come to expect openness from management, began to inquire about succession plans. The belief that the junior Alden was not functioning well enough to ensure the future of the firm and community after his departure spread. With succession unplanned and the future threatened, company morale began to decline. This decline was not reflected in sales or profit figures. However, many employees remembered it, and it was reflected in the success of the union's fifteenth organizing drive. Townsfolk and employees who doubted the future of the firm accepted unionization because it seemed to promise survival. Employees were far more concerned with the firm's future than they were with wresting day-to-day control from management. They became concerned with influencing management only after the next owners had instituted bureaucracy.

The period that included the fifteenth unionization drive and the sale of the business was acknowledged by all to have been a very dark time in Railtown's history. Reports of that time include stories of how every other window in the company's buildings had been broken during one riot. One onlooker said that she ran home crying after witnessing the senseless destruction. "It was like a war had broke out in our town," she said. The union was formalized, and with it, the separation between management and employees; deep divisions within the community formed and were openly acknowledged. Quality was sold that same year. Emotions were reported to have cooled down a bit after the firm's sale was announced. Anticipation of a new era in the company's history replaced anger and hostility. Nevertheless, many people felt a sense of loss and grief at the departure of the junior Alden. These feelings increased as employees and other community members alike learned that ensuring the future through unionization and bureaucracy had substantial costs.

The Corporal Industries Years

Corporal Industries and the Aldens had very different styles of management. The first words spoken to me during many interviews are an indication of how culturally inconsistent Corporal Industries was with Railtown and prior management: "So, you've come to study something to do with Corporal and us? it should give about the best lesson there is in how not to manage a company." The junior Alden made a statement that is consistent with the theoretical position taken in this paper. He said, "The problem was that people who were sent here didn't know how to manage a small company in a small town."

The very idea of being sold as part of a company was distasteful to many of Quality's employees. (In the remainder of this paper, Alden-era employees are referred to as *Quality's* or as the *Quality employees*. Corporal Industries' managers are referred to as *Corporal,*, *Corporal managers* and *Corporal people*.) They felt dominated almost

from the start. The Corporal manager who was put in charge of operations had been instrumental in closing the deal. He was replaced within weeks of the sale. As soon as his replacement arrived, Corporal imposed its management structure on Quality Commodity. Of Corporal's style, one retired manager said, "They never heard the old Chinese proverb that you start a journey of one thousand miles with a single step....When they came in, they pretty much rode roughshod. They developed a pretty good resentment because us country boys didn't like that."

Further evidence of Corporal's unwillingness to harmonize with local culture was provided by one interviewee, who reported that corporal's people "didn't try to fit into Railtown; they didn't care to." When individuals from Corporal's headquarters came to visit the factories, they refused to stay in either of the two local motels. Instead, they chose lodging in a larger city more than an hour from Railtown.

The biggest symbol of domination and the thing that hurt Railtown citizens the most was that Corporal destroyed every trace of the old company. This "cleansing" included the destruction of paintings of the founding family, machinery, files, and several buildings. Old, though not obsolete, equipment that Quality employees had crafted was melted down and transferred to other divisions in the Corporal conglomerate. Employees loyal to the Alden family scrambled to ferret away mementos as soon as they learned of Corporal's actions.

Corporal also attempted to implement typically bureaucratic policies. Overall direction for Quality Commodity was defined by Corporal's headquarters in the form of a five-year plan. The five-year plan included multiple operational and sales goals. Corporal seemed to require a forecast for everything.

Quality's employees did not understand the methods that Corporal used to make decisions. The goals and other results of the many analyses were nonsensical to those who had experience in the company. One manager explained that "they bogged you down in paperwork." Another reported that "they tried to turn us into paper pushers." Too much time seemed to be spent deciding what to do and too little on doing it.

Corporal placed very strong boundaries on time and space. Time was scheduled in detail. Routine meetings seemed to take precedence over substantive issues occurring on the shop floor or in the sales field. Space was also more clearly defined, and it was accorded new meaning. Corporal managers fought over office space and furniture. Office doors were locked for the first time in company history.

Perhaps the most divergent assumption about human nature that Corporal people displayed was that employees were only capable of limited growth. A Corporal manager who had been at Quality for a number of years once stated that "people in corporate headquarters told me that the people in Railtown are dumb SOBs, but after I'd been here a while I learned that they [Corporal headquarters] are the dumb SOBs." The general feeling at Quality was that the majority of Corporal people thought they were smarter and better than Quality veterans.

Corporal policies also assumed that people were basically not good. That is, people were untrustworthy, irresponsible, and self-seeking. This assumption was implied in the elaborate system of controls that Corporal tried to foster.

Another indication was that Corporal people "would not take any suggestions or ideas." One manager reported, "You couldn't tell them when you knew that they were wrong." Quality people observed dishonest and disingenuous behavior on the part of a few Corporal managers and then assumed that Corporal management was untrustworthy and self-interested.

Corporal did not want local employees to become involved with companywide issues. Through directives and other actions, Corporal made it clear that local employees were to deal only with their specific tasks. For example, managerial offices were separated, and unscheduled meetings and informal communication were discouraged. Increased conflict accompanied Corporal's attempted separation of people. One person reported that Corporal managers would "build little kingdoms, buy their people, and in two years' time, they're gone." Corporal also removed several functions from Quality's control, including research, advertising, and accounting.

Quality's identity in the community also changed. Nearly all the activities that Quality had performed for the community were discontinued. Informal representation of Quality's ownership ceased on town committees, money was no longer given to the community, advertisements disappeared from the local papers. Activities that would benefit the community were not considered a priority. As one resident stated, "Corporal had a very saddening effect on Railtown. Quality and Railtown were synonymous." Another reported that, while Corporal may have had a somewhat depressing effect, "the town pretty much acclimated itself to the new industrial companies that characterize modern corporations....We couldn't go to the industries anymore to get things done for the community." To some people, Corporal seemed like a deadly parasite that had no real interest in the well-being of Railtown.

Quality people had a difficult time understanding why Corporal managers acted impersonally and without feeling. Most Quality people interpreted impersonality as an indication of lack of caring. Other facts validated this interpretation. One Corporal manager often did not show up to work until 11 A.M. and left well before 4:30 P.M. Rumors, bolstered by powerful feelings, suggested that Corporal "didn't care about us. We were under them, just one of their plants." Others were convinced that Corporal was going to liquidate Quality. Several large layoffs and wholesale firings occurred. One manager stated that "there was a real lack of security; you didn't know who was going to go next. It was the same in the town; people were waiting for us to go under."

Teamwork and cooperation diminished. Relationships with Corporal management were specific in nature, occurring only in the business context. Unlike the Alden family days, when people shared ideas and knowledge freely, under Corporal, "if someone said that they wanted to pick your brain, that would mean that you were about to be fired." Corporal discouraged participatory behavior. Outside associations among Quality people decreased. There were no reported instances of Corporal people befriending Quality employees. There were a few Corporal people with whom Railtown folk were comfortable. However, "they didn't make up for the obnoxiousness of others."

Corporal practiced universalism. Several people described its hiring method as consisting of putting names into a hat and pulling them out at random. Corporal people had no regard for the diffuse character of relationships within Railtown. For example, people were hired who had demonstrated irresponsibility in other settings within the community, and the new hires, as well as Corporal management, were subsequently resented. Life outside Quality was unimportant to Corporal.

Short-run, self, and achievement orientations were prevalent in Corporal. Corporal managers never stayed at Quality's facilities for more than two years. More than one Quality employee said, "They came to establish a track record, and they didn't care how they did it." Once interpretation of high turnover among Corporal management became popular among Quality's employees: Quality had become the last stop before Corporal managers were fired. The combination of repeated failures initiated by Corporal and Corporal managers' limited understanding of how decisions were made prompted one Quality employee to state, "I don't think any of us could remember all the stupid things that were being done." Another employee said, "the Corporal image stood for failure, incompetence, and the like." Eventually, Quality was put up for sale. While the citizens of Railtown were apprehensive and uncertain about having yet another owner become involved in Quality, they believed that with change there was hope. Within a matter of months, the Newcastle family was making the final arrangements to acquire Quality.

Quality Commodity and the Newcastle Family

At first glance, Mr. Newcastle's academic and practical education seemed well suited to bureaucratic culture. An Ivy League graduate with an M.B.A. from a prestigious school, he had begun his career as a manager in a multinational corporation. Mrs. Newcastle was college educated. She had been primarily a homemaker until her children reached high school age. Her family had a history of female entrepreneurs. Her mother was a major contributor to recent world-changing technologies. Dissatisfaction with the management practices and politics of corporate America had led Mr. and Mrs. Newcastle to go out on their own.

Before acquiring Quality Commodity, the Newcastles had started several smaller ventures, which provided mediocre returns at best. Prompted primarily by the desire to manage a larger organization, the Newcastles began to hunt for an acquisition. Like those who had founded Railtown, the Newcastles had a history of making the most of opportunities. When Quality became available, the Newcastles quickly gauged its potential. Using a combination of intuition and financially based analyses, they decided to purchase the company.

In defining the division of labor, the Newcastles decided that Mr. Newcastle was to have primary responsibility for financial and operational management. Mrs. Newcastle was to be responsible for personnel, human resources, and marketing. They firmly decided, long before their purchase of Quality, that all major decisions about product development, company expansion, or major change would be made jointly. After mutual agreement on such decisions, they would then ask key players from the rest of the company to help them make the final decision and develop implementation plans.

The Newcastles' first actions established a clear difference between themselves and Corporal Industries. They held a factory wide meeting to explain their proposed purchase and to discuss what life would be like with new owners in control. According to employees' reports, the Newcastles, in contrast to Corporal, actually solicited, listened to, and acted on advice from everyone in the plant.

One thing that consciously bothered the Newcastles was that by purchasing the firm they were, in a philosophical sense, dominating the employees. Mr. Newcastle expressed discomfort that he had been part of a transaction in which "the workers were sold like cattle." When the Newcastles first purchased the firm, they left policies and personnel intact. Any changes that were made occurred only after consultation with the people who would be affected. As one manager put it, Mr. Newcastle "really wants people to get along with each other; he really wants to make it a team effort." Another stated, "This is the most harmonious office I've ever worked in."

The Newcastles returned pragmatic management to the company. Several people stated that Mr. Newcastle had "a real open mind." He was willing to allow people to try things without "a hundred pages of justification." Product and production ideas once again flowed from the bottom of the hierarchy.

In the Newcastles' Quality, untestable truth was defined largely by the owner, as is typical in patriarchal systems. As Mr. Newcastle said, "Ultimately, I am the boss of my business." Without any testing or discussion, the Newcastles returned the firm to its previous goals of quality products and customer service. Shortcuts in the production process that Corporal had implemented were eliminated. The attitude that everyone in the plant was member of the quality control department was adopted.

These changes were well accepted at Quality. People remembered their past prosperity as being largely the result of high quality and customer service. In a manner that resembled Mr. Alden's, Mr. and Mrs. Newcastle also sought innovations that, while costing more, noticeably improved quality. Quality's products once again became the highest-quality products in the industry.

The Newcastles also returned the sense of time and space that Quality had once enjoyed. New offices were built both at the factory and at the corporate headquarters. Both buildings are characterized by open spaces and open office doors—where doors exist at all. The Newcastles also blurred the lines that existed between Quality and Railtown. For example, the local high school's yearbooks are proudly placed on a conference room bookshelf in front of popular books on management, such as *In Search of Excellence* and *The One-Minute Manager*.

Time returned to its polychronic state. Many meetings were unscheduled, all were informal, and the number of routine meetings was so few that appointment calendars were not seen anywhere. For example, the director of quality control intermittently met with the general manager early in the morning over coffee. Further evidence came from my own experience. When I asked people if I could schedule an interview, almost everyone said, "Sure, how about now?"

Mr. and Mrs. Newcastle frequently expressed their beliefs about human nature. They believed that trust went hand in hand with the granting of

autonomy. The Newcastles also felt that, when people are allowed, they are naturally good, most are honest, and all are capable of substantial learning and growth. These beliefs were best illustrated by the amount of time and effort devoted to explaining each decision, especially the decisions that affected the overall direction of the company.

The Newcastle's style of management was reactive. While planning did occur, it was not emphasized. As one employee described the orientation toward activity at Quality, "The way we do things around here is someone asks for something to be done, and, if it's at all possible, we do it—and I don't remember too many things that were impossible!" One example of reactivity in the company as a whole was the frequency with which someone returned from a convention filled with ideas for new products, and many of the ideas were implemented.

The Newcastles were explicit about their desire for most activities to be participatory in nature. Many employees explained that they spent a good deal of time working with others. The team feeling, which had disappeared under Corporal, returned to Quality. The Newcastles were very concerned with creating a sense of family within their firm and with benefiting the community of Railtown in both the long and the short term. As Mr. Newcastle said, "I want very much to create a family system....I have attempted to allow for an environment in which a community could form. This will help me and the business and therefore the community. Quality Commodity is part of the community. It has an established place but does not take up the whole environment. It is recognized that part of them is Quality."

One action in particular symbolizes Quality's return to the community. During the Alden family days, the firm used an old steamship whistle to signal the changes of shifts and breaks. Many people in town were fond of the sound, which had become a beloved tradition. Corporal had removed the whistle early in its ownership. After the Newcastles gained control, the general manager remembered that they had hidden the whistle to preserve it from being melted down. When he returned the whistle to active duty, one newspaper headline read, "Lots of memories called up by a steam whistle's toot." An editorial in another paper gave "special thanks to those whose effort restored the old Quality whistle."

The Newcastles accepted nearly all the responsibilities that the Aldens and their company had assumed for the community. Quality once again sponsored local sports teams, bought advertisements in the local paper, made donations to local organizations, and contributed to the community in many other ways. The newspaper advertisements stressed quality, community, and teamwork; for example: "Congratulations Flames [high school team] on another Super Season — Quality Efforts of quality young men building community pride." In coordination with the local high school, the Newcastles began a work study program.

The Newcastles displayed their assumption that relationships should be diffuse by example. The entire Newcastle family worked for Quality. Moreover, Quality employed two or more members of more than fifteen local families. There was no formal organization chart. Mr. Newcastle maintained that "people have spheres of influence." People must report to many others and must individually determine to whom to give information. In this way, Mr. Newcastle tried to establish a system in which people were required to think about their role in, and their relationship to the whole company.

Particularism also worked its way back into the Quality Commodity Company. Mr. Newcastle stated that "people are judged on the basis of who they are and how they are relating to the whole and not how they are doing in their own separate sphere; their separation is de-emphasized." One employee said, "It's more like old times now than ever before; there's more interest in ya." Another commented, "We've grown so large, I'm afraid that if we grow any more, things might become impersonal." Aware of this, the Newcastles met their growth needs by expanding in other communities as well as by gradually enlarging their operations in Railtown.

Perhaps the most impressive evidence for the Newcastles' impact was union relations. Less than two years after the Newcastle family took control of the business, an internal drive started for union decertification. However, Mr. Newcastle stated that he could not endorse a decertification drive, because the union was not interfering in the daily activities of the company, because decertification drive might cause conflict among employees, and because the union still might provide some benefits and long-run security to the employees. The Newcastles' competitors were particularly distressed by this news, as the Newcastles' operation had regained the reputation of being very generous and caring toward employees. In other words, the Newcastles were setting bargaining standards that competitors had difficulty matching.

Under the Newcastle family, Quality's culture stabilized and largely returned to its state in the days before Corporal.

Figure 2. Culture of Railtown and the Quality Commodity Company

Category of Cultural Assumption	Railtown	Quality Commodity: The Alden Years	Corporal Industries	Quality Commodity: The Newcastle Years
Humanity's Relationship to Nature	Harmonize with nature	Harmony: goal of slow and cautious growth; acted as a citizen in Railtown; liberal policies toward employees halted	Domination: made many policy and product changes without seeking advice; relations with town were town; created new markets	Harmony: acted on workers' concerns, no initial changes in personnel; restored Quality's role in
The Nature of Reality and Truth	Testable truth defined pragmatically	Pragmatism: trial-and-error decision making; autonomy given for all testable decisions	Rigid Analyses: extensive documentation and forecasting required	Pragmatism: trial-and-error decision making; autonomy given for testable decisions
	Untestable truth defined patriarchically, by a council of elders	Defined by founder: Mr. Alden made all important decisions about company policy and direction	Defined in next-highest level of hierarchy: five-year plans; all decision making about policies occured in corporate headquarters	Defined by owner: Newcastles made most of the important decisions regarding overall policy and firm's direction
	Time and space are diffuse	Diffuse: no time clocks; appointments and meetings largely unscheduled; space open, and doors unlocked	Fixed: appointments formally scheduled; fights occurred over office space; doors locked	Diffuse: open offices and spaces; unscheduled meetings; no appointment books visible
The Nature of Human Nature	Basically good, capable of development, trustworthy, responsible, and accountable	Good: Mr. Alden was self-made; management never hired from outside firm; workers had high autonomy; employees held ownership in company	Bad: not concerned with employees outside work; no advice seeking; elaborate controls implemented; white collar crime	Good: time is taken to explain all decisions; teaching orientation; autonomy promoted at all levels; employees listened to, and their opinions solicited

The Nature of Human Activity	Reactive, little emphasis on planning, siezes opportunities	Reactive: no formal forecasting; new products discovered by accident	Planning: five-year plans required; quarterly forecasting	Reactive: purchase of firm and product development were responses to opportunity
	Participatory in nature	Participatory: involved employees in decision making	Individual orientation: separation of functions and offices; informal communication discouraged	Participatory: concerned with creating a "family feeling" in firm and community
	Highest-priority activities are those that benefit the collective	Benefit the collective: helped arrange housing; sponsored company activities that included the town	Benefit company: all community support disappeared	Benefit community: reestablished community support and work study programs
	Long-range time orientation	Long-range: instrumental in bringing new businesses to Railtown	Short-range:high turnover of management; short-term goals specified	Long-range:concern with quality products; invested in equipment that depressed profit in short run
The Nature of Human Relationships	Highly emotional, diffuse, particularistic, ascription and collectivity oriented	Diffuse, emotional: people interacted in many contexts, and the firm supported this; people judged in terms of who they were and how they related to the whole company; succession of son was well accepted	Specific, impersonal: teamwork replaced by destructive competition; positions in company became a rung on career ladder;community role of employees discouraged	Diffuse, emotional:sanctioned hiring of families; no formal organization chart; organization-wide meetings held; people judged on basis of who they were in relation to whole company

This happened because the Newcastles' assumptions were similar to those that historically had operated in Railtown. Figure 2 summarizes Railtown's culture and the culture of Quality Commodity during each of the three ownership periods.

The descriptions of the cultures provided here cannot be complete. It may not be possible to express the richness of culture adequately in words. This paper has attempted to provide a brief sketch of some of the important cultural aspects. The next step is to examine the effects that the various cultures had on Quality Commodity's performance.

Effects of Culture on Quality Commodity

Under Corporal, the Quality Commodity Company was often caught in the cultural cross fire between its owners and Railtown. This position led to many misinterpretations of behavior and in turn to inappropriate responses.

We have already witnessed several results of the situation in which one culture asserts itself over another culture that is incompatible, strong, and well entrenched. These results included confusion, helplessness, and anger. A dramatic example of how these conflicts affected people personally was that a manager who "didn't fit in" with Corporal and was subsequently fired committed suicide.

There were many other organizationally relevant effects. When people were asked about loyalty during Corporal's ownership, they would laugh. "What loyalty?" they asked. One manager was quite clear about the period when Corporal controlled Quality: "Loyalty was to the past rather than to Corporal or its management. I can't recall any

[loyalty]. I'm talking about the people who were local. People were responsible people. Supervisors and up, salaried people. But not because of Corporal. It was in spite of them." Several top managers and sales people quit because of cultural and managerial differences with Corporal policies.

The return of family ownership brought a return of loyalty and commitment. As a testament to the similarity in cultures, one manager who quit during the Corporal days returned to the company when the Newcastles requested his services. Employees stated that they were committed to the Newcastles and their ideals. Because the Newcastles were operating from assumptions similar to Railtown's, it was easy for townspeople to understand and support their actions, policies, and decisions. As Figures 3 through 6 indicate, the company and the employees benefited in many ways when the Newcastle family reintroduced a managerial culture that was similar to the community's culture.

Common measures of employee morale and productivity include absenteeism, turnover, and scrap rates. As Figure 3 shows, during the Alden family era, the yearly scrap rate never exceeded 11 percent. In sharp contrast, Corporal attained an unbelievable 50 percent scrap rate. As one manager stated, "Morale went bad. People were deliberately turning out a bad product. They were putting very derogatory notes in packages [that were to be shipped]." Under the Newcastle family, the scrap rate returned to the 10 percent range. Corporal's scrap rate is even more surprising than it looks because Corporal shipped goods that the Alden and Newcastle families would have considered to be scrap.

As Figure 4 shows, the pattern of absenteeism is very similar to the pattern for

Figure 3. Scrap Rates

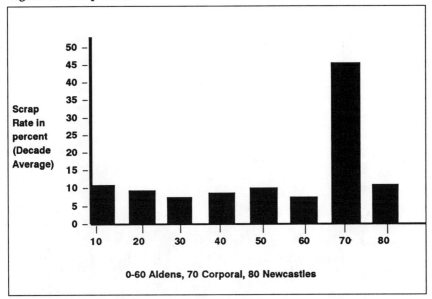

0-60 Aldens, 70 Corporal, 80 Newcastles

scrap rates. Starting with a rate of between 2 and 9 percent under the Aldens, it increased to well over 15 percent for Corporal and then returned to between 2 and 9 percent once again. (Until the year before the fieldwork for this study was conducted, when the work force was increased by 25 percent the absenteeism rate under the Newcastles had been between 1 and 5 percent.) Figures for employee turnover were not readily available from Corporal, and they were distorted by Corporal's layoffs. Setting death and retirements aside, turnover was well under 3 percent a year during the Alden period. Under Corporal, it may have jumped to between 10 and 20 percent, not including layoffs. Again the pattern reversed under the Newcastles, with turnover dropping to 3 percent or less.

Company prosperity can be measured by such indicators as sales growth and number of people employed. (Profits are not used, because they were unavailable from Corporal, and they could not be reconstructed from interview material. Indicators that rely on financial data were not adjusted for inflation. Financial data are reported in standardized terms to protect confidentiality.) As Figure 5 shows, sales growth steadily increased under the Alden family. In the first five years after the company's founding, sales increased 758 percent. By the time Corporal purchased the firm, sales had increased more than 25,000 percent. Sales decreased more than 20 percent during Corporal's ownership. However, under the Newcastle family, sales quickly rebounded. In the first year alone, sales were up 35 percent. By the end of 1985, sales had increased more than 450 percent since the Newcastles had taken control.

As Figure 6 shows, the number of employees under the Alden family grew

Figure 4. Absenteeism and Turnover

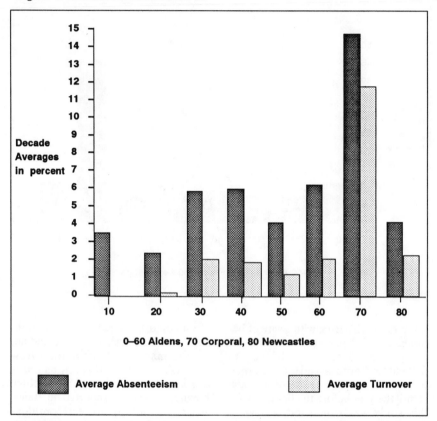

0–60 Aldens, 70 Corporal, 80 Newcastles

Average Absenteeism   Average Turnover

5,600 percent from Quality's first year of operation. During the lowest point of Corporal's cutbacks, the number of people employed dropped by more than 75 percent. Employment under the Newcastles grew 20 percent in the first year, and it had grown 300 percent overall as of December 1985. Employment figures also reflect community well-being and morale, because high employment reduces unemployment, increases the tax base, and increases local property values.

Other measures of growth and productivity, including total building space, number of production lines, money spent on new equipment, contributions to employee pension funds and insurance, dollars spent on advertising and promotion, new products introduced, and product enhancements, show a similar trend. The patterns just described vividly illustrate the relationship between ownership and a firm's prosperity.

Conclusion

This paper has explored the idea that the compatibility between firm and community culture has consequences for both the firm and the community. The case of Railtown and the Quality Commodity Company support the

Figure 5. Sales

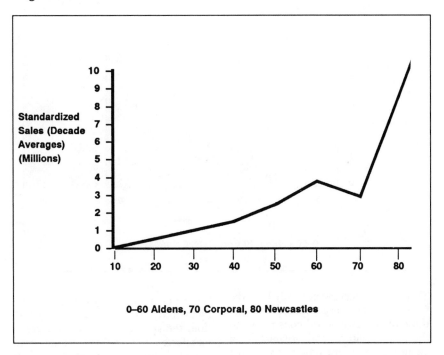

Standardized Sales (Decade Averages) (Millions)

0–60 Aldens, 70 Corporal, 80 Newcastles

premise remarkably well. The firm was initially composed entirely of people from the local community. Its owners and managers lived in Railtown. Quality Commodity firmly held and indeed shaped the cultural assumptions that were alive in Railtown. Comfortably situated within Railtown's culture, Quality Commodity was seen by the community as a resource and as a responsible and influential community member. As a result, the employees and the town displayed a great deal of loyalty and commitment to Quality. The company was treated like a trusted friend by its employees and the community, and this trust was reflected in Quality's success. Through their own behavior, the Newcastle family promoted practices, norms, and working relationships that were consistent with the assumptions of Quality Commodity, Railtown, and the Alden family.

Corporal Industries' culture was incompatible with both Railtown's culture and with the Alden's basic assumptions, which had shaped Quality's culture. Corporal's influence acted as a force that pulled the Quality Commodity Company out of the community in which it had been born. Quality personnel had difficulty understanding and responding appropriately to Corporal management. Quality's cultural assumptions led employees to misinterpret Corporal's actions. The result was low morale and the rapid failure of corporal's operations in Railtown.

Figure 6. Employment

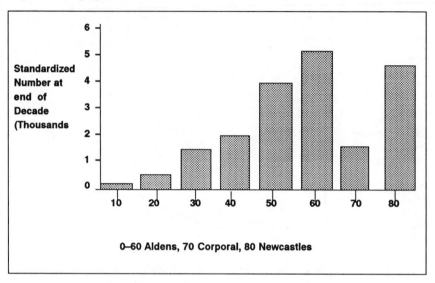

0–60 Aldens, 70 Corporal, 80 Newcastles

This paper suggests not only that the firm is part of a larger system but that the host places cultural constraints on the firm. Cultural and organizational change is therefore limited by factors that may be beyond the organization's control. Within a highly interconnected system, a change in one part of the system, such as the firm, is accompanied by changes elsewhere, such as in the community.

This paper also shows how differences in assumptions between people and between groups who must interact within larger organizational and societal contexts results in discomfort, stress, and inappropriate behavior. The paper does not intend to state that one culture is better than another culture. What its findings suggest is that cultural similarity between firm and environment is less stressful and problematic for the community and the firm than dissimilarity is.

Other factors, such as firm size, industry technology, and history and nature of the work force, may provide complementary explanations. By definition, the nature of the work force is manifested in the culture. In this case, the work force was comprised of individuals who had a fairly stable set of existing relationships. Culture also expresses history. The technology issue seems to have little bearing on the results seen in this case. Industry technology remained stable, as is evidenced by the many other firms that used similar technology.

This examination does not rule out the possibility that bureaucracies have cultures like the firms they acquire. One successful entrepreneur has started at least two large conglomerates that acquire only family businesses (Simon, 1985). And, this exploration does not rule out the possibility that family– and community–like cultures exist elsewhere than in rural areas. Research suggests that similar subcultures can be found in and around large cities (Dobriner, 1958). My research also does not say that all close communities and family firms have the culture described here. Further studies are needed to examine these other possibilities and to elaborate the factors that differentiate among situations.

One very important question that also needs further study is, Does the firm's relevant community include more than just the geographic locale and ownership? Owners and managers may also need to consider the influence of the cultures of their suppliers, distributors, and customers when managing their firms.

This line of inquiry has several implications for firms acquiring family firms, for family firms that are being sold to other firms, and for family firms that are undergoing a transfer of management. These implications spring from the central theme that sensitivity to the existing culture is critical to the success of a firm. Perhaps most important, the acquiring firm should evaluate the way in which it intends to manage the acquired firm and its community and the fit between these intentions and the cultural assumptions already in place. To do this requires an in-depth study of the cultures of all systems involved. The model types of culture presented here are a particularly useful starting point for such a study. Cultural diagnosis is a difficult and important task whenever change is planned. It is advisable to seek expert guidance.

References

Alderfer, C. P., and Klein, E. B. "Affect, Leadership, and Organizational Boundaries." *Journal of Personality and Social Systems*, 1976, 1 (3), 19-33.

Astrachan, B. M. "Organizational Boundary Management for Value Congruence." Unpublished manuscript, Yale University School of Medicine, 1975.

Bendix, R. *Work and Authority in Industry*. Berkeley: University of California Press, 1956.

Ben-Prath, Y. "'The F Connection' Families, Friends, and Firms in the Organization of Exchange." *Population and Development Review*, 1980, 6(1), 1-30.

Blood, M. R., and Hulin, C. L. "Alienation, Environmental Characteristics, and Worker Responses." *Journal of Applied Psychology*, 1969, 51, 284-290.

Clark, M. S., and Mills, J. "Interpersonal Attraction in Exchange and Communal Relationships." *Journal of Personality and Social Psychology*, 1979, 37(1), 12-24.

Dobriner, W. (ed.). *The Suburban Community*. New York: Putnam, 1958.

Dyer, W. G., Jr. "Cultural Evolution in Organizations: The Case of a Family-Owned Firm." Unpublished doctoral dissertation, Sloan School of Management, Massachusetts Institute of Technology, 1984.

Dyer, W. G., Jr. *Cultural Change in Family Firms: Anticipating and Managing Business and Family Transitions*. San Francisco: Jossey-Bass, 1986.

Etzioni, A. *The Active Society*, New York: Free Press, 1968.

Gouldner, A. W. *Patterns of Industrial Bureaucracy: A Case Study of Modern Factory Administration*. New York: Free Press, 1954.

Hall, E. T. *The Hidden Dimension*. New York: Doubleday, 1966.

Hofstede, G. *Culture's Consequences*. Newbury Park, Calif.: Sage, 1980.

Kanter, R. M. *Commitment and Community,* Cambridge, Mass.: Harvard University Press, 1972.

Lansberg, I. S. "Managing Human Resources in Family Firms: The Problem of Institutional Overlap." *Organizational Dynamics,* Summer 1983, pp. 39-46.

McCollom, M. "Organizational Culture: A Literature Review and Analysis." Unpublished manuscript, Yale School of Organization and Management, New Haven, 1983.

Merton, R. K. *Social Theory and Social Structure,* Glencoe, Ill.: Free Press, 1968.

Milgram, S. "The Experience of Living in Cities." *Science,* 1970, 167 (13), 1461-1468.

Miller, E. J., and Rice, A. K. *Systems of Organization.* London: Tavistock Publications, 1967.

Milofsky, C. "Scarcity and Community: A Resource Allocation Theory of Community and Mass Society Organizations." Unpublished working paper, Program on Nonprofit Organizations, Institute for Social and Policy Studies, Yale University, New Haven, Conn., 1981.

Parsons, T. *The Social System.* New York: Free Press, 1951.

Schein, E. H. *Organizational Culture and Leadership: A Dynamic View.* San Francisco: Jossey-Bass, 1985.

Simmel, G. *The Sociology of Georg Simmel.* (K. H. Wolff, trans.) New York: Macmillan, 1950.

Simon, R. "Thou Shalt Not Waste Deals." *Forbes,* Dec. 2, 1985, pp. 62-66.

Stein, B. A. "The Centerville Fund, Inc." A Case Study in Community Economic Control." *Journal of Applied Behavioral Science,* 1973, 2, 243-260.

Taylor, F. W. *Scientific Management.* New York: Harper & Row, 1947.

Thomas, D. A. "The Relationship Between Organizations and Their Environments: A Micro Level Perspective." Unpublished manuscript, Yale School of Organization and Management, New Haven, Conn., 1984.

Toennies, F. *Gemeinschaft und Gessellschaft [Community and Society].* C. P. Loomis, trans.) New York: Harper & Row, 1963.

Walton, R. E. "From Control to Commitment in the Workplace. *Harvard Business Review,* 1985, 63 (2), 76-84.

Weber, M. *From Max Weber: Essays in Sociology.* H. H. Gerth and C. W. Mills, trans.) New York: Oxford University Press, 1947.

Wells, L. Jr. "Misunderstandings of and Among Cultures: The Effects of Transubstantive Error." In D. Vails-Weber and J. Potts (eds.), *Sunrise Seminars: Volume 2.* Arlington, Va.: NTL Institute, 1985.

Index

Index

Index

Index

Index

DATE DUE